How to...

Speed up your network using DNS	**Chapter 5**
Use DNS, hosts, LMHOSTS, and WINS	**Chapter 5**
Understand FTP	**Chapter 6**
Use FTP	**Chapter 6**
Install FTP servers	**Chapter 6**
Work with FTP clients	**Chapter 6**
Work with your company's management	**Chapter 7**
Atone for the sins of your predecessors	**Chapter 7**
Work with the help desk	**Chapter 7**
Pick help-desk software	**Chapter 7**
Understand bridging	**Chapter 8**
Understand routing and routing protocols	**Chapter 8**
Design a router strategy	**Chapter 8**
Design a WAN	**Chapter 9**
Understand Multiprotocol Label Switching (MPLS)	**Chapter 9**
Understand SNMP	**Chapter 10**

M000216913

TCP/IP

24
seven ™

Gary Govanus

NETWORK PRESS®
SYBEX

San Francisco Paris Düsseldorf Soest London

Associate Publisher: Guy Hart-Davis
Contracts and Licensing Manager: Kristine O'Callaghan
Acquisitions & Developmental Editor: Neil Edde
Editor: Diane Lowery
Technical Editors: Don Fuller, Michelle Poole
Book Designer: Bill Gibson
Graphic Illustrator: Jerry Williams
Electronic Publishing Specialist: Adrian Woolhouse
Project Team Leader: Shannon Murphy
Proofreaders: Carrie Bradley, Ruth Flaxman, Catherine Morris
Indexer: Matthew Spence
Cover Designer: Ingalls + Associates
Cover Illustrator: Ingalls + Associates

Library of Congress Card Number: 99-64124
ISBN: 0-7821-2509-3

Manufactured in the United States of America

10 9 8 7 6 5 4 3 2 1

This book is dedicated to my favorite people in the whole world, my family. First, there is my loving, caring wife, Bobbi. Thanks for being part of my life.

Then there are my two daughters, Dawn and Denise. It has been a joy to watch you grow into the women you are today. Thanks for letting me be a part of your lives.

Finally, to the little people, my three grandchildren, Branny, C. J., and Courtney. May you grow up to take advantage of all of the vistas offered by the technology explained in this book.

I love you all!

Acknowledgments

You know, dear reader, you really don't know half of what goes on in the creation of a book. Before I started writing these things, I bought a bunch of them. I thought that the author sat down with a computer and a word-processing program and started to bang away on keys. When he or she got done with what they thought was a great book, they would send it off, and someone would pay them for their work. I was wrong.

First, it starts with a concept, and people at Sybex are great with concepts. I really can't wait for the rest of the 24seven series to come out, because I *need* them for my library. I do have an advantage over you, though—I don't have to buy this one. Once the concept is approved, they go on the search for authors. This is where Neil Edde, the acquisitions and development editor, comes into play. Neil called and asked me if I wanted to do the book, and we worked together to get the outline prepared, approved, and changed about a dozen times. Neil also spent a lot of time with me, going over material that I submitted and making sure it was ready.

Once Neil was done with me, he turned over everything to one of the Sybex Super-Women, Diane Lowery. Diane was the editor who had to keep me on schedule, check my work, make sure I really wrote in some semblance of English, and correct me when I was wrong. On the technical side, Donald Fuller and Michelle Poole took care of things. Don was the one who checked out everything to make sure it worked just the way I said it did, and he did a great job. If you get a chance, send Donald a note at `donald_fuller@ hotmail.com` and wish him well on his Cisco certification. That is not an easy course of study. Michelle came in at the end with a second read-through, and she made sure there weren't any last-minute errors that might have crept in. Thanks, Michelle!

Once the editors got done with the book, it went to the people I have never met, all the production people at Sybex. Many thanks to Adrian Woolhouse, Shannon Murphy, Jerry Williams, Carrie Bradley, Ruth Flaxman, and Catherine Morris.

Finally, I have to thank my family and friends for putting up with me during this process. Getting a book out can be stressful, and sometimes that stress showed in a lack of patience on my part. Because I have very little of it to begin with, it didn't take much to manifest itself.

Thanks also for not making me feel guilty about spending my time with my computer instead of spending time with you. I really do appreciate the sacrifices you make so I can continue to write.

So, to everyone on the team that helped with this book, thank you from the bottom of my heart.

Contents at a Glance

Introduction . . . . *xix*

Part I   **The Foundation of a TCP/IP Network**   **1**

Chapter 1   What Do You Want the Network to Do? 3

Chapter 2   TCP/IP from the Beginning 15

Chapter 3   Addressing Issues with TCP/IP 51

Part II   **Using TCP/IP Protocols to Make Your Life Easier**   **77**

Chapter 4   Using DHCP to Handle IP Addressing 79

Chapter 5   DNS and Your Network 111

Chapter 6   Using File Transfer Protocols to Ease Your Life 141

Part III   **Network Design and Planning**   **175**

Chapter 7   Atoning for the Sins of Your Predecessors 177

Chapter 8   Bridging and Routing with TCP/IP 201

Chapter 9   WAN Design Considerations 235

Chapter 10   Managing the Network Using SNMP 249

Chapter 11   The Ins and Outs of Extranets 265

Part IV   **The Road to a Successful Migration**   **291**

Chapter 12   Documentation Basic Training 293

Chapter 13   Planning for Changes 307

Chapter 14   Implementing the Plan 327

Part V   **The Connectivity Question**   **351**

Chapter 15   Using Proxy Servers to Make Your Life Easier 351

Chapter 16   IPv6 383

Part VI   **Network Security**   **405**

Chapter 17   Internal Network Security 407

Chapter 18   External Security 437

Chapter 19   Troubleshooting TCP/IP 463

Index *508*

Table of Contents

Introduction . . . . *xix*

Part I   **The Foundation of a TCP/IP Network**   **1**

Chapter 1   **What Do You Want the Network to Do?** **3**

Client/Server Implementations 3
Information Sharing 7
    Intranet Information Sharing 8
    Internet Information Sharing 8
    Internet Commerce Using S-HTTP and SSL 12
    Remote File Transfer 14

Chapter 2   **TCP/IP from the Beginning** **15**

Start at the Beginning 15
    TCP/IP Roots 17
    Internet Explosion 20
    Management of the Internet 20
    Domain Names and IP addresses 21
Networking Models 23
    The OSI Reference Model 23
    Department of Defense Model 35
TCP/IP Protocol Architecture 36
    Network Access Layer Protocols 37
    Internet Layer Protocols 37
    The Domain Name System (DNS) 40
    ARP and Address Resolution 42
    IP Routing Protocols 43
    Internet Control Message Protocol (ICMP)—or the
        Tattletale Protocol 44
    Host-to-Host Layer Protocols 45
    Process Layer Protocols 49

Chapter   3   Addressing Issues with TCP/IP **51**

IP Addressing Basics 51

IP Terminology 52

Binary vs. Decimal 53

IP Address Classes 54

Network Addresses 56

Host Addressing 63

Subnetting 64

Classless Interdomain Routing (CIDR) or Supernetting 69

How Does This Stuff Work? 70

Network Address Translation 72

DHCP with NAT 73

IPv6 75

**Part II   Using TCP/IP Protocols to Make
Your Life Easier   77**

Chapter   4   Using DHCP to Handle IP Addressing **79**

Pieces of the IP Communications Puzzle 80

MAC Address. 80

Protocol Numbers 80

Reverse Address Resolution Protocol 86

BOOTP 87

Dynamic Host Configuration Protocol (DHCP) in Depth 87

DHCP and Its BOOTP Roots 88

DHCP Address Allocation 93

DHCP Server Configuration 94

DHCP Client Configuration 105

DHCP Relay Host Configuration 107

How DHCP Works 109

Chapter   5   DNS and Your Network **111**

DNS Basics 111

DNS Components 113

Linking DNS Servers 117
Name Server Queries 118
Inverse Queries and Reverse Lookups 120
DNS Resource Records 121
Zone File. 122
DNS Clients 129
Installing DNS 131
Configuring DNS on a NetWare 5 Network 132
Configuring Microsoft DNS Server Service 134
The Future of DNS 137
Incremental Transfers of DNS information 139
Secure DNS 139

Chapter 6   Using File Transfer Protocols to Ease Your Life 141
FTP Exposed 142
FTP User Interface 143
User Protocol Interpreter (User-PI) 153
User Data Transfer Process (User DTP) 153
Sample FTP Session 155
Sun Microsystems Network File System 157
Installing and Configuring an FTP Server 159
Microsoft Windows NT 4 FTP Server 160
Internet Service Manager Authentication Options 164
NetWare 5 and FTP Services. 165
Unix and FTP Servers 169
Archie and the Fine Art of Searching the Internet 172

Part III   Network Design and Planning   175

Chapter 7   Atoning for the Sins of Your Predecessors 177
Discovering Current Problem Areas 178
Great Expectations. 179
Using the Help Desk 184

Are You in Charge of the Help Desk? 189

The Cyber Help Desk 190

The Help Desk Isn't Just for IT Anymore 193

Putting It All Together 194

Prioritize 194

Communicate. 194

Know What You Know. 195

Know and Respect Your Customers 196

Chapter   8   Bridging and Routing with TCP/IP **201**

Bridging Unmasked 202

Broadcast Basics 203

Transparent Bridges. 204

Looping—One of the Problems with Bridges 204

Source-Routing Bridges. 212

Source-Routing Transparent (SRT) Bridges. 213

Router Basics 214

Router Redundancy 216

Static Routes 218

Dynamic Routes 219

TCP/IP Routing Protocols 223

Interior Gateway Protocols. 223

Exterior Gateway Protocols 231

Chapter   9   WAN Design Considerations **235**

Design Objectives—The Future of Your Network 235

IP to the Rescue 236

Multiprotocol Label Switching (MPLS) 236

Planning for the Implementation of DHCP 237

Maintaining the DHCP Database. 239

Planning for the Implementation of DNS 239

Planning for the Implementation of WINS 241

Planning the Installation of WINS Servers 242

Maintaining the WINS Database 243

Planning for the Implementation of LMHOSTS 243

Implementation of LMHOSTS 245

Care of LMHOSTS Files 245

Planning for the Implementation of HOSTS 245

HOSTS File Basics 246

Care of HOSTS Files 247

The Final Plan. 248

Chapter 10   Managing the Network Using SNMP. **249**

SNMP Basics 250

The SNMP Managers 250

SNMP Agents 251

Management Information Bases. 251

Placement of SNMP Managers and Agents 251

Popular SNMP Software 252

How to Make Plans for Using SNMP Applications 253

Planning on Using SNMP-Compliant Hardware and Software . 254

Using SNMP in the Real World 254

How Tough Can You Make It? 254

If You Are Going to Go, Go Big. 255

It Really Is Rocket Science! 257

Customize It! 259

SMS Takes On the Y2K Issue 260

SNMP in a TCP/IP World 262

Chapter 11   The Ins and Outs of Extranets **265**

Interorganizational Internetworks. 267

The Internet 2 Project 267

Very High-Performance Backbone Network Service (vBNS). . . . 272

The Difference between vBNS and Abilene 272

Virtual Private Networks 274

VPN Tunnels and Gateways 275

What to Look for in a VPN 278

FAQs about VPNs 278

To VPN or Not to VPN 280

VPN Potholes. 281

Remote Connectivity for the VPN 286

Alternatives to VPNs 289

Part IV   The Road to a Successful Migration   291

Chapter 12   Documentation Basic Training **293**

Why Document? 294

Evaluating Current Network Environment 294

Defining Functional Requirements 295

Developing Multivendor Network Integration Plans 296

Developing Network Diagrams and Specifications 297

Changing Network Documentation 298

Developing an Implementation Plan for Deployment of a Solution 299

Locating Existing Documentation 300

TCP/IP Documentation 301

Hosts/LMHosts 304

Chapter 13   Planning for Changes **307**

Planning for Physical Layer Changes 309

Planning for New Data Link Layer Implementations 313

Bridges. .313

Ethernet Switches 313

Token Ring Switches 315

Data Link Layer Plans 315

Planning for Changes at the Network Layer 316

Develop a Strategy for Assigning IP Addresses 316

Ways to Allocate IP Addresses You May Not Have Thought Of . 319

Planning for Changes at the Transport Layer. 321

TCP. 322

UDP 322

DNS 322

Transport Layer Plans 323

Planning for Changes at the Session, Presentation, and
Application Layers 324
FTP 324
Telnet. 324
SMTP. 325
List of Things to Do 325

Chapter 14   Implementing the Plan **327**
List of Things to Do 328
Project Management 101 329
System-Design Life Cycle (SDLC) 329
Managing the Project 332
Project-Approach Phase 333
Putting the Project Definition Phase into Practice 337
Project-Design Phase 338
Determine a Routing Strategy 344
Create a Network Resource Accessibility Plan 347
Implementation Phase 347
Develop a Migration Strategy 348
Create an Implementation Schedule. 348

Part V   The Connectivity Question   351

Chapter 15   Using Proxy Servers to Make Your Life Easier. **353**
What Is a Proxy Server?. 353
Proxy Server Internet Access Support 354
Proxy Server Overview 356
How Instituting a Proxy Server Will Impact Your Network . . 356
What Can a Proxy Server Do?. 358
Proxy Servers as Routers 358
Proxy Servers as Network Address Translators 358
Proxy Servers and Caching 361
Enterprise Caching. 364

Using a Proxy Server to Control Access and Filter Packets. 370

    Using a Proxy Server to Log Connections 371

Reverse Proxying 371

    Load-Balancing 372

    Redundancy and Reverse Proxying 373

Different Methods of Proxying 373

    Application Layer Proxying 374

    Proxy Server Placement. 375

    The Proxy Connection and Communication Process 376

    The Information Exchange. 377

Application Configuration 378

    HTTP Proxy Connections 378

    FTP and a Proxy Connection 379

Circuit-Level Proxies 380

    Using Port Redirection 380

    More Powerful than an Application Proxy, More Flexible

      than a Transport Proxy, It's.... 381

Chapter 16   **IPv6** **383**

IPv6 Design 384

    IPv6 Header Format. 384

Revisions to Internet Control Message Protocol 386

    IPv6 Ping 387

The Impact on Upper Layer Protocols 388

    IPv6 in Domain Name Service (DNS) 388

IPv6 Address Architecture 389

    Address Basics 389

    IPv6 Address Notation 390

IPv6 Address Allocation 391

    Special Address Formats 391

    Multicasting and Anycasting 393

    Interdomain Routing 393

    Moving from Classless Interdomain Routing to Providers . . 394

BGP to IDRP 395

Intradomain Routing 396

Host Auto-Configuration 397

Linking Local Address. 397

Stateless Auto-Configuration of Hosts 398

Stateful vs. Stateless Configuration of Hosts 399

IPv6 Dynamic Host Configuration Protocol (DHCP) 400

IPv6 and Internet Security 401

IPv6 Encryption and Authentication 402

Transitioning to IPv6 402

Supporting Two Sets of IP Stacks 403

Dual-Stack Strategy and DNS 403

Part VI   Network Security   405

Chapter 17   Internal Network Security **407**

My Network Is Already Secure! 407

Risk Assessment 410

What Is Risk Assessment? 412

Equipment/Infrastructure Risk Assessment 414

Equipment/Infrastructure Protection 416

Data Risk Assessment 420

Intrusion Detection 421

Crackers and More 422

What Is the Point? 423

Using Security Auditing Tools 424

Trusts 426

Top Ten Things to Increase Internal Security 427

When in Doubt, Patch It 427

Implement Effective Password Schemes 428

Remove Default Accounts 429

Assigning User and Group Rights 430

Make E-Mail Secure 432

Have an Intruder-Detection Action Plan. 433
Use Encryption 433
Keep Critical Network Segments Segregated 434
Use Removable Disks and Drives 434
Monitor Information Access 435
A Final Word on Security 436

Chapter 18   External Security. **437**
Firewalls and Gateways 437
Types of Firewalls 439
Firewall Issues 444
Computer Viruses 445
Increasing Numbers of PCs Means Increasing Numbers of Viruses 446
The Cost of Virus Infection 446
Virus Prevention—Practice Safe Computing 449
Remote-Access Security 450
Remote-Access Security for the Enterprise 450
Remote-Access Security Suggestions 455
Web Page Security 459
Credit Card Processing 460

Chapter 19   Troubleshooting TCP/IP **463**
The Troubleshooting Model 464
Step One: Try a Quick Fix 464
Step Two: Gather Basic Information 466
Step Three: Develop a Plan to Isolate the Problem. 466
Step Four: Execute the Plan 467
Step Five: Ensure User Satisfaction 469
Step Six: Document the Solution, and Take Steps to Ensure It
Doesn't Happen Again 469
Quick Fixes 469
Network Connectivity 470
Problems with Configuration Files 472
Check Log Files 474

Routing 474

DNS and Name Service 476

Check the Daemons or Services 476

Solving Problems 477

Testing Basic Connectivity 477

Troubleshooting Access to the Network 481

Troubleshooting with the ipconfig/ifconfig/winipcfg Commands . 481

Troubleshooting with the arp Command 484

netstat 486

Segmenting an Ethernet Network 488

Troubleshooting Routing 491

Using tracert to Solve Problems 494

Troubleshooting Using Name Service 496

Troubleshooting with SNMP 504

Index **508**

Introduction

TCP/IP 24seven. What a topic! If you are holding this book, you are probably a network administrator who is currently working on a network that is using TCP/IP, or perhaps you are someone who wants to be an administrator on a TCP/IP network. Whatever your background and whatever the current state of your employment, I hope this book has something in it for you.

When I was approached about writing this book, I have to admit, at first it sounded like it was going to be pretty easy. Just explain TCP/IP, talk with administrators who use it, and tell their stories. That was the plan. The more I got into writing this book and the more I started talking with people who managed networks everyday, the more I began to realize that there are a lot of people who are working with TCP/IP but are not entirely comfortable with how it works. So, the focus of the book became somewhat larger, to take in not only the TCP/IP guru but also the person who needs to get a deeper understanding of the protocols and the way they all work together. I hope that I have succeeded in giving you a reference work that you can use for a long time to come.

This Book and the Development Process

During the initial development of this book, an emphasis was placed on conveying what you, as an administrator, need to know to keep your TCP/IP healthy, happy, and operational 24 hours a day, 7 days a week. I queried many experienced network administrators and asked them a few questions:

- What do you do to keep your TCP/IP network healthy and happy?
- What facts did you learn the hard way?
- What have you done wrong (and right)?
- What would you like to share with other TCP/IP administrators?

It is with this information that I assembled this book. I focused primarily on operations issues. I figured that the best way of explaining how to run a network that relies heavily on TCP/IP was to take you through all the steps necessary to design, implement, and manage an IP network. Due to the space and time constraints associated with this book, there were issues I had to avoid or only partially cover. I avoided many client/server-related issues except when necessary. I tried to keep the book as operating-system independent as possible, bringing in examples from Unix, NetWare, and NT. I know that I could write an entire book on running TCP/IP on each of these network operating systems, so I tried to stay generic.

When you are discussing TCP/IP, you have to focus on what is available and operational today. But IPv6 is looming on the horizon, and it is the subject of a multitude of books and articles. I can't predict the future about IPv6, but I put in a chapter about it anyway and how the migration will occur. I hope you get something out of that section.

Throughout this book, you will find case-studies and real-life sidebars. The sidebars contain specific situations and problems that I have encountered in the field while working with TCP/IP or problems that other people have encountered while working with TCP/IP. I felt it was important to use some special mechanism to emphasize how other companies are approaching problems. The case studies deal with more general problems and solutions that some companies have faced. In some cases, the actual names of the companies have been changed. When possible, I made sure that the companies didn't mind the publicity, and I quoted real-life examples.

Who Should Buy This Book?

If you are standing in your neighborhood bookstore asking yourself this question, then ask no further. Maybe you are just taking over a network that has an extensive deployment of TCP/IP. Possibly you have just come back from a class on TCP/IP and you want to know more. Chances are, in this age of the Internet, you are currently managing TCP/IP, and you want to know what you can do better. Perhaps you are curious about some of the pitfalls and sticky situations that can happen with TCP/IP. If you are in any of these situations, this book is for you.

Maybe you need to know how to design your network or to add new hosts or networks to your site. Are you wondering what the best management practices for a TCP/IP network are? How should you document a TCP/IP network? Have you given any consideration to what would happen if disaster strikes? How about what you can do to proactively prevent problems? If you answered yes to any of these questions, this book is for you.

This book is not for networking beginners, but it does try to cover some of the TCP/IP basics that you may have heard about but do not yet fully understand. That seems to be a common problem in the networking-industry today. Readers should have networking experience, including knowledge of network operating systems, networking hardware and software, and networking and desktop operating systems. An understanding of communications media and related technologies would certainly help.

If you are studying for certification exams, this book will be helpful but should not be considered an exam study guide. If that is what you are seeking, purchase a copy of *MCSE: Exchange 5.5 Study Guide,* by Richard Easlick and James Chellis (Sybex, 1998) or *MCSE Exam Notes: TCP/IP for NT Server 4,* which I wrote last year for Sybex. Yes, this is a blatant plug for more book sales!

Assumptions

The book is centered around IPv4. I assumed throughout this book that you are working with an Intel processor and using either Windows NT or NetWare. There is some Unix information in here, but mostly, I have tried to keep the information as operating-system independent as possible.

How This Book Is Organized

I have divided this book into 19 chapters, with the topics and complexity of the book varying from chapter to chapter. Each chapter is intended to stand on its own, but it is impossible not to spend some time building on ideas and concepts that were generated in earlier chapters. I started the book with a brief discussion of some of the things that TCP/IP could do for your network. In some cases, administrators use it because it is a default protocol or because it is necessary for Internet connectivity, but they aren't sure of the overall capabilities of the protocol suite.

When I first laid out the outline for the book, Neil Edde and I were not sure whether there should be a chapter in here describing what the TCP/IP suite actually is. We thought long and hard about it and decided that maybe we would put the information in an appendix. About a third of the way through the book, an independent technical editor did a very high-level scan of the topics covered and took us to task for not including the discussion of what TCP/IP is. So, Neil and I decided to add a chapter.

In teaching classes on networking, I have learned that there are many administrators who work with TCP/IP each and every day. They handle large networks but would like some clarification on IP addressing and subnetting. If you are the Subnet Guru, then that is a chapter you can skip! Otherwise, the information in Chapter 3 may help you out and also help in troubleshooting.

Part II focuses on using some of the major components of the TCP/IP suite, such as FTP, DHCP, DNS, and SNMP. I discuss how to implement these components, what they do, why they work well, why they may not work so well, and whether any gotchas have turned up during my research. It should be informative. You should have a complete overview of working with TCP/IP by reading the whole book. However, you are welcome to read the chapters in just about any order you wish.

Troubleshooting

With this book, I wanted to pass along as many troubleshooting tips as possible. There have been many people who answered the calls for TCP/IP tales of woe or success stories, and I have tried to name names wherever possible. Troubleshooting tips are spread throughout the book, but the largest chapter in the book, Chapter 19, is dedicated to using IP utilities and commands that try to find errors. Again, Chapter 19 is not designed for the network neophyte. It assumes that you know the difference between IRQ and DMA, and you have configured more than one host to work with IP. There will be information in there the neophyte can use, but that person may have to ask a few questions first.

IPv6

A book on TCP/IP would not be complete without a look to the future. IPv6 is really an exciting protocol, and I firmly believe that it will be the building block of the future for all forms of communications. I was fortunate enough to read a white paper from AT&T about burst technology coming to wireless communication and to find information on the next generation of the Internet. This information was based around technologies either in the TCP/IP suite or ingrained in IPv6. I think you will enjoy the chapters on IPv6 and the future of the Internet. I know those were probably the most fun sections to write. As a matter of fact, there may even be another book hiding in there somewhere.

Enjoy the book. I hope that sometime in the future I get a note from someone saying that something in the book saved them a minute or an hour or a day. Or even just, "Hey, I didn't know that!"

How to Contact the Author

Gary Govanus can be reached at ggovanus@psconsulting.com.

Part 1

The Foundation of a TCP/IP Network

Topics Covered:

- Reasons to use TCP/IP
- Client/server explained
- Using an intranet or the Internet
- The history of TCP/IP
- An explanation of the TCP/IP suite
- TCP/IP addressing explained
- Subnetting explained

1

What Do You Want the Network to Do?

The decision to use TCP/IP is usually not a conscious one. I have yet to hear of a network administrator who woke up one day and said "Hark! Today I will install TCP/IP throughout the land, just to have it there in case it is needed in the future." The decision is based on current need. The reasons people need TCP/IP are

- Client/server applications
- Sharing information/remote file transfer
- Internet information sharing

TCP/IP is not usually implemented only because you want to; you also make the decision based on having the need for it. We will cover several examples of that need in this chapter.

Client/Server Implementations

As you look around your company, you begin to notice there are a lot of strange faces coming and going. These people show up for a few days, seem to know everyone, and then disappear. When you ask, you are told these are the on-the-road sales force, auditors, technicians, installers, cleaning crews, etc. These people are affectionately known as the *road warriors*.

Road warriors, who are rarely connected to the corporate network, need to have access to e-mail. They need to access the sales automation software, and they need to enter information into a variety of databases. The policy passed down from the suits on Mahogany Row is save money: "Surely you can devise an information sharing system that will be easy to use and reliable and will not involve thousands of dollars in long-distance phone calls to a dial-up center that constantly needs attention."

To the rescue, we have TCP/IP and client/server connections. *Client/server* is one of those phrases that keeps getting tossed about but rarely gets explained. Client/server computing describes the relationship between two computer programs. One program, the client, makes a service request from another program, the server. It is up to the server to fulfill the request. Although the client/server model can be used by programs running on a single computer, it is usually found in a network situation. In that scenario, the client/server model provides a way to link programs that are distributed efficiently across different locations.

Computer transactions using the client/server model are very common. For example, to check your bank account from your computer, a client program in your computer forwards your request to a server program at the bank. That program may in turn forward the request to its own client program that sends a request to a database server at another bank computer to retrieve your account balance. The balance is returned back to the bank data client, which in turn serves it back to the client in your personal computer, which displays the information for you.

The client/server model has become one of the hallmarks of network computing. Most business applications being written today use the client/server model, including protocols like TCP/IP. Both the client programs and the server programs are often part of a larger program or application. A common implementation is the Internet. Your Web browser is a client program that requests services from a Web server. The Web server application is running on another computer somewhere on the Internet. Similarly, your computer with TCP/IP installed allows you to make client requests for files from FTP (File Transfer Protocol) servers in other distinct computers on the Internet.

Here is another example of how it works. For simplicity sake, let's use something everyone is familiar with, electronic mail. In a client/server connection, when a user wants to access their e-mail system, the client at the workstation passes a request off to the software running on the server, and the server portion gets the information and returns it to the client. In this way, the software running on the end user's computer never accesses the mail store, and what the end user's computer does not access, the end user cannot corrupt.

How Much Do You Know?

As you go through this book, you may wonder why some things that seem obvious to you are covered in detail.

I am a computer trainer by profession. I am a Master Certified Novell Instructor and a Microsoft Certified Trainer. I am also an independent trainer, meaning I work for myself and not for one of the certified training centers around the country. Those centers bring me in to teach classes that their trainers can't or won't handle, and this usually involves some pretty high-level specialty stuff. I don't usually run across new network administrators; most of the people in my classes have over five years of experience in the field or come with a college degree.

While I was working on this book, I fielded a lot of questions from students in these classes. What I noticed was that although computer professionals all over the country knew about TCP/IP and even knew how to install and configure it, they were not sure how it worked. So I took a very informal, unscientific poll to see whether I was right.

My class consisted of 13 people. The average length of their careers was about six years. There were two managers, one administrator from a network of 3,000 people, another administrator from an international network, someone from the state department of transportation, a recent college graduate, as well as a set of your basic, run-of-the-mill computer whizzes. A fairly routine cross section of the industry.

I asked the following questions and received the following responses:

- *Who can define and explain client/server computing?* 0 out of 13

- *Who knows how DNS operates?* 0 out of 13

- *Who knows how DHCP operates?* 3 out of 13 had some idea; none were completely sure.

- *Who knows how a workstation determines whether a TCP/IP packet is destined for the local segment or a remote segment?* 0 for 13

- *What IP protocols run on the routers at the office?* 0 for 13

Keep in mind these were far from noneducated people. The last question surprised me. I said that when I was first exposed to TCP/IP, I was afraid of it because I didn't understand it. I asked if anyone else felt that way. In this case 10 of 13 hands went up.

All of these people use TCP/IP every day. They install it, configure it, and make use of it. They just don't understand it. The purpose of this book is not only to work on the *how* but to answer the *why*!

Until recently, TCP/IP was not the protocol of choice among most network administrators; NetWare was the preferred network operating system, and DOS was the desktop operating system on most computers. Anyone who has ever configured a TCP/IP stack on a 286 or 386 DOS-based computer truly knows the meaning of fun: getting all that stuff to load in a very small memory space was a challenge. But then Windows NT and Windows 95 arrived. Suddenly, implementing TCP/IP was relatively painless, and whole new vistas opened up.

One group to benefit from the newfound TCP/IP popularity was the road warriors. Road warriors have always had a set of unique communication problems, such as how do you economically pass information back and forth to the office?

A variety of applications use client/server connections to make communication between field staff and the home office more efficient and cost effective. This arrangement works for a small staff or for large implementations. Here are several examples.

A company has a large and diverse sales staff. Some of these people work from desk space assigned at the regional sales offices and are linked with permanent WAN connections to the corporate headquarters. Meanwhile, there is a group of on-the-road sales people that work out of their cars and their homes. Configuring their remote dial-up connections to the headquarters is costly, time consuming, and frustrating. Most sales people are not experts at configuring their hook-ups, but they can be trained to do so.

Your company uses any one of a number of good sales automation software. All the in-house people enter their information on clients, leads, and potential sales directly into the database. What about the on-the-road folks?

Most sales automation software will have the capability to handle remote users. These users grab a copy of the database on a laptop and carry it with them wherever they go. When they make changes, these changes need to be synchronized back to the main office. By configuring a client/server connection using TCP/IP, the on-the-road staff can connect to a local Internet provider by any one of a number of methods and then send the synchronization set to the corporate office. This is the client side of the equation.

The server side comes in when the synchronization set arrives. The server portion takes the information and enters it into the main database. It then checks to see what information has changed since the last time the sales person synchronized. The server compresses the information and sends it out directly to the IP address of the workstation hooked into the Internet miles away. The client can then integrate these changes into the local database, and everyone is up-to-date.

Another implementation of client/server communication is e-mail. Most of the major groupware applications (Microsoft's Exchange/Outlook, Novell's GroupWise, Lotus

Notes, etc.) will have the ability to transfer information from a data store on a corporate file server to a workstation hooked up to the Internet using IP. Your road warriors are connected to your network, using the infrastructure of the Internet at very little cost to your organization.

What if your company doesn't use groupware? One of the most common uses of TCP/IP is for e-mail. There are a variety of standards and protocols that make accessing e-mail fast and easy, thanks to TCP/IP. Using a simple, inexpensive front end, users can access e-mail from a dial-up connection anywhere in the world. These Post Office Protocol 3 (POP3) systems may not have all the bells and whistles of the big boys, but the information gets through just the same, and that is what matters. If your company wants to have onsite e-mail, implementation of a Simple Mail Transfer Protocol (SMTP) and POP3 server is usually a painless process. Many of the server pieces are available as freeware or shareware and run on a variety of operating systems. As a matter of fact, if your network has any Linux or Unix systems sprinkled around, the piece you need may be right at hand.

Information Sharing

Today's business revolves around information. It seems that we just cannot get (or provide) enough information, yet information is everywhere. We are progressing rapidly from a manufacturing society to an information society, and as this transformation takes place, people are demanding more and more different kinds of information, and they are demanding it immediately. Terms such as *Active Desktop* or *Intelligent Search Engine* take on new meaning. If you are a geek of long-standing (meaning you have been going around the block for a few years), you remember the days when computer bulletin boards were the way companies shared information. Whenever you needed information, you dialed into a company's bulletin board. Usually the call was long distance, and it was a time-consuming, expensive task.

> **NOTE** Please take very careful note of the use of the word *geek* in this book. It will be used a lot, so we need to define terms. A geek is a computer professional who knows and loves the career path they have chosen. It is used in the finest sense of the word. My business card lists my title as geek, most of my best friends are geeks, and many of the people I admire most are geeks. Geeks come in various degrees; for example, there is the geek-wannabe, but that is a completely different story.

In the last several years, bulletin boards have all but disappeared. They have been replaced by the Internet globally and by the intranet locally.

Intranet Information Sharing

If you never have come across a corporate intranet, you may not know what they are. Think of an intranet as the Internet shrunken down to the corporate level. Here is how TCP/IP and one of its component protocols, HTTP, can help.

Contrary to popular belief, the human resources department fulfills multiple functions after you get hired. One of these functions is to write and manage corporate policies. In some companies, a revision of a corporate policy spelled bad news for a forest. Think about what would happen if a company with 100,000 employees suddenly decided to change the vacation policy from one week to two weeks after the first year. The HR department would revise the policy, write up the two-paragraph announcement, make 100,000 copies, put each copy into an interdepartment envelope, and send all 100,000 copies through the intercompany mail system. The message was effectively delivered to 100,000 employees but think of how many hours went into the work of just getting those two paragraphs into a form where people could look at it. Wouldn't it have been more efficiently delivered (not to mention more cost-effective) if the person who wrote the new policy simply saved it as an HTML document to a predesignated area, linking it on a home page to the rest of the policies. In a matter of moments, the policy is available to every member of the company, without using a single solitary piece of paper.

Now, although this *can* be an effective method of distributing information, it only works because of the diligence and planning of the information technology department. It is up to the IT department to decide where to place corporate intranet Web servers, how to train users to save documents in HTML format, and how to save these documents in the right place. It is also up to the corporate IT department to ensure the organization's staff has the applications necessary to do this simply and efficiently.

Although the setup and maintenance of an intranet are beyond the scope of this book, when you plan your IP network, you need to make sure that the Web server host has enough horsepower and disk space to handle the load. The Web server–based intranet site should be centrally located so as many people as possible can access it over a minimum number of routers.

Internet Information Sharing

At this point, your high-level design of the network has almost covered all of the people within your organization. But what about providing information to your customers and to all your potential customers? Setting up an Internet presence initially sounds like a pretty scary proposition, until you do it the first time. Once you have done so, the steps are in place, and you will find that the process is pretty painless. However, you need to be on the lookout for certain things as you begin the planning process.

To Host or Not to Host

One of the first decisions you face as a potential Internet magnate is to decide whether you want to host your own Web site or have an ISP (Internet service provider) host it for you. This is a decision you should carefully consider, even if your company has a full-time connection to the Internet.

Hosting your own Web site means that thousands of people a day can access your server, looking for information and exploring your site for all sorts of hidden gems. It also means that you are opening up your system to strangers. Someone in the media once described this as like having 10,000 people a day walk up to the front door of your house and test the doorknob to see whether it is unlocked. Not necessarily a bad thing, unless, of course, the door is unlocked. After all, your corporate Web site could be a secure window to your entire company network.

If you opt to have an ISP host the Web site for you, the responsibility for security now lies with the ISP. In addition, if someone does hack into your Web site, you may face some embarrassment, but your corporate data will be safe. The downside is the cost. ISPs do not give this stuff away for free, so it will be an added expense. The costs, obviously, depend on the ISP.

Firewall Basics

If you decide to host your own Internet site, one of the first things you should begin to explore is a good *firewall*. A firewall is a combination of hardware and software that is designed to make it more difficult for the bad guys to break in and to provide some controls when the good guys go out.

Here is how it works. A host that stands between the corporate network and the Internet is the firewall. This host can be a computer or a router. The host will have some sort of software running on it that blocks requests from getting into the corporate network or blocks inappropriate requests from leaving the network.

TCP/IP communication between hosts is based on a series of addresses. Think of these addresses as you would think of a mailing address. The addresses go from very specific to very generic. For example, if I were addressing a letter to someone, it would be in this format:

> John Doe
> Apartment 32
> 123 Main Street
> Anywhere, USA

A TCP/IP address works the same way. It starts with a port address. The port address accesses a particular service that a host has to offer. From the port address, the next section is the host address, and finally the network address.

TIP   TCP/IP addressing will be discussed in detail in Chapter 3.

Some of these services have port addresses defined by Request for Comment (RFC) 1060. Some common services include FTP, which uses port address 21; Telnet, which uses port address 23; and SMTP, which uses port address 25.

A firewall gives the network administrator the ability to shut down, change, or limit access to these port addresses. For example, suppose you worked for a financial institution. Locating the TCP/IP address of a host leading to a particular network is not rocket science, and once someone has an IP address of a host, there is a chance they can take over the host. To prevent this from happening, the firewall simply blocks the ports or moves them to an area where the unsuspecting hacker may not be able to locate them. There are 65,536 potential port addresses (2^{16}), with the port numbers below 256 being reserved for common services and the ports from 256 to 1024 being reserved for Unix-specific services. That allows plenty of room for creativity on the part of the network administrator.

Going back to the financial institution analogy, if you are the network administrator and you know the address of 208.45.13.122 is vulnerable to attack from the outside world, you will want to do everything in your power to protect it. In this case, you will install and configure a firewall. When you configure the firewall, you know that you do not want anyone to Telnet to this host, so you can shut down the Telnet port of 23 at this particular address. A true firewall controls not only the ports and addresses, it also controls direction. In our example, we would block port 23 inbound.

If you are going to use this host as both an FTP server and as an SMTP mail server, you may decide to move the FTP port from 21 to 2021 and the SMTP port from 25 to 2525. You can reassign ports to any number you choose, as long as that port is not currently being used by another service. Now, when a user wants to ftp to your new FTP server, they will have to use the IP address and the port address: 208.45.13.122:2021. As long as the user that is requesting the services has the appropriate port address and the system is configured to use that port address, the request will go through.

NOTE   This is a high-level overview of a firewall and network security. Network security is only as good as the people operating on the network. It is a lot like security on your home. If someone is bound and determined to get in, chances are they will. It is up to you to make it so difficult for them to find the appropriate opening that they choose to go play in someone else's backyard!

You can also use the firewall to block or restrict access based on other information, such as a login name or a sending IP address. Firewalls differ, depending on the complexity of the system. Usually, as the complexity and security increases, so does the cost.

TCP/IP Security Basics

As soon as you decide to hook your network up to the Internet, your security concerns skyrocket. Not only do you have to worry about all those folks that you create user accounts for but you also have to worry about all those unknown hackers in the big, bad outside world. The worst part of the security issue is that it is an ongoing issue. It will never go away. Just as soon as you fix one opening, somebody may be knocking on another opening trying to get into your network.

Although the problems of security are ever present, in the world of TCP/IP they are addressed by several RFCs. According to RFC2196, the Site Security Handbook, you should start working on security by looking at the following five areas:

1. Identify what you are trying to protect.

2. Determine what you are trying to protect it from.

3. Determine how likely the threats are.

4. Implement measures that will protect your assets in a cost-effective manner.

5. Review the process continuously, and make improvements each time a weakness is found.

The RFC continues to address the "why" of security by saying "One of the most important reasons for creating a computer-security policy is to ensure that efforts spent on security yield cost-effective benefits. Although this may seem obvious, it is possible to be misled about where the effort is needed. As an example, there is a great deal of publicity about intruders on computer systems; yet most surveys of computer security show that, for most organizations, the actual loss from 'insiders' is much greater.

"Risk analysis involves determining what you need to protect, what you need to protect it from, and how to protect it. It is the process of examining all of your risks and then ranking those risks by level of severity. This process involves making cost-effective decisions on what you want to protect. As mentioned, you should probably not spend more to protect something than it is actually worth."

Threats to a network can be broken down into three areas: unauthorized access, disclosure of information, and denial of service attacks. *Unauthorized access* is a simple concept. Somebody—an unauthorized somebody—gets access to your network and to the information on your network.

Disclosure of information is someone passing out information that you do not necessarily want released. It might be the latest plans for the hottest product ever to hit the computer market or something as simple as releasing the company phone list to a headhunter.

Denial of service is a much more insidious type of attack on a network. Due to someone messing around with your network, your users will not be able to access network services. There are a variety of network attacks that can lead to denial of service. One of the attacks is as simple as pinging a Windows NT 3.51 server with an odd-sized packet. That is enough to overload the server and deny users access to their information.

As you plan your network, you need to keep all these types of security attacks in mind. Although drawing up comprehensive security plans is a step in the right direction, you cannot effectively cover all the security holes with hardware, software, and passwords. The largest security holes are usually in the interface between the chair and keyboard.

People cause the majority of security problems. As was mentioned in RFC2196, the greatest loss of information comes from inside the company, not from outside the company. Many people scoff at this concept. After all, the network administrator has designed the perfectly secure network; no one can break in, and even if they do, there are audit trails and other things to track them down.

If you are reading this and you run or work on a company network, do a really brief security audit. Take a walk around the company. Check things out. How many of the people on your network have left their desks to go get coffee, go to lunch, or visit the rest room and have left an open network connection at their desk? How many people have their password taped to their monitor or to the underside of the keyboard or desktop? How many people are actually logged in as someone else?

Security starts at the desk. Make sure everyone, from the CEO to the newest hire, is aware of security, knows how it works, and what to do if there is a problem. Make sure everyone knows how to spot a potential problem and when to report it. Follow up on all reports. Remember, the data you save may be your own!

> **TIP**   Security will be covered in more detail in Chapter 17 on Internal Security and in Chapter 18 on External Security.

Internet Commerce Using S-HTTP and SSL

Everybody wants on the Internet. From the largest multinational corporation to the smallest home-based business, everyone is looking to the Internet as the next best way to compete in the global marketplace. Everyone is trying to become the next large cyber-seller.

With those desires come responsibility, including making sure that online transactions are secure from prying eyes.

There are several ideas you may need to implement as you plan your Internet presence. Some of these security plans revolve around Secure HyperText Transport Protocol (S-HTTP) and Secure Socket Layer (SSL) scripts. S-HTTP and SSL are designed to ensure that private communications between two computers not physically connected remain private.

S-HTTP uses any combination of three methods to ensure security: signature, authentication, and encryption. Digital *signatures* provide the sender and the recipient with the peace of mind of knowing that their communication has not been altered from one spot to another, and it also verifies the person who sent the message.

You may not recognize the term *authentication,* but if you have used Microsoft's Internet Explorer, you are familiar with the process. In this case, a digital certificate is issued by an issuing authority and is passed back and forth between sender and receiver. There are several companies around who provide this digital certificate, and when installed, it is used in the background so you may not even know it's there. It just provides a guarantee to the receiver that the real sender sent the message and nothing messed with it on the way to its destination. *Encryption* ensures that the message that is sent is garbled when it crosses the public portions of the Internet and can be reassembled correctly at the receiving end.

One of the reasons that more and more Web sites are depending on S-HTTP is its flexibility. Each transaction can have its own level of security. If your company is asking someone to send their name, address, or phone number over the Internet, you may digitally authenticate that transaction. When it comes time for the credit card number to pass across the Internet, S-HTTP will call for a higher level of security, perhaps signed and encrypted. Of course, the Web site can be designed for no security whatsoever.

Another Transport layer protocol that is used extensively is SSL. SSL can be used to secure HTTP transactions as well as other TCP/IP protocols. SSL also provides authentication, encryption, and data verification. Because SSL is application-protocol independent, it can be used with Telnet, FTP, or HTTP, and the security occurs transparently. SSL will handle all the encryption and session information, before communicating with the upper-layer protocols.

SSL is made up of two protocols: the SSL Record Protocol and the SSL Handshake Protocol. The *Record Protocol* handles encapsulation of all data. The *Handshake Protocol* is used to establish the security parameters.

Remote File Transfer

Another problem caused by having a company full of road warriors is they constantly want something. Some of the requests can be handled over the phone, but some require transferring files from one location to another.

Suppose you have a technical support engineer who is onsite at a customer's location. This customer needs a copy of the file that has a complete set of the instruction manuals for the new Super Whizbang 2000 your company sells. Of course, the technician does not have a copy of the file handy. This could be considered another area of opportunity for the IT department to shine.

If you have anticipated this need, you can set up a File Transfer Protocol (FTP) server. By putting the FTP server on the Internet or by having a dial-in capability, your engineers can simply go to the FTP site, find the file they want, and download it.

FTP works as a two-way street. Suppose that the engineer has found some documentation at a customer site and needs to make that file available for the rest of the company. In this case, the file can be uploaded to the FTP server, and the access is assured.

If you have never worked with FTP before, you may be concerned that placing information on an FTP server on the Internet means that everyone can access it. Not true! FTP has built-in security, and you can grant everyone (in the case of FTP, this is called *anonymous*) access to the files, or you can restrict who can access the files and when.

By now, you have begun to think about some of the points necessary for a successful implementation of the TCP/IP protocol. The next step is to look beyond some of the obvious reasons and look into some of the deeper design issues, such as redundancy and fault tolerance to keep the network up and running.

2

TCP/IP from the Beginning

In the last chapter, I mentioned that there were a lot of people out there who used and worked with TCP/IP every day but did not really understand how or why it works. That is the goal of this book. Chapter 1 covered some of the reasons to use TCP/IP, but before it can be implemented, you have to know which parts to use and which parts to put on the shelf.

In this chapter, we will deal with some of the history of TCP/IP and what the protocol architecture is, and we will try and break it down to some bite-sized chunks.

Start at the Beginning

There are all sorts of really trite ways we could begin this chapter. You know, things like "A journey of a thousand miles begins with a single step." Fortunately for you, I am above that kind of triteness and would never revert to such lowly tactics to start a chapter.

I knew it had to happen. More and more people are using the Internet. We, the computationally sophisticated, have reached a stage in business where we expect our suppliers to have at least an e-mail address and hopefully a full Internet presence, including Web pages and electronic commerce. A growing number of "real" people—those people who do not work in the industry every day—are using the Internet for the first time. Many of them are using the tools and utilities that at one time were only available on a limited number of computer systems (and only for really intense users!).

Generation Gap

In one of my classes, the students and I got to talking about parents. Most of us have had them, at one time or another, and some of us are still blessed with their presence. We were comparing notes on those parents who have passed the age of 80. My dad falls into that category, and he is sharp as a whip. Several years ago, Dad decided it was time that he got a computer, so he approached his son about the best way to get one. After all, he didn't need much, and his daughter-in-law had mentioned that there were all these spare parts laying around the house. Maybe his son could take a few minutes and throw one together for him. Uh-huh. His son may not be the brightest bulb on the tree, but he has learned how to take a hint. Dad soon had a 486/100 with about 32Mb of RAM, a 2GB hard drive, and a 33.6 modem. It wasn't the fastest system on the planet (and no, it did not come from parts I had laying around), but it worked just fine. I got Dad set up with his own phone line and his own Internet account, and he was off, happy as can be, surfing the Net—for a while.

It wasn't too many months later that he started to mention how "slow" his system was and how long it took to find information on the Web. Wasn't there a way to speed things up? I, being somewhat creative, managed to put him off for a short time, but it became clear that I had to do something. We finally got him upgraded to a Pentium II/350 with enough RAM and disk space to run a small file server. He also has a 56K modem, and he is back to being happy surfing and checking out his investments. If you would have told me back in 1995 or 1996 that my father would own a computer, I would have been surprised. Had you said that, in 1999, he would be out spreading the computer gospel to "all those old people" and teaching them how to use computers, I probably would have asked what you had been drinking for lunch.

Surf on, Pop. I hope it gets to the point that technology advances so that you need at least three more upgraded computers! But I am not running a T-1 to your house, no matter how slow the response is over a modem!

One sign of this growth in use has been the significant upsurge in the interest in TCP/IP as a protocol. Network systems that a few years ago shunned TCP/IP have jumped on the bandwagon and are touting the fact that the OS is using pure IP. Of course, for those of us who write books, articles, courses, and even TV shows on TCP/IP, we wholeheartedly applaud this turn of events. Before we look at what TCP/IP is, it might be worthwhile to take a few pages and examine its roots. After all, TCP/IP and the Internet seemed to be joined together from the very beginning. It was truly the protocol that would not die, and it would fight back from a United States federal government decision to kill it.

TCP/IP Roots

Prior to the 1960s, there was little computer communication. If two computers did "talk," the communication comprised simple bursts of text and binary data carried by the local telecommunication company. The *telco* infrastructure consisted of an old, circuit-switching backbone that had been around for almost 100 years. Combining the short bursts of communications that make up a discussion between two computers and the circuit-switching technology was not a match made in heaven. As a matter of fact, it was an inefficient use of what little bandwidth there was available.

Many inventions and technology changes started with the military, and this story starts there too. In 1962, an employee of the Rand Corporation, Paul Baran, had a vision of an efficient, store-and-forward data network that he included in a report to the U.S. Air Force. Baran wasn't alone in his vision. Donald Davies, working for the postal service in the United Kingdom, foresaw the same type of network. Davies even came up with the terminology packet that would describe the data units that would be sent from one computer to another. If packets are being sent over a switched network, obviously, that is a packet-switching network. According to Baran and Davies, packet-switching networks could be set up so that everything operated independently, effectively creating a redundant system and eliminating a single point of failure. Although network communication resources appear to be dedicated to a single communication channel, by using statistical multiplexing and by putting a size limit on the packet, the result is a fast, economical data network.

So how did the Internet get its start? The modern Internet began as a project of the U.S. Department of Defense (DoD). It was originally designed to interconnect DoD-funded research sites throughout the U.S. In December 1968, the Advanced Research Projects Agency (ARPA) awarded a contract to design and set up a packet-switching network to Bolt, Beranek, and Newman (BBN). In September 1969, the first node of the ARPAnet was installed at UCLA. By the end of 1969, the Internet consisted of just four nodes. By 1971, ARPAnet crossed the continental U.S., and connections in Europe followed by 1973. (Early growth would not rival the 1990s.)

With the advent of ARPAnet came the development of protocols that were new to packet switching. One of the early protocols that is still in use today is the ITU-T (formerly CCITT) Recommendation X.25. This "standard" interface encouraged BBN to start Telenet, a commercial packet-switched data service, in 1974; after much renaming, Telenet is now a part of Sprint's X.25 service.

That was fine for the packet-switching portion of the network, but what about a host-to-host communications protocol? The first try introduced in the ARPAnet was called the Network Control Protocol (NCP). As the Internet continued to grow, NCP simply couldn't keep up with the traffic load. In 1974, a more robust suite of communications protocols was proposed and implemented throughout the ARPAnet. This new suite was based on the Transmission Control Protocol (TCP) and Internet Protocol (IP). TCP and IP were originally envisioned as a single protocol. Today, the protocol suite actually refers to a large collection of protocols and applications but is usually referred to simply as TCP/IP. The versions of both TCP and IP that are currently in use were actually written in September 1981, although both have had several revisions since then. In addition, the planning specifications for a real version of IP, IP version 6 (IPv6) were released in December 1995. These specifications are nearing finalization.

TCP/IP became the *defacto* standard in 1983. The DoD mandated that all of their computer systems would use the TCP/IP protocol suite for long-haul communications, further emphasizing the scope of the ARPAnet. Also in 1983, the ARPAnet was split into two components. One component, still called ARPAnet, was used to interconnect research and development sites and academic sites; the other, called MILnet, was used to carry military traffic and became part of the Defense Data Network. That year also saw a huge boost in the popularity of TCP/IP, with its inclusion in the communications kernel for the University of California's Unix implementation, 4.2BSD (Berkeley Software Distribution) Unix.

The early Internet was beginning to grow, but it didn't look anything like what you see today. In 1986, the National Science Foundation (NSF) built a backbone network to connect four regional supercomputer centers and the National Center for Atmospheric Research (NCAR). This network, called the *NSFnet,* was not originally intended as an interconnection mechanism for individual systems. Furthermore, the "Appropriate Use Policy" defined by the NSF limited traffic to noncommercial use. The NSFnet continued to grow and provide connectivity between both NSF-funded and non-NSF regional networks, eventually becoming the backbone of what we know today as the Internet.

Although early NSFnet applications were largely multiprotocol in nature, TCP/IP was employed for interconnectivity. After all, the ultimate goal was a migration to a system where every type of computer system could connect to the Internet.

Speed on the original NSFnet was not all that great. It originally comprised 56Kbps links. It was completely upgraded to T-1 (1.544Mbps) links in 1989. Migration to a "professionally managed" network was supervised by a consortium comprising Merit (a Michigan state regional network headquartered at the University of Michigan), IBM, and MCI. Advanced Network & Services, Inc. (ANS), a nonprofit company formed by IBM and MCI, was responsible for managing the NSFnet and supervising the transition of the NSFnet backbone to T-3 (44.736Mbps) rates by the end of 1991. During this period of time, the NSF also funded a number of regional Internet service providers (ISPs) to provide local connection points for educational institutions and NSF-funded sites.

It did not take long for the NSF to decide that it really did not want to be in the Internet business. In 1993, the NSF went back to the funding of research in the areas of supercomputing and high-speed communications. In addition, there was increased pressure to commercialize the Internet. The commercial test balloon went up in 1989 when MCI, CompuServe, Internet mail services, and commercial users were linked to the NSFnet by a test gateway. Now, other people were finding out about all of the capabilities of the Internet, and they were jealous because it belonged exclusively to academic and defense department users. In 1991, the Commercial Internet Exchange (CIX) Association was formed by a union of General Atomics, Performance Systems International (PSI), and UUNET Technologies. The goal was to promote and provide a commercial Internet backbone service. Nevertheless, there remained intense pressure from non-NSF ISPs to open the network to all users.

In 1994, a plan was put in place to reduce the NSF's role in the public Internet. The new structure comprised three parts:

- Network Access Points (NAPs), where individual ISPs would interconnect. Although the NSF is only funding four such NAPs (Chicago, New York, San Francisco, and Washington, D.C.), several non-NSF NAPs were also in operation.

- The very High Speed Backbone Network Service, a network interconnecting the NAPs and NSF-funded centers and operated by MCI. This network was installed in 1995 and operated at OC-3 speeds (155.52Mbps). The high-speed backbone was completely upgraded to OC-12 (622.08Mbps) in 1997.

- The Routing Arbiter, to ensure adequate routing protocols for the Internet.

In addition, NSF-funded ISPs were given five years of reduced funding to become commercially self-sufficient. This funding ended in 1998.

In 1988, meanwhile, the DoD and most of the U.S. government chose to adopt OSI protocols. TCP/IP was now viewed as an interim, proprietary solution because it ran only on limited hardware platforms, and OSI products were only a couple of years away. The DoD mandated that all computer communications products would have to use OSI protocols by August 1990, and then the use of TCP/IP would be phased out. To further this goal, the U.S. government OSI Profile (GOSIP) defined the set of protocols that would have to be supported by products sold to the federal government, and TCP/IP was not included.

Despite this decision by the United States federal government, development of TCP/IP continued during the late 1980s as the Internet grew. TCP/IP development had always been carried out in an open environment, even though this open environment was small because of the small number of ARPA or NSF sites.

Although people were still trying to develop OSI products, these products were still a few years away. Meanwhile, TCP/IP became, in the minds of many, the real open-systems interconnection protocol suite.

The ISO Development Environment (ISODE) was created in 1990 to provide an approach for OSI migration for the DoD. ISODE software allowed OSI applications to operate over TCP/IP. During this same period, the Internet and OSI communities started to cooperate to make sure that the features of TCP and IP would be migrated into the OSI protocols. Finally, the National Institute for Standards and Technology (NIST) in 1994 decided that TCP/IP was probably not going to go away, and it suggested that GOSIP should incorporate TCP/IP and drop the "OSI only" requirement.

Internet Explosion

The ARPAnet started with four nodes in 1969 and grew to just under 600 nodes before it was split in 1983. The NSFnet also started with a modest number of sites in 1986. In RFC1296, "Internet Growth 1981–1991," the network has experienced literally exponential growth. By January 1998, it was reported that the Internet had nearly 30 million reachable hosts. Now, it looks like people are hooking up to the Internet at a rate of a new host attached every 30 minutes, and there are over 200,000 networks hooked into the Internet backbone. The growth does not seem to be slowing either. Estimates have the Internet doubling in size every ten to twelve months, and this rate of growth has been going on for the last several years.

While the Internet was growing, ARPAnet was shrinking. Everything moved over to the Internet and finally the ARPAnet was closed in mid-1990.

Management of the Internet

Once the government bowed out of the picture, who was going to run the Internet? After all, it has no single owner, yet everyone who has a host owns part of the Internet. There are some things that have to be centrally managed, such as the assignment of IP addresses or the coordination of requests for DNS names. This management is done by a variety of societies, boards, and task forces. Here are some of the major players in Internet management:

The Internet Society (ISOC)   The ISOC is a nongovernmental body providing coordination for the Internet, its internetworking technologies, and its applications. ISOC also provides oversight and communications for the Internet Activities Board.

The Internet Activities Board (IAB)   The IAB governs administrative and technical activities on the Internet. Two subgroups make up the IAB:

The Internet Engineering Task Force (IETF)   The IETF is one of the two primary bodies of the IAB. The IETF's working groups have primary responsibility for the technical activities of the Internet, including writing specifications and protocols. The impact of these specifications was significant enough that the ISO accredited the IETF as an international standards body at the end of 1994.

The Internet Engineering Steering Group (IESG)   The IESG is the other part that makes up the IAB. The IESG provides direction to the IETF.

The Internet Research Task Force (IRTF)   The IRTF comprises a number of long-term groups that are charged with promoting research regarding the evolution of the future Internet.

The Internet Engineering Planning Group (IEPG)   The IEPG coordinates worldwide Internet operations. This group also assists Internet service providers (ISPs) to work within the global Internet.

The Forum of Incident Response and Security Teams (FIRST)   The FIRST coordinates a number of Computer Emergency Response Teams (CERTs) that represent many countries, governmental agencies, and ISPs throughout the world. Internet network security is greatly enhanced and facilitated by the FIRST member organizations.

Domain Names and IP addresses

Internet hosts use a hierarchical naming convention composed of a top-level domain (TLD), a registered domain name, an optional subdomain name, and then a host name. The IP address space, as well as all TCP/IP-related numbers, has been managed by the Internet Assigned Numbers Authority (IANA).

Domain names were assigned by the TLD naming authority; until April 1998, the Internet Network Information Center (InterNIC) had authority over these names, with NICs around the world handling non-U.S. domains. The InterNIC was also responsible for the overall coordination and management of the Domain Name System (DNS), the distributed database that reconciles host names and IP addresses.

Who Is in Charge Here Anyway?

The InterNIC is an interesting example of changes in the Internet. Starting in 1993, Network Solutions, Inc. (NSI) operated the InterNIC on behalf of the NSF and had exclusive registration authority for the .com, .org, .net, and .edu top-level domains. NSI's contract ran out in April 1998. It was extended several times while this group with no management authority tried to figure out who should handle the registration of those domains. In October 1998, it was decided that NSI will remain the sole administrator for those domains but that users could register names in those domains with other firms. In addition, NSI's contract was extended to September 2000, although the registration business had to be opened to competition by mid-1999.

Meanwhile, the newest body to handle TLD registrations is the Internet Corporation for Assigned Names and Numbers (ICANN). Formed in October 1998, ICANN is the organization designated by the U.S. National Telecommunications and Information Administration (NTIA) to administer the Domain Name System.

ICANN will handle the responsibility by forming several support organizations (SOs) to manage certain parts of the Internet. These will include a Domain Name Service Organization (DNSO), an IP Address Service Organization (ASO), and the Protocol Service Organization (PSO).

While the Internet was incubating, the method of TLD assignment and management had worked well. When the World Wide Web hit the big time and became the information superhighway, questions were raised about how names can be fairly assigned without violating trademarks and conflicting claims to names. In November 1996, an Internet International Ad Hoc Committee (IAHC) was formed to resolve some of these naming issues and to act as a focal point for the international debate over a proposal to establish additional global naming registries and global top-level domains (gTLDs). In February 1997, the IAHC proposed the creation of seven new gTLDs:

- .firm for businesses or firms
- .store for businesses offering goods to purchase
- .web for entities emphasizing activities related to the WWW
- .arts for entities emphasizing cultural and entertainment activities
- .rec for entities emphasizing recreation and entertainment activities
- .info for entities providing information services
- .nom for those wishing individual or personal nomenclature

In order to clear up a potential bottleneck as businesses, industries, and even individuals apply for all these new names, the IAHC also proposed that up to 28 new registrars be established. These new registrars will be allowed to grant second-level domain names under the new gTLDs, all of which will be shared among the new registrars.

Once the IAHC had published this information, its work was done. It was dissolved in May 1997 with the publication of the *Generic Top-Level Domain Memorandum of Understanding* framework.

Networking Models

To begin the discussion of TCP/IP, it should be stated right off the bat that TCP/IP is not a protocol, although it is often discussed in those terms. It is really a suite, or collection, of different protocols that do different tasks. Before you can figure out the best way to put this stuff to use, you probably should have a good handle on what the pieces can do and how they align with similar protocols that do much the same thing.

When looking at protocols, there are two models that are commonly used, the seven layers of the Open System Interconnection (OSI) model or the four layers of the Department of Defense (DoD) model. The two models, other than having different numbers of layers, are remarkably similar. I will be referring to each model as the book progresses, so let's start by examining the OSI model. If you have any type of industry certification, you have already been exposed to this, but a refresher may not hurt. If it has been awhile since you have delved into the OSI model, we will briefly review it. If you know this stuff backward and forward, skip ahead a ways, and keep reading. I will be using the seven layers and what they do as a reference.

The OSI Reference Model

The OSI model was originally designed to provide a basis for discussion about communication on a network. Notice, that unlike TCP/IP, which is a suite of protocols, OSI is referred to as a model. A protocol is a set of rules that must (and I use that term rather loosely) be followed. A model is just that: a model. It is a reference point and nothing more. Nothing has to be written to adhere to it, but most protocols have qualities that can be generically discussed using the model.

Because we are using this model to discuss communication between nodes on a network, it only makes sense that each node is running some kind of application that has the same qualities. As a matter of fact, each layer of the OSI model communicates with its peer layer on the other node.

The seven layers of the OSI model are

- Application
- Presentation
- Session
- Transport
- Network
- Data Link
- Physical

Although these layers are just parts of the model, each layer has a set of specific tasks that needs to be accomplished.

NOTE   As you look at the seven layers of the OSI model, don't get psyched out. Many people figure it is all advanced geek and not worth knowing. As you will see for the upcoming discussions, there are times it comes in handy. Keep in mind what each layer does, and take a good close look at the name of the layer. In most cases, the name of the layer is really descriptive and should give you a clue. The people who originally came up with this stuff were great engineers and thinkers. They just didn't do marketing and packaging well, thank goodness. Otherwise, a marketing staff might have called the Application layer something like the Residuals Entrance layer!

The tasks for each layer are covered in the following sections.

Application Layer

When you see the term *application*, at least in a reference to the OSI model, don't be tricked into thinking of programs like Word, Excel, or PowerPoint. The Application layer is where the protocols and processes in charge of things, such as file and print services, database services, and e-mail, run.

In Chapter 1 we touched on the principle of the client/server connection. The Application layer provides the services for that connection. Not only is it up to the process running at the Application layer to listen and respond to requests from the client but the Application layer process has to do some advertising, as well.

Advertising for the processes will come in one of two forms, either passive advertising or active advertising. Passive advertising doesn't do much, hence the name passive. When a network service is configured, the administrator makes an entry in a database, and when something needs the service, it references the database. In more layman's terms, passive advertising is a lot like this book. It was just kind of hanging around on the bookshelf at your local bookstore waiting to get purchased. It wasn't actively trying to get purchased, it just waited until you and your credit card came along.

Active advertising is just the opposite. In this case, the service will be broadcasting messages advertising its presence on the network. These messages can take many forms, but one that might be familiar to you would be a print server on your network. The print server is really a point-to-point connection for the printer and the network. It gives the printer an interface into the network. In order to make sure the printer gets used, the print server will advertise its presence. For example, in a Novell NetWare network, the print server will periodically issue a Service Advertising Packet. This is a broadcast packet, which means every host on the network segment gets one and it lets the rest of the computers know where the print server is located.

Presentation Layer

Looking at the name, you might be surprised to find out that the Presentation layer is in charge of formatting and presenting the information from one computer to another. This is not as simple a task as it might appear. It is at this layer that many of the gateways operate.

> **NOTE** Many people think computers are magical, doing amazing things on a regular basis. You and I know they are just dumb boxes that won't do anything without proper instructions. If there is anything in computing that could be considered magical, it is a gateway. This is the smoke and mirrors of computing. A gateway is simple to describe but complex to develop. A gateway is a translator. It is the gateway that makes a mainframe computer think it is talking to another mainframe, when it is talking to a network file server. It is the gateway that will make a Macintosh think it is talking with and working with another Mac, when it is working with a Intel-based computer.

The Presentation layer is different from the lower layers. In the lower layers, the emphasis is on moving data from one computer to another. The Presentation layer, on the other hand, is concerned with the representation, or the *syntax*, of data during transfer between two communicating application processes.

To achieve true open-systems interconnection, a number of common, abstract-data syntax forms have been defined. The International Standards Organization (ISO) defined a general abstract syntax suitable for the definition of data types associated with most distributed applications. This became known as *abstract syntax notation number one* or ASN.1. The data types associated with ASN.1 are abstract data types, and an associated transfer syntax has been defined.

At present, only one transfer syntax notation exists in OSI: the Basic Encoding Rules (BER) of ASN.1. As experience with applications using BER grows, new transfer syntax notations, such as those that include data compression or encryption, will be defined.

Syntax conversion may be the major role of the Presentation layer, but its role in the communication process does not stop there. Because it performs operations on all data prior to transfer and on all data that is received, the Presentation layer is responsible for data encryption and data compression.

Session Layer

The Session layer is the place in the communication hierarchy where the conversation is maintained. It is the applications running at the Session layer that establish the conversation, manage the conversation, and end the conversation when it is over. The Session layer applications also reestablish the conversation if it is broken for some reason.

Session layer services are application-to-application based, and the services at this layer are designed to provide for the step-by-step setup and tear-down of application dialogs.

As part of this service, the Session layer also provides points to synchronize the application data flow. This is one of a series of checks that makes sure the sending computer is not overwhelming the receiving computer with data. To make sure that this process occurs flawlessly, the Session layer will provide a mechanism for the two computers to negotiate the rules of exchanging data between applications.

Examples of Session layer services include

- Hypertext Transfer Protocol (HTTP)
- Simple Network Management Protocol (SNMP)
- Network Basic Input/Output System (NetBIOS)

Transport Layer

Have you ever heard about one of those middle-management types that takes all the credit for all the hard work of the people they manage? Many people have bumped into someone like this in their career. Notice where the Transport layer sits? Right in the middle of the seven layers of the OSI model. The Transport layer is just like that middle manager. The Transport layer hides all hard work done by the lower layers when it passes the conversation up the line.

Actually, while the Transport layer hides the work of the lower levels of the OSI model, it does some valuable work on its own. It is at the Transport layer that name- and address-resolution occurs. There is some high-level connection and transaction addressing happening here as well as the development of packet segments.

The Foundation of a
TCP/IP Network

PART 1

Finally, the Transport layer is responsible for some connection services, such as segment sequencing, error control, and even end-to-end flow control.

Network Layer

When you think of the term *network,* you think of this large conglomeration of computers strung out all over a company. The amazing thing is they can all talk to each other and access resources anywhere on the network. Now take that vision one step further, to the Internet. With the Internet, you can establish communication with a computer or a host thousands of miles away. How does it do that? How does one computer located on the Lower East Side of Upper YourTown get to see a Web page on a computer located in Upper West Side of Lower MyTown? Things that happen at the Network layer make that communication possible. This layer is where all the routing protocols work and play.

The Network layer is one busy little puppy. For starters, it has some addressing work to accomplish. Whenever you assign a network address, either by subnetting in TCP/IP or by binding IPX to a network card, you are creating a Network layer address.

Switching also falls into the bailiwick of the Network layer. It is up to protocols operating at this layer to take care of handling packet-switching, message switching, and circuit switching.

When we get to Chapter 8, you will see how some of the Network layer protocols handle tasks such as discovering which route a packet should take and how the routers and bridges on your network make that decision.

Anytime there is route discovery taking place, a connection is established between two computers. Whenever there is a connection, negotiations need to take place. At the Network layer, the systems have to negotiate Network layer flow control, error control, and the sequence of the packets they send and receive.

Finally, some gateways operate at the Network layer, so some translation happens down here.

Data Link Layer

The Data Link layer has a important job to do. Whenever information is sent out over a network cable, the information is put into something referred to as a frame or a packet. There are other synonyms for *packet* (depending on the layer), but they all mean the envelope the message is sent in. Think of the Data Link layer as the mailroom of the communication process. It is up to the Data Link layer to take all the mail coming down from above and put it into some kind of envelope so it can go out. It also has responsibility for working with the incoming messages, too. At this point, it opens the mail, finds out who it is addressed to, and then sends it on its way up the corporate ladder until it lands on your desk.

Actually the Data Link layer has so much to do, it is broken down into two sublayers: the Media Access Control (MAC) layer and the Logical Link Control (LLC) layer.

Media Access Control Sublayer   In the MAC sublayer, the network determines whether the logical topology of the network (as opposed to the actual physical topology of the network) is a ring or a bus type. Once it has determined this, the MAC layer protocols know how to put the data frame on the network. The protocol can use the following methods:

Contention   When you think of the contention method, think of the old party-line phones, with multiple people accessing the phone network at the same time. The same is true with Ethernet. More than one system can try and place a frame on the network at the same time.

Token Passing   There used to be a kids' game that had a wonderful purpose, to keep only one child talking at any given time. In this game, something was passed from child to child, and the only time someone could speak would be when they were holding the object. This is the same as a token-passing network. A 3-bit token is passed from node to node. Each time the node gets the token, it checks to see if there is data attached to it. If there is, the node can check to see whether the data is addressed to it. If there isn't, the node can attach information, or it passes the information to the next node down the line. A very civilized way of accessing a network.

Polling   With the polling method of access, you must have some type of central control unit. This central control unit goes completely around the network and asks each node whether it has something to say. If the node does have something to say, it replies at that time. If not, the central control unit will move on to the next node. This, I would imagine, is the equivalent of not speaking unless you are spoken to!

Finally, it is up to the MAC sublayer to handle physical device addressing. Also known as the MAC address, this is the hardware address that manufacturers add to their network cards. It is usually hard-coded into the card, and there is very little you can do to change a MAC address.

LLC SubLayer   The LLC sublayer is responsible for transmission synchronization and for some connection services. Transmission synchronization falls into three categories:

Asynchronous   When you think of asynchronous communications, think of modems. Each device sends each frame separately. Each byte that is sent starts with a start bit and ends with a stop bit to indicate that the transmission has started and ended. This is a mature method of sending messages but not completely reliable. Error-correcting is done with the help of a parity bit.

Synchronous   With synchronous communications, the sending and receiving hosts time their communication using a transmission or framing clock. Rather than depending on start and stop bits to indicate communications, this communication is synchronized by the clock. This method uses SYN or SYNC control characters to make sure the two sides agree. Synchronous transmission is a more efficient method of transmitting large blocks of data, because it has eliminated a lot of the overhead costs associated with asynchronous communications. It is faster and more efficient.

Isochronous   In this case, there is a constant fixed frequency transmission clock to create time slots. In this case, the hosts monitor the network for free time slots. If it finds one, the data is transmitted.

In the area of connection services, once again we see that there is concern that one system will overflow the other with information. There is some LLC layer flow control of data and some very basic error control.

Physical Layer

This is the layer that is responsible for actually connecting systems, so the other layers can get the little 1s and 0s out onto the network. It is the Physical layer that electronically converts a 1 or a 0 to an impulse and then sends that signal over the network when the timing is right. That is not an easy task. It is up to the Physical layer to determine what type of connection is being used, the physical topology of the network, whether the network is using digital signaling or analog signaling, and how the bits are synchronized. As you can see, the Physical layer is the busiest layer of them all!

Connection Type   There are two basic types of connections that the Physical layer recognizes: a point-to-point connection or a multipoint connection.

Point-to-point connections   A point-to-point connection is easy to imagine. Think about being able to go behind one host and grab a wire that can be traced directly back to another host. Think of a computer and a local printer, and you have the perfect point-to-point connection.

Multipoint connections   Again, multipoint connections are easy to visualize. Imagine one host connected to many hosts; for example, following the network cable hooked to your computer through the wall, into the wiring closet, and through the wiring closet directly to the concentrator. Here, your computer is hooked to a multiple of different systems.

Physical Topology   All computer networks rely on either point-to-point connections or multipoint connections. Multipoint connections come in various fashions, all of which can be grouped into the single category of physical topology. The breakdown of the categories within the category include

> **Bus topology**   A physical bus topology typically uses one long cable as a backbone. Computers are attached to the backbone using BNC T-connectors. Backbones are terminated on both ends to remove the signal from the wire after it has passed all the devices. Figure 2.1 shows an example of bus topology.

Figure 2.1   Bus topology

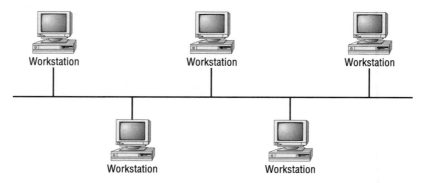

Ring topology   The physical ring is a circular topology or a closed loop using point-to-point links. Each device connects directly to the ring through an interface device and a drop cable. Signals are passed from device to another device in only one direction. Signals are repeated or regenerated at each device so signal degradation is minimal. Figure 2.2 shows an example of ring topology.

Star topology   Physical star topologies use a central device with drop cables extending in all directions. Each networked device is connected via a point-to-point link to the central device called a *hub, multiport repeater,* or a *concentrator.* Figure 2.3 shows an example of a star topology.

Figure 2.2   Ring topology

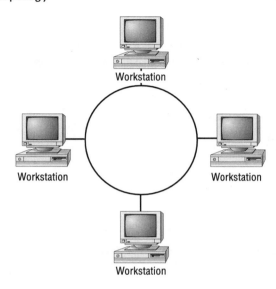

Figure 2.3   Star topology

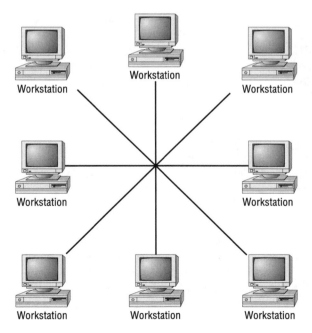

Mesh topology   In a mesh topology, each device requires an interface to every other device. As you can see in Figure 2.4, that would not always be possible on a major network. Mesh topology is used in organizations where redundancy is important. It is usually configured in a hybrid configuration, where only the most important nodes are meshed together.

Figure 2.4   Mesh topology

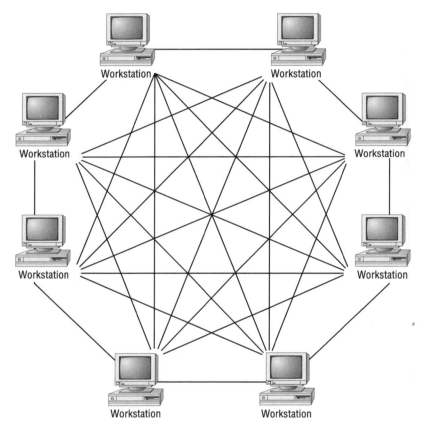

Cellular topology   Cellular topology is a combination of wireless point-to-point and multipoint strategies that divide a geographic area into cells. Each cell represents a portion of the total network area in which a specific connection operates. Figure 2.5 shows an example of a cellular topology.

Figure 2.5   Cellular topology

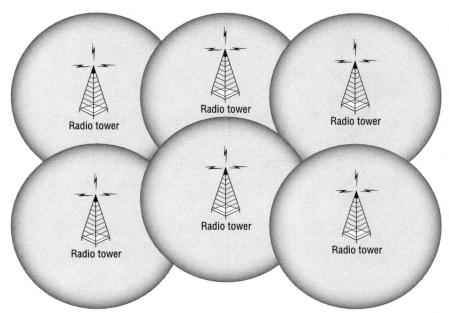

Digital Signaling   At the lowest forms, every decision a computer makes is based on a 1 or a 0. When two computers communicate, they also do it with 1s and 0s; these bits are transmitted by either electrical impulses or electronic waves, called *digital signaling*. In computer networks, digital signaling is accomplished by pulses of light or electric voltages. Each pulse creates a discrete state, either on or off. These states can then be measured and turned into a 1 or a 0. Figure 2.6 shows an example of a digital signal.

Figure 2.6   A digital signal

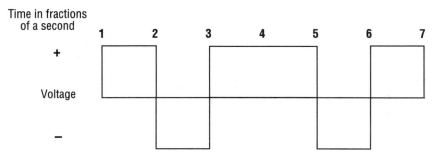

Analog Signaling   While a digital signal is a discrete state (on or off), an *analog signal* comes from reading the state of an electrical wave. In this case, it is not the presence of the signal that is measured, but the amplitude, the frequency, or the phase of the wave. Figure 2.7 shows an example of an analog signal.

Figure 2.7   An analog signal

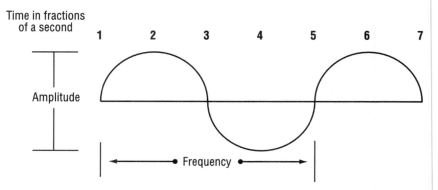

The amplitude of the wave would be the height or depth of the wave. The frequency of the wave would be how many waves occurred in each time period, and the phase of the wave would be which cycle (plus, minus, or neutral) the wave was in when sampled.

Bit Synchronization   Whether using analog or digital signaling, the two computers have to agree on when to sample the wire. Obviously, the sending and receiving computers need to be in complete synchronization for this process to occur properly. This is referred to as *bit synchronization*. There are two methods of synchronization, and these methods are similar to the upper layers.

   Asychronous   In asynchronous communication, bits are transmitted in intermittent signals. When no data is being transmitted, no signals are sent. Timing is managed by having the transmitting device send a single start bit onto the media immediately before transmitting data. When the receiving system senses the start bit, it immediately starts its internal clock. This will continue until a stop bit is sent.

   Synchronous   Synchronous bit streams use some form of embedded timing signal in the communication. This signal may take the form of a guaranteed state change (plus to minus or minus to plus) at a specific time, or there may be a separate clock signal.

Department of Defense Model

The seven layers of the OSI model provide a model for the discussion of protocols and what each layer accomplishes, but there really isn't any protocol written exactly to the OSI model. As with all good models, similar processes may be available, and whenever you discuss communication in the TCP/IP protocol suite, it is common to switch models. The TCP/IP protocol suite is actually mapped to the four layers of the Department of Defense (DoD) model. To keep things relatively simple, I explained the seven layers of the OSI model to compare how it works with the DoD model. The seven layers seem to break down the communication channel in more reasonably sized bites! Figure 2.8 shows you how the two models compare.

Figure 2.8   DoD and OSI models

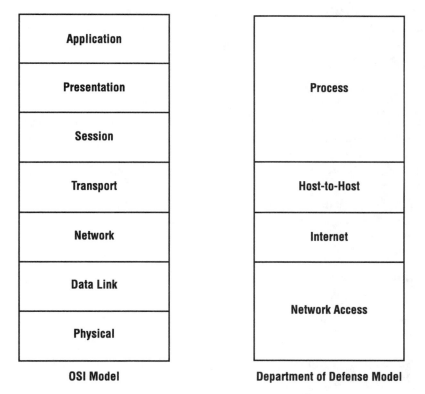

As you can see, the Network Access layer maps out to the Physical and Data Link layers of the OSI model. This layer handles accessing the media, framing, and communicating. The Internet layer is on par with the Network layer of the OSI model. This is where routing occurs and where you will see the discussion of the routing protocols. The Host-to-Host layer handles end-to-end flow control. It is at the Host-to-Host layer that name and address resolution occurs as well as some high-level connection and transaction addressing. The Host-to-Host layer also does the development of packet segments.

Finally, you have the Process layer. The Process layer fulfills all the functions of the Session, Presentation, and Application layers of the OSI model.

The TCP/IP suite is usually mapped out to the DoD model. It is time to dig into the suite and see what it is actually made of.

TCP/IP Protocol Architecture

When TCP/IP first started, it was most commonly associated with the Unix operating system. Although Unix and IP have been developed separately, they have been linked since the days of 4.2BSD Unix with the bundling of the TCP/IP protocols with the operating system.

TCP/IP protocols began to achieve general acceptance with the release of Microsoft's Windows 95. Prior to the release of Windows 95, the job of configuring TCP/IP on a machine running DOS was not a project for the faint of heart. TCP/IP is now available for most widely used operating systems. Native TCP/IP support is provided in NetWare version 5, OS/2, OS/400, and Windows 95/98/NT as well as most Unix variants. Table 2.1 shows how the TCP/IP protocol suite maps out to the DoD model.

Table 2.1   TCP/IP and the DoD Model

Process Layer	Telnet	FTP	Gopher	SMTP	HTTP	BGP	POP	Finger
Host-to-Host Layer	TCP			UDP		OSPF		
Internet Layer	IP			ICMP				
Network Access Layer	Ethernet		Token Ring	FDDI		X.25		Frame Relay
	SMDS		ISDN	ATM		SLIP		PPP

Network Access Layer Protocols

TCP/IP protocols have been designed to operate over most local- or wide-area network topologies and infrastructure. Although each network operating system is configured differently, IP messages can be transported over all of the technologies shown in Table 2.1 as well as numerous others.

Two of the underlying interface protocols are particularly relevant to TCP/IP. The Serial Line Internet Protocol (SLIP) and Point-to-Point Protocol (PPP), respectively, may be used to provide Data Link layer protocol services where no other underlying data-link protocol may be in use, such as in leased-line or especially in dial-up environments. Most commercial TCP/IP software packages for PC operating systems include these two protocols. With SLIP or PPP, a remote computer can dial in directly to a host server, using a dial-up medium, such as Remote Access Service (RAS), and connect to the Internet using IP rather than be limited to just an asynchronous connection.

SLIP was the earliest implementation of the dial-up protocols. It was soon replaced by PPP, which also provides support for simultaneous multiple protocols over a single connection and has enhanced security mechanisms, such as CHAP and PAP, data compression, and a dynamic bandwidth allocation for occasions when you might be running over ISDN.

Internet Layer Protocols

Here is where we start getting into the meat of the TCP/IP stack. The Internet Protocol (IP) was defined in RFC791. It was written to provide services that are roughly equivalent to the OSI Network layer, making it a very routable protocol.

The Internet Protocol (IP)

IP provides a *datagram* (connectionless) *transport service* across the network. This service is sometimes referred to as *unreliable* because the network does not guarantee delivery nor notify the source host system about packets lost due to errors or network congestion.

> **NOTE**   As we talk about datagrams and packets flying over the wire, there are four terms whose usage might be misunderstood. *Connectionless* and *unreliable*, *connection-oriented* and *reliable*. In regards to connectionless and unreliable protocols, think of what happens when you use the mail service to mail a letter. You take the letter down to the post office and drop it in a box. Once it hits the box, there is no way to track the letter until it gets to its destination. The operation is connectionless. (You aren't having regular conversations with the receiver, and the receiver is not going to notify you when the letter arrives.) It is unreliable because there are no guarantees. The postal service will make its best effort to get the letter there, and it usually arrives safely 99 percent of the time, but there are rare occasions when it doesn't work. A connection-oriented and reliable protocol would be when you send a letter by a commercial delivery service, such as Airborne Express or Federal Express. In this case, you can trace your packet from the time it was picked up until the time it was delivered.

IP's messages (and the messages of other protocols that operate at the Network layer) are contained in things called *datagrams*. A datagram can contain a complete message or one fragment of a message. The datagram may be up to 65,535 bytes (octets) in length. IP does not provide a mechanism for flow control.

> **TIP**   When discussing datagram movement, *flow control* becomes important. Flow control is the act of coordinating how fast one machine can send information to another machine. Something has to control the speed of the movement of messages, otherwise a Pentium III computer would simply overwhelm an XT with information that it couldn't process fast enough to complete the communication.

The basic IP packet header format is shown in Figure 2.9.

The format of the diagram is consistent with the definition found in the RFC. Each row represents a single 32-bit word; note that an IP header will be at least five words (20 bytes) in length. The fields contained in the header and their functions are

> **Version**   This identifier specifies the IP version of the packet. The current version of IP is version 4, so this field will usually contain the binary value 0100. IPv6 header information would contain a 0110. Other version numbers of IP have also been assigned.

> **Internet Header Length (IHL)**   This identifier indicates the length of the header in 4-octet or 32-bit words. A minimum-length header is 20 octets, so this field always has a value of at least 5 (0101).

Figure 2.9   IP packet (datagram) header format

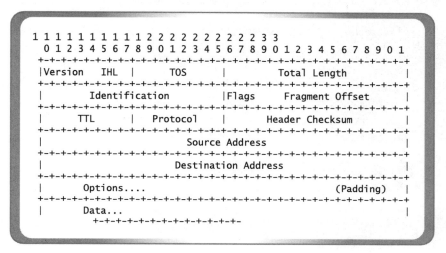

Type of Service (TOS)   This identifier allows an originating host to request different classes of service for packets it transmits. TOS is usually not used in IPv4. The TOS field can be used by the sending host in response to a service request across the Transport layer/Internet layer service interface. It can specify a service priority (0–7), or it can request that the route be optimized for cost, delay, throughput, or reliability.

Total Length   This identifier indicates the length (in bytes or octets) of the entire packet, including header and data. Given the size of this field, the maximum size of an IP packet is 64KB, or 65,535 bytes. In practice, packet sizes are limited to the maximum transmission unit (MTU) or the largest size a particular transport medium can carry. For example, the largest size packet that can be on a Token Ring network is 4,202 bytes, and on an Ethernet 802.3 network the largest size is 1,518 bytes.

Identification   Used when a packet or a message is fragmented into smaller pieces while crossing the Internet, this identifier is assigned by the transmitting host so that different fragments arriving at the destination can be put back together in the right order.

Flags   These identifiers are also used for the fragmentation and reassembly of the packet. The first bit is called the *More Fragments* (MF) bit and is used to indicate the last fragment of a packet. Once this flag has been set, the receiver knows the last fragment has arrived, and the packets can be reassembled. The second bit is the *Don't Fragment* (DF) bit, which suppresses fragmentation. The third bit is unused, so you can always expect to see it set to 0.

Fragment Offset This identifier indicates the position of this fragment in the original packet. In the first packet of a fragment stream, the offset is 0; in subsequent fragments, this field indicates the offset in increments of 8 bytes.

Time-to-Live (TTL) This identifier shows a value from 0 to 255, indicating the number of hops that a packet is allowed to take before being discarded within the network. Every router that sees this packet will decrement the TTL value by one. If the TTL reaches 0, the router determines that it is handling a lost packet and discards it.

Protocol This identifier indicates the higher layer protocol contents of the data carried in the packet; options include ICMP (1), TCP (6), UDP (17), or OSPF (89). A complete list of IP protocol numbers can be found at the IANA's list of protocol numbers.

Header Checksum This identifier carries information to ensure that the received IP header is error free. Remember that IP provides an unreliable service, so this field checks only the header rather than the entire packet.

Source Address This identifier gives the IP address of the host sending the packet.

Destination Address This identifier gives the IP address of the host intended to receive the packet.

Options A set of options may be applied to any given packet, such as sender-specified source routing or security indication. The option list may use up to 40 bytes (10 words) and will be padded to a word boundary. IP options are taken from the IANA's list of IP option numbers.

NOTE Sending and destination IP addresses are always 32-bits in length. When an IP address is assigned to a host it is typically written as a sequence of four numbers, representing the decimal value of each of the address bytes. Because the values are separated by periods, the notation is referred to as dotted decimal. A sample IP address is 203.15.210.17. A complete explanation of IP addresses is found in Chapter 3.

The Domain Name System (DNS)

Yes, the Domain Name System is an application-level protocol. Yes, we are discussing Internet layer protocols. Yes, this discussion is out of place. The reason I am placing this section here is to lay the groundwork for the Address Resolution Protocol (ARP). If you don't understand DNS, ARP will be really mysterious.

You can attach to any host of the Internet in two ways. The first way, and the most efficient, is to simply type in the IP address of the host you want to reach. Although this may be the most efficient solution, it is definitely not the most practical. The other method, and the most practical, is to access the host by typing in the host's name; for example, www.sybex.com. Most IP hosts will have both a numeric IP address and a name. This option is convenient for most people, but it causes a lot more work for the sending system because the name must be resolved back to a numeric address for routing purposes. IP does not understand names; it only understands IP numerical addresses.

Previously in this chapter, we talked a little about the domain-naming structure of the Internet. In the early days of the ARPAnet, every host on the network maintained a file, called HOSTS.TXT, that contained a list of all hosts on the network. This file included the IP address of the host, the host name, and any and all alias names. At that time, when the ARPAnet was a small and intimate group, this was all that was needed for name-to-address resolution. When the network growth rate was slow, this worked fine, but as things picked up, it was simply not an adequate solution.

> **NOTE** The HOSTS.TXT files are still found on Unix systems, although the files are usually used to reconcile names of hosts on the local network to cut down on local DNS traffic. On Microsoft Windows 95/98 systems, there is a file called HOSTS.SAM that can be found in the c:\windows folder. This is a sample HOSTS file that can be used to speed up name-to-address resolution of popular sites.

To keep up with the rapid rate that new names were being added to the Internet, the Domain Name System (DNS) was created. The DNS is a distributed database containing host name and IP address information for all domains on the Internet. A single authoritative name server exists for every domain (e.g., .com) that contains all DNS-related information about the domain. In addition, each domain also has at least one secondary name server that also contains a copy of this information. Thirteen Root servers around the globe maintain a list of all of these authoritative name servers.

Suppose that you are using your Internet browser and you decide to look for www.sybex.com. Your computer needs to search the Internet in an attempt to obtain an IP address based upon the URL www.sybex.com. In this case, your computer issues a DNS request to a local name server. The local name server may be able to respond to the request with information that is either configured or cached at the name server. If the local name server cannot respond, it becomes necessary for the local name server to forward the request to one of the Root servers. The Root server, then, will determine an appropriate name server to handle the request. The DNS request will then be forwarded to the domain's name server, in this case, the name server handling the .com domain.

Like all good databases, there has to be more than just the name and the address. After all, if your company has an Internet presence, it probably has several servers hooked to the Internet that perform various functions. These functions may be things like a Web server, an Internet connection for your e-mail system, or a server dedicated to remote access of files using the File Transfer Protocol (FTP). Name servers have to contain information on several different types of servers, such as

A-record   An address record that maps a host name to an IP address.

PTR-record   A pointer record that maps an IP address to a host name.

NS-record   A name server record that lists the authoritative name server(s) for a given domain.

MX-record   A mail-exchanger record that lists the mail servers for a given domain. As an example, consider the following e-mail address: ggovanus@ psconsulting.com. The psconsulting.com portion of the address is a domain name, not a host name, and mail has to be sent to a specific host. The MX-records in the psconsulting.com name database specifies that the host *mail.psconsulting* .com is the mail server for this domain.

Assuming you pressed enter at the end of your request for the information on www.sybex .com, your system would send the request to a local name server, the name server would continue forwarding the information up the ladder until an A-Record would point you to a specific IP address. Once you have that IP address, we can get back to our discussion of Internet layer protocols and look at the Address Resolution Protocol (ARP).

ARP and Address Resolution

Many IP implementations run on hosts commonly interconnected by Ethernet local-area networks (LAN). Every transmission on the LAN contains the local network or the Medium Access Control (MAC) layer address of the source and destination nodes. MAC addresses are 48-bits in length and are nonhierarchical, so routing cannot be performed using the MAC address. MAC addresses are never the same as IP addresses.

NOTE   Just in case you missed it, MAC addresses are covered in the discussion of the Data Link layer of the seven layers of the OSI model, earlier in this chapter.

When you need to send a datagram to another computer on the same network, your system has to know both the IP and MAC addresses of the intended receiver. Without this information, the destination IP address cannot be placed in the IP packet, and the destination MAC address cannot be placed in the LAN MAC protocol frame. It would be like sending a letter without addressing the envelope and hoping that the postal service can somehow magically direct your missive to the right place. The MAC and IP addresses are essential.

Unfortunately, the IP process may not know the MAC address of the intended receiver. This is where the Address Resolution Protocol (ARP) comes into play. ARP is described in RFC826, and it provides a mechanism so that a host can learn a receiver's MAC address when knowing only the IP address.

The process is simple. When we are dealing with two computers on the same network, your computer or host sends an ARP Request packet in a frame containing the MAC broadcast address (MAC destination address of all 1s); the ARP request advertises the destination IP address and asks for the associated MAC address. Every station on the LAN reads the broadcast but only the host that recognizes its own IP address will send an ARP Response with its own MAC address. ARP messages are carried directly in the LAN frame, and ARP is an independent protocol from IP. The IANA maintains a list of all ARP parameters. In addition, other address resolution procedures have also been defined, including

> **Reverse ARP (RARP)**   This procedure allows a diskless processor to determine its IP address based on knowing its own MAC address.

> **Inverse ARP (InARP)**   This procedure provides a mapping between an IP address and a frame relay virtual-circuit identifier.

> **ATMARP and ATMInARP**   These procedures provide a mapping between an IP address and ATM virtual path/channel identifiers.

> **LAN Emulation ARP (LEARP)**   This procedure maps a recipient's ATM address to its LAN Emulation (LE) address. The LE address takes the form of a MAC address.

IP Routing Protocols

As an OSI Network layer protocol, IP has the responsibility to route packets. It performs this function by looking up a packet's destination IP network identifier in a routing table and forwarding the packet based on the information in the table. But it is routing protocols, and not IP, that populate the routing tables with routing information. There are three routing protocols commonly associated with IP and the Internet: Routing Information Protocol (RIP), Open Shortest Path First (OSPF), and Border Gateway Protocol

(BGP). OSPF and RIP are primarily used to provide routing within a particular domain, such as within a corporate network or within an ISP's network. Because the routing is inside the domain, these protocols are generically referred to as interior gateway protocols. The Border Gateway Protocol version 4 (BGP-4) is an exterior gateway protocol because it is used to provide routing information between Internet routing domains.

TIP   For more information on routing, see Chapter 8.

Internet Control Message Protocol (ICMP)—or the Tattletale Protocol

The Internet Control Message Protocol (ICMP) is the piece of the TCP/IP protocol suite that is responsible for notifying the sender of IP datagrams about problems. This protocol is really important when you remember that IP runs in a connectionless environment.

As you have browsed the Internet or otherwise worked with TCP/IP, you have probably bumped into ICMP without even knowing it. The ICMP message types include

Destination Unreachable   This message indicates that a packet cannot be delivered because the destination host cannot be reached. The reason for the nondelivery may be that the host or network is unreachable or unknown, the protocol or port is unknown or unusable, fragmentation is required but not allowed, or the network or host is unreachable for this type of service.

Echo and Echo Reply   These two messages are used to check whether hosts are reachable on the network. One host sends an Echo message to the other, optionally containing some data, and the receiving host responds with an Echo Reply containing the same data. These messages are the basis for the commonly used ping command.

Parameter Problem   This message indicates that a router or host encountered a problem with some aspect of the packet's Header.

Redirect   This message is used by a host or router to let the sending host know that packets should be forwarded to another address. For security reasons, Redirect messages should usually be blocked at the firewall.

Source Quench   This message is sent by a router to the sending host to indicate that it is experiencing congestion, usually due to limited buffer space. When this occurs, the router will start discarding datagrams.

TTL Exceeded   This message indicates that a datagram has been discarded because the TTL field reached 0 or because the entire packet was not received before the fragmentation timer expired.

Timestamp and Timestamp Reply   These messages are like the Echo messages, but they place a timestamp in the message. This provides a way for systems to measure how long remote systems spend buffering and processing datagrams. It also provides a mechanism so that hosts can synchronize their clocks.

ICMP messages are carried in IP packets.

Host-to-Host Layer Protocols

The TCP/IP protocol suite comprises two protocols that correspond roughly to the OSI Host-to-Host and Session layers; these protocols are called the Transmission Control Protocol (the TCP in TCP/IP) and the User Datagram Protocol (UDP).

Transmission Control Protocol

TCP provides a virtual-circuit or connection-oriented communication service across the network. TCP includes rules for formatting messages, establishing and terminating virtual circuits, sequencing, flow control, and error correction. Most of the applications in the TCP/IP suite operate over the reliable transport service provided by TCP.

In TCP, the data unit is called a *segment*. The name came about because TCP does not recognize entire messages. It merely sends a block of bytes from the byte stream between sender and receiver. The fields of the different segments are shown in Figure 2.10.

Figure 2.10   TCP segment format

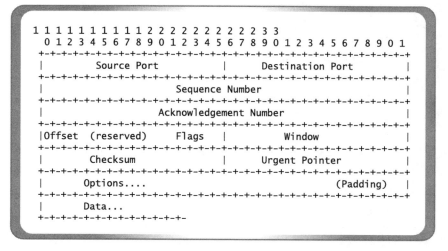

The functions of the different segments are as follows:

Source Port and Destination Port   These functions identify the source and destination ports for the end-to-end connection and higher-layer application.

Sequence Number   This function contains the sequence number of the segment's first data byte in the overall connection byte stream. Since the sequence number refers to a byte count rather than a segment count, sequence numbers in contiguous TCP segments are not numbered sequentially.

Acknowledgment Number   This function is used by the sender to acknowledge receipt of data. This field indicates the sequence number of the next byte expected from the receiver.

Data Offset   This function points to the first data byte in this segment; this field indicates the segment header length.

Control Flags   This set of flags control certain aspects of the TCP connection. The flags include

Urgent Pointer Field Significant (URG)   This flag indicates the current segment contains urgent (or high-priority) data and that the Urgent Pointer field value is valid.

Acknowledgment Field Significant (ACK)   This flag indicates the value contained in the Acknowledgment Number field is valid. This bit is usually set, except during the first message while a connection is being established.

Push Function (PSH)   This flag is used when the transmitting application wants to force TCP to immediately transmit the data that is currently buffered without waiting for the buffer to fill; useful for transmitting small units of data.

Reset Connection (RST)   This flag immediately terminates the end-to-end TCP connection.

Synchronize Sequence Numbers (SYN)   This flag is set in the initial segments used to establish a connection, indicating that the segments carry the initial sequence number.

Finish (FIN)   This flag is set to request normal termination of the TCP connection in the direction the segment is traveling; completely closing the connection requires one FIN segment in each direction.

Window   This function is used for flow control, and it contains the value of the receive window size, which is the number of transmitted bytes that the sender of the segment is willing to accept from the receiver.

Checksum   This function provides basic error detection for the segment.

Urgent Pointer   Urgent data is information that has been marked as high-priority by a higher-layer application; this data, in turn, usually bypasses normal TCP buffering and is placed in a segment between the header and "normal" data. The Urgent Pointer, valid when the URG flag is set, indicates the position of the first octet of nonexpedited data in the segment.

Options: This function is used at connection establishment to negotiate a variety of options. This includes options such as the Maximum Segment Size (MSS). MSS is the most commonly used option. If it is not set, the MSS defaults to a size of 536.

The Complete IP Address

What actually is the port address used for? Assume that the TCP/IP address is like a business phone number. When a person calls that number, they are at the beginning of the maze you call your company. In order for that person to get any worthwhile information, they need to be directed to a specific person, at a given extension. The same is true with applications. When an application makes a request for a specific service from a specific IP address, it must get to the right service. It does this by not only going to the correct IP address but looking for the service at the right port address. The higher-layer TCP/IP applications are referred to by what is called a *port identifier* in a TCP or UDP message. The port identifier and IP address together form a *socket,* and the end-to-end communication between two hosts is uniquely identified on the Internet by the 4-part address that includes the source port, the source address, the destination port, and the destination address. Well-known default port numbers include

Port #	Protocol	Application	Purpose
20	TCP	FTP	Remote transfer of data
21	TCP	FTP	Control
23	TCP	Telnet	Remote control of a host
25	TCP	SMTP	Mail Transfer
43	TCP	whois	Identification
53	TCP/UDP	DNS	Name resolution
70	TCP	Gopher	Access to remote hosts
79	TCP	finger	Information about a user
80	TCP	HTTP	Web access

The Complete IP Address *(continued)*			
110	TCP	POPv3	E-mail
161	UDP	SNMP	Network Management
162	UDP	SNMP trap	Network Management
520	UDP	RIP	Routing

TIP   For more information on TCP/IP ports, refer to RFC 1700 at the
www.netsolutions.com.

TIP   The IANA maintains a list of all TCP option numbers.

User Datagram Protocol (UDP)

UDP provides an end-to-end datagram or connectionless service. Some applications, such as those that involve a simple query and response, are better suited to the datagram service of UDP because there is no time lost to virtual-circuit establishment and termination. UDP's primary function is to add a port number to the IP address to provide a socket for the application. The UDP datagram format is shown in Figure 2.11.

Figure 2.11   UDP datagram format

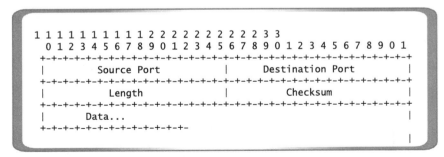

The fields of a UDP datagram are

Source Port   This field identifies the UDP port at the source side of the connection. The use of this field is optional in UDP and may be set to 0.

Destination Port   This field identifies the destination port of the end-to-end connection.

Length   This field indicates the total length of the UDP datagram.

Checksum   This field provides basic error detection for the datagram.

UDP does offer some advantages over TCP. As you can see from the figure, there is a lot less to a UDP datagram than there is to a TCP datagram. That means less overhead. Because UDP is connectionless, it also means a more effective use of the bandwidth.

Process Layer Protocols

This is the richest layer of the protocol suite and probably the layer you are most familiar with. The TCP/IP Process layer protocols support the applications and utilities that make up the Internet. Table 2.2 describes some of the more commonly used protocols. The discussion may not be in depth, because many of these are handled individually later in the book.

Table 2.2   Common Process Layer Protocols

Application	Purpose
Telnet	Telnet is short for Telecommunication Network. It is a virtual-terminal protocol allowing a user logged on to one TCP/IP host to access other hosts on the network. Telnet is routinely used for such tasks as remotely configuring routers or running applications on different hosts on the network.
File Transfer Protocol (FTP)	The File Transfer Protocol allows a user to transfer files between local and remote-host computers.
Archie	Archie is a utility that allows a user to search all registered anonymous FTP sites for files on a specified topic.
Gopher	Gopher is a tool that allows users to search through data repositories using a menu-driven, hierarchical interface, with links to other sites.
Simple Mail Transfer Protocol (SMTP)	The Simple Mail Transfer Protocol is the standard protocol for the exchange of electronic mail over the Internet. SMTP is used between e-mail servers on the Internet or to allow an e-mail client to send mail to a server.

Table 2.2   Common Process Layer Protocols *(continued)*

Application	Purpose
Hypertext Transfer Protocol (HTTP)	The HTTP is the basis for the exchange of information over the World Wide Web (WWW). Various versions of HTTP are in use over the Internet, with HTTP version 1 being the most current. WWW pages are written in the Hypertext Markup Language (HTML), which is an ASCII-based, platform-independent formatting language.
Finger	Finger is a tool that is used to determine the status of other hosts or users.
Post Office Protocol (POP)	The Post Office Protocol provides an interface between a user's mail client software and an e-mail server; POP is used to download mail from the mail server to the client and allows the user to manage their mailboxes. The current version is POP3.
Domain Name Service (DNS)	The Domain Name System defines the structure of Internet names and their association with IP addresses. It also provides an association of mail and name servers with registered domains.
Simple Network Management Protocol (SNMP)	The Simple Network Management Protocol defines procedures and management information databases for managing TCP/IP-based network devices. SNMP is widely used in local and wide-area network environments. SNMP version 2 (SNMPv2, RFC 1441) adds security mechanisms that are missing in basic SNMP, but it is also very complex; widespread use of SNMPv2 has yet to be seen.
The Packet Internet Groper (Ping)	Ping is a utility that allows a user at one system to determine the status of other hosts and the time it takes to get a message to that host. Ping uses ICMP Echo messages.
Traceroute	Traceroute is a tool that displays the route that packets will take when traveling to a remote host.
Whois/NICNAME	Whois and NICNAME are utilities that search databases for information about Internet domains and domain contact information.

3

Addressing Issues with TCP/IP

One of the most challenging aspects of operating a TCP/IP network is managing IP addresses and keeping track of what goes where. This is especially true for the new TCP/IP administrator or for someone who has just been given the task of handling the IP addresses. This chapter will be devoted to trying to make that task a little easier and to give you some hints and tips on some IP calculation tools that are available on the Internet.

IP Addressing Basics

Talk about misunderstood! Talk about confusing! Yep, IP addressing can be all of that. Even the most experienced people sometimes suffer from brain-overload when it comes to figuring out which IP addresses belong on which subnet. Because I don't want to make too many assumptions about where you are in the "curve," this section will be a brief review of IP addressing issues and how the process of getting a packet from one location to another actually works.

NOTE   If you have IP addressing down cold, you may want to just skip over this chapter and move on to Chapter 4, in which I'll discuss DHCP.

IP Terminology

It seems like every part of the computer industry has its own set of acronyms, terms, and definitions. Protocols are the same way. Before we can get started with a discussion of IP addressing, we need to make sure we are all talking about the same things.

Anytime we are interested in getting information from one host to another, three things come into play: the name of the host, the address of the host, and the route to the host. The name of the host is just the unique identifier that has been placed on that object. It is location independent, meaning that even if the address changes, the name will remain the same. Radia Perlman, in the book *Interconnections—Bridges and Routers* (Addison Wesley, 1994), likens the name to a social security number. Your social security number will stay the same, even if you move all over the country.

The address of a host may change, if the host changes location. An example of this would be your postal address. While your social security number will stay the same, your postal address changes each and every time you move.

The route is dependent on the location of both the source and the destination hosts. If two sources want to get to the same destination, chances are they may take different routes. If the destination changes location, the routes will most definitely change. Keeping with the analogy of a person on the move, when you move to a different home, the directions that you have given all of your friends to get to your house are now worthless. The route has changed.

You probably already know that an IP address is a 32-bit address that is usually described as 4 octets in length. Just to be sure, let's break it down:

Bit (Binary Digit)   The smallest unit of data on a computer. A bit has two possible states, usually referred to as a 1 or a 0.

Byte   Usually, a unit of data that is 8 bits in length. There have been some computer systems that have used 18-bit bytes and even 6-bit bytes. For the sake of this book, a byte will be 8 bits in length.

Octet   A unit of data that is always 8 bits in length. It takes four octets to make up an IP address.

All ones: (all 1s)   A condition where are all the bits in an octet are set to 1. This results in the octet having a value of 255.

All zeros (All 0s)   A condition where all the bits in an octet are set to zero.

Least significant   This can also be described as low order. Although the terms are impressive, they mean those bits starting from the right. For example, if we referenced the four least significant bits, it would be the first four bits from the right-hand side of the octet.

Most significant   This can also be described as high order. Although the terms are impressive, they mean those bits starting from the left. For example, if we referenced the four most significant bits, it would be the first four bits from the left-hand side of the octet. It can also be used to describe the bit or data unit that, if you were to take it away or change the value, would have the most impact on the equation.

Host   A host is defined as anything that can have an IP address. It could be a printer, a computer, a print server, a file server, one network card in a router, or anything that can have an IP address is a host. In addition, some hosts are referred to as multihomed. This means that a particular host may have multiple IP addresses associated with it.

Network   The network portion of the IP address designates which network segment a particular host resides on. Each IP address is made up of a network segment and a host segment.

Binary vs. Decimal

As you know, computers are digital beasts. They are discrete in their design, meaning there are no gray areas. At the computer's most basic level, there are only two states, on or off. These states are trigged by 1s and 0s.

An IP address is made up of four octets of these 1s and 0s. While you may see the IP address of 192.2.6.10, that is not what your computer sees. Your computer takes these decimal numbers and breaks them down into the binary equivalents.

So, as mentioned above, an octet is really a grouping of eight 1s and 0s. In binary, the placeholders have different values than you may be used to. For example, in every day decimal life, we all know what 100 signifies. You can visualize 100 objects. In binary though, 100 is really 4. Here is the way the conversion table for 100 looks:

128	64	32	16	8	4	2	1
0	0	0	0	0	1	0	0

To see how the conversion table works, let's look at the number 183 and see what that would break down to in a binary conversion.

128	64	32	16	8	4	2	1
1	0	1	1	0	1	1	1

The number 183 can be broken down to 128+32+16+4+2+1. Looking at the chart you can see that the binary equivalent of 183 is 10110111.

IP Address Classes

As you begin to examine IP addresses, the first thing that you will need to identify is the class of the address. When the people who control the IP addressing scheme developed the class structure, they opted to create five classes (Classes A–E), though only three are used in commercial networks. To figure out which class of account your IP address falls into, break down the first octet into binary.

Class A

If the most significant bit is a 0, this is a Class A address. It doesn't matter what any of the other bits in the first octet are set to, with a 0 in the left-most column, you are working with a Class A address. Since the first octet determines address class, this means that any address where the first octet is less than 128 is a Class A address.

NOTE   The address 10.34.27.65 is a Class A TCP/IP address. If you were using the default subnet mask of 255.0.0.0 for a Class A address, the network portion of the address would be 10.0.0.0 and the host portion of the address would be 0.34.27.65.

It does not take a rocket scientist to figure out that there can only be 128 Class A network addresses in the universe (0 to 127), so these are pretty scarce. As a matter of fact, they were gone a long time ago. Each Class A network can have 16,777,216 (2^{24}) unique host identifiers.

NOTE   Not all Class A networks are created equal. With the advent and use of firewalls, Proxy servers, and Network Address Translation (NAT), checking the IP address of the host that you are using may not be indicative of the class of network you are really working on. These topics—firewalls, proxies, and NAT—will be discussed in later chapters.

Class B

If the first two most significant digits of your IP address are 10, then you have a Class B IP address. In addition, the Class B IP address reserves the first two octets of the address for the network portion, and the last two for the host portion. Class B network addresses range from 128.0.0.0 to 191.255.0.0.

NOTE   The address 130.34.27.65 is a Class B TCP/IP address. If you were using the default subnet mask of 255.255.0.0 for a Class B address, the network portion of the address would be 130.34.0.0 and the host portion of the address would be 0.0.27.65.

Doing the math, we find that Class B can have 16,384 networks and 65,536 (2^{16}) unique host identifiers per network.

Class C

A Class C IP address sets the three most significant digits of the first octet to 110. In addition, the Class C IP address uses the first three octets to signify the network address and the last octet to signify the unique host address. A Class C address will range from 192.0.0.0 to 223.255.255.255.

NOTE   The address 200.34.27.65 is a Class C TCP/IP address. If you were using the default subnet mask of 255.255.255.0 for a Class C address, the network portion of the address would be 200.34.27.0 and the host portion of the address would be 0.0.0.65.

There are 2,097,152 Class C networks and each Class C network can have up to 256 (2^8) host identifiers per network.

Class D

The last two classes of IP addresses may not have much of an impact on your life. The Class D address has the first four significant bits set to 1110. A Class D IP address ranges from 224.0.0.0 to 239.255.255.255 inclusive. You may have noticed something here. If all the bits in the last three octets are being used (remember 255 signifies all 1s) where the heck does the host address come from? Good observation! In a Class D network, all the addresses are reserved for multicast group usage. In a multicast operation, there is no host or network, there is only the group, and once you are a member of the multicast group, you get the same information as everyone else in the group.

Class E

A Class E address has the first four significant bits set to all 1's. In this case a Class E address will fall in the range of 240.0.0.0 to 255.255.255.255. Class E addresses are reserved for future use.

Network Addresses

Yeah, yeah, okay, so there are three types of general use addresses; what difference does that make? Actually, it makes a lot of difference. Because an IP address is broken down into two parts—a network address and a host address—you will have to figure out how many IP addresses you will need to run your network.

Life would be wonderful if all you had to do was simply bring up your inventory program, figure out how many computers, printers, concentrators, print servers, and routers you had that needed an IP address, and start from there. Unfortunately, it is not quite that simple. First, you need to figure out how many *network* addresses you need, and then you need to look at how many hosts you have on each network. That brings up the question, what constitutes a network?

So What Constitutes a Network?

In RFC950, "Internet Standard Subnetting Procedure," J. Mogul and J. Postel suggested that reasons for different networks were the following:

Different technologies   Many local-area networks (LANs) start out as one thing and end up as something completely different. For example, if you manage a LAN that has one primary file server with an ArcNet segment, a Token Ring Segment, and two Ethernet segments, each of these segments would constitute a different network.

Limits to size and distance   Most LAN technologies have some sort of electrical specifications that they must adhere too before the degradation of signal becomes so severe that it becomes impossible to use.

Traffic   Just like the freeway you use to drive to work, a LAN or WAN connection can have so much traffic that it is difficult to get a signal from Point A to Point B without a collision. In this case, it is often preferable to break up the segment by adding a router, a switch, or a bridge and creating another "network."

Point-to-point links   Suppose you have two regional offices, one in Chicago and the other in New York. In this case, the link between the sites, even though it would not be populated, would still be considered a network.

For examples of these procedures at work, let's look at some illustrations. Figure 3.1 shows the concept of multiple technologies.

Figure 3.1   Differing technologies

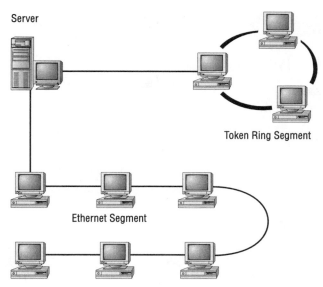

In this figure, you will notice that the single server is providing services to both an Ethernet segment and a Token Ring segment. In this case, the Ethernet segment would require a network number, and the Token Ring segment would require a network number. Figure 3.2 shows the concept of size and distance limitations.

Figure 3.2   Size and distance limitations

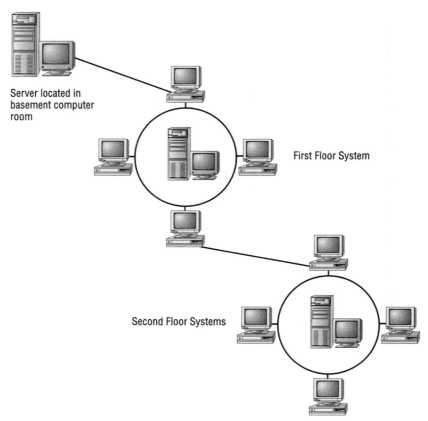

Server located in
basement computer
room

First Floor System

Second Floor Systems

In this example, the server is located in the basement computer room. A single network segment runs through all the computers on floor one and all the computers on floor two. When you add a new computer to the last office on floor two, you find that the service for the entire network goes from bad to worse. You have just exceeded the distance limitations. Luckily, though, this is one of those problems that is easy to solve. Figure 3.3 shows one of the ways around the problem. In this case, the administrator simply divided one network segment into two, effectively halving the distances involved, and network performance increased.

Figure 3.3   Solving the distance problem

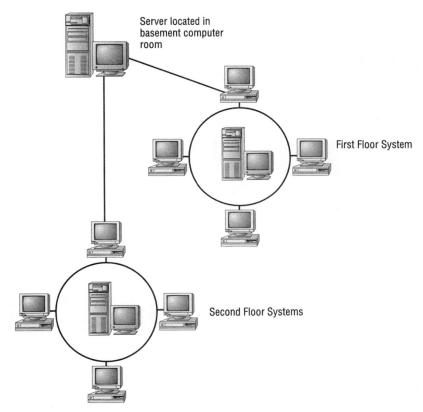

Server located in
basement computer
room

First Floor System

Second Floor Systems

The same kind of thing can be done with network congestion. Depending on who you talk to, some specifications say that you can have more than 1,000 nodes or hosts on a single Ethernet segment. Now, that may be true in theory. It may even be true in an environment where switches are used instead of regular old concentrators. In many of the locations where I have worked, if you get more than 75 to 100 workstations on a particular network segment, collisions are going to occur, and those collisions will dramatically affect network performance. A solution to this issue is to add another network card to the server, put in another concentrator, and divide up one network segment into two.

Finally, there is the case of the point-to-point connection, as shown in Figure 3.4.

Figure 3.4   Point-to-point links

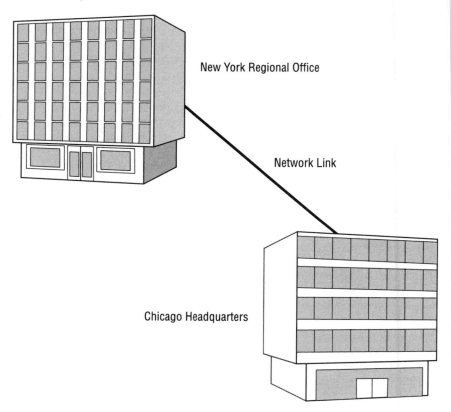

Here, we have two offices in two cities connected by a wide-area network link. This link will require its own network number.

Now the tough part comes into play: figuring out the types and numbers of addresses that you will need.

Figuring Out How Many Networks You Have

The question looks simple enough. Just exactly how many networks do I have? Depending on the network operating system that you are using and even the protocols that you have on the network, there may be several ways of telling how many networks you have.

The best way of determining the number of networks that you manage is to look at a network map and check out the documentation that you have on the network. You know, that really, really up-to-date map that shows where all the workstations are, where all the servers are, how many network cards each server has in it, and, if there are routers and bridges on your network, what they route and bridge. If you don't have a network map, you should probably skip ahead to Chapter 12 to find out more about documentation basics. In the meantime, Figure 3.5 shows a simple network map.

Figure 3.5   A simple network map

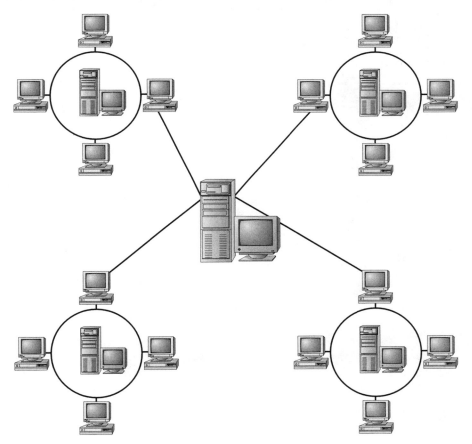

With this layout, you can see that there are four separate and distinct networks, one for each network card in the file server. The server may be a little stressed, but as far as the administrator having to answer a trick question, no problem.

Now let's take a look at something a little more complicated. In the case of Figure 3.6, you will see that things quickly get a lot more complicated.

Figure 3.6   A complicated network map

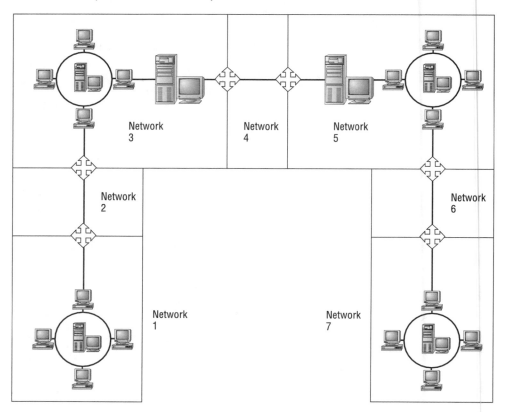

As you look at this diagram, work with me here and make several assumptions. Each router is using two interfaces. Each server (part of Network 3 and Network 5) has one interface. Also, remember this diagram is designed to show how to figure out how many networks you have, not necessarily how to properly design a network. It is pretty ugly, isn't it? Anyway, back to the demonstration.

Starting at the lower left-hand corner, Network 1 is sort of off in its own little world. It is, in fact, using the services of a server, but that server is not necessarily on the same network segment. The boundary for Network 1 runs right up to where it connects with the first router interface.

Network 2 links the two routers. It is a point-to-point connection that is not populated, but it still counts as a network. Network 3 picks up at one of the router interfaces on both sides of the network. Remember, we assumed that the server only had one interface card. That means the minibackbone is defined by the link between the two routers.

Network 4 is another point-to-point connection between routers. Network 5 looks like a mirror image of Network 3 and Network 6 mirrors Network 2. Finally, we end up with Network 7. When you look at your network map, if there is a change in technology or a change in the configuration of the backbone, you have another network.

Host Addressing

Documentation shows that you have seven networks. But what about hosts per network segment? In this case, it is back to the drawing board to figure it out. For the sake of simplicity, let's assume that you have varying numbers of hosts per network. The network with the most hosts is Network 5, which has 25 hosts on it. Each host on a network segment needs a unique IP address. That means that each network address must be able to handle at least 25 host addresses.

At this point, you can take a look at the break down of address classes. Because you only have a maximum of 30 hosts on a network, you fall well into the Class C range, so all you have to do is apply for seven Class C network addresses, and you will be ready to go. Does it seem a waste to not use at least 225 (255-30) addresses per network? After all, for just your company, you will be wasting at least 1,575 addresses. There has got to be a better way!

> **TIP** IP addresses are available from the InterNIC or from your local Internet service provider. To get the form to petition the InterNIC for a block of IP addresses, download `ftp://rs.internic.net/templates/internet-number-template.txt`, fill out the form, and send it back in. There are a few Class B addresses available, but you will have to jump through lots of hoops to prove you need a Class B. Class C addresses are available, and your ISP is usually the quickest way of getting a block. You only need an official IP address if your network is going to be hooked up to the Internet. If your network is completely internal, with no plans ever to hook into the outside world, grab your favorite Class A address and go, because no one will ever the know the difference.

There is a better way of more effectively using IP addresses, and it is called *subnetting*.

Subnetting

A Class C network address will allow you to have up to 255 hosts on a single network segment. You may have a network segment that has 255 hosts on it, but in reality, the chances are your network will be similar to the sample. You will probably have multiple network segments with a manageable number of hosts per segment. Subnetting lets you share the wealth. You can take a particular network address and break it down into multiple network addresses.

> **NOTE**   When we talk about subnetting and subnet masks, I am going to use examples based on a Class C address. This is because the numbers are smaller, and chances are the addresses you apply for today will be Class C.

You know that you have seven networks with a maximum number of 30 hosts on any network segment. The company is not in a major growth stage, and any growth that occurs will probably be in those areas that have fewer than 30 hosts. You call up your ISP, ask for some IP addresses, and explain the situation. The ISP calls back and says your new network IP addresses are 206.15.143.0. and 208.46.28.0. When you ask about the other six networks, the ISP simply says "subnet" and hangs up the phone.

Subnetting is the art of taking part of the host address and using it to provide more network addresses. This has another implication. Because having more network addresses is a good thing, we are lowering the number of host addresses per network, and we are making more efficient use of the addresses we have been assigned.

As discussed previously, all IP addresses are made up of two parts, a network portion and a host portion. A Class C network address uses the first three octets to designate network and the last octet to designate host. It can be shown this way, in which N is for network and H is for host:

NNNNNNNN.NNNNNNNN.NNNNNNNN.HHHHHHHH

To create a subnet mask, we simply change some of those Hs to Ns and use the resulting numbers for network addresses. The formula for determining how many Hs need to get switched to Ns is $2^x - 2 = Y$, in which x is the number of bits being used for the network and Y is the resulting number of networks. We also have to keep in mind the number of hosts on each network segment. To figure out the number of hosts a network can support, use the same formula, only this time the x is the number of bits remaining for a host and Y is the number of hosts.

To see how it works, let's see what happens when we borrow two bits from the host portion for the network. The address will look like this:

NNNNNNNN.NNNNNNNN.NNNNNNNN.NNHHHHHH

This means we will have 2^2-2, or 2, potential networks with 2^6-2, or 62, hosts on each network. That is not going to work real well, because even if we apply the same subnet mask to both addresses we have been given, we do not have enough network addresses; we need at least seven.

Taking another bit makes our address look like this:

NNNNNNNN.NNNNNNNN.NNNNNNNN.NNNHHHHH

Using the formula again, we have $2^3-2 = 6$ for the number of networks and $2^5-2 = 30$ for the number of hosts. At this point, we are still short potential networks, but if we subnet down any farther, we will drop below the number of hosts we need. This means that we need to subnet both IP addresses, stealing three bits from the host portion for network bits. It will give us a total of 12 potential networks and 30 hosts per network.

Now we have to decide how to express this subnet mask to the world, and more importantly, so TCP/IP understands what you have done. By default, the subnet mask for a Class C address is 255.255.255.0, which means the first three octets are used for network addresses and the last octet is used for a host. We decided to use the first three bits of the last octet for the network and the last five bits for the host. Looking at our conversion chart again, we have to place 1s in the first three most significant bit positions, leaving 0s in those positions designated for the host.

128	64	32	16	8	4	2	1
1	1	1	0	0	0	0	0

If we add 128 + 64 + 32, the result is 224. In this case, our subnet mask is now 255.255.255.224.

All that is left to figure out is which networks get assigned which IP addresses and which host addresses work with which network addresses. Because we are using the first three bits for a subnet mask, we can configure those bits in the following eight ways (a binary count).

000
001
010
011
100
101
110
111

Right now, you are probably asking yourself why we show eight potential subnets, but the answer above says only six. In most cases, using all 1s or all 0s for an address is not allowed. Some operating systems and some routers cannot handle all 1s or all 0s in a subnet mask, so we will assume these are currently unusable.

That means in *usable* network numbers, we have

001

010

011

100

101

110

because these are the only valid configurations of these three bits. Let's bring our chart back, and see how this plays for the network numbers. In this chart, I am going to use an *H* to show it is part of the host address and not significant in this calculation

128	64	32	16	8	4	2	1	Equals
0	0	1	H	H	H	H	H	32
0	1	0	H	H	H	H	H	64
0	1	1	H	H	H	H	H	96
1	0	0	H	H	H	H	H	128
1	0	1	H	H	H	H	H	160
1	1	0	H	H	H	H	H	192

The addresses again were 206.15.143.0 and 208.46.28.0. Using the addresses from the ISP and the subnet mask information from the chart above, our potential network addresses are:

206.15.143.32	208.46.28.32
206.15.143.64	208.46.28.64
206.15.143.96	208.46.28.96
206.15.143.128	208.46.28.128
206.15.143.160	208.46.28.160
206.15.143.192	208.46.28.192

> **TIP**   Subnet masks are expressed in one of two ways. The subnet mask will
> look something like 255.240.0.0 for a Class A address, 255.255.240.0 for a
> Class B address, or 255.255.255.240 for a Class C address. To make notations
> easier, another method was devised using a "/n" method. In this case, a /24 indi-
> cates no subnet mask, /25 would equal a .128, /26 would equal .192, /27 would
> be the same as .224, /28 would provide the same results as a .240 mask, /29
> would be the same as .248, and /30 would give the same number of hosts and net-
> works as a subnet ending in .252. To put this another way, our network address
> of 206.15.143.32 with a subnet of 255.255.255.224 can also be expressed as
> 206.15.143.32 /27.

Now that we have the network addresses, we can assign them to a specific network and
begin to allocate host addresses. For the sake of simplicity, let's assign 206.15.143.32 to
Network 1. As a reference, Figure 3.7 shows another copy of the network map.

Figure 3.7   A network map

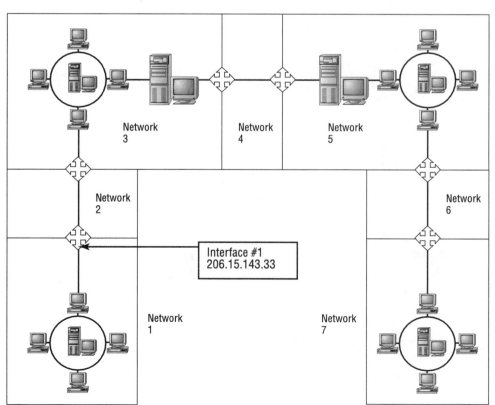

More by convention than anything else, the router interface fronting the network will usually get the first IP address of the set. In Figure 3.7, I have marked this with an arrow: Interface #1 and the appropriate IP address of 206.15.143.33. (The first calculated address defines the subnet ID, and the last address in the same subnet range is reserved for broadcasting. Neither of these addresses can be used for hosts. To arrive at the address, I know that the last octet is designated for the host, but the three most significant bits are taken up with the subnet mask. In this case, I am using the following chart for the network address:

128	64	32	16	8	4	2	1	Equals
0	0	1	H	H	H	H	H	32

To figure out the limits of the host addresses on the network, I have to shift my emphasis from the network portion to the host portion. We already know that this network is going to start with 32, so we can change our emphasis by marking the first three significant bits with an N and concentrating on the last five, like this:

128	64	32	16	8	4	2	1	Equals
N	N	N	0	0	0	0	1	32 + 1 = 33
N	N	N	1	1	1	1	0	32 + 30 = 62

Again, because we can't have all 0s or all 1s in our host address, the range of addresses will go from 33 to 62. Our first block of IP addresses is 206.15.143.33 to 206.15.143.62. The rest of the host address ranges for the first assigned network address will be:

206.15.143.65 to 206.15.143.94

206.15.143.97 to 206.15.143.126

206.15.143.129 to 206.15.143.158

206.15.143.161 to 206.15.143.190

206.15.143.193 to 206.15.143.222

I will let you figure out the host addresses for the second address as practice.

NOTE This same procedure can be done for Class A and Class B addresses. Because the number of bits available for subnetting is large, the number of networks is exceptionally large and difficult to demonstrate in a format like this!

Is It Worth It?

You may be a TCP/IP power user, able to convert binary to digital and back again in your head, with the ability to figure out host ranges without any help. But that is not always the case. Some of the people you would most expect to be able to handle this procedure, can't.

There have been cases of Internet service providers (ISPs) who have provided clients with invalid IP addresses. On a very simple network configuration of under 10 work-stations, I called the ISP and asked for a block of IP addresses. The information I received back was rather surprising: I was told the Class C IP address assigned to our network was XXX.XXX.XXX.0. I thought that was an interesting assignment, and it became more interesting when I asked for the subnet mask, and the response was a noncommittal, confused "huh?" Needless to say, what should have been a simple configuration turned into a long and arduous task as the person in charge of ISP configurations learned all about subnetting the hard way!

Classless Interdomain Routing (CIDR) or Supernetting

Classless Interdomain Routing (CIDR) is more commonly known as *supernetting,* and it can be used to consolidate several Class C network addresses into one logical network address. CIDR was defined in RFC1518/1519, and some special circumstances are required to use supernetting. The IP network addresses that are to be combined must share the same high-order bits, and the subnet mask is "shortened" to take bits away from the network portion of the address and add them to the host portion.

Let's look at an example of how this works. The Class C network addresses 199.199.5.0, 199.199.6.0, and 199.199.7.0 can be combined by using a subnet mask of 255.255.252.0 for each:

```
199.199.5.0   (11000111.11000111.00000101.00000000)
199.199.6.0   (11000111.11000111.00000110.00000000)
199.199.7.0   (11000111.11000111.00000111.00000000)
MASK 255.255.252.0 (11111111.11111111.11111100.00000000)
```

When a router makes a routing decision, only the bits covered by the subnet mask are used, thus making these addresses appear to be part of the same network for routing purposes. Any routers in the network must support CIDR. An advanced routing protocol, such as OSPF, supports CIDR; RIP does not.

How Does This Stuff Work?

Now that you know that each host on a network that is going to be using TCP/IP needs a unique host address assigned to the proper network, let's look at *why* this is necessary. This is not an exercise in bookkeeping, although it can be that. It is necessary for successful communication between two IP hosts.

When you install and configure the TCP/IP protocol stack to work on a computer, you assign that computer a valid IP address. You also define a subnet mask, provide the address of the gateway (or router) out of the network, and also provide two or more addresses to DNS servers somewhere out on the Internet. This is at a minimum! Now the "source" computer, the one you are sitting at, is ready to rock and roll. To test it, you decide to take a look at your favorite Web site, www.that's-a-Web-site.com. When you press enter, you are kicking off an involved process that results in seeing the home page (hopefully) of www.that's-a-Web-site.com.

Assuming you don't have WINS and LMHOSTS configured (just to keep this as simple as possible), the first thing your system will do is "parse" or read the HOSTS file to see if that's-a-Web-site.com is listed. If it's not, your system knows it has to access the DNS servers provided in the configuration information. The protocol creates a packet with a source address (your computer's address) and then tries to find the DNS server. It gets the information from it's configuration of what IP address the DNS server is located at. Your computer then compares the network portion of its address to the network portion of the destination computer's address. This is done through a process of boolean logic called *ANDing*. If the network portion of the addresses is the same, your computer knows it has a local address on its hands. If the network portion is not the same, then your computer recognizes that this is a remote address. It is not up to your computer to keep track of where every remote address in the world is located, and who are you anyway to ask it to do such a thing? At this point, your computer will show you who is boss by passing off the whole mess to the defined gateway or router. The packet that is sent to the router still has the source address of your computer and a destination address somewhere out there. The router will take the information and begin to trace the best way to get to the destination address.

The important thing in this example is that if the IP address does not match the network the host is really on, the ANDing process won't know what is local and what is remote, and all the routers on the net probably won't be able to find you again. This means you can't talk to anyone, and people can't talk to you either.

Spend $100, Open Mouth, Insert Foot

I was working on setting up a Web server, and I had an officially approved IP address for this Web server. It looked like it was communicating with the outside world, because I could go to the server and ping outside my local network. I could even ping the server from my laptop, as long as I was on the same network. The problem showed when I tried to dial in to an ISP and ping my server from the outside. It wouldn't work.

Of course, I first blamed my ISP. I called him and asked him just what the heck was going on that he was blocking my network from Internet access. He proceeded to ask what exactly was in my iced tea, because he could see my Web page just fine. He even described it.

At this point, it was obviously a server-configuration problem on my part. I had screwed something up, so I called tech support for my Network Operating System (NOS) and asked them to check it out. They charged me $100, pinged my server, opened my Web page, and described it to me. Hmm…curiouser and curiouser. While I had them on the phone, I dialed in to my nationwide ISP (I travel a lot, so I have a local ISP and a nationwide ISP. Yes, it does become confusing!) and tried finding my server. No such luck. The NOS tech support person and I then ascertained that it must be something my nationwide ISP was doing to block my Web site.

I called the nationwide ISP tech support, explained the problem, they pinged my server and described my Web site. I was still not convinced. The tech support guy came back on the line and said it was my problem. He said if I blew away my static IP address that I used when I attached to the network, Windows would now know not to use the static gateway and only go with the DHCP information that was provided when I dialed in. Of course, this answer was absurd. There should be *no* connection between the static IP address I have for my network card and the DHCP address I get when I dial in. After I protested much too much, he told me to try it anyway and hung up. So I cleared out my static IP address. I went into winipcfg and cleared all IP addresses, I called my nationwide ISP while not attached to my network, and then I opened a browser, typed in the appropriate IP address, smuggly sat there, and said to myself, "See that doesn't…errr, ummmm, dang." It was a Windows problem.

The moral of the story is Windows 95 and Windows 98 get confused with multiple IP addresses. If you can't get to a local IP address when you are out of the office, make sure all the vestiges of your old IP address are long gone.

Network Address Translation

When I first started working with TCP/IP, a lot of talk was going around about how the available TCP/IP network and host addresses were being used up at an alarming rate. The fear was that sooner or later, the world would run out of IP addresses, and IP network communication as a whole would come to a grinding halt. Although discussions are still in the works about how to extend IP addressing, solutions were found in other methods, most commonly, Proxy servers, firewalls, and Network Address Translation (NAT). By using a combination of some or all of these tools, the network administrator is able to have his or her very own addressing scheme and to heck with the rest of the world. Here is how NAT works.

Look at Figure 3.8. In this case, we have a router connecting a network to the Internet. It has already been discussed that as soon as you hook your network to the Internet, you have to come up with individual host addresses and registered IP addresses with a subnet mask, and you have to make sure that everything is absolutely perfect, otherwise bad things will happen.

Figure 3.8   A network connecting to the Internet

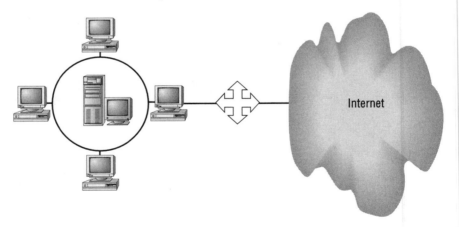

If you have the ability to use NAT, you may only need to have a few registered IP addresses, and all the rest, you use almost any addressing scheme you choose. In the example shown in Figure 3.8, you may need to have one registered IP address for the router. Depending on the type of NAT software you are using, everything else behind the router can have any IP address you want to assign. The only IP address that is visible to the Internet would be the IP address of the router; everything else would be invisible.

e more specific, we know that our gateway to the Internet needs to have a "real" ned IP address, and that IP address must remain the same. After all, because the hosts e company side of the router are going to be accessing that gateway, it would not : well if the IP address were constantly changing.

hy do all the hosts on the company side of the router need to have a valid IP address? answer is because all hosts on the Internet have to have a unique IP address. But what if you have met that criteria with a valid IP address on the gateway, why would all the hosts on the company side of the router need to have a registered IP address? The answer is they don't. With software such as Microsoft's Proxy Server or Novell's BorderManager or even the default software that comes with an Ascend router, you can enable NAT, and every computer on the company side of the gateway can have *any* valid IP address. The gateway "hides" the host IP address. When a packet comes to the gateway, it remembers where the communication came from, and then places its (the gateway's) valid IP address in the source address field of the packet. When the packet comes back, the gateway readdresses the packet for the appropriate "hidden" host and sends the information on its way. Truly another gee-whiz technology!

In Part 6, we will discuss some implications of using NAT with Proxy servers and firewalls as well as a method for security. Using NAT is definitely a way to ease the addressing problems on a busy network.

TIP Many other commercially available firewall and Proxy server implementations also include NAT as a standard feature. However, even though NAT is included, it is usually disabled by default.

DHCP with NAT

The description of NAT and its benefits may have caught your attention. It may also have raised some more questions. One of the most common questions asked about NAT is whether you can still use some of the other management features with NAT, things such as Dynamic Host Configuration Protocol (DHCP). The answer is yes.

By using some commonsense network design, it is possible to combine the features of NAT with any other combination of services needed for the TCP/IP network. For example, if you have need for an Internet presence and you want to host your own Web page that is available to everyone on the Internet, this host is going to need a static, registered IP address that everyone else in the world can see. However, if you also want to have an intranet presence where you are sharing information only among employees and everything they are going to be looking at resides behind the firewall, there is no reason why the host running the intranet Web server can't have a NAT-assigned address. Keep in mind that the intranet Web server host will need to have a static IP address, just so everyone else can find it!

DHCP also works just fine with NAT. With DHCP implementations, not only can you assign an IP address but you can also point to WINS servers, gateways, and DNS servers. All of this information can be passed down to hosts using DHCP, as long as the basics are adhered to. A DHCP broadcast request cannot pass a router (unless the router is configured with a helper address), so if a DHCP server resides on a different network segment, there must be a DHCP relay agent configured to pass the request from one segment to another.

Even though you are using NAT instead of a series of registered IP addresses, you still must make sure that each network has its own set of appropriate addresses. Admittedly, it does make it much easier when you can decide to use IP address 10.1.0.0 with a subnet mask of 255.255.255.0 for your addressing scheme. Now you have 65,534 networks with 255 hosts on each network, but you still have to get the right host addresses with the right network addresses to get communication to work smoothly.

Implementing NAT on routers allows the use of a *NAT pool*. A NAT pool contains multiple registered Internet addresses. NAT works exactly as previously described, but multiple gateways are used to enhance throughput.

IP Calculators

Calculating IP network and host addresses can be a time-consuming job. You have probably figured out that somewhere out there, someone has probably programmed all this information into a great little software package that is available for download as freeware, shareware, or even really cheapware. Here are some places you may want to look.

Microsoft's Calculator   If you are using any of Microsoft's 32-bit operating systems, e.g., Windows 9x or Windows NT, the calculator that is included with the OS will allow you to perform binary-to-decimal and decimal-to-binary conversions. Very rudimentary and you will still have to do a lot of the work by hand, but it is available, and the price is right.

IP Subnet Calculator, version 2   The Net3 Group from Minnesota offers a great freeware IP calculator. It will provide you with all sorts of information about your network and IP addresses. If you enter in the IP address of your network and the subnet mask, it will break down the host addresses that can be assigned to each network. It does

> **IP Calculators** *(continued)*
>
> decimal-to-hex conversions, so if your network operating system prefers FF.FF.FF.F8 to 255.255.255.248, you can handle it. It will also reverse-engineer an IP address. If you enter in the IP address and the subnet mask, it will tell you what network address the IP address should be assigned to. The IP Subnet Calculator is available from www.net3group.com.
>
> **Tech Help Computer Services**   At the THCS Web site, there is an online subnet calculator that does much the same stuff that the Net3 Group's calculator does. The advantage here is that it is run off the Internet, so there are not a lot of utilities crowding up your hard drive. The disadvantage is that it is run off the Internet, so it is not on the hard drive of your laptop when you need it. Check it out at www.thcs.com/netcalc.html.
>
> **Cheap Shareware**   I found several (two or three) decent IP calculators at www.winfiles.com. These were of the shareware variety, and prices ranged from $15–$30. If you know of any other good IP calculators, let me know. My e-mail address is ggovanus@psconsulting.com.

IPv6

You may have heard it referred to as IP version 6, IPv6, or even IPng (for IP next generation). IPv6 is the next iteration of IP addressing. Gone are IP addresses with 32-bit, dotted-decimal notation. Instead, things are going to get somewhat more complicated.

IPv6 is defined in RFC1883, "Internet Protocol, version 6 (IPv6) Specification," written in December 1995. In that document, the authors explained the reasons for a new addressing scheme. Those reasons fell into five logical boundaries.

Expanded addressing capabilities   The current IP addressing standard, IP version 4, uses a 32-bit address space. IPv6 is going to push that address space out to 128 bits. Currently, using IPv4, the possibility exists of 4.3×10^9 unique hosts on the Internet. With the explosive growth of the information superhighway, unique IP addresses are becoming an endangered species. With IPv6 and its 128-bit capabilities, there will be the possibility of 3.4×10^{38} unique host addresses.

Frame header format simplifications   The size of the header on each IP frame is going to increase. This increase is necessary because of the increase in size of the source and destination addresses. Because this increase was inevitable, the designers simplified the overall header to try and reduce the overhead.

More support of extensions and options The flexibility of the IP datagram will increase and further reduce overhead.

Flow-labeling capability Assignment characteristics will assist in managing data or traffic flow.

Authentication and privacy capabilities Extensions are added to help with authentication concerns.

It does all come down to one reason: there are simply not enough addresses left to go into the future, so there must be a new way to handle the problem.

You are going to see some strange types of IP addresses showing up when IPv6 begins to be implemented. The preferred form of address representation is one in which the octets of the address are represented in pairs and are shown in hexidecimal format, separated by colons: for example, 7B2A:98D2:0000:3456:FE23:4C18:78AC:1234 will be a valid IP address.

During the transition between IPv4 and IPv6, a mechanism has been put in place to allow the version 4 addresses to be absorbed into the v6 cousins. Although little has been written about a proposed time schedule for the implementation of version 6, it would seem to make sense that DNS specifications and DHCP would be updated in advance of the changeover.

Part 2

Using TCP/IP Protocols to Make Your Life Easier

- Using DHCP and BOOTP
- To relay or not to relay
- Using FTP for fun and profit
- Search and you may find using DNS

4

Using DHCP to Handle
IP Addressing

Assuming you now have the basic concepts of TCP/IP down, it is time to dive into the alphabet soup that makes up the protocol suite.

One of the protocols that is widely used today is the Dynamic Host Configuration Protocol (DHCP), which is used to pass out information to workstations—such as an IP address, the address of a gateway or Proxy server, and even the addresses of some domain name system servers on the Internet. It is one of those tools that when used right can simplify your life. When you misuse it or when it is not configured properly, it can cause some periods of stress that may not be desired.

Entering the world of DHCP is entering the world of servers, clients, relay agents, protocol numbers, port numbers, well-known services, BOOTP, ARP, RARP, and BOOTPFWD. See what I mean about alphabet soup? Before you can figure out how best to use it, you should figure out how it works. Before you can figure out how it works, you should know what all those pieces that make up DHCP do. So we will start there!

Pieces of the IP Communications Puzzle

Chapter 3 addressed some of the issues of IP addressing. To fully understand the complexity of what goes on when a packet or datagram is moved from one location to another, it is necessary to delve deeper into the nether world of addressing.

Each host that is attached to the network has an address that is several layers deep. In Chapter 3, we talked about manually assigning an IP address like 207.45.16.23 to a host. That address (with the appropriate subnet mask) is really made up of two different parts: the network address and the host address. If the host using the address of 207.45.16.23 had been assigned the default Class C subnet mask of 255.255.255.0, this host would be located on network 207.45.16.0 and have a host address of 0.0.0.23. That is the highest level of the address, the so-called Network layer address. Addressing goes deeper, into the heart of the network card. In each TCP/IP communication that occurs, information is addressed to a host on a particular network. Once the information gets to the right network number, the host ID needs to be resolved to an address that identifies a particular network card. This is called the *Media Access Control* or MAC address. Once the information arrives at the right network card, it has found the right host. At this point, a protocol is communicating with a specific host. But there is yet another layer. All that remains is to find the right process running on that host to handle the communication. This part of the address is called a *service* or *port address*. In order to fully understand how this works, it should be explored in a little more detail.

MAC Address

If you were to take the addressing down a level, the next address you would have to access is the MAC address. The MAC address is a hardware-level address that is assigned to a network card when it is manufactured. For example, a MAC address would look something like 00:20:78:15:0a:ed. In most instances, this number cannot be changed. Unless you are involved in some heavy-duty protocol analysis, you will probably never have to look at or find the MAC layer address.

Given these two addresses, we would have a host address of 207.46.16.23 that is assigned to a network card with the MAC address of 00:20:78:15:0a:ed. These two addresses can be used to route information from one host to another.

Protocol Numbers

Once the datagram or the packet arrives at our destination host, it must be delivered to the appropriate user or to the appropriate process. As the data moves up or down the layers of the DoD/OSI models, something must be there to make sure the appropriate protocol at the appropriate level gets the information. The distribution system must be able to transfer data from many applications into a few transport protocols and then move from the transport protocols into the Internet Protocol. Taking multiple sources of data and combining them into a single data stream is called *multiplexing*.

When the data arrives at its destination, it has to be taken apart again. This is called *demultiplexing*. In order to accomplish this task, IP uses protocol numbers to identify transport protocols. The transport protocols then use port addresses to identify applications or processes.

Some protocol numbers and some port numbers are called a *well-known service*. Well-known services are the oldies but goodies network protocols, such as FTP and Telnet that are commonly used throughout the Internet. The protocol numbers and the port numbers allocated to these well-known services are documented in an RFC called Assigned Numbers. Examples of some of these well-known protocols are found in a text file called PROTOCOL found in the \Windows directory of a Windows 9x–based machine.

The following shows the contents of a PROTOCOL file.

```
# Copyright (c) 1993-1995 Microsoft Corp.
#
# This file contains the Internet protocols as defined by RFC1060
# (Assigned Numbers).
#
# Format:
#
# <protocol name> <assigned number> [aliases...]   [#<comment>]


ip          0       IP          # Internet protocol
icmp        1       ICMP        # Internet control message protocol
ggp         3       GGP         # Gateway-gateway protocol
tcp         6       TCP         # Transmission control protocol
egp         8       EGP         # Exterior gateway protocol
pup         12      PUP         # PARC universal packet protocol
udp         17      UDP         # User datagram protocol
hmp         20      HMP         # Host monitoring protocol
xns-idp     22      XNS-IDP     # Xerox NS IDP
rdp         27      RDP         # "reliable datagram" protocol
rvd         66      RVD         # MIT remote virtual disk
```

How are protocol numbers actually used? If you were to take a look at an IP packet, the protocol number is a single byte in the third word of the datagram header. I have captured a TCP packet using Microsoft Windows NT 4 Network Monitor. The packet is shown in Figure 4.1.

Figure 4.1   TCP packet capture

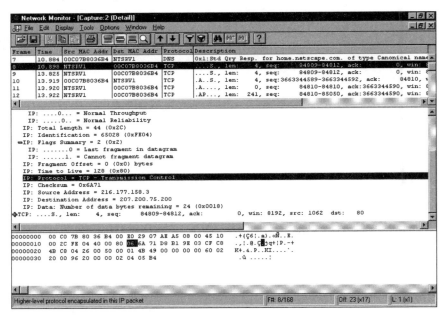

If you look closely, you can see the packet is defined as a TCP packet, and the protocol number is 6.

Service Numbers

After the packet or datagram has been passed to the right transport protocol, the transport protocol is responsible for getting the data to the right application process or network service. Here, when I say *application process,* don't think of applications such as Microsoft Word or Excel, think of applications such as File Transfer Protocol (FTP) or Simple Mail Transfer Protocol (SMTP). The confusion with this stage of the process occurs because there are so many darn names for it. We can call it *application process* or *network services,* but in the real world, these are all identified by port numbers.

As with most things in communication, there are two sides to every story, and this is no different. There is a *source* port address (where the information is coming from) and a *destination* port address (where the information is going to). This information is contained in the first header of each TCP segment and UDP packet. Just like the protocols being listed, there is a listing of some of the more common port addresses or services in a file called SERVICES located in the \Windows directory of Windows 95/98 workstations. The following is a part of a sample of the SERVICES file.

```
#

# This file contains port numbers for well-known services as defined
by

# RFC1060 (Assigned Numbers).

#

# Format:

#

# <service name> <port number>/<protocol> [aliases...]   [#<comment>]

#


echo        7/tcp
echo        7/udp
discard     9/tcp      sink null
discard     9/udp      sink null
systat      11/tcp
systat      11/tcp     users
daytime     13/tcp
daytime     13/udp
netstat     15/tcp
qotd        17/tcp     quote
qotd        17/udp     quote
chargen     19/tcp     ttytst source
chargen     19/udp     ttytst source
ftp-data    20/tcp
ftp         21/tcp
telnet      23/tcp
```

```
smtp         25/tcp     mail
time         37/tcp     timserver
time         37/udp     timserver
rlp          39/udp     resource      #resourcelocation
name         42/tcp     nameserver
name         42/udp     nameserver
whois        43/tcp     nicname       # usually to sri-nic
domain       53/tcp     nameserver    # name-domain server
domain       53/udp     nameserver
nameserver   53/tcp     domain        # name-domain server
nameserver   53/udp     domain
mtp          57/tcp                   # deprecated
bootp        67/udp                   # boot program server
tftp         69/udp
rje          77/tcp     netrjs
finger       79/tcp
link         87/tcp     ttylink
supdup       95/tcp
hostnames    101/tcp    hostname      # usually from sri-nic
iso-tsap     102/tcp
dictionary   103/tcp    webster
x400         103/tcp                  # ISO Mail
x400-snd     104/tcp
csnet-ns     105/tcp
pop          109/tcp    postoffice
pop2         109/tcp                  # Post Office
pop3         110/tcp    postoffice
portmap      111/tcp
portmap      111/udp
nntp         119/tcp    usenet        # Network News Transfer
ntp          123/udp    ntpd ntp      # network time protocol (exp)
```

tcprepo	158/tcp	repository	# PCMAIL
snmp	161/udp	snmp	
snmp-trap	162/udp	snmp	
print-srv	170/tcp		# network PostScript
exec	512/tcp		
login	513/tcp		
who	513/udp	whod	
shell	514/tcp	cmd	# no passwords used
syslog	514/udp		
printer	515/tcp	spooler	# line printer spooler
talk	517/udp		
ntalk	518/udp		

Figure 4.2 shows a captured packet heading out to do a DNS look up. If you look closely, you will see that the packet shows DNS using port 53, which matches the SERVICES file.

Figure 4.2   DNS captured!

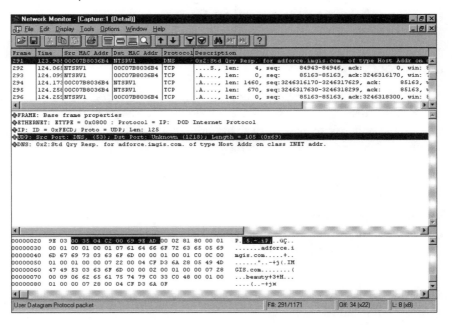

Now, just like there are well-known protocols, there are well-known ports, and these are pretty standard. For example, SMTP is port 25, and Telnet is allocated to port 23. There are other types of ports in use also; these are called *dynamically allocated ports*. These are addresses that the port numbers are assigned on the fly, on an as needed basis.

Here is how it works. Let's say that I want to telnet to a different host. When I execute my Telnet command, my system will randomly allocate a port to the process. When it sends the command out, the destination address will contain Telnet's well-known port of 23, but the source address will include my system address and my randomly assigned port address. Now, there is a unique channel for the Telnet session.

Say, for example, the source of the request has an IP address of 208.45.13.26. When that host starts the Telnet session, it is randomly assigned a port address of 1699. When 208.45.13.26 sends the packet, it directs the packet to the destination at 192.34.22.99 at the Telnet port of 23. When that host at 192.34.22.99 responds, it uses the destination port address of 1699 and a source port of 23. Hence, the system can keep the lines of communication open and conversations straight.

So, now we have communication using an IP address and the appropriate ports. But how does the MAC address come into play, and what does this all have to do with DCHP? Back at the beginning of this chapter I told you it would be alphabet soup, and I also told you we would explore the building blocks before getting into DHCP. Hang with me!

Reverse Address Resolution Protocol

Address Resolution Protocol (ARP) takes an IP address and resolves it to a MAC address. The Reverse Address Resolution Protocol (RARP) takes a MAC address and resolves it to an IP address.

A RARP server maps the physical address to an IP address for a client that doesn't know its own IP address. The client sends out a broadcast (meaning the packet goes to every host on the network segment, not to an individual host). The broadcast packet contains the client's physical address (the terms MAC address and physical address can be used interchangeably) and a request to see whether any system on the network knows what IP address is associated with that physical address. The RARP server responds with a packet that provides the host's IP address. Although RARP is a useful tool, it provides only an IP address. There are still other values that need to be configured before the system can be a really hard-working host on the Internet. The next step up the protocol food-chain is the bootstrap protocol or BOOTP.

BOOTP

BOOTP is described in RFCs 951 and 1532 as an alternative to RARP. The RFCs also talk about all those times when BOOTP is appropriate and RARP isn't. The original specification for BOOTP allowed for different vendors to extend the protocol to match their needs. These extensions were originally formalized in RFC1048. RFC1048 has been updated from time to time, and the current BOOTP definition is contained in RFC2132.

Many people will recognize BOOTP as the vehicle that allows a diskless workstation to obtain an address and get information that will allow it to access network services. BOOTP works this way: a client will broadcast a single packet that is called a *BOOTREQUEST packet*. This packet must contain, at least, the client's physical network address or MAC address. The client sends the request out as a limited broadcast message to the address of 255.255.255.255, and a port address of 67. Once the client has completed these tasks, it sits back and waits for a response from the server. If the response does not come in a specified period of time, it will retransmit the request. Both transmissions use UDP as the transport protocol.

When the server gets the client request, it responds with a BOOTREPLY packet addressed to port address 68. Does this seem to fly in the face of the information discussed above, where I stated that communication between a network service and a client usually involved a well-known port address and a randomly generated host address? It does seem to be somewhat of a dichotomy, doesn't it? It would seem that way at first blush, but it really isn't. Remember, the client is in the process of booting. It doesn't have all of its information or protocols loaded yet, so the communications have to remain simplistic. Do you also see that we have another problem? The client that is booting is trying to get an address. Because it can provide only its hardware address, communication is still going to be difficult.

When BOOTP sends out its reply, it addresses that reply to port 68 on all hosts. When the hosts receive the packet, it will check for the MAC address. If the MAC address matches the client's address, the client now has the essential information it needs to be a contributing member of the network. BOOTP can provide all essential TCP/IP configuration options.

Dynamic Host Configuration Protocol (DHCP) In Depth

If you are really into such things and want to find out more about it, DHCP is defined in RFCs 2131 and 2132. As you would expect, DHCP is designed to be compatible with

BOOTP. As you would also expect when different protocols are designed to interact, some problems can occur, but we will get to that later. First, let's address DHCP basics.

A DHCP system can be made up of as many as three parts:

DHCP Server   The DHCP Server is the provider in this relationship. The DHCP server is the piece of the puzzle that provides all the configuration information the client may need. Not only that, the DHCP server tracks the requests for addressing information and leases them to clients, which means it has adminstration work to do, as well.

DHCP Client   The DHCP client is the requestor in this relationship. The DHCP client asks the server to give it the information it needs to be a contributing part of the network.

DHCP Relay Agent   As you read in the description of BOOTP, in the address assignment process, there are a lot of broadcast messages flying around the network. Broadcast messages work well on the same network segment. The issue with broadcast messages comes in when a router is involved. When a router gets a broadcast message, it discards it (unless programmed otherwise). If your DHCP server is on one side of a router and your DHCP client is on the other side of the router, the request for services will never get through. Therefore, you, the network administrator, have to install a DHCP relay agent on the same side of the router as the client. The DHCP Relay Agent just hangs around waiting for a client to ask for a DHCP address or to renew a lease. The agent then takes the information and passes it on to the DHCP server directly. Think of the DHCP Relay Agent as a very important middleman.

DHCP and Its BOOTP Roots

Much of what you are about to read is similar to what went on with the BOOTP scenarios. As a matter of fact, you can sort of consider DHCP to be BOOTP with an attitude. DHCP really expands BOOTP in two areas:

- The configuration parameters that a DHCP server can provide include everything that is defined in the Requirements for Internet Hosts RFC. DHCP can provide the client with a complete set of DHCP configuration values.

- DHCP permits the automated allocation of IP addresses.

If you remember, back in the discussion of the BOOTP packets, I mentioned that the protocol was left open for vendor implementation. DHCP makes use of the area designated for vendor extensions to provide a complete set of configuration options. The options field has been expanded to 312 bytes from the original 64 bytes that were part of the BOOTP process.

Table 4.1 is a list of some of the options available that a DHCP server can pass to a DHCP client.

Table 4.1   DHCP Options

Code	Option Name	Meaning
0	Pad	Causes subsequent fields to align on word boundaries.
255	End	Indicates end of options in the DHCP packet.
1	Subnet Mask	Specifies the subnet mask of the client subnet. In the Windows NT 4 implementation, this option is defined in the DHCP Manager Create Scope or Scope Properties dialog box. It cannot be set directly in the DHCP Options dialog box.
2	Time Offset	Specifies the Universal Coordinated Time (UCT) offset in seconds.
3	Router	Specifies a list of IP addresses for routers on the client's subnet.
4	Time Server	Specifies a list of IP addresses for time servers available to the client.
5	Name Servers	Specifies a list of IP addresses for name servers available to the client.
6	DNS Servers	Specifies a list of IP addresses for DNS name servers available to the client. Multihomed computers can have only one list per computer, not one per adapter card.
9	LPR Servers	Specifies a list of IP addresses for RFC1179 line-printer servers available to the client.
12	Host Name	Specifies the host name of up to 63 characters for the client. The name must start with a letter, end with a letter or digit, and have as interior characters only letters, numbers, and hyphens. The name can be qualified with the local DNS domain name.

Table 4.1   DHCP Options *(continued)*

Code	Option Name	Meaning
15	Domain Name	Specifies the DNS domain name that the client should use for DNS host-name resolution.
23	Default Time to Live	Specifies the default time-to-live (TTL) that the client uses on outgoing datagrams. The value for the octet is a number between 1 and 255.
27	All Subnets Are Local	Specifies whether the client assumes that all subnets of the client's internetwork use the same Maximum Transfer Unit (MTU) as the local subnet where the client is connected. 1 indicates that all subnets share the same MTU; 0 indicates that the client should assume some subnets might have smaller MTUs.
28	Broadcast Address	Specifies the broadcast address used on the client's subnet.
29	Perform Mask Discovery	Specifies whether the client should use Internet Control Message Protocol (ICMP) for subnet-mask discovery. 1 indicates that the client should perform mask discovery; 0 indicates that the client should not.
30	Mask Supplier	Specifies whether the client should respond to subnet-mask requests using ICMP. 1 indicates that the client should respond; 0 indicates that the client should not respond.
31	Perform Router Discovery	Specifies whether the client should solicit routers using the router discovery method specified in RFC1256. 1 indicates that the client should perform router discovery; 0 indicates that the client should not use it.

Table 4.1   DHCP Options *(continued)*

Code	Option Name	Meaning
33	Static Routes	Specifies a list of IP address pairs that indicate the static routes the client should install in its routing cache. Any multiple routes to the same destination are listed in descending order or priority. The routes are destination/router address pairs. (The default route of 0.0.0.0 is an illegal destination for a static route.)*
35	ARP Cache Timeout	Specifies the timeout in seconds for ARP cache entries.
37	Default Time to Live	Specifies the default TTL that the client should use when sending TCP segments. The minimum value of the octet is 1.
38	Keep Alive Interval	Specifies the interval in seconds that a TCP client should wait before sending a *keepalive* message on a TCP connection. A value of 0 indicates that the client should not send keepalive messages on connections unless specifically requested by an application.
44	WINS/NBNS Servers	Specifies a list of IP addresses for NetBIOS Name Servers (NBNS).
46	WINS/NBT Node Type	Allows configurable NetBIOS over TCP/IP (NetBT) clients to be configured as described in RFC1001/1002, in which 1 = b-node, 2 = p-node, 4 = m-node, and 8 = h-node. On multihomed computers, the node type is assigned to the entire computer, not to individual adapter cards.
47	NetBIOS Scope ID	Specifies a text string that is the NetBIOS over TCP/IP Scope ID for the client, as specified in RFC1001/1002. On multihomed computers, the scope ID is assigned to the entire computer, not to individual adapter cards.

Using TCP/IP Protocols

PART 2

Table 4.1   DHCP Options *(continued)*

Code	Option Name	Meaning
51	Lease Time	Specifies the time in seconds from address assignment until the client's lease on the address expires. Lease time is specified in the DHCP Manager–Create Scope or Scope Properties dialog box. It cannot be set directly in the DHCP Options dialog box.
58	Renewal (T1) Time Value	Specifies the time in seconds from address assignment until the client enters the renewing state. In Windows NT 4 Systems, Renewal Time is a function of the Lease Time option, which is specified in the DHCP Manager–Create Scope or Scope Properties dialog box. It cannot be set directly in the DHCP Options dialog box.
59	Rebinding (T2) Time Value	Specifies the time in seconds from address assignment until the client enters the rebinding state. On a Windows NT 4 system, rebinding time is a function of the Lease Time option, which is specified in the DHCP Manager–Create Scope or Scope Properties dialog box. It cannot be set directly in the DHCP Options dialog box.

*Routers have the capability of setting a Default route of 0.0.0.0. The default route is mapped to an IP address, and any packet destined for a route that is not in the router's table is forwarded to the IP of the default route.

You probably are never going to mess with any of these, but it is nice to know that they are available. This is far from an exhaustive list of options; if you don't see what you need, check out some of the RFCs or even the documentation for your particular operating system and see whether it can do what you need it to do.

DHCP Address Allocation

The main reason that network administrators will set up a DHCP server is to provide a method for hosts to receive the automatic allocation of an IP address. DHCP actually allows IP addresses to be assigned one of three ways:

Manual Allocation   The network administrator maintains control over addresses by specifically assigning them to clients using the client MAC address. This is how addresses are assigned in BOOTP. In Windows NT, this is referred to as a Client Reservation.

Automatic Allocation   The DHCP server does it all. Once it has been configured, the DHCP server is in charge of passing out all the addresses from an address pool. The network administrator has configured it and forgotten about it. The addresses do not expire.

Dynamic Allocation   The server assigns an address to a DHCP client for a limited period of time, called a *lease*. The client can return the address to the server at any time, but the client must request a lease extension to retain the address for longer than the original lease. If the lease expires, the server gets the lease back.

Dynamic allocation is probably the configuration you hear about the most, and it can be a real time-saver. It is useful in most cases, but occasionally, it is something to be avoided like the plague!

NOTE   There are certain pieces of equipment that should not be configured to use Dynamic DHCP. This equipment includes mail servers, Web servers, name servers, login hosts, routers, and other online gear that is always expected to be in the same place. Make sure they are configured to use manual allocation addressing, or assign the host a static IP address and be done with it.

The problem of hosts moving around because of Dynamic DHCP is such an issue that the IETF is currently working on a set of standards that will make DNS dynamic. If and when the new plan goes into effect, any host that provides services will have its IP address dynamically updated in DNS. Then, when a user wants to access the device, DNS will have the correct address.

When you look at the implementation of DNS at most sites, you will find a mixture. Some systems have static IP addresses, some systems have dynamic allocation, and some systems have reserved addresses from DHCP. It is a kind of hodgepodge.

Using TCP/IP Protocols

PART 2

Sometimes It Works, and Sometimes It Doesn't, Part I

Lee Vine, a Senior System Engineer with Microage in Minneapolis, has had some interesting experiences with DHCP. Before Lee went to work for Microage, he was called out to a client site where the TCP/IP communication seemed to be going south in a hurry.

The system was laid out so all information would be provided by a DHCP server. The problem was that although the DHCP server was succeeding in passing out the IP addresses, it just passed them out twice.

Now, because IP addresses have to be unique within the same network, two machines having the same IP address generally falls into the bad category. Some desktop operating systems, such as Windows NT, will be kind enough to tell you when two systems are sharing an IP address. Others, such as Windows 95/98, won't. Troubleshooting that system can be somewhat of a challenge.

Luckily for Lee, once he discovered the problem, the solution was as simple as downloading and installing a patch to the DHCP server. He used FTP, but we can't talk about that yet, because it is covered in Chapter 6.

DHCP Server Configuration

As mentioned earlier in this chapter, in order for DHCP to work properly, up to three different components need to be configured. It would be nice if all the major manufacturers did everything exactly the same, but they don't.

In this section, we will take a high-level overview of configuring a DHCP server on a NetWare 5 server, a Windows NT 4 Server, and even take a look at a Linux implementation.

Novell NetWare 5

Once Eric Schmidt became Novell's Chief Executive Officer, it was almost inevitable that Java and IP would be in NetWare's future. It took a couple of years, but NetWare 5 makes good use of Java; it is designed to work in a pure IP environment, an IPX environment, or a mixed environment. Many of NetWare's rather stodgy old utilities have been upgraded to take advantage of the new technologies. One of the changes Novell has made has been to link DNS and DHCP management into a single tool called the DNS/DHCP Management Console.

The DNS/DHCP Management Console is a Java application that provides a graphical user interface and allows administrators to configure and manage IP addresses and name services through Novell Directory Services (NDS)–based DHCP and DNS objects. Because the management console is a Java-based utility, it can be launched from within the NetWare Administrator utility or as a stand-alone utility on a Windows 9x or NT client.

> **NOTE**   The installation of the DNS/DHCP Management Console requires two steps. The first step is the installation of the software from the file server console; the second step requires the management console to be set up on the workstation. Because the management console is already listed on the Tools menu of the NWADMIN utility, you would think there would be an easier way to get it to install. Maybe in NetWare 5.1.

Once you have successfully installed the DNS/DHCP Management Console, it is available through NWAdmin. Figure 4.3 shows the new Tools menu.

Figure 4.3   Tools menu from NWAdmin

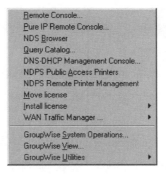

When you kick-off the DNS/DHCP Console and select DHCP options, you are presented with the detail screen shown in Figure 4.4.

Figure 4.4   DHCP Management Console detail screen

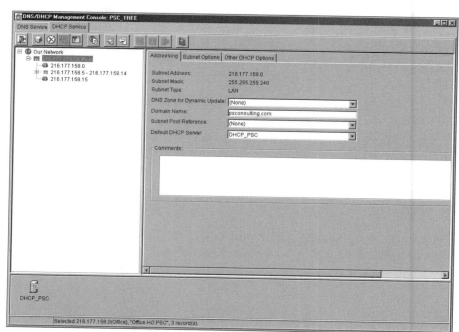

Notice you are looking at the Addressing tab, which gives some general details of the subnet. To create a new DHCP Object, click on the Create button (which is the little box on the menu bar), which will present the menu shown in Figure 4.5.

Figure 4.5   DHCP Creation objects

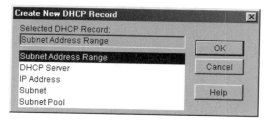

Notice that you can use this tool to create a new subnet, define a new DHCP Server, and create address pools.

Figure 4.6 shows the options that are available for this particular subnet. In the case of this subnet, there is nothing fancy, just the usual lease period of three days. Note that this is where BOOTP compatibility can be defined.

NOTE   Lease periods will be described later in this chapter.

Figure 4.6   Options for a particular subnet

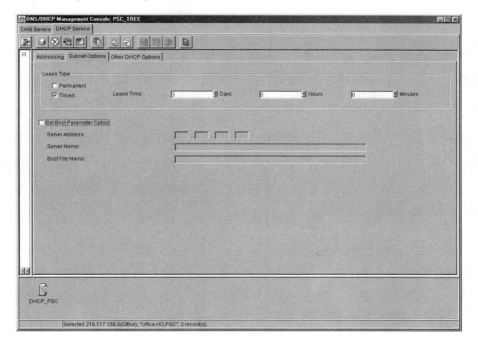

Earlier in the chapter, there was a table with a long list of DHCP Options and what they did. You may have noticed that there is a tab marked Other DHCP Options. Clicking on that tab brings up Figure 4.7, which I must admit isn't too impressive at first glance. Notice, however, that there is a Modify button at the bottom of the screen.

Figure 4.7   The Other DHCP Options tab

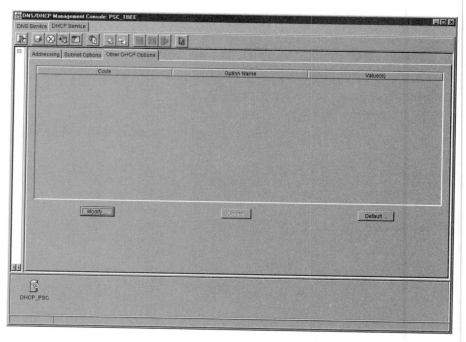

If you click the Modify button, your screen will resemble Figure 4.8. You may notice that some vendor-specific settings are used in this figure, primarily the NDS tree name.

Once you have completed your modifications, the Other DHCP Options screen looks a little more impressive, as you can tell from Figure 4.9.

Once you have configured the DHCP system the way you want it, the next step is to start the DHCP server process. To start the process, you should access the file server console and type **DHCPSRVR**.

Figure 4.8   The Modify DHCP Options dialog box

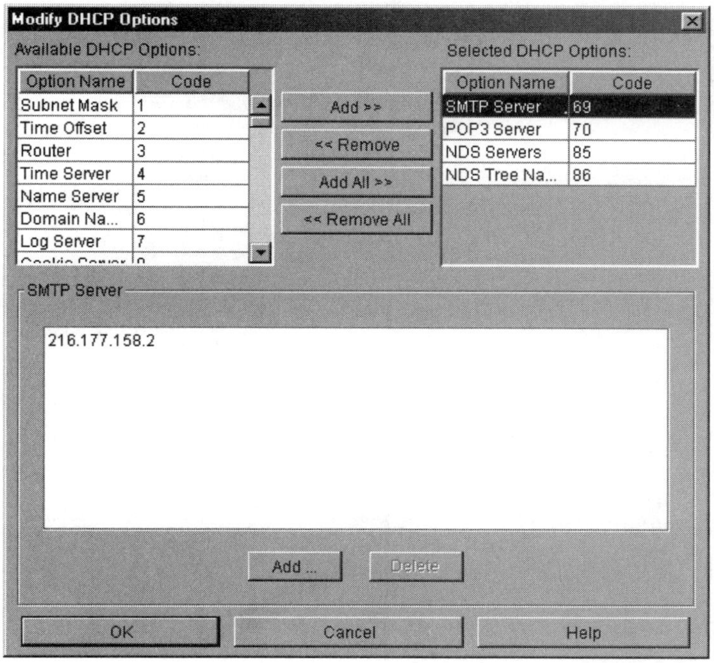

NOTE   This description is not intended to show you how to install and configure DHCP on a NetWare 5 network; instead, it's an overview of some of the utilities and screen shots. For more information on the installation and creation of a DHCP server on a NetWare network, refer to the Novell Documentation or to the Novell Web site at www.novell.com.

Figure 4.9 The Other DHCP Options tab with some actual options

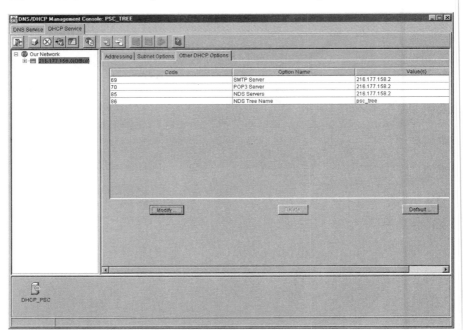

Sometimes It Works, and Sometimes It Doesn't, Part II

Sometimes it is the simple things that can cause problems.

Lee Vine has had an experience with corruption in the sys:etc\dhcptab file. He wasn't sure how it got corrupted because it can be introduced via a server ABEND, power outage, or even by manually editing the file. In the NetWare 4.11 world, changes to DHCP configuration should be made through the DHCPCFG.NLM on the server, not by other means.

Somehow, the DHCPTAB file became corrupt, and every time Lee started the server, it would get to the point of loading DHCP and come to an abnormal end, or ABEND. In the world of NetWare, an ABEND is the same as the Windows NT Blue Screen of Death.

When Lee set out to research the problem, he found that DHCPSRVR uses two configuration files: DHCPTAB.LWG and DHCPTAB. DHCPTAB.LWG is a copy of DHCPTAB that is held in memory; DHCPTAB is not held in memory. When changes are made to the DHCP configuration via DHCPCFG, the server updates DHCPTAB.LWG and then creates a new DHCPTAB file based on what is in memory.

Sometimes It Works, and Sometimes It Doesn't, Part II *(continued)*

Each time a new DHCPTAB file is made this way, the previous DHCPTAB file is renamed to DHCPTAB.SAV, and a new DHCPTAB file is written, including the recent changes in DHCPCFG. You can also get previous copies of the DHCPTAB.SAV file by using FILER to salvage DHCPTAB.SAV.

Sometimes a VREPAIR will fix the file corruption. In other cases, the file is too far gone, and you must rename a DHCPTAB.SAV file to DHCPTAB and then reload dhcpcfg or dhcpsrvr. These files are ASCII files and should not contain any "garbage" characters. The last line of the file should be a comment warning you not to delete the file.

Lee also discovered that he had to make sure that DHCPIO.NLM, DHCPSRVR.NLM, and DHCPCFG.NLM were unloaded when he performed the rename, restore, and rename operations. When restoring a DHCP configuration from DHCPTAB.SAV files, to preserve any configuration changes that you may have made up to that point, always use the most recent DHCPTAB.SAV file that is known to be noncorrupt.

Microsoft Windows NT

Installation of the DHCP server on an NT 4 server is pretty straightforward. From the Control Panel, opt for Network, then choose Services, and click Add. Scroll down until you find the DHCP service, highlight it, click a button, put in the CD, and you are on your way. After the service has been installed, it makes sure that you have a static address on the server that is going to be running DHCP Server, and then it has you restart the computer. Once the computer has come back on line, all that remains is to configure the scopes and the options using DHCP Manager. To access DHCP Manager, go to Start ➤ Programs ➤ Administrative Tools ➤ DHCP Manager.

Firing up the DHCP Manager will bring up a blank screen that is shown in Figure 4.10.

To begin, select your server's IP address from the left side (you may have to open Local Machine) of the screen, and select from the main menu Scope ➤ Create. You will notice that this screen has the starting point and ending point of the pool, along with the ability to exclude addresses from the middle of the pool as you see fit. You can also add to the excluded range on the fly if necessary.

Figure 4.10 The DHCP Manager starting point

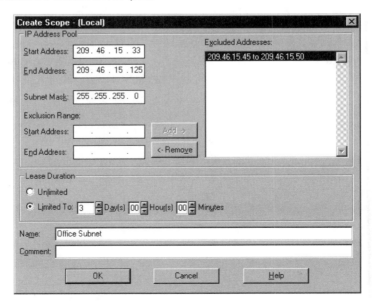

Figure 4.11 shows the screen with some information ready to be put in place.

Figure 4.11 Almost a usable DHCP pool

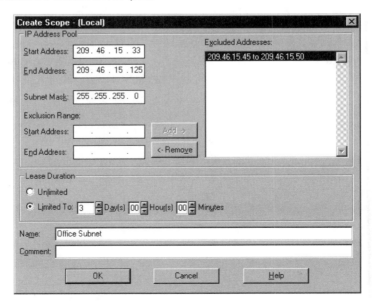

Actually, if this were a small network with no routers and no Internet connections, this DHCP pool would be usable. If, however, you have gateways installed or want to provide DNS server addresses, then you will have to go to the DHCP Options as shown in Figure 4.12.

Figure 4.12   The DHCP Options dialog box

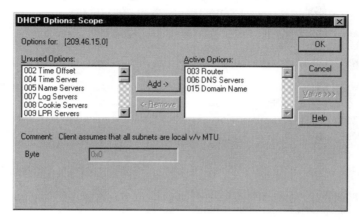

Once the options have been configured with the appropriate IP addresses of the gateways and the DNS servers, if you click on OK until you exit back to the first screen, you can activate the server at your convenience.

DHCP and Windows 2000

With Windows 2000, Microsoft has enhanced its implementation of DHCP over what had been used in NT 4. According to the folks in Redmond, Washington, the new version of DHCP will integrate DHCP with DNS, provide enhanced monitoring and statistical reporting for DHCP servers, handle multicast address allocation, and have new vendor-specific and new class ID option support. In addition, it will have the ability to detect when a rogue DHCP server has suddenly shown up on the network. DHCP will be integrated into the Active Directory, and it will support clustering services. The DHCP Manager will also be improved.

DHCP and Unix

DHCP on Unix comes in several flavors. One of the commonly used, free versions of a DHCP server is the Internet Software Consortium (ISC) Dynamic Host Configuration Protocol Daemon or the DHCPd. It even works with Linux.

If It Seems Too Good to Be True, It Probably Is

Dan Dillman and St. Cloud Technical College in Minnesota got bitten by the infamous Microsoft DHCP implementation problem.

Dan is a network administrator from a small college campus, and he was complaining about DHCP. It seems that when he was running his DHCP server from a Linux box, he would have trouble passing information to Windows clients. When he investigated, he surmised that the problem arose from those "vendor specific" implementations of the protocol.

Windows DHCP clients are notoriously picky. To get DHCP to work with Windows clients, DHCP must be able send packets to an IP destination address of 255.255.255.255. Linux insists on changing that into a local subnet broadcast address, which results in a DHCP protocol violation. Many DHCP clients ignore the problem and get on with things. Microsoft clients are famous for choking. Because of that, the client will not see the DHCPOFFER message from the server.

Consider this just a word to the wise.

Configuration of DHCP using DHCPd is done through a text file called dhcpd.conf. A sample dhcpd.conf file is shown below.

```
default-lease-time 6000;
max-lease-time 72000;
option subnet-mask 255.255.255.0;
option routers 192.46.15.254;
option domain-name-servers 192.46.15.253, 192.46.15.252;
option domain-name "mycoolcompany.com";

subnet 192.46.15.0 netmask 255.255.255.0 {
  range 192.46.15.15 192.46.15.155;
  range 192.46.15.175 192.46.15.225;
}
```

This configuration will result in the DHCP server giving a client an IP address from the range of 192.46.15.15 to 192.46.15.155 or from the range of 192.46.15.175 to

192.46.15.225. The IP address will be leased for 6,000 seconds, if the client doesn't ask for a specific time frame. Otherwise, the maximum allowed lease will be 72,000 seconds. The DCHP server will let the client know that the client should use 255.255.255.0 as the subnet mask, its router/gateway is found at 192.46.15.254, and it can find DNS servers at 192.46.15.253 and 192.46.15.252.

DHCP Client Configuration

At this point of the process, we have a DHCP server configured, but we do not have any clients configured. Again, configuring a Windows 32-bit operating system client to handle TCP/IP using DHCP is a straightforward matter.

Windows 95/98/NT

When you install a Microsoft 32-bit operating system and install the TCP/IP protocol, the install program assumes that you are going to be using DHCP. Figure 4.13 shows the Network Neighborhood ≻ Properties ≻ Configuration window, listing the TCP/IP protocol.

Figure 4.13   Protocol configurations

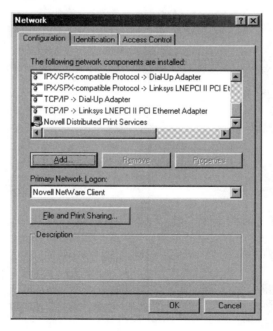

If I highlight TCP/IP and select properties, you will see in Figure 4.14 that the option is selected to make the workstation a DHCP client.

Figure 4.14   DHCP client selection

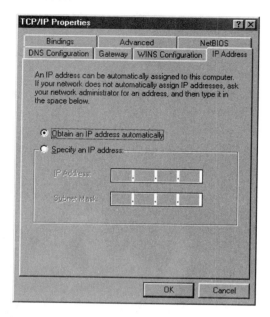

Windows 95/98 and the Road Warrior

As you have seen, you can pass various information to the DHCP client, including the location of DNS servers and the addresses of gateways. If you deal with traveling users that use an Internet service provider dial-up service, there can be some problems.

When the end user logs into the local network with a laptop configured either as a DHCP client or with a static address, the laptop has information on the local network, including a gateway. When the end user takes the laptop on the road, and dials into an ISP, the system will receive an IP address with a gateway for the TCP/IP dial-up adapter. The laptop now has two complete IP configurations, one for the network card and one for the dial-up adapter. When the user is working on the Net, everything is fine until they issue a request to go to a service that would be local if they were on the LAN. When this happens, for whatever reason, Windows does not use the gateway defined in the dial-up adapter but tries to use the gateway defined for the NIC. Because the system is not attached to the LAN segment, the gateway cannot be used, and the road warrior can go anywhere on the Net *except* back to the office!

Windows 95/98 and the Road Warrior *(continued)*

The problem can be solved by running winipcfg and releasing the DHCP information for the NIC. They may need to restart the computer. This is one of those little nagging problems that can cause premature gray hair.

Unix Client Configuration

About the only thing that is standard about the Unix client configuration is that you will have to get the DHCP client daemon DHCPcd. Usually, the developer of the version of the operating system has it either on the installation CD or on their Web site. Once you have gotten your hands on the client, it is best to RTFM and follow the directions provided.

DHCP Relay Host Configuration

The last piece of the DHCP puzzle is the DHCP relay host. Configuration of the host varies, obviously, and I will take a look at both Novell's implementation using NetWare 5 and Microsoft's using NT 4.

Novell NetWare 5

NetWare 5 handles relays a couple of different ways. First, it opts for the "Let someone do it" approach. In this case, it expects the router that you have in place to be able to run the BOOTP relay agent or forwarder. The BOOTP relay agent is provided with the IP address of the nearest DHCP server, and it then listens for DHCP requests. If it hears a DHCP broadcast request, it forwards it to the DHCP server on the behalf of the client. As far as the client is concerned, the router is the DHCP server.

What if there isn't a router or if you are using a NetWare 5 server as your router? In that case, you would run a NetWare Loadable Module (NLM) called BOOTPFWD.NLM. This NLM has the following start-up options.

Server= Specifies the IP address of the nearest DHCP server.

Log= Specifies whether the BOOTPFWD.NLM creates a log to the console or to a file.

File= Specifies the name of the log file.

The load statement for the BOOTPFWD.NLM is

```
LOAD BOOTPFWD SERVER=192.46.15.254 LOG=YES FILE=SYS:\ETC\BOOTPFWD.LOG
```

TIP   BOOTPFWD and DHCP server should not be loaded on the same server.
They both use UDP port 67, and only one service at a time can access that port.

Windows NT 4 Configuration of a Relay Agent

Configuration of the NT 4 DHCP relay agent is done through the Network Services
screen. You first have to add the service to your NT server and then restart the server.
Once that has been accomplished, your Network services screen will look like Figure 4.15.

Figure 4.15   The Services tab with the DHCP Relay Agent loaded

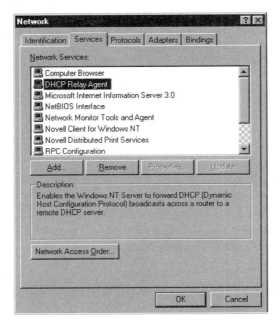

As the Relay Agent was being installed, it made sure that it had the IP address of at least
one DHCP server. This was done on the DHCP Relay tab of the Microsoft TCP/IP properties as shown in Figure 4.16.

Figure 4.16   The DHCP Relay tab of the TCP/IP properties

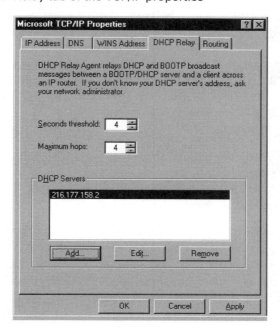

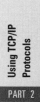

Once the computer has been restarted, it becomes a relay agent on its network segment and will forward the appropriate request to the DHCP server.

NOTE Depending on the router that you are using, you may be able to avoid configuring a DHCP or BOOTP relay agent. Although, in theory, a router will not forward a broadcast message, many routers have a BOOTP forwarder service available as part of the standard configuration. It may be disabled by default, but it may be there. If it is, you will have to decide which is easier to configure to be a relay agent: the router or a host.

How DHCP Works

All the pieces are in place. We have a working DHCP server and a DHCP client. To keep it simple, we will assume that everything is on the same network segment. Now how does the IP address get from the DHCP server's scope to the workstation?

When a workstation is turned on, its recognizes the need for an IP address. At this point, the workstation broadcasts a lease request, called a *DHCPDISCOVER message*. The client has no idea what the IP address of the DHCP server is, so the DHCPDISCOVER message is a broadcast message, meaning that every client on the subnet will receive the packet. If nothing responds to the request, the workstation will send the lease request four more times, at 9 seconds, at 13 seconds, at 16 seconds, and then at a random number of seconds. If the client still doesn't get an answer, it will continue to issue lease requests every five minutes.

When a DHCP server receives a lease request, it answers by sending back an IP Lease Offer or a DHCPOFFER packet. The offer packet is also sent as a broadcast message, because at this point, the client does not have an IP address. The DHCP offer will contain an IP address and subnet mask, the hardware address of the DHCP client, the IP address of the DHCP server, and the duration of the lease.

Back at the client side, the client receives the DHCPOFFER packet. If you have multiple DHCP servers on a subnet, the client may receive multiple offers. The client accepts the first offer it receives by sending back a packet called the *DHCPREQUEST packet*. The DHCPREQUEST packet tells the successful DHCP server that the workstation is taking it up on its offer. All of the other servers realize the offered IP address can be returned to the scope to be used by another workstation.

The process has not been completed. The DHCP server still needs to verify the successful lease. The server sends back an acknowledgment in the form of a packet known as a DHCPACK. This confirms the address and other configuration information. Once the client receives the DHCPACK, the client can initialize TCP/IP, and the communications begin.

What if the client is unsuccessful in its lease, or it is trying to renew a lease that has expired and the number has been reassigned? In that case, the DHCP server will send out a DHCPNACK. When a client gets a DHCPNACK, it knows it is back to square one, and it starts the process over again.

Once the client has the acknowledged configuration information, it can keep that address until the system shuts down, or the address is released manually. Like all leases, this one has to be renewed. The default lease period is three days. After 50 percent of the lease time is up, the client will attempt to renew its lease. If the DHCP server is up and working, the client gets a new lease on the address. If, however, the DHCP server is down, the client can still keep using the address, because the lease will not expire for another 36 hours. DHCP clients also attempt to renew their leases on start-up by broadcasting their last leased IP address. If the address hasn't been given out, it will be reassigned.

5

DNS and Your Network

Talk about simple yet elegant protocols, the domain name system (DNS) really fits the bill! When the Internet was young and the number of hosts few, systems connected to the Internet relied on a text file to resolve host names to IP addresses. This text file, called the HOSTS file, is still used in some instances today. As the Internet continued to grow, and it became more and more obvious that some type of system was needed to regulate and locate host names, DNS was born. DNS is evolving as we speak. DNS was originally designed as a way to keep track of host names that were assigned to hosts with static IP addresses. As connectivity to the Internet has changed, many companies require a dial-up connection to the Internet, meaning the host accesses a DHCP address that changes with each connection. First, we will look at how DNS worked at the beginning; next, we will look at some of the ways DNS is evolving with Dynamic DNS; and then we will look at ways that you can use DNS in your environment.

DNS Basics

DNS is a static, distributed, hierarchical database system with millions of registered, unique domain names. Each domain name needs to be unique within its section of the database. Some of the top-level domain databases commonly used are included in Table 5.1.

The top level of the domain database hierarchy is known as the *<root>,* which is usually represented by a trailing period in the domain name. If you have never seen a domain name

Table 5.1   Top-Level Domain Names

Top-Level Domain	Description	Examples
.com	Commercial	Microsoft.com Psconsulting.com Compaq.com
.gov	Governmental	Whitehouse.gov Senate.gov
.mil	Military	Army.mil Navy.mil
.edu	Education	Umich.edu (go blue!) UMN.edu
.net	Network services	InterNIC.net Earthlink.net
.se	Sweden	www.stockholm.se
.au	Australia	www.smh.com.au

with the trailing period, something that would look like sybex.com., don't worry about it. The trailing period is so common that it's ignored.

The Internet uses these domain names to create logical divisions. Within these divisions, individuals or companies can apply for a domain name or several domain names of their choice. If the name is available, it will be assigned. Once the domain name has been assigned to the company, it is up to the network administrator to manage the domain or subdivide it further. As you will see later in the chapter, domains can be broken down into what are called *zones,* or the administrator may decide to have just one zone and assign DNS names at the host level. When domains are broken down to the host level, the host name added to the domain name is referred to as a *fully qualified domain name* (FQDN).

A FQDN starts at the host level and works its way back completely through the DNS hierarchy, left to right, smallest to biggest. For example, the registered domain name for my publisher is sybex.com. As part of sybex.com, they may have a host that is named FRED. The FQDN for that server would be fred.sybex.com. As long as all the host names within a domain are unique, all FQDNs are unique.

> **TIP** If your network is not connected to the Internet, you can still use DNS, you just don't have to worry about a unique domain name. Host names still have to be unique, however.

At this point in the discussion, I should probably issue a few disclaimers to make sure there is no confusion. To be able to use a FQDN, you have to apply (and pay) for the privilege. In the past, applications for domain names were made to a group called the InterNIC, but now, applications can be made through a company called Network Solutions at www.networksolutions.com as well as through various other sources.

Domain is a commonly used term in the networking community. Microsoft uses domain to indicate a grouping of managed hosts. Novell, in its GroupWise product, uses domain to indicate a clustering of post offices or e-mail services. There is absolutely no connection between what Microsoft calls a domain, what Novell calls a domain, and what Network Solutions calls a domain. These are three completely different things.

Also, if you are familiar with Microsoft Windows NT, you probably know about WINS. Although DNS has a similar function to WINS, it is not be confused with WINS. WINS resolves NetBIOS computer names to IP addresses. DNS resolves host names to IP addresses. There are some other differences. For example, WINS maintains a single dynamic database, whereas DNS traditionally has distributed, static databases. A WINS name space is flat; the DNS name space is hierarchical. WINS operates at your network level; DNS, although it can be configured to operate at your network level, was designed to work at the Internet level. When configured to work at the local network level, DNS can also communicate with other DNS servers on the Internet to provide an Internet-level name resolution.

> **NOTE** Whenever there is a discussion of DNS, you will come across the term BIND. It stands for the Unix-based Berkeley Internet Name Domain servers, which provide name resolution at the Internet level. For more information, the definitive tome on DNS is *DNS and BIND*, by Paul Albitz and Cricket Liu.

DNS Components

The domain name system is broken down into three different components:

- Resolvers
- Name servers
- Name space

Using TCP/IP Protocols

PART 2

Resolvers and Name Servers

The first part of the DNS is the *resolver*. A resolver is any host on any IP network that needs to look up a domain name. That pretty much covers any host on an IP network that is connected to the Internet, doesn't it? When the resolver sends its query out to the name server, it attempts to connect to the name server using UDP. If your network has a problem with UDP, the resolver can fall back to using TCP.

Domain Name Space

The domain name space is another way of referencing the top-level domain names. The responsibility for each of these top-level domains can be delegated to a separate entity, and the database is distributed over many name servers. These databases are distributed partly by 13 Root servers that are maintained by the InterNIC. These 13 servers are the authorities for top-level domains. These Root servers also know how to contact the name servers for each of the other domains.

***

TIP All name servers have a list of the Root servers' names and IP addresses.

***

Each of these top-level domains have name servers that are the authority for that particular domain. These servers are distributed all over the world and are typically operated by governments.

Registering a Domain Name

Probably the most difficult part of registering a domain name is finding one that is currently not being used. The easiest way of handling that is to sit down and make up a list of the names you really want and then fire up your browser and point it to http://www .networksolutions.com/. Once you get to the Network Solutions homepage, you will be able to type in the names you want and get an immediate response as to whether they are available. If they are available, you can reserve the names for two years or register the names for three years. The costs vary. Figure 5.1 shows the results of a search on Network Solutions.

Figure 5.1 Nobody has govanus.com yet! Imagine that!

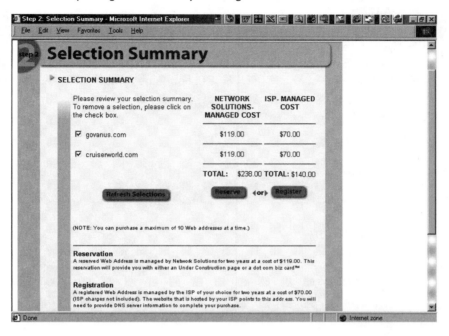

The trick of registering a name is that you must provide the addresses of two name servers available on the Internet. These name servers are the ones that will contain your host information. Your name servers will contain all the host data for your domain, such as `www.govanus.com`, `mail.govanus.com`, and `ftp.govanus.com`. What if you don't have two name servers attached to the Web and you still want to have your own domain name? This is usually not a problem, because there are thousands of ISP's out there who would be more than willing to host your domain name for you. This, of course, will come at a cost. In the area of the country where I live, the application fee goes from $70 for three years to about $300 for two years.

Once you have your second-level domain registered, you can further subdivide it, if you see fit. You have to contact the entity that hosts your domain name and provide them with information such as subdivision name and TCP/IP address. That way, you can have a name like `corporate.govanus.com`, or `mn.govanus.com`.

Domains versus Zones

I mentioned zones a few pages ago. A zone is the part of the domain name space that a particular name server is responsible for. Looking at Figure 5.2 will give you an idea of what I mean.

Figure 5.2   Second-level domain server with subdomains and name servers

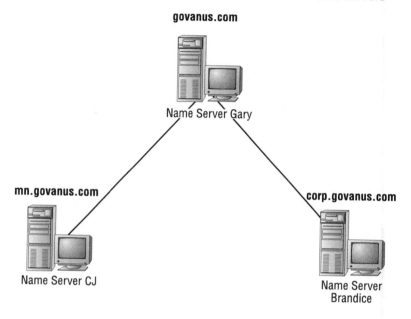

As you can see from the diagram, the name server Gary is responsible for the govanus.com domain. Meanwhile, the name server CJ is responsible for mn.govanus.com, and the name server Brandice is responsible for the subdomain corp.govanus.com.

This approach provides several advantages: it improves performance; you can divide up network traffic to heavily accessed sites or regionalize the traffic by geographic location. This method also gives some degree of fault tolerance. There are several servers carrying the load, and if one server should have a problem, your entire DNS structure won't come down. Dividing up your wide-area network (WAN) into zones also helps to distribute management functions across several layers.

The actual domain data, meaning the host name and the associated IP addresses, is stored in a text file called the *zone file* or the *zone database file*.

DNS Server Roles

When DNS is installed on a potential name server, it is installed as a *caching-only* computer, but when DNS is configured as part of a zone, there can be different server roles.

Caching Only   The caching-only computer contains no zone files, but users can still query it for host names. When the server learns a host name and address, it caches this information for a designated period of time.

Primary Name Server   The primary name server gets all of its zone data from local files. Any changes to a zone are done at the primary name server level.

Secondary Name Server   A secondary name server gets its information from another name server across the network. This provides for DNS redundancy. If you position the servers carefully, you can also speed up DNS access for remote locations and reduce the load on the primary name server. A secondary name server is really a copy of its primary name server or of another secondary name server.

Master Name Server   A secondary name server must receive its information from another name server. The information source can be a primary name server or a secondary name server. When you designate a source name server, that server becomes the master name server for the receiving secondary name server.

When a secondary name server starts up, it contacts the master name server and initiates a zone transfer of information for that server. (The zone files are copied.)

Forwarder   When a name server has been configured, you can define other servers as forwarder servers. When your name server cannot resolve a name, it checks with one of the forwarder servers rather than going through standard name resolution and checking with Root servers.

Linking DNS Servers

The concept of the forwarder and the concept that the DNS servers will query each other when there is missing information sounds simple enough. The question that jumps to mind, however, is how do these local DNS servers know where to go to get the information. When you design your DNS system, you must make sure your DNS servers know about each other and other DNS servers on the Internet. How do you do that?

Actually, that part is a no-brainer. Later in this section, when the DNS server is installed, you will see how each of the operating systems handles this issue. As you can see in Figure 5.3, a complete list of the Root servers is part of the DNS/DHCP Management Console utility for NetWare 5.

Figure 5.3 DNS/DHCP Management Console utility showing Root servers

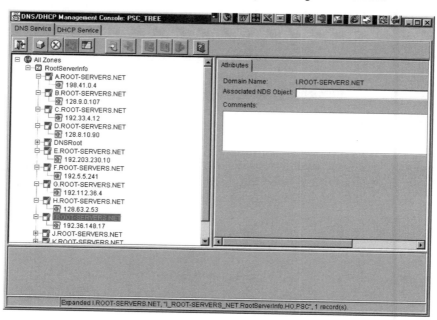

When the DNS service is installed in Windows NT 4, a file named cache.dns is created. This file comes complete with all the root server's IP addresses already installed. If your DNS server is connected to the Internet, it should help resolve DNS names with the information provided at installation.

What if your network is not connected to the Internet and you still want to use DNS? How can you link one server to another? In both NT 4 and NetWare 5, you start by creating a new host in your primary zone. To do this, you will need the host name of the DNS server that will be asked for help and its IP address. Once the host has been created, create a resource record of type NS pointing to the new DNS host. Now, when your DNS server has a problem resolving names, it will look to the other DNS server for help.

Name Server Queries

At the beginning of this chapter, I said that the DNS system was a static, distributed, hierarchical database system of millions of registered, unique domain names. The term *distributed* means that no single name server in DNS has a complete copy of the domain name space database. This is possible because of two types of resolution technology.

Recursive   The *resolver,* or the client, asks the server for a specific address. The client instructs the server to go find the address if it doesn't possess it.

Iterative   Name servers will typically do an iterative query. In this case, if a name server cannot answer the query from its own zone database or cache, it will consult a root server. The root server will transfer the query down to a top-level server, which passes the buck off to a second-level domain server. About this time in the process, the query reaches the right spot. The second-level domain server will return the answer to the original name server, and that name server sends the answer back to the resolver. The client then connects directly to the destination via the IP resolved by the iterative query.

Look at Figure 5.4 to see how this works.

Figure 5.4   Queries—you really can get there from here!

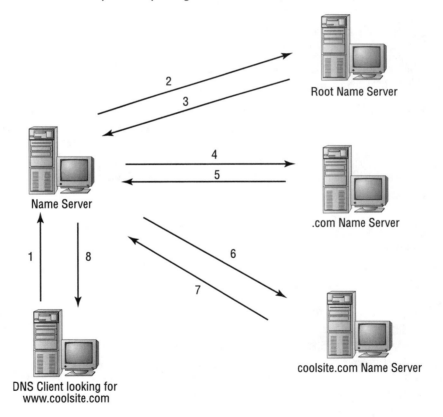

In step 1, the DNS client wants to know where www.coolsite.com is. It issues a recursive query to the name server computer. The name server computer checks its database and does not have an entry for www.coolsite.com, so it sends an interactive query to the root name server (or its ISP) in step 2. The query asks for the address of a name server that handles requests for addresses in the .com domain. The root server responds, in step 3, with the address of the .com name server. In step 4, the name-server computer contacts the .com name server looking for the name www.coolsite.com. In step 5, the .com name server replies that if you want that information, you will have to check with coolsite.com name server and here is the address. In step 6, the beleaguered name server sends another message to the coolsite.com name server, asking where www.coolsite.com is actually located. In step 7, the coolsite.com name server sends the appropriate address back to the name server, and the name server returns the address to the DNS client. Now, and only now, can the DNS client actually find the www.coolsite.com home page. And you wondered why the Internet was sometimes slow!

Inverse Queries and Reverse Lookups

The last section talked about how you can locate an IP address if you have the FQDN. What happens if you already have the IP address and you are looking for the FQDN? Are you out of luck? Not in the least.

There is a special purpose domain that has been set up to take care of inverse queries of this nature. It is called the in-addr.arpa zone. Now, you may not be sitting around with tons of IP addresses that you want to resolve to FQDNs, but this is a common practice for things such as mail servers. As a matter of fact, some mail servers will deny access to hosts that don't have a registered FQDN. Some application servers, such as FTP, will not allow you to log in unless you have a registered FQDN.

Security and FQDN

You may have already run into the issue of getting denied service because your FQDN was not registered. You just may not have known it.

Have you ever tried to download a product like the Netscape browser over a dial-in connection? The last time I tried, I had the option of downloading a 128-bit version of Netscape. This encryption method is available to people within the United States, but because of the laws and treaties regarding encryption, it cannot be exported. When I tried to download the software, the FTP agent at Netscape did a reverse lookup on my IP address and could not verify that my host had a FQDN registered in the U.S. Hence, I was denied service and had to take the alternative 64-bit version.

What about reverse queries? These are based on the fact that domain names get more specific when read right to left and IP addresses get more specific when read left to right. For this reason, domain names in a Reverse-Query file are reversed. In this case, if your network address was 208.15.140.0, the inverse-query zone would be 140.15.208 in-addr.arpa. Notice the address is reversed, and in-addr.arpa is added to the right side of the address to indicate it is a reverse lookup.

> *TIP* When creating zones, you should also create a reverse-lookup zone for any IP addresses you are managing.

DNS Resource Records

Over the past several pages, I have continued to talk about the DNS database and all these registered names. When you create a DNS server and define a zone, the information is kept in a zone file. A zone file (or text file) contains all of the resource records for the zone the DNS server manages. It is usually named after the zone, with an extension of .dns. When you enter information into the zone file, you are creating DNS entries for your network. This can be done using any text editor or a graphical utility. In the case of DNS, you can use DNS Manager to add the information to an NT network or the DNS/DHCP Manager tool in NWAdmin on a NetWare 5 network. Whatever tool you use, you will be adding resource records to the DNS database.

There are many different types of resource records that can be added to a DNS database. Each record has a type designator assigned to it, and each record provides a different service. Table 5.2 provides a summary of some of these records.

Table 5.2 Summary of Resource Records

Record Type	Record Name	Description
SOA	Start of Authority	The SOA record is always the first record in the database file. This record indicates the server is an "authority" on host names.
NS	Name Server	This record points to another DNS name server. If the local DNS name server cannot resolve the name, it will forward the request to the other servers.

Table 5.2 Summary of Resource Records *(continued)*

Record Type	Record Name	Description
A	Address	An A record maps the host name to the IP address.
CNAME	Canonical Name (Alias)	An alias is just an alternative name to a host.
PTR	Pointer	Maps the IP address to the host name. The reverse of an A record.
MX Record	Mail Exchanger	An MX record dictates where to send e-mail to any specific domain name.
RP	Responsible Person	If you use the InterNIC's Whois utility, you will see that each domain name has a responsible person listed. This is where it gets the information.

Zone File

The zone file is the file that will be replicated between all the masters and the secondaries.

SOA Record The first record in any database file is the Start of Authority (SOA) record. The SOA record entry is

```
IN SOA <source host><contact e-mail><ser.no.><refresh time><retry
time><expiration time><TTL>
```

Source host The host on which the file is maintained.

Contact e-mail The Internet e-mail address for the person responsible for the domain's database file.

NOTE Instead of writing the @ symbol in the e-mail name as would normally be done, the @ must be replaced with a "." when placed in the zone files. In other words, the e-mail address garyg@psconsulting.com would be garyg.psconsulting.com in the zone file.

Serial number   The version number of this database file. This number should increase each time the database file has been changed.

Refresh time   The elapsed time in seconds that a secondary server will wait between checks of its master server to see whether the database file has changed and a zone transfer should be requested.

Retry time   The elapsed time in seconds that a secondary server will wait before retrying a failed zone transfer.

Expiration time   The elapsed time in seconds that a secondary server will keep trying to download a zone. After this time limit expires, the old zone information will be discarded.

Time to live   The elapsed time in seconds that a DNS server is allowed to cache any resource record from this database file. This is the value sent out with all query responses from the zone file when the individual resource record does not contain an overriding value.

Resource Record Tidbits

Sometimes, a resource record will be longer than a single line in a text file. If this is the case, parentheses must enclose the line breaks.

In a zone file, the @ symbol represents the root domain of the zone, e.g., psconsulting.com. The "IN" is the class of data and stands for Internet. Although there are other classes of data available, none of them are in widespread use.

If there is a domain name in the database file that does not end with a period ".", it will have the root domain appended to the end.

Here is an example of a SOA record:

```
@ IN SOA nameserver1.psconsulting.com garyg.psconsulting.com. (
1; serial number
10800; refresh in three hours
3600; retry in one hour
604800; expire in seven days
86400); time to live one day
```

Name Server Record   The name server record lists the name servers for this domain, allowing other name servers to look up names in the domain. The name server entry is

```
<domain>IN NS <nameserver host>
```

For example,

```
@ IN NS nameserver2.psconsulting.com
@ IN NS nameserver3.psconsulting.com
```

Mail-Exchanger Record   The mail-exchanger record tells the system which host processes e-mail for this domain. There can be multiple mail-exchanger records. If this is the case, the resolver will attempt to contact the mail servers in the order of preference from the lowest value (the highest priority) to the highest value (lowest priority). A sample of a mail exchanger record is

```
<domain> IN MX <preference><mailserver host>
```

For example,

```
@ IN MX 1 mailserver0
@ IN MX 2 mailserver1
```

In these examples, if you sent an e-mail message to garyg@psconsulting.com, delivery would be attempted for garyg@mailserver0.psconsulting.com and then delivery would be attempted at garyg@mailserver1.psconsulting.com.

The Host Record   A host record associates a host name with an IP address within a zone. It should include entries for all hosts that require static mappings, including workstations, name servers, mail servers, etc. These are the most common records within the database file when static addressing is used.

The sample entry looks like this:

```
<host name> IN A <ip address of the host>
```

or it looks like this:

```
courtney  IN  A  192.55.192.43
brandice  IN  A  192.55.192.44
CJ        IN  A  192.55.192.45
Mail      IN  A  192.55.192.130
```

The CNAME Record   As mentioned previously, the CNAME can also be considered an alias. A sample record would look like this:

```
<host alias name>  IN CNAME <host name>
```

For example,

```
Server1     IN A 192.55.192.46
FTP             CNAME Server1
WWW     CNAME        Server2
```

Other DNS Files

Besides the zone database files, there are several other types of files that are routinely used with Unix DNS name servers.

Reverse-Lookup File   In order for the Reverse-Lookup file to handle inverse queries effectively, there must be a Reverse-Lookup file for each IP network address whose host you manage. These files contain the PTR records that provide IP-address-to-host-name lookups. An example of an entry in the Reverse-Lookup file would be

```
100.200.192.in-addr.arpa
55.157.in-addr.arpa
```

These entries indicate a Class C and a Class B network.

Cache   The Cache file contains a listing of the names and the IP addresses of the Root servers. This file does not need to normally be updated. Below is the sample cache file from ftp://rs.internic.net/domain/named.cache.

```
;       This file holds the information on root name servers needed to
;       initialize cache of Internet domain name servers
;       (e.g., reference this file in the "cache  .  <file>"
;       configuration file of BIND domain name servers).
;
;       This file is made available by InterNIC registration services
;       under anonymous FTP as
;           file            /domain/named.root
;           on server       FTP.RS.INTERNIC.NET
```

```
;         -OR- under Gopher at    RS.INTERNIC.NET
;             under menu          InterNIC Registration Services (NSI)
;               submenu           InterNIC Registration Archives
;             file                named.root
;
;         last update:    Aug 22, 1997
;         related version of root zone:   1997082200
;
;
; formerly NS.INTERNIC.NET
;
.                           3600000  IN  NS    A.ROOT-SERVERS.NET.
A.ROOT-SERVERS.NET.         3600000      A     198.41.0.4
;
; formerly NS1.ISI.EDU
;
.                           3600000      NS    B.ROOT-SERVERS.NET.
B.ROOT-SERVERS.NET.         3600000      A     128.9.0.107
;
; formerly C.PSI.NET
;
.                           3600000      NS    C.ROOT-SERVERS.NET.
C.ROOT-SERVERS.NET.         3600000      A     192.33.4.12
;
; formerly TERP.UMD.EDU
;
.                           3600000      NS    D.ROOT-SERVERS.NET.
D.ROOT-SERVERS.NET.         3600000      A     128.8.10.90
;
; formerly NS.NASA.GOV
;
```

```
.                         3600000      NS      E.ROOT-SERVERS.NET.
E.ROOT-SERVERS.NET.       3600000      A       192.203.230.10
;
; formerly NS.ISC.ORG
;
.                         3600000      NS      F.ROOT-SERVERS.NET.
F.ROOT-SERVERS.NET.       3600000      A       192.5.5.241
;
; formerly NS.NIC.DDN.MIL
;
.                         3600000      NS      G.ROOT-SERVERS.NET.
G.ROOT-SERVERS.NET.       3600000      A       192.112.36.4
;
; formerly AOS.ARL.ARMY.MIL
;
.                         3600000      NS      H.ROOT-SERVERS.NET.
H.ROOT-SERVERS.NET.       3600000      A       128.63.2.53
;
; formerly NIC.NORDU.NET
;
.                         3600000      NS      I.ROOT-SERVERS.NET.
I.ROOT-SERVERS.NET.       3600000      A       192.36.148.17
;
; temporarily housed at NSI (InterNIC)
;
.                         3600000      NS      J.ROOT-SERVERS.NET.
J.ROOT-SERVERS.NET.       3600000      A       198.41.0.10
;
; housed in LINX, operated by RIPE NCC
;
```

```
.                         3600000    NS    K.ROOT-SERVERS.NET.
K.ROOT-SERVERS.NET.       3600000    A     193.0.14.129
;
; temporarily housed at ISI (IANA)
;
.                         3600000    NS    L.ROOT-SERVERS.NET.
L.ROOT-SERVERS.NET.       3600000    A     198.32.64.12
;
; housed in Japan, operated by WIDE
;
.                         3600000    NS    M.ROOT-SERVERS.NET.
M.ROOT-SERVERS.NET.       3600000    A     202.12.27.33
; End of File
```

The BIND Boot File   Found on Berkeley Internet Name Domain (BIND) DNS servers, this file tells the name server software where to find Zone Database files, Reverse-Lookup files, and the Cache file. This file is not defined in an RFC and is not needed to be RFC-compliant.

These files control the startup of the DNS server. Commands must start at the beginning of a line, and no spaces may precede the commands. Some of the commands that may appear in a Boot file include Directory, Cache, Primary, and Secondary. The syntax for each command follows:

Directory Command

```
directory <directory>
```

A sample of this command would be

```
directory c:\winnt\system32\dns
```

Cache Command

```
cache . <filename>
```

A sample of this command would be

```
cache . cache
```

Primary Command

```
primary <domain> <filename>
```

A sample of this command would be

```
primary psconsulting.com psconsulting.dns
```

Secondary Command

```
secondary <domain><hostlist><local filename>
```

A sample of this command would be

```
secondary test.psconsulting.com 192.55.192.124 test.dns
```

That sums up the configuration and operation of the traditional DNS servers. Now let's turn our attention to the other side of the relationship, the client.

DNS Clients

As mentioned previously, DNS on the client side fulfills the role of a resolver. It starts the process to resolve a URL to an IP address. When you install TCP/IP on your computer, and you configure that computer to talk with the outside world, your computer can pretty much find any computer that is hooked to the Internet, if you have the destination's IP address. TCP/IP knows what to do with an IP address; it has no problems with 208.45.15.137:1677. But when you start requesting names, such as www.sybex.com, that gives your computer a reason to pause.

When you throw a URL at TCP/IP, it knows that the only way it can actually get you there is to resolve that URL to an IP address. Your computer has several places to look locally. It can check memory cache, it can check a HOSTS file, and if you are on an NT network, it can check for a WINS entry. Assuming that the IP address for www.sybex.com is not found in any of these places, your host has to look to the outside world for information.

In the last chapter, we talked about DHCP sending out broadcast requests for information and the problems involved in that process. Because broadcast requests may not get forwarded over a router, the request your workstation will send to the name server must be a directed request. That means if your system is going to ask a question of my system, you better have the IP address of my system. In the case of DNS, these addresses are provided as part of the IP configuration process, either using DHCP or static addressing.

Here is an example of what I mean. My lab network has NT, NetWare, and Linux hosts available. My current DHCP service runs on the NetWare 5 system. Figure 5.5 shows the

Global Options screen from the DHCP configuration page. (We discussed the DNS/DHCP Management utility in Chapter 4.) In this figure, you will notice that every workstation on the subnet served by this server receives the same two addresses for DNS servers.

Figure 5.5   Global Options from DHCP Management Console

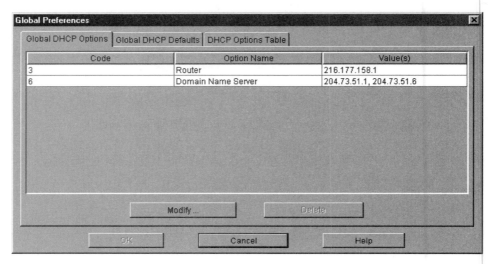

NOTE   Because my lab is very small, I use the DNS servers that my ISP provides. If I wanted, I could have my little slice of the DNS pie in my own lab by configuring a DNS server to run on my network. We will look at how to create a DNS server using NT and NetWare later in this chapter.

Because the information is being passed down by DHCP, I don't have to configure anything on the workstation, as is shown by Figure 5.6.

My system has the address of a pair of DNS servers, so it will send a directed request to the first server on the list asking where www.sybex.com is located. If that server can answer the request, it will send back the information. If not, the DNS server (depending on how it's configured) will probably send the request up to another DNS server. This will continue until one of two things happens: either the request will be fulfilled or the request will hit the root server.

If the request is fulfilled anywhere along the line, your host will receive the IP address of the host where the URL resides. If the request gets all the way up to the root server and it cannot answer the question, you will receive a 404 error, *Server Not Found*.

Figure 5.6   Client implementation showing DNS disabled

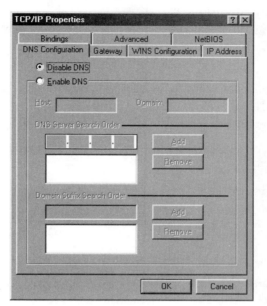

TIP   Receiving the ever-famous 404 error does not mean the server does not exist. The connection to the Internet may be temporarily down, or the system may simply be too busy to answer. The best solution, if you are sure of your URL, is to try again.

Installing DNS

Have you been getting a lot of complaints about the Internet being slow? When you try to access a URL, do you notice that it takes forever to get there, even slower than when you dial in using a 14.4 modem? Do you want to control your own DNS records and take it out of the hands of your ISP? Do you have an intranet with several servers? Any one of these reasons may be enough for you to decide that you want to maintain your own DNS server. In this section, I will look at installing and configuring DNS on a NetWare 5 platform and on a Windows NT 4 platform.

Configuring DNS on a NetWare 5 Network

When DHCP was installed in the last chapter, it installed the DNS/DHCP Manager that is used to configure the DNS servers. In NetWare 5, DNS information is stored in the Novell Directory Services (NDS) so it will be replicated throughout the network.

Zone data is stored in NDS and is replicated just like any other information in the tree. This means that all NetWare servers can access DNS data from NDS, providing fault tolerance and load balancing. With NDS, you can make changes to the DNS zone from anywhere on the network.

DNS Zone objects in NDS can represent three kinds of zones:

- A standard DNS zone
- An `in-addr.arpa` zone
- An `ip6.int` zone

All zones must be either a primary zone or a secondary zone.

Designated Servers

A *designated server* is a server that is assigned to service a DNS zone. If the server is assigned to the Primary Zone object, it will be tasked to

- Look to NDS to resolve names into IP addresses
- Add and delete resource records
- Update the zone serial number

In the majority of cases, your server will be set up to be a secondary DNS zone server. In this case, it will receive zone transfers from a master name server, usually at the site of your ISP. Once the DNS secondary server gets the information, it will then be replicated throughout the NDS structure of your network.

A DNS Server object is created from within the DNS Service tab of the DNS/DHCP Management Console. Figure 5.7 shows the dialog box to create the server.

Figure 5.7 DNS server creation

After the DNS server has been created, it is then linked to the NDS Server object. Creation of the DNS server is just one step in the process. You must also have a Zone object created. The zone is also created using the DNS/DHCP Manager tool. Figure 5.8 shows the Create Zone screen.

Figure 5.8   The Create Zone screen

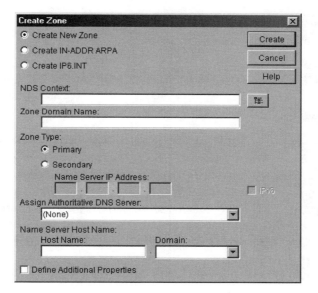

The Create Zone screen is pretty self-explanatory, but there are some *gotchas*. For example, the zone domain name. You would think that you would enter in your zone and your domain name. If you are creating a primary domain, that is fine, but in most cases, you will be working with secondary zones to mirror your ISP's domain name servers. In the case of creating a secondary zone, the domain name must match the name of the domain being replicated from the master name server. You must also provide the IP address of the master name server.

Once this has been completed, you can start the DNS server by typing **NAMED** at the server console and pressing Enter. When NAMED is loaded, information from the master name server will be replicated to your secondary server.

Using TCP/IP
Protocols

PART 2

Why Create a Secondary Server?

In a word, *speed*. If you look back in the chapter to the section on name-to-address resolution, you will see a diagram that indicates packets are flying all over the Internet trying to resolve a name to a number. If you can bring a mirror image of one of those servers to a network segment near you, you are eliminating at least one of the steps across the Internet.

Configuring Microsoft DNS Server Service

DNS on NT runs as a server service. Therefore, it must run on an NT server rather than on an NT workstation.

TIP   DNS is also one of those server services that have been patched a couple of times, so it would probably be a good idea to reapply the latest NT Service Pack (SP3 or greater) as well as any DNS-related patches. If you are running NT on an Intel platform, at least one additional patch is available at Microsoft's post-SP3 FTP site. The URL is ftp.microsoft.com/bussys/winnt/winnt-public/fixes/ usa/nt40/hotfixes-postsp3/dns-fix. Two files are on this site: one is for the Alpha installation of NT, one is for an installation on an Intel server. If you are installing on an Intel system, the file name is dnsfix_i.exe.

Installing DNS server is a matter of accessing the Control Panel and going to Network Services. When you reach the Network Services screen, click add to bring up a list of services that can be installed. Figure 5.9 shows DNS highlighted.

Figure 5.9   DNS Installation

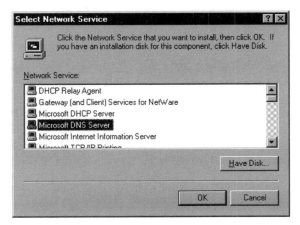

After the DNS Server service is installed, you will notice there is another new utility on the Administrative Tools (Common) menu, called *DNS Manager*. You start the configuration of DNS by defining the computer as a DNS server in DNS Manager. Once you have defined the server, you will notice in Figure 5.10 that immediately under the server is the word *Cache*.

Figure 5.10   Domain Name Service Manager

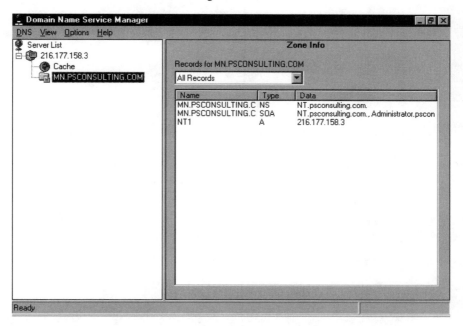

When you first create a DNS server, it is a caching-only server. As a caching-only server, it will not maintain any of the DNS database, but it will help resolve names by contacting other DNS servers. Does this sound like too much middle management? Not really, because once the names have been resolved, the DNS caching server stores the queries in memory as part of cache. Each entry has a TTL. (Doesn't everything?) If you want to see the entries in your cache, simply go to the Domain Name Service Manager, and click Cache.

Besides the information that the DNS server has been able to ascertain for itself, it also caches entries in a file called `cache.dns`. This is just a text file that contains information on where DNS should go to find top-level servers to resolve names to IP addresses. Figure 5.11 shows all the Root servers stored in cache for name resolution.

Figure 5.11 Root servers already in cache

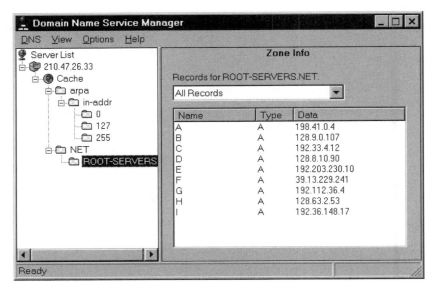

After you create the zone, you will notice that several records are added for you. Looking at Figure 5.12, you will see that an SOA record and an NS record were created for my server.

Figure 5.12 Domain Name Service Manager with default zone records

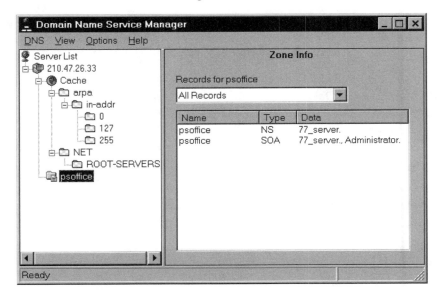

After you have created the zone, your DNS server is fully configured. You can now add records to the database or integrate DNS into the network with other name services.

Integrating DNS with WINS

WINS and DNS are sort of the same but sort of different. Both services resolve names to IP addresses, but the types of names and the way the resolution occurs is very different. The databases are different also.

DNS works with host names. On a Windows-based machine, by default, the host name is the computer name. On non-Windows machines, such as those Unix boxes that are popping up all over the place, there is no such thing as a NetBIOS computer name, there is just the host name. Somehow, it has to be possible to meld the best of both worlds.

You can configure a DNS server to use a WINS server to resolve just the host-name portion of the FQDN. Here is how it works. Suppose the DNS server for `psconsulting.com` received a request for `ntmail.psconsulting.com`, and the DNS server did not have an entry for the host name `ntmail`. At that point, DNS would ask the WINS server for the IP address of the WINS client `ntmail`. If WINS had the client information, it would pass the information back to the DNS server, which would then forward the information to the client.

One of the benefits of configuring DNS and WINS to work together is that it makes DNS appear almost dynamic. Because many companies are now relying on DHCP to assign IP addresses, host names will need to change from one IP address to another. In a DNS environment, where the address table is static, this can lead to chaos. WINS is a dynamic system, so it will help resolve the host name with the current IP address, whether the client is using DHCP or a permanent address.

> **TIP** The only way DNS and WINS can work together in this manner is if the host name and the NetBIOS computer names are the same throughout the network.

Integrating WINS and DNS is done through the Zone Properties page of the DNS zone. When completed, the WINS integration creates a WINS resource record in the primary zone file. This is a record that cannot be added manually.

The Future of DNS

The reoccurring theme through this chapter seems to be that DNS works very well, but it is somewhat rigid for the way today's world operates. For each DNS entry, it appears there needs to be at least one static IP address. If you want to register your own DNS name, you need to provide two DNS name-server static IP addresses that are visible from the Internet. In today's world, the technology exists to have a server on the Internet that is accessible by dial-up communications. The problem is when you establish a dial-up connection, you receive a DHCP address which changes with each call. What is a small company to do?

Actually, there are several services on the Internet that will allow you to register a DNS name, manage that name, and still have your servers connect to the Internet via dial-up.

> **TIP**   For a list of the companies that provide this service, I suggest you do a search on dynamic DNS using your favorite search vehicle. I use Copernic 99 Plus from Copernic Technologies (www.copernic.com/), and when I did an all-words search, I received 87 separate hits.

DNS dynamic update is an IETF standard. As you can see from Figure 5.13, choosing a DNS dynamic server is part of the DNS Management Console for NetWare 5. Dynamic DNS updates is a feature that Microsoft will implement in Windows 2000.

Figure 5.13   The DNS Management Console

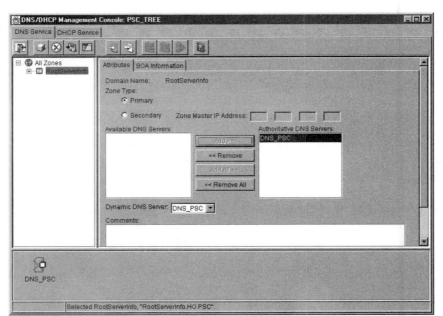

Information Gathering on the Internet

Throughout this book, I have been mentioning and quoting Request for Comments. If you would like a list of the RFCs or if you want to search out a particular RFC, start at http://ietf.org/rfc.html.

If you would like to find out more information on dynamic DNS, check out the specifications at http://ds.internic.net/Internet-drafts/drafts-ietf-dnsind-dynDNS-09.txt.

Finally, for everything you wanted to know about the RFC process and the secret handshakes it takes to get RFCs published, take a look at ftp://ftp.is.co.za/internet-drafts/draft-bradner-handshake-03.txt.

Incremental Transfers of DNS information

Another emerging standard is the incremental transfers. This will allow for the rapid propagation of changes to a DNS database. This is designed to reduce latency and decrease the amount of data sent during a zone transfer.

The reduction in data is handled through two mechanisms. Notification will actively notify servers of a change to a zone file. The notification is accomplished by the NOTIFY extension of DNS. Now that the servers have been notified, only the information that has changed will be sent.

NOTE If you would like more information on the Incremental Transfer Protocol, see the Internet draft at http://ds.internic.net/Internet-drafts/drafts-ietf-dnsind-ixfr-06.txt.

Secure DNS

One of the issues that arises with dynamic DNS and incremental transfers is security. How is the system to know who really has access to the DNS records for a particular name space? Extensions to the DNS are described in the IETF draft, *DNS Protocol Security Extensions—30 January 1996*. These extensions will provide services to security-aware resolvers or applications through using *cryptographic digital signatures*. These digital signatures are included in secured zones as resource records. Security can even be provided with non-security-aware DNS servers.

The extensions also allow for the storage of authenticated public keys in DNS. This storage of keys can support general-public, key-distribution services as well as DNS security. The stored keys enable security-aware resolvers to learn the authenticating key of zones as well as those for which they were initially configured. Keys that are associated with DNS names can be retrieved to support other protocols. In addition, the extensions provide for the optional authentication of DNS protocol transactions.

NOTE   For more information on Secure DNS see `http://ds.internic.net/Internet-drafts/draft-ietf-dnssec-secext-09.txt`.

NOTE   If you would like to stay on top of the changes, you can subscribe to the DNS workgroup mailing list from the `http://ietf.org` Web page.

6

Using File Transfer Protocols to Ease Your Life

It happens often: a remote user calls your phone because they need a particular file they cannot get access to via e-mail or through their dial-up connection. Or perhaps a customer needs a particular document about a particular product you have to offer that they saw on the Web site, but they need to have a hard copy of the information sent to them immediately. Now, I am not saying these are unreasonable requests or even requests that you can't, won't, or shouldn't handle, but they are requests that the user can handle themselves. With the TCP/IP protocol suite, there are actually three protocols that will help you to transfer files.

If you have worked in this industry for more than a week, you have downloaded a file from somewhere using the File Transfer Protocol (FTP). It is easy to do, but like many things that are easy to do, more is going on in the background than you may think. FTP works in conjunction with Telnet to log you into a remote FTP server and then to provide for the transfer of files. FTP also provides for security in the access to the directory structure.

Trivial File Transfer Protocol (TFTP) is kind of FTP-lite. It offers you the ability to be able to transfer files from here to there, but you had better know where here and there are when you start! With TFTP, you cannot browse directories or do anything fancy; it is designed to just give and receive files. TFTP also lacks the security of FTP. If the file is available to the general public, you can use TFTP to get it. If there is security involved, TFTP is not going to be able to help you.

Finally, there is the Network File System, or NFS. NFS allows two different types of file systems to interoperate. Imagine, if you will, what happens when a server running Windows NT needs to share a file with a Unix host. If the NFS server side software is running on the NT server and the NFS client software was running on the Unix machine, NFS on NT would store the Unix files in RAM where they would be accessible to the Unix hosts. Even though the two file-system definitions are different, both sets of users would be able to use the file.

NOTE   File transfer is not the same thing as remotely executing a file. That uses a completely different set of TCP/IP Application layer protocols.

FTP Exposed

When you examine the protocol traffic statistics of the Internet, FTP is the most widely used TCP/IP application protocol. Because it is one of the oldest TCP/IP protocols, nearly every commercial TCP/IP product has some form of FTP support.

FTP is defined in RFC959. When you think about file transfer, you obviously have some place you are transferring the file from and somewhere you are transferring the file to. The place the file is being transferred from is referred to as the Server-FTP, and the place that is requesting the file transfer is referred to as the User-FTP. On the User-FTP side of the equation, there are three components that make up the building blocks for a successful file transfer. Take a look at Figure 6.1, which is a representation of how FTP works.

As you can see, with any good communication model it takes two sides to make a conversation. On the User-FTP side, there is the User Interface (UI), the User Protocol Interpreter, and the User Data Transfer Process. The Server-FTP features the Server Protocol Interpreter and the Server Data Transfer Process. Let's take a look at the User-FTP side first, starting with the User Interface.

Figure 6.1   File Transfer Protocol model

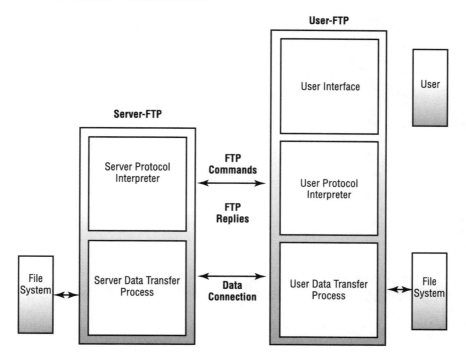

FTP User Interface

The FTP User Interface takes on many faces. You can access FTP from most Internet browsers: if you have the client software available on your host, you can access FTP from the command line, or you can use any one of a number of commercially available freeware, shareware, or software versions of the front end. No matter how the User Interface hides or masks the process, each one is still using the same set of defined ftp commands.

> **NOTE**   For simplicity sake, think of FTP this way. When you see FTP in all capitals, think of the protocol, the server, or the user interface. When you see ftp in lowercase letters, think of the command-line utility that is used to initiate file transfer between two hosts.

Now, we will cover ftp and the ftp command set later in the chapter, but Figure 6.2 is one way that your users are using ftp without even knowing it.

Figure 6.2 FTP using Internet Explorer 5 as a UI

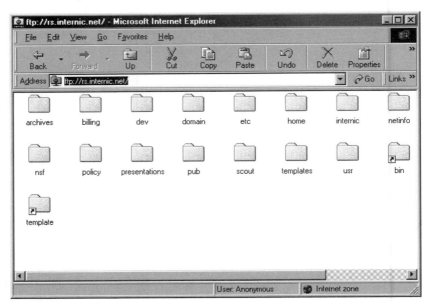

Internet Explorer, Netscape, and most other browsers provide a simple way for users to be able to take advantage of some of the functionality of FTP. Unfortunately, these UIs work only one way: you can get data from an FTP server, but you can't put anything back.

Some users spend a lot of their time uploading, downloading, and managing files using the ftp command. For these people, the FTP process is made easier to use because of some dedicated shareware, freeware, and software solutions. Many of these feature drag-and-drop technology or the ability to resume a file transfer after an unscheduled interruption.

Some of the more popular models with the reviewers include Bullet Proof FTP, CuteFTP, FTP Control, and FTP Voyager. I only chose those UIs that provided the ability to both upload and download files using FTP.

TIP Did you know that many browsers can handle more than one download at a time? I didn't either. For example, Internet Explorer can handle up to four downloads at the same time. Just start one download, find the next file you want, and start that download. It can help you shuffle file transfers if you have over four connections going at the same time.

Bullet Proof FTP

Bullet Proof FTP is a shareware utility available at www.bpftp.com. You can download a 30-day trial version for free; if you want to register the program, the going rate is around $30, which is a one-time charge and the upgrades are free. Figure 6.3 shows the UI for Bullet Proof FTP.

Figure 6.3   Bullet Proof FTP User Interface

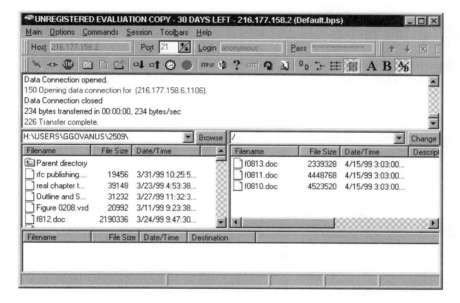

CuteFTP

CuteFTP is another shareware program. For some reason, this User Interface did not seem as "busy" to me as the interface to Bullet Proof. The CuteFTP file icons were descriptive, as well, meaning they pointed to the creating program. You can see what I mean in Figure 6.4.

Figure 6.4 The CuteFTP User Interface

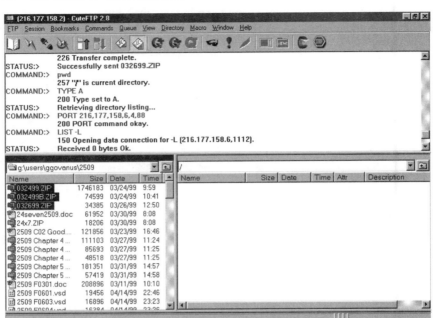

The icons come with a price though. CuteFTP is available from www.cuteftp.com and registration will cost approximately $35 for a single user license. There are discounts available for multiple licenses.

FTP Control

FTP Control is a shareware program from the Netherlands. It is available from www.transsoft.com. There are several versions of FTP Control, and along with those versions, you have several pricing structures.

- The Lite version is $10. The Lite version offers basic FTP functionality, including server profiles, FTP browsing, and file transfers.

- The Professional (Pro) version is $29. The Pro version offers Favorites/Bookmark handling, MRU support, proxy support, the ability to resume an interrupted transfer, remote commands and attribute settings.

- The Pro Power Version is $49. The Pro Power version unlocks the full potential of FTP Control. Additional features in this version are Zip file handling; scripting facilities; multiple, simultaneous open FTP sessions; distributable EXE file generation from scripts; transfers between remote servers ("cross-servers transfer"); and fast encrypt/scramble and decrypt/descramble capablilities.

The user front-end for FTP Control is shown in Figure 6.5.

Figure 6.5   FTP Control from Transsoft

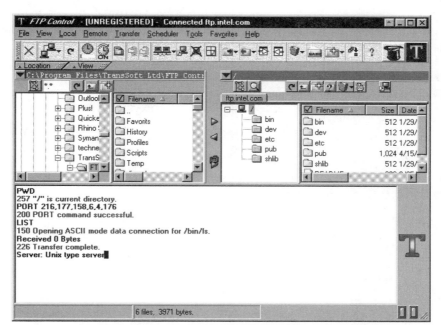

FTP Voyager

The last User Interface I will show you is FTP Voyager. Several things about the install were interesting. The first one is shown in Figure 6.6.

Figure 6.6   FTP Voyager installation screen

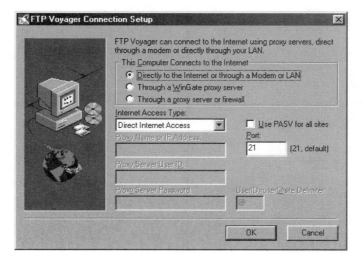

Notice the little check box off to the right-hand side that asks whether I want to use PASV for all transfers. PASV stands for *Passive mode* and the use of this command allows FTP to work through a firewall that refuses incoming TCP connections that are assigned to arbitrary ports. Figure 6.7 shows the Voyager User Interface.

Figure 6.7 Voyager User Interface

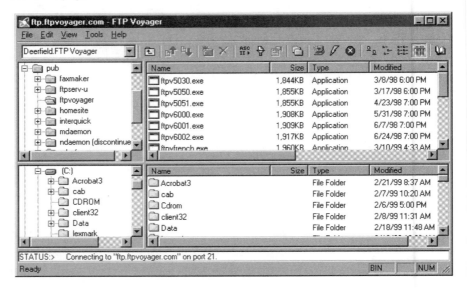

NOTE PASV can also come into play when designing Web documents with Microsoft Front Page. Front Page does not like FTP in Passive mode.

FTP Voyager is available as shareware from www.ftpvoyager.com. If you choose to buy it, the cost is around $38; if you buy multiple copies, the price will go down.

FTP-PM

FTP-PM is a Graphical User Interface that is designed to work with OS/2. It allows users to both upload and download files (if the servers allow it) by using a drag-and-drop method. File-transfer methods need to be specified, whether in ASCII or binary mode.

FTP Commands

For those hard-line, die-hard Unix folks, or even for those of us that grew up on the command line, there is nothing quite like doing it yourself. For those types, it is nice to know that they can always fall back on the command-line `ftp` command. Depending on your familiarity with the command line, entire `ftp` sessions can be managed without ever entering a Graphical User Interface (GUI). To those who are only used to point-and-click, this ability might be kind of scary. The syntax to open or start an `ftp` session is

```
ftp [-v] [-n][-I][-d][-g][-s:filename][hostname]
```

A breakdown of the parameters follows:

-v   Suppresses the display of remote-server responses.

-n   Suppresses autologon upon initial connection.

-i   Turns off interactive prompting during multiple file transfers.

-d   Enables debugging, displaying all `ftp` commands passed between the client and the server.

-g   Disables filename globbing, which permits the use of wildcard characters in local file and path names.

-s:filename   Specifies a text file containing `ftp` commands that will automatically run once the `ftp` session starts. This switch is used instead of the redirection indicator (>).

hostname   Specifies the host name or IP address of the remote host Server-FTP. The host, if specified, must be the last parameter on the line.

The `ftp` command simply opens a session between the User-FTP and the Server-FTP. Once the communication session has been established, the user must authenticate into the Server-FTP, and this may be done using *anonymous* FTP. Anonymous FTP allows the user to access a machine without having a formal account on that host. The anonymous Server-FTP may contain software, documents of various sorts, files to aid in configuring networks, graphic images, and almost any other type of information you can imagine.

> **NOTE**   Although some Server-FTP implementations are configured to use user names and passwords, most don't. FTP specifications call for the password to be sent over the wire in clear text, meaning that the password is not encrypted or protected. Anyone with a sniffer could capture the password for a specific user. To prevent this from happening, Server-FTP sites will usually have a user created with the name of Anonymous. To create a connection when prompted for a user name, type **anonymous**. The password for the session would be your e-mail address, for example, garyg@psconsulting.com. Although this process obviously provides no security whatsoever, it allows the system administrator with the capability to track who has accessed the Server-FTP and which files they accessed.

Using TCP/IP Protocols

PART 2

Once the FTP session has been established between the Server-FTP and the User-FTP, the prompt on your screen will resemble this:

```
ftp>
```

This prompt will be followed by a blinking cursor. The server is obviously waiting for some input in the form of a command. Some of the commands necessary to run an FTP session are contained in Table 6.1.

Table 6.1 FTP Session Commands

Command	Purpose
!	Runs the specified command on the local computer.
?	Displays descriptions of ftp commands. ? is used for help.
ascii	Sets the file-transfer type to ASCII, which is the default.
bell	Toggles a bell to ring after each file-transfer command is completed. By default, the bell is off.
binary	Sets the file-transfer type to binary.
bye	Ends the FTP session with the remote host and exits ftp.
cd	Changes the working directory on the remote server and returns to the command interpreter.
debug	Toggles debugging. When debugging is on, each command sent to the remote host is printed, preceded by the string --- >. By default, debugging is off.
delete	Deletes files on remote hosts.
dir	Displays a list of a remote's directory files and subdirectories.
disconnect	Disconnects from the remote host retaining the ftp> prompt.
get	Copies a remote file to the local host using the current file-transfer type.
glob	Toggles filename globbing. Globbing permits use of wildcard characters in the local file path or path names. By default, globbing is on.

Table 6.1   FTP Session Commands *(continued)*

Command	Purpose
hash	Toggles hash-sign (#) printing for each data block transferred. The size of the data block is 2,048 bytes. By default, hash is off.
lcd	Changes the working directory on the local host. By default, the current directory on the local host is used.
literal	Sends arguments, verbatim, to the remote FTP server. A single FTP reply code is expected in return.
ls	Displays an abbreviated list of a remote directory's files and subdirectories.
mdelete	Delete multiple files on a remote host.
mdir	Displays a list of a remote directory's files and subdirectories. mdir enables you to specify multiple files.
mget	Copies remote files to the local host using the current file-transfer type.
mkdir	Creates a remote directory.
mls	Displays an abbreviated list of a remote directory's files and subdirectories.
mput	Copies local files to the remote host using the current file-transfer type.
open	Connects to the specified FTP server.
prompt	Toggles prompting. FTP prompts during multiple file transfers to enable you to selectively retrieve or store files; mget and mput transfer all of the files if prompting is turned off. By default, prompting is on.
put	Copies a local file to the remote host using the current file-transfer type.
pwd	Displays the current directory on the remote host.
quit	Ends the FTP session with the remote host and exits ftp.

Table 6.1   FTP Session Commands *(continued)*

Command	Purpose
quote	Sends arguments, verbatim, to the remote FTP server. A single FTP reply code is expected in return. quote is identical to literal.
recv	Copies a remote file to a local host using the current file-transfer type. recv is identical to get.
remotehelp	Displays help for remote commands.
rename	Renames remote files.
rmdir	Deletes a remote directory.
send	Copies a local file to the remote host using the current file-transfer type. send is identical to put.
status	Displays the current status of FTP connections and toggles.
trace	Toggles packet tracing; trace displays the route of each packet when running an ftp command.
type	Sets or displays the file-transfer type.
user	Sends new user information.
verbose	Toggles Verbose mode. If on, all FTP responses are displayed. When a file transfer completes, statistics regarding the efficiency of the transfer are also displayed. By default, verbose is on.

Once the ftp session has been started and the commands are passed using either a GUI or the command line, it is time to move to the next level of the user side of the equation, the User Protocol Interpreter.

TIP   Downloading files takes time—everyone knows that. Why fight the crowds? Using several of the FTP clients listed above, you can schedule your downloads for late nights, when traffic is minimal. The busiest times of the day on the Internet are between 3 P.M. and 5 P.M., Eastern time, and in the evening between 7 P.M. and 11:00 P.M., Eastern time. So if you have a large file to download, try doing it late at night or early in the morning.

User Protocol Interpreter (User-PI)

When a session is started, the User-FTP internally assigns a port address and initiates the control connection. The control connection follows the Telnet Protocol. At the initiation of the user connection, standard ftp commands are used by the User-PI and transmitted to the server process via the control connection. Standard replies are sent from the Server-PI to the User-PI over the control connection in response to the ftp commands. The ftp commands specify the parameters for the data connection; this includes the data port, the transfer mode, the representation type, and the data structure. It also defines the nature of file-system operation, initiating file storage, file retrieval, an append to a file, or a file deletion.

> **NOTE**   FTP uses two separate, well-known port addresses as well as two randomly assigned port addresses. The User-FTP Interface initially assigns a random port for its communications, and this port number is used to connect to the Server-FTP port number 21. This is designated for FTP control of the communication session. The data that is to be transferred passes from another self-assigned port on the User-DTP to port number 20, which is designated for the transfer of FTP data, on the Server-DTP. This means that two port numbers are used for the two logical communication paths: the control path and the data path.

The Relationship between the FTP User PI and Telnet

The User PI uses the Telnet Protocol to establish the control connection. This connection can be achieved in two ways: the User-PI or the Server-PI may implement the rules of the Telnet Protocol directly in their own procedures; or the User-PI or the Server-PI may make use of the existing Telnet module in the system.

The use of the existing Telnet module is the preferred approach because of the ease of implementation, the ability to share code, and the efficiency of modular programming. Efficiency and independence suggest that implementing the rules of the Telnet Protocol directly may make the most sense. In reality, FTP does not rely heavily on the Telnet Protocol.

User Data Transfer Process (User DTP)

The User-DTP or its designated process should "listen" on the specified data port, and then the server side can initiate the data connection and data transfer in accordance with the parameters specified in the command string. The data port need not be in the same host that initiates the ftp commands via the control connection, but the user or the User-FTP process must ensure a "listen" on the specified data port. It should also be noted that the data connection may be used for both sending and receiving.

Files are transferred only via the data connection. The control connection is used for the transfer of commands, which describe the functions to be performed, and the replies to these commands. Several commands are concerned with the transfer of data between hosts. These data-transfer commands include the MODE command, which specifies how the bits of the data are to be transmitted, and the STRUcture and TYPE commands, which are used to define the way in which the data is to be represented. The transmission and representation are basically independent.

A "What If" Data Transfer

The previous scenario adequately defines how a user can transfer files from a remote host to a local host or vice versa. Now let's play a quick game of What If. What if a user wants to transfer files between two hosts, neither of which is a local host. In this case, the user sets up control connections to the two servers and then arranges for a data connection between them. In this manner, the information controlling the session is passed to the User-PI, but data is transferred between the two-server data-transfer processes. Figure 6.8 shows this server-to-server interaction.

Figure 6.8   Server-to-server interaction

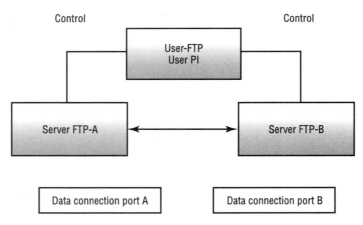

FTP requires that the control connections be open while data transfer is in progress. It is the responsibility of the user to request the closing of the control connections when finished using the FTP service, whereas the server takes the action. The server may abort data transfer if the control connections are closed without a command.

TIP Sometimes, it is not what you download that determines the speed of the process but from where you download. Most major FTP sites make use of mirror sites. You know the ones, every time you try to download a file, you get this list of 15 to 20 sites to choose from. If you are like me, you blindly select the cities closest to your hometown, because you want to minimize the distance that the little packet has to travel. Unfortunately, everyone else in the region is hitting the same server, and performance can really degrade. Break away from the crowds, and choose a server on the other side of the world. Think about it: while it is prime-time downloading where you are, it is the middle of the night on the other side of the world, and those servers are probably not overworked.

Sample FTP Session

As an example of the way you can work with FTP, here were the instructions given to a beta tester of Windows 2000. The object was to go out to a beta site that was accessed with a user name and password and to download all the files necessary to install Windows 2000. The following list shows the FTP session results:

```
C:\ftp ntbeta.microsoft.com
Connected to ntbeta.microsoft.com
220 ntbeta Microsoft FTP Service (Version 3.0)
User (ntbeta.microsoft.com: (none)):985123
331 Password required for 985123
Password:
230-Welcome to the Windows 2000 Beta FTP Server.
**Unauthorized use of this server is prohibited.**
230 User 985123 logged in
ftp> cd/outgoing/nt5/build2000/x86/2000.pro
250 CWD command successful
ftp> bin
200 Type set to I
ftp> prompt off
Interactive mode Off
ftp> mget *.*
```

Using TCP/IP
Protocols

PART 2

Notice all those little numbers after each command has been entered. They are called *FTP server return codes*. Table 6.2 has a list of some of the more common codes.

Table 6.2 FTP Server Return Codes

Code	Meaning
119	Terminal not available; will try mailbox
120	Service ready in *nnn* minutes
125	Data connection already open; transfer starting
225	Data connection open; no transfer in progress
150	File status okay; about to open a data connection
151	User not local; will forward to user@host
152	User unknown; mail will be forwarded by the operator
250	Requested file action okay, completed
200	Command okay
211	System status, or system help reply
212	Directory status
213	File status
214	Help message
220	Service ready for new user
221	Service closing Telnet connection
226	Closing data connection; requested file action successful
227	Entering Passive mode
230	User logged in; proceed
331	User name okay; need password
332	Need account for login

Table 6.2   FTP Server Return Codes *(continued)*

Code	Meaning
350	Requested file action pending further information
450	Requested file action not taken; file unavailable
421	Service not available; closing Telnet connection
425	Cannot open data connection
426	Connection closed; transfer aborted
530	Not logged in
532	Need account for storing files
550	Requested action not taken

Sun Microsystems Network File System

Sun Microsystems released Network File System (NFS) in 1985 as part of the Sun Operating System, which was included on Sun workstations. Since then, NFS has been adopted and adapted to many computing platforms, including PCs, minicomputers, and large mainframes.

NFS is based on the client/server model in which the client is the local computer that runs the application, and the server is the computer that manages the file or application programs. There may be vast distances between the client and the server, but that does not matter to NFS. NFS provides transparent access to files regardless of their location. In addition, any machine can be either the client or the server.

Another advantage of NFS is that users can access files regardless of the operating system under which they are stored. Therefore, NFS allows directories and files to be shared between a Windows NT computer and machines running Unix, DEC VAX, VMS, MVS, or the Apple Macintosh operating system. If all those machines are running NFS, NFS assures access to files.

The basis for the Sun protocols is the UDP and IP transport protocols. These traditionally operate on a number of LAN/WAN interfaces. Because NFS relies on UDP and UDP is a connectionless transport, NFS must make some allowances for errors. The NFS client/ server model uses a stateless protocol in which one operation (or state) must complete successfully before another operation even starts. When a client makes a request, it has to wait for the server's response. If the server does not respond or delays its response, the client will simply repeat the request. A server crash will not have an impact on the client, other than to slow down the client interface, or in a worst case scenario, give the impression that the server has become hung up. If the client has successfully received the application file, then the client/server interaction is complete. If the client has not received the file, it will continue to send the file request until the server is reinitialized. It can be said that the process is persistent, if nothing else.

Several protocols help to make up the Sun NFS suite, and these protocols are made up of three separate modules: the Remote Procedure Call (RPC), the External Data Representation (XDR), and NFS. These three sit on top of UDP and IP, as shown in Figure 6.9.

Figure 6.9   The NFS protocol stack

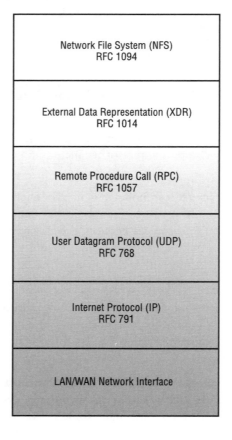

The first layer on top of UDP is the Remote Procedure Call. The RPC establishes a logical connection between the client and the server. In this case, the client sends a message to the server and then waits for the server's reply. The server's reply must include the results of the requested procedure.

The External Data Representation layer, or XDR layer, provides all the functions of the OSI model's Presentation layer. It describes and encodes the data that is transferred to and from the client and the server. The NFS Protocol defines the file, the directory structure, and the procedures for the client and the server.

Why Institute NFS?

There is no such thing as a simple network. Each network is made up of pieces that are designed to do a specific job, and it is your job to make these work together seamlessly. If your network has Unix hosts or Linux systems, interspersed with Windows NT or Windows 98 systems, then making file transfer easier is just one of the reasons to use NFS. NFS also provides for robust printer sharing between platforms. If you have Unix hosts that need to print to a non-Unix printer or a Windows NT host that needs to print to a printer hooked to a Unix computer, chances are you are using (or will be shortly) some form of NFS.

Installing and Configuring an FTP Server

Because we now have the user side of the equation pretty well covered, we can move on to the FTP server side. Again, there are shareware as well as other versions of FTP servers, some with more bells and whistles than others. There are also my favorite kinds of FTP servers, and those are the free kind!

> **TIP** Be sure your users know that FTP sites can be added to their favorites for quick access. If the site requires a user name and a password, they can be added to the URL to provide seamless access. For example, `ftp://username-:password@ site_address` should get them through the door.

An FTP server product comes with Microsoft Windows NT 4 and Novell NetWare 5, and it can be configured to run on most Unix hosts. Let's take a look at how some of the systems are configured.

Microsoft Windows NT 4 FTP Server

The FTP server service on a Windows NT 4 server can be installed when the operating system is installed. It is part of the installation of the Internet Information Service. If you look at Figure 6.10, you will see the IIS 3.0 Setup screen.

Figure 6.10   IIS 3.0 Setup screen

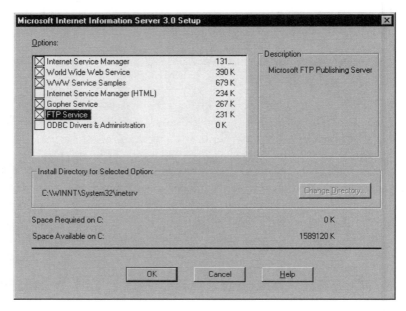

Once FTP has been installed, it shows up on the IIS Manager screen shown in Figure 6.11.

Figure 6.11   The IIS Manager with FTP

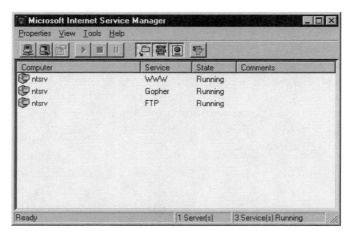

To actually manage FTP, you have to double-click on the FTP entry in the IIS Manager window to get to the FTP Services Properties window shown in Figure 6.12.

Figure 6.12   The FTP Services Properties window

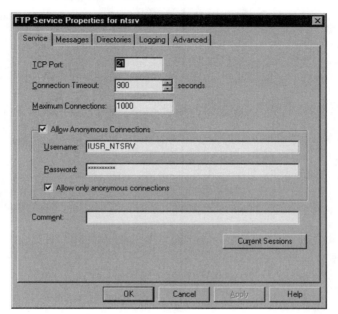

Notice that there is a check box to allow only anonymous entries to the system. If you uncheck that box, you can move over to the Advanced tab on the FTP Services Properties window. If you look closely at Figure 6.13, you will see that you can allow or disallow access based on a host address.

> **WARNING**   One of the limitations of the FTP server is that its password is sent over the wire in clear text, meaning it is not encrypted. Any person on the network with a network sniffer can capture the password packets and know the password for that specified user. This is one of the reasons that many FTP servers allow only anonymous access and do not try to limit the access to the server.

Now, from this it may appear that the Microsoft FTP server only allows people to log on anonymously or from a specific workstation address. That is not the case. FTP can always use user-level security, meaning the user must log on to gain access to the FTP server using a defined user name and password. The Internet Information Server FTP service can use the Windows NT user account database to authenticate users logging on. Remember, all FTP transmissions are in clear text, thus exposing user names and passwords.

Figure 6.13 The advanced tab of the FTP Services Properties window

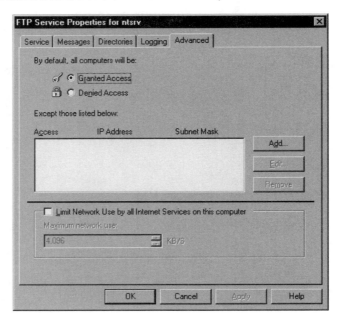

To turn this potential security risk into a feature of FTP, the marketing folks at Microsoft put this spin on the anonymous user logon: "The problem of exposed passwords is eliminated when an FTP server is configured to permit anonymous logons. Anonymous logon requires the user to type **anonymous** as their user name and their Internet e-mail address as their password. Anonymous users get access to files under the IUSR_*computername* account." That came from the April 1999 version of Microsoft *TechNet*. I am not sure how that washes with a network administrator's desire to protect certain files, but I may be missing something! FTP is configured for anonymous access by default.

TIP You can make an alternative FTP utility your default, instead of browsers such as Microsoft Internet Explorer or Netscape Navigator. To do that using a Windows 95/98 system, double-click the My Computer icon, go to the View menu, and select Folder Options. Select the File Types tab in the Options dialog box, and select URL:File Transfer Protocol in the Registered File Types list box. Click the Edit button, and open the Edit File Type dialog box; select the open line in the Actions text box, and click the Edit button. In the Editing Action for Type box, use the Browse button to select the FTP program you want, deselect the Use DDE option, and click OK.

If a user does authenticate to the network using a predefined user name and password, it is called a *request containing credentials*. A request containing credentials is one of the following:

An FTP client logs on with a valid Windows NT user name and password. This requires that the FTP service check box labeled Allow Only Anonymous Connections be unchecked.

A WWW (HTTP) requests header contains a user name and a password. This is HTTP basic authentication.

If a WWW browser that supports NTLM (Windows NT native) authentication is used, an anonymous client request will be denied access to a resource. In this case, the browser automatically sends the Windows client's user name and password to the Internet Information Server Web server using the encrypted NTLM protocol.

When an Internet Information Server service receives a client request that contains credentials (a user name and password), the anonymous-logon user account is not used in processing the request. Instead, the user name and password received by the client are used by the service. If the service is not granted permission to access the requested resource while impersonating the specified user, the request fails, and an error notification is returned to the client.

If the request comes from a WWW (HTTP) client and the anonymous request fails because the anonymous-logon user account does not have permission to access the desired resource, the response to the client indicates which authentication schemes the service supports. This is determined by the configuration of the WWW service-authentication features. If the response indicates to the client that the service is configured to support HTTP basic authentication, most Web browsers will pop up a User Name/Password dialog box and reissue the anonymous request as a request with credentials, including the user name and password entered by the user.

Suppose a Web browser supports NTLM authentication. (This can be a large supposition because Microsoft Internet Explorer does, but Netscape Navigator and Communicator do not.) Now, if the Web service is configured to support NTLM authentication and an anonymous WWW request fails due to permissions settings, this will result in automatic use of the NTLM Protocol. The browser will be sending a user name and encrypted password from the client to the service. The client request will then be reprocessed, using the client's user information. The user account obtained from the client is the one that the user is logged on with. Because this account, including its Windows NT domain, must be a valid account on the Web server machine, NTLM authentication is most useful in an intranet environment, in which the client and server machines are in the same, or trusted, domains.

Internet Service Manager Authentication Options

In addition to the anonymous-logon user-name and password fields, the Internet Service Manager Service property page contains several authentication options.

For WWW, the options are as follows:

Allow Anonymous   When this box is checked, anonymous connections are processed, and the anonymous-logon user name/password are used for these connections. When this box is unchecked, all anonymous connections are rejected. In this case, basic or NTLM authentication can be used to access content.

Basic   When this box is checked, the Web service will process requests using basic authentication. Basic authentication sends Windows NT user names and passwords across the network without encryption. This box is unchecked by default for security reasons.

Windows NT Challenge/Response   When this box is checked, the service will honor requests by clients to send user account information using the Windows NT Challenge/Response (NTLM) Protocol. This protocol uses encryption for secure transmission of passwords. The NTLM authentication process is initiated automatically as a result of an 'access denied' error on an anonymous client request.

The following authentication options are for FTP:

Allow Anonymous Connections   When this box is checked, FTP logons in which the user enters a user name of 'anonymous' will be processed. These anonymous connections will be processed on behalf of the Windows NT user account specified on the Service property page. When this box is unchecked, users will be required to enter valid Windows NT user names and passwords to log on to the FTP service.

Allow Only Anonymous Connections   When this box is checked, user logons with a user name other than anonymous will be rejected.

Other Authentication Issues

One other piece of the authentication puzzle is not used on every connection but might come in handy.

SSL SSL is a WWW feature that supports data encryption and server authentication. All data sent to or from the client using SSL is encrypted. If HTTP basic authentication is used in conjunction with SSL, the user name and password are transmitted after being encrypted by the client's SSL support software.

INTERACTIVE and NETWORK Users

If you use the predefined Windows NT user accounts INTERACTIVE and NETWORK for access control, your use of these accounts may affect client access to some resources. In order for a file to be accessed by anonymous client requests or client requests using basic authentication, the requested file must be accessible by the INTERACTIVE user. In order for a file to be accessible by a client request using NTLM authentication, the file must be accessible by the NETWORK user.

Log On Locally User Right In User Manager, when configuring a Windows NT user account to be used either as the Internet Information Server anonymous-logon account or as a user account specified by client requests using HTTP basic authentication, be sure that the user account is granted the Log on Locally user right. This is specified in User Manager's Policies menu.

Customizing FTP Server

When a user connects to an FTP server, they may not even know where they are or what they are doing there. One way to solve that problem is by providing site information. You can add a welcome message, an exit message, or even a directory contents message. The personalization can be done through the Messages tab of the FTP service page.

NetWare 5 and FTP Services

As with most services in the new NetWare, there are about three or four different ways to install Unix support services to run on a NetWare 5 server. The easiest way I found is through the NWCONFIG screen and Install Other Products. Once FTP is installed, it is managed using the familiar UNICON.NLM interface. I say familiar, because this interface and utility hasn't changed much in the last several revisions of NetWare.

Selecting the FTP Service Process from UNICON will bring up the menu options shown in Figure 6.14.

Figure 6.14 UNICON FTP selections

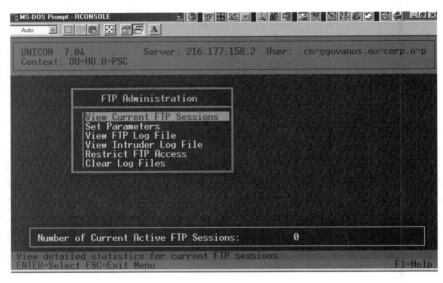

Not really too much to look at there, but if you choose the Parameters page shown in Figure 6.15, there is more to configure.

Figure 6.15 Parameters page of UNICON

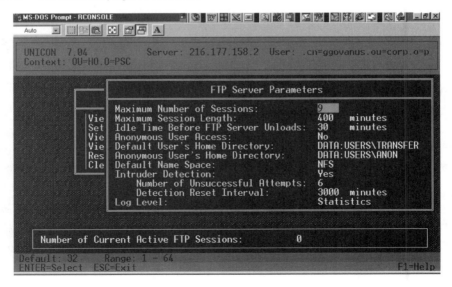

Notice again that you can choose to allow anonymous users access to the FTP server, or you can have the server for only your network users. If you decide to allow real users to access the page, they will have to authenticate using their Novell Directory Services name and password.

Security for the FTP service is not very complicated. Other than NDS, other options are configured using a simple text file called the restrict.ftp file. The following is an example of the file:

```
#                      FTP Server Access Control File
#
#  This file determines who can access files through the ftp
#  server. The user name must be specified to gain access. The
#  default configuration allows all users access.
#
#  Syntax:
#
#  <username> [ACCESS=DENY,GUEST,NOREMOTE,READONLY]
#             [ADDRESS=<hostname>,<hostgroup>]
#
#  <username> All users.
#                      e.g. "*"
#             All users from a NDS context.
#                      e.g. "*.OU=sales.O=acme"
#             NDS user relative to the default context.
#                      e.g. "bill"
#             Complete Canonicalized NDS name.
#                      e.g. ".CN=Admin.O=acme"
#
#             <username> is required and must be the first field in
#             the line.
#
#  ACCESS=    This option limits user access to the server. This
```

Using TCP/IP
Protocols

PART 2

```
#                    option is case sensitive and is not required.
#
#        DENY        Denies access to the server. This parameter
#                    overrides a previously declared global access.
#
#        GUEST       Restricts the user to the home directory on the
#                    server running the FTP server.
#
#        NOREMOTE    Restricts the user to the local server. User cannot
#                    access any remote servers.
#
#        READONLY    Restricts the user from storing any files on the
#                    server.
#
#   ADDRESS=    This option restricts access for users from a specific
#               host or set of hosts (hostgroup). This option is
#               case sensitive and is not required.
#
#   Examples:
#
#   1. The following example specifies that all users have access to
#      the local server but cannot access remote NetWare servers.
#
#   * ACCESS=NOREMOTE
#
#   2. The following example specifies that all users from the OU
#      called SALES have full access, but must connect from the host
#      <hostname>.
#
#   *.OU=SALES.O=ACME ADDRESS=hostname
```

```
#
#    3. The following example specifies the user ADMIN cannot access
#       the FTP server.
#
#    .ADMIN.O=ACME ACCESS=DENY
#
#    The following default entry of "*" allows all users access to
#    ftp server.
# *
.CN=GGOVANUS.OU=CORP.O=PSC
```

In this case, the only user who is allowed access to the FTP server is
`.CN=GGOVANUS.OU=CORP.O=PSC`. A password is required on the account.

Unix and FTP Servers

So far, we have been talking about using operating systems that come with Graphical
User Interfaces or with menu-driven installation routines. When you start talking about
Unix, these things can change. Setting up an FTP server to handle anonymous FTP ser-
vices can be a little complicated.

FTP Server Creation Overview

To complete the task, follow these steps:

1. Add the user named `ftp` to the `/etc/passwd` file.

2. Create an `ftp` home directory that is owned by the user `ftp`. This directory should
   be configured so that it cannot be written to by anyone.

3. Create a `bin` directory under the `ftp` home directory that is owned by `root`. This
   is another directory that cannot be written to by anyone. The **ls** program should
   be placed in this directory and changed to Execute-Only mode, which is mode 111.

4. Create an `etc` directory in the `ftp` home directory that is owned by `root`. Again
   this directory cannot be written to by anyone. There should be a special `passwd`
   and `group` file in that directory, and the mode of both files should be changed to
   read only, or mode 444.

5. Create a `pub` directory in the `ftp` home directory. This directory should be owned
   by `root`, and the only object that can write to the directory is `root` (mode 644).
   Unless it is absolutely necessary, don't allow remote users to store files on your

FTP server. The only times users should be allowed to store files on your FTP server is if the host is on a private network, not connected to the Internet. If you must allow users to store files on the host, change the ownership of the directory to ftp and the mode to 666 (read and write). There should only be one directory where anonymous FTP users can keep files.

FTP Server Creation, Step by Step

If you are new to Unix or just unfamiliar with some of the commands to accomplish the previously mentioned tasks, here is how it's done.

First of all, we need to create a ftp directory and some associated subdirectories. Because this directory is going to be associated with a user, we will place the directory under the /usr directory.

```
mkdir /usr/ftp
cd /usr/ftp
mkdir bin
mkdir etc
mkdir pub
```

Now, a copy of **ls** needs to be placed in the /usr/ftp/bin directory and have its permissions changed.

```
cp /bin/ls /usr/ftp/bin
chmod 111 /usr/ftp/bin/ls
```

Once this is done, a group should be created that will be used only by anonymous FTP. This group will have no other members. For the sake of simplicity, and also because it will help me to remember why I created the group, I will call it anonymous. This group will be created by using a text editor and making an entry in the /etc/group file. This entry should also be added to another file created and named /usr/ftp/etc/group that contains just this one single entry:

```
anonymous:*:15:
```

Next, we have to create the user named ftp. This is done by placing an entry for the user in the file /etc/passwd. You will also need to use your text editor to create a filename /usr/ftp/etc/passwd that contains only the ftp entry. The entry for both files should look like this:

```
ftp:*:15:15:Anonymous ftp:/usr/ftp:
```

> **NOTE** These examples use a Group ID (GID) and a User ID (UID) of 15. These are only random choices: you can pick any GID or UID that is not currently being used by your system.

If we were to use the `cat` command on the /usr/ftp/etc/passwd and on the /usr/ftp/etc/group files, it would show:

```
cat /usr/ftp/etc/passwd
ftp:*:15:15:Anonymous ftp:/usr/ftp:
cat /usr/ftp/etc/group
anonymous:*:15:
```

After both these files have been edited, both files can be set to mode 444 by using the following commands:

```
chmod 444 /usr/ftp/etc/passwd
chmod 444 /usr/ftp/etc/group
```

Now you need to set the appropriate ownership and mode for each of the directories. If you were logged on to the system as root when you created the /usr/ftp/pub, /usr/ftp/bin, and /usr/ftp/etc directories, nothing more needs to be done to them.

```
cd /usr/ftp
chmod 644 pub
chmod 555 bin
chmod 555 etc
cd ..
chown ftp ftp
chmod 555 ftp
```

To grant access to other users that upload files to the pub directory, make the following changes:

```
chown ftp pub
chmod 666 pub
```

For most Unix systems, the task is done, you should have an FTP Server. Before making the grand announcement to the world that the FTP service has been started and is available to anyone at anytime, it would probably be a great idea to check your work and make sure it functions as advertised.

Archie and the Fine Art of Searching the Internet

Archie is another one of those aspects of TCP/IP, like the ftp command, that are great to know about but will not be used on an everyday basis. At least that will be true for the vast majority of us.

Archie is a service that helps you to locate a file, a program, or other information you need. Archie has access to information servers that contain information about hundreds of FTP servers and thousands of files scattered all over the Internet. In other words, if you are looking for the file myfile.zip, you tell Archie, and Archie will tell you which FTP servers have the file. Although Archie started out just doing FTP files, it has been expanded to include all the World Wide Web directories and resource listings.

There are Archie servers available at (http://www.bunyip.com/products/archie/world/servers.html).

> **NOTE** I bet you're wondering, "Where does the name Archie come from?" The word archives is the origin of the name Archie. Traditionally, commands on Unix systems tend to be relatively small, so the name came to life when someone simply decided to drop the v and the s from archives. That is another one of those little known facts you can use the next time you are playing Trivial Pursuit.

Once you find the Archie server you want to use, you can telnet to it and log in using the user name archie and no password. When you get an archie> prompt, typing a simple **help** will get you a full set of interactive commands.

Archie can also be used by e-mail. To start with, you send an e-mail to Archie at any one of the Archie servers (archie@archie.internic.net). The text of the message should contain a valid archie e-mail command. To get a valid list of archie e-mail commands, send a message containing the help command to one of the Archie servers. If you are interested in the Archie servers, Figure 6.16 shows you a listing of the all the Archie servers worldwide.

Figure 6.16   Archie server listing

Probably the easiest way for most people to use Archie is through a Web browser. If you point your favorite Web browser to `http://archie.bunyip.com/archie.html`, you will have an opportunity to try Archie. Just so you don't close this book and run right out to try it, here is a sample of the Archie search page in Figure 6.17.

Figure 6.17 Archie search page

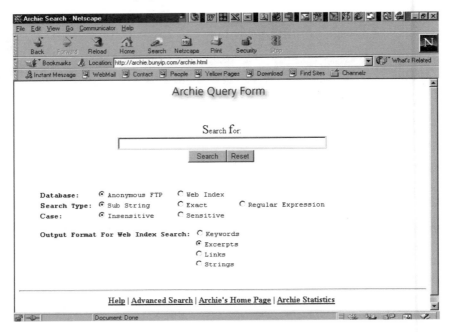

If you have to make files or information available, chances are FTP is going to be a part of your life. Even if you don't need to set up an FTP server, knowing how one operates will help you when you troubleshoot end-user problems when downloading files. It may also help you provide alternative methods for accessing just the right download.

Part 3

Network Design and Planning

- Working with management
- Working with the help desk
- Planning your work and working your plan
- Designing a WAN
- The future of the Internet
- How to be proactive rather than reactive using SNMP
- Creating your very own extranet and VPN

7

Atoning for the Sins of Your Predecessors

How about if we take a short break from the really techie stuff and look at something that is just as important to the career of a good network administrator. There are times when your interaction with the carbon-based units that work on your network is actually more important than the interface you have with the silicon-based units. These next couple of sections may not be entirely about TCP/IP, but there may be something here you can take away. If you are interested only in the technical stuff, this would probably be a great chapter to mark for reading at another time.

Every time you take over a new job, whether it comes with a change of companies or just a change of responsibilities, it comes with a honeymoon period. The honeymoon period—that wonderful period of bliss where you cannot do any wrong. By the same token, you may have noticed that when someone leaves the company, suddenly all of the woes of the world can become tagged to that person. This chapter will discuss how to milk the honeymoon period for all it is worth and how to make sure that when you leave for bigger and better things, the people left behind will only have good things to say about you.

Discovering Current Problem Areas

How did you get your job? What happened to the person who previously sat in your cube? Did they get promoted? Did they take a new job with a different company? Were they asked to leave? Why is this important to you and your current position? What if you are reading this book after being in your current position for a while? What does all this have to do with you? Actually, plenty.

When you take over a new job, much is expected. You are the hero or heroine, riding in on the charger, protecting the land from evil and making sure that the network will work the first time, every time. A great concept that no one can live up to over the long haul, but one that can help you to establish yourself as the network guru your boss knew they hired.

When you first walk into a new position to manage a new network, it is important to realize that the person who was there before you probably did a lot right. It is also important that you remember computing is one of those fields in which the same task can usually be done about a dozen different ways, and there is no "right way" or "wrong way" to do something. The definition of success is "it works," meaning it meets or exceeds the customers' needs. To take it a step further, the definition of success in network administration is "it works when the customer says it works."

That is a pretty tough definition, isn't it? At first blush, you may think it's unfair. After all, how many of the sales road warriors know *anything* about TCP/IP and all the work you are going to have to do to make files remotely available using FTP? Although you and I may have a long and fascinating discussion about this very topic, in the shape and scheme of the real world, it simply doesn't matter. What matters is the sales people and road warriors are singing your praises when the FTP server is up and working, because when it works, everything is great.

It is also important to keep in mind that not everything works. In the words of the famous bumper-sticker writer—well, maybe to paraphrase just a bit—stuff happens. Not everything you try is going to work the first time. It may not even work the fiftieth try. But sooner or later, you will get it to work. When things do not succumb to your magic touch the first time, remember the perception that people around you have about the work you do. You are truly a wizard. You are working with things that mere mortals (non-IT people) feel they have no right understanding. Though they may not understand it, it does not mean they cannot complain when it doesn't work or doesn't fulfill their expectations. They can, and they will. That is why perception is so important.

Great Expectations

Because you are expected to be the heroic knight (or knight-ette) who comes in to save the day, you'd best be able to locate the dragon pretty darn quickly. How can you find out what the biggest issues are around the company? More importantly, who decides what constitutes biggest?

That last question may seem to be rhetorical. The biggest problem is obviously that problem that affects the largest number of people for the longest time, right? That might make sense to you and me. But we may be wrong. Usually the "biggest" problem is something that causes the most people to gripe. In some cases, it may not even be a "problem" that you can fix, it may be an expectation.

For example, a friend took a new job, which came with all sorts of new responsibilities. Most of the responsibilities were fun—you know, the kind of back-room stuff that some geeks really like: building servers, installing operating systems, laying out security, figuring out addressing schemes, designing subnets, things like that. With the good, came the bad, however; in this case, it was the company's e-mail system.

Whenever anybody talked about the e-mail system, it was in derogatory terms. End users had problems printing out their calendars: they couldn't print the calendar out in the format they wanted, and the calendar's printing wasn't adaptable to the end user. For example, the chief executive officer of the company wanted to print a calendar in Week or Month view, but the e-mail program wouldn't do that.

So my friend set to work researching that issue. It didn't take long to figure out. When he called tech support and said his CEO was having a problem printing a monthly view of the calendar, the tech support's answer was that for as long as this program had been around, there had never a monthly view of the calendar that you could print. At least not a company-supported monthly view. There was some shareware that would do the trick, but it was not written and designed by the manufacturer.

Now my friend had a problem. The people in his company were expecting the e-mail package to do things it was never intended to do. Does that mean there is a problem with the e-mail package? Can't be. It was simply an issue of setting expectations. Had the expectations been set at the beginning, things may have worked out differently. As it was, the company upgraded to the newer version of the e-mail package, and it did all the things the people in the company wanted, so they were finally happy. Sometimes problem solving is simply setting or changing expectations.

So, what is your biggest problem? Your biggest problem is whatever your boss tells you your biggest problem is. You may have a DHCP server down, and IP addressing may be unavailable to 250 different hosts, making communication impossible for everyone on that segment of the network. If your boss says your biggest problem is making sure that the CEO's secretary's printer has paper in it, that becomes your biggest problem. It ain't fair, but whoever said life was fair?

Don't Sweat the Small Stuff

If left to your own devices, what are some of the ways you can determine the areas of opportunity on your new network? In case you are not familiar with the term *areas of opportunity,* that is marketing-speak for which problems can you tackle to make yourself look really good in a hurry.

Discovering some of these problems may require some data mining on your part. Usually, many of the problems become apparent as you find your way around the company. As you begin to meet people, you discover that everyone is very anxious to talk with the newest network person on the block. Most of those conversations start out with "How soon are you going to fix [*fill in the blank*]?" or "When will the new [*insert name of product or service*] be ready?" These are the kind of things that will give you a really large hint of what needs to be done.

If that doesn't do it for you, there are other places you can look. Most network administrators that I know will work with their companies' help desk but only if it is absolutely necessary. The administrators often seem to think that the help desk should be able to solve all the routine problems of the day. In an ideal world, that is the way it would be. Unfortunately, we don't live in an ideal world. Some of the problems the help desk faces on a routine basis may be things you can help with; you won't know it until you ask. Now may be a really good time to do so.

In most companies, the people that work the phone support desk are usually not the most network-savvy people in the company, because that is not what they are trained to do. They are trained to help end users with the typical end-user problems. You know the ones: if you plug it in, reboot it, or put paper in it, half the problems of the world will go away. But in some cases, end users may actually have problems you can help with.

Imagine, for example, that you are having lunch with Brandice from the help desk. As you begin to eat, she looks at you sheepishly and says, "Gee, while I have your attention, can I ask you about this really puzzling problem I have?" Being the nice person you are, you take a deep breath, put down your sandwich, and say sure.

The situation begins with C. J., who keeps having trouble getting to the Internet. The problem occurs on the rare occasions when C. J., an outside salesperson, brings his laptop into the office and plugs it into the docking station. The laptop is running a version Windows 98. Whenever C. J. dials into the local ISP, everything looks and works fine. As a matter of fact, when he is plugged into the docking station, he can access the corporate intranet and even ping addresses outside of the firewall. But when he fires up the browser, nothing seems to work.

Up until now, the preferred solution has been to have users dial the ISP whenever Internet access is necessary. Because C. J. is used to this, he doesn't seem to mind, but it is a nagging little thing that doesn't make sense. Any ideas?

You are about to make Brandice look really, really good. You smile knowingly and suggest she call C. J. back and tell him to check the TCP/IP configuration for the Network Interface Card (NIC). Because he can access the intranet and even ping the outside world, you know that TCP/IP is configured and working for the NIC. The gateway configuration is also correct because C. J. can access the outside world with a ping command. So it has to be something that is browser- or Domain Name Service–related. Tell Brandice to check the DNS addresses for the TCP/IP Protocol bound to the NIC. The DNS lookup addresses for the NIC may be wrong, probably because of an inverted number pair or something similar. Brandice comes away with a smile, you will probably get credit somewhere down the line, and there is another happy end user. Sometimes, it is the simple things that make a difference.

Because you understand the way that a packet gets routed to the Internet, you know that the client has to be doing some kind of name lookup to access an Internet Web site. You also understand that people can have fat fingers, and it is easy to mistype an IP address. Because the DNS lookup address for the dial-up connection may be provided by the ISP, it may be completely different than the address you are currently using for the company network. Checking the DNS address, correcting it, and restarting the computer will make all the difference in the world.

Understanding Expectations

Expectations are funny things. Everyone has them. They are what makes communication such a fascinating thing. Someone once said that anything that is really important can be said in under 15 seconds, usually in one sentence. Think about it. These are some of my favorites:

- I'm pregnant (or not).
- I'm from the IRS.
- I love you.
- I want a divorce.
- Will you marry me?

See what I mean? Do you wonder how expectations fit into these topics? Let's take a look at the first one. Assume we are overhearing a conversation of a young couple that has

Network Design and Planning

PART 3

been happily married for a few years, have great jobs, and really want a child. The phrase "I am pregnant" brings great joy, because the expectation is for a long and happy life together. Now, let's assume that the person uttering the phrase is someone very young, in her late teens. The father is nowhere to be found, and she is facing a life of raising and supporting the child by herself. Although the phrase may still be the source of joy, there can be expectations of a life that has been changed, and dreams that may have to be postponed. There may be a sense of fear and desperation also. Same phrase, different results, depending on expectations.

You and your users can have the same communication issues. Expectations need to be set, and they need to be maintained and nurtured. Proper setting of expectations can be a real stress reliever. I call it my 4-hour rule.

Before I became a consultant, I had a real 9-to-5 job. (It was a pretty frightening experience, so I started to work for myself.) I was a network administrator, just like you. I ran around configuring networks and servers, made sure workstations could access resources, and did most of what you probably do on a daily basis. It was routine most of the time, with periods of panic thrown in just for grins and giggles, to make sure I was still awake.

I was also considered somewhat of a hardware kind of guy. Whenever someone had something they needed added to a server, I usually got the call. Most of the time, again, it was routine stuff: adding memory or throwing another hard drive in the machine to add more storage, etc. Early in my "hardware guy" career, I learned an important lesson: There is nothing I can do on a server (or any computer for that matter) that requires less than four hours of allocated time. Absolutely nothing at all. Ever. For those of you that work with consultants, I should be quick to point out that the 4-hour rule has nothing to do with billable hours either!

Here is what I learned. First of all, you must go on the premise that Murphy's Law is always in effect. For those of you that may have been out of touch, Murphy's Law of the Universe states that anything that can go wrong, will go wrong, at the worst possible moment. To offset that law, you have the Williams's Law, which states that the way to tell a good network administrator is to measure their level of paranoia. Those that are very paranoid are very good and vice versa. I was very paranoid. I was also prone to make mistakes. One of the early mistakes I made was telling people exactly how long I thought a job should last. For example, for those of you that are hardware people, you know that adding memory to a computer is usually not a difficult job. As a matter of fact, if the main board manufacturer and the case manufacturer put some thought into the design of the system, it should take 30 minutes. That is on a slow day, when you have to look for your screwdriver. If things go right, probably less time than that. So I would tell people, thereby setting their expectations, that this job would be done in 30 minutes. Then I would get into it and find out that the case used the one screwdriver bit that I did not have with me. When I got into the case, I found that to access the open memory slots, I had to remove every hard drive and CD in the computer and dismantle the case completely. Total elapsed time to do the 30-minute job was about 2 1/2 hours. As far as the customer was concerned, I was an idiot. The fact that the memory was installed, the server was brought back up, and everything worked fine was immaterial. I had taken over two hours to do a job that should have taken 30 minutes. After several occurrences like this, I came to the realization that I really was an *idiot*. Not because I didn't know how to work with hardware, but because I didn't know how to work with people.

The next time I had a memory install, I told the customer to plan on the task taking four hours. I explained that several things could occur that would slow the process down even farther, but I figured that if the computer gods were shining on us, we would be out of the building four hours after we got there. Of course, I would get into the project and find out that the case used the one screwdriver bit I did not have with me. When I got into the case, I found that to access the open memory slots, I had to remove every hard drive and CD in the computer, and dismantle the case completely. Total elapsed time to do the 4-hour job was about 2 1/2 hours. As far as the customer was concerned, I was a genius. The fact that the memory was installed, the server was brought back up, and everything worked fine was immaterial. I had taken just over two hours to do a job that should have taken four hours. After several occurrences just like this, I came to the realization that I really was a genius. Not because I knew how to work with hardware, but because I had found one little lesson in working with people.

The 4-hour rule is simple. No job, no matter how simple or how small, takes less than four hours, ever. If I think a job is really complicated, I will mentally figure out my best estimate for the amount of time it is going to take, and then double it, at a minimum. If I think the job is really complicated, with lots of ways to screw it up, I may even triple it. That way, I am almost certain to finish early and be a genius. I have found that I really like being a genius a lot better than being an idiot. Use the 4-hour rule. You will find you will like it a lot better, too.

Expectations can be set many ways. Expectations can be set in what you say to people, but they can also be set in the way you act around people. End users want to think you are a computer god or goddess. They attribute certain characteristics to you that you may or may not actually have. For example, in the mind of the end user, if you are the network person hired to manage all the routers, you know all about computers. If you know about computers, then you must know everything there is to know about software. If you know everything there is to know about software, than you know how to remotely change the font on a linked spreadsheet stored on a host on the other side of world using a noninte-grated word-processing program. For your sake, don't even try to tell them that you have no clue of how to do that. They will look at you like you think you are too good for them and you are just blowing off their problem.

It gets worse. Heaven forbid if you list MCSE or CNE or some such title after your name because when you make a computer pronouncement, it comes directly from the heavens and should be etched in stone and kept for all time. You have those letters after your name, so you must know everything there is to know about computers, and whatever you say is 100 percent accurate every time on every subject. That is an awesome responsibility, and one that you shouldn't take lightly.

Now, for those of you that don't have the MCSE or CNE after their name, I am going to let you in on a highly guarded secret. This is probably breaking some kind of geek code, but I feel confident enough in my geekness to get away with this. I have both the MCSE and CNE after my name. As a matter of fact, I am an instructor, so I have Master CNE, Master CNI, and MCT after my name. I have written books helping people to become MCSEs, and I have helped write network encyclopedias. I have written books on TCP/IP. I have done all this, and yet not only don't I know everything about computers, the stuff I don't know far exceeds the stuff I do know. Just because somebody has all those fancy letters after their name doesn't mean they know everything. Hopefully, it means they are smart enough to recognize what they don't know and can get help to solve the current problem from someone who does know.

Don't be afraid to say you don't know. If a problem really has you stumped and you cannot figure it out, tell the user or administrator that you simply don't know the answer to this one, but you will find out. Then set their expectations. Tell them you will get back with them inside of *x* hours, and then *do it*. Call them, e-mail them, see them, but do something within that time period, even if it is to tell them you still don't know. Let them know what you have done to try to discover a solution to the problem and what the results were, but tell them something, and make sure it is the truth. The customer will respect and trust you for it. You are setting reasonable expectations, and you are meeting those expectations. That is building confidence in the customer. Confidence is a good thing!

Using the Help Desk

Earlier in this chapter, we looked at using help-desk calls to try to locate bigger TCP/IP problems. Keeping an ongoing relationship with the folks on the help desk (assuming you are also not the help desk) will make your job easier in the long run.

Working with the help desk can be a two-edged sword. You will gain lots of insights into the problems of your network and the vision of the users on your network. You will also be accessible to the help-desk staff for those really pesky "Oh, since you are already here..." kind of calls. The good outweighs the bad.

How organized is your help desk? With some companies, the help desk is a source of pride. Every call is logged and categorized so trends may develop. If a new problem arises, the problem and the solution are all documented in a searchable database, so the next time it occurs, someone will not have to reinvent the wheel when they try to solve it. These systems are a joy to behold and even more of a joy to work with. If you are a network administrator in this kind of an environment, chances are reports are already being generated that show whether the problem was desktop- or network-related. If it was desktop-related, it may not apply to you; if it is network-related, it may.

Keep in mind that with reports, someone has to analyze the data in them to see what they show. Help-desk reports can be a great source of information; you should take the time to read and analyze them and, more importantly, try to see the forest for the trees.

Things to Look for from the Help Desk

You have been put on the distribution list for the help-desk reports. You have tried to analyze the numbers of calls, the breakdown of calls, and how the calls relate to your department. After a while, your head starts to spin, and you begin to think that purchasing stock in the company that manufactures your favorite brand of aspirin might not be a bad idea. Where do you go from here?

Invest in a good spreadsheet program to put the information into, and start looking for trends. If you are new to the company, see if you can find reports that your predecessor may have overlooked or left lying around. Try to get a history established as soon as possible.

Start with the basics. How many calls has the help desk handled that were truly network-related over the last year? Is the number of calls per month increasing or decreasing? You may have to rework some of the figures here. Many help-desk systems will break down desktop vs. network types of calls, but sometimes the line may be fuzzy, especially for an inexperienced person on the help desk. For example, an end user calls up and says that he cannot access files or applications on the network. He swears that he really did log on to the network, but the help-desk person has the user restart their computer, log on to the network, and try to access resources. Once the restart was completed, everything worked as advertised. Is that a network problem, a desktop problem, or a problem with the carbon-unit interface between the chair and the keyboard. The answer is, it depends. It could very well be an end-user problem. The user shut his computer off the night before, came in the next morning, and turned it back on. The user thought he had logged on successfully, when, in fact, the logon failed. In this case, it is an end-user error.

Suppose, however, you notice that during a one-month period, several calls like that came from a particular network segment. The calls were usually grouped; perhaps on a particular Tuesday morning, ten users from a particular subnet called in to report losing a network connection. Some of the users shut off their machines the night before, but others didn't. Now, the cause may not be the end user. It may be a failing hub or MSAU. In this case, analyzing the numbers and types of calls from that particular subnet may give you a heads up on being proactive in solving the problem.

There are other ways for which you can analyze trends. For example, look at the total number of justified network calls. The number of calls will fluctuate month to month, but you are looking for trends. Is the number of justified network calls going up or is it (hopefully) going down? If the number of network calls is going up, is it increasing at a rate that reflects the growth of your network, or is it going up at an unreasonable pace? In looking at your documentation, was there an event that may have caused a temporary anomaly in the reporting? Let's look at some examples.

You notice that the number of justified network calls has climbed from an average of 10 per month in January to an average of 15 per month in November. Upon further review, you remember that back in January, there were 200 users on the network. Since that time, your network has grown, the company has done an acquisition, and now you have 400 users on the network. In this case, the size of your network has doubled and the number of calls has only increased by 5 per month. Looks like you are doing a wonderful job. Make sure to bring your spreadsheet to your next annual review!

Now, let's assume that you are filling out your spreadsheet, and you notice that the number of calls went from 10 in January to 100 in February. Now is the time to review the documentation for any network outages that may have occurred in February. You may have forgotten the ice storm that downed the telephone lines providing you with communication between your office and a remote office. Perhaps the ice storm knocked the power out in your main computer center, and all the servers had to be stopped temporarily. This, of course, severed the network connections between the server and workstations and prompted the help-desk phones to ring incessantly. This is an act of God and not your fault!

Finally, you notice that the number of justified network calls has climbed from an average of 10 per month in January to an average of 15 per month in November. Upon further review, you remember that back in January, there were 200 users on the network. Since that time, the network has added a couple of new users but certainly not enough to warrant a 50 percent increase in the number of calls to the help desk. Maybe it is time to look deeper to see whether there is an issue that needs addressing.

Commonality   As you analyze the help-desk reports, try to get as much information about the incident as possible. Try, also, to group the calls as best you can. What is the same about the calls? What is different? Are the network calls coming at a particular time of the day or certain day of the week? People calling Monday morning to complain that the network is slow or that they lost their network connection over the weekend may not be such a big deal. After all, most Monday mornings are usually high-traffic times. If your network is scheduled to do a full backup every Sunday night, you may have it configured to sever network connections with anyone who hasn't logged out on Friday night. In either case, the complaints and the calls are justified but not your problem! You have to determine whether the calls are part of a trend and then determine what is causing the trend. Once that has been established, then decisions have to be made about how to handle the problem.

The problem with commonality is that it might not be easy to spot. As a matter of fact, appearances may be deceiving. Does your company have a corporate standard when it comes to equipment purchases? Many companies claim to have a corporate standard, but in effect, the standard is whatever carries the cheapest price tag on any given day. Many times it is a sign of good business to save money wherever and whenever possible. Other times it may be the case of false frugality.

For example, the new chief information officer for a company was trying to make a case for corporate standard equipment. She wanted to specify a certain manufacturer of computers for the desktop, and she wanted all the peripherals to be from the manufacturer's approved list.

The purchasing agent wanted the freedom to be able to shop the market and get the best prices on equipment. Besides, even if they were to standardize on a particular computer brand, the brand the CIO suggested was several hundred dollars more expensive than the clone brand he was currently pricing from a local manufacturer. These clone machines were "just as good" as the other systems, and with tech support right out their backdoor, what could be better. The CEO was tempted, but to placate the CIO, she decided to bring one of the clones in for a test. The CIO got the test machine in and ran it through its paces. It performed flawlessly with Windows NT Server—not the most forgiving operating system—and all additional tests went off without a hitch. The acquisition meeting was held, and the CIO attempted to make a case for the brand-name computers. The purchasing agent trotted out the results of the tests on the clone and sung the praises of his selection. In this case, the CEO decided she was on safe ground okaying the purchase of 20 of these new machines. The CIO countered *her* test results by saying that the test results were more or less meaningless, because the configuration they tested would not be the configuration they received. The clone manufacturer was famous for making sure that each of the machines contained whichever parts they had on hand during any given day.

The order was placed, the computers delivered, and sure enough, problems developed almost immediately. None of the components in the computers they received matched the components in the test bed machine. As a matter of fact, upon closer inspection, it turned out that very few of the 20 machines ordered had the same components.

The company tried to repair the computers and update them one at a time. That didn't work. Finally, all 20 computers were boxed up and returned to the manufacturer. The name brand systems were ordered, put in place, and worked just fine. While the corporate in-fighting was taking place and while the powers-that-be were squabbling, the end users were the ones who couldn't do their work. They were caught in the middle.

In the case above, it was obvious which machines were causing the problems. What if the situation were changed somewhat and instead of buying a complete system, the purchasing agent bought generic brand network cards. Now, these cards may work just fine, or they may not. But if these cards are placed in your inventory as replacement parts when things go wrong, it will be difficult to remember where they were installed. In this case, you may have a TCP/IP problem with a network card-driver. The problem may exhibit itself from across the network, on all the computers that have the generic-brand card installed. The problem, and the solution, may be staring you in the face, but unless you have some way of knowing which computers those network cards are installed in, it may take a while to recognize the answer.

The case is not being made here for a standardization for a particular product or manufacturer. A case is being made for some form of standardization, period. Always using a particular brand of network card is going to make it easier on the installer and easier on the troubleshooter. It will probably make it easier on the purchasing person, also, because now they can buy in bulk!

Things for the Help Desk to Expect from You

So far, we have looked at how the help desk can help you do your job. Using their records and their reports, talking to their staff can give you a really good idea about the state of your network. If you are new to the position, you can use this invaluable resource to help determine your priority list for making things better on the network. Surely there has got to be some way for you to repay the help desk for services rendered. One of the ways is by sharing your wealth of knowledge and experience with those not as fortunate as you.

Now, many of you are going to be saying things like, "Yeah, sure, I have all the time in the world to be training people on the help desk. Let's see, I can give up sleep." Training the help desk people, especially in matters of TCP/IP, may be a great investment in having more free time. The more calls the help desk can troubleshoot and stop before they reach your pager, the better!

Are You in Charge of the Help Desk?

In addition to your responsibilities as network god or goddess, you may have been assigned with the task of overseeing the help desk. If your company is small, you may be not only the network god or goddess but also the help desk. If that is the case, then good luck; you will probably never make it completely through your list of things to do. Isn't it wonderful to know that each day will be filled with new challenges, and boredom won't be an issue?

Depending on the size (and budget) of your company, there may be some ways to reduce calls to the help desk. Some of these revolve around software solutions; others revolve around thinking "outside of the box" and coming up with really unique solutions.

One of those unique solutions involves the computer operators license. After all, the discussion has been around for years, and no one has ever done anything about it: if you can license people to do something such as drive cars, shouldn't you be able to license them to do other things, as well? The first time I heard the topic, the licensing was for raising children, but we will not get into that.

Recently, I read an article about a company that issues their end users Desktop Drivers Licenses. Each user is required to take certain tests to prove a certain level of computer competency. If that person has proven they have the skills to operate at a certain level and they call the help desk with a question that they should be reasonably able to answer, they are "ticketed" for wasting the help desk's time.

Certifying is done through self-study courses, online tutorials, or CD-ROMs and text-books. The courses can cover e-mail, software applications, or even printer operation. If your users aren't excited about getting a license, you may try tying it to a bonus, a gift certificate, or even a paid day off.

For the IT manager, another benefit of the program is being able to quantify end-user competence. Often, senior management does not want to pay for end-user training. If you can prove how many people need it, based on a fair and equitable standard, it may help you justify the cost.

Maybe user licensing is not the way your company wants to go. I have to admit, it sounds like a great idea, but it seems like it would be a nightmare to administer. I also think there would be some customer-service issues, such as when you tell an executive senior vice president in charge of everything that they are asking a question they should already know the answer to. I am not sure, but somehow I could see that become an issue.

Network Design and Planning

PART 3

The Cyber Help Desk

Some companies are turning to software solutions for their help desk. Many of these programs are written and designed to learn the answer to frequent end-user questions. But anytime you start talking about intelligent software, you are also talking about a fairly large price tag. That is certainly the case in most of the examples I located. Prices start at around $5,000 per seat for McAfee's product and go up from there. Let's take a look at three similar products.

McAfee's Total Service Desk

TSD runs on a Windows NT platform. It contains three different modules: Help Desk, PC Medic, and the Zero Administration Client. The product itself is sold as either HelpDesk, which requires a current SQL Server installation, or HelpDesk EZ SQL, which comes with a 15-user version of SQL Server.

HelpDesk Module TSD is designed to help you automate PC- and LAN-problem reporting, resolution, and recording. It also provides some troubleshooting help for the person running the phones. Here is how it works: when a phone call comes in, the help-desk analyst opens an incident. When the incident is opened, it is given a unique activity number and is stamped with a date and time. The analyst is then given a contact box and can fill in the name of the caller. The database searches and locates all users with a similar spelling. The user is also assigned secondary information, such as a phone number and an address, to make sure the appropriate user is selected. When the analyst locates the appropriate user, a call history is generated and displayed.

The analyst then types in a description of the problem. The program will search through the solution database for similar incidents. A list of problems similar to the description is presented, and the analyst can select one that most closely matches the caller's issue. HelpDesk then provides a detailed procedure to solve the problem.

HelpDesk comes with a database that offers about 30,000 problem resolutions for a wide range of topics. There are solutions to common application problems, hardware troubleshooting, and operating-system errors. In addition, you can create your own unique knowledge base using an express authoring tool.

PC Medic PC Medic is a workstation diagnostic utility that watches over system resources and provides suggestions to increase system performance. It works to prevent system crashes, it tries to restart hung applications, it resolves conflicts between peripherals, and if it finds a problem, it will report the problem directly to the HelpDesk module. This communication between modules is done via IP, so it will even work on remote workstations. Once the information gets to HelpDesk, it enters in the information the same way a help-desk support person would.

Zero Administration Client   With the ZAC Enterprise Console, you can manage a LAN, control software distribution, and manage a user's desktop. When the console is brought up, the screen is divided into two views, a Scope view and a Results view. The Scope view displays all the installed modules, such as the Virus Scan Security suite and the ZAC suite. If you click on one of the modules, information about the module will show up in the Results view. It will also provide an integrated hardware and software inventory. Output from ZAC can be managed by creating custom reports using Crystal Reports 4.5.

Follow Up   As part of the HelpDesk module, there is an Activity information screen. This screen can be used to list all open calls and the person that has been assigned to solve the problem. The software package is versatile, but with versatility comes complexity. It does require lots of training before rollout.

NetManage SupportNow

NetManage is a unique concept in help-desk support tools. Most companies try to aim their product at as large a segment of the market as possible, but NetManage has decided to specialize by focusing on software development companies. The theory is that these companies will then embed SupportNow modules in the new products as a value-added feature.

NetManage also has a product called OpTime that is geared to the corporate market. Both products will provide real-time interactive help to end users. In both products, help-desk personnel can connect to troubled computers by one click of a drop-down menu. Although this is a convenient feature, reviewers point out that it is also one of the product's shortcomings. If you are the help-desk person, you have no way of knowing who is still in the queue waiting for help and how long they have been there.

SupportNow is also unique in that it is designed to work in environments where firewalls are in place. The SupportNow server is placed on the outside of the firewall, and both the technician and the client can access the server through outbound ports, making sure that firewall security remains in place.

Most help-desk packages will allow an administrator to take over the desktop to effect change. In some companies, this is viewed as a two-edged sword. Technicians love it. They don't have to run all over the planet trying to find out what is going on with a computer. They can just take it over and run whatever tests and diagnostics they see fit. The client is understandably concerned over their lack of control. In some companies, the decision was made to not use remote-management software because members of senior management felt they couldn't be sure whether an MIS person was looking over their shoulder as they typed. It was an unreasonable stance, to be sure, but one that was valid

Network Design and Planning

PART 3

in the minds of the folks who could say no. With SupportNow, the client decides how much control the technician can have. The technician can be given access to just an application or to the entire computer.

Self-Service Approach

The previous two examples of help-desk software are great if you happen to have an extra $40 or $50 thousand dollars lying around in your budget. Isn't there another way?

One of the things that many companies are doing to take advantage of the roll out of TCP/IP is to create, maintain, and update a corporate intranet to disseminate information. The intranet is a perfect way to provide users a way to get quick answers to support questions while keeping help-desk support costs in line.

One company I have heard of was a financial institution with 6,000 employees that has created an intranet with a self-service support site using just Web browsers. The site serves about 300 users each week.

The site is designed to help users troubleshoot things such as printer problems, application hang-ups, and problems with the company's proprietary trading and quote system. The system is designed so trouble tickets can be submitted for problems that cannot be solved quickly, and the help desk has the ability to log and monitor the trouble tickets.

This intranet site is more than just a list of frequently asked questions (FAQs). It has over 3,000 packaged and custom-built how-to scripts that help users fix everyday problems.

As with everything, there is a catch. Asking a user to go to a Web-based help site is like asking an administrator to go to the tech-support page of a company's Web site. Great idea, but it is usually not the first thing on the list of things to try. When there is a problem with a computer, people want to talk with other people, not with a computer. Searching through a knowledge base can be a time-consuming process. People feel that is just easier to call the help desk, wait in the queue, and then explain their problem to a real person. For the technology to work, people have to be trained to look to technology first and then go to the phone.

Besides taking care of users, the self-service help desk also helps to take care of the company. A company based in Burlington, Massachusetts, has reported that they were able to handle a 100 percent increase in the number of help-desk requests without adding any employees to that department. Because this company had plants in Texas and California as well as Massachusetts, the cost savings were rather large. Other companies have found that there were specific cases when the Web-based system shined.

It is wonderful to have all these services available. They are only beneficial if the users actually go out and access them. Some companies actively promote their intranet sites, having promotions, such as scavenger hunts, to show off their wares. Other companies will advertise the site using a ticker on the intranet home page to show how many visitors have accessed the site or how many new solutions are currently available.

The Help Desk Isn't Just for IT Anymore

One of the problems I have always found about working in the corporate environment is that when someone has a really good idea, someone else always seems to borrow it, change it, or otherwise want to get in on the good stuff. Several companies are reporting that the Web-based help desk is so successful that the IT department can't keep it for itself anymore.

This is one of those ideas that when you see it, you immediately stop and say, "Why the heck didn't I think of that?" The Web-based help desk is designed for people to find information and solve problems based on a set of defined criteria. Once the information is located, then a step-by-step approach can be taken to solve the problem. Why not use that same philosophy for those nontechnical areas of the company?

Let's start with human resources. Many companies issue a human-resources policy manual. This manual lists the things the employee can and cannot do, gives the break down of benefits provided by the company, and lists what the user has to do to access those benefits. How many times have you been confronted with a problem such as "I want to take a vacation day, but I don't know how to do that." This is perfect for the Web-based help-desk system. It is an easily definable problem, solved by a simple set of step-by-step procedures.

This opens up entirely new vistas to Web access and design. If I want to take a vacation day, I should be able to determine whether I have worked enough this year to warrant the day off. That information can be accessed through the Web.

What if you need to take a sick day or find out the company's holidays? How about being able to access how much overtime you have worked this pay period? All of these are valid uses for the help-desk site.

Using the help desk to sift through the piles of paperwork can be expanded to other areas as well. What about the accounting department? Have you had to fill out an expense report lately? Some of those reports can be confusing, especially if you are an infrequent traveler.

> **NOTE** Maybe this same idea could be rolled out to the government. For example, in Rockdale County, Georgia, 60,000 daytime users can plug into the county Web site for help on how to apply for a building permit or how to book events at a local park. This eliminates the need to go stand in line for what seems like hours. It frees up the clerical people to do real work, rather than hand someone a form to fill out, and is just more efficient all the way around.

When you think about these examples, there are many similarities. Each has to do with paperwork that is done on an infrequent basis. In the case of the Web-based help desk, everything seems to revolve around just answering questions. It doesn't even matter who the questions come from!

Putting It All Together

So, what can you do to make sure that your newfound career path leads to fame, fortune, and great annual reviews? If you are just starting out at a new company, you have to work hard to make the most of the new opportunity you have been given. To do that, there are several things you need to set perception and expectation at reasonable levels.

Prioritize

First of all, find out what your superiors expect. They have their agenda for what things they think need to be done to your network, and you may already have a priority list in place, as well. When judging the two lists, remember the golden rule, "Them's that got the gold make all the rules." See if there is a way that you can blend the two lists together to make sure that everything gets done. If there is a conflict between what you think should be done and what your superiors think should be done, see whether you can blend the projects to make sure they both get done.

Communicate

Communication is important. Communicate between your department and your superiors, your customers, and those within your own department. If your superiors know what your agenda is, they can ask the questions they feel need to be answered on the progress of the agenda. They can see what strides you are making to finish the project on the time line that you projected. If that time line has to change, make sure you inform them. Also, make sure to tell them why the change was necessary. In a perfect world, you would have the opportunity to start a project and work on it through completion without distraction. Make sure the people above know what kind of fires you have to put out, what those fires did to your time line, and what steps you took to make sure they do not reappear.

Open lines of communication with other areas of the company. Too often the IT department is viewed as a separate world, filled with people who speak a different language and work with machines everyone uses but few understand. If this is a picture of your corporate workplace, try to break down some of those barriers. Those are your customers out there. They are saying things about your network and about the IT staff. Whether you are listening or not is irrelevant, because somebody is listening. Your department may be the best in the business, but if your customers aren't convinced, you could be facing an uphill battle.

If you have ever worked in a company where there was poor communication, you know how insidious it can be. For example, an IT department does not do a good job of communicating with the rest of the company. Perhaps there are not enough people in the department, so those that actually talk to the customers or work at the desktops are constantly running behind schedule. These folks feel that they just want to do their job, avoid any small talk, finish the task at hand, and move on to the next problem.

That is all very understandable, and your staff is probably getting lots done. Unfortunately, they may be viewed as aloof or socially challenged. When someone doesn't take the time to show your customer what is going on with their desktop, the customer is going to feel slighted. If the customer feels slighted, there is a sense of resentment and soon that opinion starts to spread. People talk, and the reputation of the IT department can suffer. When that information gets to management, and if they hear it over and over again, sooner or later they will believe it. You may have all the facts and figures to disprove this theory, but it is all a matter of perception. Make sure everyone on your staff knows how to communicate with the customer.

Know What You Know

The flip side to this topic, and probably the more important side, is know what you don't know. If you don't know, say you don't know. Get help from someone who does know. Recognize your field of expertise, understand your strengths, and work with them. On the flip side, understand what you don't know, and if you see yourself getting in over your head, call for help!

What about those times when you are thrown into the deep end? You know something major will break down sooner or later, there will be is no expert around to fix it, and you will be the last great hope for survival of the network. While the same philosophy applies, in this case you have no choice; you have to jump in with both feet and try to save the day. What do you do then?

Network Design and Planning

PART 3

Know your limitations, read the manual, and most importantly, do everything in your power to leave yourself an out. If you are not sure what is happening and you are the one who has to fix it, make sure you document what you are doing and only do one thing at a time. That way, if you notice things going from bad to worse, you can go back a step or two and reestablish the base line at just bad.

Know and Respect Your Customers

This book is written to appeal to a large number of network administrators all over the world. You each have your own unique networks, and your users are all individuals, no two of them are exactly a like. However, there are some similarities you should keep in mind when you deal with them.

There are some fields that attract the type of person who is very self-assured and intelligent. Because of these characteristics, these people feel they have a handle on the inner workings of their world and everything in it. When a technician comes up to fix a computer, these are the people who feel it is necessary to "help" the technician fix the system. Now, in reality, many of these people don't know a network card from a video card, but they have to help. It is up to the technician to make sure that

- These people stay out of the way.
- These people are heard and the suggestions acknowledged (if not used).
- The problem gets fixed without ruffling any feathers.

It is also important to know who you work for. A friend of mine, a network administrator, and I began to talk one night over a few frosty, cold beverages. Often in these situations, network administrators start talking about the people they work with and the individual challenges they present. This administrator stands out because of the way he was able to grasp his constituency and what he did to work with its idiosyncrasies.

My friend worked for a state supreme court, which provided many network-planning challenges. First, there was a definite pecking order. Actually, that oversimplifies the situation; there were several pecking orders that had to be acknowledged and maintained. The supreme court had justices. It oversaw the appellate courts and the probate courts as well as managed several other levels of courts. In the pecking order of judges, the best stuff had to go to the supreme court justices. The appellate court judges had to have better stuff than the probate judges. You get the picture. This all had to be done on the sly, because if you asked any of the judges whether this pecking order was in place, they would swear it wasn't—until you violated it.

The other pecking order revolved around the judges' staff. The staff of the Chief Justice had priority over the staffs of the other justices and so on down the line. Again, the pecking order had to be maintained but not in an overt fashion. This meant that the staff had to be very careful about the types of machines they placed in offices. If a "lower order" employee received hardware that was better than a "higher level" employee, there was trouble. This was solved with a *very* large chart in the IS department offices that listed the maximium (rather than minimum) hardware requirements for each level within the court system.

Many of us who have worked in the computer industry have worked with people who felt that they were gods and expected to be treated like it. So when it came to supporting a justice, you had to be very respectful and listen carefully while this person told you exactly what was wrong with their computer; then you could go off and fix it your own way.

How can you take advantage of the mistakes that were made by your predecessor? We can all learn from history, and most of us can learn from our mistakes. It takes a real pro to be able to recognize areas where others may have done well, or where things could have been done a little differently, and change them.

Identify those areas that need to be addressed, come up with a solution to the problems you encounter, lay out a path that you can take to solve those problems, and then follow the path. Communicate with people along the way. Let them know of your successes and your failures. If you have a failure, let people know what you are doing to implement Plan B.

Network Design
and Planning

PART 3

The Case of the Misplaced Port

Courtney is having a problem getting in through the corporate firewall. She is trying to get her e-mail off the POP3 server that is hiding on the other side of the firewall. Courtney has no difficulty finding the firewall and is able go through it to perform other tasks, but when she tries to hit the POP3 server, things come to a halt in a big hurry. Larry, manning the help desk, has checked Courtney's login name and password; everything is spelled right and in the right case, but things still don't work. What should they do?

Solution

The problem is probably a misplaced port. A firewall is designed to block access to the corporate network from the outside world, so most administrators move the default port addresses around to make access from outsiders difficult. If you are unfamiliar with port addresses, think of them this way. Assume that the IP address of the host you are trying to contact is the phone number for the main receptionist at your company. If I were to call that number and start to ask questions about the TCP/IP layout and de-

sign, I would not get many straight answers. Instead, I would need to access your extension to get the information I required. The same is true with an IP address. The IP address is like the main switchboard. Requesting a particular service is done through a port address, or extension number. In order to complicate the lives of hackers everywhere, people who install firewalls often change the default port addresses to close known holes in a firewall. If I call you and I get the wrong extension, I won't get much satisfaction. If I call and ask for the right extension, the world opens up for me.

Make sure the end user is using the correct port address, and more importantly, the correct syntax.

Port addresses are usually expressed like this: $109.46.15.98:1677$. It is easy to make that colon a semicolon. It is also hard to "see" that mistake. Your eye tells you it is right when you look at it, because you are checking the numbers. It usually takes someone else to come by and point out the discrepancy.

The Expert

Dan Dillman is a member of the Information Technology team at St. Cloud Technical College in St. Cloud, Minnesota. The college was having some network problems. Dan felt he was in over his head, so they started looking for an expert.

One person came highly recommended. The network at SCTC is NetWare-based, running IP and IPX at the desktop. It is like most networks, with a little of everything on it, including NT, Unix, and Macintosh. But the network was not running as efficiently as Dan thought it should, so he looked to someone who had 14 years of experience in the field. This person had a Master CNE and a long list of success stories to his credit. The person came in, evaluated the server and the applications that were running and started to make some changes.

The changes that the person made to server parameters were great. They all made perfect sense, followed the Novell Tech Notes to a tee and helped solve some of the nit-picky problems the network had been experiencing. Then the Master CNE went into the GroupWise configuration and started making changes there. At this point, the Master CNE with 14 of years experience was in over his head. He may not have known he was in over his head, but he was, and it showed.

The Master CNE proceeded to make some changes to the GroupWise system that reflected the way he felt GroupWise operated. He was confident in his statements and gave the appearance of competence. Because of this, Dan allowed him to make changes to the system. Shortly after making the changes, the Master CNE left the building. Shortly after that, Dan started to notice that his phone began ringing. People were complaining that the e-mail was not going through. Upon investigation, Dan found that all the e-mail messages going to all the users in one particular area had stopped being delivered. Although Dan knew the reasons why, he didn't trust himself. So Dan called another Master CNE. This one had GroupWise experience and understood the inner workings of the system. When Dan told the story of what happened, he said, "I am not sure he should have done this, but this is what was done." Dan used that phrase several times during the phone call, and in every case, Dan was right and the original Master CNE was wrong. The settings were changed back to the originals, mail started to flow, and people in the kingdom were happy again. Unfortunately, not enough of them know to thank Dan for making that happen.

8

Bridging and Routing with TCP/IP

In this chapter, we will look at various issues that you will need to face as your network grows. We will start by looking at *bridging*. Bridging is a Data Link layer (oh, no, not more about those damn seven layers of the OSI model) event that can be used to expand the size of some of your network segments. We will look at the different types of bridges and the advantages of each type. We will also explore how to lay out bridges to avoid any potential problems.

If your network becomes large, you will need to look at adding a router. In our discussion of routing, we will discuss the different types of routing methods available and the various protocols that are in use on networks today. We will examine the pluses and minuses of each and look at how each protocol accomplishes its job. By using these protocols properly, you can design an efficient network infrastructure and even protect yourself against some communication failures. These failures can be averted by providing a second set of routes that a packet may take around your network; this is called *providing a redundant link*. Before we get the cart before the horse, let's look at the basics of bridging.

Bridging Unmasked

As segments on your network grow, traffic builds and performance starts to decrease. You need to increase performance but not spend a ton of money. One solution to solve the problem is to use a bridge. There are several different styles of bridges, but Figure 8.1 shows some bridge basics.

Figure 8.1   A bridging diagram

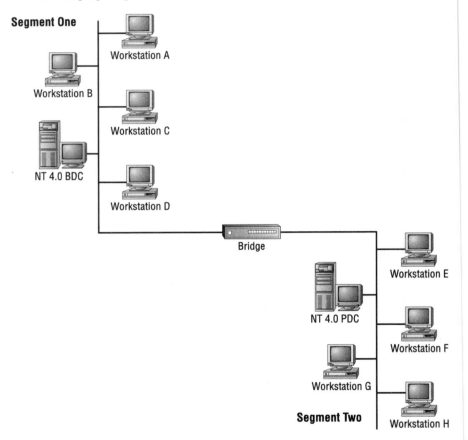

The diagram shows two segments joined together with a bridge. Bridges are devices that can increase the total throughput of a LAN segment by keeping frames on the local segment local and filtering frames that belong to other LAN segments. Bridges have other benefits, which include the following:

- Bridges work independently of all upper layer protocols. Therefore, they can forward or filter frames from many different protocols. Protocols that cannot be routed (NetBEUI and NetBIOS) can be bridged.

- Bridges can increase the media distance and device limits on a LAN because the signal is filtered and repeated to the appropriate segment.

Look closely at Figure 8.1. Each of the workstations is labeled, and the two servers are a *primary domain controller* and a *backup domain controller*. The bridge resides in the middle. The bridge is referred to as *semi-intelligent device*. Unlike a router, which takes an active part in learning about its environs, a bridge is more of a passive learner. In addition, the bridge doesn't want to know about the whole world, it just wants to know about its little piece of the world.

Broadcast Basics

On a network, when one device wants to talk to another device, it puts the packet onto the network. When the packet traverses the network, every host on the segment gets to look at it to see whether it is the designated recipient. If it is the designated recipient, it grabs the packet and acts on it. As you will read later in the chapter, every packet that is sent contains both a source address and a destination address.

In Figure 8.1, let's assume we have just brought the bridge on line, and it is in what is called *learning mode*. The bridge knows what it is supposed to do, but it doesn't know anything about its environment, so all it can do is sit back and wait. Workstation H decides that it needs information from the BDC, so it sends out a packet addressed to the BDC. When the packet hits the bridge, the bridge looks at the packet and examines its source address. In this case, the bridge knows the information is coming in through Segment Two. So it can make an entry in its database that says Workstation H resides on Segment Two. When the BDC responds, the bridge sees that packet, as well. It glances quickly at the packet's source address and knows that it is coming off of Segment One. Now, let's say Workstation D sends a packet addressed to the BDC. In this case, the bridge grabs the source address and makes a note in its database that Workstation D is on Segment One. It now looks at the destination address and finds that the packet is going to its old buddy the BDC. Because both the BDC and the workstation are on the same segment, the bridge will prevent the packet from hitting Segment Two, thus eliminating some unwanted traffic.

When you think about using a bridge, you should follow the 80/20 rule. In this case, the bridge should be placed where 80 percent of the traffic is local and only 20 percent of the traffic is remote or crossover. Figure 8.1 shows the perfect scenario for a bridge. Because there are NT servers on both segments, chances are most of the segment traffic will revolve around those two systems.

In concept, there are three types of bridges. There is the *transparent bridge*, the *source-routing bridge*, and the *source-routing transparent (SRT) bridge*. We will look at all three and then explain why the bridging technologies have merged.

Transparent Bridges

Some things in life are easy to use. Transparent bridges fall into that category. You plug in cables from the different segments, turn them on, and watch them go to work.

Transparent bridges are so named because the sending device is unaware that the target device might live on a remote segment. The sending device also has no idea there are any bridges between it and the receiving device. In other words, because the bridge does not make its presence known, it is transparent.

NOTE   Transparent bridges are also known as *learning bridges*.

Looping—One of the Problems with Bridges

Fault tolerance is always a good thing to have in any network situation. If a key component breaks, life goes on without a problem. In Figure 8.2, two network segments are connected by two bridges.

Figure 8.2   Network Segments Connected by Two Bridges

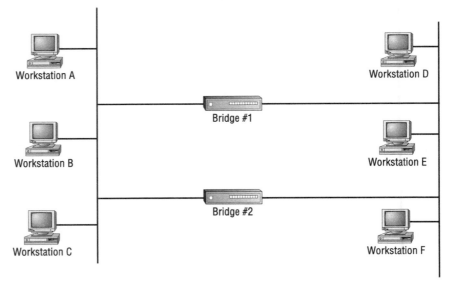

Segment One   **Segment Two**

Although fault tolerance can be a good thing, if your bridges are improperly configured, you could have a problem called *looping*. Here is how looping can occur: Workstation A transmits a packet to Workstation F on Segment Two. Both Bridge 1 and Bridge 2 copy the packet and let it go through to Segment Two. There is no entry in either database for Workstation A because this is the first time it has sent a packet through the bridge, and both bridges add the information that Workstation A is on Segment One.

Keep in mind that one bridge will be somewhat faster than the other. We are talking computer terms here, so the speed issue may be milliseconds, but that is enough. Assume that Bridge 1 forwards the packet to Segment Two a fraction before Bridge Two. Because Bridge Two has no way of knowing the packet off of Segment Two really came from Bridge One, Bridge Two copies the packet from Segment Two. Now, Bridge Two checks its database, and finds that it thought Workstation A was on Segment One. But, according to the packet of information it just received, it's obvious that Workstation A is really on Segment Two. So, Bridge Two mistakenly changes its database to reflect the fact that Workstation A resides on Segment 2. Once that update has been made, the bridge then forwards the packet onto Segment One.

Meanwhile, Bridge One is still fat and happy, though not for long. It gets the packet that Bridge Two sent out and figures that Workstation A is really on Segment Two, and the screwup is almost complete.

We now have those packets floating around on Segment One. The bridges both see those packets and readjust databases to reflect that Workstation A is back on Segment One. Unfortunately, the loop has been completed and will continue.

This scenario shows that bridges are *unintelligent* devices. They are not capable of generating a packet and finding out where this host actually resides. They are not even smart enough to figure out that there is a problem moving the same host from one network segment to another over and over again. Bridge looping causes broadcast storms, which will degrade system performance dramatically or, more than likely, down the system entirely. The looping problem can be prevented by using the Spanning Tree Protocol.

Spanning Tree Protocol

The Spanning Tree Protocol is a bridge hierarchy protocol that organizes routes between network segments with redundant routes. It is designed to eliminate loops. The protocol assigns one of each pair of redundant bridges to be the designated bridge and the other to be the backup.

The Spanning Tree Protocol also provides communication between bridges. When the bridges start talking, they can automatically detect a route failure and then reconfigure the network on the fly.

The benefits of the Spanning Tree Protocol include

- The dynamic configuration of paths between routes. (This eliminates bridging loops.)
- The dynamic reconfiguration of routes in case the primary bridge fails.
- Automatic backup.

At the top of the spanning tree is something called the *root bridge* (see Figure 8.3). The root bridge is the bridge that is responsible for sending configuration messages on a routine basis. These messages are then pushed down the line to all the designated bridges. These messages cause the spanning tree to recognize when something on the network has changed and the network needs to be reconfigured.

Figure 8.3 The Spanning Tree Protocol layout

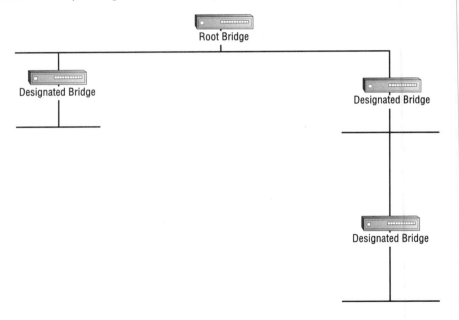

The root bridge may reside logically at the top of the spanning tree, but the only way it gets its designation as the leader of the pack is with some help from the network administrator.

Growing a Spanning Tree The Spanning Tree Protocol works with a packet called a Bridge Protocol Data Unit (BPDU), which is how the bridges can communicate with each other. Bridges will then dynamically pick a root bridge, designated bridges, and backup bridges for all the routes between segments.

The bridge with the lowest bridge identification number (Bridge ID) will become the root bridge. In the entire spanning-tree network, there can only be one root bridge. Because you are designing the network and you know how you want the communication between segments to occur, you can designate the root bridge by manually configuring the bridge IDs for your network. After all, why gamble with your job?

Root bridges should be set as close to the physical center of the network as possible. By doing so, if there is a segment or bridge failure, reconfiguration will be minimized.

> **TIP**   Because it is important to be able to manually set the bridge IDs and the costs of the ports on the bridge, you should make sure that the bridges you buy can be managed with an SNMP solution. This should be done before the purchase, so it will have to go on your list of things to do.

Now that you have configured a bridge ID, it is time to turn the bridge on and see how it works.

Bridge Elections   When a bridge comes on line, it has to establish itself within the tree. It has to make sure that a root bridge has been designated and that all the routes have been designated. It does this by broadcasting a frame (see Figure 8.4).

Figure 8.4   A bridge broadcast frame

DEST ADDR	SRCE ADDR	DSAP	SSAP	BPDU	CRC	MAC HEAD	LLC HEAD	BPDU	CRC

That sure is a mish-mash of acronyms, isn't it? Let's take a look at what each one means.

Dest Addr (Destination Address)   This means where the frame is headed.

Srce Addr (Source Address)   This means where the frame is coming from.

DSAP (Destination Link Service Access Point)   A service access point is the address that can be used to identify this process to another system on the network. The destination link is the Data Link layer address that this communication is going to.

> **NOTE** Computer communications have what seems like an endless series of addresses. The addresses get more and more specific as you climb the OSI ladder. Rather than go into great detail in this book on each type of address, maybe we can agree that there are more levels of addressing than we need to worry about. As long as the communicating entities know what a DSAP and an SSAP are, we're fine with what we need to do.

SSAP (Session Service Access Point) The SSAP is a unique subaddress that identifies this particular conversation between two bridges.

BPDU (Bridge Packet Data Unit) The fields of the BPDU will be explained below in Figure 8.5.

CRC (Cyclic Redundancy Check) A checksum used to show whether the packet has been damaged in transit.

MAC Header (Medium Access Control Header) A MAC header shows how the system has accessed the media.

LLC Header (Logical Link Control Header) The LLC Header gives information needed by the peer at the Logical Link Control layer.

> **NOTE** The Data Link layer of the OSI model is made up of two sublayers: the Media Access Control layer and the Logical Link Control layer. The Media Access Control layer is what controls the access to the media. The Logical Link Control layer begins the process of managing the communication.

Each BPDU portion of the frame is made up of several fields. Figure 8.5 shows these fields.

Figure 8.5 A BPDU configuration message

CONSTANTS	TCA,TC FLAG	ROOT ID	PORT COST	BRIDGE ID	MISCELLANEOUS

The fields of the BPDU are

Constants The Constants field defines the protocol, the version of the protocol, and the type of message.

TC and TCA Flag   TC is the Topology Change Notification Flag; TCA is the Topology Change Notification Acknowledgement Flag.

Root ID   This field gives the root bridge ID.

Port Cost   The Port Cost field defines the cost of the path to the root.

Bridge ID   This field shows the identifier of the bridge sending the message.

Miscellaneous   These fields include

Port ID   If two bridges are trying for the position of root bridge and they have equal bridge IDs, this field can be used as a tie breaker.

Message Age   This field shows how long since the last configuration message was sent.

Maximum Age   This field shows how long before this message gets deleted, otherwise known as Time to Live.

Hello Time   This field shows the time elapsed since the last configuration message was received from the root.

Forward Delay   This field shows the delay time before the bridge goes the next step after a topology change has been detected.

When the bridge that is coming online sends these frames out, it wants to be the root bridge. After all, we would all love to be the big, big boss with no one to answer to. Because it wants to be the root bridge, it advertises itself as that fact to all the other bridges in the tree. But remember, the lowest bridge ID is the winner. Who sets the bridge ID field? You do. So, when the new bridge comes online, it will broadcast out its information. If there is a designated root bridge already on the system and its bridge ID is lower than the new kid on the block, it will immediately send out a frame with that information. As the frame gets copied to all segments, each bridge will readjust its place in life.

Once the election of the root bridge is over, the system now has to determine the designated bridges.

Designated Bridges   If there are multiple bridges handling communications between the same segment, one of those bridges must be the designated or preferred route. The bridges go through yet another selection process of sorts, this time looking at the Port Cost field. Just like in the election for the root bridge, the designated bridge is elected by having the lowest cost. Because the root bridge is the main bridge, it has a port cost of 0. When it sends out a BPDU to the other bridges on the network, each bridge increments the port cost by one and accepts that as its own. Figure 8.6 will show you what I mean.

Figure 8.6   Port Costs

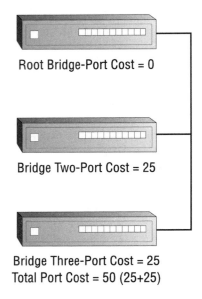

Root Bridge-Port Cost = 0

Bridge Two-Port Cost = 25

Bridge Three-Port Cost = 25
Total Port Cost = 50 (25+25)

In this case, the root bridge has a designated port cost of 0. It sends its BPDU down to Bridge 1. The first bridge has been configured with a port cost of 25. It then takes the port cost and adds it to the port cost of the root bridge, giving it a port cost of 25. The BPDU is then sent down the line. Bridge 2 gets the packet. It has a designated port cost of 25. It looks at the BPDU and sees that the cost factor of 25 has been passed down to it. The bridge adds in its port cost, and now it has a cost of 50. Once the process is completed, the bridge with the lowest cost to the segment becomes the designated port, and the other bridge becomes its backup.

Cost is a techno-geek computer term that simply means *preference*. The lower the cost, the more a route or path is preferred. In routers, cost is inversely proportional to bandwidth. The higher the bandwidth, the lower the cost. What does all this mean? It means that given two paths to a destination, the route with the lowest cost (highest bandwidth) is simply the preferred path.

Just because a backup bridge doesn't appear to have any work to do, it is still monitoring traffic on the line. It is kind of like an understudy in a play. The understudy doesn't really want anything bad to happen to the person who has the role, but by the same token, they sure would like to get out there and strut their stuff. The backup bridge monitors the line, and if it notices that there hasn't been a BPDU on the segment for a while, it will assume the designated bridge is down. If that happens, it is time for the backup bridge to spring into action.

The backup bridge first has to let the rest of the world know that it is taking over. It does that by broadcasting a Topology Change Notification (TCN). The TCN will continue to be broadcast until the designated bridge answers or the root bridge receives and acknowledges the change.

Once the root bridge has acknowledged the change, it has to notify all the other bridges that there is a new kid on the block. It sends out a BPDU every two seconds with the Topology Change Flag set, and sooner or later, this BPDU makes its way to all the bridges on the network.

Ideal Spanning-Tree Environment

Now that you know how it works, take a look at the way the spanning tree should be configured. Figure 8.7 will give you a good idea of the suggested layout in a multiple segment environment.

Figure 8.7   An ideal spanning tree

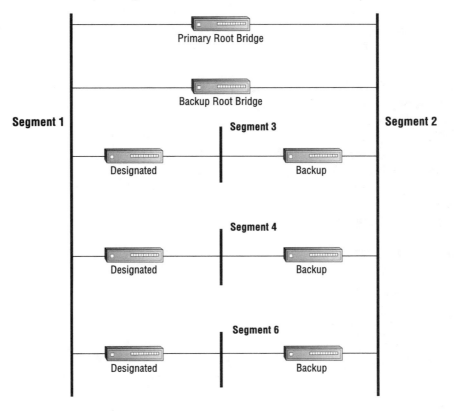

As you can see, in a perfect world, there will be a redundant route to each and every segment, and a frame will never have to travel through more than two bridges during normal operations. If something bad happens, a frame should still never have to travel through more than three bridges.

The spanning-tree topology can offer your network the following advantages:

- There will be a minimum amount of delay introduced by having a maximum of three bridges in any route. The delay is caused by filtering activity of a bridge.

- If something were to happen to a bridge, the time to reconfigure the network would be minimal because TCNs from a backup bridge do not have to cross more than one segment to reach the root.

- Almost immediate topology changes because the BPDUs are forwarded only one level away from the root bridge.

Source-Routing Bridges

With a transparent bridge, the bridge learned about the network. In a network that uses a source-routing bridge, it is no longer up to the bridge to maintain a filtering database. In this case, each device on the network is responsible for maintaining its own dynamic table of routes to the devices it wants to talk with.

> **NOTE** Source-routing bridges are normally found in Token Ring networks.

When one host wants to communicate with another host on the network, it starts the process by broadcasting a "hello frame" addressed to the target device. As the hello frame travels from ring to ring, each source-routing bridge adds new route information to the route information already stated by the frame. In this way, the path from the source to the destination is built dynamically as the frame makes its way across the network (see Figure 8.8).

Figure 8.8   Token rings joined by a source-routing bridge

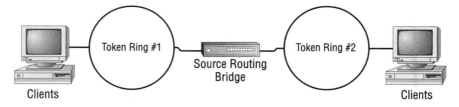

In Figure 8.8, Workstation A needs to communicate with Workstation B. It sends a hello packet, and as the frame passes from Ring 1 to the bridge, routing information is added to the frame. As the frame passes into Ring 2, more information is added to the header. Now, Workstation B is ready to respond to Workstation A. Because of all the information that was gathered on the trip over, Workstation B can address the frame with the appropriate routing information already in place.

The routing information that each workstation maintains is held in RAM; the routing information is a dynamic table. Entries will remain in the table for as long as the workstation is powered on and is a part of the ring. There is a limit to the size of the table, and when that limit is reached, entries will be overwritten on a first in, first out (FIFO) basis.

Source-Routing Transparent Bridges (SRT)

Don't you just love history? Sometimes, you have to be amazed at the way computer networks developed. At one time, back in the early days of networking, the proponents of source-routing bridging took it before the IEEE 802.1 committee. (The IEEE 802.1 committee looks into Ethernet standards.) The source-routing folks wanted their standard to compete against transparent bridging as the preferred method to connect two LANs together at the Data Link layer. The IEEE 802.1 committee wasn't swayed by the source-routing arguments, so they adopted the standard for transparent bridging. The source-routing aficionados were not to be denied. They took the concept to the 802.5 (Token Ring) standards committee, and there they found favor.

Life went on. Source-routing bridges evolved, as did transparent bridges. Suddenly, there came a time when someone discovered that you may have to link two extended LANs, one using source routing and the other using the transparent bridge. The SRT bridge was born.

At this time, however, there still was the source-routing bridge, the transparent bridge, and the SRT bridge. The tricky part of SRT operations is that the bridge needs to decide when to add routing information and when to skip the whole process (see Figure 8.9).

Figure 8.9   SRT in action

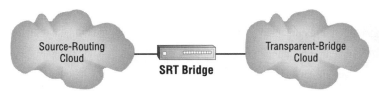

Source-Routing Cloud — SRT Bridge — Transparent-Bridge Cloud

In the case of Figure 8.9, if the packet arrives from the transparent-bridge cloud, and the bridge determines that the packet is going back into the cloud, nothing needs to be added or removed. If, however, the destination address is on the source-routing side of the world, then the bridge will forward the packet, using a route that it has already cached in memory. If there is no entry in cache, the bridge can do one of the following:

- Forward the packet to all segments.
- Forward the packet as a source-routing packet.
- Cache the packet, and try to discover the route.
- Drop the packet, try a discovery procedure, and hope that the source will resend the packet.

Does this seem to you to be getting overly complicated really quickly? If it does, you are absolutely right.

Source-routing transparent bridges have unsolvable problems. Notice the fourth option above that states the bridge can simply drop a packet and hope for the best. That option is otherwise known as a black hole where things enter and are never seen again.

In addition, it has been mentioned several times that there was a strategy to discover routes. The problem arose when there was no standard way of route discovery. Each bridge manufacturer did it a different way. That spelled *chaos* if you had more than one type of bridge on your network.

The proponents of source-routing bridging were the first to give it up. Source routing would be removed from the 802.5 standards. Instead, source routing would become an "enhancement" for transparent bridges. At this point in the history of computing, theoretically there are three types of bridges, but physically there are two: the transparent bridge and the SRT bridge.

What about if your network grows too large for a bridge or you want to connect your network to the Internet? Bridges won't work here, so we will move up a layer of the OSI model into the network layer and take a look at routers.

Router Basics

A very knowledgeable computer professional called me several months ago and asked a great question. She was really hesitant to ask, and it took me a while to pry the question out of her, but she wanted to know what it was exactly that a router did. She had installed routers, configured a few for Internet connectivity, but the actual inner workings of a router remained somewhat of mystery.

In its most basic form, a router routes. Now, think about that statement before you say "Duh!" A router routes packets of information from your desktop to another system somewhere on the "network." In this case, a network can be defined as anything from a LAN with multiple segments, to the Internet. It is up to the router to get the packet from one host to another.

Routers have the capability to learn routes to other network segments. The way that routers get this information varies, depending on the protocol, but it is important to recognize that routers maintain this information in something called a *routing table*. This table is stored on each router, and the table has to be routinely updated to make sure the routes haven't changed due to network conditions. The way these routing information tables are updated and maintained and the way the routers make decisions on the paths the packet should take are what makes routers and routing protocols different. We will be examining several of these protocols in this chapter.

Now, let's take a high-level overview of how a packet gets from one spot to another on a network. For example, I opened my Web browser and typed in the URL of my favorite Web site, **www.sybex.com**. When that occurs, my browser recognizes that it is going to have to "resolve" the name www.sybex.com to some kind of IP address, such as 209.1.78.150.

NOTE Each host on the Internet has its own unique host name (e.g., www.sybex.com) as well as a unique IP address (e.g., 209.1.78.150). Resolving a name simply means looking up the name in a database and matching it to the associated IP address.

How does the browser resolve the address? It looks at the source host's TCP/IP configuration and finds the first address of a DNS server. In the case of my system, it looks to a DNS server at 204.73.51.1. My host can also create a packet specifically addressed to 204.73.51.1. This is called the *destination address*. The packet is designed to ask the DNS server for the whereabouts of www.sybex.com. Because the DNS server will need to know where to respond, my workstation also appends or attaches the IP address of my workstation as the source address of the packet.

When this packet is ready to be sent, TCP/IP looks at the destination address and determines that this address is not on the same subnet or network segment as my host. Because the source and the destination are not on the same subnet, the destination address is changed to reflect the address of the "gateway" to the next network segment or to the outside world. In this case, the gateway will be the same as a router interface. The system looks to the configuration information again, and comes up with the address of the gateway. This specific address is added to the packet, and the packet is shipped off to the gateway/router.

When the router receives the packet, it looks at where the packet is going and figures out the best way to get there. It makes this determination by examining its routing table and finding the best path to the ultimate destination. Usually, this path is taken one step, or *hop,* at a time. The router now redirects the packet to the next step, adding a specific IP address to the packet and sending it on its way to the next router.

When the packet reaches the next router, the process continues. The packet merrily skips its way across the Internet to its destination. Each time the packet crosses a router, the router increases the metric or hop count, so that the Internet is not overcrowded with lost and misdirected packets. If the hop count hits a certain point (usually 16 for IP RIP routing protocol), the packet is declared lost and is discarded (not forwarded).

When the packet finally gets to its destination, the DNS server acts on the request for information about www.sybex.com. It resolves the name to an IP address for the particular type of requested information, for example, if the request is WWW-based it is forwarded to the WWW server's IP. The requested information is repackaged and the requestor's IP address is appended to each packet, and sent back to the original source IP address. The data packet goes from the responding server to a router and starts skipping its way merrily across the Internet back to my machine. It is important to note that the packet coming back does not have to take the same path as the original request. It may bounce all over the world before coming home to roost on my computer. The important thing is not how it gets back, as that it *does* get back. This is what I like to call a very serious *gee whiz.*

Given this basic routing information, it makes sense to plan your network design to make it easier for packets to traverse the infrastructure. This means keeping the bandwidth sufficient so that routers can communicate and protecting against a total network failure in the event of a temporary interruption in service to one of your leased lines. Redundancy, then, is having a backup plan. If one of your routers or one of your leased lines goes out to lunch, your system has a backup plan to make sure communication continues. It may not be as fast or as efficient as the primary route, but communication still goes through.

Router Redundancy

Up until this point, we have talked about the ways that routers handle moving packets from one area to another. It seems that these machines can and will make all the decisions if you let them. But how does a machine know that you have a grand network design and you want to build in certain paths in case of problems on the network? Surely, you believe that with proper planning you should be able to make sure there are multiple routes going to any location. If the truth were to be told, you would probably even want these things to provide some sort of load balancing along the way. In other words, if the route from A to B to C was *really* busy, the router would redirect the packet from A to D to C. You can take the initiative and plan your routes so you have some degree of load-balancing.

Depending on the routing protocol you are using (and we will be discussing these protocols later in this chapter), there may already be a certain degree of intelligence for path selection. For example, the Open Shortest Path First (OSPF) algorithm that decides which route a packet will take factors in the speed of the link each interface is attached to. This means that faster links are weighted differently than slower links, so if a particular route were to go down, the next fastest route would be selected for the packet.

Although that may provide some sense of well being, computer people tend to be somewhat anal retentive and controlling, so you will probably want to know what is going to happen if something goes down. After all, the job on the line here is yours!

What we are looking for, in the end, is a safe and predictable path from one end of our network to another. It doesn't necessarily have to be the same path every time; it just needs to be safe and predictable. You should be able to take a look at your network at any time, and by knowing which links are up and which links are down, figure out how a packet from Network A will get to Network B. This is important for several reasons. First, you have to make sure that communication goes on in the event of a minor disaster. Secondly, you need to know the way the packets are *supposed* to flow in order to figure out why they are not going that way. Take a close look at Figure 8.10.

Figure 8.10   Redundant network design

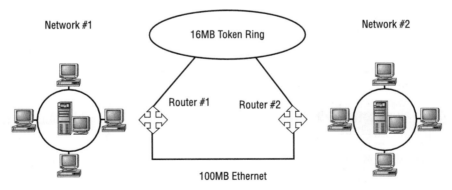

In this diagram, we have two networks, connected by a 100base-T Ethernet segment. Because of location, the networks are also joined by a Token Ring segment, providing a perfect example of redundancy. When the Ethernet segment is up and working, packets fly along at tremendous speeds. If something goes wrong, the design says to reroute the packets over the Token Ring segment, and Network 1 is still connected to Network 2. The only trick here is to make sure the routers use their dynamic routing protocols to full advantage until something goes wrong. Then the system should jump in with the backup plans.

Unfortunately, there are as many ways of accomplishing this task as there are routers, networks, and protocols. When you get down to the basics, it boils down to cost. In the case of routers and routing protocols, this is what is referred to as a *route metric*.

As you will see in the discussion of the different protocols, the router somehow determined how many hops it is away from all its neighbors.

NOTE A *hop* is defined as the passage of a data packet between two network nodes, or routers. Hops are measured in hop counts, and each time a packet crosses a router, its hop count is incremented by one.

These hops can be either the entire cost of using a particular route or a major contributing factor. In one protocol, the Routing Information Protocol (RIP), the cost of the route is entirely based on hops. In Open Shortest Path First (OSPF), other things play a part, such as the speed of the links and a predefined link cost. We seem to be getting a little ahead of ourselves, so let's take a closer look at the different types of routes we can define.

Static Routes

Static routes are routes devised by humans for machines. For example, take a look at the network diagram in Figure 8.11.

In Figure 8.11, you have four routers. In a static-route situation, the network administrator must determine the best way to get from Network 1 to any other network. Let's assume that you have decided the best way for information to get from Network 1 to Network 4 is through Router 1 and Router 3. You manually enter in the route paths on each router and life goes on, until there is a problem with Router 3. Now, looking at the diagram you notice that packets can still get from Network 1 to Network 4 through Router 2 and Router 4. Unfortunately, your system may never know it, because you didn't enter the information into the routing-information tables.

Static routing works best on small networks or on networks where the route selection is dependent on extenuating circumstances, such as security. You can imagine the work that would be necessary if your network had ten routers instead of four. In that case, any time a change was made to the layout of the network, you could plan on spending some serious time reconfiguring and testing router tables. The chances are this is not how you would normally choose to spend your time.

Figure 8.11   A network map without routing defined

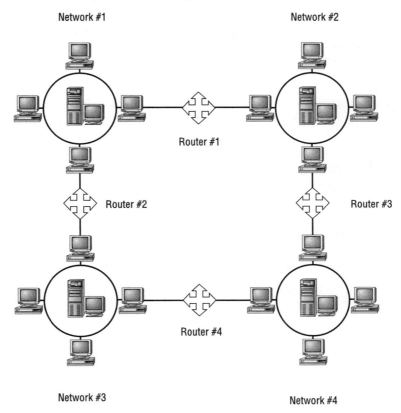

Dynamic Routes

The way around having to do all that work is to make use of dynamic routing protocols. With dynamic routing, the routers get together and share information. When all that information is put to good use, a picture of the entire network exists and then just has to be maintained.

But how do the routers actually learn about the network? There are two generic ways dynamic routers gather information: distance-vector routing and link-state routing.

Distance-Vector Routing

In distance-vector routing, each router must maintain a router-information table that contains the distance from itself to every other router on the network. These distances are ascertained by combining information from all surrounding neighborhoods.

A router is really nothing more than a specialized piece of computer hardware. Like most computer hardware, when it is first turned out, it really doesn't know much. Just like the PC on your desk, it goes through a power-on self-test and then boots an operating system that gives it some basic information. At this point, the router knows that it needs to find out where everything else on the network is located, so it starts off the process by telling the rest of the world everything it knows about itself.

Each router is configured with its own ID. In addition, it is configured with a number that it will use to "cost" each link. Because the cost can be configured by the system administrator, we will keep it simple and say the cost will be one. Now, when the router boots up, it only knows where it is located, so it will use that as a starting point and assign itself a distance vector of 0. After all, it doesn't have to go anywhere to get to itself. The router does not know who it's nearest neighbor is or where the neighbor lives, so it will set a random value of "infinity" for the distance to all the other destinations. Once it has these two pieces of information, it is time to tell the world; it broadcasts out a packet with its hardware address and the two costs it has established, zero and infinity (see Figure 8.12).

Figure 8.12   Another network map to define distance-vector routing

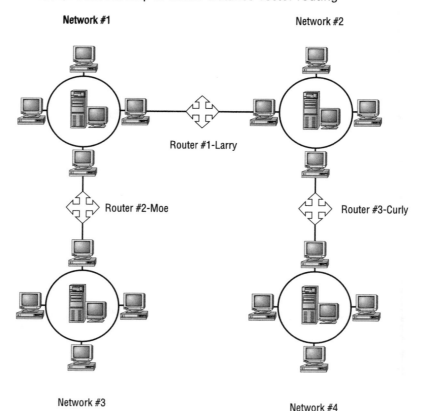

For simplicity sake, let's name our routers Larry, Moe, and Curly. Assume that router Larry has been down, the router version of a coffee break. This leaves routers Moe and Curly to do all the work, and they are not happy about it. When Larry comes back online, it knows about Networks 1 and 2. It sends out a distance-vector packet that says "Hey, here I am, I am zero hops away from Networks 1 and 2, and I don't know where anything else is."

Moe gets this information. Now, Moe *also* knows where Network 1 is, because Moe is connected to Networks 1 and 3. As far as Moe is concerned, those two networks are "local," meaning Moe has a connection to each. Moe will see to it that each network has a distance vector of 0. Moe takes a close look at the information it's received from Larry. Moe doesn't have to do anything with the information on Network 1, but the information on Network 2 is new and different. Moe figures that to get to Network 2, a packet will have to go past Larry. Moe adds this information to its routing-information table and sets the distance vector to Network 2 at 1. Meanwhile, Moe needs to share information with Larry. Moe sends back its routing-information table, and now Larry knows that Network 1 and Network 3 are available through Moe. Larry assigns Network 3 a distance vector of 1, because any packet going to Network 3 will have to pass through Moe.

Curly and Larry go through the same types of gyrations. Curly knows from Larry that Network 1 has a distance vector of 1. Larry learns from Curly that Network 4 will have a distance vector of 1. After it has assimilated all that information, Larry sends information to Curly that says, "Hey, Moe knows where Network 3 is. If you want to send a packet to Network 3, send it to me, and I will forward it to Moe." Curly puts this information in its routing information table and adds another hop, so Network 3 is two hops away from Curly. Larry shares Curly's information with Moe, and now the network routing tables have converged, which means everybody knows about everybody else.

For the time being. Until something changes. Each of the routers needs to be vigilant, so communication continues until one of the routers learns about something else or some of the information changes. If something changes, the whole process begins again.

If this process seems long and involved, it is. That is one of the problems with distance-vector routing. Every router has to figure out where everything else is independently. It is a long and arduous process that can seem to take forever. When you are operating in the modern day world of exceptionally fast links and a topology that can change drastically at a moment's notice, this is unacceptable.

Count to Infinity

Unfortunately, distance-vector routing does have other problems. One is called Count to Infinity.

Larry--------------------Moe----------------------------Curly

Here is how Count to Infinity works. In this example, both Larry and Moe want to find out how far it is to Curly. After a period of time, Moe figures that it is one hop to Curly, and Larry figures it is two. Everything is great as long as Curly doesn't go out to lunch. Let's assume Curly skips out and stops working. Moe can't find Curly, so Moe asks Larry if Larry knows how far way Curly is. Larry says, "Sure, Curly is two hops away." Moe takes this information, figures it can route any packets to Curly through Larry and adds a distance vector of 1; now Moe thinks Curly is three hops away. Meanwhile, Larry can't find Curly. Larry asks Moe, and Moe tells Larry that Curly is just three hops away. Larry adds one, puts the route to Curly at four hops through Moe, and the Count to Infinity is on. What we've just described is *router looping,* in which the Count to Infinity actually stops the looping. In the world of routing, infinity equals the protocol's maximum hop count +1 or 16 for IP RIP. It brings the issue to the forefront rather quickly. However, there are some solutions to router looping.

Split Horizon   Split Horizon basically says that if Larry sends information to Curly through Moe, then Larry does not need to know what the distance is from Moe to Curly. All Larry needs to know is that to get to Curly, it should send the information to Moe. So Larry makes an entry in its router information table that the distance to Curly is infinity. If Moe asks, the routers do not need to Count to Infinity, it is already there.

Poison Reverse   With Poison Reverse enabled, all routes learned from a network are advertised back as unreachable. So if Moe tells Larry how to get to Curly and Moe comes back to Larry for directions to Curly, Larry tells Moe you cannot get there from here!

Link-State Routing

The other generic form of routing is link-state routing. With link-state routing, each router needs to be friendly. It will go out and find out about its neighbors and learn their names. Once the router knows this information, it constructs a *link-state packet,* or LSP, which has all of the names of its neighbors and their associated costs.

These LSPs are then broadcast to all the other routers. Each router stores the information it has received from all of its neighbors, and a complete map of the network is assured.

These LSPs are broadcast at routine intervals as well as when a router discovers that there is a new neighbor, the cost to an existing link has changed, or when a link to a neighbor has gone down.

Which is a better generic protocol: a link state or a distance vector? In her book *Interconnections—Bridges and Routers* (Addison Wesley, 1994), Radia Perlman shows that the two methods of route discovery are close on memory, bandwidth consumed, computations required, and robustness. She feels that when it comes to functionality, link state rules the day.

- Link state can discover the topology of the network easier than distance vector.
- Troubleshooting is easier, because a single router can be asked to show the entire database.
- Implementation in simple environments is more practical in link state.
- Convergence is faster.
- In link state, after its neighbors are determined, only changes to its routes are transmitted as updates. Distance Vector Protocols transmit their entire routing tables typically every 30 seconds.

TCP/IP Routing Protocols

Distance vector versus link state. Static versus dynamic. What makes all this stuff really work? Now that we have covered the generics, it is time to take a close look at some of the specific TCP/IP routing protocols. As we do this, we will try and compare some advantages and disadvantages of each.

TCP/IP routing protocols can be broken down into two types: Interior Gateway Protocols (IGPs) and Exterior Gateway Protocols (EGP).

Interior Gateway Protocols

IGPs are the protocols that route packets within your network. Some of the most popular IGP protocols are RIP, OSPF, and IS-IS. There are some other proprietary protocols that you may be working with, including IGRP and EIGRP.

RIP

RIP is the TCP/IP implementation of a Distance Vector Protocol. The advantage of RIP is that it is relatively simple to install and configure. The disadvantage is that it is a Distance Vector Protocol and subject to Count to Infinity problems and slow convergence. RIP also suffers because of its extensive use of bandwidth. Every 30 seconds, the routers on the network broadcast a list of all the routes they know about and their associated costs. That is a lot of traffic for information that does not change frequently. RIP is a great protocol for small networks. But, depending on the source, if your network has more than 15 routers, you will probably need to look at other protocol implementation. RIP starts to degrade in performance after seven routers. RIP does not transmit the route's subnet mask, therefore it only supports classfull addressing (default subnet masks).

RIP Redundancy   RIP is a simple protocol. It really doesn't know or care about things such as the speed of the links it is connecting or even what the traffic looks like on any of its links. All RIP cares about is that if a packet wants to go from Network 1 to Network 2, it needs to pass through two routers, and 100Mb/second is just the same as 16Mb/second. As far as RIP is concerned, a packet delivered is a packet delivered and hang the speed issue. As a matter of fact, RIP is so indiscriminate as to pass the packet using the first route it hears about. That will be the path, no matter what, until it finds a path with a lower cost or if a path fails for some reason.

This makes control of the router particularly difficult. You cannot reasonably predict which path the router will hear about first, so you have to take control of the router by adjusting the metrics along one path to be better or worse than the metrics of another.

Take a closer look back at Figure 8.10. In this case, we want a packet to usually go over the Ethernet route, but we want the Token Ring route to be available just in case. In this example, you would adjust the cost of the Token Ring interfaces to be a number greater than the metric of the Ethernet segment. When the router determines the cost, Ethernet always wins, no matter when the router discovers the path. If the Ethernet segment should suffer some form of failure, however, the Token Ring path would be there for instantaneous backup.

RIP II

RIP II is an updated version of RIP, providing some additional support in the following areas:

Authentication   With RIP II, you can use a password for authentication or supply a key that can be used to verify the routing information on the router.

Variable Length Subnet Masks   A variable-length subnet mask can be given to each destination, allowing for an increased number of hosts and subnets available on your internetwork.

Next Hop Address   The routing table can be configured with the IP address of the next router that should be used to reach a destination. This helps prevent occurrences where a packet takes the long way to get to a particular network.

Multicast Packets   Only a RIP II router will be listening for packets addressed to 224.0.0.9 or multicast packets. This will help ease the load on those systems that are not listening for RIP II packets.

RIP II is a Link State Protocol and not a Distance Vector Protocol.

Open Shortest Path First (OSPF)

OSPF is the Link State Protocol that is usually used on an IP network. As was mentioned above, with a Link State Protocol, a router is responsible for finding out about its neighbors. What better way to meet your neighbors than to say "hello," and OSPF starts out its conversations with a hello packet.

The hello packet is designed to get and maintain information from neighbors. When information is returned, it is added to the routers' routing information table. The hello packet serves several purposes:

- It announces the router, including the router's IP address and subnet mask.
- It determines who the routers' neighbors are.
- It establishes the time interval at which each router will send out its packets. This is used to determine whether a router has gone down or not.
- The hello packet identifies a Designated Router (DR) and a Backup Designated Router (BDR). A DR has the highest priority on the network. The BDR is next in line. If a new router comes on line with a higher priority that the DR, it will just have to wait its turn. The DR remains in place until it becomes inactive. Then the BDR takes its place, and the new router becomes a BDR. These priorities are configurable.

At this stage of route discovery, the DR and the BDR have been elected, and all the routers have met their neighbors. The problem now is to take all of this information and put it into some reasonable, workable format. This is when the synchronization of the link-state advertisement database takes place.

Prior to synchronization, routers are talking in a one-way state. After the databases have been synchronized, routers go into a 2-way, full-neighbor state, and each router is said to be adjacent with its neighbor. Figure 8.13 shows the way this synchronization occurs.

Figure 8.13 Establishing Adjacency

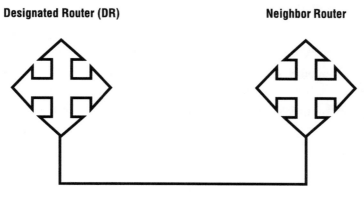

Designated Router (DR)   **Neighbor Router**

Two-Way State

Network Design
and Planning

PART 3

1. As we join the communication already in progress, the neighbor router has contacted the DR and sent through a database description packet (DDP). Just for safekeeping, the BDR gets a copy of the DDP also. For now, the neighbor is just sending though a summary of what it knows, not the complete entry.

2. Once the DR and the BDR have received the summary DDP, they check out the data contained and make sure that they have all the same up-to-date information that the neighbor has.

3. If the neighbors DDP has more information than the DR, the DR will send through a Link State Request (LSR) for more information on the route that is in question.

4. The router that receives the LSR responds by putting all its current information into a Link State Update (LSU) packet and sending it back.

5. Once the information has been received and acted upon, the requesting router (the DR in this example) will send back a Link State Acknowledgement (LSA) packet.

After this communication takes place, the two routers will switch their state of readiness to the full neighbor state. Now that all the information on the network has been gathered, the question remains, how is it used?

Selecting Routes   How does the router turn the results of the polling process in the link-state advertisement database, into a routing table? The first process is to assign a cost to each interface. OSPF takes a look at the database and determines how many routers a packet has to cross to get to a given network. Once it has that information, it can assign a total cost to each path. What happens if there are several paths to a network? In that case, the path with the lowest cost (highest bandwidth) is designated the "best" path, and that information is added to the routing information table. Once this has been completed, the routing-information table needs to be upgraded only when there is a change.

Now, when a packet hits the router, the router can figure out the path to the destination network and send the packet on its way.

OSPF Specialized Terms   When the time comes to configure a router using OSPF, you should be aware of some of the terms that may crop up. The most common terms are

Autonomous System (AS)   A grouping of routers that swap routing information using a common routing protocol. These routers are in a single administrative unit.

Autonomous System Border Router (ASBR)   An ASBR is a router that exchanges information with other autonomous systems. An ASBR will pass information along to the other routers in its autonomous system as information about external systems. For example, the router that connects a network to the Internet will be an ASBR.

Area   In a very large enterprise consisting of hundreds of routers, an area is a logical division of the network, usually based on things like departments, buildings, or geographic sites. When using OSPF, an area can be likened to an AS. Areas are designated to provide easier administration and faster convergence.

Backbone   A backbone is a logical area to which all other areas are connected. The backbone is required and always uses a designated area or 0. Routers that attach to the backbone are called *area border routers* or ABRs. An ABR supplies information for all the routers within the area and acts as a front end into an area. If ever there is a heavyweight when it comes to routing capability, it should be the ABR.

Stub Area   A stub area is an OSPF area that uses a default route, intra-area routes, and interarea routes. It does not broadcast external routes and cannot contain an ASBR. The stub area's ABR advertises itself as the default router (for its area) to all external destinations.

Transit Area   A transit area is an area containing more than one ABR.

Advantages of OSPF   When you have a choice, OSPF is preferred over RIP for the following reasons:

Support for Larger Internetworks   RIP can't route to more than 15 other routers. OSPF can handle 65,535 hops.

Variable-Length Subnetting   The LSAs (Link State Announcements) not only contain information about the address of the router but also contain information about the subnet mask of the network. Because of this functionality, OSPF can handle an increased number of subnets and host addresses.

Rapid Convergence   OSPF is quicker on the uptake when a change occurs. There is also no Count to Infinity problem with OSPF internetworks.

Reduced Internetwork Traffic   RIP sends out its routing-information table every 30 seconds. OSPF transmits updates only when there are changes and, by default, transmits its entire routing table every two hours.

OSPF Redundancy   As you know by now, OSPF is different, more advanced, and more sophisticated than RIP. OSPF does care about bandwidth, albeit in an offhand kind of way. Each link in the network is given a cost by the protocol. The cost is determined to be 10^8/bandwidth. The costs for several types of links are shown in Table 8.1.

Network Design and Planning

PART 3

Table 8.1 Default OSPF Costs

Link Bandwidth	Default OSPF Cost
56kbps serial link	1,785
64kbps serial link	1,562
T-1 (1.544Mbps)	65
E-1 (2.048Mbps)	48
4Mbps Token Ring	25
Ethernet	10
16Mbps Token Ring	6
FDDI or Fast Ethernet	1

Because the Fast Ethernet segment has a lower default cost than the 16Mbps Token Ring, the OSPF router will take the Ethernet segment as long as it is available. As a matter of fact, OSPF is so sophisticated that if both our segments had been 100Mb Ethernet, OSPF will try to do some form of load balancing. According to our scenario above, this is just what we want: redundant links without the pain and hassle of messing around, reconfiguring the routers.

There may be other reasons, such as security or even network politics, that may determine whether you change the OSPF metrics. In the example above, however, it wasn't necessary.

Intermediate System to Intermediate System (IS-IS)

When the International Standards Organization (ISO) came up with a routing standard for a connectionless network protocol (CLNP), IS-IS was the result. It is primarily used by Digital's DECnet networks. As a matter of fact, IS-IS is the precursor to OSPF.

To understand IS-IS, we have to define several terms and several different routing protocols. In the Open System Interconnection (OSI) parlance, an end system is a nonrouting network device where an intermediate system (IS) is a routing device. A particular routing domain is called an *area,* which is similar to the discussion on OSPF. In any particular area, all end systems have full access to all other end systems.

Connection vs. Connectionless

As we discuss protocols, there are a couple of concepts that should be explained in more detail, that of connection-oriented protocols and connectionless protocols.

A connectionless protocol is one that will dump the packet on the wire and hope that it gets there. It will do some checking to make sure the packet arrived, but with connectionless, the protocol makes its best effort for delivery. Connection-oriented protocols, on the other hand, establish a link with the receiving host and don't break the link until the conversation is completed.

When you think of connectionless protocols, think of the mail system. When you want to send a letter to someone that is important, you take the letter to a postal box, drop it in, and trust in the postal service to make sure it arrives without a hitch.

Now imagine that the letter you are mailing is really, really important, such as the winning lottery ticket in the $56,000,000,000 lotto. Are you going to trust that letter to the postal service and hope for a best effort delivery? Definitely not. You are going to make sure that you get a signed receipt every time something or someone touches the note. That is an example of a connection-oriented protocol. And like the neighborhood post office, special handling costs extra. Connection-oriented protocols come with extra baggage and larger overhead.

Network Design and Planning

PART 3

The ISO defined several types of intermediate system protocols.

- The first was designed as part of ISO 9542, the ES-IS protocol to be used with CLNP. ES-IS defines how an end system talks with an intermediate system.

- ISO 10589 defines IS-IS, or intermediate systems–to–intermediate system, intra-domain routing protocol. This protocol defines how routers talk to other routers in the same domain.

- IDRP is the IS-IS interdomain routing protocol. This lays out how routers communicate with routers in other domains.

ISO 10589, the IS-IS protocol, is a Link State Protocol defined for DECnet that can operate over a variety of subnetworks, including LANs, WANs, and point-to-point links.

IS-IS is broken down even farther into Level 1 and Level 2 routers or ISs. A Level 1 IS knows how to communicate with other Level 1 ISs in the same area. To route between areas, you would need a Level 2 IS. Interconnecting the Level 2 systems will form the network backbone.

IS-IS was defined as an OSI-specific protocol. Because OSI-specific protocols and TCP need to coexist, IS-IS needs to be run in both worlds. This is called *dual IS-IS,* and its primary advantage is to run with reduced CPU utilization. Dual IS-IS only runs the routing algorithm once, with only one set of routing updates sent. It is a useful protocol on backbones with various types of traffic.

Interior Gateway Routing Protocol (IGRP)

You haven't been hanging around the world of computers very long if you haven't heard the name Cisco. Although Microsoft may have a corner on the software market, Cisco is one of the power players in the router market. As a power player, Cisco can define its own rules, or in this case, define a proprietary routing protocol.

IGRP is a Distance Vector Protocol that uses a one-dimensional vector based on four elements. The elements that go into choosing the best path include

- Bandwidth
- Delay
- Load
- Reliability

IGRP was designed to replace RIP with a protocol that would scale with network growth. Table 8.2 shows some of the features of IGRP:

Table 8.2   IGRP Features

Feature	Description
Configurable Metrics	Metrics involved in the algorithm responsible for calculating route information may be configured by the user.
Flash Update	Updates may be sent out prior to the default time setting. This occurs when the route metrics change.
Poison Reverse Updates	Implemented to prevent routing loops. The updates place a route in *holddown*. Holddown means that the router will not accept any new route information on a given route for a certain period of time.
Unequal-Cost Load Balancing	Allows packets to be shared and distributed across multiple paths.

Enhanced IGRP (EIGRP)

Although IGRP was good, Cisco felt it could be better. EIGRP is designed to resolve some of the problems with IGRP.

EIGRP is a hybrid, or a mix, of a link-state routing and distance-vector routing. IGRP would send out an entire routing table when changes are made in the network, but EIGRP will only send out the change. The features of EIGRP are shown in Table 8.3.

Table 8.3 Features of EIGRP

Feature	Description
Route Tagging	Distinguishes routes learned via different EIGRP sessions.
Formal Neighbor Relationships	Uses the Hello Protocol to establish peering.
Incremental Routing Updates	Only changes are advertised instead of the entire route table.
Classless Routing	EIGRP support subnets and variable-length subnet masks.
Configurable Metrics	Metric information can be set through configuration commands.
Equal Cost Load Balancing	Allows traffic to be sent equally across multiple connections.

Exterior Gateway Protocols

One problem with the IGP protocols was that they wouldn't scale up beyond the enterprise network, so the EGPs were introduced.

In the previous examples, the routing protocols have been area-based, or Interior Gateway Protocols (IGPs). Now it is time to look at what happens if you need to use what is called an Exterior Gateway Protocol or EGP. An EGP is like an IGP with an attitude. The differences are in the amount of details that are being handled.

IGP needs to get granular. It needs to know which subnet a particular host is on so that traditional routing can occur. EGP on the other hand, is designed to remove some of this granularity. After all, if you are sending out a packet all the way to the other side of the world, each and every router this packet crosses does not need to know about the inner workings of your subnet's structure.

EGPs are different because of the amount of information they share with other routers. These "other" routers are not administered by the local staff, so the same level of trust is not needed as there would be with an IGP. The last difference depends not on trust but on administration. Because you have little control over what an EGP gets information from, you do not want to have to contact some higher authority every time you want to make a change to your network. An EGP allows you to have that autonomy.

The two most common EGPs are the Exterior Gateway Protocol (EGP) and the Border Gateway Protocol (BGP).

NOTE Don't you just love acronyms? Yes, in fact, one of the two most common EGPs is EGP. And to think, real people think geeks talk funny!

Both EGP and BGP employ the concept of the autonomous system. An autonomous system is nothing more than a group of networks under the control of some central form of administration. This means that any network or any router will belong to just one autonomous system. Because the EGP sits on the fence between the autonomous system and the outside world, it hides the details of the autonomous system from the rest of society. The EGP figures that if a packet comes addressed to a router in the autonomous system, it can pass it off to any router on the inside, and it will be delivered.

This is not as simple a process as it may seem. As a matter of fact, each autonomous system is identified by a unique 16-bit number. These autonomous system (AS) numbers are assigned by the same folks who give you your official IP network addresses. If you feel you need one, check with your ISP on how to get it.

Border Gateway Protocol

The first of the EGPs is really the latest. BGP was written to overcome some of the problems that the earlier Exterior Gateway Protocol exhibited; BGP was written to detect routing loops and to use a metric to add some intelligence to any routing decisions.

BGP can actually be used as an IGP or an EGP. If there are two BGP neighbors that are being used to communicate across domains, those systems must reside on the same physical network. Setting up BGP routers to handle this is essentially an interior communication and is done to ensure both routers have a consistent view of the domain and to determine which router will actually be the connecting point to or from the external domain.

BGP handles update messages that are made up of network numbers and domain path pairs. The domain path is a string of domains that a packet must go through to reach the specified network. This is the update packet, so how does the router get its original set of data? This comes from an exchange of the entire routing table. Any change to the routing table is passed along as an incremental change. Although a BGP router may maintain several paths to a particular destination, only the most optimum path is shared with other routers.

Exterior Gateway Protocol

EGP is the forefather of BGP. Although it has some shortcomings, it was the primary routing protocol for the Internet. This protocol, which is used to communicate between "core" Internet routers, was defined in RFC904 in 1984. The core routers grew in scope to form what is now the backbone of the information superhighway.

EGP uses a very simple design. It does not use metrics and cannot make any intelligent routing decisions. EGP updates contain information about the accessibility of a particular network. In other words, it tells the world that a particular network is accessible through a certain router.

Updates to the routing tables are sent at certain intervals. Each router indicates the networks that it is directly attached to. Routing tables are built based on this information.

EGP does have several shortcomings. It cannot deal with routing loops. The EGP updates are very large and very cumbersome, and because it does not make intelligent decisions, its influence in the Internet community was slowly phased out.

9

WAN Design Considerations

A good, well thought out design can contribute to important work issues, such as a stable network, and to peaceful evenings and weekends when your pager does not go off. You should be able to take the information from the previous chapters and rough out some type of a design for your wide-area network (WAN). Ask yourself some questions, such as is my network big enough that I need to create an area? Do I need to apply for an autonomous system number and to make use of BGP routers? How can I design my metrics, or how can I lay out my routers to make sure that I have multiple paths to the same areas, guaranteeing redundancy and minimizing downtime? As you make your design choices, considering these questions is a good place for you to start.

Design Objectives—The Future of Your Network

Not all of us get to design a network from the beginning and decide what will be needed over the next ten years. Most of us are probably working with a network that is already established. But either way, you have to work with what you have, so you should always look to the future any time expansion or reconfiguration comes up. The signs are there, the times are changing, and with the changing times, comes more stress on your network.

Let's look at some ways the experts predict how IP will be used in the future.

IP to the Rescue

It wasn't all that long ago that the only people using TCP/IP and the Internet were researchers, government contractors, or military people. My goodness how times have changed!

Rumors and speculation abound as to the ways IP will be used in the future. Think about this: someone figured out that with new IP addressing standards, there could be as many as five IP addresses for each square meter of land on earth. Notice, I didn't say *dry* land, just land. Now, I have never run the numbers, and I don't really plan to, but for whatever reason, a lot of IP addresses are going to be floating around.

IP is taking over the enterprise-wide network, and not just in the traditional networking areas either. New standards by the Internet Engineering Task Force (IETF) will simplify data storage and ease the use of IP over satellite links. When that happens, IP will become the protocol of choice for both cable and broadcast television. In many areas of the United States, cable modems are bringing 10MB/Sec Internet access into the home. When that type of access is available everywhere, voice and video communication will become commonplace. With the progress being made in wireless technology, I can see the day coming when newborns will be issued an IP address, and that address will be used for all forms of communications.

The latest technology just hanging out in the weeds, waiting for acceptance, is to use the Internet for voice communications. Why should telephony require all these extra wires? If I have Internet access to my office, why can't I piggyback onto that for telephone calls? The technology is already there. Acceptance is a little slow in coming.

What does this mean to you? If you are an IT manager or a network administrator, it means that the nightmare of fighting with the alphabet soup of protocols may be soon coming to an end. When that happens, you will be responsible for managing voice, video, and data being transmitted over the very same media.

All of these new implementations call for new technologies. Some of them are already available, such as local-area network (LAN) switches that contain multiple-packet queues. Some systems are working with an IP packet header that contains a precedence field, and there is the emerging Multiprotocol Label Switching (MPLS) standard.

Multiprotocol Label Switching (MPLS)

MPLS was originally presented as a way of improving the speed of routers when forwarding packets to other networks. It is now emerging as a crucial standard technology that offers capabilities for large-scale IP networks. Traffic engineering—giving network operators a way to dictate the path that traffic takes through their network—and Virtual

Private Network support are examples of two key applications where MPLS is superior to any currently available IP technology.

The secret of MPLS lies in the generation of a short, fixed-length "label" that acts as a shorthand representation of an IP packet's header. This is similar to the way a zip code is a designator for a small area of a city in a very large country. MPLS can use that label to make forwarding decisions about the packet. IP packets have a field in their header called the *destination address*. That field contains the address to which the packet is to be routed. Traditional routed networks process this information at every router in a packet's path through the network. (This is also known as *hop-by-hop routing*.)

When the IP packets enter the network, the MPLS router analyzes the contents of the IP header and selects an appropriate label with which to "encapsulate" the packet. Part of the great power of MPLS comes from the fact that this analysis can be based on more than just the destination address. At all the subsequent nodes within the network, the MPLS label, and not the IP header, is used to make the forwarding decisions for the packet.

MPLS is an emerging technology. So what about some of the planning you should do for the network you have in place today?

Planning for the Implementation of DHCP

In Chapter 4, we had an in-depth discussion of the Dynamic Host Configuration Protocol (DHCP). If, by some chance, you skipped that chapter, you probably already know how DHCP can help simplify your task of assigning and managing IP addresses. Although DCHP is a powerful tool, it does come with its own set of *gotchas* that should be addressed at the planning stage.

When a potential DHCP host comes online, it "knows" that it is supposed to go out and either acquire a TCP/IP address from a DHCP server, or it knows that it is supposed to renew its lease on its current DHCP address, which is both a good and a bad thing. It is a good thing because the potential host will go out and look for an IP address; it is a bad thing because the potential host has no clue where to begin looking. When in doubt, broadcast.

When the host comes up, it sends out a broadcast message asking for an IP address. Depending on which DHCP server gets the request first, the DHCP server will respond with a packet offering an IP address to the potential host. The host accepts the offer, and it is now an official IP host, able to communicate with other systems using TCP/IP. The situation works well, as long as the network designer remembers that, as a rule, broadcast messages do not get routed. That means the DHCP server needs to be either on the same subnet as the potential host or in constant contact with a DHCP server using a DHCP relay agent.

The DHCP relay agent has a deceptively simple job. It has the actual TCP/IP address of the DHCP server. It also resides on a subnet that does not have a DHCP server. If there is no DHCP server on a segment when a potential host comes online and asks to lease a TCP/IP address without the DHCP relay agent, the request falls on deaf ears. In this case, the relay agent grabs the broadcast request and addresses it to the DHCP server. Because this is a specific address, the packet will be routed to another network. The DHCP server will answer the request with a lease offer and forward it back to the relay agent. The DHCP relay agent will address the packet to the potential host looking for a TCP/IP address and send a directed packet, using its MAC address, to that piece of equipment. The potential host will accept the offer, and another host is online.

When designing your network, remember a DHCP server or a DHCP relay agent must belong on every network segment. Take a look at Figure 9.1 to see what I mean.

Figure 9.1   DHCP Server and Relay Agents

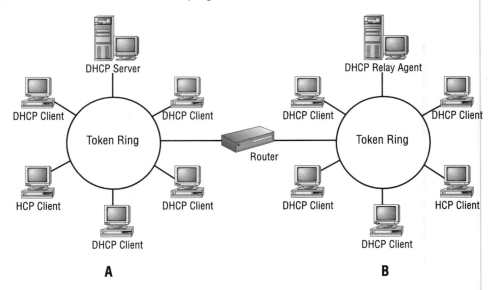

As you can see from the diagram, Ring A has the DHCP server, and Ring B has a DHCP relay agent. In this way, hosts on both rings can access the same DHCP server. Keep in mind that these DHCP servers can pass out more information than just the IP address. They can be configured to pass out things, such as the default gateway address, the addresses of DNS servers, and much more.

NOTE   For more information on DHCP, see Chapter 4.

Maintaining the DHCP Database

DHCP works off of a series of databases, and like most databases, they can become corrupt. To protect yourself against these kinds of calamities, make sure you maintain the databases regularly. Depending on the kind of network operating system (NOS) that you have dishing out the DHCP addresses, this maintenance may take on several different forms. For the sake of simplicity, let's look at how to maintain a DHCP database on an NT 4 server.

Backing up the DHCP Database

Once DHCP Services have been installed on an NT server, the DHCP databases are automatically backed up hourly to the \%SYSTEMROOT%\SYSTEM32\DHCP\BACKUP\JET directory. The intervals are configurable through registry entries.

Restoring the DHCP Database

The DHCP databases can be restored in a variety of ways. First, the database will automatically be restored for the DHCP server, if the server determines the data is corrupt while the server starts. You can force the restore with a registry entry or by simply copying the backup directory listed above to the \%SYSTEMROOT%\SYSTEM32\DHCP directory.

Compacting the DHCP Database

Information about addresses that have been leased, leases that have expired, and leases that are about to expire can change the layout of the DHCP database and require the database be brought back into size. With NT 4, this process is completed automatically.

Planning for the Implementation of DNS

To me, Domain Name System (DNS) and routing are the two really "gee whiz" aspects of the Internet. All network communication revolves around two pieces of equipment having something to say, communicating over some kind of media, and using a set of rules or protocols. Networking at the most basic level. The problem with that definition is it does not explain how these two pieces of equipment find each other out there in the big, bad world.

When we look at the world's largest TCP/IP network, the Internet, we realize that each computer has several ways of being addressed. First, there is a host name, for example, xyz.novell.com or abc.microsoft.com. The host name gives a user-friendly name to a host somewhere on a particular network, and the host name gets mapped to a TCP/IP address. For example, `xyz.novell.com` may be `192.34.22.148` and `abc.microsoft.com` may be `156.33.21.111`. Finally, that address gets *resolved*, or matched up, with a hardware-specific address, such as 00-60-08-02-4D-D1. When someone opens a browser and types **xyz.novell.com**, that name gets resolved to the IP address of 192.34.22.148. A packet gets addressed to the network that the host resides on, and when the packet gets to the network, it is redirected to hardware address 00-60-08-02-4D-D1. But how does it know the IP address in the first place?

NOTE   If you read Chapter 5, "DNS and Your Network," some of this may be a review.

This is where DNS comes in. DNS is a distributed database stored all over the Internet. Each section of the database stores a certain amount of information. It is important to know that each computer that stores DNS information knows where other DNS computers reside. When you make the request for `abc.microsoft.com`, your browser knows to look in a couple of places for the information. If the browser doesn't find it in WINS, LMHOSTS, or the HOST file, it has to turn to DNS. The computer looks to its IP configuration and accesses the address of a DNS server. It then sends a directed packet (a specifically addressed packet, not a broadcast packet) to the DNS server asking for name-to-address resolution. When the DNS server gets the packet, it will answer whether it knows the whereabouts of the name. If not, it will keep pushing the request farther up the tree of servers until there is an answer.

How does your network enter into this worldwide scope of magic? As a network administrator, you are always looking for ways to speed up communication on your network. After all, if you do something particularly brilliant today, you might not have to hear "God, the network is slow today!" tomorrow. We would all like that.

One way you might want to see about speeding up the response of requests to the Internet is to create a local DNS server. This is a particularly valuable tool, if your network is hooked up to an intranet as well as the Internet. Here is how it works. You establish a DNS server on your local network. In your DNS database, you enter the host names and IP addresses of all the local, important hosts as well as the IP addresses and host names of all the important company suppliers, most frequently used Web sites, e-mail servers, etc. Then you also make sure that your DNS server is pointing to a powerful DNS server on your ISP's network, just in case your DNS server does not have all the information it needs.

When you configure your DHCP server, make sure that one of the DNS addresses it provides points to your local server. When someone opens a browser and asks for a host name stored in your DNS server, the response back with the appropriate IP address is almost immediate.

Because a DNS request is a directed request, you do not need DNS servers on every network segment. You may decide you do not need a local DNS server at all, and that is perfectly all right. It is just something to speed up network access.

> **NOTE** Although it will never replace DNS, Proxy servers do somewhat of the same thing on the fly. Any request heading out to the Internet will travel through the Proxy server. The Proxy server is the host making the actual request to the Internet, and it then passes the returned information back to the originating system. The Proxy server keeps track of requests and will also cache the most frequently used Web pages or pages you request it to precache. When a user requests the home page for www.microsoft.com, the Proxy server will return the page stored in its memory, saving all that traffic over the Internet.

If you do opt for a DNS server, remember it needs to be updated with the names of your new local hosts, along with their new IP addresses. If you have a large WAN, placing several DNS servers throughout the company will also speed up communications.

Planning for the Implementation of WINS

If the Internet has DNS to resolve host names to TCP/IP addresses, what does a Windows NT network have to resolve NetBIOS computer names to IP addresses? It is WINS, or Windows Internet Name Service.

WINS works this way: one system on the network is designated as the WINS server. When a WINS client starts up, it knows the address to the WINS server either because it is set in the WINS Configuration folder in TCP/IP Properties or because it was attained from the DHCP server. The first thing the client has to do is "register" with the WINS server to let the rest of the network know it is around. When the client comes on line, it directs a packet to the WINS server, which lets the server know that the new kid on the block wants to register a name. The WINS client provides all kinds of information for the server, such as its source address and the Name to Register. Once the WINS server has received the packet, it responds with a Name Registered packet as well as notification of the name's Time to Live, or *TTL*. Of course, this is assuming the name that was requested was not already in use by another computer. If some other computer on the network has already registered your computer's name, the new WINS client will be refused access to the network.

NOTE If this happens, the system administrator will probably spend long periods of time late at night trying to figure out why this new computer won't connect to the network when everything looks like it should attach perfectly. Then some young punk (or a punk-ette) fresh out of school will walk by and point out to the seasoned IT veteran that perhaps naming a computer JOE (or MARY) may not be such a wise idea. After all, there is probably more than one Joe (or Mary) in the office, and they know for a fact that one of them is already using that computer name. Of course, at this point the wily IT veteran looks over at the wet-behind-the-ears little punk (or punk-ette) and says something to the effect of, "Really good, I wondered how long it would take you to spot that!" Not that the above scenario has ever happened, and even if it did, it would not have happened to the author of this book, and the punk-ette would not have been his 24-year old daughter who was still learning how to install an operating system and a video card. Nope, that would never, ever have happened!

Whenever you have a TTL, you must have some form of renewal and release. Of course, WINS has that covered also. All these systems are registered in the WINS database, so how does another system access these items? In this case, when a system needs a network resource and knows where it is located, it will simply ask for it. When the request comes through for a printer hanging off that mythical computer MARY, the WINS server looks up the address in the database and returns it to the requesting system. At that point, the system that needs the resource can direct a packet to the appropriate address and get the services it needs.

Planning the Installation of WINS Servers

Although WINS is usually an asset to a network, it is not always the case. For example, if you have a large Unix installation and a few systems using NetBIOS, chances are it would be easier to configure the DNS server to point to the NetBIOS hosts. Unix hosts can be added to the WINS database as a *static mapping,* but the host name must be capitalized (Unix host names do not have to be capitalized) and cannot exceed 15 characters.

If your network is a large NetBIOS shop and WINS is in your future, you will probably want to have at least two WINS servers in the network. Although your network may be small enough for one system to handle the load, two gives you the advantages of fault tolerance in case one of the servers goes down.

As with most installations, bigger/faster/more memory is usually better. With a two-server implementation, your network, according to Microsoft, will be ready to handle up to 10,000 clients. When you configure the clients, point 5,000 clients to the first server as a primary WINS server, and point the second 5,000 clients to the other server as the primary WINS server. The first 5,000 will use the second server as a secondary WINS server, the second 5,000 will use the first server as the secondary WINS server. This is a manual configuration for fault tolerance!

Because all these clients will be sending directed messages to the WINS servers, it should be obvious that each server must have a static IP address. The WINS systems do not have to be domain controllers.

Maintaining the WINS Database

Unlike the DNS database, which is replicated and distributed, the WINS database resembles the DHCP systems that need some attention. Always remember that the sign of a really good administrator is the level of paranoia they have. The more paranoia, the better the administrator. When in doubt, back up.

Backing Up the WINS Database

Backups of the WINS database become automatic after a 24-hour period lapses and a backup directory has been specified. The specification takes place in the WINS Manager Mapping menu, after selecting Backup Database.

Restoring the WINS Database

Just like the DHCP server, if the WINS server notices that the data in the database is corrupt, it will replace it. This occurs when the WINS server comes up. You can also manually force database restoration by using WINS Manager, or by deleting some files in the \%SYSTEMROOT%\SYSTEM32\WINS directory.

Compacting the WINS Database

Again, just like the DHCP database, these databases can get somewhat out of hand. In the case of the WINS database, the JETPACK.EXE utility should be run anytime the WINS database gets over 30MB in size.

Planning for the Implementation of LMHOSTS

Above, we talked about the dynamic way to resolve NetBIOS names to IP addresses. There is another way to ensure that Windows computer name-to-address resolution takes place using a static file or table called the LMHOSTS file. The LMHOSTS file was the precursor to WINS. With Windows NT, the LMHOSTS file performs well and does what it is supposed to do without too many problems. However, the thing that should concern you is whenever something or someone says the word *static*. Static usually translates into work for someone, and that someone looks exactly like you.

Some of you TCP/IP veterans may recognize the similarity to the HOSTS file. The HOSTS file is still used, but the LMHOSTS file offers some increased functionality; while the HOSTS file is "local" serving one machine, an LMHOSTS file can be networked, having several different computers refer to it for information.

An LMHOSTS file is a rather simple file. First of all, it does not have an extension, it is simply LMHOSTS. Here is an example of an LMHOSTS file:

```
125.2.74.3     Brandice   #Print Server
125.2.74.27    CJ         #Application Server
125.2.74.33    Dawn       #PRE        #source LMHOSTS Server
125.2.74.35    Denise     #PRE
#INCLUDE \\thatbox\public\lmhosts
#INCLUDE \\thisbox\private\lmhosts
```

> **TIP**   Text beginning with the # sign are treated as statements or comments. The lines with #INCLUDE indicate that the system will go to those resources and include the LMHOSTS file they find there.

When the NT server comes up or boots, it looks for an LMHOSTS file and parses the file prior to a user logging onto the network.

One of the ways that you provide for distribution of work is to use block-inclusion statements. A block-inclusion statement doesn't actually go out and merge the contents of one LMHOSTS file into another LMHOSTS file; instead, it is like a pointer to another resource. For example, in the sample LMHOSTS file above, when the NT server is coming up, it will add the information in its LMHOSTS file. It will then check out DAWN and DENISE and load whatever entries it finds there in memory.

The LMHOSTS file uses predefined keywords to perform various tasks. These keywords are

#PRE   This keyword defines which entries should be initially preloaded as permanent entries in the name cache. Preloaded entries help to reduce network traffic, because it eliminates the need for broadcasts. Entries with #PRE tag are loaded automatically.

#DOM [domain_name]   This keyword facilitates domain activity, such as logon validation over a router, account synchronization, and browsing.

#NOFNR   This keyword avoids using NetBIOS-directed name queries for older LAN MANAGER systems.

#BEGIN_ALTERNATE and #END_ALTERNATE   This keyword defines a redundant list of alternate locations for LMHOSTS files. Using this keyword is also the recommended way to #INCLUDE remote files, using a UNC path to ensure access to the file.

#INCLUDE   This keyword loads and searches NetBIOS entries in a separate file from the default.

#MH   This keyword adds multiple entries for a multihomed computer.

Problems with LMHOSTS

I was talking with a friend recently who worked at a large, nationwide financial institution. When the subject of LMHOSTS files came up, she began to tremble and shake, almost uncontrollably. It seems their network was originally configured to use LMHOSTS, and as the network grew and grew, the nightmare of keeping these manual configurations grew and grew.

The company finally abandoned LMHOSTS for WINS, and life is now somewhat better, as long as no one mentions the *L*-word!

Implementation of LMHOSTS

If you opt to use the LMHOSTS system, documentation is the key. Make sure people know what is needed to go where and which server points to which other system. An intricately designed, well-run system can have problems if someone decides to rename, move a server, or heaven forbid, change an IP address.

Care of LMHOSTS Files

Because LMHOSTS is simply a series of text files, they can be backed up using your regular tape backup system. This is not a database system, so nothing has to be compacted.

Planning for the Implementation of HOSTS

Back when TCP/IP was young and the Internet was still the bailiwick of eggheads and generals, the way to resolve host names to IP addresses was through the use of a text file called HOSTS. This file was stored in a cryptic directory structure (usually \etc) that provided all the information any system would ever need. Of course, that occurred back in the days when a PC had a single 5.25" floppy drive that handled a 360K floppy, and that was all the storage we had.

As the Internet grew, the HOSTS file became more and more difficult to keep up, and other methods were devised. The HOSTS file still has uses, and you will undoubtedly come up against it somewhere in your IT career.

HOSTS File Basics

Just like the LMHOSTS file, the HOSTS file is a text-based file, made out in tabular form, that lists the IP address and the host name for a variety of computers. The HOSTS file can be an exceptional aid in handling the "Gosh, the Internet is really slow today" comments.

The HOSTS file received a lot of work from various Unix utilities, such as FTP, Telnet, and Ping, when it was necessary to resolve a host name. Below is a sample of a HOSTS file taken from a Windows 98 workstation.

```
# This file contains the mappings of IP addresses to host names. Each
# entry should be kept on an individual line. The IP address should
# be placed in the first column followed by the corresponding host
# name.
# The IP address and the host name should be separated by at least one
# space.
#
# Additionally, comments (such as these) may be inserted on individual
# lines or following the machine name denoted by a '#' symbol.
#
# For example:
#
#   102.54.94.97   rhino.acme.com   # source server
#   38.25.63.10   x.acme.com    # x client host

127.0.0.1  localhost
209.46.15.104 psconsulting.com
217.177.156.16 mail.xyzcompany.com
```

When the system needs to access the HOSTS file, it will begin "parsing" or reading the file in, line by line, until it finds an entry it can use. This does simplify things, somewhat, because if you add multiple entries, it won't matter. For speed of access, the most used entries should be at the top of the list.

If the HOSTS file is the only method of name-to-address resolution and the address is not in the HOST file, you will receive a NO SUCH HOST error. This is not necessarily catastrophic. If you are sure the host is actually there, go into the file, and make sure you check its spelling. Even if you have access to a spell checker, several editors and proofreaders, as well as other people just looking over your shoulder, you can still misspell a word. Always check syntax because it will cause problems.

If the HOSTS file does contain the entry, then the communication continues as before.

> **TIP**   Here are some ways that the HOSTS file on local machines can help speed up Internet access. Suppose the people in your company all spend a lot of time at a particular Web site. Every time they issue a request for www.coolsite.com, the name has to be sent out to the DNS server and pushed up or down the Internet until it is located. This process can take a while. But if you add the IP address of the www.coolsite.com site to your HOSTS file, you can save everyone some time.

> **TIP**   By the way, if you are looking for the HOSTS file on a Windows machine, don't look in the /etc directory. Try the \Windows directory for a Windows 95/98 machine. For Windows NT 4, the HOSTS files is located in the \%SYSTEMROOT%\system32\drivers\etc directory.

Notice that the HOSTS file does not have some of the sexy predefined KEY terms that the LMHOSTS file has. The file is just plain and utilitarian. It also has to be propagated by hand, copying it from one location to another location to another location to another location. Now you know why the networking gurus came up with DNS!

Care of HOSTS Files

Because a HOSTS file is simply a text file, it can be backed up using your regular tape backup system. This is not a database system, so nothing has to be compacted.

Syntax and documentation is the key. If you spell it right, the commands will find it.

Network Design and Planning

PART 3

The Final Plan

The IP network you design today is going to be the network you live with for a long time. Taking some time to properly design and lay out your network will pay off in the long run.

As with anything in computing, design is a tricky thing. As you have seen in this chapter, the technology is changing rapidly, and the decisions you make today will have to stand the test of time for tomorrow. The important thing is to make sure that your network does what it needs to do to serve its customers in the most efficient method possible today. A well laid out network will lend itself toward upgrading to new technologies such as MPLS, gigabit Ethernet, and even storage area networks.

10

Managing the Network Using SNMP

So often, it is the lot of the network manager to spend their lives putting out fires. You never know where they are going to crop up next; you just know the fires will start, and you will be called out to fight them. It can be a lonely job, but, hey, that is why you get paid the really big bucks!

Simple Network Management Protocol or SNMP can be used not only to help you put out fires but also to predict where fires are going to break out. Does this sound like something that might be useful to you?

Tip for a Network Manager

A friend noticed that every time he walked across a particular floor of his office building, he was besieged with an outbreak of the "Oh, by the way" syndrome. Because most of the problems were of a routine nature that could have been handled by a call to the help desk, he was looking for a way to cross that floor without having to explain eight or ten times why a mouse works a whole lot better if the little ball is kept down against the mouse pad.

> **Tip for a Network Manager** *(continued)*
>
> To solve this problem, he found an old, beat-up clipboard. From the bottom of one of the piles on his desk, he found an old, well-worn legal pad, which he added to the clipboard. He then scribbled some stuff on the top sheet of paper, nothing fancy, just something that looked good. After this was completed, he would grab the clipboard each time he walked across the office floor. He would study it intently, and people would believe he was so remarkably busy that they would not bother him. When he did not have his clipboard with him, he would routinely refer to the trek across the office as travelling with a target on his back!

SNMP Basics

SNMP gathers all sorts of information from around your network, puts it into some form you can use, and presents it to you in a format you can handle. This information can be presented in the form of a report or in real time, meaning that you can set the system up so if a particular segment of the network has too much traffic on it, an alarm will go off, and you can be notified. Although this sounds really simple, and it is, there are a few more components and procedures that you need to be aware of to make the most of SNMP.

The SNMP Managers

SNMP makes use of two types of hosts to accomplish management tasks. The first type is the designated manager. The SNMP manager acts just like good managers everywhere. It is exceptionally nosey, constantly asking questions that demand answers, and all the information ends up in a report somewhere. Because most SNMP systems issue reports only on demand or when there is a problem, chances are the statistics that are gathered by the SNMP manager will end up never being used. Does this sound familiar? SNMP is also like middle managers everywhere, whose discussions tend to revolve around a vocabulary that has no place in the real world. SNMP has a vocabulary all its own, and to start with, if you see the acronym NMS, it stands for the Network Management Station—a fancy way of saying the PC is running the management piece.

An SNMP manager or NMS is a computer dedicated to performing the management task. The manager will have a static IP address, so all the other agent computers can find it and return information when the manager gets nosey. The manager is usually not a server or a router, because these hosts have better, more important server stuff to do than spend time poking around a network.

The SNMP manager operates using three specific types of operations: Get, Get-Next, and Set operations. A Get operation is simply a request for information. As the manager, the SNMP system asks another host (running the SNMP agent software) for a specific value, such as how much disk space is still available, or how many packets have been routed today?

The Get-Next operation is a request for the next value. If the manager is looking through a table of values, the Get-Next operation just returns the next value from the table.

The last operation is to set or change a value. Because most agents are rather protective of the values they have, these are usually marked read only, so the Set operation is rarely used.

SNMP Agents

The SNMP agent software is designed to provide the SNMP manager with whatever information it needs. Because the only systems that have information the manager wants are critical pieces of hardware, an agent is running on something like a server, a router, a printer, or a concentrator. Besides all the other work that these systems perform, an agent will require the operation of what is called a *trap*.

A Trap operation keeps track of when an extraordinary event occurs. For example, this event can be the server coming online or going offline.

Management Information Bases

Any time you have effective communications you have a tacit understanding between the sender and the receiver about what is being communicated. The same is true with SNMP. This understanding comes from the use of Management Information Bases, or MIBs. A MIB is a set of objects that can be managed, along with information about those particular devices. Some MIBs are common, for example, the Internet MIB II defined in RFC1212. This MIB defines 171 common objects that can be polled for either configuration information or problem calls.

Other MIBs are specialized, depending on the management piece the SNMP system is using. An example would be a LAN Manager MIB II, which has definitions for 90 objects, including logon information, session or user information, and other statistical information.

Windows NT 4 also contains MIBs for DHCP that defines the objects used to monitor the activity of a DHCP server as well as a WINS MIB, for WINS Server activity.

Placement of SNMP Managers and Agents

If you operate or plan to operate a large network, and you are going to use SNMP, you will need to break down the network into reasonably sized chunks, otherwise, the information you receive from the SNMP manager will be so overwhelming as to be meaningless. SNMP already has the resources in place to handle this. It is called an *SNMP community*.

A community is simply a defined group of hosts. Each of these hosts is running the SNMP agent software. When communities are defined, they are named, and in providing a community name, a very limited degree of security is defined. Whenever a request for information is received, the systems will check the community name. An agent will not accept a request from any SNMP management agent outside of its own community.

But because an agent will not do this, don't think for a minute that an agent can belong to only one community. Most agents are servers or routers, and most servers or routers perform different functions, so each agent can report to multiple managers in several communities.

Popular SNMP Software

Because many of the most popular network operating systems don't come with a native SNMP manager, we will have to keep this discussion somewhat generic. Let's assume that you have a fairly large network, and you are looking to manage the network with a popular software package. You have to sit down and decide exactly what kind of information you want to receive from the SNMP manager. First, you should look at the different types of servers on your network. You probably have file and print services, database services, mail services, and maybe even a communication server. You want an SNMP manager to keep track of all the server stuff going on. This includes logons/logoffs, password verifications, whether the server is up or down, little inconsequential things like that. Because you may want to gather information about the servers, you may decide to make all servers a part of one community.

You may also have a problem network segment or building. This segment or building may consist of a variety of servers, printers, concentrators, e-mail gateways, and a router or two for good measure. Because this is also an area you will want to track, you can make this a separate community.

Here is how SNMP works:

1. Any time something happens on a host machine running the SNMP agent, if it is defined by an active MIB, the host keeps track of the information. Like all good "employees," it doesn't report on all its activities until it is asked. Asking what each agent has been doing is the responsibility of the SNMP manager.

2. The nosey SNMP management system sends out a request to a particular agent. This request can be done in the form of a host name or in the form of an IP address.

    If a host name is used, it is resolved to an IP address using DNS, a HOSTS file, WINS, LMHOSTS, or a broadcast.

3. Now that the notification is received by the agent, an SNMP packet has to be formed by the manager with the appropriate request for information on an object or a set of objects. The community name is added to the packet for validation. Once the packet is complete, it is sent on to the agent's IP address.

4. The SNMP agent receives the packet, verifies the community name, and verifies the source host name or IP address. Once the verification has been completed, the request is passed down to the appropriate software piece, and the statistics are tallied.

5. An SNMP packet is formed at the agent with the new found information and routed back to the SNMP manager with the requested information.

Network design should not revolve around SNMP, but it will be one of the issues that will need to be addressed. When you look at your network map, common sense will prevail. You will not put a network manager on a segment with limited bandwidth and expect that manager to handle the information on hundreds of agent hosts.

How to Make Plans for Using SNMP Applications

If you are in the enviable position of deciding which network management suite you want to use, you can start off by making a list of everything you want the program to do for you. This will include managing or monitoring your NT servers, your NetWare servers, and your e-mail implementation as well as the complete list of Unix and Linux hosts. Once you have an all-encompassing list, you can go out and make informed decisions about which products will be right for you.

> **WARNING** Before purchasing the product, be sure to look at what is going to have to be done to configure the agents. The management aspect might be a simple installation, but configuring all those servers to report back to the management host may be a different story. This is just a word to the wise. You never want to look your boss straight in the eye and say the project will be completed tomorrow, only to discover that several hundred settings need to be changed on servers around the network.

Planning on Using SNMP-Compliant Hardware and Software

If you already have an SNMP manager configured on your network and you are planning on a major hardware/software upgrade or purchase, make sure that the MIBs the new system uses are compliant. There is nothing more frustrating than finding out that all your new stuff does not necessarily work well with all of your old stuff. This is not a long involved process; usually, it amounts to reading the manuals and documentation that come with the agents or the managers.

Keep in mind that if you are planning on making major purchases, some of the equipment may come with its SNMP agent software.

SNMP software comes in a bevy of shapes and sizes. Some software, such as Nortel's Optivity or Hewlett-Packard's OpenView, is designed to handle SNMP and do it very well. Some companies write their own SNMP code to handle various situations, and then there are the SNMP + packages, such as Systems Management Server from Microsoft or ManageWise from Novell. These packages do some SNMP stuff, but they were designed with a larger network management scheme in mind.

Using SNMP in the Real World

Some of the case studies that I was able to find were quite extensive and explicit. Some held back certain pieces of information. In any case, there is something to learn from each one.

How Tough Can You Make It?

The first case study involves a local municipality that is the customer of Data Systems West of Woodland Hills, California. Vice President Phil Mogavero provided the information.

Network Integration

There was a time when people kept talking about their Novell networks or their Windows NT networks. In this Data Systems West (DSW) case study, the city in question was probably close to what your WAN looks like, a sort of hodgepodge of equipment and operating systems all designed to do a specific job. The trick was to get them all to work together.

> **Network Integration** *(continued)*
>
> Here is the DSW description of the network: "DSW is in the process of deploying a network backbone which collapses 100MB segments from Cisco Catalyst 5000 switches supporting Police, Fire, City Hall, Information Services, and Public Services into a Cisco 7513 router placed in the Data Center." The report goes on, "Each Catalyst 5000 switch, positioned within each building, feeds 100MB and 10MB Virtual Local Area Networks (VLANs) via Fiber Risers to Bay Networks hubs. Network management is accomplished with a Hewlett-Packard Unix system supporting multiple X-Terminals, which are running HP OpenView Node Manager, HP Operations Center, Bay Networks Optivity, and Cisco Works. This allows the city full visibility into their entire network infrastructure and support for systems activities via the Operations Center."
>
> In addition, each department is deploying a NetWare file server, providing access to Microsoft Office and other applications. The system is using GroupWise as its e-mail package and integrating Cheyenne Fax Serve to provide faxing to the desktop. Remote users can access the city via a Citrix Application server.
>
> For security, DSW instituted a SUN system Firewall/1, with a Netscape Proxy server, Security Dynamics SecureID for token authentication services via a Sun ACE server, and the Cisco AS5200 for inbound access via ISDN and analog phone lines. The complete case study is available at www.dsw.net/www301seccase.html.

Network Design and Planning

PART 3

The thing that I find most fascinating about the DSW case study is the integration of different technologies to get the job done. In Networking Hardware 101, it seems that it is drummed into the student that hardware standards and software standards are good, diversity is bad. In this case, you have Cisco switches and routers working with Bay hubs and SUN ACE servers, being managed by Cisco, Bay, and HP SNMP implementations. Throw in NetWare, Unix, and the occasional Citrix communication server, and it sounds like the perfect opportunity for one tech support desk to point the finger at another and say, "It's not our fault the network isn't working, call *X*." Fortunately for DSW, that is not the case.

If You Are Going to Go, Go Big

The next two case studies are provided by John Napier of www.openview.org. John was quick to point out that the case studies were provided to him by various integrators across the country, and he was the one responsible for compiling them. He also said, "One thing I better make clear, www.openview.org is not an HP affiliated or sponsored Web site. I sell OpenView solutions and use the Web site to inform clients and potential clients."

For the first case study, let's pick an Internet service provider; specifically, let's pick AT&T WorldNet. This case study was provided to the OpenView organization by Net-Source Partners (www.nspartners.com).

True Enterprise Management

Talk about a challenge: NetSource Partners was challenged with helping AT&T WorldNet manage one of the world's fastest-growing Internet services. They had to provide 7 x 24 reliability, leave room for rapid network growth and deployment, as well as keep the costs down. Does this sound somewhat familiar?

The management domains were laid out as

Service Management   End-to-end management of a service, such as e-mail

Application Management   Management of particular applications, such as registration and account creation

System Management   Management of the computing platforms

Network Management   Management of the network infrastructure

Element Management   Management of the networking components, in this case Cisco Routers

In addition, the SNMP management system also had to handle the following functions:

Fault Management   Alarm reporting, recovery, and trouble ticketing

Performance Management   Performance monitoring and thresholding functions

Configuration and Control Management   Asset management, start and stop control management

Data Management   Backup and recovery

Security Management   Security monitoring and auditing

These goals were met by integrating and customizing several off-the-shelf packages from a wide variety of vendors. The primary platform support was provided by HP OpenView.

Although the task of taking care of the network needs of AT&T WorldNet seems daunting enough, the next case study blows me away. Okay, okay, it's a really poor pun. I was just trying to see if you were awake!

It Really Is Rocket Science!

I have been in some computer operations centers that make you think you have just entered the United States National Aeronautics and Space Administration (NASA) Mission Control Center in Houston, Texas, during a space shuttle mission. Suppose you *were* managing the network for NASA and you were responsible for the network that supported voice, video, and data from all U.S. spacecraft, both manned and unmanned. Your network would be the one that NASA uses to communicate with the space shuttle. I think we would all agree that in this case, downtime is not an option, and the word *Ooops* will never, ever be uttered, even in jest.

This is another case study provided by John Napier at `www.openview.org`.

Houston, We Are Avoiding Problems

Talk about a challenge! Vishai Desai oversees and manages a multinational and multivendor network. Back in the first half of the 1990s, he was given the task of taking a largely proprietary, specially designed and constructed computer network (albeit outdated) and turning it into something that would last NASA for the next 15 to 20 years. His mandate was clear: "Make this happen using primarily off-the-shelf and shrink-wrapped products." The days of contract customization for NASA were over. To make matters even more challenging, he was dealing with a network in flux.

As Desai began the project, he listed everything he knew about the network. He then listed everything he didn't know. He finally came to the realization that for this network to do what it was supposed to, the key piece was the network-management piece. When everything was said and done, this was going to be the piece that maintained uptime at 99.98 percent. If things couldn't be managed properly, life would be a nightmare.

Because the caveat was *off-the-shelf and shrink-wrapped*, the protocol was TCP/IP. This meant management would be handled using SNMP and taking a standard off-the-shelf product and customizing it to NASA's needs. (Yes, there are plenty of MIBs available, but some of the equipment that NASA uses is not necessarily something you would find in a home-based business).

Houston, We Are Avoiding Problems *(continued)*

As the transition began, new equipment appeared and was migrated into the network, such as CSU/DSUs from Digital Link Corp. of Sunnyvale, California, which were used to hook into T-1 lines from AT&T.

Meanwhile, Desai was looking at SNMP management packages. There were a bunch, and most were weeded out, leaving HP OpenView. OpenView was selected, not necessarily for what it would do out of the box, but for what it had the potential to do. OpenView supported many third-party applications, but it also had the ability to be customized. HP OpenView, straight out of the box, is a lot like IBM's Lotus Notes. When you first install it, it doesn't look like much. Its strength comes from its ability to adapt to the world around it. In this case, displays had to be redone, MIBs had to be written, and the product had to be taught to do exactly what was expected of it.

Desai then had to come up with a list of applications to interface with OV, such as a trouble-ticketing package and the relational-database software to go with it. Asset management software was integrated into the package as well as remote monitoring software for the FDDI links.

How critical were the specs? How would you like to manage a network where if a problem occurs while data is being transmitted from space, the policy states the outage can last for *one minute*! But if information is just coming over the Web and an outage occurs, the policy says you have plenty of time to fix it, up to two hours.

SNMP was also configured so the team could keep a close eye on security. This meant that the software piece must keep track of all the firewalls and other security gear on the network.

The final project worked so well, NASA issued a directive to consolidate other networks. The standard had been set.

Even though your network probably doesn't rival NASA's for complexity, there should be some things here that even the administrator of the smallest network can take to heart. Here is the network administrator for a multinational network being told to drag the old network into the new century, do it with stuff that is readily available (read *cost-effective*), get it done immediately, make sure *everything* stays up while you are doing it, and see to it that the unexpected is expected and can be handled. Sounds impossible, doesn't it? Yet you are probably doing the impossible every day.

The real problem comes in *after* you do the impossible. Somebody wants you to do it again, and this time, they expect more!

Customize It!

Some companies want to go from proprietary to off the shelf. Other companies want to take the trend the other way and hire someone to make their SNMP package do exactly what they want it to do. One of those companies is WorldTalk, a vendor of messaging, groupware, and directory services integration software from Australia. In this case, CiTR of Milton, Australia, came to the rescue.

Six Months from Alpha to Visa

A friend once defined the cycle that software development goes through as the passage from alpha to Visa. Alpha code is where someone, usually in marketing or management, says, "Sure, we can do that!" when, in fact, nothing in the current product line remotely resembles a solution for the problem. *Alpha* means an idea has been born.

Beta code is what the software developers turn out the first time. The code does what it is designed to do in their environment, so now its time to test it in the real world. Usually about this time, the specifications for the project are completely revamped, and it is back to the drawing board.

Finally, we hit Visa code. *Visa code,* otherwise referred to as Gold, is the code where someone can lay down a Visa card and walk away with a software package.

The challenge CiTR faced was that a client, Worldtalk Corporation, had decided to add some remote-management functionality into its NetJunction product. CiTR was called to develop a Windows NT–based SNMP Manager called *NetOps,* which allows administrators to manage several NetJunction servers and all of their components.

NetJunction is a router product that runs on HP-UX9000 servers and provides connectivity to different types of systems, such as

- Banyan Vines
- DEC
- EMC2
- HP OpenMail
- IBM PROFS and IBM SNADS

Six Months from Alpha to Visa *(continued)*

- Lotus cc:MAIL and Lotus Notes

- Microsoft Mail and Exchange

- Novell GroupWise and MHS

- QuickMail

- SMTP/MIME

- X.400, X.500, and LDAP

The NetJunction solution will be completely NT Server–based, designed for small- and medium-sized enterprises and departments. The first release was to integrate Exchange with Lotus Notes and cc:Mail, using a graphical user interface (GUI).

In addition to management, an administrator can also track messages and gather statistics. Statistical analysis includes

- Number of messages per hour

- Number of directory records added per synchronization cycle

- Date of last synchronization

- Number of nondelivery reports (NDRs)

CiTR managed to pull off this incredible cross-platform programming feat in just six months using SNMP.

This information came from John Gottschalk at j.gottschalk@citr.com.au.

So far we have seen how SNMP applications can be molded to perform a variety of different tasks. One of the great things about SNMP is its flexibility. It is so flexible that even network operating systems that were not inherently written around TCP/IP try to come up with products to do the same kinds of management tasks.

SMS Takes On the Y2K Issue

Microsoft's implementation of Systems Management Server, or SMS, is a *sort of, kind of, type of* SNMP. Windows NT has long included an SNMP agent piece that will report to an SNMP manager, but it has lacked a true SNMP manager. SMS helps by translating Windows NT events into data that can be captured by network-management systems. Some SNMP events can be captured by SMS and then stored in an SMS database.

SMS has four primary functions in a Windows NT environment:

- Hardware and software inventory collection
- Software distribution
- Shared application management
- Remote support

The way SMS can be implemented varies, and some very creative ways have been found. Nancy Winnick Cluts wrote a white paper on SMS and the Year 2000 issue, based on a presentation given at the Microsoft Global Summit of 1998.

SMS/Y2K

SMS 2 has a feature that will allow it to check database applications for the compliance level of Y2K issues. SMS breaks compliance down into three levels:

- Compliant
- Noncompliant
- Compliant with issues

SMS also provides some standard built-in queries and reports that can be generated based on comparison of the Y2K database and installed software. In addition, you can customize your Y2K reports.

SMS can take the issue one step further. If it finds noncompliant software, it will use the Y2K database to determine whether or not a software patch is available. If there is a patch available, SMS can package the patches and help with the downloading.

From the hardware side, SMS will also check the hardware BIOS for Y2K compliance.

Although this is a great start, Microsoft is quick to point out that SMS still has some limitations. SMS checks the applications "header" for version information, so if this information is not provided in the header or it is a DOS application, SMS can't help you. There is also an issue with applications that are integrated into an operating system, for example, Internet Explorer and Windows NT.

The last limitation is one that occurs with all databases. Because some of the new patches and fixes come out regularly, the Y2K SMS database may not be totally up-to-date. This may return an error message reflecting a problem you have already fixed.

Network Design
and Planning

PART 3

SMS is a great management tool. It is just not totally SNMP-compliant.

SNMP in a TCP/IP World

Of all the pieces of the TCP/IP protocol suite, SNMP is the most flexible. This protocol has been molded into several off-the-shelf implementations that will help you manage a network, large or small. As we have seen, some of the functions that SNMP can perform include:

- **Reporting**   An SNMP manager can gather information about the state of the network. It can report on available bandwidth, e-mail activity, the number of packets crossing a router, the status of any number of agents, etc.

- **Alarms**   As a system administrator, you have a pretty good idea what the acceptable performance standards are for your network. You can use SNMP to make sure you are notified when some of these standards are violated or when a mission-critical piece of equipment fails.

- **Planning**   You can use your SNMP implementation for planning purposes. If you know how your network operates now, given a certain set of criteria, you can project how the network will operate in the future if you improve or change your configuration.

- **Proactive Maintenance**   Watching the performance of certain key pieces of hardware can tell you when things start to degrade. Wouldn't it be wonderful to make plans to fix something before it breaks?

Case Study: Optivity Put to Good Use

According to Larry Johnson of SCP Global Technologies of Boise, Idaho, Nortel's (formerly Bay Network's) Optivity let him do the job of several people.

Prior to working at SCP Global, Larry worked at an air force military hospital outside of the Boise area. His network consisted of eight SCO Unix boxes, one router for the building, and another router linking the hospital with Defense Data network. The network was hooked together using a fiber-optic backbone, consisting primarily of Synoptics equipment. Because Optivity came with the Synoptics equipment, it made sense to put it to good use.

Larry reported that all the Synoptics equipment showed up on the management console in a "what you see is what you get" format, with several different management tools available for each piece of equipment. Non-Synoptic equipment may not have been as graphical, but he was still able to monitor and manage all the network links and hubs from the central console.

From Larry's perspective, having an SNMP system in place meant some peace of mind. Because he was basically the only person on site managing the network, he could set the manager to automatically page him if a catastrophic event occurred. In addition, the Central Office could also monitor and manage the network if Larry was not available.

Larry said he found one of the main reasons for using SNMP software was to manage the bandwidth he had available over the WAN links. He said that with SNMP, he could spot problems before they actually became too troublesome.

24*seven* **CASE STUDY**

11

The Ins and Outs of Extranets

Much has been said throughout this book about the Internet and about intranets. As technology has grown, the access to information of all sorts has become a given. More and more users are requiring access to all sorts of information; information stored on the local-area network, data from a storage-area network on the other side of the wide-area-network link, and information that is available publicly or privately from sources on the Internet. Sometimes, the information that is the most difficult to access is the information that should be the easiest to get. For example, the Acme Widget Manufacturing Company has just signed a long-term deal with the Ajax Top-Notch Marketing company to put together catalogs and brochures, manage the vendor show sites, and generally help Acme to become the number one widget manufacturing company in the world. The goal here is for people who need widgets to think of Acme, the way people who need tissues think of Kleenex. Acme Widget is on its way to becoming a household name.

What is the first thing the folks at Ajax are going to want? They will need information on the company, who their customers are, who buys the most widgets, what is the hottest season for widgets, how many different types of widgets does Acme make, and probably a thousand other questions. Each question has an answer, and the answer is located right there on the Acme computer system. Of course, Ajax is on the other side of the country. There is no dedicated connection between Ajax and Acme or between Ajax and its 100 other customers. The people at Ajax can't imagine why they don't have access to the Acme data; after all, they have immediate access to all sorts of data with their other accounts. It must be a hardware issue.

Actually, it's not.

This scenario between Acme and Ajax really boils down to the ability to assemble information and make it available to people who need it, people who want it, and people who have the rights to have it. These are the basic principles of the extranet. The extranet provides a seamless access to applications and data, regardless of the underlying platforms or any intervening networks. The information will be provided in a manner appropriate to whatever platform a company chooses to use.

As the name implies, the extranet is really a network that transcends the Internet. Take a look at Figure 11.1.

Figure 11.1 An extranet, where users of separate intranets can use the Internet as a communication channel.

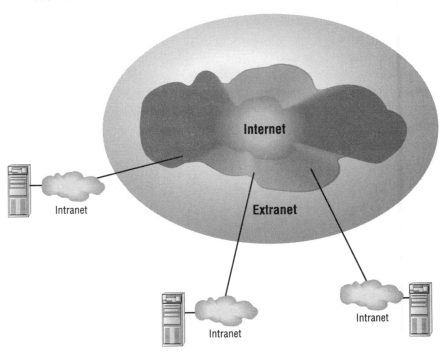

The extranet bypasses corporate boundaries and even bypasses the Internet. Relevant information is made available to people in each of the companies, no matter which sources need to be accessed. No matter where the information is hiding, the extranet can locate the information and present it in a useful form to the end user.

In order for an extranet to work, it must provide seamless interoperability. This means data must flow across networks, hardware platforms, and software architectures as though the communicating systems were directly connected. This must occur with platform independence. When this occurs, the end user and the application developers are freed from the confines of using a specific platform. This is what happens every time you decide to go out to the Internet to check the latest stock prices for Acme Widget. When you connect to your favorite quotation site, you have no idea whether the system on the other end of the connection is using Windows NT, Unix, NetWare, Solaris, or CP/M. It simply doesn't matter. The user controls what information is retrieved from where, how frequently, and how it is displayed and used.

The extranet simply extends the concept of the organizational network beyond the boundaries of the organization. As a matter of fact, it really extends the concept of the corporate organization to include a vast, ever-changing organization made up of dozens of companies all working together for the common good. Let's refer to this as *interorganizational internetworking*.

Interorganizational Internetworks

What we are really talking about here is just an extension of the concept of the Internet. When companies connect to the Internet and put up a Web page, an FTP server, or even a mail server that gives users access through a Web browser, they are making information available to people from anywhere in the world. The interorganizational internetwork takes this theory one step further, giving users access to secure information and making sure the information stays secure. This obviously requires increased administrative duties, even across organizational boundaries.

The Internet 2 Project

If you are going to try something like this, you might as well go big. That is what was attempted with the Internet 2 Project.

The Internet 2 Project began in 1996. Representatives of 40 educational institutions announced a project to create a high-performance internetwork of universities and research organizations. By the dawn of the year 2000, there will be more than 120

Network Design and Planning

PART 3

charter organizations (primarily universities) and more than 30 partner- and affiliate-member organizations.

The stated objective of this august group was to create a high-performance, broadband internetwork to link their organizations. In addition, this internetwork would foster the development of applications to make such networks more efficient. Some of these applications would include

- Multimedia, multicasting applications required for distance learning and remote-classroom applications.
- Virtual access to national laboratories and supercomputing facilities.
- Access to large bodies of simulation or observed data of the type required for astronomical, geophysical, or meteorological research.
- Remote medical consultations and diagnoses for research purposes.
- Access to large volumes of financial and commercial transactions for real-time economic analysis.

In order to accomplish these lofty goals, the design specifications had to be state of the art and had to offer

- Support for high-bandwidth networking applications
- Use of IP version 6 (but with backward compatibility to IP version 4)
- Support for a high degree of interoperability by providing access to a wide range of client devices

This means that above all else, Internet 2 must be interoperable with the existing Internet. It must use object-brokering services and software components that will work with a large population of users and connect 100 or more organizations from the start. In other words, this is the extranet to beat all extranets. Let's look at how the Internet 2 Project can be scaled down to meet the needs of smaller organizations.

Internet 2 Design Principles

The Internet 2 Project preliminary engineering report presented the following principles after their initial deliberations:

- Use available, well-supported, and reliable technologies instead of creating new ones, wherever possible.
- Use industry standards instead of proprietary solutions and generally maintain the network as openly as possible. This principle includes sharing performance information with other members.

- Build the network as reliably as possible, making use of redundancy. The objective is to avoid any single point of failure that might result from reliance on any single service provider, hardware manufacturer, or software publisher by building in backup routes and using alternative vendors to the greatest extent possible.

- Build the basic network functions before adding more advanced functions. The project is sufficiently complex that it would be counterproductive to start adding advanced new features before implementing the base set of features.

- Become a production network, not an experimental network or research test bed.

- Complement, not compete against, commercial networks. Any Internet 2 services provided by commercial Internet service providers must remain separate from access to commercial networks such as the Internet.

As you look over these principles, they all make as much sense for the design of the Acme to Ajax project as they do for the Internet 2 Project.

Organizational Linking

There is much more to the Internet 2 Project than stringing cable and configuring some routers. Charter members of the project were required to make commitments that included some serious financial support to the project. According to the Internet 2 Project Web page, estimates of the cost for member institutions were set at approximately a half-million dollars a year for the first few years of the project. There was also a commitment of as much as $25,000 per year for administrative and support expenses.

Money wasn't the only thing that was required. Charter members also had to commit to

- Providing executive-level support to the project-management effort.

- Helping build application-development and network-services project teams to support the project.

- Implementing end-to-end broadband Internet access so that project developers can build, test, and use Internet 2 applications.

Management of the project is done through steering committees and working groups. Member organizations can participate in various project meetings, depending on the membership level.

Internet 2 Infrastructure, What Makes It Work

As you read about this technology, you may be wondering, "Okay, but how am I going to make this thing work?" Figure 11.2 shows an example of how the project was supposed to look.

Figure 11.2   The Internet 2 Project architecture uses high-speed, high-bandwidth gigapops to link campuses to a connectivity cloud.

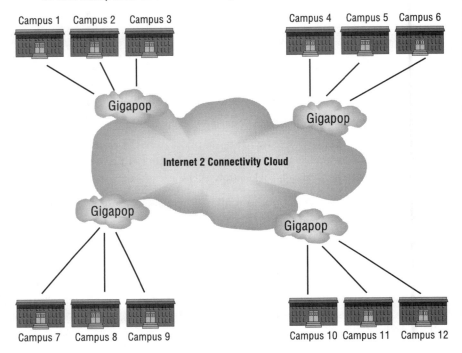

Back in 1996 when the project started, the connectivity cloud held some to-be-determined, high-speed, high-bandwidth data-communication services. The project hadn't determined how it was all going to work, but the plan for access was to be provided through gigapops, or *gigabit capacity points of presence,* that would serve Internet 2 members within the same region.

Internet 2 Applications

What has happened since then? The Internet 2 Project has been divided up into several different areas. The first area is still called Internet 2. This is the push to develop applications to run over the high-speed network.

University of Michigan and I-2

The University of Michigan in Ann Arbor is one of many universities participating in the Internet 2 Project. The university expects the quality and speed of Internet 2 to reflect what will be expected from future networks. In this case, the university is hoping to provide immediate access to video resources, and the ability to interact via video in real time with better quality than can be obtained from a regular television set.

In 1999, the university had several projects underway, including secure videoconferencing, working with an electron microscope, meteorological forecasting, and support for archeological research.

The secure videoconferencing project at the University of Michigan's Center for Information Technology Integration (CITI) set a goal to use off-the-shelf hardware, use public videoconferencing software, and do as much work as possible to make the results available to the largest number of end users. The project was designed to test encryption performance problems and investigate cryptographic protocols and smart card-key exchange algorithims.

NOTE If you decide to go digging for some of this information on your own, you will find the acronym QoS in various places. QoS stands for *Quality of Service*. According to various releases about Internet 2, the project is being driven by the "shortcomings of the commodity Internet." Because the current "commodity Internet,"—i.e., what you and I use every day—is so rife with shortcomings, the designers of Internet 2 are striving to make sure that Internet 2 has an exceptionally high QoS.

Abilene Project

The next part of the Internet 2 Project has been dubbed the Abilene network. The Abilene Project is the most advanced research and education network in the United States. It began nationwide operations, providing high-performance network services to 37 universities, in February of 1999. The project acts as a test bed for Internet 2 applications, including distance learning, tele-medicine, and digital libraries that are projected to become commonplace in the future. The Abilene Project is a joint venture between the universities and Qwest Communications, Cisco, and Nortel Networks. It is valued at over $500 million.

Abilene spans 10,000 miles and operates at 2.4 gigabits per second. This is about 45,000 times faster than your average 56K modem.

Very High-Performance Backbone Network Service (vBNS)

Meanwhile, back in 1995, the National Science Foundation and MCI launched the vBNS. It was the product of a five-year agreement to provide a high-bandwidth network for research applications. The vBNS started life as a nationwide network that operated at a speed of 622 megabits per second (OC12 speed) using advanced switching and fiber-optic techniques. These techniques combine Asynchronous Transfer Mode (ATM) and Synchronous Optical Networks (SONET) and allow high-speed, high-capacity voice, data, and video signals to be combined and transmitted "on demand." In January 1999, the OC-48c, 2.488Gbps link was brought online to production-based traffic.

The vBNS was designed, like the Internet 2, to support the scientific and research communities. It originally provided a high-speed connection between NSF supercomputing sites and connections to Network Access Points. At this time, it is only available for selected research projects that have a need for high-bandwidth use. It is not used for general Internet traffic.

The Difference between vBNS and Abilene

When Abilene came online in early 1999, it was providing throughput at 2.4 gigabits per second, matching the speed of vBNS. According to the vBNS Web site, www.vbns.net, the differences between the two are

- Abilene uses management and engineering from various partners, whereas vBNS has an engineering team dedicated to the advanced deployment of IP services and functionality.

- vBNS has a 7x24 Network Operations Center.

- vBNS interconnects national and international sites.

- vBNS access and utilization is restricted to NSF designated organizations.

- vBNS does not provide access to the commercial Internet access.

- vBNS also supports advanced routing services, including Native Multicast and Native IPv6.

Cooperation between vBNS and Internet 2

Both of these versions of the next Internet are up and working and both serve the educational and research communities, so you would think there would be some overlap, and there is. Fifty-three of the Internet 2 university members have received grants to provide acquisition of connections to the vBNS.

How Is vBNS Being Used?

The Earth Systems Science Center at Penn State University is using the vBNS to execute a water-cycling model for predicting the impact of global change on water resources and human activites. The ESSC uses remotely sensed and field data to track the global water cycle, gaining new insights into the processes that shape the Earth's surface and define change.

Carnegie-Mellon University is using vBNS to study earthquakes. The "Quake" project is not trying to predict when the next big shake is coming; instead, they are trying to determine more specific conclusions. They are investigating situations such as if an earthquake hits Los Angeles, which parts of the city are the most vulnerable? Which seismic frequencies will be amplified most by the soil? The answers to these questions will aid city planners when it comes time to set building codes and will provide architects with a better understanding of earthquakes.

The University of Illinois at Chicago and the University of Pennsylvania are working together in the National Scaleable Cluster Project (NCSP) to develop cluster computing. Cluster computing involves grouping workstation computers or similar systems together to provide supercomputer-like performance without linking into an actual supercomputer center. It would be like having a supercomputer on your desktop. An offshoot of this project has led to exploration of data-mining applications. Data mining is being used to find significant patterns within data provided by high-energy physics. The University of Pennsylvania is also using their facility for real-time brain-imaging techniques using magnetic-resonance imaging.

Network Design and Planning

PART 3

So, you say that you don't work at a research institute or an educational institution? Although the thought of 2.4 gigabits to the computer room is exciting, chances are your boss would balk at the monthly bill? You are not alone! But there are some things coming out of these models that can be applied to your business, including the *virtual private network,* or VPN.

Virtual Private Networks

A VPN is like an extranet, only smaller. A VPN uses encryption and authentication to secure a private channel across a public network, such as the Internet. These private channels, as shown in Figure 11.3, can link two or more remote networks or connect a host to a remote network.

Figure 11.3   Virtual private networks link networks and hosts using encrypted channels transmitted across the Internet.

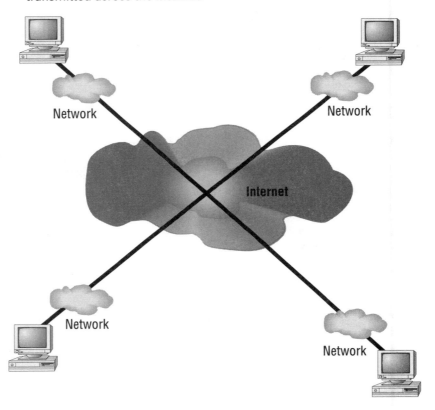

When the VPN is used to link two networks, it provides a channel that can carry all traffic between the two networks. VPNs usually operate by encapsulating regular IP traffic inside an encrypted IP channel. The VPN transmits the encrypted, encapsulated packets directly to the remote VPN, which decrypts the datagrams and forwards them to their final destination located somewhere on the remote network.

VPN Tunnels and Gateways

VPN products come in two flavors: those delivered as part of a firewall gateway, and those delivered as stand-alone tunneling solutions. In either case, remote access to the main network is possible either from a satellite network (e.g., a branch office or a business partner) or from an individual host.

VPN products typically offer two types of servers: one server allows you to securely connect a client computer to a server in a private network using the Internet as the backbone; the other server allows you to connect two private networks together and still support confidential organization-to-organization communications. In both scenarios, the end point of the connection must be a Tunnel server that supports authorization, authentication, and management.

VPNs May Not Be Immune to Outside Interference

The joy and the agony of working with network systems is that everything changes so fast; just when you think you have a handle on things, everything is different. Although software and hardware vendors do their best to ensure that everything is compatible, sometimes it works, and sometimes the unexpected happens. This is the tale of one of those cases: the rollout of Microsoft's Internet Explorer 5 and Netscape's Netscape Navigator 4.51.

It seems the browsers had a bad habit of disabling or wiping out the tunneling features so prominent in a VPN. The hiccup didn't last for long: Microsoft jumped on top of the problem and issued a work-around.

Microsoft tunneling is done using the Microsoft's iteration of the Point-to-Point Tunneling Protocol, or PPTP. This protocol has been around since the days of Windows 95 when an addition was made to Dial-Up Networking (DUN). The installation of the new generation of browsers seems to exacerbate a problem with PPTP. According to BugNet, there were a few tweaks that were necessary to get IE 5 to handle tunneling properly.

BugNet says

- Running on a Windows 95 or 98 platform, the browsers IE 5 and Navigator 4.51 would have difficulty opening Web pages on a server via tunneling until the work-around was applied.

- Running on an NT 4 client, Navigator and IE 4 would open Web pages just fine, but IE 5 wouldn't open Web pages on a Windows NT client without tweaking.

VPNs May Not Be Immune to Outside Interference *(continued)*

What was the work-around? When it was first reported in the versions of DUN, Microsoft published a support article at support.microsoft.com/support/kb/ articles/q222/9/36.asp. According to Microsoft, a VPN connection may hang or never be established if the properties of the connection show your VPN's host server name instead of the IP address. If that is the case, you would have to change your host name to an IP address for your tunneling connections.

BugNet found that the work-around fixed most of the problems with tunneling. It also found that PPTP filtering had to be turned off to get IE 5 to support tunneling on NT 4 clients. You can check out their findings at www.bugnet.com/analysis/browser_ pptp.html.

For more information on tunneling and how to set it up in a Microsoft environment, see the Microsoft support Web site at support.microsoft.com/support/kb/ articles/q221/1/19.asp.

What Is Tunneling?

Tunneling allows information to be passed between one computer and another over a public network, such as the Internet. This provides the same kind of services as if the two computers were on the same private network. The process of sending information through the tunnels is simple. After the client and the server have been authenticated, information is encrypted by the sender, encapsulated into TCP/IP data packets, and sent across the Internet as unreadable and unrecognizable data. Once the packets reach the final destination, they are reconstituted and then decrypted into a readable form.

A system that is running either the client software or the server software may act as a tunnel client, but only the server side may act as the Tunnel server, which means it provides management capabilities.

Is the Data Really Safe?

Many tunneling systems employ the RSA Public Key Cryptosystem for user authentication and session key exchange as well as the RSA RC4 Symmetric Stream Cipher for bulk data encryption. The Cryptographic identity and keys are tied to the user, leaving the IP address free to be dynamically assigned. Once the authenticated tunnel session is created, the Tunnel server and the tunnel client automatically switch from public key encryption to RC4-based secret key encryption to perform bulk data encryption and transfer. In some cases, the tunnel client and server will change session keys at regular intervals.

Some components, such as the Alta Vista Tunnel, support the options' use of Security Dynamics' SecurID authentication tokens to authenticate the identity of the users. The tunnel administrator designates a tunnel to require SecurID authentication. When a tunnel client connects, the Tunnel server instructs the tunnel client to prompt the user for SecurID credentials. This information is sent to the Tunnel server for processing. (The Tunnel server is an ACE client acting as a proxy to the tunnel clients.) The tunnel client is then allowed to either connect or be disconnected. The Alta Vista tunnel clients also support NEWPIN and NEXTCODE modes to complete the SecurID implementation.

Because of federal regulations, products within the U.S. can use 128-bit encryption, whereas international versions support a 56-bit or 40-bit version. If a multinational tunnel is being created, automatic arbitration reconciles any encryption differences transparently. This enables both the tunnel client and the server to operate in the highest common encryption key mode that is supported. This method earns the product the classification of ITAR (International Traffic in Arms Regulation) Controlled.

Data Compression

VPNs use data compression to reduce redundancy in data representations. This decreases storage space and communication costs and increases performance. Data compression is usually an optional service. The server side will usually have it enabled, but it is up to the outbound system to determine whether compression will be used or not. If both tunnel systems have compression enabled, then compression will be used. Otherwise, the tunnel traffic is not compressed.

Integration with the Private Network

Most of the VPN systems will take advantage of the infrastructure of the private network. For example, if the private network has a DNS server installed, the Tunnel server should automatically add that for users running the tunnel client. The tunnel administrator can select the DNS server for all tunnel client connections. If the client is running a 32-bit Windows operating system, the private network's WINS server can be specified for WINS resolution.

Tunnel Management

Management utilities vary with implementation. For a sample, let us continue to look at Alta Vista's Tunnel software. In this case, the software provides a management key feature as well as a graphical user interface to simplify the management tasks. This can eliminate the need for a dedicated administrator. In a client-to-server tunnel, the server performs all the tunnel management. In the server-to-server or organization-to-organization tunnel environment, either server can perform the following management tasks:

- Connection authorization
- Public key generation and management

- Tunnel parameter management
- Dynamic assignment of tunnel clients
- Tunnel-related routing change monitoring
- Tunnel-usage statistical-report generation
- Tunnel deletion

How Does It Work with a Firewall?

You may be asking yourself, "This all sounds fine and good, but I have a firewall. How does this work with a firewall?" Most companies connected to the Internet employ firewalls to protect the information on their private networks from Internet invaders. Because most VPN software works with encryption and authentication already, it really assists in network security.

What to Look for in a VPN

You may be sold on the functionality of a VPN, but what about your boss or the chief financial officer? How do you sell them on VPNs being a great way to connect your office to some outlying area in the middle of somewhere?

The first thing you can do is start talking the language that CFOs and other managers all seem to agree on.

FAQs about VPNs

When potential users were asked about VPNs, they voiced concern over several areas. The first should be expected: what does it cost? After that, they seemed to be most concerned with performance, security, and ease of use.

What Does It Cost?

On average, VPNs can reduce the cost of traditional remote-access solutions between 30 and 70 percent. Because of the flexibility of the VPN, it can be used to support your sales force, telecommuters, and even executives wandering around the country. To put it simply, with a VPN, access to your network is simply an Internet connection away.

What Is the Performance Like?

Whenever anyone asks about performance, the stock answer has to be, "It depends." So much goes into the equation, it is really hard to generalize. When we discuss VPN performance, concerns are two-fold. First, no matter what the upper-level applications do, down where the work is done, it is still IP. IP is connectionless, meaning it is a best-effort protocol. It will do its best to get something through, but there are no guarantees. The first concern then revolves around dependability. The second issue revolves around security. No one doubts that VPNs can be secure, but the questions are about the performance hit that security is going to cause. In other words, will all that security slow the network down to a crawl?

The IETF and others have several proposals under discussion to address these issues. On the subject of network performance, one proposal is IP Differentiated Services (diffserv). Diffserv will prioritize traffic over a WAN so that different "levels of service" are offered on an IP network. Network traffic would be tagged according to the level of service required from the network. Carriers would then use these tags to prioritize traffic and meet their performance guarantees.

On a different front, Multiprotocol Label Switching (MPLS) makes use of guaranteed QoS features found in Asynchronous Transfer Mode (ATM), which already underlies many ISP networks. MPLS adds a special label to the layer-two traffic that describes how it should be switched through the underlying network. Many vendors are already shipping products that make use of both diffserv and MPLS implementations. A number of ISPs are testing and piloting these offerings. By combining both diffserv and MPLS, IP providers can now offer VPN users service-level agreements that include assured performance.

Now, that is all fine and good for the service provided by the ISP. We all know that the speed of the transmission can be lightening fast on the outside of our building, but the connections on the inside of the building need to support that increased quality of service. VPN customer premise equipment (CPE) is also being enhanced to provide wire-line encryption speeds. Early VPN equipment created bottlenecks, but the vendors have fought to solve these problems. Some of the tolls that have been brought to bear include data compression and hardware-encryption acceleration. CPE devices are now capable of supporting data throughput in excess of 100Mbps.

Data Security

The next major concern for most people installing a VPN is data security. Recently, there has been a great deal of work completed by the IETF's security working groups. This work has turned out the framework of the Internet Protocol Security, or IPSec. IPSec defines a standard method for encrypting and authenticating communications to create secure "tunnels" that are capable of passing over IP networks. The protocol supports a number of encryption and authentication schemes, including the triple-strength DES (3DES) encryption algorithm. IPSec has become the security protocol of choice for VPN implementations.

Ease of Use

The easier it is to use, the more it will be used and the less administration needed. Managers all over the world love less administration. VPNs, unlike their frame relay cousins, do not require a permanent virtual-circuit mapping between each pair of network nodes. They do require a security relationship be defined and established between each pair of hosts that may need to communicate. This means that administrators have to configure the rules that users will use to communicate with each other. This also means a tremendous number of configurations.

Part of the burden has been eased by initiatives such as the Public Key Infrastructure (PKI). PKI allows VPN managers to configure and manage VPN users from a single, centralized database. The database contains the security keys that are used between each communicating pair. Many of the PKI implementations include automated key generation and templates. These features enable VPN managers to create, configure, monitor, or destroy keys as needed.

The people who sell VPNs have it in their best interest to improve the usability of VPN management tools. Some vendors even offer VPN management systems that provide service providers and IT managers with a single view of the entire VPN implementation. Service providers can also offer different levels of configuration control.

Is a VPN a WAN Replacement?

The easiest and surest way to save money would be just to pitch out the old WAN and then install a VPN, right? Well, according to a survey done by TeleChoice, Inc., of Boston, only about 6 percent of organizations with VPNs use them exclusively. Most IP managers view the VPN as being an adjunct to their WAN, not a replacement for it. Many people are using the technology for a single purpose, such as remote access, international connections, or for an extranet. The driving force behind most of these decisions has been cost savings.

To VPN or Not to VPN

You have heard all the reasons why people use a VPN, so now it is up to you to decide whether you have the need to implement this kind of technology. If you do, then the next step is to figure out who is going to install it and which technology you are going to use.

One of the first decisions is whether or not to outsource the installation and management. Many service providers deliver packaged or custom VPN solutions that come complete with design, integration, monitoring, support, reporting, and performance guarantees. Some organizations that have implemented home-grown VPNs have decided that the managed solutions may be preferable. Any time you institute a new technology, there are going to be unforeseen hassles and expenses. With a technology as robust as this, having someone install it who has done it before and understands how to get the most out of it may go a long way to ensuring that you maximize your investment.

If you have a small network and really need a VPN but can't afford to have someone come in and install one for you, there are always some tried-and-true solutions. Earlier in the chapter, I mentioned that Alta Vista had a VPN solution. In addition, both Novell and Microsoft offer products that can provide this type of functionality.

VPN Potholes

There is a downside to everything, and VPNs are no different. Even though VPNs are becoming more straightforward, it is still necessary to find the right solution for your organization, which may not be completely straightforward. In many cases, the organizational and managerial issues with a VPN are almost as significant as the technological challenges.

In a survey done by the International Network Services of Sunnyvale, California, three quarters of the respondents were satisfied with the currently available VPN products, but nearly half said inadequate product capabilities (as opposed to business requirements) is the greatest barrier to improving a VPN's capabilities. Another third said that staff training and justifying the costs and benefits of VPNs to upper management were additional barriers.

Security and Tunneling

Mention the subject of VPN security and you are sure to get a discussion going. Earlier in the chapter, third-party alternatives were discussed as a method of ensuring that the VPN communications were safe. When working with VPNs, remember the key word in the title is *virtual*. While the concept is a secure pipe leading from one computer to another, in reality, individual packets can take any route in getting from point A to point B. The encrypted channel is not a fixed pipe but a dynamically shifting, encrypted communication path that may travel all over the world to get from one spot to another.

Most VPNs are designed to be server-to-server types. In this case, only the organization's perimeter is protected from the Internet. There is no end-to-end or desktop-to-desktop security provided. This subject is only beginning to be explored by the designers of VPNs. When it arrives, it will provide protection throughout the organization and will use more than the bottom two or three layers of the OSI model.

Security Protocols

IPSec is a layer-three (Network layer) protocol suite that creates a standard platform for security on a VPN. There are underlying protocols that all contribute, such as the standard Layer Two Tunneling Protocol (L2TP). L2TP is an extension to the Point-to-Point (PPP) protocol that merges the best features of two other tunneling protocols: Layer Two Forwarding (L2F) from Cisco Systems and Point-to-Point Tunneling Protocol (PPTP) from Microsoft. L2TP is an Internet Engineering Task Force (IETF) emerging standard, currently under codevelopment and endorsed by Cisco Systems, Microsoft, Ascend, 3Com, and other networking industry leaders.

To see how L2TP security is implemented, let's look at the protection offered by Cisco's implementation. According to information from the Cisco Web site, Cisco offers

Authentication, Authorization, and Accounting (AAA), which includes

- Support for username/password or Dialed Number Identification Service (DNIS) to determine authorization to the Access VPN services. In other words, when you dial into the VPN, your security will be checked by either the username and password you enter or by verifying the phone number you dialed from. If you dial from an unauthorized phone number, you don't receive access to the network.

- User authentication support that includes Password Authentication Protocol (PAP), the Challenge Handshake Authentication Protocol (CHAP), Microsoft CHAP (MD4-CHAP), and One-Time Password.

- A per user configuration support, including per user provisioning of IP address assignment, static routes, and access filters.

- Accounting that can be performed on the L2TP Access Concentrator (LAC) and the L2TP Network Server (LNS), which includes connection, start/stop, and full logging information of failed connection attempts.

- Remote Authentication Dial-In User Service (RADIUS) and enhanced Terminal Access Controller Access Control System (TACACS+) support.

- AAA support and CiscoSecure global roaming server (GRS), providing proxy and translation of Access-VPN roaming user authentication.

IPSec   IPSec provides data confidentiality, integrity, and authenticity among participating peers in a network. Cisco provides full encapsulating security payload (ESP) and authentication header (AH) support. IPSec is available from Cisco on network-access servers and router platforms as well as the PIX firewall. IPSec is also available on Windows 95 and Windows NT 4 with the RavlinSoft IPSec software.

IKE   The Internet Security Association Key Management Protocol, formally known as ISAKMP/Oakley, provides security association management. IKE authenticates each peer in an IPSec transaction, negotiates security policy, and handles the sessions keys exchange. Cisco has been leading the IKE standardization effort.

Cisco Encryption Technology (CET)   CET is the original network-based encryption solution.

Certificate Management   Cisco fully supports the use of X.509-V3 certificates for device authentication as required by IKE.

Quality of Service   Cisco IOS software supports IP precedence, priority queuing, and custom queuing; Weighted Fair Queuing (WFQ); Weighted Round Robin (WRR); Generic Traffic Shaping (GTS); Committed Access Rate (CAR); fragmentation and interleaving; Autonomous Boarder Router (ABR); Weighted Random Early Detection (WRED); IP precedence; and Border Gateway Protocol 4 (BGP4) precedence propagation. Leveraging IP precedence with multiple tunnels to a given LNS, service providers can offer enterprise users differentiated tunnels with varying bandwidth levels.

Address Allocation and Management   L2TP provides full support of dynamic IP address allocation from an IP address pool maintained by the enterprise, including full support of the private addresses defined in RFC1918. L2TP also supports dynamic address allocation from the DHCP server. Cisco IOS software supports network address translation (NAT) while preventing internal "inside addresses" from being published to the outside world.

Redundancy   The Cisco L2TP implementation provides a backup capability, allowing multiple LNS peers to be configured with backup LNSs. If the connection to the primary LNS is unreachable, the NAS (LAC) will establish a connection with a backup LNS.

Scalability   The Cisco L2TP implementation supports unlimited sessions on each LAC and can support more than 2,000 sessions per each LNS on a Cisco router platform. Other Cisco implementations provide support for over 8,000 sessions.

When using the Cisco L2TP implementation of load sharing and stackable LNS features, multiple LNSs can perform load-sharing across multiple tunnel connections between one LAC and the LNSs. The statistical load-sharing capability across multiple LNSs provides added reliability and scalability. The stackable LNS feature has additional support for multilink PPP sessions. One of the LNSs will take responsibility for assembling segmented packets for each session across the multiple tunnels.

Management   For enhanced fault management, the Cisco L2TP implementation includes support for the L2TP SNMP MIB prior to the availability of the IETF standard MIB. MIB support provides full failure codes and reports the reasons for a disconnection. L2TP also includes a full suite of messages that can be sent to a Syslog server. This set of capabilities provides a full end-to-end troubleshooting solution for Access VPNs built on L2TP.

Security Concerns

Not all VPNs are created equal, and not all VPN implementations have the same levels of security. There have been several VPN discussions about Microsoft's implementation of the Point-to Point Tunneling Protocol (PPTP) not providing adequate security.

Counterpane and Microsoft

Bruce Schneier is the president of Counterpane Systems, a Minneapolis-based cryptography and computer-security firm. In June 1998, he sent out a press release that announced that his company had discovered flaws in Microsoft's implementation of a communications protocol used in many commercial VPNs. These flaws lead to password compromise, disclosure of private information, and server inoperability in VPNs running under Windows NT and 95.

According to the press release, "PPTP is an Internet Protocol designed to provide the security needed to create and maintain a VPN over a public Transmission Control Protocol/Internet Protocol (TCP/IP) network. This raises serious concerns as most commercial products use Microsoft's Windows NT version of the protocol. While no flaws were found in PPTP itself, several serious flaws were found in the Microsoft implementation of it."

"Microsoft's implementation is seriously flawed on several levels," according to Schneier. "It uses weak authentication and poor encryption. For example, they use the user's password as an encryption key instead of using any of the well-known and more secure alternatives," explained Schneier.

"VPN implementations using PPTP products require management control software at both ends of the tunnel as well as a cryptographic analysis of the system," said Wray West, chief technology officer of Indus River Networks, a supplier of remote access VPNs. "Most implementors do not have the specific in-house cryptographic expertise to discern the subtleties that are often the root of security breaches in today's commercial servers. They rely on their vendors and information security providers to build robust, secured products."

According to the team that did the cryptanalysis, there are at least five major flaws in this implementation. They are

Password hashing   Weak algorithms allow eavesdroppers to learn the user's password.

Challenge/Reply Authentication Protocol   A design flaw allows an attacker to masquerade as the server.

Counterpane and Microsoft *(continued)*

Encryption   Implementation mistakes allow encrypted data to be recovered.

Encryption key   Common passwords yield breakable keys, even for 128-bit encryption.

Control channel   Unauthenticated messages let attackers crash PPTP servers.

A host of additional attacks were identified, including bit-flipping, packet resynchronization, passive monitoring of Microsoft's PPTP, and PPP (Point-to-Point Protocol) packet negotiation spoofing—all compromising further the intended security of any VPN. The cryptanalysis work on Microsoft's implementation of PPTP was conducted by Bruce Schneier of Counterpane Systems and expert hacker Peter Mudge.

According to Mark Chen, CTO of VeriGuard, Inc, a Menlo Park–based computer-security company, "The flaws in this implementation are quite amateurish." Chen continued, "A competent cryptographic review would have prevented the product from shipping in this form. "

"This should serve as a caution to VPN implementors and users," said David Wagner, a student at the University of California, Berkeley." There are a lot of corporate security officers out there who will be very glad the 'good guys' found this first." Last year, Wagner, along with Bruce Schneier and John Kelsey of Counterpane Systems, discovered a major flaw in the privacy protection used in cell phones.

Schneier and Counterpane Systems provide consulting services in cryptography and computer-security issues. The firm has consulted for clients on five continents. Schneier invented the Blowfish encryption algorithm, which remains unbroken after almost four years of public testing. Blowfish has been incorporated into dozens of products, including Symantec's Your Eyes Only and McAfee's PCCrypto. Schneier is also the author of five books on cryptography and computer security, including *Applied Cryptography*, the definitive work in this field. He has written dozens of magazine articles, presented papers at major international conferences, and lectured widely on cryptography, computer security, and privacy.

In the spring of 1999, Schneier was asked if Microsoft had taken steps to close the holes in their implementation of PPTP, and he said they had made some strides, but the strides were "not enough."

Network Design and Planning

PART 3

Remote Connectivity for the VPN

If you decide to go ahead with a VPN, one of the first issues facing you is how to hook up your remote users. Depending on where the users are located, you should have plenty of choices. VPNs can be constructed with analog modems, ISDN, xDSL, and even cable modems. You will probably be tearing your hair out trying to figure out which service is best for you.

As with most decisions, the best way to approach it is from the beginning. Take a look at some of the other things you may have to consider.

IP Addressing

Is your VPN going to use dynamic or static IP addresses? Although dedicated IP addresses are not necessary, they do make some security issues easier to handle. With a static IP address at both ends, it is relatively easy to institute such things as packet filtering and authentication. Static addresses also make it much easier for applications to function, especially those applications that rely on an IP address to identify the user or resource. Ping, FTP, HTTP and point-to-point IP telephony are examples of applications that require you to know the address of the host you are trying to reach.

Always-On Internet Connectivity

An always-on connection is a connection to the Internet that is always up. If you can afford an always-on connection, you will be opening a broad vista of applications that you can use, such as remote backup software, remote software maintenance, and many of the IP telephony capabilities, including IP voice or video.

If you do not have the capability of always-on, the network would somehow have to know who and where you are and be capable of initiating a session. If you are connecting permanent remote sites, always-on should be close to mandatory.

What about Bandwidth?

When you start making decisions about bandwidth, you will have to select the service that will fill your needs now and in the future. But the question comes into play of how exactly do you figure out how much bandwidth you need? Good question, but unfortunately, there is no easy answer. If you can't figure out how much bandwidth you are using now, how can you come close to predicting what you will be using in the future? If your luck at predictions is anything like mine (ask my stockbroker, she takes all my orders, and does exactly the opposite. I have made that woman really wealthy!), just about the time you feel you have a good handle on the bandwidth usage of your company, someone will come along and demand that there be desktop video for each and every host on the network.

When you look at bandwidth, it is not just the data moving over the wire. There may be an entire suite of services that each office on your VPN needs. Do you want to add analog voice and faxing to the mix? If you do, then the solution you may be looking for includes simultaneous data and switched analog connectivity.

When you talk about bandwidth, you are really talking about throughput. If you are thinking that 56Kbs or 128Kbs is really fast, for most applications you are probably correct. However, VPNs may change all that.

When you install a VPN, you are taking away some of the throughput and using it for overhead, such as security, protocol tunneling, and possibly telephony applications and video. All of a sudden, the laws of physics that state that Nature abhors a vacuum come into play, and all the throughput you thought you had is gone. When it comes time to talk throughput, more is always better than less.

What about Cable Modems for the Remote Sites?

One of the reasons VPNs are established is to provide communication with remote sites. With the growing popularity of telecommuting, somebody's home suddenly becomes your next remote office. Because cable modems are showing up in the most unlikely places, let's see how they stack up against the criteria just laid out.

The first criterion was a dedicated or static IP address. This requirement depends on the cable provider. Some providers offer static IP addresses, while others force you to use a dynamic address. Most cable providers will provide either, though the static address usually comes with an added charge. The requirement for static addresses will probably change once users can be located by some kind of directory service, but that is still a few years off.

The next requirement was always-on, and cable modems can provide a dedicated channel.

As far as bandwidth requirements go, cable modems have been the subject of some debate. Cable modems are capable of delivering up to 10Mbps if you are hooked in through an Ethernet card. They are usually slower going upstream, but this should not be a major issue. The bandwidth needed for a cable modem should be adequate for now, as long as all your neighbors haven't signed up, too. Just like an Ethernet LAN, cable modems require users to share the transmission media. This means the more users you get, the less bandwidth there is available to each individual user.

This is one of the things the cable industry is working on. One solution is to reorganize the networks as more subscribers are added. This means that fewer subscribers would be served by any single cable head-end. Keep in mind, this is just a plan, and it has not been tested yet.

It appears that cable modems may fit the bill. They do have bandwidth, they provide coverage (if you can get one!), and the cost seems to be running under $50 per month. But the problems with cable modems are pretty severe in the areas of security, reliability, and customer service.

I Can See Yours, Can You See Mine?

The progress of rolling out cable modems across the country has been slow. Most cable providers are taking it slow for a reason.

In Apple Valley, Minnesota, Charter Communications started testing cable modems with a beta program. To qualify as a tester, all you had to do was call the cable company, and Charter would come out and install the modem, giving you very fast Internet access. It sounded like a dream come true.

Just before the company was going to take the new service live, there was a glitch. It seems that one resident was poking around and discovered that once his cable modem was installed, he not only could find things on his computer but could see things on other people's computers, too. Such as his neighbor's computer. He found that he was seeing things he really didn't want to see, so he went to the city council to complain, and Charter Communications had to go back to the drawing board.

The moral to this tale is security is obviously an issue with cable modems.

At this time, there really isn't any kind of standards-based security solution. Many of the modem manufacturers, including Motorola and Nortel, include some form of encryption and authentication with the modem. The security is usually based on the 56-bit Data Encryption Standard (DES). This may be okay for everyday home use, but it falls very short of the triple DES security usually included with most VPN gear.

When security is finally implemented, it should be based on standards, should be interoperable, and should be transparent. Some ISPs have now begun to bundle full-blown VPN functionality with cable-access service.

Then there is the marketing piece. Cable providers will have to convince the public that they are able to meet the reliability standards that are necessary to run a home office. This will probably come in the form of some level of service agreement that will cover both network performance and customer service.

Should you use cable modems? If they are available in your area, they are certainly a viable alternative; they certainly fit the bill when it comes to being cheap and plentiful.

Alternatives to VPNs

Although VPNs are definitely becoming a tried-and-true network strategy, it does not mean that they are right for every implementation. Each case must be weighed separately.

One of the things to take into consideration is the flow of your current and future network traffic. This evaluation should consist of volume, content, origination, and destination information that can help determine how your network infrastructure needs to grow. The requirements then flow into budgetary requirements, which can then be compared with the promised cost savings of a VPN. That is where things get complicated. Because VPNs are a relatively new technology and because there are new services hitting the market every day, trying to get a firm grasp on the market and cutting the up-front and secondary costs of the VPN may take some effort. In addition to everything else, product and carrier costs change quickly.

As with most new installations, you should select product vendors who sell devices that fit into your network architecture and can be supported by your current staff. If you decide to outsource, again look for solutions that match your business needs for network reliability, geographic coverage, security protocols, and billing systems.

Network Design and Planning

PART 3

PSINet and Galaxy Scientific Corporation

How would you like a partner that would save you lots of money, almost immediately? According to reports published in *Computer-World,* that is what happened with Galaxy Scientific Corporation and PSINet. Glenn Botkin, Galaxy's manager of information services, was working diligently to find a way to link more than 20 remote offices together. He had decided that the best way of handling the problem was to spend $160,000 to erect firewalls at six major sites as part of a VPN. Just before he was to ink the deal, Botkin found that PSINet was offering a service that could save the company tons of money.

Prior to installing the VPN, communication between the sites was done using dial-up connections at a cost of almost $4,000 per month. When Botkin wanted to link the offices together, he wanted each office to have access to corporate information resources. The offices also needed access to business-critical systems such as time keeping and accounting. Of course, e-mail was important, and it needed to be sent directly to the Internet rather than to a dial-up connection. He also wanted the solution to handle about 50 remote users.

Botkin decided to work with PSINet and take advantage of their intranet service. With the intranet service, Galaxy's sites would be linked together via PSINet's backbone. Even though the network is part of the Internet, PSINet data packets never leave the ISP's portion, so the company could offer service-level guarantees. Galaxy connects to PSINet through a permanent virtual circuit (PVC).

This solution is different from traditional VPNs. Because the data never leaves PSINet's backbone, the data is not encrypted. Even though the data hasn't been encrypted, PSINet spokesman Mike Binko says security is still tight. The data is switched rather than routed, so it's virtually impossible to hack into data travelling across the network.

One of the advantages from Galaxy's point of view is management. All management tasks are handled by PSINet. Galaxy tells PSINet what kind of information is coming in and going out of each location, and then all Galaxy has to do is monitor the information to make sure their instructions were implemented.

The cost of the six PVCs and some ISDN lines to take care of smaller offices is about the same cost as the dial-up connections: around $4,000 per month. According to Botkin, the company feels it is saving money by improving efficiency and allowing for greater collaboration between employees. Using the new VPN, the company was able to put together a bid for a $250,000 contract in a matter of days. The bid had come in at the last minute, and instead of requiring several people to meet at a central location, all the work was done over the network.

Part 4

The Road to a Successful Migration

- Why and how to document your network
- Using the seven layers of the OSI model to plan an upgrade
- Implementing the plan
- Making sure your upgrade is done on time, or better yet, early

Documentation Basic Training

Hard to believe, isn't it? Right here, in print, in a *geek* book for goodness sake, the author is *swearing*. Imagine, using that horrible *D* word in mixed company. Why children may actually be reading this book, and to think, there is going to be an entire chapter on *documentation*? Isn't that enough to get the book banned in several states?

Sybex is brave. They will let me write this chapter. As a matter of fact, the acquisitions editor even encouraged it. Scary, huh?

True Confessions, Yet Again

The problem with writing books like this is that people I know read them. Now, some of them are looking at the heading of this chapter and are probably dying laughing. Gary, writing about documentation? Yeah, right. That's like Dennis Rodman writing on fashion.

Okay, so maybe I have never been known as the greatest keeper of documentation. Who better to tell you about the evils of sin than a sinner? Believe me, I can attest to all the time I would have saved if I had taken a few minutes to document my work. I always meant well. Documentation was always right up there on the top of my list of things to do. As a matter of fact, many times I started it, by writing down all sorts of worthwhile stuff on a small piece of paper, which went into my shirt pocket. The shirt

True Confessions, Yet Again *(continued)*

pocket was emptied onto the dresser, and sometimes I even managed to salvage some of the stuff before my wife threw it way. Why just the other day, I came across a note that said RC4, NE2, I3, P300, and N8022. If I could just remember if that NE2000 card, with the IRQ of 3 and the port of 300, went into the server on RenCen 4 or one of the workstations located on Network 8022, I would sleep better at night. Of course, since the date on the note was four years ago, I guess I wasn't too worried about it.

Now, at least, I don't feel like such a hypocrite. And Don, you can stop laughing!

Now that true confessions are out of the way, let's begin.

Why Document?

Suppose, just suppose, that after you have scoured the bookshelves, the Internet, and the intranet, you find that perhaps there is no network documentation, and you figure that having some would make your life easier. You are probably right! Reasons for creating documentation are discussed further in the following sections.

Evaluating Current Network Environment

It never fails. Someone is always asking you for that bit of information that you just don't seem to have. If all calls to the support lines are documented and tabulated, you will have a handle on the state of your network environment. You may even be able to spot trouble areas before they become troublesome.

I Really Can Do Some Things Right!

Throughout the first four chapters of this book, I documented some of those moments when I was not too proud of my performance. There have been some victories, though, and one of them even involved documentation that I created by my very own self—amazing as that may seem.

Network file servers always seem to run out of disk space. I was constantly seeing administrators run through the halls chasing management types down the hall for a signature for a new disk drive because the old one was full. I decided to do something about that. I started a spreadsheet, and every Friday afternoon before I went home, I had a series of tasks that made me look really busy, but in reality, they were a wind down leading to the weekend.

I Really Can Do Some Things Right! *(continued)*

As I worked with my spreadsheet, noting the amount of free space left on each volume, I noticed a trend start to develop. Each and every week, we used about 50 megabytes of disk space. I also knew that I never, ever wanted to fall below 500MB of free disk space. One day, looking at my spreadsheet, I noticed that there was 850MB of disk space on a particular hard disk. I then wrote a purchase order for exactly what I wanted and hand carried it to my manager. I placed it on her desk and asked for a signature. With 850MB of free disk space, she wondered why I needed more. I explained that we were using about 50MB each week and that we should never fall below 500MB. I also said that by filling out the paperwork now, it would give the PO time to go through the proper channels. The purchasing department would have time to get the best price, get delivery when we wanted it, and provide me with enough time to schedule and install the hard drive without causing panic in the cubes. She was fairly shocked that a network administrator could be proactive instead of reactive. I managed to live off that and milk it for healthy salary increases for quite a while!

There are other reasons for maintaining documentation on the state of your network. Even though many of us feel like we are the last outpost on the planet doing this kind of work, that may not necessarily be the case. As a matter of fact, there may even be other people in the same company doing the same kinds of work that you do. Wouldn't it be wonderful if through some strange quirk of fate, all of you actually communicated?

Think about the way documentation could make your life easier. How many times have you gone about fighting and looking for a solution to a particular problem, only to become frustrated, angry, and perhaps even use words that you wouldn't want your mother to hear? I don't know about you, but this has happened to me at least once. If that wasn't frustrating enough, there are times you go back to the office and start to discuss all the issues you had with that problem. About this time, someone would walk in and say something like, "Hey, I just solved that yesterday by doing…." That sure would have been nice had it be documented somewhere, so you could have found it.

Defining Functional Requirements

Working on and thinking about documentation will give you the opportunity to get a broader prospective of your network. You are almost forced to see the forest and not just the trees. In doing so, you may notice bottlenecks or potential areas of concern starting to rear their ugly heads.

The Road to a Successful Migration

PART 4

In Chapter 10, I talked about SNMP and all the wonderful things it can do for you. One of the areas where SNMP has helped has been in the area of baselines.

How Much Bandwidth Is Enough

Most companies have a connection to the Internet. If you have a small company, your connection may not be all that fast—perhaps it's an ISDN using one 56KB channel. Because your company is small, it works well enough, and everyone is happy. You have access to SNMP, so you set up your system to check the number of packets flowing across your ISDN router, and you keep a record of the "normal" amount of traffic going to the Internet. As a matter of fact, you make a point of actually graphing the information. You have established a baseline for Internet traffic.

Now the company starts to grow. The more the company grows, the more Internet traffic increases. All of a sudden, people on your network begin to complain that Internet traffic is painfully slow. It may be time to open up the other 56K channel of the ISDN line or even upgrade to a faster technology. When you approach management about the problem, the first reaction might be why do we need to do this? Can you prove it's a problem? Because you have the documentation to show how things used to be, how things are now, as well as how you are utilizing the available bandwidth, you will able to answer all management questions with hard and fast facts.

Developing Multivendor Network Integration Plans

One of the most difficult decisions a network administration team has to face is when to get another vendor involved. At some point or another, we have all been locked in one of those finger-pointing, troubleshooting sessions. If you can test equipment before bringing it online or document what happens when you introduce a new vendor into your production environment, it will help you with decisions later.

SNMP Promo

In Chapter 10, there is an in-depth discussion of Simple Network Management Protocol and its various uses. In that chapter, there are several examples of how different companies managed to integrate different technologies to make their network work. In each case, extensive testing was involved before the insertion into the production environment. Why is all this testing necessary, anyway?

SNMP Promo *(continued)*

Someone once said that the wonderful thing about standards is that we have so many of them. The same can be said for any implementation of TCP/IP. Depending on the network operating system (NOS) you are using, you may be using any of a number of implementations of IP. Microsoft does its own thing with IP, Novell does its own thing with IP, and of course, Unix handles IP a little differently than either Microsoft or Novell.

It doesn't stop at the NOS. Hardware has different implementations of different protocols, as well. Check out any book on Cisco routers and the protocols they employ, and you will see the word "proprietary" several times. This is why testing is so important. If you have a network that revolves around a set of Cisco routers, all using Interior Gateway Routing Protocol (IGRP) or Enhanced Interior Gateway Routing Protocol (EIGRP), your network may hum along. But what happens when you decide to add a router from a different company into the mix?

Checking the hardware documentation is a start. Make sure that before you buy the hardware, it is compliant with the things you want to do and there is not a better way of doing something. Even if you have configured something exactly like this six months ago, technology changes so fast that there may be a better, cheaper, faster solution available now that you don't even know about.

Once you have verified that the new piece of equipment should work with your current configuration, try and get something to test. Set up a testing lab, if possible, and make it as realistic as you can. Try to test the new stuff with the old stuff under as close to a real-life load as possible. When you do the final project install, make sure you plan on leaving yourself an out. Murphy's law plays a big part in any redesign of an infrastructure. Having things start to go wrong without a safety net can lead to a very upset stomach and several sleepless nights. Try to avoid that at all costs.

I know, this sounds dull and boring. But dull and boring can be good sometimes— take it from someone who has been on the edge several times. That is the subject of another book!

The Road to a
Successful Migration

PART 4

Developing Network Diagrams and Specifications

Network maps and layouts were discussed previously, but some of the benefits may not have been mentioned. Having an up-to-date network diagram, with specifications about how the network is configured and laid out, will help you lay the ground rules for expansion and for replacement of key components. We all know that our memories used to be a lot better than they are now. It is nice to have a central repository of information on the topology and specifications of the network. It also helps in troubleshooting. There have been occasions when it seemed like the entire WAN was beginning to collapse in on itself. However, with a network diagram, it showed that all the diverse links were actually communicating through a central point. Our troubleshooting steps switched from "Oh, my gosh, the sky is falling," to "What is wrong with that router?"

Changing Network Documentation

If you have worked in networking for any length of time at all, you know the adage that end users lie. Always. Without exception. Now, they may not know they are lying, but, in fact, they usually are. Think about the last time you went out to troubleshoot a problem. The first question I usually ask is what have you done to my network/computer/ router/segment lately? The answer I invariably get is "*Nothing.*" By probing a little deeper, I usually find that there may have been something done that unintentionally caused the problem. For example, new software was unintentionally installed or a new modem installed and there was one part left over when the installation was done. Unfortunately, that one part was the network card, so network communication for that host was at a standstill! If additions and changes are documented, you can solve the problem faster than if you were Detective Columbo.

Network Management 101

It can be such a simple thing: an ongoing electronic journal kept by all members of the data processing department; perhaps an old fashioned three-ring binder kept in the computer room. Something to keep track of what has changed or what will be changing on a network. Some companies have even gone so far as to have computer documentation stored at each desk. That seems pretty radical, but they say that it works. Any time a change is made to a specific computer, something should be added to the journal. If you have updated a driver, added a new network card, installed the latest patch from Microsoft, removed a program, or changed the system in any way, it should be written down somewhere. Then, if a problem occurs on the machine, whoever is designated to fix it has an idea what it is you have done.

Keep a simple log sheet that tells what you did and why you did it. If there are problems, make sure they are documented also. After a while, trends may develop, and when a trend develops, you can take a proactive stand on the issue.

Developing an Implementation Plan for Deployment of a Solution

Documentation shows the problem, and you know the potential solution. But that solution may not be as simple as you would like. The final process may take time to roll out enterprise-wide. Using your documentation and history will show what needs to be done and what sort of time frame should be allowed for that to occur.

Lights, Camera, Rollout

You have decided to make a major change to your network. You have researched the change and tested the proposed solution. Everything seems to work just fine. Whatever little glitches have shown up have been taken care of, and now it is time to schedule and do the official rollout on the production network. I've already quoted the infamous words of Donald Williams, consultant for Compuware in Minneapolis, many times, but they bear repeating: "You can tell how good a network administrator is by the level of paranoia they exhibit." Let's take it small first.

When doing extensive changes to a network, it is usually a good thing to start small. If you can limit your exposure, you can also limit the catastrophe potential. You can also increase the odds that if something goes wrong, you can get out of it and go back to the status quo.

Taking it small has other advantages. No matter how much you test, how much you plan, and how much you are ready for a rollout, things will go wrong. Stuff happens, especially in networking. By limiting your exposure, you can, hopefully, fix the problems of the few and learn for the sake of the many. After doing multiple small rollouts, you will learn where a problem may lie and also how to fix it when the problem arises. It then stops being a problem and is just another step in the process.

This leads us back to the subject at hand, documentation. Every time a problem and a solution comes up, it should be documented. Every time a rollout is completed, there should be a postmortem done with all the people that took part. The postmortem should cover what you did, what worked, what didn't, what you did to fix what didn't, and then what you could do differently to make the whole procedure work more smoothly.

The Road to a
Successful Migration

PART 4

Locating Existing Documentation

Documentation is a drag. Let's face it, we did not get into this industry to do paperwork. We got into this industry because it was fast-paced, with something new every day. Challenges appear at a moment's notice, and it is up to you to put the fire out immediately, if not sooner. Where in the world does sitting down and filling out paperwork fit into this scenario? Right at the top of the priority list.

Documenting a network, even if it is small, can be a lot of work. When you think of all the questions that someone could ask about your network, you want your documentation to be able to answer them. Where in the world do you start?

Start by figuring out what is already available. You may think it will be easier to just dive right in and start over, but that is not always the truth. Many times, when you locate a WAN/LAN map of the network, it may be out of date, but it gives you a really good place to start. It may also give you the history about why some things were done the way they were done.

> **TIP**   Some of these may seem beyond the scope of a book on TCP/IP. Because TCP/IP is such an open protocol and because it is so widely used, it is the one where problems may show up first.

These are things that you as a network administrator will have to look for:

WAN/LAN Map   Depending on the detail, if you have one of these, you are off to a great start. A WAN/LAN map is simply a map of your network and how it is laid out. This should include topology (Ethernet, Token Ring, and FDDI), routers, bridges, concentrators, servers of various shapes and sizes, and even the number of workstations on each segment. A good map may include network numbers, speed of the segment (10Mbps vs. 100Mbps, 4Mbps vs. 16Mbps), and the IP addresses of the key static components.

IP Address Worksheet   This can be a breakdown of the addresses available for a particular subnet as well as any default assignments that have been made by policy. An example would be that the first available address in a subnet is always reserved for the gateway, and servers always have an address within the first ten host addresses on a subnet.

IS Policies   Sometime, somewhere, someone may have laid down some policies for the way the information services department should be run. This may include host/server naming standards, when a network segment is split, network layout standards, e-mail system standards, browser/Web server standards, and Internet or intranet policies.

Software Licenses   In many companies, this can be the toughest thing to do. If you are fortunate, you may work for a large company that has negotiated with software manufacturers for site licenses for all its software. If this is the case, you have it made. For those of us who live on the other side of the tracks, making sure a network is legal is becoming more and more of a headache every day.

Virus Protection Policies   These are statements that include what should be scanned how often, whose responsibility it is to make sure that all virus definitions are up to date, and how a new definition will be rolled out to all the hosts on a network.

Security Policy   This information explains what to do in case of an internal or an external attack. This should include who to notify and what steps should be taken to find out if anything has been tampered with.

E-mail Policy   If you are going to use the SMTP and POP3 Protocols, or any other e-mail system for that matter, you should have written policies in place that explain to your users that the company owns the e-mail system. Anything that can be written and sent by e-mail can be saved and read by lots of other people.

Internet Policy   Just what is and is not an acceptable use of the Internet? As you know, the darn thing can be quite addicting. Some companies have a strict limited-use policy; other companies have a hands-off policy. Is there a written policy for your network?

As you can see, there are quite a few things that may be included in the documentation of your network. If you have scrounged through the bookshelves and have come up with the documentation, this might be the time to check it out and make sure that it is still valid. For example, if the written Internet policy limits downloads to less than 1MB because at 2,400 baud it ties up the phone, you may want to change this to reflect the new installation of a T-1 line.

TCP/IP Documentation

So far, we have mentioned several things that should be done for the entire network, but what about specifically for the TCP/IP part of the system? There are several areas you will want to look at, including configurations, addressing and subnets, DHCP, HOSTS/ LMHOSTS, and routers.

Configurations

Each operating system has its own peculiarities. When you configure TCP/IP on a Windows NT 4 server, pointing the system to the Internet is done with adding an IP address to a tabbed section of a configuration window. The same is true for pointing the system to appropriate DNS servers. If you are performing the same task on a NetWare 4 or 5 server, there are three or four different ways of accomplishing the same task, depending on the way the server is configured. None of these are as simple as the configuration of an NT server, at least the first time you do it. Once you can configure *anything* semicomplicated the first time, help yourself to learn by experience, and write it down.

Besides helping you remember the way you solved the problem the last time you faced it, configuration documentation also leads to a certain sense of well being that comes from consistency. If you know that each time something is done, it is done the same way, it will help you to explore where problems lie.

Configuration documentation is also great for reference. It is amazing the number of times companies or administrators will purchase the latest and greatest SuperWhizBang 10,000 to run as part of a network segment, only to find the network segment cannot handle the load. Had the administrator checked the documentation beforehand, that important detail would have been discovered before any money was spent.

Addressing and Subnets

In the previous chapter, we discussed the fact that each host must have a unique network and host address. Each host on the same network segment must have the same network portion of its address, otherwise things go to hell in a handbasket. Once you have devised your network addressing scheme and once you know which network address and which host addresses are going to be assigned to which segment, why not write that information down? What a concept! It is such a simple thing—I cannot understand why more companies don't do it.

As a system administrator, you know a lot about your network without having to refer to the documentation. You know the basic layout in your head. You probably know where the various segments meet up and how it is laid out. You know the tough stuff! It is the easy stuff that will screw you up each and every time. Write down your addressing scheme and assign the network addresses to various network segments. If you have more network addresses than you have segments, make a note of that. Leave the information somewhere so you find it the next time you have to split a segment into two. That way you will not be playing the age-old game of, "I think I left off at...."

DHCP

This ties in very closely with the addressing and subnetting sections. If you have a section of a network that is being serviced by a DHCP server, you should know the range of addresses you are letting that server manage. You should also know which of the addresses assigned to that subnet you are *not* letting DHCP manage. Each subnet may have routers, servers, printers, or something that requires a static IP address. When you configure DHCP, make sure that you leave yourself some room for these static addresses. Don't let DHCP manage the entire block; be sure to reserve some special-case addresses.

Once you have reserved the special-case addresses, make sure you document when and where you assign them. The rule states that each host must have a unique IP address. Some operating systems, such as NT Server, will make a big deal if it spots another host with the same IP address. Other operating systems, including NetWare, may just post a message on a console screen that says it has detected another system with the same IP address and then just stop working with IP. It makes troubleshooting more difficult than it should be. Be careful.

Keep track of how many hosts you add to a segment. It's really easy to forget that you created a subnet and made sure that DHCP server would handle the allocation of 30 IP addresses, until you add host number 31 and can't figure out why it is not getting an IP address and access to the Internet. It seems like a simple thing, but sometimes when I troubleshoot, I overlook the simple things and go right to the really hard stuff.

But then, there is the really bizarre.

Darn Newbie Strikes Again.

Randy Cook, Certified Novell Engineer (CNE) and Certified Novell Instructor (CNI), of Productivity Point International of Jacksonville, Florida, had this story to tell.

"I walked into my office one afternoon to find Jason, a Microsoft Certified System Engineer with Internet (MCSE+I) and a Microsoft Certified Trainer (MCT) cursing a Windows 98 box and a DHCP Server. He explained to me that he had been working on this for over two hours and could ping any computer with the server except for the 98 box, and the 98 box could ping any computer on the network except the DHCP server. He released the IP address from the Windows 98 machine and renewed it. The DHCP server would give the client an IP address but would then refuse to talk to it. Sometimes the ping would find no address; sometimes it would show the TTL had expired, and the packet had died prior to reaching its destination. With three Microsoft Engineers now deeply involved and unwilling to simply use another host, it had become a personal vendetta. Operating systems were reinstalled, service packs were applied, and protocols were removed and reapplied. A 17-year-old high-school intern had come in to watch the top engineers in the company analyze BOOTP packets, responses, and ARP caches. After several minutes of peeking over the shoulders of the experienced technicians, the young intern blurted out the answer to the problem that years of experience had prevented the engineers from seeing: 'That's pretty cool, they both have the same MAC address!' There were two identical Ethernet cards, with the same manufacturer, same model, and the same hardware address!"

Hosts/LMHosts

If you have opted to bypass the DNS method of resolving host names to IP addresses, that means you may be using HOSTS or LMHOSTS. Make sure you document what you want in each file and the syntax for each. Quite often, problems occur and communication is lost for the silliest little thing. Of course, the same is true with DNS!

The Case of the Missing Period

Be careful where you tread. The path that seems so clear may harbor unseen terrors.

I recently changed ISPs. The level of service that I received from one was not what I needed. It was not the fault of the owners, it just wasn't working out. I called around and found a company that could meet my needs, provide me with the service I required, and had a tech who really knew his stuff. We coordinated and worked together, and soon my Internet connection was up and smoking, except for my e-mail server. E-mail was going out, but nothing was coming in. This indicates a problem with the DNS record. We checked the DNS, and sure enough, it needed to get switched over to the new ISP for management. After getting that done, everything looked good. I left town and was gone for four days. There was no e-mail when I got back. Hmmm...there must be a problem.

I called my ISP, who said, "We did what we had to do; it has to be a problem on your end." We went back and forth over this topic; I even told them I sent myself an e-mail message from a different account, and it got bounced by their server. Eventually they said, "Oops." It turns out when the definition for the DNS record was typed in, a period was left out. That means a strange domain name was appended to mine, and everything became undeliverable. As soon as the period was added, mail began to flow, and everything worked!

When dealing with HOSTS files, check syntax first. You would be surprised at the creative ways things can be spelled or the ways numbers can be transposed. You also run into the problem of editing a HOSTS file with a text editor that *insists* on adding a .txt to the end of every text document. Funny thing, in the exacting world of computers, HOSTS and HOSTS.TXT are not the same things.

When using an LMHOSTS file, especially when you are going out and including statements from files on other machines, make sure access to those machines is assured. Try to limit the number of levels that your systems have to go to get the information from an LMHOSTS file. If your system is getting information from another system, which is getting information from a third system, the pyramid does not take long to collapse if something can't communicate. Document what goes where and when and how it gets there. If you can have a "standard" file, so much the better.

Routers

Static routes or dynamic routes? Dynamic routes can be pretty painless. If you have documented the router configuration and how it is put together, as long as nothing changes, you should be in great shape.

Static routes require you to know not only how the router is configured but also how the router table is laid out. If you make a change to one router, everything has to be updated. If the documentation of the static route table fails to be updated and a router goes down unexpectedly, you may have segments of the network that are locked out and cannot be reached. That can be one of those career-limiting moments in one's life.

What Have You Done Lately?

The first rule of troubleshooting is to determine what is different. If everything has worked properly in the past, and suddenly things start going south, what has changed? There is usually something that has had an impact on the environment. It can be something new being introduced, some change made to a setting, or even an environmental change.

Introducing something new to a network can produce unexpected results. For example, I once had a print server installed on a Token Ring network. This print server plugged right into the network, and the printers plugged right into the print server; within a mere matter of minutes, you *should* have output and happy end users.

I called facilities and asked that a line be installed for the print server. They asked where I wanted it, and I gave a very general description of the location. I told them that I would put the box where I wanted to line to be run, so they would know exactly where the wire should go. I did what I was supposed to do: I dropped off the box. Facilities did more than what they were supposed to do: not only did they install the wire, they took the print server out of the box, plugged it into the electrical outlet, and plugged it into the newly installed cable running to a 4Mbps multiple-station access unit (MSAU). Great job, folks! Unfortunately, I had never configured the print server. The default was a 16Mbps data transfer rate. Bad things happened.

The positive side of the story was I knew exactly what had changed on my network. Had I really checked the network map and reminded myself that this was the only 4Mbps ring left in the company, I would have saved myself and the users on the network segment some stress.

13

Planning for Changes

Let's assume that you have just been assigned a fairly large network to rework. You are going to redefine the network infrastructure and then figure out what needs to be done. You know one major implementation that is going to be made: you are going to be installing TCP/IP on all the desktops and on all the servers. Network operating system communication seems to be going to IP, so you want to stay on top of things. Why are we making all these assumptions? This chapter is designed to show you how to plan a major TCP/IP upgrade. Without an upgrade to plan, this would be a really short chapter!

Decision one has already been made—that you are going to have to support a multiple protocol environment. This single decision is going to drive many of the other plans and choices you are going to make. You should know that as soon as you, or someone above you on the corporate food chain, have decided that your network is going to be upgraded, you are entering into very dangerous waters. While this is an exciting time, it is also a time to be *very* careful. There are certain rules of network computing that seem to work like the law of gravity.

Gary's Laws of Network Computing

Over the years that I've made changes to networks and listened to other administrators, I have unscientifically determined that there are forces acting in the universe that we, as mere mortals, have no control over. Here is a brief listing of what I have discovered:

1. Murphy's Law states that anything that can go wrong will go wrong. It will also happen at the worst possible moment. This law is always in effect.

Gary's Laws of Network Computing *(continued)*

2. When it comes to major network upgrades, Murphy was an optimist.

3. William's Law states that the way to judge the skill of a network administrator is to determine their level of paranoia. The more paranoid, the better the network administrator.

4. The chance of success for a project is inversely proportional to the visibility of the project and the proximity of your annual review.

5. Most end users are computationally challenged.

6. All end users lie. System administrators, at times, prove they are the best end users!

7. The computer skill of an end user is inversely proportional to the user's position on the Organizational Chart. People low on the ladder (like IS people) need to know a lot. People high on the ladder don't have to know much. They are too busy doing management stuff to worry about it.

8. The type and quality of a computer that an end user is given to use is also inversely proportional to the user's position on the Organizational Chart. The person residing at the top of the chart will have a computer that will rival most servers on your network. This is so they can print out their e-mail, quickly. The people that do the real work will have machines with serial numbers in the low 100s.

9. People hate change. They may say they don't, but they do. Whenever you make changes, people will whine. The volume of the whining is in direct proportion to the number of changes.

10. Most middle managers, if they receive pressure from above, will fold like a cheap suit. This is why, if you are making several major changes, get the final okay and signature from someone way high up the organizational ladder. That way, whenever you receive the inevitable question, "What dummy approved this project anyway?" you can nip the conversation in the bud. It is amazing how quickly the cooperation you receive goes from 0 percent to 100 percent when people find out the CEO of the company is really behind your project.

Given these laws of the universe, you can see that you are about to embark on a treacherous path. Your project could possibly affect everyone in the company. This means it is highly visible. Depending on exactly what you are going to do, it could mean lots of change for people. We know how well users react to that. Given a choice, people will not be dragged from their comfort zone, so we have to make this process as painless as possible. This can be accomplished with planning, and testing, and planning, and more testing.

Because the tasks involved in this process can be extensive, let's break them down into a manageable format. We already talked about the seven layers of the OSI model back in Chapter 2, so that should be a good reference point.

Planning for Physical Layer Changes

Everything at your Physical layer can also be described as the infrastructure. It is what we spent Chapter 12 talking about. All that documentation! So break it out, and let's take a look at it. First of all, we have to look at the high-level overview of the company. Figure 13.1 is a map of your organization.

Figure 13.1   Corporate map

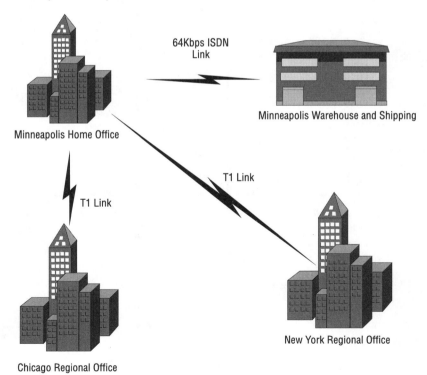

As you can see, you have the Minneapolis home office linked to the New York and Chicago regional offices with T-1 lines. The warehouse and shipping departments are housed in a separate building, via a 64Kbps, single-channel ISDN link.

Although it is important to know what the corporate infrastructure is, it is also important to know what it serves. That requires an inventory; you have gone through the documentation and found that information. The inventory for the Minneapolis headquarters is found in Figure 13.2.

Figure 13.2   Minneapolis inventory

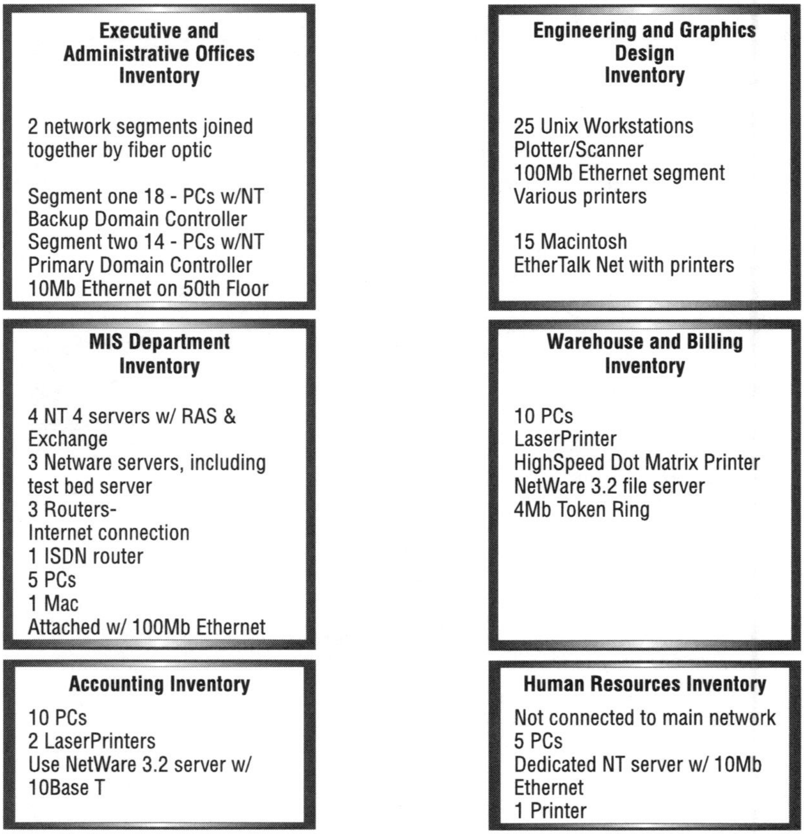

Executive and Administrative Offices Inventory	Engineering and Graphics Design Inventory
2 network segments joined together by fiber optic Segment one 18 - PCs w/NT Backup Domain Controller Segment two 14 - PCs w/NT Primary Domain Controller 10Mb Ethernet on 50th Floor	25 Unix Workstations Plotter/Scanner 100Mb Ethernet segment Various printers 15 Macintosh EtherTalk Net with printers

MIS Department Inventory	Warehouse and Billing Inventory
4 NT 4 servers w/ RAS & Exchange 3 Netware servers, including test bed server 3 Routers- Internet connection 1 ISDN router 5 PCs 1 Mac Attached w/ 100Mb Ethernet	10 PCs LaserPrinter HighSpeed Dot Matrix Printer NetWare 3.2 file server 4Mb Token Ring

Accounting Inventory	Human Resources Inventory
10 PCs 2 LaserPrinters Use NetWare 3.2 server w/ 10Base T	Not connected to main network 5 PCs Dedicated NT server w/ 10Mb Ethernet 1 Printer

It is apparent that, like most modern-day shops, yours has a mixture of stuff. There is some NT stuff, there is some NetWare stuff, there is some Unix stuff, and there is some Mac stuff. It is up to you to make sure all that stuff fits together. As you look through the inventory, you can also make note of the fact that some of these systems are connected together using Token Ring, some of them are connected using Ethernet, and there is FDDI thrown in for good measure. You have a little bit of everything, don't you? Why, the human resources department isn't even connected to the main network. That may have to change!

There is also the issue of the Chicago office and the New York regional office. Before we can make any great decisions on those offices, you need to see what their inventory looks like. Figure 13.3 shows both Chicago and New York's inventory.

Figure 13.3   Regional office inventory

```
                    Chicago Regional Office Inventory

        50 PCs
        2 - NT servers
                1 Server used for RAS connections
                1 Server used for Exchange
                1 BDC
        1 - Novell Server
        16Mb Token Ring network
        1 Router
        15 Printers
        2 Scanners
        1 Videoconferencing system
        Connected to the Internet
```

```
                    New York Regional Office Inventory

        50 PCs
        2 - NT servers
                1 Server used for RAS connections
                1 Server used for Exchange
                1 BDC
        1 - Novell Server
        16Mb Token Ring
        1 Router
        15 Printers
        2 Scanners
        1 Videoconferencing system
        Connected to the Internet
```

Now, for the sake of simplicity, both the regional offices are exactly alike. They attach to the home office via a T-1 line. They have a couple of NT servers to do RAS and Exchange, and they have a NetWare server to do file and print services. Because each regional office is primarily another sales arm of the company, they have plenty of printers, scanners, videoconferencing, etc. They both have a connection to the Internet, and they are both running on 16Mb Token Ring.

Because you are just dealing with the physical layer at this point, is there anything that stands out from a communication point of view? T-1 links to offices that serve only 50 people should be plenty of bandwidth unless they configure it to run videoconferencing all day, every day over the T-1 connections. If so, the connections for the regional offices are covered.

What about the link to the warehouse and shipping department? It is running a 64Kbps ISDN link that is fiscally conservative to serve 10 people. They also have their own server and Token Ring network. Because that information is not listed, we can only assume that they have to access the Internet through the main office, so that could be an issue.

If you look closely at the engineering and graphics design department, it's clear that part of that department is segmented off by itself. It's time the Macs joined the real world and hooked into the main network. They need to be upgraded, and supporting another platform when it is not absolutely necessary is an inefficient use of corporate resources. Getting rid of the EtherTalk network is a decision you probably won't mourn.

Is there a decision that has to be made here? It depends on how strict your view of the term "corporate standard" is, and it also depends on how deep the pockets are. If there is growth in the future of the company, there may be some thought given to changing everyone over to 100Mb Ethernet. After all, if it is good for the IS Department, shouldn't it be good enough for everyone?

That would mean upgrading 32 PCs on the 50th floor, 15 Macs, 10 PCs in the warehouse, 10 PCs in accounting, and 5 PCs in human resources. All the machines in the regional offices will have to be upgraded, and the offices themselves will have to be rewired. That could be somewhat costly. But, what the heck, I am spending your company's money, and as a consultant, that is something I am really good at! We will go for it, but on a scheduled rollout basis.

At this point, you should make a note on your list of things that need to get accomplished to schedule and deploy 100Mb Ethernet throughout the company. After we review the Physical layer implementations, that list of things to do should also include adding HR to the network and switching the Macs over to the main network.

There are a couple of other ways that you could be spending the company's money at the Physical layer. For example, you could upgrade to SNMP-compliant switches instead of hubs. Hmmm, maybe that should be studied.

Planning for New Data Link Layer Implementations

One of the things that I find interesting about the seven layers of the OSI model is the farther up the model you get, the more expensive the equipment. Usually, the more expensive the equipment, the greater chance it will slow communication down. I will cover this subject a little later.

Taking a look at the inventory again, there doesn't seem to be a whole lot that we have to worry about at the Data Link layer, at least in this scenario. In your world, however, you may have need of something called a *bridge*.

In looking at the layout of your offices, you notice that there are two Ethernet segments connected between the executive and administrative offices. Given the number of PCs on each segment, the amount of traffic that this segment is going to generate is not going to be massive. For the sake of argument (and to make explaining the purpose of a bridge a whole lot easier), let's assume that there were lots of PCs on each segment and the throughput was very slow. You wanted to speed things up, keep the packets flowing, and do it at a minimal cost.

> **NOTE** As with anything in computing, there are probably a dozen ways to accomplish the same task. In this case, I am going to choose to solve it with a bridge. It does not necessarily mean it is the only way to solve the problem, the "correct" way to solve the problem, or the most efficient way to solve the problem. I am just choosing this solution for the sake of an example!

Bridges

As you remember from Chapter 9, there are several types of bridges, so it will be up to you to decide which one to use. That will go on your growing list of things to do.

Bridging is not without its problems. Both Ethernet and Token Ring have addressed some of the issues with bridging and have located other ways of handling the problem.

Ethernet Switches

Ethernet has always been a popular choice for people designing a LAN. The reasons were pretty obvious.

1. It was inexpensive.
2. It was a stable technology.

The Road to a Successful Migration

PART 4

3. It was inexpensive.

4. It was a mature technology.

5. It was inexpensive.

6. It was easy and worry free for adds and moves.

7. It was inexpensive.

Looking at the list, you would pretty much think that Ethernet had it all, and it was time for the Token Ring folks to pack it in. But Ethernet had its drawbacks. Some of them were pretty serious for a LAN segment of any size. If you read the specs, you would know that theoretically an Ethernet segment could have over 1,000 workstations; if you also worked in an Ethernet environment and carried a pager, you realized that theory was great. Reality said that if you put between 75 to 100 workstations on a single LAN segment, packet collisions would skyrocket and performance would drop off the face of the earth. It was not a good situation.

If your network segment grew to more than 100, you used to have a couple of choices: you could add a bridge, or you could subdivide the segment. You could also throw the whole LAN away and start over with something faster, but this option involved rewiring the building, replacing the network cards in each host, and replacing hubs, routers, bridges, and print servers. This option was usually discussed for the amount of time it takes to read this sentence and then discarded. It was just too darn expensive.

Because the alternatives were too expensive, another solution was developed. As is so often the case, nature abhors a vacuum. Switching hubs were born to fill the void. A switching hub can be considered a really high-speed sophisticated bridge. Figure 13.4 illustrates the switching hub concept.

Figure 13.4 Switching hub layout

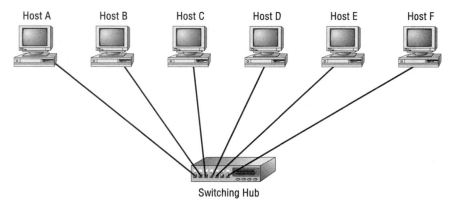

Switching Hub

Anytime a frame comes into a regular Ethernet concentrator, that frame is rebroadcast to every host plugged into the concentrator. With a switching hub, the hub learns the MAC layer address of every host plugged into the concentrator. When a frame arrives, the switch looks at the MAC address of the destination host. If that host is attached to that switch, the switch then sends the frame only to the host it is addressed to. Each port on the switching hub can be attached to a single high-volume user, or a server, or to a multiport 10BASE-T hub. The devices that have been connected to each port define a collision domain in which devices compete for bandwidth only with other devices on the same port.

Token Ring Switches

Until recently, Token Ring switches were not really in demand. Token Ring operated at 16Mbps, and with the high utilization inherent in regular Token Ring, there just didn't seem to be the need.

Token Ring switches do offer many of the same benefits as Ethernet switches. These include

Easy installation   A great plug-and-play solution for an overworked Token Ring backbone.

Performance   With a Token Ring switch, you can use the high-speed backplane to provide full 16Mbps connections between any two ring segments at any time.

Hop reduction   Switches can ease design restrictions by reducing the hop count in a wide-area network. All segments attached to the same switch see the switch as a single bridge hop. If the number of bridge hops is reduced, it speeds up the overall communication.

Increased server bandwidth   Network boards in servers can be connected directly to switch ports, allowing the full 16Mbps bandwidth between the server and any workstation.

Full duplex   Some Token Ring switches can boost server bandwidth by providing full-duplex connections to full-duplex server boards.

When you start looking at Data Link layer solutions for network congestion, it comes down to bridges or switches.

Data Link Layer Plans

Here is something else for the list of things to do. Do you want to employ a bridge between the executive and administrative sections of the LAN? With so few people on the two segments, it probably isn't necessary at this point, especially if you are going to 100Mbps Ethernet. As you begin your plan for growth, that may be something you want to take a look at. We will move it to your list of things to do.

The Road to a
Successful Migration

PART 4

Planning for Changes at the Network Layer

You know that IP is a routable protocol, and with all the offices you have spread out all over the United States, some routing is involved already. (Routing at the Network layer was discussed in more detail in Chapter 8.) Although the routing system seems to be in good shape, there may be some ways to make your life easier by planning for the proper implementation of assigning IP addresses.

Develop a Strategy for Assigning IP Addresses

This is such a popular subject it is even addressed in RFC1219, "On the Assignment of Subnet Numbers." When you first set up your IP network, you can determine exactly how many subnets you have now. You can speculate about how many subnets you will need in the future, but even the best of us do not come equipped with a crystal ball. If you use the strategy outlined in RFC1219, you can modify the way you subnet your network without having to reassign any IP addresses.

RFC1219

The theory is simple. Subnets should be assigned by placing ones only in the leftmost portion of the masked address. Host addresses should be assigned by placing ones only in the rightmost bits of the IP address. This way, there is a buffer of bits bordering the division of the subnet and the host that are all set to zero. If, at a later date, you have to go in and resubnet the network, adding additional bits to the mask should not require reconfiguring the IP address on any host.

Here is an example of what I mean. For the sake of simplicity, I will say that your company has been assigned a Class B address. After calculating the numbers, you decide that all you need to use now is the first four bits of the third octet for your subnet mask. The last octet can be saved for host addresses. You check the paperwork and determine that your new IP address is 164.47.0.0. The subnet mask that you are going to be using will be 240. If we lay out the subnet mask in a grid, it will look like Table 13.1.

Table 13.1   Potential Subnet Mask

11111111	11111111	11110000	00000000
Network	Network	Subnet	Host

Because there will be four bits masked for the subnet, we have 14 potential subnets. They can be laid out like Table 13.2.

Table 13.2   Potential Subnets

128	64	32	16
0	0	0	1
0	0	1	0
0	0	1	1
0	1	0	0
0	1	0	1
0	1	1	0
0	1	1	1
1	0	0	0
1	0	0	1
1	0	1	0
1	0	1	1
1	1	0	0
1	1	0	1
1	1	1	0

I laid this table out according to the way we are taught to count, moving from right to left, filling up all the spaces from 0 to 9 before going into the 10s column. But that is not the way the suggestion tells us to do it.

Table 13.3 takes a look at the same potential subnets, this time going from left to right, leaving 0s in the rightmost column.

Table 13.3   Following the Rules

128	64	32	16
1	0	0	0
0	1	0	0
1	1	0	0
0	0	1	0
1	0	1	0
0	1	1	0
1	1	0	0
1	1	1	0

I think you get the picture. Looking at this table then, the first network that you would start filling in would be network 164.47.128.0. Your natural inclination (at least my natural inclination) would have been to start at 164.47.16.0.

Given these rules, you would start assigning network numbers in the following order: 128, 64, 192, 32, 160, 96, and 224.

What about hosts? Host addresses are supposed to be assigned from the farthest right side of the column, moving up. It would look something like Table 13.4.

Table 13.4   Host Assignments

128	64	32	16	8	4	2	1
0	0	0	0	0	0	0	1
0	0	0	0	0	0	1	0
0	0	0	0	0	0	1	1
0	0	0	0	0	1	0	0
0	0	0	0	0	1	0	1

Table 13.4   Host Assignments *(continued)*

128	64	32	16	8	4	2	1
0	0	0	0	0	1	1	0
0	0	0	0	0	1	1	1

Again, you get the picture. Here, however, we are counting the "right way." We are starting at one and progressing up the numerical chart.

By using this plan, addresses such as 164.47.224.7, where several 0 bits exist on the border between the subnet and the host address, will find their way onto the same subnet and node address when any of the following subnet masks are applied:

- 255.255.255.0
- 255.255.254.0
- 255.255.255.128

If you look at it another way, an address like 164.47.225.128 will produce different values for subnet and host addresses for each of the masks listed above.

There are other ways of laying out an addressing scheme.

Ways to Allocate IP Addresses You May Not Have Thought Of

There is always another way, isn't there? In this section, we will take a few quick looks at the different ways people have decided to allocate IP addresses on their networks.

Give 'Em More Than They Need

In this scenario, you take a look at the network segment and determine how many host or node addresses you could possibly need on that segment. At that point you subnet the network to give that segment the maximum number of IP addresses they will ever need. This is a very common method of IP address allocation.

Work Group Allocation

Take your average ordinary Ethernet network and divide it up into workgroups. Each workgroup should have the majority of its resources located internally to the workgroup. In this case, the subnet mask is assigned to best allocate the number of hosts each work-group needs. Figure 13.5 shows an example of workgroup numbering.

The Road to a
Successful Migration

PART 4

Figure 13.5   Workgroup addressing

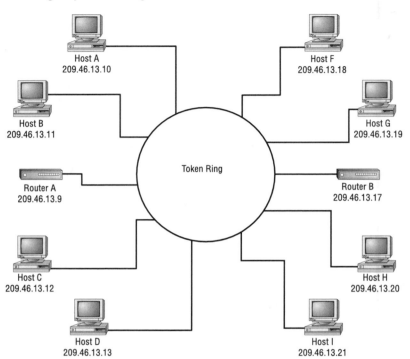

There are several advantages to the workgroup method:

- You are keeping much of the IP traffic as local as possible.
- Static IP addressing depends on the group you work with, but it makes for easier identification of where problems reside.
- You can have smaller pools of IP addresses to track with a larger number of networks to assign.

But there is a disadvantage to the workgroup method:

- You will have increased traffic through a router. Anytime a workgroup member needs to communicate with a resource not native to the workgroup, the router is invoked.

Point-to-Point Addressing

Some router manufacturers do not offer an option for an unnumbered IP interface. If this is the case, then each end of the point-to-point link must have an IP address. In this case, subnet the system down as far as it will go while still allowing two hosts per subnet. Figure 13.6 shows an example of a point-to-point link.

Figure 13.6   Point-to-point numbered connection

Router A
209.46.13.5
255.255.255.252

Router B
209.46.13.6
255.255.255.252

Pooled Addresses for Dial-In

Now, here is an interesting problem for you. You are running an Internet service provider. That ISP sells mainly dial-up connections, and while you have several thousand subscribers, you have absolutely no idea how many of them will be dialing in at the same time. How do you handle the blocking out of those IP addresses? One suggestion is to treat the dial-up pool as separate point-to-point links that are terminated on a single device. In this case, the server would dynamically assign the IP addresses with a subnet mask of 255.255.255.252. The terminal server would also have to be configured to find the router.

Network Layer Plans

When you look at the protocols of the TCP/IP suite that operate at the Network layer, IP is the main protocol on which you will have an impact. Two other common members of the IP family operate at this layer. Both the Address Resolution Protocol and the Internet Control Messaging Protocol work at the Network layer, but you probably are not going to have much control over these.

From the Network layer, the main thing to add to the list of things to do is to decide on a network-addressing scheme.

Planning for Changes at the Transport Layer

Three major protocols of the TCP/IP suite operate at the Transport layer: Transmission Control Protocol (TCP), User Datagram Protocol (UDP), and Domain Name Service (DNS). It is an interesting mix, because TCP and UDP operate as Host-to-Host Protocols. A Host-to-Host Protocol delivers data to and receives data from peer Host-to-Host Protocols. While TCP and UDP are transparent to the user, DNS actually provides a service that your end user can see and understand.

TCP

TCP provides a full-duplex, connection-oriented transport of information between two hosts. Sounds impressive and it is.

> **NOTE** Terminology plays a big part here. *Full-duplex* means that conversations between the two hosts can go both ways, simultaneously. This is like a phone call. A connection-oriented protocol means that anytime a communication is opened between two hosts, the systems keep it open the entire time of the conversation, and they keep checking on the status of the packets they send. Think of the protocol as being really careful with your information.

TCP is also in charge of synchronizing the packets that are sent out over the network. When a message is too large to be handled in just one packet, the message is broken up and placed in several packets. These packets are then sent over the network, but the packets may not arrive in the same order they were sent. Something has to be able to reassemble them in their original order. This is the job of TCP.

Again, you will not really have an impact on TCP. The applications you use will access it and use it if it is available.

UDP

UDP is a connectionless Transport protocol. To understand connectionless, think of the postal service. When you drop a letter in the mail, you really hope it gets there, but you can never be sure. The same is true of UDP. It puts the packet on the network, sends it off on its merry way, and hopes for the best. It is so confident that the packet will arrive that it does not even check for delivery.

Although TCP is more careful than UDP, UDP gets the job done faster.

DNS

Now here is something that is going to be added to your list of things to do. You are going to have to decide whether you want to maintain a DNS server within the walls of your network.

We are all familiar with DNS names. They are things like `microsoft.com`, `novell.com`, and `whitehouse.gov`. These are great, user-friendly implementations that make it easier for real people to find their way around the Internet. It's great for real people, but for TCP/IP, it just means more work.

When you or someone on your network types **http://www.sybex.com** on their browser and presses return, all TCP/IP cares about is resolving that URL to a real IP address. Remember your basics, TCP/IP does not understand *names,* it only understands *IP addresses.* It gets that IP address by looking it up using DNS. If TCP/IP cannot find the address locally, it will go out and ask a DNS server. If the DNS server cannot answer the question, the DNS server will keep pushing the question up the line until somewhere there is an answer. Now, if the request goes all the way up the line and there is no answer, a 404 Host Unknown error will be returned.

So, how can you use DNS, and why should you worry about it? First of all, DNS is nothing more than a distributed database. Bits and pieces of this database are stored all over the world. You can create a DNS server on your network and have all your users point to that server. Whenever they have a URL to look up, the DNS server is where they will look first. This is a great solution if your users are constantly going out to a set number of sites on the Internet that never change their addresses. This can also be a great solution if you have a corporate intranet, because you can direct where your users go to look for information. If none of these situations match your business, you are probably better off pointing your users' computers to the DNS server your ISP suggests and being done with it.

There are other reasons you should be concerned about DNS. If your company is hooked up to the Internet, and if you have your own DNS name, e.g., `sybex.com`, `microsoft.com`, or `sun.com`, there is a DNS record on your company stored somewhere on the Internet. You may have control over that record, or your ISP may have control over that record, but you should know this information.

DNS records are important if you want to set up your own Internet Web server. In that case, the DNS record will have to be altered so that it points to the host running your Web server. Also, if you want to receive Internet mail at your own POP3 server, the MX record associated with your account will have to be changed.

Transport Layer Plans

Most of the plans you will have to make at the Transport layer revolve around DNS. Do you want to host a DNS server? Does your company have a DNS name, and if not, do you need or want one? If you have a DNS name, who hosts it, and what does the record look like?

Planning for Changes at the Session, Presentation, and Application Layers

Why are we taking the last three layers together? The remaining protocols that we have to look at map out across all three layers. Remember, TCP/IP wasn't originally written to map to the OSI model, it was written against the DOD model, and it only has four layers.

In this section, we are going to look at File Transfer Protocol (FTP), Telnet, and Simple Mail Transfer Protocol (SMTP). Because we are now operating at the Application layer, a lot of the underlying mystery will be removed because you have probably used each of these protocols, whether you know it or not.

FTP

Have you ever downloaded something from the Internet? Does the address `ftp://ftp .microsoft.com` look somewhat familiar? FTP is the File Transfer Protocol, and like the name says, it is used to transfer files from one location to another. This can be done using a Unix session with special commands or through a browser. The front end of FTP commands, those things that the users see, are getting friendlier and friendlier, but the functionality stays the same.

Why would you need FTP? Do you have to provide files to employees or customers? How are they connecting to your site to download these files? Hosting an FTP server may be just the answer. Not only will an FTP server make your files available to the outside world, the FTP server has enough security built in to prevent unwanted visitors from accessing your data. For more information on FTP, see Chapter 6.

Another option to consider and add to your list of decisions to make is whether you need and want an FTP server to provide file access.

Telnet

Telnet is the Terminal Emulation Protocol. Telnet is a bonus. When you start installing and configuring native TCP/IP devices, you are going to need some way to connect to the device to issue its commands. If you are lucky, you may have an SNMP management and agent piece that will allow you get into the configuration utility. Or maybe the hardware is sophisticated enough to have its own installation utility. If not, you are probably going to be using Telnet.

Telnet is versatile. You can establish Telnet sessions over the phone. If there is no phone connection and your device is accessible to the Internet, you can establish a Telnet session over the Internet. Finally, if you can, make a direct connection to some device using a null modem cable. In any of these situations, you can establish a Telnet session with a remote host.

Telnet is so versatile, most communication suites, including Microsoft's dial-up networking, will let you establish a Telnet session. This one is a no-brainer. You don't have anything to do, you just know that it is there and have a null modem cable around if you need it.

SMTP

Do you have an e-mail address? If you do, you have used Simple Mail Transfer Protocol or SMTP. SMTP takes e-mail from your desktop and somehow gets it to mine.

E-mail is one of the biggest reasons companies are connecting to the Internet. It is getting so that some customers will not do business with people who do not have (and use) an e-mail account.

SMTP options you will have to consider include, is your company going to use Internet mail, what package are they going to implement, and what does that mean to your hardware configurations?

List of Things to Do

We have gone up the seven layers of the OSI model and have examined all sorts of issues. Now you have to make some decisions. As we went through the chapter, these are the things that still need to be addressed:

- When do you want to schedule and deploy 100Mbps Ethernet throughout the company?
- When do you want to add HR to the network?
- When do you want to switch the Macs over to the main network?
- Do you want to upgrade to SNMP-compliant switches instead of hubs?
- Do you want to buy a bridge?
- If you buy a bridge, how can you make sure that the bridge can be managed with an SNMP solution?
- Which network addressing scheme do you want to use from the Network layer?
- Do you want to maintain a DNS server within the walls of your network?
- Do you want to host a DNS server?
- Does your company have a DNS name, and if not, do you need or want one?
- If you do have a DNS name, who hosts it, and what does the record look like?

- Do you need and want an FTP server to provide file access?
- Is your company going to use Internet mail?
- What mail package are you going to implement?
- What does the e-mail rollout mean to your hardware configurations?

These and many other questions will be answered in Chapter 14, when our schedule starts to come together.

14

Implementing the Plan

I suppose this chapter could be renamed as something like "The Compendium of Really Trite Phrases and Analogies," because it will be. After all, try as I might, I just can't come up with a better way to say "Plan the work, and work the plan," or "A journey of a thousand miles begins with a single step." So I won't try.

To set the stage for the material that follows, several presumptions must be made. First, I have mentioned William's Law several times. But in case you missed it, William's Law states that the way to judge the skill of a network administrator is to determine their level of paranoia. The more paranoid, the better the network administrator. This brings to mind another set of laws that are extremely applicable to this chapter. These were devised by that seer and prophet, Murphy. Murphy states unequivocally:

1. If anything can go wrong, it will.

2. If there is a possibility of several things going wrong, the one that will cause the most damage will be the one to go wrong.

    a. Corollary: If there is a worse time for something to go wrong, it will happen then.

3. If anything just cannot go wrong, it will anyway.

4. If you perceive that there are four possible ways in which something can go wrong, and you circumvent these, then a fifth way, unprepared for, will promptly develop.

5. Left to themselves, things tend to go from bad to worse.

6. If everything seems to be going well, you have obviously overlooked something.

7. Nature always sides with the hidden flaw.

8. Murphy was an optimist.

Murphy went on and on; as a matter of fact, he diversified. There are laws of technology, laws for cops, and even laws for love. But the laws I've just mentioned pretty much cover things. In this chapter, I will take the list of things to do that has been garnered over the last several chapters and see how we can use William's Law to minimize the effects of Murphy's Law. Keeping those two laws in the forefront while you work through any project will help you immensely!

List of Things to Do

Any good project must start out with a list of things to do. So, just to make sure everyone is clear on the tasks, in the last chapter we have gone up the seven layers of the OSI model, examined the issues, and devised a list of changes to the network that are being considered. We have also covered VPNs, so you will want to take a look at that option, too. Now we are at that stage of the process where the rubber hits the road (see, I warned you, inane trite sayings will abound in this chapter!) and you have to make some decisions. These are the issues that you still need to address:

- When should you schedule and deploy 100Mbps Ethernet throughout the company?
- When do you want to add HR to the network?
- When do you want to switch the Macs over to the main network?
- Do you want to upgrade to SNMP-compliant switches instead of hubs?
- Do you want to buy a bridge?
- If you buy a bridge, how can you make sure that the bridge can be managed with an SNMP solution?
- Which network addressing scheme do you want to use from the Network layer?
- Do you want to maintain a DNS server within the walls of your network?
- Do you want to host a DNS server?
- Does your company have a DNS name, and if not, do you need or want one?
- If you do have a DNS name, who hosts it, and what does the record look like?
- Do you need and want an FTP server to provide file access?
- Is your company going to use Internet mail?

- What mail package are you going to implement?
- What does the e-mail rollout mean to your hardware configurations?
- What about the possibility of a virtual private network to link the company with its partners?

Sounds like a pretty impressive project, doesn't it? If nothing else, it sounds like job security for quite a while. The next question that probably leaps to mind is "Where in the world do you start?"

Project Management 101

When you enter into the world of project management, you begin to realize that somebody, somewhere, took that trite saying about the journey beginning with a single step pretty darn literally. Project management helps you to take a large, seemingly insurmountable project and break it down into smaller tasks. Each completed task is one more step along the journey. In network administration terms, this process is called a *system-design life cycle*.

System-Design Life Cycle (SDLC)

In order to gain a broad view of how to go about designing, implementing, maintaining, and revising a large information system, let's break down the SDLC. This tool is used throughout the electronic-systems industry, so you may have come in contact with it somewhere before.

Figure 14.1 shows a linear approach to a system-design life cycle. You may have seen this chart in the past, but it may have had different names or styles. Most examples, though, will have several steps in common that identify the procedures that relate to the development phases of

- Analysis and specification
- Design
- Implementation
- Maintenance

Figure 14.1   System-design life cycle

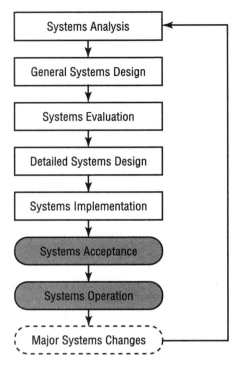

System Analysis and Specification

Projects begin with analysis and specifications. This is called the Project Approach Phase. During this phase, project requirements and scopes are determined. This phase should include the following steps:

1. Recognize and state the underlying business need.
2. Describe the high-level goals, constraints, and resource requirements.
3. Gather general information about the project through interviews, surveys, and so on.
4. Prepare preliminary schedules.
5. Agree on the project charter.
6. List team-member responsibilities and assignments.

General System Design and Systems Evaluation

After the analysis and specification phase is completed, the project moves into the design phase. In the design phase, you begin to design a solution based on the identified needs. The design phase usually includes the following steps:

1. Identify generic steps.
2. Evaluate alternatives.
3. Review documentation, and apply alternatives.
4. Design a specific solution.

Detailed System Design, Implementation, and Operation

Once the decisions are made, and the hardware is purchased, you can begin the implementation. Implementation may also take place in stages, so you should handle the implementation phase with these steps:

1. Define implementation-specific milestones.
2. Develop and test a working solution.
3. Implement a pilot solution.
4. Test the pilot solution, and obtain management acceptance.
5. Document the system or solution, and train users.

Maintenance

Once the new solution is in place, it will be up to you to maintain it. Up until this point, any decision you made was based on why and how you should build the system. In this phase, there are tasks to make sure you made the right decisions.

This is an often-overlooked phase of the process, mostly because it starts the day you turn the solution on and ends the day you turn it off. This phase does more than determine how the system is working; it also determines when you start the entire SDLC process again.

At the very least, you should do the following:

- Establish ongoing checkpoints and associated system-performance reports.
- Perform maintenance until the costs become excessive.
- Retire or replace the solution.

As we take our list of things to do and begin to lay out the implementation of the project, you will see that several of these areas have substantial subtasks that need to be performed before we can move on to the next phase. We will cover each of these as we get to that specific phase.

Managing the Project

As you can see from the list of things to do at the start of the chapter, much of the gathering of information has been completed. This means the project will kick off with an organizational tone designed to bring this project some scope and depth.

To give you an idea of how we can use the four phases of the project to determine the procedures involved, look at Figure 14.2.

Figure 14.2 The design and implementation process

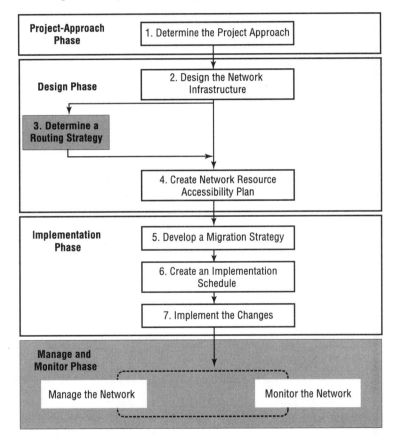

This is a very high-level overview of the procedures that must be accomplished to reach the final goals of the network-upgrade project. The monumental project is beginning to take on some formation and direction and almost seem manageable. As I have said a few times in this chapter, a journey of a thousand miles…oh, heck, you know what I mean.

Project-Approach Phase

This phase has only one procedure: to determine the project approach. Figure 14.3 illustrates this subsection.

Figure 14.3   The project-approach phase

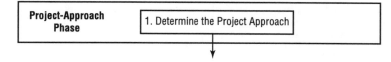

The first procedure involves the following steps:

1. Assemble the project team.

2. Gather business information related to the tasks at hand.

3. Train the project team, if necessary.

4. Determine the scope of the design process.

5. Do some preliminary scheduling.

By accomplishing these tasks, the team can help set realistic expectations for the project time line. This helps to avoid any miscommunication or misunderstanding later in the cycle. When you organize a project this way, you are also figuring out the kinks and what each individual team member will be contributing.

Project-Approach Phase Tasks

Referring back to our list of things to do, you can see there will plenty to do during the project-approach phase. First, there are several decisions that have to be made:

- Should you upgrade to SNMP-compliant switches instead of hubs?
- Should you buy a bridge, a switch, or a router?
- Do you want to host a DNS server?
- Do you need a DNS name?
- Do you need FTP?
- Do you need e-mail?
- Do you need a VPN?

The team that you put together in the project-approach phase is going to be responsible for making some heavy-duty decisions. In addition, many of the decisions can be very costly if the proper decision isn't made. If the wrong decision is made, your company may lose not only money but also productivity, and this is usually far more costly to an organization than just the money.

Assemble the Team   As you start to create a list of resources available to you, take a look at the members of the network team your company has assembled. In some companies, this may be as simple as looking in a mirror. In other companies, you may have the ability to pick and choose from dozens of employees spread all over the world. Lucky you!

If you're in the latter group, try to pick people that can help you out in this process. Stretch the boundaries of your thinking a little bit when you look for potential allies. Go beyond your IS staff to look for people in unlikely places. For example, you may want to include a friendly end user on your team. There will usually be at least one person on the staff whom others will turn to as an unofficial help desk. This is the power user who can whip through all the desktop applications that you just know how to install. This power user may be able to bring a desktop perspective to some of the decisions you make that you may not have considered. More importantly, this power user brings with them credibility for your project. You are about to inflict change on the entire staff. If you are lucky, the change will be invisible. If you are not so fortunate, your users are going to be facing some new applications with a new look and feel, and they are going to have to learn new stuff. People resist change. They especially resist change that is going to be forced upon them for reasons they may not clearly understand. When this happens, it is really nice for those people to think they have an ally on the team looking out for their best interests. When the changes start to happen, and people may experience some loss of service or confusion because of the new products, telling them it is all for the best might not be as comforting coming from you as from one of their peers.

Another person you may want on your team is a member of senior management—especially if you are planning on major changes and the costs could be significant. At some point, you are probably going to have to go and fight for the budget. You may be more likely to get the funds your project needs if there is a friend in high places. There are a few other reasons that you want a member of senior management on your team. The other members of the management team may be reluctant to ask questions about the work you are doing for fear of looking foolish. Although they do not want to look foolish in front of you, they may not feel so squeamish about professing their technological ignorance in front of their peer. After all, they are both managers, so they speak the same language and probably suffer from the same phobias; they are expected to know how to do management stuff, not technology stuff. You know that, and I know that, but when you breathe the rarified air of mahogany row, sometimes you begin to feel like people expect you to know everything.

The final reason for having a member of senior management on your team is rather sneaky and underhanded, but so be it. I have heard many stories from network administrators who come to their bosses with great ideas. These great ideas usually cause some pain for end users. When the middle manager is approached, it sounds like a really good idea, and they give it their blessing. You run out and institute the idea, and it starts causing pain. Someone may get in your face about the changes, but more than likely, they will go to your boss or your boss's boss and complain. When this happens, some management types tend to fold like a cheap suit, and you are left holding the bag. In this case, the advantage of having a high-level manager on the team is to refer these problem cases directly to the corner mahogany-row office. Once word gets around that this project has the blessing of the powers that be, many of the complaints about change will magically disappear.

What about outside resources? Many companies have at least one consultant on staff or on retainer. Could that person contribute, or are there resources at that person's company that can be brought into the action? What about other trusted partners? Suppose you have a particular vendor you do business with regularly, and this vendor will probably get the majority of the orders for the new equipment. If the vendor is in on the project from the beginning, they will have a better idea how to help you. They may also know about products and services that are available that may have passed you by, or they may know of a new product that has more capabilities at the same price. Someone from the outside may be an ideal candidate to help.

Gathering Business Information   Much of this was done as part of the chapter on planning. You went through the seven layers of the OSI model, recognized what you needed, but more importantly, found out what you had. Finding out where you need to go is definitely a lot easier when you already know where you are.

Training the Project Team   How much training is going to be necessary for the project team, and will it really be necessary? It depends. If you are planning on installing a single Cisco router in your office and if you have every intention of having a consultant come in and configure it for you, as well as provide routine maintenance, it would be pretty silly to send someone out for the complete Cisco certification. If, however, you are installing 100 Cisco routers and one person is going to be in charge of installing, configuring, upgrading, and maintaining all of them, then training becomes vitally important.

On a Personal Note

I do a lot of training, and I see a lot of people come through my classes. The people that come through my classes usually fall into one of three categories. Category one we can call the old pro. This is the person who has been around the block and has fought their way through whatever problems they have faced. They may be taking on another new challenge, or they simply want to upgrade their skills on current products. For whatever reason, they are there to learn. They are also battle-scarred and usually somewhat bitter, but they are better people for it.

The second category of people that come into my classes have absolutely no clue what the job entails when it is given to them. They pretty much accept their bosses' logic that because everyone in the office came to them for answers about Word and Excel, they must know about computers. And because they know about computers, they are the perfect choice to be the LAN Administrator/Web Page Editor/E-Mail Supervisor/WAN Specialist (pick one or two). By the time I get them, they are really bitter.

Finally, there are those people who are just starting out in a new position. These are the people who are learning how to do the job before they are given the responsibility of doing it on a production system. These people may actually come in and screw up my network during class. As a matter of fact, many of them do. Better my network in a controlled environment than your network with real live people trying to do real live work. Although there may be an up-front cost to training, your company may reap the benefits in ways they never realized. Your network may stay up because a former student has learned from their mistakes and knows better than to crash the network. Anyway, if they come to class and notice it's me, tell them to say "Hi."

One of the issues with training has always been, gosh, if I train them, I make them more marketable, and they will take that training and go find another job. It could happen. There are several ways around that, however, from having employees sign a form saying they are financially responsible for any training they receive if they leave the company within one year, to having them sign a noncompete clause. However you decide to handle it, training still pays.

Determining the Scope of the Design Process   This can be a sticky point, simply because you are now being asked to actually define the project. How much are you going to do as part of this project? Will it be all of the items listed on the to-do list presented earlier in the chapter? Or will it be a pared-down version of that list, say, for example, to take just the infrastructure segment of routers, bridges, and switches, and leave the Internet connectivity, the potential intranet, and VPN alone for the time being. This is the part of the equation when you start taking a good close look at what you want to do, what you have to do, what you can afford to do, and what you really can do. Anyone who has ever worked on a project with any magnitude knows that those four things can be remarkably different.

Doing Some Preliminary Scheduling   At this point in the process, the scheduling you do will probably be preliminary. It may amount to bringing the team together and getting a good idea of when people are going on vacation, so you can begin to plan around those dates. It may even be something as broad as "We need to get this done by the end of the year." This tentative completion date gives you something to shoot for, and sometimes that is all that is needed to keep a project on track. Another one of those trite phrases to keep in mind is "It's not a goal until it is written down and committed to." Set your goal, but be sure to give yourself plenty of time to accomplish your tasks.

Putting the Project Definition Phase into Practice

Now, obviously, I am not really going to upgrade a network here, but at the end of each of the sections, I will lay out some ideas about how I would proceed from that point.

With this project, because I am a consultant and spending your money, I will take on all the tasks previously listed. Some of these will need to be researched, so we will start the research process in the next phase of the project.

First, I would assemble a team of specialists to help. I will need someone within the organization to help ease the project through the rocky path of the budget process. I will also need an Internet/intranet person to work on the Web server and the home pages. Having a router person around would be nice, but I may be able to scam one of those on an hourly basis from the vendor who is going to sell me the equipment. I want the technical person from a good multipurpose vendor to be a part of this team, too. Then, there will be the grunt workers. These will be the people that will be heading out to the desktops and doing some work on each machine if necessary. I will make sure they know the basics of each desktop system I am using: Windows 98, Windows NT, Windows 2000, OS/2 Warp, and the Mac OS. Each team member may not be trained on each operating system, but I will have specialists who can handle the job.

For scheduling, let's assume (we are going to be doing a lot of that in this chapter) that we are currently in January, and we want to get the project done by the end of the year. This requires a project manager. If you are not a project manager or your company does not have a project manager, take each task that has to be completed and write it down on an index card. When all the index cards are done, lay them down, placing them in first-task-to-last-task order. When you're certain they are in the proper sequence, place the task's completion date on the bottom of each card. Now, add the name of the person or the team that is responsible for completing each task. Enter the information on each card into a project-management tool.

In Figure 14.4, you will see that we have opened a project and have scheduled it for completion by the end of the year. This type of chart is called a Gantt chart and is one of the standards of the project-management field. So far, the only tasks that I have added are finding the project team, training the project team, and gathering information. The rest of the tasks that go along with our project will be filled in later.

Figure 14.4 A beginning Gantt chart

ID	Task Name	Start Date	End Date	Duration	Jan 00
					31 1 2 3 4 5 6 7 8 9 10 11 12 13 14 15 16
1	Network Upgrade Project	1/1/00	12/29/00	260d	
2	Assemble the project team	1/3/00	1/7/00	5d	
3	Train the project team	1/10/00	3/31/00	60d	
4	Gather necessary network information	1/3/00	1/14/00	10d	

At the top of the Gantt chart, I have our project listed as taking the entire year. Under that, I have begun to devise the subtasks associated with the project, the first being to assemble the project team. With the team assembled, I have allocated the first quarter of the year 2000 for training the team. Finally, we have a ten-day period to gather information necessary to start making decisions.

This should about cover the first phase of the project, so let's move ahead a couple of weeks, and start the next phase.

Project-Design Phase

Take a look at Figure 14.5 to give you kind of a refresher about what is involved in the design phase. As you can see, there is not a lot to do in this section, just redesign the network so that people all over the company can get access to it. Oh yeah, this is not a problem, this should be a piece of cake that can be knocked out in about a 15-minute meeting. *Not!*

Figure 14.5 Overview of the project-design phase

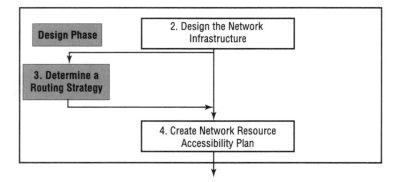

As you can see, some procedures at this phase may be conditional. For example, if you were managing a small network with a router to access your Internet connection, designing a routing strategy would not make much sense. That is why this procedure is off to the side.

At this point, it would be a good idea to review some of the facts about the infrastructure from Chapter 13. Figure 14.6 shows a map of the corporate side of the company, headquartered in Minneapolis.

Figure 14.6   A corporate map of the network

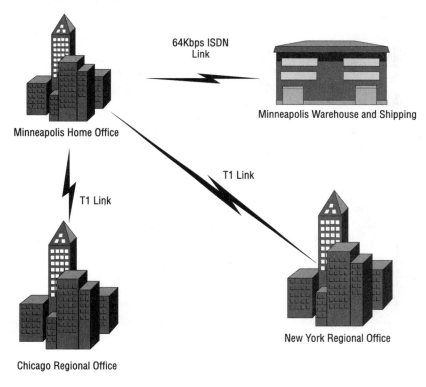

Figure 14.7 is a listing of the Minneapolis inventory.

Figure 14.7   The Minneapolis computer inventory

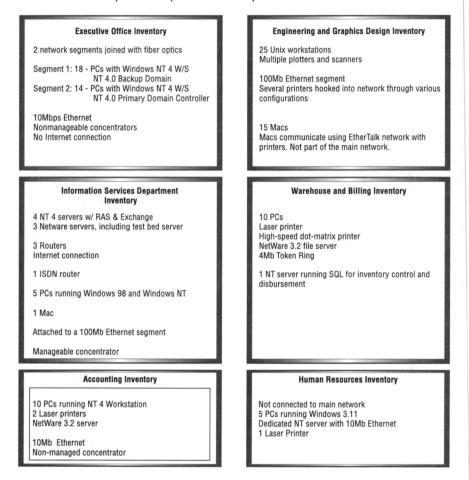

Figure 14.8 is an inventory of the regional offices' computer equipment.

Combined with the list of things to do from the start of the chapter, we should have enough information to give our upgrade teams something to start working on.

Design the Network Infrastructure

The first thing the team should be doing at this step of the process is to refer back to the list of things to do. Specifically, the issues to handle include

- Specifying, defining, and preparing to move to 100Mbps Ethernet throughout the company.

Figure 14.8   The regional offices' computer inventories

```
Chicago Regional Office Inventory

50 PCs with a variety of desktop operating systems
3 - NT 4 servers
        1 Server used for RAS connections
        1 Server used for exchange
        1 BDC
1 - Novell server
16Mb Token Ring
1 - Router
15 Printers
2 Scanners
Videoconferencing system
Connected to the Internet
```

```
New York Regional Office Inventory

50 PCs with a variety of desktop operating systems
3 - NT 4 servers
        1 Server used for RAS connections
        1 Server used for exchange
        1 BDC
1 - Novell server
16Mb Token Ring
1 Router
15 Printers
2 Scanners
Videoconferencing system
Connected to the Internet
```

- Adding human resources to the network.
- Switching the Macs in the engineering department to PCs.
- Making a decision on SNMP.
- Making a decision for bridging versus routing.
- Deciding on a network-addressing scheme.
- Deciding on hosting DNS servers and applying for a DNS name.
- Deciding whether you need FTP.
- Deciding whether you need e-mail.
- Will there be a VPN link in your future?

SNMP   Again in this section, as plans are made, assumptions will be made. Simple Network Management Protocol operations are in your future, whether you want them to be or not. More and more of the equipment that is designed and manufactured today is SNMP-compliant, removing the choice. In this case, it makes sense to go with the flow and implement it during this upgrade. The issue now remaining is which SNMP package to implement and at what cost? I have added some of the tasks to the Gantt chart that will be necessary for the team to accomplish in completing the preparations for SNMP implementation (see Figure 14.9).

Figure 14.9   The Gantt chart with SNMP tasks

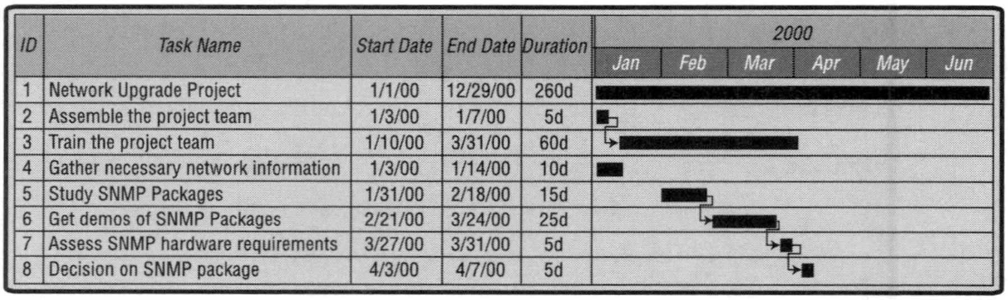

ID	Task Name	Start Date	End Date	Duration	2000 Jan	Feb	Mar	Apr	May	Jun
1	Network Upgrade Project	1/1/00	12/29/00	260d						
2	Assemble the project team	1/3/00	1/7/00	5d						
3	Train the project team	1/10/00	3/31/00	60d						
4	Gather necessary network information	1/3/00	1/14/00	10d						
5	Study SNMP Packages	1/31/00	2/18/00	15d						
6	Get demos of SNMP Packages	2/21/00	3/24/00	25d						
7	Assess SNMP hardware requirements	3/27/00	3/31/00	5d						
8	Decision on SNMP package	4/3/00	4/7/00	5d						

Routers vs. Bridges   The network is configured now with routers at each of the main sites. The only place a bridge may be appropriate is between the two network segments in the executive and administrative offices. Everywhere else has either its own segment or a router to handle the traffic. With just 32 PCs between the two fiber-optic segments, running on 100Mbps Ethernet should be more than adequate to handle the traffic. Adding a bridge to the segment at a later date will always remain a possibility. Because this does not require a change, nothing will be added to the Gantt chart.

Internet Connectivity   The next decision involves the Internet. Each of the three main offices has a direct connection to the Internet. The only offices that don't have a direct connection are the warehouse and billing departments, but that building has access through the home office connection. The link between the two sites is a single ISDN channel. Depending on the amount of traffic that is going to be going across that line, it will need to be upgraded to at least a dual-channel ISDN connection. One more task to add to the Gantt chart is to study the throughput or usage of the ISDN connection. Figure 14.10 shows the Gantt chart after the update.

Figure 14.10   The Gantt chart with the ISDN task added

ID	Task Name	Start Date	End Date	Duration	2000 Jan	Feb	Mar	Apr	May	Jun
1	Network Upgrade Project	1/1/00	12/29/00	260d						
2	Assemble the project team	1/3/00	1/7/00	5d						
3	Train the project team	1/10/00	3/31/00	60d						
4	Gather necessary network information	1/3/00	1/14/00	10d						
5	Study SNMP Packages	1/31/00	2/18/00	15d						
6	Get demos of SNMP Packages	2/21/00	3/24/00	25d						
7	Assess SNMP hardware requirements	3/27/00	3/31/00	5d						
8	Decision on SNMP package	4/3/00	4/7/00	5d						
9	Study ISDN connection to Warehouse	2/28/00	3/31/00	25d						

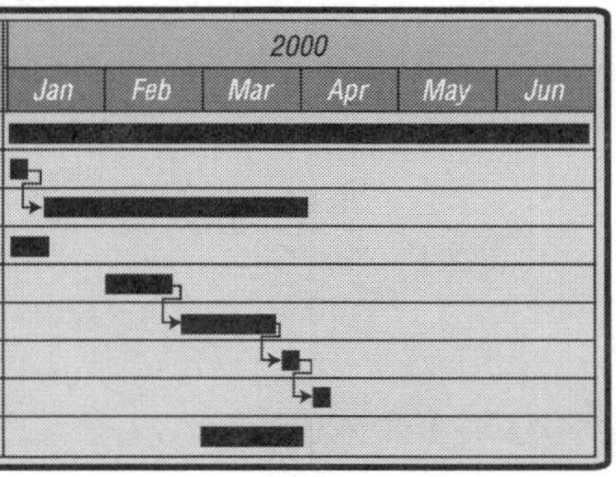

IP Addressing

Because all of the offices are currently connected to the Internet, it implies that at least some of the desktops have IP addresses assigned. It is time for another assumption, and this will be that your company has in fact rolled out Internet access to the entire organization, which also means some sort of IP addressing scheme is in place. In looking over the network documentation, I found that you are currently assigning IP addresses statically. For the sake of the project, though, because we are reviewing everything, let's have the project team revisit the network and decide whether you need to make any changes. In particular, the team should study using DHCP to manage IP addresses, whether the company should apply for more addresses to manage growth, and whether the company is a candidate for using a Network Address Translator (NAT).

The Gantt chart has been updated, as you can see in Figure 14.11.

Figure 14.11   The Gantt chart with TCP/IP addressing issues added

ID	Task Name	Start Date	End Date	Duration	2000 Jan	Feb	Mar	Apr	May	Jun
1	Network Upgrade Project	1/1/00	12/29/00	260d						
2	Assemble the project team	1/3/00	1/7/00	5d						
3	Train the project team	1/10/00	3/31/00	60d						
4	Gather necessary network information	1/3/00	1/14/00	10d						
5	Study SNMP Packages	1/31/00	2/18/00	15d						
6	Get demos of SNMP Packages	2/21/00	3/24/00	25d						
7	Assess SNMP hardware requirements	3/27/00	3/31/00	5d						
8	Decision on SNMP package	4/3/00	4/7/00	5d						
9	Study ISDN connection to Warehouse	2/28/00	3/31/00	25d						
10	Study IP addressing scheme	2/28/00	3/31/00	25d						
11	Decision on NAT	4/3/00	4/7/00	5d						
12	Lay out DHCP implementation	4/3/00	4/7/00	5d						
13	Design new IP addressing plan	4/3/00	4/14/00	10d						

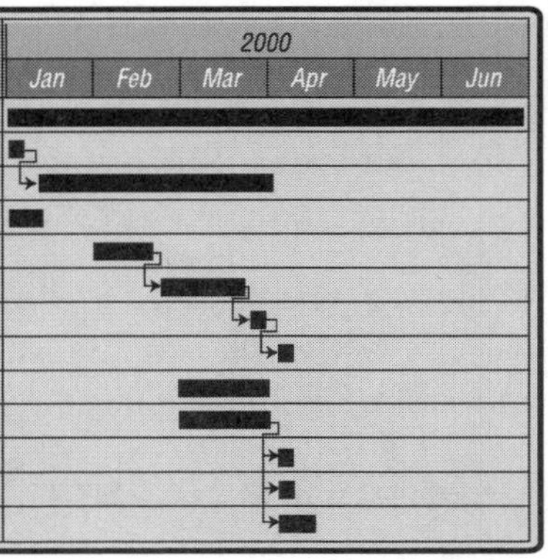

The Road to a
Successful Migration

PART 4

DNS Configuration

Up until this time, our sample company has not had a need for its own DNS name. After all, there was no e-mail package, and the company didn't have or need a Web site, so why go to the hassle and expense of applying for a DNS name?

Times have changed. More and more customers are asking for e-mail addresses rather than fax numbers or phone numbers. Customers don't understand why simple documents or communications cannot be carried out by e-mail instead of more costly methods. Therefore, it is time to drag our sample company into the new millennium kicking and screaming.

The domain-name piece won't be tricky, just time-consuming. Someone has to go to http://www.networksolutions.com and keep trying domain names until they find one that isn't taken, and then grab it. Sounds easy, doesn't it? But this is a company, so that means all the management people and marketing people will want to be involved in choosing just the right domain name. For this piece, we will allow 60 days.

While we are hassling over the domain name, the study can be going on as to which type of e-mail package the company really needs. The company is relatively small, so it could get by just using a POP3 client such as Internet Explorer, Netscape, Eudora, etc. The company is also growing, so it may want to look at integrated packages that provide scheduling, document management, task management, forms, workflow, and other services. This would involve the installation of a program such as Lotus Notes, Microsoft's Exchange Server, or Novell's GroupWise. Installation of any one of these products is going to involve a steeper cost than a POP3 client, but it may be worth it.

Finally, there is the placement of a DNS server. Because the company is so spread out, and because there is no intranet, the corporate decision was made to skip adding a DNS server to the sample network and just go with the DNS servers from a local Internet service provider.

It is time to upgrade the Gantt chart again, with the DNS piece and the e-mail issues. Check out Figure 14.12 to see how we are coming.

FTP

In the case of the current implementation plans for the sample company, the decision has been made that there is no justifiable reason to install FTP. Of course, this decision can be revisited at a later time.

Determine a Routing Strategy

The network map is laid out with a hub-and-spoke type of network infrastructure. With a hub-and-spoke plan (otherwise called a star configuration), the network looks like Figure 14.13.

Figure 14.12 The Gantt chart for DNS and e-mail

ID	Task Name	Start Date	End Date	Duration	2000
					Mar Apr May Jun Jul Aug
1	Network Upgrade Project	1/1/00	12/29/00	260d	
2	Assemble the project team	1/3/00	1/7/00	5d	
3	Train the project team	1/10/00	3/31/00	60d	
4	Gather necessary network information	1/3/00	1/14/00	10d	
5	Study SNMP Packages	1/31/00	2/18/00	15d	
6	Get demos of SNMP Packages	2/21/00	3/24/00	25d	
7	Assess SNMP hardware requirements	3/27/00	3/31/00	5d	
8	Decision on SNMP package	4/3/00	4/7/00	5d	
9	Study ISDN connection to Warehouse	2/28/00	3/31/00	25d	
10	Study IP addressing scheme	2/28/00	3/31/00	25d	
11	Decision on NAT	4/3/00	4/7/00	5d	
12	Lay out DHCP implementation	4/3/00	4/7/00	5d	
13	Design new IP addressing plan	4/3/00	4/14/00	10d	
14	Research potential DNS Names	4/17/00	5/12/00	20d	
15	Apply for new DNS Name	5/15/00	5/26/00	10d	
16	Research E-Mail Package	5/1/00	6/23/00	40d	
17	Acquire E-Mail Package	6/26/00	7/7/00	10d	
18	Train administrators on E-Mail	6/26/00	8/18/00	40d	

Figure 14.13 Hub-and-spoke, or star, network topology

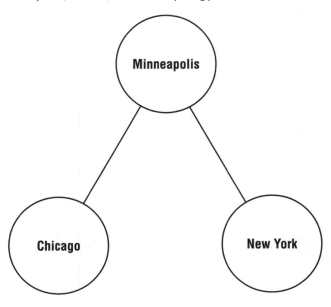

In this case, any traffic that needs to go from Chicago to New York must pass through Minneapolis. The advantage to this configuration is cost. If there is minimal traffic flowing from Chicago to New York or back again, it is not beneficial to maintain a permanent connection between the two offices.

The disadvantage of this layout should be obvious. If something were to happen to the Minneapolis hub, Chicago and New York would be isolated. There is no built in redundancy. The other disadvantage would be speed. Because there is no direct link, if the routers in Minneapolis get really busy, response time could suffer.

After looking at the diagram, one proposed solution would be a virtual private network. This is an option because

- Both sites have access to the Internet.

- Both sites have a router.

- If the current layout is hub-and-spoke, the traffic must not be sufficient to warrant a full-time direct connection between the two.

Other than a possible VPN, there is not a lot of routing strategy to define for this network. If the company wanted to provide redundant routing, it could add backup systems. Given the costs involved in the project so far, I am guessing that it will postpone redundant routing for a couple of months, at least.

A VPN is going to take a while to study. The team will assign it to a subcommittee and give it plenty of time to work on the problem. Because this is a redundancy effort, it may not have as high a priority as others. Figure 14.14 shows the Gantt chart with the latest additions.

Figure 14.14 The Gantt chart after VPN update

ID	Task Name	Start Date	End Date	Duration	2000					
					Jan	Feb	Mar	Apr	May	Jun
1	Network Upgrade Project	1/1/00	12/29/00	260d						
2	Assemble the project team	1/3/00	1/7/00	5d						
3	Train the project team	1/10/00	3/31/00	60d						
4	Gather necessary network information	1/3/00	1/14/00	10d						
5	Study SNMP Packages	1/31/00	2/18/00	15d						
6	Get demos of SNMP Packages	2/21/00	3/24/00	25d						
7	Assess SNMP hardware requirements	3/27/00	3/31/00	5d						
8	Decision on SNMP package	4/3/00	4/7/00	5d						
9	Study ISDN connection to Warehouse	2/28/00	3/31/00	25d						
10	Study IP addressing scheme	2/28/00	3/31/00	25d						
11	Decision on NAT	4/3/00	4/7/00	5d						
12	Lay out DHCP implementation	4/3/00	4/7/00	5d						
13	Design new IP addressing plan	4/3/00	4/14/00	10d						
14	Research potential DNS Names	4/17/00	5/12/00	20d						
15	Apply for new DNS Name	5/15/00	5/26/00	10d						
16	Research E-Mail Package	5/1/00	6/23/00	40d						
17	Acquire E-Mail Package	6/26/00	7/7/00	10d						
18	Train administrators on E-Mail	6/26/00	8/18/00	40d						
19	VPN between Chicago and NY	2/28/00	5/19/00	60d						

Create a Network Resource Accessibility Plan

In looking at the list of things to do, there are several that fall under this category. First of all, the entire network needs to be converted to 100Mbps Ethernet. Because there is such a hodgepodge of stuff out there, there will be some issues surrounding just this piece.

Adding to the mix, human resources has to be wired and configured for network access, and the people in the graphics department are going to have to give up their Macs.

NOTE   Macintosh users, please do not revolt and slam the book. It wasn't my decision! Don't shoot the messenger!

That transformation will involve some end-user training as well as translation between Mac and PC. Because this part of the plan will be involved, I have created a new Gantt chart for the network access team. It is shown in Figure 14.15.

Figure 14.15   The network access Gantt chart

ID	Task Name	Start Date	End Date	Duration	2000 Jan	Feb	Mar	Apr	May	Jun
1	Network Accessibility	1/2/00	6/16/00	120d						
2	Check wiring of all Ethernet Sites	1/2/00	2/11/00	30d						
3	Take bids on renewing Token Ring sites	1/2/00	2/11/00	30d						
4	Get bids on new concentrators and NIC	1/31/00	3/10/00	30d						
5	Buy PCs to replace Macs	4/3/00	6/23/00	60d						
6	Train Mac user on PCs	4/3/00	6/23/00	60d						

Implementation Phase

This is where the rubber hits the road. Take a look at what has to be done in this section. Figure 14.16 shows the implementation phase.

Figure 14.16   The implementation phase

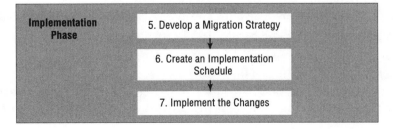

This is the phase where the fun starts. Up until now, it has been mostly meetings and maybe some testing, but the implementation phase is where things start to happen.

Develop a Migration Strategy

At this point you should know what you want to do. Hardware and software, operating systems, everything should be decided. All that is left to do is place the orders and wait for everything to come rolling through the back door. Once it arrives, of course, it has to be installed. Now comes the migration strategy.

Migration varies so much with each individual site that it would be impossible to develop even a sample migration policy. I can give you the benefit of acquired wisdom. Unfortunately, these points are not attributable to any one person. It is a gathering of knowledge.

- When migrating, if at all possible, start small. Remember back to the start of the chapter when I quoted Murphy? Murphy is an optimist. When you start small, it follows that if something goes wrong, it is easier to fix 10 systems than 10,000.

- When migrating, if at all possible, start with people who expect to feel pain and understand the process. This usually means the IS team. Migrate them, and then move on to the others after you have the kinks worked out.

- When developing a migration strategy, if at all possible, leave yourself an out. When you develop the strategy, see if there are ways of implementing the new technology while leaving the old technology online or nearly online. It is comforting to know that if something dies, you can always go back.

- Although the mantra of real estate is location, location, location, the mantra of migration should be back up, back up, back up!

- Expect the best, prepare for the worst. Prepare a strategy for every possible known occurrence that could cause you problems. Have backup plans, backup hardware, and personnel, just in case.

Create an Implementation Schedule

It was very early in my career as a hardware guy that I learned one of my most valuable IS lessons: Everything will take longer than you think it should. This is a law, similar to the Law of Gravity. I discussed this law, known as the 4-Hour Rule, in Chapter 7, in the section "Understanding Expectations."

A few other points about scheduling. People hate change. Always. However, they don't hate change nearly as much if they know what is coming. Be open with the people you are going to affect, before going in to make the changes. They may not understand that a new set of routers will make their life better because of new routing protocols. They will understand, however, that you told them what was going to happen during the changeover. They do appreciate that. It may make your life somewhat easier.

Plan on holding hands after the migration piece is completed. If you are going to upgrade an office, don't fly in on Friday night, upgrade the office, and leave on Sunday. Fly in Friday, be visible, do the upgrade, and be visible Monday, just to make sure things are going just as they are supposed to.

Make sure you have enough people trained to do the tasks they are assigned. Also, make sure you have a chief. Just one per crew is fine, someone who understands the whole picture and has the authority to handle things if there are problems. We all work in the computer industry. You know as well as I do that for every job you do, there are six to ten different ways of approaching that job. In many cases, there is no "right" way to do a job or "wrong" way to do a job, there is just your way and my way. As long as it works as advertised in the end, life is good. You should have one person to direct traffic and make sure things are consistently done the same way. That way, if there is any troubleshooting to be done, the technician may have an easier time if they know that everything is configured the same way.

Finally, document what you do, how you did it, what you did right, and what you would change the next time. If you do all these things on a small basis first, by the time you hit the big sites, the tasks will be second nature, the problems will be expected, and things will go smoothly.

Now you are on your own. If you have followed most of the advice from this chapter, you and your team should do just fine!

Part 5

The Connectivity Question

- Proxy servers defined
- Proxy servers and performance
- Proxy servers as firewalls
- IPv6 defined
- IPv6 addressing
- IPv6 implementation

Using Proxy Servers to Make Your Life Easier

You have heard of Proxy servers. Your company may even have a Proxy server. If it does, you know that one of the purposes of a Proxy server is to decrease response time to requests from the Internet. In other words, it is designed to make life easier and faster for the people on your network.

What Is a Proxy Server?

Proxy servers come in various shapes and sizes, running on different operating systems and providing different features and functionality. In simplified terms, a Proxy server operates in typical client/server mode. When a client application (a browser) makes a request for an object on the Internet, a Proxy server on the private network responds by translating the request and passing it to the Internet. When a computer on the Internet answers back, the Proxy server caches the response and passes it back to the client application on the computer that made the request. Pure client/server computing.

The Proxy server is a gateway between the private network and the Internet. The Proxy server allows you to make requests to the Internet and receive responses, but it does not allow access to your network by unauthorized users.

> **NOTE**   The term *gateway* is tossed around a lot and rarely explained. At times, things that happen inside a computer can best be described as PCM, or pure computing magic. A gateway is close to that. A gateway is special software, or a computer running special software, that acts as a translator between two different systems. It is up to the gateway to make each system think it is talking with a peer, when, in fact, the exact opposite is the case. For example, if a laptop computer is hooked into the network and is communicating with a mainframe, it is a gateway of some sort that makes that communication happen.

Proxy Server Internet Access Support

Proxy server access software, must, by design, support all the Internet access protocols, including things like HTTP, FTP, streaming audio, streaming video, chat, mail, and news. Most will support a variety of transport protocols and not limit themselves to only TCP/IP. Most will also be able to support some form of IPX/SPX on the private network side of the cloud. Figure 15.1 shows how a Proxy server would relate to the networks it was connecting.

Figure 15.1   Proxy server connecting a network to the Internet

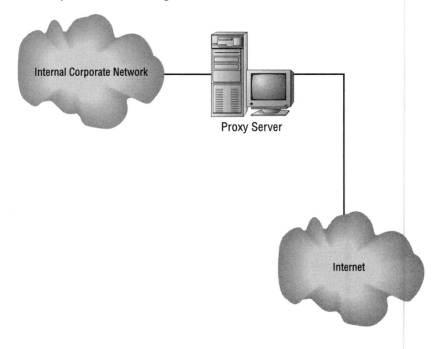

When you install a Proxy server, you are creating an intranet. The Proxy server computer will have two network interfaces. One of the interfaces will connect back to the local-area network, and the other will be connected to the Internet. In this case, the Proxy server is what is connecting your network to the outside world. Intranet applications do not directly access an operating system's Transport Protocol driver when moving data from one system to another. Instead, intranet applications usually rely on an intermediary service called the *sockets driver,* which, in turn, communicates with lower-level components such as the TCP/IP transport drivers. This communication path makes applications more portable because the sockets driver application programming interface (API) is transport-, as well as operating system–, independent. Most Windows-based intranet applications are designed to use the Windows Sockets API. Microsoft provides a WinSock driver for each Windows operating system, but some third-party vendors provide their own implementations.

When a Windows-based intranet application communicates, it creates application-specific commands, and passes these commands off to the WinSock driver. The WinSock driver then passes the command off to lower-level components; for example, when you open Internet Explorer and decide to go to www.sybex.com, your browser will create the appropriate HTTP command and pass them to the WinSock driver. The WinSock driver passes them to a transport driver, such as TCP/IP, and that driver delivers the HTTP command to the Web server.

A Proxy server acting as a gateway between LAN-based clients and servers on the Internet can move commands by one of two ways:

- The Proxy server receives the application protocol commands (HTTP, for example) from clients and forwards them to the servers on the Internet. The Proxy server must understand the application's protocol but does not need to know the client's operating system.

- The Proxy server receives WinSock API calls from the Windows-based client and passes those API calls to the Proxy server's WinSock driver. The Proxy server then passes the calls to its TCP/IP driver, which delivers the commands to the Internet server. This client and server must be Windows-based so the client can create Windows Sockets API calls and the server can implement them, but the Proxy server does not need to understand the application-level protocol.

Proxy servers may be able to perform both functions.

The Connectivity Question

PART 5

Proxy Server Overview

Proxy servers abound on the market today, and while they all operate in somewhat the same manner, each has its own unique qualities. In general, though, many of their characteristics and how they function are the same.

The Proxy server is a service that runs on a host computer. When it manages the only connection between the LAN and the Internet, a Proxy server can provide the following benefits:

Blocks inbound connections The Proxy server allows LAN clients to initiate connections to Internet servers but does not allow Internet clients to initiate connections to LAN servers.

Restricts outbound connections The Proxy server authenticates application users against user-level security and can restrict outbound connections in several ways, including by user, application protocol, TCP/IP port number, time of day, or the destination's domain name or IP address.

Forwards numerous protocols The Proxy server acts as a gateway for Internet protocols, including HTTP, FTP, RealAudio, VDOLive, Internet Relay Chat (IRC), and mail and news protocols.

Logs outbound connections The Proxy server can gather and store information about connection attempts so that administrators can track the clients' use of Internet resources.

Translates application protocols 32-bit Windows client systems can deliver WinSock API calls to a Proxy server using NWLink, and a Proxy server can implement those API calls and communicate with Internet services using TCP/IP.

Improves application performance A Proxy server can cache frequently accessed resources, so subsequent client requests are satisfied by the Proxy server instead of the Internet server.

Cuts Internet connection costs Proxy server's caching ability reduces the traffic to the Internet connection and provides content during off-peak hours.

Because applications will behave differently when using a Proxy server, they must be reconfigured. Web browsers will need to be reconfigured but won't require additional resources.

How Instituting a Proxy Server Will Impact Your Network

The Proxy server sits between your network and the Internet, which means everything that sits behind the Proxy server should be concealed from the outside world. Sometimes this is a good thing; at other times, it can be a real problem. For example, what if you have a Web server running behind the Proxy server? In this case, you certainly want users to be able to penetrate the Proxy server to get to the Web server. The same can be said of e-mail servers and database servers. This section will examine how some of these services can be affected once you start a Proxy server.

In Chapter 8, I talked about different methods of connecting network segments together. This included bridges, routers, and hubs. A Proxy server is a connection device, but it connects with a level of intelligence found at the Transport layer of the OSI model and above. A Proxy server can actually look inside the packet at things that routers and bridges consider nothing but payload. The Proxy server can analyze the data and then make an intelligent decision about what to do with the data.

At the Transport layer of the OSI model, circuit-level proxies handle connections based on either a TCP or a UDP port number. At the highest layer of the OSI model, the Application layer, the proxy will transfer data between clients and servers, processing the information with the knowledge gained from application-specific commands.

Real-Life Proxy Server Implementations

At Krause Publications in Iola, Wisconsin, Microsoft's Proxy Server allowed them to deploy their Internet connections with less time and money spent on software and servers, lower bandwidth leased lines, and spend less time on administration.

Prior to instituting Proxy Server, the company allowed Internet connections through dial-out connections. But they found this method was costly, a security nightmare, and impossible to track. By instituting Proxy Server and Internet access, they were able to cut costs on paper and postage for subscription notices, product information, catalogs, event calendars, and other items.

In order to provide affordable Internet access, Krause opted to use a fractional T-1 line. The company used the bandwidth-saving features of Proxy Server to make this work. The cost for the 348Kbps fractional T-1 is almost $25,000 a year less than the cost of a full T-1.

Krause also had concerns about Internet security. Because Microsoft's Proxy Server supports the Secure Socket Layer (SSL) protocol, their fears were eased. With SSL tunneling providing an encrypted path between the client and ISP server, it meant that they had achieved the goal of secure communication.

As for the main purpose of running a Proxy server, Krause is running a Web cache containing more than 500MB of information with a 27 percent log/cache hit ratio and an average of 1,165 URLs cached at the same time.

What Can a Proxy Server Do?

Connectivity is not the only purpose that Proxy servers have. Proxy servers also perform security, caching, logging, and IP address translation. Devices operating at a lower level of the OSI model can perform some of these functions, but none can do it all. This section will look at how a Proxy server fulfills each of these roles.

Proxy Servers as Routers

When you look at the primary purpose of the Proxy server, theoretically, a router could replace it. As a matter of fact, when it comes to routing, a Proxy server is not nearly as efficient. A Proxy server is slower than a router, it is more expensive than a router, and it requires more attention from your administrative staff than a router. If you are going to use a Proxy server only to connect your network to the Internet, save yourself some time, money, and grief, and buy a router.

Proxy servers provide value by giving you access to features beyond what a typical router can provide. These additional features are what make a Proxy server worth the money and are what will be discussed in the following sections.

> **NOTE**   Do not overlook the fact that a Proxy server performs all the functionality of the standard router.

Proxy Servers as Network Address Translators

RFC1918 (Address Allocation for Private Internet) suggests that it would be wise for network administrators to use "private" IP addresses for local-area networks. Using private IP addresses instead of public IP addresses will help ease the shortage of IP addresses around the world. This means that instead of assigning each and every node on your network a public IP address, a company will only receive enough public addresses to cover those systems that are directly connected to the Internet.

Without a Proxy server, this recommendation has been difficult to implement. After all, systems on the local network still need to access the Internet, and therefore they will need a valid IP address. This is where a Proxy server can come to the rescue.

A Proxy server is capable of receiving requests from a private IP address on a private LAN, getting the information from the public Internet, and returning it to the original user. Figure 15.2 will give you an idea of what I mean.

NOTE   What is the difference between a public IP address and a private IP address? A public IP address is one that is assigned and managed by InterNIC. A private IP address is any valid IP address that you would like to use (as if you were not even hooked up to the Internet). Think about it. Remember in Chapter 3 when we talked about addressing and the hassle of figuring out which subnets you could use and how many hosts you could have on a particular subnet? With private addressing, suddenly Class A addresses are back in vogue. A business that I know of in Minneapolis is using NAT, and they have 20 different subnets. To make life simple, their addressing scheme is 10.x.y.y with a subnet mask of 255.255.0.0. Network addresses run from 10.1.0.0 to 10.21.0.0, and host addresses start at 1 and go to whatever number is necessary. Thanks to NAT, this company is certainly not in danger of running out of addresses anytime soon.

Figure 15.2   A Proxy server working with private IP addresses

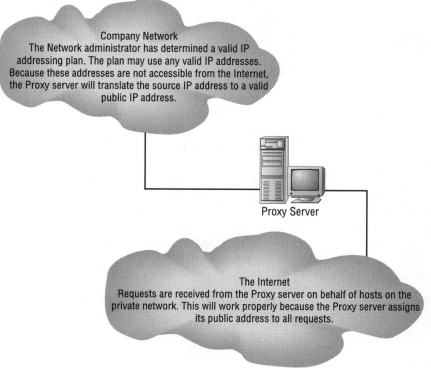

Not only is establishing NAT good for the cyber-ecology (okay, I just made that phrase up—think it will stick?), not only is NAT good for reducing the IP addressing stress level of network administrators, but it is also good for security. Because the IP addresses on the LAN aren't visible to the outside world, no one on the LAN is capable of bypassing the Proxy server. Likewise, no one from the outside can hack his or her way in, because the Proxy server is acting like a firewall. Finally, the InterNIC has not assigned IP addresses to your network, so routes do not exist in the InterNIC's routers.

Hiding Internal Addresses

Many times during this book, I have mentioned that for each and every opportunity presented in the daily life of a network administrator, there are several different ways to conquer it. NAT may be one way of handling the following scenario.

At a small company in the Midwest, the network administrator was faced with a challenge. Inside the company, one of the most popular applications had evolved to the point that it ran most efficiently and securely on TCP/IP. This posed somewhat of a problem, because none of the workstations were using IP. Our fearless LAN guy took a look at the problem and decided that DHCP would be a really quick fix. Because the workstations were running Windows 9x or Windows NT, a little work needed to be done but not a whole lot. DHCP could pass out the IP addresses, and life would be good again. Because the network was not connected to the Internet, any old IP address would do, so he used the simplest approach he could think of. He knew enough about IP addressing to be dangerous but not enough to be good, just was enough to get by.

He remembered reading something about all 1s in an IP address not working really well, so he started his numbering scheme at 2.0.0.0. He only had 75 workstations on a single network segment, so he let things go with DHCP assigning addresses from 1 to 200.

Soon the network grew, and he had to make some changes. He had several network segments, and his network numbers still started with 2, but the second number was random. He had meant to document, but he never got around to it. And rather than go back and check which numbers *had* been used, he grabbed any numbers he thought of to use. He started at 2.1.0.0, and then he went to 2.2.0.0. The next time, he couldn't remember which numbers he used, so he assigned 2.250.0.0; after that, he still couldn't remember which numbers he used, so he went to 2.135.0.0, and so it went.

About this time, someone got the bright idea that the company needed to hook up to the Internet. When the LAN administrator heard this, panic set in. Visions of the work necessary to reassign all these network addresses, host addressing, and subnets were enough to turn him to drink. Then he heard about a Proxy server and NAT. This solution could be the way out of a sticky situation.

See what I mean about having more than one way to solve a problem?

Figure 15.3 shows how the solution worked out in real life.

Figure 15.3   Burying your mistakes behind a Proxy server

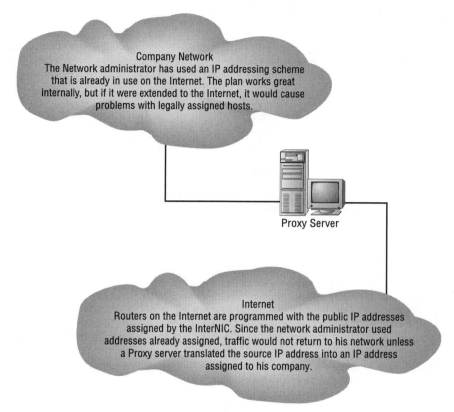

Company Network
The Network administrator has used an IP addressing scheme that is already in use on the Internet. The plan works great internally, but if it were extended to the Internet, it would cause problems with legally assigned hosts.

Proxy Server

Internet
Routers on the Internet are programmed with the public IP addresses assigned by the InterNIC. Since the network administrator used addresses already assigned, traffic would not return to his network unless a Proxy server translated the source IP address into an IP address assigned to his company.

Proxy Servers and Caching

These days, everyone is concerned about bandwidth. If you are leasing a high-speed connection, your payment may be based on how many packets are sent and received. If packets aren't a cost factor, then performance is usually an issue. You may be bogging down your router or putting a strain on your current connection to the Internet. One way to reduce traffic is to configure a Proxy server that is local to the LAN and enable caching.

TIP   Caching is available only on Proxy servers that operate at the Application layer.

Setting up a Proxy server helps not only the performance and Internet traffic leaving your site but also your ISP. It is in your ISP's best interest to reduce traffic. If you are paying for a connection by usage, think about what their bill must be like. In many cases, ISPs set up Proxy servers to connect their customers to the Internet. Figure 15.4 shows what that looks like.

Figure 15.4 How an ISP would use a Proxy server

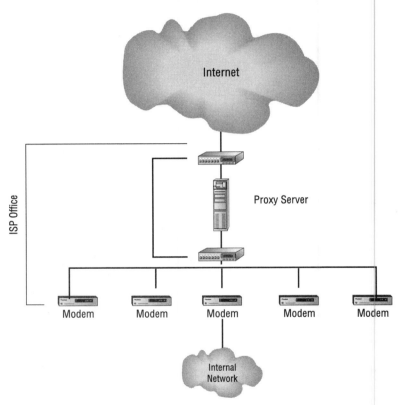

Caching is an Application-layer procedure, and therefore, it is sophisticated. When looking at caching, keep in mind that no two Proxy servers do it the same way. The following sections list some of the ways that Proxy servers can cache.

Protocol Caching

A Proxy server receives the majority of its use from Web pages, so it would make sense that most Proxy servers will support caching of HTTP. Support for other protocols varies.

FTP is a protocol that can be cached easily, but support is limited. Some of the major Proxy servers (Microsoft Proxy Server, Netscape Proxy Server, WinGate, and Novell's BorderManager) are all supporting the caching of FTP.

When you choose a Proxy server, choose which protocols you want cached, and make sure your final decision fits the bill.

Proactive Caching

The types of caching we have been discussing so far has been reactive. In other words, I go to www.sybex.com, and the Sybex home page is cached at the local Proxy server. What happens if the Sybex home page is changed, or if the proxy cache expires? The next time someone reloads it, it has to be recached to the Proxy server. Waiting for a client to request a popular Web page before reading it into cache makes the most efficient use of network bandwidth, but it increases the latency by forcing the end user to wait while the page is retrieved. We all know how much an end user likes to wait!

Proactive caching helps to eliminate the amount of time people spend waiting on pages to be refreshed after expiring. The Proxy server keeps a list of the files in its cache, and when one of those files begins to approach its expiration date, the server will ask the Internet Web server for a newer version of the file. In this way, the cache will get a newer version of the file without ever making the user wait for the update. To make this process even sweeter, the Proxy server should be capable of timing these requests so they occur during nonpeak hours. This can, however, be a two-edged sword. On one side, we have reduced wait time for the end user, and on the other side, we have increased traffic or even wasted bandwidth.

Proactive caching can be configured on some Proxy servers. In this case, the network administrator can specify which pages should be upgraded on a regular basis. They can also support batch updates, in which Web pages are routinely downloaded during off hours and made available in cache during working hours.

Proactive caching has one purpose and one purpose only, and that is to reduce the time that a user has to wait to receive a Web page. If your company is on a reduced-bandwidth utilization kick, this may not be the solution for you.

Security Noncaching

If a Web page has any kind of authentication on it—for example, you have to type in a name and password to retrieve the page—most Application layer Proxy servers will not cache it. The Proxy server will recognize the header fields in the HTTP command set and will not cache that page. Although this will slow down some future requests for the page, it increases the security level for those pages.

Many Proxy servers were designed this way. The Proxy server has no way of determining who is supposed to access those pages, so it basically ignores the page. There are some servers that will cache the page anyway, and because of that, subsequent requests may be served directly from the cache, bypassing an authentication mechanism.

Enterprise Caching

In a large computing environment, just one cache server is not going to cut it. In cases where multiple caching servers are used, the system can be set up so the Proxy servers cache pages at many different levels. It is also possible that each Proxy server on the network store only one copy of any particular file on the Internet. This level of intelligence is included in some, but not all, Proxy servers. It is called *hierarchical and distributed caching*.

Hierarchical and distributed caching are important for the scalability of the system. It is very important for large organizations but not so important for small- to medium-sized networks. Hierarchical caching divides Proxy servers up into multiple layers. The first-level Proxy server will query the Internet directly, and the second level will simply query the first-level server. There are very few cases in which going to a third level of proxy caching makes any sense.

In the Microsoft implementation of a Proxy server, each server can handle a maximum of 2,000 clients. The Proxy servers can be chained together for as many clients as needed. A request from, let's say, a client attached to the fifth server in the chain for a page that is not in its cache will be forwarded to the most likely server to cache that page in the chain. If that server does not have the page, the request is forwarded directly to the Internet.

Distributed caching is similar to a disk array. It combines multiple Proxy servers into one functional array so the servers can share a large load and divide the load as evenly as possible between them. Simply, all of the array's disks are combined together to work as one very large cache. Figure 15.5 shows a distributed and hierarchical caching.

Figure 15.5   Distributed and hierarchical caching

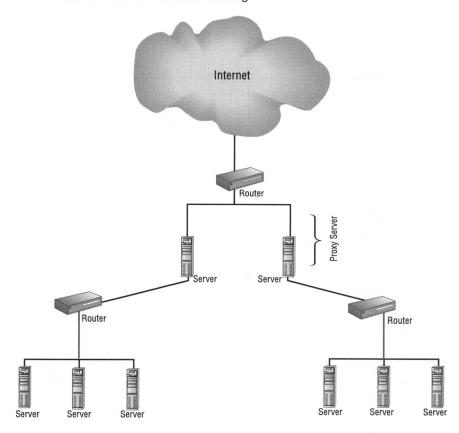

Proxy Server Implementation, Part One

How would you like this for a challenge? You have been assigned to manage a corporate Web site dedicated to computer professionals that receives over 1 million hits a day. The Web site is obviously strategic to the company: it provides visitors with a view of the company and with up-to-date information about its products, solutions, programs, and channel partners. It is also an interactive site, so communication can take place between the visitor and the company. Because it is the Web site of one of the largest computer networking companies in the world, it needs to be secure, up 24 hours a day, 7 days a week, and have exceptional performance.

Proxy Server Implementation, Part One *(continued)*

That was the task given to the team during the evolution of Novell's corporate Web site.

The solution revolves, not surprisingly, around Novell's BorderManager product. At the present time, the only servers located within the "no man's land" in front of Novell's inner firewall are two BorderManager servers that are configured as Web accelerators. These servers handle all requests for cacheable objects, including all HTML pages and graphic files. Ninety percent of the Web traffic aimed at www.novell.com is handled by the BorderManager servers and off-loaded from the Web servers.

If you are interested in performance statistics, Novell says that one BorderManager Web server accelerator is sufficient to handle the equivalent of five T-3 lines (32MB of payload per second). The benefits that Novell has seen from its BorderManager implementation include the following:

Enhanced Company Image Even though every Web site on the Internet is accessible around the globe, the reality is that international bandwidth and performance can prevent a target market from making full use of your site without pain. Using a proxy cache, Novell is able to distribute its caches into areas where bandwidth is a problem. Because this is accomplished with a low-cost PC system and little administrative burden, Novell considers its globally friendly solution a winner.

Simplified Management and Control All of the accelerator caches are 100 percent hands-off autonomous systems. No one has to look at them for any reason, they just run. In this case, BorderManager servers can be distributed to remote locations without the company having to provide backup technical expertise.

Performance and Scalability The performance characteristics of BorderManager allow Novell the flexibility of keeping their main Web site centralized and still meet the needs of content authors around the world.

Lower Costs Novell enjoyed an immediate savings when they were able to cancel an order for three SUN Enterprise 3000 servers. They also reduced costs by placing BorderManager servers at sites around the world. Because the caching at these international sites are handling 90 percent of the requests they receive, a substantial amount of traffic is removed from the corporate headquarters site in Provo, Utah.

Internet Cache Protocol (ICP)

At its most basic, proxy caching was designed to run on a single system. Hierarchical and distributed proxy caching is really an afterthought. In fact, if you have two independent Proxy servers on the same network, they may have as much as 80 percent of the same information in their caches. If nothing else, this is a lot of wasted disk space! In addition, each Proxy server still needs to make original requests to the public Internet, which does not take advantage of the files that may be stored on the server right next door.

To clean up this problem, Proxy servers may use the Internet Cache Protocol or ICP. This is the protocol that allows a group of Proxy servers to share cached documents with each other and brings some sort of order to the chaos. For example, what happens, in a multiple Proxy server environment, when someone requests a document that is not in cache? Which server goes and gets the document, and how is the document shared with the other servers?

In order to make the most effective use of the system, an organization would have to implement a hierarchical caching system. Within each part of the network, the level-two Proxy servers act as the first line of support for Internet requests. Between these servers and the Internet, an array of level-one Proxy servers will handle all the requests that come in from the level-two servers. This architecture allows for caching on each part of the network, thereby reducing network traffic between segments. It is the ICP that makes it all work.

How are the clients configured? The clients are configured to query a Proxy server for data that exists on the Internet. As far as the client is concerned, the entire proxy array looks like one big Proxy server, because that single proxy is always used as an interface into the larger ICP array. In fact, if the client asks the ICP proxy for information it already has in cache, it responds just like a single Proxy server. The magic starts when the request is not already in cache.

When the ICP server discovers that it does not have a requested Web page, it will check with its neighbors in the array. If they do have the data on hand, it will be returned to the requesting Proxy server, which will return it to the client. Because the request was answered from proxy, a request to the outside network was avoided.

If none of the neighboring proxies has the information, the ICP proxy will send the query up the ladder. If hierarchical caching has been configured, the next Proxy server up the ladder may be another ICP array that can handle the request. If not, the request is passed to the Internet and handled in the same way a regular proxy request is handled. When the data is returned, it is cached so the request will be fulfilled faster in the future. If a hierarchy exists, the data will be cached at each level as it moves its way down through the proxy ladder.

While ICP takes Proxy servers to the next level, it does not come without its trade-offs. First, members of an ICP array will cache duplicate information, which wastes disk space and memory. The longer the servers remain members of the array, the more duplication of cache occur.

Second, with a proxy array, there is built-in latency. If one server doesn't have the information, it has to request information from all the other servers in the array before finally determining that the stuff you want isn't in cache. Then, and only then, will the Proxy server go out to the Internet and find the requested information. So, because of this, ICP Proxy servers become more inefficient as another Proxy server is added to an array.

Finally, the array allows for scalability but does not provide for redundancy in any way. If one of the Proxy servers fail, all the clients that point to that server will lose their connection to the Internet.

Cache Array Routing Protocol (CARP)

CARP is a protocol designed to atone for the sins of ICP. CARP allows content to be cached on a proxy array without duplication. In addition, it specifies an algorithm that can be used to determine which Proxy server the information should be stored on, if it is already cached. This way, the Proxy server does not have to query all the servers in the array, just the specific server. Figure 15.6 shows how a CARP cache array might work. As you can see from the figure, the hashing algorithm is based on the URL of the cached information.

CARP also allows for some redundancy. If a Proxy server that is a member of the CARP array stops responding for a specific amount of time, it can be removed from the array automatically. Documents that it had cached may be distributed to other members of the proxy array. CARP is a Microsoft-supported product, and Microsoft is currently going through the motions of making CARP a legitimate IETF-endorsed protocol.

CARP proxying capabilities are only important for those networks that are handling large amounts of traffic (greater than 20Mbps) and implementing an array of Proxy servers. CARP is supported by Microsoft's Proxy Server 2, Netscape Proxy Server, and others. Each supports CARP functionality, though in slightly different implementations.

CARP avoids the overhead of having to query all the member servers in the array for information. Therefore it has positive scalability. The more systems you add to a CARP array, the faster and more efficient it becomes.

CARP does all this using the HTTP protocol. This is an advantage, because you do not have to add another protocol to the network. Any time a new protocol is added to the network, administration overhead increases. In addition, the new protocol may require

Figure 15.6   A proxy array using CARP

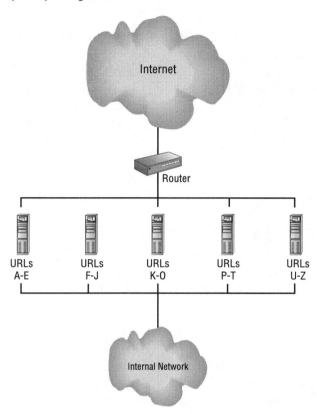

changes to the firewall and may not work through some gateways. Because CARP uses HTTP for the exchange and transfer of information, most networks will not have to make any changes.

CARP Configuration

Before you can configure CARP, you have to create a CARP array. This will assemble all the CARP Proxy servers into something called an *array membership list*. The members on this list are checked on a regular basis to make sure they are still alive; if they stop responding, they are removed from the list.

After the servers are added to the array, each CARP server performs a hash on the names of its neighboring Proxy servers. A hash is simply a way of converting data into a series of numbers, making the information easier for the computer to handle. Once the hash is completed, it is stored away for later use, when it will be used to determine which server has which URL.

When a client issues a request for a specific URL, the Proxy server that receives the request *hashes* the URL. A hash of the URL is combined with the hash of each Proxy server's name. Using the hash value, the Proxy server is able to determine which Proxy server in the CARP array would be storing the information. The Proxy server then queries only that member of the array for the information. It does not even need to check its own cache. If the queried Proxy server has the information, it is returned. If not, the queried Proxy server retrieves the information from the Internet, caches it, and returns it to the first proxy. The first proxy will then return it to the client.

If a single server is removed from a CARP array, the other servers in the array communicate with each other and redistribute the cache the missing server has been carrying. In this way, CARP arrays include some form of redundancy. It also helps make administration easy, because no manual changes are necessary when removing a system from the array.

CARP also has the ability to increase cache hits for an enterprise through a CARP hierarchy. This can be combined with the distribution method described above. This method allows multiple arrays of CARP systems to query the same servers in the event of a cache failure.

> **NOTE**   For more information on CARP, look for the Microsoft white paper titled *Cache Array Routing Protocol and MS Proxy Server version 2.0* on the TechNet CDs or on Microsoft's Web site at www.microsoft.com/proxy/guide/carpspec.asp.

Using a Proxy Server to Control Access and Filter Packets

One of the reasons many companies have not taken advantage of the Internet is because of the misguided belief that it is populated by nothing but porn sites. Others feel that if they connect to the Internet, their employees will turn into mindless entities spending the entire day surfing the Net and not getting any work done. The best method for reducing the chances for users to misuse an Internet connection is to implement filtering at a Proxy server.

Most Proxy servers allow the administrator to set up filters that will limit access to Web sites that might not be appropriate to the workplace. All Application layer Proxy servers support this feature. It is a key component to ensure that people are making the most productive use of the Internet. Most administrators don't make use of the filtering capabilities, but it is there if you need it.

Another form of filtering is called *content filtering*. This type of filtering is available on all types of Proxy servers, but the Application layer servers offer the most extensive filtering capabilities. In this case, they can filter the actual content being transferred, not just the location being accessed.

As with everything in computing, different Proxy servers offer different levels of content filtering. Most servers will allow source-IP filtering, which means it will filter out any information from a specific IP address. Unfortunately, the purveyors of the sites you may want to filter know how the filters work, so they routinely change addresses.

Application layer Proxy servers give a more intelligent filtering, disallowing incoming information because of URL, content type, and HTML content. Some Proxy servers, such as Netscape's, even include the ability to scan incoming content for viruses. Although this is a useful feature, it does increase the amount of overhead needed and increases processing time.

Content filtering is useful, but you first have to suspect that your users are abusing the Internet privilege. There are ways of finding out exactly what your users are doing on the Web.

Using a Proxy Server to Log Connections

Because all Internet traffic must pass through the Proxy server, the Proxy server can log all requests that it processes. This information is useful in several ways. First, you can use it to track usage, billing, bandwidth analysis, and even needs analysis. It can also be used to locate those users who are consuming large amounts of your bandwidth or for the location of those Web sites that need to be filtered.

Reverse Proxying

If proxying is such a good thing for those people using a private LAN, you would think that it could also be used to help people trying to get an inbound connection. When a Proxy server handles a request from a host on the Internet coming into a private network, this is called *reverse proxying*. Figure 15.7 shows an example of a reverse proxy.

Figure 15.7   Reverse proxying

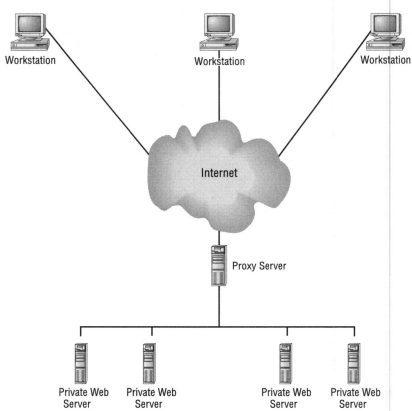

Why would you want to institute reverse proxying? First of all, by using reverse proxying, you can grant some access to your internal resources for users on the Internet. This maybe something as simple as granting access to your Web server. In this case, the Web server would be housed on the internal private network, hidden behind a proxy. The proxy would be configured to act as a reverse proxy, accepting connections from the public Internet, and forwarding them to the Web server. In this way, you can make use of the filtering and security issues that might not otherwise be possible if the Web server were on an external network.

Load-Balancing

What happens if your Web site is so popular, you need to have multiple Web servers capable of keeping up with all the hits? A Proxy server can help with load-balancing. In this scenario, the Proxy server can be configured with one IP address, and it could distribute incoming queries equally between all of the servers. Because all requests are funneled through a single Proxy server, only a single DNS entry is required on the Internet. The entire burden is not placed on a single server, allowing for increased scalability and performance.

Redundancy and Reverse Proxying

With reverse proxy redundancy, the Proxy server is intelligent enough to recognize the fact that one of the Web servers has failed and is no longer responding. If one of the Web servers fails, the Proxy server will no longer submit requests to that server. Clients connecting to the Web servers through the Proxy server will not notice a change in service.

How Can I Use Reverse Proxying?

Reverse proxying is used for high-end fast networking for load-balancing and fail-safe purposes. Because speed is a high priority, the system that provides reverse proxying is very specialized. One example is Cisco's LocalDirector, which is a hardware-based Proxy server capable of forward and reverse proxying.

Software-based solutions, such as those available from Microsoft, Netscape, and Novell, are not as efficient, but they work well for sites that are not overloaded. All of these offer reverse proxy capabilities, but they are much slower than specialized hardware-based solutions.

Different Methods of Proxying

As you have no doubt surmised by now, Proxy servers come in all different shapes, sizes, configurations, and price points. Application layer proxies offer the most control over a specific set of Internet protocols, but they tend to be rigid and generally do not adapt well to changes in technology. Server-dependent Transport layer proxies are less intelligent but more flexible. Although they work with the Internet protocols, they do not have any application-specific intelligence.

Another type of Proxy server requires a change to the client's IP stacks as well as the server's configurations. This allows for unlimited flexibility but must be implemented separately for each client operating system. This system seems problematic because it would limit any future upgrades as well as limit the number of desktop operating systems a network administrator can roll out.

If you are not confused enough, many Proxy servers will implement a combination of these features. One example is Microsoft's Proxy Server, which can be an Application layer proxy and a client/server proxy. A big part of choosing which Proxy server is best for your implementation is choosing the unique feature set that best suits your environment. In order to make a wise decision, you have to understand each of the types of proxying available.

Application Layer Proxying

Of all the different types of proxying methods, the Application layer proxying is the best known. (It is also known as the classical application proxy.) In this method, the proxy system sits between the traditional client and the server. The client must be configured to direct its requests to the proxy and inform the proxy of the final destination. The proxy has to act as both a client and a server, though its implementation is not as complex as either.

The Proxy server must be able to do several things.

1. It must be able to accept connections from the clients.
2. It must be able to understand the clients' requests and determine the final destination.
3. It must locate and initiate a session to the destination server.
4. Once these connections are established, the Proxy server is responsible for relaying information between the clients and the final destination.

Depending on the implementation, the system can be very simple or very complex. The simple proxies establish a connection and pass all the data directly to the final destination server. More sophisticated systems are capable of caching, filtering, logging, and even optimizing the data that passes through them.

The complete proxy process starts when a client on the internal network asks for some information. This request is truly internal to the network; the source address is the IP address of the client, and the destination address is the internal network interface of the Proxy server. Take a look at Figure 15.8 to see an example of how this process starts.

When the client contacts the Proxy server, it will use a connection-oriented, Transport layer protocol (TCP). Therefore, the two systems must perform a standard three-way handshake to begin communications. Because the Proxy server and the client are on the same LAN (usually), there may be some latency added to this step, but it shouldn't slow the process down too much. If it does become a burden, you may be able to reduce the time

Figure 15.8   Accepting a client connection

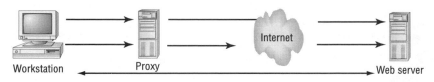

factor by enabling HTTP Keep-Alives. When these have been enabled, the client will be able to maintain a single TCP connection with the Proxy server for all external Web communications, even if they are on entirely different external servers.

Because the Proxy server is both a client and a server, it must be able to accept incoming client connections. In TCP/IP, this means the server must be listening to a specific UDP or TCP port. This should not normally cause any problems. If you would like to use the Proxy server as both a Proxy server to a specific application and a server for that application, however, then you may have a problem.

For example, a problem would occur when you decide to run a Web server on the same system that you are going to use as a Proxy server. In this case, either the Proxy server or the Web server can claim TCP port 80. To use both a Web server and a Proxy server on the same system, you have to configure one of these products to use an alternate port. The exception to this rule is Microsoft's Proxy Server. Because the Proxy Server is part of the Internet Information Server (IIS), it is capable of distinguishing between requests destined for the local machine and requests destined for a remote machine.

Proxy Server Placement

Because one of the advantages of running a Proxy server is the protection it gives to your internal network, it is usually placed at the edge of the network. In this way, the Proxy server separates the client from the Internet or other external network. Although this works well for security purposes, it complicates naming and name resolution.

For example, if the client on a private LAN is requesting a Web page from a Web server on the Internet, the client probably can't resolve the DNS name to an IP address. In this case, it is simply not the client's job to do the resolution. The client will probably only have access to DNS entries that relate to the private network. Therefore, it is up to the Proxy server to be able to receive requests for servers using the DNS name, and then the Proxy server has to resolve the DNS entry to an IP address.

This capability will allow an end user to use a Web browser that has been configured to use a Proxy server to issue a request to go to `www.sybex.com` rather than to enter the exact IP address. Although the client does not need to be able to resolve the name of the destination server, it does need to be able to locate the Proxy server. For that reason, either DNS should be configured on the LAN or IP addresses should be used.

Proxy Server Implementation, Part Two

Proxy servers come in various shapes and sizes. So far, I have mentioned solutions from Microsoft, Novell, Netscape, and WinGate. Other companies have Proxy servers, and some of them have been molded into specialized solutions. David Hunt, the marketing and communication manager of JDL Technologies of Edina, Minnesota, talked about one of the implementations of JDL's K-12WORLD CyberLibrary.

JDL specializes in providing solutions to school districts. In this case, JDL was working with one of the top 100 school districts in the United States, the Lee County School District in Florida. It serves over 55,000 students, 7,000 teachers, 65 schools, and 12,000 computers.

The network is configured to take advantage of frame-relay technology and a caching Proxy server at each school in the district. Any computer trying to access the Internet must use the Proxy server.

The Lee County MIS department did their own testing and realized that with a Proxy server, 30 students were able to access the Internet simultaneously. Paul Del Prete, who is the network manager for the Fort Meyer's, Florida–based school district, says that Proxy servers have boosted network access from 30 percent to 70 percent.

Besides giving administrators local control over access to both the Internet and the school district intranet, it also increased the usage of the intranet. The Proxy server serves as an internal Web server, allowing some pages to be published only at the school level and others that can be published district-wide.

The infrastructure has gone from being a tool to being mission-critical. Teachers want their e-mail, their grade books, and access to the Web sites.

The Proxy Connection and Communication Process

The process starts out when the client contacts the Proxy server and informs the Proxy server which Web page it is interested in obtaining. If the Proxy server does not have the Web page, it must resolve the DNS name to an IP address and contact the Web server to retrieve the requested information. This portion of the process is shown in Figure 15.9, where the Proxy server is working directly with the Web server. The Proxy server does not need much of the intelligence housed at the internal client, because it is merely forwarding a request.

Figure 15.9   A Proxy server acting as a client to the Web server

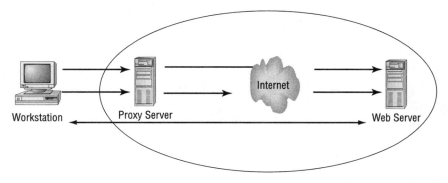

When the Proxy server talks with the Web server, it is using a connection-oriented protocol such as HTTP. When the communication begins, there is a standard three-way handshake that must be negotiated. Again, this may add latency to the communications, but it can be avoided in certain circumstances. Most of the HTTP Proxy servers have the option to use the HTTP Keep-Alives when it is communicating with a Web server. This can decrease the wait time in those cases in which the Proxy server has to retrieve information from an Internet Web server but has retrieved other information recently. This is a Proxy server plus, because an entirely different user may have started the original connection, making the overall transaction faster than it would have been if each user queried the Internet server directly.

All of the information and traffic that passes between the Proxy server and the final destination server use IP addresses. If the Proxy server is connecting to a host on the Internet, outgoing traffic will contain the source IP address of the Proxy server's public interface. The destination IP address will be that of the Internet Web server.

The Information Exchange

At this stage of the communication process, all that remains is for the Proxy server to get the requested information and get out of Dodge. To do so, the Proxy server needs to pass a request to the Web server without modifications. This stage of the communication process is shown in Figure 15.10. During this process, certain fields and TCP and IP headers will have to be modified, but normally things running at the Application layer are not changed.

The Connectivity Question

PART 5

Figure 15.10   Proxy server retrieving information from a Web server

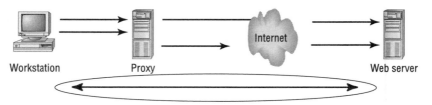

There is, however, an exception, and that is an HTTP proxy. An HTTP proxy will add its own message-header field for each messages it relays. This header field is called VIA, and it is used to notify both the clients and the servers that the message has passed through a proxy.

Application Configuration

When you are using an Application layer Proxy server, it has to be configured for each different application. For this reason, most of the Proxy servers that work at this layer only support a small set of application proxies. The most popular are HTTP and FTP, the two most common applications used on the Internet. Occasionally, Gopher will be supported. The configuration of these Proxy servers is dependent on having a detailed knowledge of the workings of both the protocols and the proxy methods they employ.

HTTP Proxy Connections

If ever there was an Application layer protocol that is *really* used, it is HTTP. It has been called on to do yeoman-like work with the explosion of the Internet and the World Wide Web. As the WWW grew and specialized applications, such as a Proxy server, appeared, HTTP needed to change with the times. HTTP had the Proxy protocol added as specified in RFC1945 and RFC2068. The Proxy protocol provides an Application layer gateway between the client and the server, allowing its browser to reach the Web servers without speaking directly to each other.

Why are proxies necessary? When groups of users from the same network visit Web pages, they may visit the same Web pages. This means that the same data is being transmitted from the Web server over and over again. The HTTP Protocol takes into account client-side caching and server-side caching controls, but it does not help cache data between users that may be closer to each other on the network than they are to the Internet Web server. When a proxy is placed at the boundary of an organization's connection to the Internet, that proxy is capable of implementing caching for all of the users on the internal network. Therefore, if one of the users goes out and accesses www.sybex.com, the next user who visits that site will probably get the information from the Proxy server instead of from the Sybex Web server.

Proxy servers can help make up for the inefficiencies of transferring data using HTTP. The HTTP proxies can also add a great deal of network security. They can allow full HTTP access to the Internet, or they can stop all inbound traffic. By putting the Proxy server at the boundary of your network, you can give users full access to the Internet but eliminate any chance of someone connecting to their computers from the Internet.

FTP and a Proxy Connection

Let's face it, Proxy servers were created to work with HTTP. FTP is an afterthought. Therefore, the FTP connections are not as clear-cut as the HTTP proxies. First of all, the standards for proxying FTP are not detailed in RFC959. Instead, vendor-specific implementations of FTP proxies have been created. These proxies fall into two categories: Conseil Europeenne pour la Recherche Nucleaire (CERN)–style proxying, and everything else.

CERN-style FTP proxies trick the systems into thinking they are really working with HTTP. A CERN-style FTP proxy will simply encapsulate the FTP request inside of HTTP. In that case, the FTP client submits a request to get information from a URL that starts with `ftp://`, such as `ftp://ftp.microsoft.com`. Both Netscape Navigator and Microsoft Internet Explorer support CERN-style proxying. Because these are the two most popular FTP clients, CERN-style proxying is the most likely to be used.

As mentioned above, CERN-style is not the only method of proxying an FTP connection. Some are more sophisticated than others, but they all have one thing in common, and that is they lack FTP client support. For example, if your system is using a WinGate Proxy server (www.wingate.net), it will support FTP connections, but it requires the end user to have knowledge of the Proxy server and how to use it. The user connects an FTP client directly to the Proxy server. The WinGate Proxy server has been configured to listen for the FTP connect and return a greeting message as any good FTP server would. Because the Application layer Proxy server requires knowledge of the final destination server, the user has to supply that FTP server's name to the Proxy server. For an inexperienced end user, things are about to get dicey.

The user will be prompted for a username by the FTP client application, and the user must enter the username in the correct format, for example, `anonymous@ftp.microsoft.com`. The WinGate proxy interprets the name, initializes a connection to the `ftp.microsoft.com` server and submits the username `anonymous`. After this, the WinGate server steps back into Transfer mode and sends the information back and forth between the client and the Proxy server. WinGate will also watch out for FTP commands that initiate data transfer because those will require the Proxy server to listen on additional ports.

This method has the advantage of working with any FTP client, but it may be a problem for the average person on your network. For example, if you have your average end user out there playing on the Net and wanting to download a file, they would have to launch an additional FTP client and submit the username and server name in the format above. Somehow, it seems much easier to click on the hyperlink.

Circuit-Level Proxies

Application layer proxies work great—with HTTP. As you have seen, working with FTP can be a challenge. With other popular Internet protocols, such as POP3 and SMTP, Application layer proxies don't work at all. Very few of the new protocols support any kind of Application layer, unless the new protocols make use of HTTP. In addition, Application layer proxying places a heavy strain on the Proxy server. The Proxy server has to do more than simply pass traffic to and from clients, it has to process each command filter and take care of any proxy directives that exist before sending the information on to the client. If the server retransmits the information on the external network, it must rewrite headers for the first four layers of the OSI model. In other words, Proxy servers at the Application layer are able to handle less traffic and fewer connections than other types of Proxy servers. If you want to bypass this problem, you have to start moving down the seven layers of the OSI model.

Some Proxy servers operate at the Transport layer. From the Transport layer, the Proxy server is capable of handling either TCP or UDP packets from clients on the internal network and sending them out to another network interface card connected to the external network. When the packets are resent, both the source and destination IP addresses are changed. Depending on the server configuration, the Transport layer packet headers may also be rewritten. The communication process with a Transport layer Proxy server is shown in Figure 15.11. The Proxy servers keeps track of its connections and can return information to the client when it hears back from the server it is proxying for.

Circuit-level proxying tends to be vendor specific, and each vendor does things just a little bit differently.

Using Port Redirection

The easiest way to make circuit-level proxying work is to redirect ports or forward ports to a different port address. This is truly the sledgehammer approach to proxying; it is simple to understand and doesn't require much from the software developers.

It works this way. The network administrator configures the Proxy server to listen for inbound connections on a specific TCP or UDP port address. At the same time, the administrator specifies an outboard IP address and port number. When a client wishes to connect to the external network, it connects to the Proxy server using the port number specified for inbound connections. The Proxy server opens an outbound connection to the destination IP address and port number that the administrator configured earlier. Once the connection is established, all data forwarded to the internal connection is then forwarded out to the external network.

Figure 15.11 The circuit-level proxy acts as a gateway from the Transport layer.

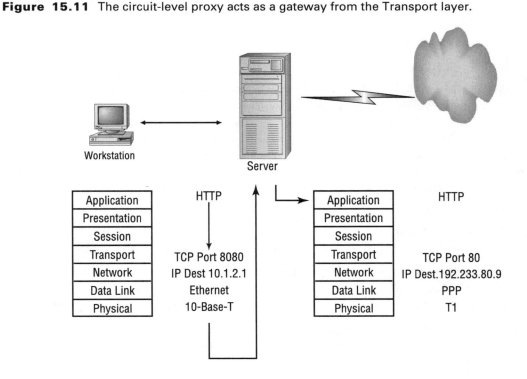

Port redirection is reliable and simple to configure, but it does not scale well. You may have to configure several redirections for each user on the network. If the user wants to access a different Proxy server, the configuration will have to be changed. Port redirection is not even included in Microsoft Proxy Server. It is available in some shareware solutions and in most versions of Unix.

Transport layer Proxy servers will serve POP and SMTP.

More Powerful than an Application Proxy, More Flexible than a Transport Proxy, It's…

SOCKS. As in WinSock proxy. SOCKS is the most powerful and flexible proxy protocol around. It allows the internal network clients to have full network connectivity to the server on the external side of the Proxy server.

SOCKS was originally set up to be a firewall technology, but it has been pushed into service as a proxy protocol. When you use a SOCKS Proxy server, the end user does not need to have any knowledge of the SOCKS Proxy server to use it, as long as the applications the client is using are written to take advantage of SOCKS. Server-side applications see a SOCKS client just as they do any other client, because the SOCKS proxy handles all the translating.

The Inner Workings of SOCKS

SOCKS works at the Session layer of the OSI model by redirecting network connections from an internal network to an external network, which is really the definition of a Proxy server. Applications use SOCKS in a way that is similar to the way applications use Win-Sock. Unlike an HTTP proxy, which can connect a server to a DNS address, a SOCKS connection requires a legitimate IP address. Therefore, clients on the internal network must have the capability of resolving DNS addresses on the external network. Most Proxy servers that support SOCKS also provide DNS services.

Once the application knows the IP address of the Destination server, it makes a request to SOCKS to communicate with the Application server. This request will include the IP address of the server, information about the type of connection, and the user's identity.

This is different from other Application layer Proxy servers because SOCKS will work with any client that has been programmed to use the SOCKS application-programming interface. It will not work at all if the client has not been programmed to use SOCKS.

If the client requests it, the SOCKS client will start a connection with the SOCKS Proxy server. By default, this uses TCP port 1080. If the Proxy server is listening in on the same port, it will initiate a connection to the final destination server.

The last step in the communication process is to send the information from the client to the server, passing through the SOCKS proxy. The SOCKS Protocol does not require any additional bandwidth; the SOCKS Proxy server remembers where to forward the traffic from the client.

Microsoft's Proxy Server includes a WWW proxy (HTTP), a SOCKS proxy, and a Win-Sock proxy.

NOTE   SOCKS is the best option for networks that incorporate both Unix and Windows systems. For more information on SOCKS, check out the Web site at www.socks.nec.com.

16

IPv6

Earlier in this book, I mentioned that there was some concern that the world was running out of IP addresses. I also mentioned that the Internet powers that be were addressing that very problem. The solution has had several names, including IPng and IPv6. The IPng (next generation) project is finished, and it is now referred to as IPv6 (IP version 6).

The decision-making process for the new version of IP started back in 1992. A decision had been made that the 32-bit IP address designed in 1978 was proving to be too short. The Internet was in danger of running out of network numbers, routing tables were getting too big, and there was a chance that network addresses would dry up. The biggest issue decision makers had to face was estimating the future size of the Internet.

The Internet Activities Board (IAB) started with the basic hypothesis that the Internet should connect all the computers in the world. Now, that sounds like a lofty enough goal, but the trick was defining "all the computers in the world." At one time, there were 200 million computers in the world, but that number was growing at a tremendous rate. As the discussions continued, the scope of the hypothesis changed. Rather than connecting every computer in the world, it should be possible for every person in the world to be connected. By the year 2020, that could mean over 10 billion people or 10 billion computers.

Then someone in the discussion group pointed out that each person may be served by more than one computer. After all, computers are in cars, and they are predicted to be in washing machines and refrigerators before too long. There is no reason these computers shouldn't be connected to the Internet. That way, when your car needs some repairs, it can e-mail your mechanic about work that needs to be done. If cars, refrigerators, microwaves, and dishwashers can have computers, how about pacemakers or lightbulbs? In this case, a figure of a hundred computers per human is not unrealistic. One hundred computers for each of 10 billion people would be a 1,000 billion computers on the Internet in 2020. Some of the people participating in the discussion said even that number was a bit narrow. When the smoke cleared, the target for IP was set at 1 quadrillion computers (10^{15}) connected through 1 trillion networks (10^{12}). That is a lot of computer networks. I guess there will be no shortage of work for IP experts over the next few years!

IPv6 Design

The current version of IP, IPv4, was designed to handle 4 billion addresses. Obviously, the jump between 4 billion computers and 1 quadrillion was quite substantial, and there had to be some serious changes in the way IPv6 worked. However, IPv4 was a very good design, and there was no reason that IPv6 should not keep most of its characteristics. Besides, with such a large installed base, the changes had to be backward-compatible to all the equipment out in the field still running version 4. IPv4 was not perfect, and 10 years of experience did bring out some of the challenges of using the protocol. In this case, IPv6 is not a derivative of IPv4, but it is an improvement.

IPv6 Header Format

The best place to start any discussion is at the beginning, and the beginning of IPv6 is the packet header. The IPv6 packet header is composed of a 64-bit header, followed by two 128-bit IPv6 addresses for source and destination, for a total length of 40 bytes. The first 64 bits are composed of the following:

- Version fields (4 bits)
- Class (8 bits)
- Flow label (20 bits)
- Length of "payload" (16 bits)
- Type of the next header (8 bits)
- Hop limit (8 bits)

Figure 16.1 shows you an example of the new IPv6 header.

Figure 16.1   The IPv6 header

Version	Class	Flow Label	
Payload Length		Next Header	Hop Limit
Source Address			
Destination Address			

The new header is in fact much simpler than the header for version 4. The new version counts six fields and two addresses, whereas the old version had 10 fixed header fields, two addresses, and some optional fields. The only field that has kept the same meaning and the same position is the version number, which is the first four bits of the packet.

IPv6 Simplifications

Although the version 4 header was as good as it got back in 1975, over 20 years later, people know there is a better way to do things. When the specifications for IPv6 were completed, there were three major simplifications:

- A fixed format was assigned to all headers.
- A header checksum was no longer needed.
- The hop-by-hop segmentation procedure was removed.

One field removed from IPv4 was the variable-length option field. Instead, extension headers are appended after the main header.

When people first look at this list, they question the removal of the header checksum. After all, isn't more error-checking better than less? The advantage of its removal is to ease the cost of header processing. It was determined that the checksum did not need to be checked and updated at each relay. Of course, there is an obvious risk that undetected errors may result in misrouted packets, but the risk is minimal because most encapsulation procedures include a packet checksum. There are also checksums in the media access control procedures of IEEE-802 networks, in the adaptation layers for the ATM circuits, and in the framing procedures of the Point-to-Point Protocol for serial links.

Other procedures have been changed, as well. For example, in IPv4, a specific fragmentation procedure allowed large packets to be sent without worrying about the capacities of the relay points. These large packets would be chopped up into adequately sized fragments if that was needed. The recipients would wait for the arrival of these segments and then reconstitute the packet. This sounded great in theory, but in reality there were some lessons to be learned. The primary lesson was that the unit of transmission should also be the unit of control. When you try to transmit large packets over a network that can only carry small segments, the successful transmission of the packet depends on the successful transmission of each segment. If only one segment is missing, the whole packet must be transmitted again, resulting in an inefficient use of the network.

With IPv6, all hosts will learn the maximum acceptable segment size through a procedure called *path MTU discovery*. If they try to send a larger packet, the network will reject the packet. As a consequence, there is no need for IPv6 to worry about segmentation control flags or a fragment offset. For the record, the networks are supposed to be able to carry a payload of 536 octets, according to the 1996 specifications.

IPv6 New Fields

Two new fields available in IPv6 were not around in version 4: the *flow label* field and the *class* field. Both were designed to facilitate the handling of real-time traffic. The subject of real-time traffic is still new enough that revisions were taking place regularly. For example, the class field started life as a 4-bit field called *control bits*. These bits were designed as a priority field that could have sixteen possible values, ranging from 0, which was the highest priority, to 15, the lowest priority. Research and experience proved that a 4-bit field was not enough. The field was enlarged to 8 bits and then renamed to class.

The flow label is used to distinguish packets that require the same treatment. In other words, the packets are sent from a given source to a given destination with the same set of options.

Revisions to Internet Control Message Protocol

If you are going to completely revise the specifications for the core protocols, it makes sense that some of the other protocols in the suite will have to be revised. One of the protocols that have undergone revision is the Internet Control Message Protocol or ICMP. The revision has followed the same guidelines as that of the Internet Protocol itself. The protocol started off by being streamlined. The functionalities that were present in the IPv4 ICMP, but were no longer needed, were removed. Then the protocol was made more complete by adding the multicast control functions that were found in the IPv4 Internet Group Membership Protocol, IGMP. Some formats were extended to carry the larger fields of IPv6. When all was said and done, ICMP was new and different, and it was not compatible with the previous version. If you examine an ICMP packet, you will see the header type has been changed to a Type 2 instead of a Type 1. Type 2 headers were originally used for IGMP IPv4 packets.

All IPv6 ICMP messages have the same general format, made up of a type, code, checksum, and a variable-length body. The checksum is computed according to the general IPv6 rules. It covers the ICMP packet and the fixed fields of the IPv6 header. The precise format of the message body, as well as the different values of the code parameter, depends on the ICMP type. Currently there are 14 different ICMP types. Table 16.1 lists the types of control messages available in IPv6.

Table 16.1   IPv6 ICMP Message Codes

Type	Definition
1	Destination unreachable
2	Packet too big
3	Time exceeded
4	Parameter problem
128	Echo request
129	Echo reply
130	Group membership query
131	Group membership report
132	Group membership reduction
133	Router solicitation
134	Router advertisement
135	Neighbor solicitation
136	Neighbor advertisement
137	Redirect

Codes 1 through 4 are error messages. Codes 133 to 137 are used for auto-reconfiguration procedures. Codes 128 and 129 are used for the IPv6 equivalent of Ping.

IPv6 Ping

Because ICMP has changed, the way systems deal with the familiar Ping function will also change. As mentioned in Table 16.1, it is now an echo-request and an echo-reply message. These messages both have the same type of format. When IPv6 wants to trigger an echo from a remote node, it sends an echo request. The echo reply will be sent to the source

The Connectivity Question

PART 5

address of the incoming packet. The ICMP echo-reply message will be almost identical to the incoming message. The only differences will be the type field, which will be set to 129, and the checksum field, which will be recomputed.

The Impact on Upper Layer Protocols

Although the impact on the upper layer protocols appears to be kept to a minimum, the implementation of Transport Protocols, such as TCP and UDP, will have to be updated to take into account the larger addresses and the new format of the ICMP messages. The new definition of addresses also has an impact on the applications themselves. For example, DNS will now have to return a long IPv6 address instead of the condensed IPv4 address. This means that the applications will have to push the information to the Transport Protocols down through the programming interfaces.

IPv6 in Domain Name Service (DNS)

Browsers and other applications should be able to normally manipulate domain names such as www.sybex.com, rather than messing with a numeric addresses such as 10.2.4.6. Actually, when compared with an IPv6 address, most applications would love to deal with 10.2.4.6. An IPv6 address looks something like 1a03:9:2b:3c:5:7ec3:de09:5b73, so it is obvious that people are going to be relying more on DNS and DHCP when IPv6 is finalized.

An IP address is normally obtained through a DNS lookup. DNS is the distributed database that stores resource records for each Internet domain. These records are identified by a type, and the type is designated by a literal acronym in the documentation and by a type number on the DNS query and response packets. With IPv4, addresses are stored in records of Type A, and each record contains a 32-bit address. A new resource record has been defined for IPv6. Because the new resource record contains one 128-bit address and, as such, is four times larger than the current Type A record, its type has been set to AAAA.

The DNS databases also contain a numerical hierarchy that is used for retrieving the name of the host when the address is available. You can get the IPv4 address of a domain name by reversing the order of the components and appending the domain name with in-addr.arpa. Servers use this reverse name to retrieve the real domain name associated with an address. A similar service is defined with IPv6. The problem with an IPv6 address is that it does not have any natural boundaries, like a subnet. The separations between the provider and the subscriber, the network and the subnetwork, and the subnetwork and the host identifier do not have to fall on a 32-bit, 16-bit, or even on an 8-bit boundary. The numeric names are thus built by first representing the address as a sequence of hexadecimal digits (or nibbles), reversing their order, separating them by dots, and then appending the suffix `.IP6.INT`. According to the rules, the IPv6 address of `432:0:1:2 :3:4:567:89ab` will be represented in DNS as `b.a.9.8.7.6.5.0.4.0.0.0.0.3.0.0.0 .2.0.0.0.1.0.0.0.0.0.0.0.1.2.3.4.IP6.INT`.

IPv6 Address Architecture

The biggest difference between going from IPv4 to IPv6 is the enlarged address format. Going from 32 bits to 128 bits guarantees that there will be thousands of billions of hosts, but it also provides room to insert more degrees of hierarchy than the basic three layers of a network, subnet, and host offered by IPv4.

Address Basics

Throughout this chapter, I have stressed over and over again that IPv6 is based on the same architecture principles as IPv4. Like IPv4 addresses, the new IPv6 addresses identify an interface connected to a subnetwork, not a workstation, and a station that is multi-homed will have as many IP addresses as it has interface cards. One big difference between IPv4 and IPv6 is that version 6 routinely allows each interface to be identified by several addresses to facilitate routing or management.

IPv6 addresses will belong to one of three categories:

- Unicast
- Multicast
- Anycast

Unicast addressing is just a fancy name for a point-to-point connection. These addresses identify exactly one interface. A packet sent to a unicast address will normally be delivered to that one particular interface.

A *multicast address* identifies a group of interfaces. A packet sent to a multicast address will normally be delivered to all the members of the group.

An *anycast address* also identifies a group of workstations or interfaces. The difference between a multicast address and an anycast address comes in the transmission process. Instead of being delivered to all members of the group, packets sent to an anycast address are normally delivered to only one point. That point would be the nearest member of the group. This facility did not exist in IPv4.

IPv6 Address Notation

As I mentioned before, an IPv6 address is made up of 128 bits. The designers chose to write these 128 bits as eight 16-bit integers, separated by colons. Each integer is represented by four hexadecimal digits, as in

ABCD:EF98:7654:3210:FEDC:BA12:3456:7890

Hexadecimal notation is one of those things that are great for computers, but we humans find it a bit difficult to manipulate. Some people seem to think that this unfriendliness is an advantage, because you want users to concentrate on DNS names, not addresses. But these people may not have the system managers' best interests at heart. To make the lives of system managers a little easier, there have been some facilities put in place for abbreviations.

First of all, in the beginning, many of the 128 bits will go begging. They will simply not be needed. So, in our real IPv6 address, there will probably be a lot of zeros, such as

2490:0000:0000:0000:00B1:0700:200C:4171

The first rule of abbreviation is that you can skip all the leading zeros in each hexadecimal component. This means a component will be 0 instead of 0000, or B1 instead of 00B1. So, looking at the address above, it would be

2490:0:0:0:B1:700:200C:4171

This address can be shortened even further. The specification says that inside an address, two colons can replace a set of consecutive null 16-bit numbers. This is called the *double-colon convention*. In the previous example, we can now get rid of the three consecutive null numbers with a double colon. The address will now look like:

2490::B1:700:200C:4171

The double-colon convention can be used only once inside an address. So, if your address were 0000:0000:0000:ABCD:1234:0000:0000:0000, it could be abbreviated as

::ABCD:1234:0:0:0

or as

0:0:0:ABCD:1234::

For backward-compatibility, your standard IPv4, 32-bit address can be converted into a new IPv6 address by adding 96 zeros to the front of the address. This can be written as ::10.2.3.4.

IPv6 Address Allocation

How are these new IP addresses going to be assigned, and what effect will those assignments have on things such as routing? The first IPv6 addresses will be allocated according to what is called an *aggregatable plan*. Aggregatable global unicast addresses are composed of the 3-bit prefix 010 followed by four 16-bit components.

The second component of the address is called the *Top Level Aggregator* (TLA). The Internet Assigned Numbers Authority (IANA) will allocate the ranges of the TLA to various continental registries, which could then further subdivide the ranges to national or even regional registries. A TLA need not be an actual provider of services. It could be an "exchange point" that is used to join a set of secondary providers. At the core of the Internet, the routing tables will need to have one entry per TLA and are not expected to contain any information except the routing information inside the TLA. The size of the TLA is just 13 bits, because more than 8,192 exchange points and backbone providers are not expected. (The exchange points and backbone providers are those parts of the Internet infrastructure that Internet service providers hook into.) If this number seems small, it is. As a matter of fact, it is smaller than the size of the current Internet routing table.

The third address component identifies what is called the *Next Level Aggregator* (NLA). The NLA is 32 bits long and will be structured by long haul providers to point to the second-tier providers or site identifiers.

The fourth component of the address is the *Site Local Aggregator* (SLA). This is a 16-bit identifier that is normally allocated to a link within a site. The site itself is a very small part of the addressing hierarchy. If a site needs to be renumbered after changing a provider, the TLA and the NLA may change, but the SLA and the Interface ID will remain the same.

The last component of the address is the *interface identifier*. This is a unique assignment to the interface connected to that link. The two basic decisions about the interface identifier are

- The identifier length will be 64 bits long, even on links that only connect a small number of stations.
- Most of these identifiers will be based on the IEEE EUI-64 format. This format is the evolution of the old IEEE 802 48-bit address.

Special Address Formats

As is the case with IPv4, there are some special types of addresses reserved in IPv6. There are five different types of unicast addresses defined:

- Unspecified addresses
- Loopback addresses

The Connectivity Question

PART 5

- IPv4-based addresses
- Site local addresses
- Link local addresses

Unspecified Address

An unspecified address is composed of 16 null bytes, which could be noted simply as two colons (::). This address is used as a source address by a station that has not yet been configured with a regular address. It can also be used in control messages where the presence of an address is semantically required, but no address is available. It can never be used as a destination address.

Loopback Address

The loopback address of 0:0:0:0:0:0:0:1 is used by a node to send a datagram to itself. This address and the unspecified address can never be assigned to an interface.

IPv4-based Address

It is possible to construct an IPv6 address by attaching a null prefix of 96 0 bits to a 32-bit IPv4 address. These addresses will be noted by combining the double colon combined with the dotted-decimal notation found in IPv4, such as ::222.111.123.24. These types of addresses will be used during the transition period between version 4 and version 6.

NOTE   The reserved prefix of eight 0 bits is common to the unspecified address, the loopback address, and the IPv4-based address.

Site Local Address

What can you do if your company wants to use TCP/IP but is not hooked to the Internet? The site local addressing prefix of 1111 1110 11 has been reserved for this purpose. A typical site local address will consist of the prefix, a set of zeros, a subnet ID, and the interface identifier. The last 80 bits of the site local address will have the same format as the last 80 bits of the aggregatable address, with the subnet ID being the same as the site local aggregator.

Link Local Address

The link local address can best be described as the merging of a site local address and a host address. It will be covered in more detail in the section "Host Auto-Configuration."

NOTE   Site local addresses cannot be routed to the Internet.

Multicasting and Anycasting

IPv6 was designed to take advantage of the deployment of multicasting and anycasting available on all IPv6 nodes. Multicast addresses were put into a format that all routers should recognize, incorporating the functionality of IPv4's Interned Group Management Protocol into the new Interned Control Message Protocol for IPv6.

> **TIP**   *Anycasting* is sending to the nearest member of a group of servers; *multicasting* is sending to a group of hosts at the same time.

Multicast Routing

Multicast routing over the Internet is still a topic of research. At this time, the procedure is still considered to be state of the art. It is so new that there are predictions about changes to come in the future. These predicted changes are as follows:

- There is a project to add one or several source-address fields in the report to indicate that one wants to listen to a specific subset of sources within a group.

- There is a similar project to add several source-address fields in its termination to indicate that one is not interested in several of the group's members.

- Certain multicast routing protocols require additional messages to determine which of the link's routers will relay the packets for a specific group.

Anycast Routing

Although multicasting is a well-tested technology, when the specifications for IPv6 were written, anycasting was still a research project. The principle of anycasting is simple. Instead of sending one packet to a given server, send a packet to a generic address that will be recognized by all servers of a given type. Once it has been delivered to the specified server, you have to trust the router to deliver the packet to the nearest of these servers. One could use anycasting to find out the nearest name server, the nearest file server or the nearest time server.

There is no specific anycast format in IPv6. Hosts treat anycast addresses in exactly the same way as a unicast address. The load is on the routing system, which has to maintain one route for each anycast address that is active in a given site.

Interdomain Routing

Back when people were predicting that the explosive growth of the Internet would kill it, one of the reasons given was the potential gigantic size of the routing tables. With today's Internet, if a router wants to figure out the best routes toward all destinations, it has to maintain an entry for each network of the Internet in its routing table. Most routers do not do this, because their tables are already too large. They only maintain precise routing tables for a small subset of the Internet, and they use default routes to get to other networks.

Although this approach will work for smaller companies, it is not viable for the backbone routers in the transit networks of Internet providers. They *have* to maintain complete tables.

The solution to the dilemma is to aggregate several routing entries. This means that there must be some form of hierarchy for the addresses and that there is an interdomain routing technology that can take advantage of that hierarchy. In IPv6, this will be done using provider addresses, because these addresses have a good relationship with the network's topology. Routes can be exchanged through the Interdomain Routing Protocol (IDRP). Users that have specific constraints will be able to build tunnels or use a routing header to build up transit routes that fit their requirements.

Moving from Classless Interdomain Routing to Providers

When you start to talk routing in IPv6, much of the groundwork was done with Classless Interdomain Routing or CIDR. CIDR was an effort to curb the explosive growth of routing tables. Using CIDR, IPv4 addresses are not considered to be composed of fixed-length network numbers. Network numbers are now replaced by variable-length prefixes. These prefixes are allegedly assigned in some sort of coordinated way. If everything were to work according to plan, it would be possible to replace all the individual entries in a given location (say a country) with a common prefix.

I said allegedly, because networks do not really follow any type of boundary. The route used to get to any network depends on how those networks attach to the Internet. Any addressing plan based on political or geographical boundaries would not allow for aggregation.

An addressing plan will allow for aggregation if it reflects the network topology. This was the main argument for choosing provider-based addresses for IPv6. In other words, all customers of a single Internet service provider will be routed through this provider's network. Outside the network, it is sufficient to enter a line per provider in the routing table. Provider-based addressing solves the routing table explosion by adding a Provider layer on top of the Network layer in the addressing hierarchy.

NOTE When you read the last paragraph, the immediate question that should have jumped to mind is "What happens if I change my ISP?" The answer is automatic configuration, which I'll cover later in the chapter in the section "Host Autoconfiguration."

BGP to IDRP

Back in Chapter 8 where I covered routing, I also discussed autonomous systems and the Border Gateway Protocol. The autonomous system and the BGP are really the building blocks of the IPv4 Internet. For a refresher, an autonomous system is a collection of sub-networks all managed by a single entity. It may be the network formed by an Internet service provider or the network formed by one very large company. It also includes the interior-routing procedures for managing routing within the system.

BGP-4, the current version of the Border Gateway Protocol, supports the routing-table procedures required to work with CIDR. These procedures together are referred to as a Path Vector Protocol. It allows border routers that link two adjacent autonomous systems to announce paths. A path is described using a set of attributes that include the list of autonomous systems that the path traverses and also a list of network prefixes that it reaches.

BGP was designed specifically for the Internet. It is designed and optimized to handle 32-bit addresses. It is so in tune with the 32-bit addressing structure that it could not be upgraded to work with IPv6. Because of this, the Exterior Gateway Protocol used with IPv6 is the Interdomain Routing Protocol (IDRP). IDRP was considered a good candidate for the task because

- It does not show any dependency on the Open System Interconnection (OSI) family of protocols.
- It was defined from the beginning for multiprotocol routing and is capable of computing tables using several families of addresses.
- It is based on the same path vector family as BGP and includes a superset of BGP's functions.

Many of the designers of BGP also worked on designing IDRP. If you look closely at the differences between BGP and IDRP, you will see that many of them revolve around terminology and that there are only four major differences:

- BGP messages are exchanged in a TCP connection; IDRP protocol units are carried by the bare datagram service.
- BGP is a single-address-family protocol; IDRP can work with several types of addresses.
- BGP uses 16-bit autonomous system numbers; IDRP identifies a domain by using variable-length address prefixes.
- BGP describes the full list of autonomous system numbers that a path passes through; the IDRP concept of Routing Domain Confederations can be used to aggregate this information.

Intradomain Routing

Because IDRP will be used to route packets around the Internet, which protocol is going to be used to handle routing duties on the interior network? The job of the Interior Routing Protocol is to compute routes and maintain connectivity within a routing domain or an autonomous system. In this case, there is no need to invent a new technology. Both Open Shortest Path First (OSPF) and Routing Information Protocol (RIP) can be updated to work with IPv6. Other protocols, including IS-IS and EIGRP, are also expected to be updated to work with IPv6.

OSPF

OSPF is the recommended Intradomain Routing Protocol. It is a Link State Protocol, so all routers maintain a copy of a database that contains link-state records describing the status of the network. This protocol has been used for years and has constantly been upgraded. The IPv6 version of OSPF is a simple translation of the IPv4 version, requiring minimal changes to accommodate the new address format.

OSPF for IPv6 will run between IPv6-capable nodes. The link-state database will not be shared with the IPv4 database. The two protocols will operate in parallel rather than trying to achieve integrated routing.

The IPv6 version is obtained by applying minimal changes to the IPv4 version, with just the replacement of all occurrences of the 32-bit address with the 128-bit addresses used in IPv6.

RIP

Once again the design committee opted for a simple transformation of a simple protocol to take the longer addresses into consideration.

RIP is a simple Distance Vector Protocol. The length of the path is equal to the number of hops on the path, whatever the speed or delay of these hops. In some conditions, RIP relies on counting to infinity to eliminate loops. Paths whose metrics exceed the conventional value of infinity (usually set to 16) are considered to be lost and are discarded. RIP cannot be used on a network in which paths are longer than 16 hops. The only advantage to RIP over OSPF is that it is very simple and can thus be implemented in cheap routers that could not support a fully functional protocol like OSPF. RIP is perfect for networks that are small and simple.

In the IPv6 version of RIP, the packet is made up of a 32-bit header, a set of addresses, and metric pairs describing reachable destinations. As in RIP for IPv4, only two commands are defined: one for requests and one for responses. A 128-bit IPv6 address and a subnet mask—that is, an octet containing the number of valid bits in the address—describe each destination. RIP processes in UDP datagrams exchange RIP messages.

Host Auto-Configuration

It's nice to know that the people on the design committee for IPv6 actually worked for a living, using the protocol as well as designing how it should work. Early on in the discussions, the topic of auto-configurations came up. The group used two metaphors to refer to the problem: the "dentist's office" and the "thousand computers on the dock."

The dentist's office is a familiar scene. There is someone who can afford to buy several computers, but they are not trained computer specialists. They can basically take the computer out of the box, plug in the connectors, switch it on, and expect it to work. One of the requirements was for IPv6 to be this simple to operate, even if the dentist isn't connected to the Internet or there isn't a router in the office.

The thousand computers on the dock is a metaphor based on a recurring nightmare. One thousand computers have just been delivered and are waiting on the unloading dock. It's 2 P.M. on Friday, and the deadline for having the entire network up and working is the end of the afternoon. Configuration of each computer should be as automatic as possible.

As the specification process progressed, other needs appeared. Setting up a machine once and forever is not sufficient. It is imperative that it is easy to change addresses dynamically, even to the point of changing ISPs. Each machine should be able to receive several addresses from several different providers. There are also security and management requirements, not to mention some design decisions. Address configuration should be an integral part of any IPv6 implementation. It should come in a Stateless mode, meaning the addresses would be automatically assigned without the need of any special services. There should also be a Stateful mode using the IPv6 version of DHCP.

Linking Local Address

So how will this automatic configuration and reconfiguration work? The plan says that as soon as the network interface card (NIC) is initialized, the host can build its address by taking a well-known link local prefix and adding a unique token or a number that is unique to the host on this link. The model for this "unique" token is the 64-bit unique Ethernet address that is burned into each and every Ethernet adapter. Ethernet addresses are supposedly unique worldwide. Knowing that the interface comes out of the box with a unique address means that you can plug it into any Ethernet cable anywhere and be assured that there would not be a collision based on addressing.

The advantages of this plan should be self-evident. There is simpler network management as well as the possibility of connecting Ethernet segments by learning bridges. According to the designers of Ethernet, worldwide uniqueness is assured. A manufacturer is sold a range of addresses. The manufacturer then programs each interface with its own unique worldwide address.

The 802 committee of the IEEE has generalized the Ethernet solution over many different types of local networks. They have standardized it on Token Rings, FDDI Rings, and even radio networks.

There is no requirement for the Internet addresses, or even link local addresses, to have anything in common with the MAC address of the Ethernet card. The only mandatory characteristic is uniqueness, that only one interface uses that address on a given link. For networks where there is no IEEE-802 address available, a unique token will have to be derived from other sources, such as from another computer board, or from another interface used to attach the station to another link, or even from a number selected at random.

Link local addresses can only be used on the local link. They will not be sufficient for managing a large network.

Stateless Auto-Configuration of Hosts

When an IPv6 node first comes up, it starts by trying to initialize and join all of the nodes in the multicast group. This is done by programming their interfaces to receive all the packets sent to the multicast address, FF02::1. The host will send a solicitation message to the routers on the link, using the router's address of FF02::2 and setting the source address to their own local link. The hop count is set to 255.

The solicitation message is an ICMP message of Type 133. The code is set to zero. The solicitation message can include various options, using one octet for type, one octet for length, and a variable number of octets for the value. The only option that is mandatory is the Link layer address of the source; i.e., the Ethernet or Token Ring address.

When a router receives a solicitation, it is supposed to reply with a router advertisement message. This message is sent toward the Link layer address of the requestor, using the content of the source-address option as a media address.

Router Advertisements

A router advertisement is also an ICMP message. This message can contain several parameters that can be found in a fixed position in the advertisement header or as a variable-length option. The parameters are used to manage auto-configuration and for neighbor discovery.

NOTE   Neighbor discovery replaces the IPv4 protocols for address resolution and for router discovery.

Router advertisements are not only sent in response to solicitations. Routers can also transmit them at regular intervals on the host's multicast address. If they receive a solicitation at a moment when the interval between repetitions has almost expired, they may choose to respond by multicasting their advertisement instead of sending a directed message.

The soliciting station is supposed to wait for a response. To protect itself against transmission error, it will repeat the request if it does not receive a response after a reasonable period of time. It will not repeat the request more than three times. Failure to receive a response after three attempts indicates there is no router on the link. The station can then only communicate with other stations on the same link. It will use the link local address.

Yeah, But, What If There Is a Duplicate Address?

Auto-configuration is great, as long as there are no duplicate addresses. In theory, each network interface card comes out of the box with a unique MAC address. That is a great theory, but unfortunately, it isn't always so. Some manufacturers of low-cost devices are known to use unregistered addressing. Resorting to random numbers can cause problems, especially when the random number generator isn't all that it is supposed to be. Because duplicate addresses can cause severe problems, a facility had to be built in to detect and report these errors as soon as possible.

The detection of duplicate addressing in IPv6 uses the neighbor-discovery procedure. Once an address has been configured, the host sends out a solicitation message towards that address and waits for one second. If another station has been configured with the same address, it will reply and advertise its link layer address. At this point, the host will know that its number is not unique, and it has to try again. It either picks a new number or displays an error message and asks for a human to intervene.

The procedure is not perfect. The absence of a reply may be caused by the loss of the initial solicitation. Stations are supposed to try the solicitation several times before being assured of the uniqueness of the token.

Stateful vs. Stateless Configuration of Hosts

While stateless configuration has many advantages, it does have two disadvantages:

- Inefficient use of address space
- A lack of network access control

Automatic address configuration only manages the configuration of addresses. The actual configuration of a host requires more than just an address configuration. Although the neighbor-discovery method will also allow hosts to recognize gateways and local subnet information, they must still discover the location of DNS servers.

The Connectivity Question

PART 5

Stateless auto-configuration may also ease the task of industrial spies and hackers. The idea behind Plug and Play is that a legitimate user can take the machine out of the box, plug it in, and have it work. This also means that if a hacker were to move a computer within the same premises, that person would be able to plug it in and run it as if it were a legitimate local user.

Lifetime of Addresses

Addresses obtained through stateless or stateful configuration will have a limited lifetime. In a stateful configuration, the lifetime will be provided by the address server. In a stateless configuration, the lifetime of the address will be derived from the lifetime of the prefix, based on a router's advertisement.

An address whose lifetime has expired becomes invalid. It can no longer be used as a source address or as a destination address. To protect against this happening, IPv6 addresses will have two lifetimes: a preferred lifetime and a valid lifetime. An address whose preferred lifetime has expired should not be used. An address whose valid lifetime has expired will become invalid. When a TCP process starts a connection, it knows the destination address, but it can choose any of the local addresses as its source address. It should pick the one that has the longest preferred lifetime.

Hosts are expected to be getting router advertisements continuously and will examine the prefixes in these advertisements. If the prefix is already known, they will use the valid and preferred lifetimes contained in the advertisements to update the lifetimes obtained when the address was configured. If they learn of a new prefix, a new address will be configured. This way, the address continuously evolves. Both valid and preferred lifetimes can be set to infinity.

IPv6 Dynamic Host Configuration Protocol (DHCP)

In Chapter 4, I mentioned some of the issues that have to be faced with IPv4 DHCP. A DHCP server or a relay agent has to be present on each subnet in order for the protocol to fulfill its role.

In IPv6, the version of DHCP solves these problems by taking advantage of two IPv6 capabilities: the possibility of hosts to build up a link local address and the availability of multicasting.

When a host needs to be configured, it tries to locate a local DHCP server by sending a "DHCP solicitation message" to the "all DHCP server and relay agents" address. The source address will be the host's link local address. If a DHCP relay agent receives the request, it fills in the "relay address" with the global or site local address of the receiving interface and then ships the message back out to the "all DHCP servers" address. The servers will reply, sending an advertised message to the relay address if it was present in the solicitation message or directly to the client address.

The advertisement message contains a variable number of "extensions" or configuration information that may be used by the client. A host can get several advertisement messages in response to its solicitations. If it does not receive a response, it will resend the request until it simply gives up. The DHCP agents will also broadcast advertisements regularly, notifying systems that the configuration server is now available. Once it has received an advertisement, a host will then select an agent and a server and will request configuration parameters by sending a "request" message.

Request messages are never multicast. They are sent to a specific server, either directly or through a specific agent. Requests will be relayed by the agent and then received by the server. The server will send a reply to the agent, and the agent will then relay the reply to the link local address of the host.

The extension fields of requests and replies contain the list of parameters or "extensions" that the server should provide. The most important extension is the address extension. The address extension will provide an IPv6 address to the host and can provide both the valid and preferred lifetimes of the specified address. The extension will also contain the domain name to which the address is associated. In addition, DHCP can now configure an AAAA DNS record for the host.

Other extensions that can now be configured include the following:

Time Offset   Specifies the differential between universal (GMT) time and the local time.

Domain Name Server   Provides the addresses of directory servers.

Static Route Extension   Contains a list of address pairs, each composed of the address to a destination and of the corresponding next hop.

TTL   Time to Live, which is the same as the maximum hop limit.

Maximum Message Size   Specifies the maximum message size a host is willing to accept.

IPv6 and Internet Security

One of the issues that constantly arises whenever a discussion revolves around the Internet and TCP/IP is security. Tales of hackers, crackers, and other nefarious sorts abound. Password cracking became a hobby, and password sniffing, spoofing of addresses, and stealing of connections became a sport. Security was a big issue in the design of IPv6. These new security measures are one of the features that are going to drive companies toward instituting the new protocol.

IPv6 Encryption and Authentication

The IPv6 specifications include two security payloads: the authentication header and the encrypted security payload (data). The authentication header provides a procedure by which the recipient of a packet can guarantee that the source address is authentic and that the packet has not been altered during transmission. The encrypted security payload guarantees that only legitimate receivers will be able to read the content (data) of the packet. Both procedures are based on the concept of security associations.

Security Associations

In order for security to work, both the sender and the receiver have to agree on a key, on the encryption algorithm, and on a set of parameters such as the lifetime of the key or the details of the way the algorithm is used. This set of agreements is the basis for a security association between the sender and the receiver. When packets are received, they can only be verified or decrypted if the receiver can link them within the context of the security association. The IPv6 authenticated and encrypted packets all convey a Security Parameter Index (SPI).

When packets are sent to a unique receiver via a unicast address, the receiver chooses the SPI. The SPI that is used for each partner's host will be a parameter of the security context. Each station must remember the SPI used by the partner to identify the security context.

When packets are sent using multicast addresses, the SPI is common to all members of the group. Each member should be able to match the combination of group addresses and the SPI with the key algorithm and other parameters. The SPI is normally negotiated as part of the key exchange procedure.

Encrypted Security Payload

The authentication header does not transform data. Data remains in the clear, subject to sniffer attacks. When confidentiality is desired, the Encrypted Security Payload (ESP) header should be used.

The precise format depends on the particular encryption algorithm being used. The default algorithm suggested by the specification will be the Cipher Block Chaining mode of the Data Encryption Standard (DES-CBC).

Transitioning to IPv6

The transition between IPv6 and IPv4 will follow what is described as the dual-stack strategy. Basically, an IPv6 Internet will be deployed in parallel to the existing IPv4 Internet, borrowing some of its infrastructure. At the beginning, all IPv6-capable hosts will also be IPv4 capable, to retain connectivity with the existing Internet. The choice to use either stack will depend on information provided in the name service.

Supporting Two Sets of IP Stacks

The similarity between IPv4 and IPv6 ensures that only minor developments are needed to transform an IPv4 station into a dual-stack, IPv6-capable host. The list of required upgrades includes

- IPv6 code, basic IPv6, ICMP, and neighbor-discovery code
- The handling of IPv6 within the Transport Protocols TCP and UDP
- Modifications to the Sockets or WinSock libraries to support IPv6 addresses and IPv6-interface extensions
- The interface with the name service

Although the support of the two stacks shouldn't be difficult, the trickiest part of supporting two stacks will be the need to manage two different sets of addresses. The designers of IPv6 feel that with the neighbor-discovery procedures of IPv6, this task should be almost invisible to the administrator.

Router support of IPv6 should be slightly more complex. The router must be equipped with IPv6-packet forwarding code, the IPv6 routing protocols, and the IPv6 Management protocols, not to mention the transition mechanisms. For a router, there is very little overlap between IPv4 and IPv6. Because most routers can handle multiple protocols, the lack of overlap should not be a problem.

Dual-Stack Strategy and DNS

The dual-stack strategy relies heavily on the Domain Name System. The dual-stack host will have several address records in DNS, one A record for the IPv4 address, and one AAAA record for the IPv6 address. When browsers are configured, they can be configured to search for IPv6 records first and then for IPv4 addresses. This list will then be returned to the host. At that point, the host will pick the best address out of the returned list and use that address in the TCP connection request or as a destination address for UDP datagrams. The Dual Stack Protocol will have to decide to use either the IPv6 address or the IPv4 address if it is a mapped address.

The deployment process between DNS for IPv4 and IPv6 will be an ongoing process. As an increasing proportion of the Internet hosts receive IPv6 addresses and document them in DNS, the transition will take place naturally.

For more in-depth information on IPv6, see the second edition of *IPv6, The New Internet Protocol* by Christian Huitema (Prentice Hall, 1997).

The Connectivity
Question

PART 5

Part 6

Network Security

- Keeping the baddies out
- If the baddies are working from the inside, how to make sure they can't do any damage
- How to fix it if it breaks
- How to figure out what broke in the first place

17

Internal Network Security

You knew that any book designed for system administrators on TCP/IP had to have at least one chapter on security in it, didn't you? Because everyone associated with this book is trying hard to make sure it is worth every penny you paid for it, we are not only going to give you one chapter on security, we are going to give you two chapters on security. When you start talking about security, people immediately assume that you are protecting your system against attacks from the outside. Studies have shown that the biggest risk to computer data comes from inside the firewall.

Because there are going to be two chapters on security, one for internal security and one for external security, the firewall is a pretty good dividing line, so that is where the line will be drawn. This chapter will concentrate on things from the desktop to the firewall; Chapter 18 will concentrate on how to protect your system and your Web presence from outside attacks.

My Network Is Already Secure!

Any discussion of security has to start with a couple of war stories, just to prove that a network is only as secure as its weakest link. A colleague of mine specialized in checking out networks for security leaks. He had several ways of attempting to gain access to the system, but he usually found that with major companies, his best tool was the telephone. He was a nationally renowned speaker, and he would usually start off his speech to computer professionals by asking who felt they had a completely secure network. In most cases, people sheepishly look to the ground and probably think, "If I had a completely secure network, I wouldn't have to be here!" Every once in a while, though, someone would hold up a hand, and that is when the fun would begin.

Security Case Study Number One

This speaker usually carried around a $100 bill. Now, while that may not seem like a lot of money, he had a way of phrasing things to make it seem like an awful lot of money. He would bet the person who raised their hand that he could break into their network in 24 hours or less. If he couldn't do it, he would send the person the $100 bill. If he could do it, the person would have to donate $100 to the speaker's favorite charity. He would usually seal the deal by pointing out that the company was getting a routine security check for far under the going rate. All the security person needed was the name of the company and a phone number.

On one particular occasion, a member of the audience took the speaker up on his claim and provided the name of the company and the phone number. The bet was that the security person could infiltrate the network and get into an area where some serious damage could be done, all in less than 24 hours. The two synchronized their watches, and the clock started ticking. At that point, our security expert began his lunchtime talk. After his talk, the expert went back to his hotel room, took a shower, changed clothes, made a few business-related phone calls, and then decided to start working on the bet.

The first phone call he made was to the company's main switchboard. He told the operator that one of the company's sales staff had been out to see him just a couple of weeks before, and while he hadn't needed their product at that time, he certainly did now. The problem was he had lost the information on the salesperson. Would it be possible for him to get the name and phone number of the salesperson? Now this company was like most businesses. It was more than willing to do whatever was necessary to get the customer's money. So the receptionist proceeded to give the speaker the name, address, phone number, cell number, pager number, e-mail address, and anything else necessary to contact the salesperson.

Once the speaker had that information in hand, he waited a few minutes and called back, this time asking for the IT department. When he got in touch with someone from IT, he pushed himself off as the salesperson. He told the harried IT staffer that he had done a typical salesperson stunt by deleting all the information necessary to dial in and get his stuff. What should he do? The person from IT had everything under control. The speaker told the IT person that he wasn't in his office, but at a hotel, and gave the IT person the phone and room numbers. The IT person had a sheet of instructions on how to configure a dial-up connection on his computer, so he faxed it immediately while they were still on the phone. The intruder was so thankful, he made sure to ask the IT person for his name and the name of his boss, so he could send a thank you letter and tell the boss how appreciative he was of all the support he had received. The IT person was feeling pretty proud of himself for being so responsive to the end user, so he was happy to provide all that information and more.

Once the speaker hung up, it was all over but the shouting. He ran down to the hotel front desk, got the fax, came back up to his room, and called the company back, asking for the accounts receivable department. Once he had someone on the phone from A/R, he went into his pitch. "Hi, I'm (insert name of IT person), we are doing some work on the accounting package, and I need to log in as your user account to do some testing. Would you please give me your user name and password?" The accounting clerk didn't think anything of it and passed along the information.

At this point, the speaker hooked up his laptop, dialed into the RAS server, logged on as the accounting clerk, went into the clerk's e-mail account, and sent a note to the head of security asking that the check be sent to his favorite charity. The amount of time needed to access the system was under five hours, using nothing more than a telephone.

In this case, security policies were in place, but they were easily circumvented.

Security Case Study Number Two

I was doing a network upgrade for a small mutual fund company headquartered in the Midwest, and they used an older Novell system. Whenever I did an upgrade on the network, one of the first things I would always check was security. When I went to the server console to see who was logged in, I found 25 users logged in the network, and 24 were logged in as Supervisor with full rights to everything. One was logged in using her login name, which was okay because she was a Supervisor equivalent. When I was asked the senior management about this, I was told that the only way a particular piece of software would work was if everyone was logged in as Supervisor. Their consultant had told them so. Besides, they didn't need things like usernames and passwords because they were all family, it was a small company, and the management trusted everyone.

When I went to lunch with management, the members of senior management commented on having a new temp worker at the receptionist desk, filling in for a member of the family that was on maternity leave. I quickly pointed out that this temp, whose name they did not know, was logged into the network and had full access to every file on the network, including customer lists, customer financial information, and even the holdings that made up the mutual-fund portfolio. Needless to say, we started instituting login names and passwords, with restrictions, that afternoon.

Security Case Study Number Three

Unemployment rates are at an all-time low. Finding and hiring good people is exceptionally difficult, especially with the limited budgets you have to work with. When you make an offer to a potential hire, your HR department is selling more than a salary and benefit package. They have to sell what a great place this is to work, what exceptional people these are to work with, how great the laissez-faire management style is to work under, and all those intangibles that don't show up on the deposit ticket. It is hard work, but every once in while, they manage to land a really, really good person.

In this case, the person was hired in the marketing department. She was put in charge of several new and exciting projects that were just getting off the ground. She was given access to all sorts of research-and-development information, she was given access to advertising strategies, and she was given full run of the place. She proved to be a godsend. Everything she did, she did on time, she did under budget, and she did well. The company was lucky to have her.

So was your competitor. It turns out she was paid to get a job at your company by your competitor. You behaved exactly as expected. You gave her the full run of the place, and she passed along everything she learned to your competitor.

These examples do not create a pretty picture. Unfortunately, at more and more companies, these are the rules, not the exceptions! Scary, isn't it? Are you blushing yet? When I relate these stories, there is usually one person who comes up to me later and wonders if I have been inside their company. It appears that not every company has strict security guidelines!

Risk Assessment

Businesses all over the world are spending millions of dollars to make communications between employees easier and faster. As a by-product, consumers and partners have access to previously unheard of amounts of information. This is a one of those dichotomies that can make a network administrator go crazy, because while you want data to be available, you don't want it to be *too* available!

News stories abound about security breaches, viruses, hackers, and worms invading networks where they are not wanted. Some are invading holes that could be described as administrative oversights. An administrative oversight is one of those things that happen while you are working hard to build and deploy a more responsive network. In addition to the administrative oversights, there are known holes to operating systems, newly discovered holes to operating systems, and new operating systems coming out regularly. Many of these new operating systems handle security in a slightly different manner than they did in previous versions. To make your life even more difficult, the number of free hacking utilities on the Internet abound, making it easy for even a computer novice to exploit known security holes.

When the Melissa virus struck companies around the world, causing an e-mail meltdown in some locations, the media attention it received was unparalleled. There were some other facets of the attack that were unique. First of all, the amount of resources that were devoted to finding the person allegedly responsible for the outbreak was unheard of. When the person suspected of kicking off the virus was finally tracked down, he was arrested and charged with committing major crimes. That may not have been a first, but it was certainly uncommon.

Very few security violations are ever brought to trial and successfully prosecuted. Usually, legal evidence is insufficient to prove that a crime has been committed. Furthermore, companies are just now realizing that they can be held criminally liable if their computer systems are used to launch a break-in at another company—regardless of whether or not the perpetrator is an employee of the company.

To further complicate things, the foundations of many of the database applications are vulnerable to attack. Oracle will often have a guessable default password for their administrative accounts. Middleware technologies like MQSeries frequently use well-known usernames and passwords to communicate between computers, and these passwords get transmitted in clear text across the network. Some packaged applications like SAP R/3 use hard-coded usernames and passwords to access the master administrative accounts.

Data warehousing and storage-area networks are growing in popularity daily. With both of these technologies, corporate information is gathered from various business applications into a central site, where people can access that information. Some of the access is secure, other parts just rely on anonymous FTP. Although vendors address each of these issues, many times the solutions are never implemented because the IT staff is already overworked taking care of simple configuration issues.

Risk assessment is essentially a two-pronged study. The first study involves the network infrastructure and hardware. The other study looks at the software applications and data that the infrastructure is used to access. In the hardware arena, you will be doing an inventory, listing not only the types and functions but also the necessity of the equipment to the continued operation of the company. Because you are dealing with hardware here, much of your work may already be done from your current, up-to-date documentation.

On the application and data side, it is a little different. If you are going to try to proactively protect a network and look for security holes that affect data and software applications, there are four major approaches you can take:

- Risk assessment using a network probe
- Risk assessment using intelligent agents
- Intrusion detection using network probes
- Intrusion detection using intelligent agents

Each of these approaches will be covered later in the chapter. Let's start by looking at some of the things you should take into consideration when you begin your risk assessment audit.

What Is Risk Assessment?

At its simplest, risk assessment is figuring out how vulnerable your data is and applying some sort of criteria to judge how important pieces of data are to your network. Now, I know network administrators feel that all the information stored on their networks is absolutely vital to the health and well-being of the corporate infrastructure. This is a great attitude to have. But let's face it, chances are the data that is amassed to support the new rollout of the company's next great product is really more important than the agenda for last month's Employee of the Month committee meeting.

Some risk-assessment firms suggest that your company inventory its equipment and data using a scale. The scale could look something like Table 17.1.

Table 17.1   Risk-Assessment Table

Rating	Data	Hardware
High	A critical concern to the system	Uptime must equal 100%
Medium	An important concern, but not necessary to the continued operation of the company	Uptime may be less than 100%, but should be higher than 98%
Low	Some minimal level of security is required	Uptime is not a major concern

There may be other concerns that enter into your decisions when it comes to data. For example, depending on your business, confidentiality, integrity, and availability may come into play. For example, if you are working for a company doing top-secret government work, the data may have not only a high rating but also a high-level of confidentiality, whereas its level of availability would be low. Table 17.2 shows confidentiality considerations for data.

Table 17.2   Example of Confidentiality

Evaluation	Comment
High	The data contains proprietary business information and other financial information, which, if disclosed to unauthorized sources, could cause a financial loss or adverse legal action to the user's organization.
Medium	Security requirements for assuring confidentiality are of moderate importance. Having access to only small portions of the information has little practical purpose.
Low	The mission of this information is to be available to the general user at all times. None of the information requires protection against disclosure.

Table 17.3 shows an example of integrity considerations.

Table 17.3   Integrity Considerations

Evaluation	Comment
High	This application or system runs a financial transaction system. Unauthorized or unintentional modification of this information could result in fraud, under- or overpayments of obligations, or fines or penalties resulting from late or inadequate payments.
Medium	Assurance of the integrity of the information is required to the extent that destruction of the information would require significant expenditures of time and effort to replace. Although corrupted information would present an inconvenience to the staff, most information and all vital information is backed up by either paper documentation or on computer media.

Table 17.3   Integrity Considerations *(continued)*

Evaluation	Comment
Low	The system mainly contains messages or reports. If these messages or reports were modified by unauthorized means, employees would detect the modifications. These modifications, if undetected, would not be a major concern for the organization.

Table 17.4 shows the kinds of availability considerations that should be taken into account.

Table 17.4   Availability Considerations

Evaluation	Comment
High	Unavailability of the system could result in the inability to meet obligations that could cause work stoppage and a failure to meet mission-critical requirements. The system requires 24 x 7 x 365 access.
Medium	Information availability is of moderate concern to the mission. Availability would be required within 24 to 72 hours. Information backups are maintained at off-site storage and they would be sufficient to carry on with limited office tasks.
Low	The system serves primarily as a server for e-mail for a small population. Messages are usually duplicated and can be easily replaced. Should the system be unavailable, users would have alternative connections available.

The type of systems that you operate, the information that you store, and the level of availability, integrity, and confidentiality that you have will determine the type of risk assessment survey that you should perform.

Equipment/Infrastructure Risk Assessment

This study really has many names. Some companies call it auditing the network, other companies begin a Tiger Team, some companies call it disaster-recovery planning. The whole thing boils down to being able to play several serious games, such as

- What if...
- How do we protect...

- How quick can we...
- Is there a better way to...

When doing risk assessment or disaster recovery, you need to be creative and approach concerns from a variety of angles. For example, many companies' answer to a disaster is to have a pair of mirrored drives in the only file server. That is a fine solution if one of the hard drives should fail. But what if the drive controller should fail? What if the motherboard should fail? What if the building should catch on fire? What if the building were completely destroyed by fire? What if the entire block was consumed by fire? What if the entire city was without power? You get my point.

They Thought They Had the Fire Thing Covered

One of the scariest situations that can occur is a fire in a high-rise office building. One person that I spoke with told me a story that happened to him. It was a Monday morning, and he was working in an office building in New York City when the fire alarms went off. There really was a fire, and it was one floor above his company's offices.

When the alarms went off, everyone did what they were supposed to, which was clear out of the building. They all trundled down 15 floors and watched as the fire engines pulled up and the battle began. The IS team started talking about what was going to happen after the fire was contained. Fortunately, the firefighters put the fire out quickly.

After reentering the building, the first issue that was discovered was from the person in charge of the tape backups. The good news was the complete tape backup had run the night before and had completed successfully. The bad news was the person had not had an opportunity to get the tapes off the tape machines and send them to the off-site storage unit. The good news was the fire was mostly contained to the floor above. The bad news was the computer room halon unit kicked off. The good news was the halon stopped whatever incursion the fire caused. The bad news was the fire department had to go into the computer room to clean up the area. The good news was, they didn't do any damage, and the tapes were right where they were left, in perfect condition. The bad news was the fire department discovered asbestos in the make-up of the computer room. No one was allowed in the room and nothing, including the tapes, was allowed out. This could definitely be considered an "Oh, darn" situation (or perhaps something stronger).

The good news was the backup from the week before was good, and the company had a plan to replace all hardware within 48 hours. By the end of the week, the company and all employees were back to work.

When approaching risk assessment, be creative in terms of risk. It is not just someone deleting files, the power going out, or the building catching fire. There are all sorts of risks that need to be addressed, for example

- Tornadoes and hurricanes
- The 100-year flood that is never supposed to flood the main street of a town in North Dakota
- Explosions

It is a sad commentary on the state of the world, but one company has even planned the layout of the offices with a terrorist act in mind. Not only are there plenty of emergency exits spread throughout the building but there are also hidden knock-out panels in otherwise solid-looking walls that will lead to the outside of the building. If people are locked in a room and the terrorist is not with them, they can knock out one of the panels and make an escape. Unfortunately, this precaution was taken using hindsight. Someone had already lost her life before this was put in place.

Once you have a list of the disasters you need to prepare for, the work can begin.

Equipment/Infrastructure Protection

Now comes the interesting part. You have your list of equipment and the matrix that shows how each piece serves the company. Start plugging in disasters and designing a plan to meet the needs of the organization.

Here is an example. Take a look at the equipment in the computer room. This equipment has a high degree of security with corresponding high degrees of availability and integrity. These systems cannot go down, ever. So you start planning disasters. A thunderstorm hits and knocks out the power to the building. How do you protect against that? Purchase an Uninterruptable Power Supply (UPS) and a generator, and you are back in business.

Now suppose that the thunderstorm turned into a tornado, how would you protect against that? How would you protect against the building blowing up? You have taken all normal precautions, but over and above everything else, the network must remain online, and the data must be secure. It gets trickier quickly.

What Happens to Old Schools?

Have you ever wondered what happens to old school buildings? Not necessarily those old wooden buildings from *Little House on the Prairie* but those old sturdy brick buildings such as dear ol' P.S. 59. You know the ones I am talking about! Two stories, lots of room, every city in America seems to have an old one around somewhere. Someone has invariably turned them into an office building, an apartment complex, or an antique mall. There are many different uses for them.

One upper Midwest company is in the habit of buying old school buildings and turning them into nondescript data centers. They purchase the building, gut parts of the interior, and build a mirror image of their data center. They run all the appropriate lines and connections to the old school and bring the system online to mirror their primary data center. Several of these sites are scattered around the countryside, though the neighbors may not even know what goes on in there because there aren't any signs.

In this case, a company will have covered all the bases. If something were to happen where the main computer center was rendered inoperable, business would go on as usual. Because of the built-in redundancy, any one of the centers can act as a standalone computer center and keep the company's vital business operations going.

Your company may not have the need of such an elaborate risk-management system. It's also expensive. Your equipment may not have the same degree of security necessary as this particular business, but everything on your network should be protected.

Here are some things to think about. Although most of these issues may seem very obvious, each is a problem that has been experienced out in the field:

- Make sure important computers are placed in safe, secure environments. Placing a file server, with monitor and keyboard, in the main company lobby is not a wise idea. Placing a file server in the company break room, directly under the coffee maker, is a disaster waiting to happen. Yes, companies are this foolish. I could name names.

- Make sure network components are behind locked doors in a ventilated, air-conditioned, humidity-controlled environment. Although putting the network components in the unventilated, non-air-conditioned wiring closet may save space and money, it is a death warrant for the components.

- Make sure you have adequate ancillary equipment. Servers should be plugged into UPS systems that are capable of keeping the server up until someone can politely bring it down, or the UPS should be able to shut the system down automatically. Make sure the UPS you are using *conditions* the power as well as provides a backup source of power. You would like to believe that the power coming from the power generating plant is clean, noise free, and without power spikes. You would also like to believe in the Easter Bunny. The worst case of power damage to a system that I repaired was at a power-generating station. The file server took a spike and blew out the main board. The nice part about it, from my perspective, was troubleshooting had never been easier. The smell of fried silicon is one odor that is easy to identify.

- The mantra of all good network administrators should be back up, back up, back up. It is the first line of data defense, and because it is so routine, mundane, and boring, it is often overlooked. If you are working without a good backup and you are doing a relatively dangerous operation, you will get that sinking feeling in your stomach when Murphy's Law comes into play.

More True Confessions

This one, though, wasn't my fault.

I was doing an e-mail migration from one version of a popular e-mail program to another. I was brought in as the consultant on the project to do the initial migration and make sure things were working right.

I started working with the network manager and his staff. As soon as we started getting into stuff that could lead to data loss, they kicked off a backup. After the backup was completed, we checked it by verifying a file. Everything was good to go, so we did.

We started the process by migrating a key component to the new version. While the system was working through the migration and database upgrade, we decided that patience was called for at this juncture, so we went to dinner. When we got back, we checked the server screen to see the progress of the work we were doing, and while flipping through open windows, the network manager got a funny look on his face and then turned pale. It seems that while we were at dinner, the normal daily backup kicked off at 9 P.M., and it was set to overwrite whatever tape was in the system. The tape that was in the tape backup unit was the e-mail backup tape we made before the process started. The tape was now useless, so there was no going back. Our safety net had been removed.

More True Confessions *(continued)*

Luckily, everything worked just fine, and the migration went through without a hitch. I must admit, that was one night when I missed a lot of sleep for not being more careful and insisting on physically holding the tape in my hands.

- Limit access to the locked computer room. Do not put a single key in a central location so that everyone can get to it. Pass out individual keys, use a card-reader entry system, use a button pad, do something to make sure that not everyone has access to the computer room. Be sure this is done before something bad happens.

The Story of the Thief with Good Timing

One of the people I worked with spent a weekend upgrading a file server for a new client. They went all out, adding a fancy new internal tape backup unit, upgrading the memory, adding more disk space, putting in faster controllers, creating a RAID system, you get the picture. At the end of Saturday night, everything was working fine, so my friend kicked off the tape backup job and went home to play with his family, congratulating himself on a job well done.

When he arrived to work on Monday morning, he had a dozen voice-mail messages, all from the company he had been at over the weekend. Panic had ensued, because people could not authenticate into the file server. As my friend took the long drive back to the site, all he could think about was, "Okay, what could I have possibly screwed up?" When he arrived at the site, he ran in, grabbed the key from the central repository, and rushed back to the computer room. When he threw open the door, he saw why there was a problem.

No wonder people couldn't authenticate to the server. The server had been stolen, complete with the new internal tape backup unit, and the last known good backup.

Redundancy in Network Links

One of the most often overlooked aspects of risk management is the links between offices. While all the hardware may be protected to the fullest extent, a network line going down can effectively stop your business. Make sure that you take this into consideration as you plan your disaster-recovery scheme. In addition, make sure that there is an alternate way of getting there from here.

Redundancy not only applies to lines coming into the building but also applies to the routes defined to get from one office to another.

Data Risk Assessment

As I mentioned earlier, there are basically four ways of checking whether your data is at risk. These methods are diagrammed in Figure 17.1.

Figure 17.1   Data Risk Assessment Tools

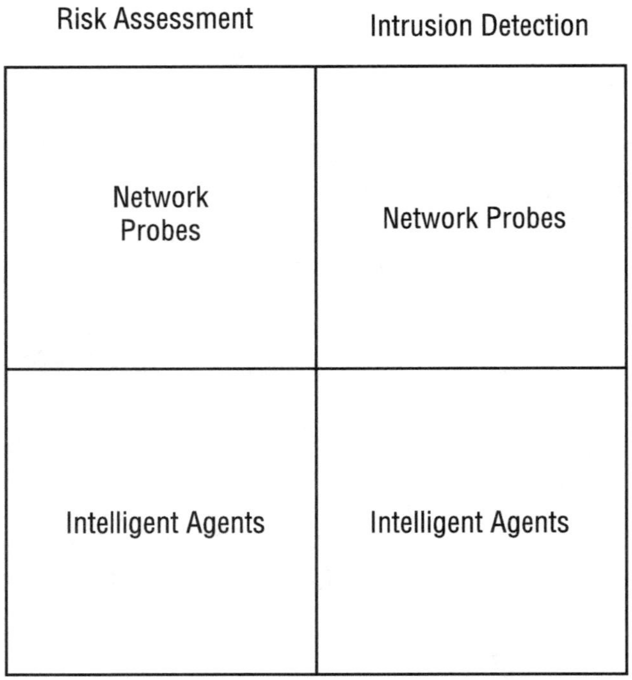

Risk Assessment   Intrusion Detection

| Network Probes | Network Probes |
| Intelligent Agents | Intelligent Agents |

Risk Assessment Using Network Probes

If you were to go back to the bookstore where you bought this book, you would find any number of computer books written about network security. Most of these books come complete with a CD-ROM, and many come with links to areas of the Internet where you can get utilities to attempt to break into your own network. Many of these probes are exceptionally easy to deploy. Once deployed, a network probe launches a break-in attempt across a network from a central computer and then documents which attempts were successful. This approach effectively simulates how intruders would attempt to find potential vulnerabilities. Because the software only has to run on a single machine, using network probes does not involve supporting individual operating systems or distributing and installing software on each and every computer.

The network-probe approach has several inherent weaknesses. Hacker attacks hit one computer and one security vulnerability at a time. It can take a single computer a long time to assess the risks to a large number of systems. Sometimes it is impossible to distinguish between the legitimate and illegitimate use of this type of product on the systems being attacked. Even more of a concern is that all the information gathered about security holes is subject to eavesdropping when it is transferred back to the central computer in clear text across the network.

Risk Assessment Using Intelligent Agents

An alternative technique is to deploy intelligent agents that reside on individual computers. These agents contain security policies that define the vulnerabilities to look for and how to correct them automatically. This is a feature that is not found with network probes. Security policies can be defined to check for potential vulnerabilities in databases, middleware and business applications, and operating systems. These agents are considerably more thorough than products that simply attack a computer from another computer on the network. Risk assessments can be scheduled and run on multiple computers in parallel, thereby speeding up the process. Most agents have a low overhead with regard to network traffic, so companies can afford to run risk assessment across the enterprise on a daily basis. The agents will also typically encrypt the results before transmitting their reports back to the central management interface. This means the information is not subject to eavesdropping.

Just like the network probe, the intelligent agent has some problems. For example, it still cannot exactly mimic what an intruder would do. The most effective method is to use a combination of network probes and intelligent agents. The issue here is that very few vendors will offer both in a single product. As the security market becomes more sophisticated, the tools will be enhanced to provide cryptographic identifications of the person using the product, canned security policies for major applications, and more sophisticated vulnerability checking.

For example, if a risk-assessment tool penetrates a computer system and steals passwords, it would then go out and revisit other computers that have not been successfully penetrated and try to use the passwords on these systems.

Intrusion Detection

If you have done your homework, your network may be close to impervious. However, that won't stop people from trying to get into the system. You should still document break-in attempts to gather legal evidence. One way of doing that is to implement an intrusion-detection system that is capable of identifying an attempted break-in while it's occurring.

Intrusion Detection Using Network Probes

Two distinct approaches can be used to detect attempted intrusions. The first uses network probes and involves actively monitoring all network activity from a centrally located computer on the network. Network traffic is inspected, and suspicious activity is immediately reported to security administrators. This approach is easy to implement, but network probes can mistake legitimate traffic for illegitimate traffic and vice versa. Network probes cannot detect an intrusion attempt penetrated across an encrypted connection, such as a VPN.

Intrusion Detection Using Intelligent Agents

The other approach to detecting intrusions is to deploy intelligent agents on every system and periodically check any audit trails produced by the operating systems, databases, and applications. Audit trails contain information about various attempts to access a computer system and whether those attempts were successful. Although intelligent agents can detect intrusions coming across an encrypted network connection, the intrusion may be detected well after the fact. This delay is caused by the frequency with which an agent examines the audit trail. An audit trail is also the first thing intruders will modify once they have successfully penetrated a computer or applications. Additionally, many administrators disable audit-trail facilities because of the excessive CPU and disk space they require.

Intelligent agents can also detect intrusions by actively monitoring all the possible network connection points on the computer where it resides. The agent continuously checks to see whether anyone is attempting to circumvent the standard access methods and exploit any known vulnerabilities, such as anonymous FTP or back doors in the electronic-mail daemon. This approach consumes more CPU time than simply monitoring the audit trails and requires the intelligent agent to have knowledge of any new security vulnerabilities that may have been recently discovered by the computer system's vendors.

Crackers and More

One of the really great parts of my job as a certified computer trainer is that I get to meet all types of interesting people with fascinating jobs. One person I encountered worked for On-Track Computer in Minneapolis. On-Track is a data-recovery service, and when you screw up and erase data so that it absolutely cannot be retrieved, they will figure out how to get it back. Of course, you also get back a very large bill, but that is okay. The person I met was in charge of the virus-protection division of On-Track. All day long, his job was to try to locate viruses and try to figure out how to defeat them. When we got to talking about the people who write viruses, he said that usually these people were young males, under the age 20, who were in need of a date. Since that oversimplification was passed out, things have changed somewhat. Although the socially inept young person can still be a problem, the ones who are far more dangerous are those who know the ins and outs of the latest security auditing and cracking tools. These people also know how to modify these tools for specific attacks and can write their own programs. This is the type of person who not only reads about the latest security holes but also personally discovers bugs and vulnerabilities. This is a data-deadly person who can strike and hide their tracks without a hint of a trail.

What Is the Point?

These supercrackers have gone beyond the old scenario of trying to get into a site just because it is there. Now, there is a purpose. That purpose could be personal monetary gain, a hit-and-run attack to gather specific information, a challenge to get into a major or prestigious site, or just to receive some notoriety amongst their peers. These supercrackers are hard to find, harder to stop, and hardest to keep out of your site for good.

How Do They Do It?

There are literally hundreds of ways to hack into a system. Some groups have even written software that was designed to help you gather information about your particular system. One of the most popular programs around is Security Analysis Tool for Auditing Networks (SATAN). SATAN examines a remote host or set of hosts and gathers as much information as possible by remotely probing Network Information Service (NIS), finger commands, Network Facilities Services (NFS), File Transfer Protocol (FTP) and Trivial File Transfer Protocol (TFTP), Remote Program Execution Daemon (REXD) and other services. SATAN uses this information and includes the presence of various network information services and potential security flaws. These flaws come in the form of incorrectly set up or configured network services, well-known bugs in the systems or network utilities, or just poor policy decisions.

The goal of any incursion is to gain information. Information comes from various sources, certainly from using the commands and utilities just mentioned to their best advantage. For example, using the finger command will show the cracker who is logged into the host and whether the user is active or idle. If the user is idle, chances are no one will notice the break-in. Finger has various command-line switches that can be employed to find out very interesting things about a host. This information can include account names, home directories, and the name of the host the account last logged in from. Another command that is added to this information is rusers. This command will provide information on logged-in users.

The Unix command showmount is another very powerful command. When run against a remote host, this command will show which file systems are shared or exported. If a user finds that the mounted file system is Network File System (NFS), the remote user can create a guest account in the local password file. Once the user guest has been created, you can put an .rhosts entry in the remote guest-home directory. This will allow you to log in to the target machine and not have to provide a password.

There are other methods for accessing a host. For example, if the host has anonymous FTP enabled, it may be misconfigured. There may be a complete copy of the /etc/passwd file in the anonymous FTP ~ftp/etc directory. If the home directory of FTP is writable, you can remotely execute a command to mail the passwd file back to yourself. You get the point. For someone that is knowledgeable, your network could be an open book.

Using Security Auditing Tools

Unix, Linux, NetWare, and Windows NT/2000 are all vulnerable to attacks and have well-documented security holes. These holes can usually be fixed by applying the appropriate patches, but this requires almost full-time dedication to searching Web sites and patch lists to ensure that you are using the most recent iteration of all the patches. When you get one thing patched, another thing pops up to make you vulnerable again.

NetWare and NT are not nearly as "open" as Unix and Linux, but they're still vulnerable. Unix is a fairly secure operating system, but there are several books explaining security holes within a site.

There is no way that a software solution can reasonably be expected to identify all security problems on any system. In this section, I will focus primarily on the Unix system and the Computer Oracle Password and Security System (COPS). COPS was written back in the early 1990s and is considered the bellwether for Unix security standards.

COPS is a collection of programs and shell scripts that attempt to address as many of the Unix security problems as possible. The main goal of COPS is prevention. It tries to anticipate and eliminate security problems by making sure people don't get a chance to compromise security in the first place. COPS is made up of a variety of smaller programs that perform different tasks. For example, one part of COPS checks "vital" system directories to see whether they are world-writable. The directories listed as critical include the following:

- /
- /etc
- /usr

- /bin
- /Mail
- /usr/spool
- /usr/adm
- /usr/etc
- /usr/lib
- /usr/bin
- /usr/spool/mail
- /usr/spool/uucp
- /usr/spool/at

In this case, COPS reads through a configuration file (`dir.chklst`) that contains all of the potential danger spots and then compares each of the directory modes with a bit mask to see whether it is world-writable. The program that performs this task is `dir.chk`.

COPS checks vital system files to see whether they are world-writable, to see whether those same system files are world-readable, and to see whether all files in the system are qualified for SUID status. COPS will check the password files, looking for null passwords, an improper number of fields, nonunique user IDs, nonnumeric group IDs, blank lines, and nonalphanumeric user IDs. It will also check the passwords of the users on the system, comparing the encrypted passwords found in the `/etc/passwd` file with the encrypted login ID and all single-letter passwords.

In addition, COPS looks at the `/etc/group` file, where it looks for groups with passwords, an improper number of fields, a duplicate number of users in groups, blank lines, and nonunique group IDs.

COPS then goes in and starts checking the root path and making sure that many of the files are world-writable. It examines commands and looks at data files.

Results from Running COPS

Not surprisingly, the results of running COPS varies from system to system and from site to site. Some results were consistent (and these results show that there is a reasonable amount of security concern for all of the machines tested) but were not necessarily the fault of Unix. After all, different vendors and administrators have varying opinions on how a machine should be set up.

Trusts

Another issue of security is *trust relationships*. The problems involved with trusts seem to cross operating-system boundaries. It doesn't matter if a cracker is entering an NT system, a Unix system, or a Novell system; if the trusts are not set up properly, getting access to one account can grant access to the entire network.

The word *trust* is used whenever there is a situation when a host that allows remote access can permit a local resource to be used by a client without password authentication, when password authentication is normally required. In the Unix world, there are many ways a host can trust. Using the .rhosts and hosts.equiv files allow access without password verification. Window's servers will allow remote systems to use and abuse privileges, and export files can control other files via NFS.

Nearly all of these access methods rely on the client IP address to host-name conversion to determine whether or not a service is to be granted. In the simplest method, the file /etc/hosts is used as part of a direct lookup. Today, the hosts file has become more or less obsolete; systems are using DNS, NIS, or both for name lookup service. A reverse lookup occurs when a server has an IP address and needs the host name for verification.

Although the concepts involved in trust relationships are well understood by most system administrators, the dangers of trusts and the practical problems they represent is one of the least understood problems of the Internet. This goes beyond the obvious hosts.equiv and .rhosts files; NFS, NIS, and windowing systems are based on the concept that well-known sites are trusted in some way. What is not understood is how networking so tightly binds security between what are normally considered disjointed hosts.

Any form of trust can be spoofed, fooled, or subverted. This is especially true when the authority that gets queried to check the credentials of the client is outside the server's administrative domain or when the trust mechanism is based on something that has a weak form of authentication.

The problem is compounded if the intruder can convince the target host that he or she is coming from a trusted host. It is now sufficient just to find out which hosts are trusted by the target. This task is often helped by examining where system administrators and system accounts last logged in from.

Two methods can be used to prevent such attacks. The first method is the most direct. If your site doesn't use a trust, you won't be vulnerable to host spoofing. The other strategy is to use some form of cryptographic protocol. Using a secure RPC protocol is one method. Although secure RPC has been "broken" cryptographically, it still provides better assurance than RPC authentication schemes that do not use any form of encryption. Other solutions include both hardware, such as smartcards, and software, such as Kerberos.

Top Ten Things to Increase Internal Security

Here is a list of ten things you can do to increase the internal security of your network. It is not an all-inclusive list by any means. It is not designed for networks where everything must be 100 percent secure every day. This is designed for average networks (if there is such a thing). Take a look at the list, and see whether something here can help you.

1. When in doubt, patch it.
2. Implement effective password schemes.
3. Make default accounts inaccessible.
4. Assign user and group rights appropriately.
5. Make e-mail secure.
6. Have an intruder-detection action plan.
7. Use encryption.
8. Keep critical network segments segregated.
9. Use removable disks and drives.
10. Monitor information access.

When in Doubt, Patch It

There are several different philosophies about patching computers. Many people take the philosophy that if it ain't broke, don't fix it. They contend that more often than not, a patch will fix one thing and break another.

The other philosophy says that if a major hardware or software vendor has gone so far as to issue a patch, chances are they have seen some problems and are trying to fix them. Many times the fixes exceed the list that is contained in the readme file, or the patch is designed to fix one thing, and when it does, it also corrects about a dozen other things along the way.

Hardly a week goes by without some group taking credit for finding a security hole in some operating system, browser, or application. Thankfully, the manufacturers are quick to spot these holes, confirm them, and usually issue a patch. It only works if you apply it.

Get in the habit of checking for the latest patches for whatever operating systems, browsers, and applications you use. If new patches come out, especially if they concern security, apply it. You will be better off in the long run.

Implement Effective Password Schemes

I live in Minnesota, the home of Minnesota Mining and Manufacturing, otherwise known as 3M. To network administrators everywhere, 3M is the company that has unwittingly done the most to undermine network security. After all, they produce Scotch tape and Post-It notes.

Starting in Network Administration 101 at the local technical college, would-be system administrators are taught that unique logon names and strict password policies are the first line of defense in your corporate network. If these two things are easily compromised, any other security measures are not very effective.

Password Minimum Size

Set a minimum number of characters for a password. All the major network operating systems allow administrators to do this. The reason you are setting a minimum is to make it more difficult for someone to guess a password. The more letters you require, the harder it will be for someone to guess a password; but keep in mind, it will also be harder for users (including you) to enter. So you need to reach a happy medium. You want to have your password minimum set to the maximum number of letters your users can remember without writing it down. Many companies seem to feel that six or seven letters in a password is a happy medium.

Password Makeup

Stress to your users that their passwords should contain letters and numbers. Common names should not be allowed. If you really want to be security conscious, find a program that will randomly generate a series of letters and numbers and have that program assign all the passwords. You may also want to get a copy of some cracking code and run it on your system. The cracking code will go out and test passwords against a dictionary. If it finds a word that it recognizes, it makes a note of that entry.

NOTE   Books devoted to security often contain a cracking code on an included CD.

Passwords should be changed frequently, and passwords should be unique, meaning your users cannot use the same password over and over again.

User Education

Make up a security policy, and stick to it. Passwords *must* be kept private. Any user caught giving out a password should be subject to some sort of disciplinary action. This discipline should be part of the written policy the employees sign when they start working for the company.

You are probably saying to yourself, but what about my system? My users have to remember a logon name and password for an NT domain, a username and password for a NetWare system, a password for the mainframe, an e-mail password, a PIN for the voice-mail system, and three passwords for software access. How can you ask them to change these regularly, keep them unique, and still remember them? This is a tough question, especially because the password policy is the thing users will complain about the most. So what do you do?

Ultimately, your job in the IS department is to protect the data. That is why these sections on security are written. The whole system is designed to protect the data. It is true that a user has a lot to remember and passwords can be an irritant. It is also true that the same user who screams the loudest about having so many passwords to remember is the same end user who can quote the batting average of their favorite baseball player over the last ten years, replay their five best holes of golf, stroke for stroke, knows which beanie babies are scarce and how much each one sold for, and can remember what they planted in their garden last year and what the crop outcome was. Sorry, folks, it is hard to feel sorry for people having to remember ten extra sequences of numbers and letters when they can already handle this amount of vital information.

Audit the passwords, check them regularly, and police them. Have no sympathy for people who forget and even less for anyone giving out their password or leaving an open computer connection.

Different Strokes for Different Folks

Password policies can be fluid things. Depending on your network, you may have several levels of password security. For example, a clerk in the word-processing department may not have the same level of access to sensitive information as the head of the payroll department. In this case, the password restrictions can be set differently for the clerk than for the payroll manager.

> **TIP** For an interesting article on passwords, see the 1985 work from the Department of Defense, titled the *Department of Defense Password Management Guideline* at alw.nih.gov/security/FIRST/papers/password/dodpwman.txt.

Remove Default Accounts

For Windows NT/2000, there is Administrator; for NetWare 5, there is Admin; for NetWare 3.x, there is Supervisor; and for Unix, there is root. In each case, there is a default user that has powerful rights to the entire system. The problem is not that these users exist, the problem is that everyone who has ever worked on a network knows they exist. The first line of network defense is the username/password. You must match a valid username with a valid password. If someone already knows half of the equation, the second half is easier to break.

Change the Name to Protect the Innocent

Change the name of the administrative user, or even remove the user. In NT, the administrator account cannot be removed, only renamed. In NetWare 4.x and 5.x, renaming or removing is not difficult to do. In NetWare 3.x, you cannot rename or remove the Supervisor account; it is there to stay.

TIP   Before removing an administrative account, make sure there is another account somewhere in the system with full rights. You want to protect the system, not make it unreachable.

Supervisor Passwords

Would it surprise you to know that the easiest account to break into is the administrative account? Common sense tells you why. How many people are in your IS department with access to the administrative account? If the number is more than one, we have a communication issue. Typically, the super-user account gets a password during the creation of the system. It is rarely, if ever, changed, simply because it would involve communicating with too many people. You might forget one, and that person would be the one who needs it during an emergency. So to "protect the system," the super-user never has the password changed.

Moreover, it is well known that the most common passwords on administrative accounts are GOD, Supervisor, Administrator, and Password. Short, sweet, easy to remember, and easy to crack. If your password is not one of these, how about the name of the company, the phone number of the company, the address of the company, the name of the company president, or something else common to the entire system? I bet there is someone blushing right now.

If you cannot remove or rename the account, certainly make the password difficult to guess.

Assigning User and Group Rights

You haven't been in networking very long if you haven't heard the horror stories about networks where everyone logging in was given supervisor or administrator rights to everything. When asked why, the IS department said it was easier.

User and group rights are a complicated issue, simply because many administrators don't fully understand how they work. In addition, in these days of mixed networks, you have to understand not only how file-system rights work in an NT environment but also how these rights interact with the NetWare system, the mainframe, and any Unix or Mac systems.

No matter which network operating system you use, group rights are a key management concept. Effective network management is democratic. Doing unto many rather than doing unto one at a time makes the life of an administrator easier.

File System Rights

Data is placed on a network to share. That is the reason the network was created. Your challenge is to determine, with the help of management, who gets to share what data and what they can do with the data they have access to.

That means the question is not whether we want to share data, but whom we want to share data with. Most networks have some sort of shared area, where anyone and everyone can store and retrieve data. Some of that data may not be appropriate for everyone to have access.

How does a network administrator handle this problem? Usually, the issue is solved by the creation of workgroups and workgroup-storage areas. The most difficult part of this security scheme is trying to figure out who belongs to which workgroup. This is usually a lot more difficult than it sounds.

As you plan these areas, have some of the groups overlap. For example, the budgeting department will probably need to have some idea about how much money is brought in during a certain time period as well as how much money is going out. This will involve read-only access to both the accounts-receivable and the accounts-payable sections.

Different NOS, Different Security

The trick is to know the limitations of each of the security systems you are working with. You will also be expected to know how the different NOSs work together to give people access to information.

When instituting a new file-system plan, it is always a good idea to lay it out on paper. You would be surprised how many holes you can find when you put it in graphical form. You will also be able to spot those areas of overlap when one person should belong to two different groups with opposite needs.

This scheme will also give you the opportunity to test out the effects of your assignments. It is always best to spot problems before they are put into production. For example, the CEO really doesn't need to know that you *almost* blocked their visibility to all sales and accounting data.

Unique User Directories

One area where the group concept definitely will not work is the unique user directory, or the home directory. Every user gets one, and every user stuffs it full of all sorts of things.

Each of the major network operating systems has the facility to create a user directory when you create the users. This directory will be a repository for the end user's stuff; the end user will have full access to this directory. It is up to the end user to police this home directory. The responsibility of the administrator is to back the material up and make sure the area adheres to the corporate disk-space management policies.

Make E-Mail Secure

In corporate America today, the three largest-selling LAN/WAN groupware solutions are Microsoft Exchange, Novell GroupWise, and Lotus Notes/Domino. Because these are the big three, we will concentrate on them.

The three packages have many things in common. They are all groupware, so you can do more than just send e-mail. Because they are LAN/WAN-based, messages are stored in a central location called the *message store*. They all use some form of client/server connection, relying on TCP/IP to connect the client with the agents that can access the message store.

These entire solutions store messages in different types of databases, and the messages and attachments are all encrypted when they are sent and when they are stored. It would appear that sending and storing messages across a corporate network is relatively secure. Just choosing one of these packages puts you on the right track for securing your internal e-mail. The major security "holes" come from the person sitting behind the keyboard.

Each of the packages has the ability to have a password placed on the e-mail client. In other words, a user cannot access the message store until they enter in the appropriate password. Some of the packages allow this password to be synchronized with the network logon password, allowing the user to access both the network and the e-mail with a single password. This is a two-edged sword. Although it is more convenient for the end user, finding one password gives the potential cracker access to the network and e-mail resources for the end users. Administrators may be reluctant to impose yet another password on users; but for the most important users, it may be necessary. After all, what if some sly little devil manages to go into the CEO's mailbox and read all the mail, or even worse, send mail to various people within the organization.

The End User and E-Mail Security

The biggest source of security leaks inside an organization is the end user. End users tend to be really lax when it comes to things such as making sure they have closed out of all network sessions before leaving their desks. Many people will fire up their e-mail client when they first get into work in the morning and never shut it down completely. It is always there and waiting. This is very convenient for the end users and also very convenient for someone who wants to peek inside the e-mail account. Stress to your users that they must close down their systems at night.

Have an Intruder-Detection Action Plan

Many companies spend a lot of time planning security and testing security, but they never ever check to see if their security plan has been breached. Even worse, they have no clue what to do if sensitive data has been compromised.

The time to decide what you are going to do is before the event happens. This is especially true of sensitive corporate material that you may not want viewed from inside the company. Lay out a security policy for sensitive data. Audit the data to make sure it cannot be accessed by unauthorized people. Determine what the penalties will be for unauthorized access. Make sure there is a reporting procedure in place, and everyone from the CEO on down knows the policy and how to implement it.

TIP   Make sure your security policy has some provision for network administrator access. There may be times when an administrator needs to have access to that particular section of the network to do their job. Ensure that there are ways for the administrator to gain permission for temporary access.

Use Encryption

The world of data encryption is changing. More than 20 years ago IBM designed the earliest version of what has become known as the Data Encryption Standard (DES). DES is currently used on Unix machines for password encryption.

Here is how DES works: DES takes the information and encodes it using a one-way operation called a *hash*. While the hash is not foolproof, decoding it is a complex task that will eat up resources. For example, it has been estimated that a password can be encoded almost 4,100 different ways. Here is what was said by the National Institute of Standards and Technology (NIST), in the publication "Data Encryption Standard (DES)" from the *Federal Information Processing Standards Publication 46-2,* published in 1993:

"The cryptographic algorithm DES transforms a 64-bit binary value into a unique 64-bit binary value based on a 56-bit variable. If the complete 64-bit input is used and if the 56-bit variable is randomly chosen, no technique other than trying all possible keys using known input and output for the DES will guarantee finding the chosen key. As there are 70,000,000,000,000,000 (70 quadrillion) possible keys of 56 bits, the feasibility of deriving a particular key in this way is extremely unlikely in typical threat environments."

This was written back in 1993; in the late 1990s, computing power has grown and cracking DES is coming closer and closer to reality. To solve this problem, the United States Federal Government and the NIST are now working on replacement standards, and the NIST is currently in the process of evaluating standards.

Strong 128-bit encryption is available in Microsoft Internet Explorer and Netscape Navigator. The algorithms for strong encryption are well known. The most widely accepted is RSA Data Security's encryption scheme using a public key and then decrypting by the recipient using a private key.

Keep Critical Network Segments Segregated

Earlier in the chapter, the problem of trust relationships was discussed. A trust relationship is formed when network segments are joined to produce larger, more diverse networks.

This network expansion is a good thing for administration. If you have one large network, instead of a dozen small networks, it is easier for a centralized group of information-technology professionals to manage and administer the network.

From a security point of view, bigger is not always better. If a hacker gains access to one section of the interconnected network, the hacker will have access to the entire network. If, however, certain network segments are deemed to be security risks, it might prove to be a wise idea to keep them segregated. You may want to ensure that the network segment is self-sufficient and keep it apart from the rest of the WAN. It will not ensure invincibility, but it will reduce the risk of a network segment being attacked from within.

Use Removable Disks and Drives

People cannot get access to information that they cannot find, so when in doubt, hide the information. That sounds really straightforward, doesn't it?

Typically with critical special projects, data is stored on some kind of file server. The information is backed up, and a copy is kept at a secure off-site location, but the information is still on the file server and susceptible to attack. Recently, there have been advances in hardware that allow for storage of data on removable devices. The removable media can be removed from the system and stored in a safe place, such as a locked, fireproof, heat-resistant safe.

Several companies have come out with removable devices that can store up to 5GB of data. Hard drives are removable, so the entire drive can be removed from the system and stored in a safe place.

Monitor Information Access

Auditing, or logging, is the practice of keeping track of who is doing what where on your network. Auditing programs are designed to track who logged on to the network at what time, how long they stayed on the network, and what they did while they were connected.

Most network operating systems support some form of auditing or logging. Both Microsoft Windows NT/2000 and Novell NetWare have an auditing or a logging function built in. In both cases, the auditing can be customized to track certain events rather than try to track everything that is happening on the network.

Who Should Be the Auditor?

Because auditing is the practice of tracking who is accessing what information, and because the network administrator is the person with the most rights on the network, the designated network auditor should *not* be the system administrator or any member of the IS team. Putting someone with full rights in charge of auditing is kind of like having the fox watch the henhouse. The person in charge of auditing should have the rights necessary to access any section of the network, but usually, the auditor can just look and not touch. The auditor can track who has accessed a file but cannot see the contents of the file. In this case, the auditor will know that someone was playing in the payroll data files but will not have the rights or permissions to enter and read these files.

What Should Be Audited?

The network auditor should be instructed to keep track of the data in the sensitive areas of the company, but auditing can involve much more. For example, the auditor may decide to track all system logins between the hours of 5 P.M. and 8 A.M., just to see whether any strange activity happens during the off hours.

Auditors should also be versed in hacking techniques. It helps if you understand the person who may be trying to access the network. This will let the auditor know to watch out for any accounts where there are repeated refused logins because of bad passwords or for anyone trying to access the /etc/passwrd file on a Unix system.

Auditors should try to track any activity that is not normal. Of course, the definition of normal tends to change from company to company. Your auditor has to make that call and stick to it. The auditor should also be aware that doing random checks on random events is probably a wise idea. Because random checks may be made, this information should be published so that everyone knows about it. That way, if something does show up, there will be no surprises. It is also a proactive way of stopping problems before they start.

Auditors should also be involved in software-licensing decisions. Most of the auditing programs available include tools for protecting your company against running unlicensed software.

A Final Word on Security

The cheapest and easiest form of security is employee education. Any security plan is only as good as the employees carrying it out. If anyone within the organization sees anything suspicious, there should be a reporting method in place, and every report should be handled promptly and taken seriously.

Employees should also know that there are penalties for violating corporate security and that these penalties will be enforced. Too often, threats are made and are proven to be empty. Once that happens, all the policies in the world aren't worth the paper they are written on.

Security is important to your company. Do not assume you network is safe, do not assume that all the threats will come from the outside. Make sure you have operational plans in effect before an event occurs so you know what to do when an attack happens. After all of your data has been compromised, now is not the best time to come up with a security plan.

18

External Security

In some of the previous chapters, I have touched on issues of protecting your network from the big, bad, outside world. This was especially true in the chapter on Proxy servers. In this chapter, we will take an in-depth look at the security issues surrounding the Internet. There are many ways to protect your network from outside attack, but it seems that as soon as you do, another new threat appears.

People traditionally define attacks from the outside as coming from hackers or crackers sneaking their way into your network from the Internet in all sorts of underhanded ways. But they are not the only people who can harm your network. There's the person who writes viruses. There's also the person who takes advantages of holes in remote-access connections or the people who find a way to scam information from those who are trying to buy your product off your Web page. In this chapter, I will look at all these possibilities and offer some suggestions.

Firewalls and Gateways

One of the first lines of defense for your network is a firewall. A firewall sits between your network and the outside world, and it helps protect your network by keeping the bad packets out and making sure the good packets go where they are supposed to.

At first glance, firewalls and gateways may seem an odd combination of topics. A firewall brings to mind a rather rigid set of rules and specifications that make a judgment every time a packet comes through the system. A gateway, on the other hand, brings to mind smoke and mirrors. A gateway is something that translates from one "language" to another.

Firewalls 101

A firewall is any device designed to prevent users outside your network from accessing your network. It is usually a combination of hardware and software, and many firewalls can perform multiple tasks. The first thing to understand about firewalls is why they are necessary.

As we discussed in Chapter 8, Bridging and Routing with TCP/IP, your network needs a router to connect to the Internet. This router knows where the Internet is, and when it receives a packet destined for the outside world, it passes the packet on. Because the router is a key part of Internet communications, every other workstation must point to it as part of its TCP/IP configuration. Because all these other workstations are going to be looking for the router, the router must have a static IP address.

Static IP addresses can be wonderful things. When a router is assigned a static IP address, every workstation inside the network can find that address and use that system as a portal to the Internet. Tricky things, portals. Not only do they let things out but they also let things in. Somehow there has to be a method of protecting what comes into the network. That is the job of the firewall. Figure 18.1 shows where a firewall would be positioned.

Figure 18.1   Firewall positioning

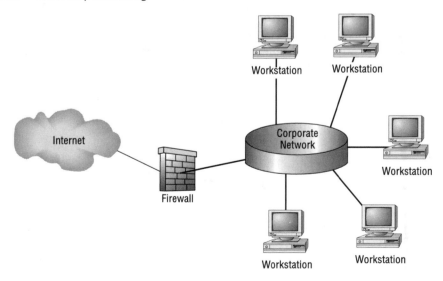

When packets are sent to and received from the Internet, one of the ways these packets are identified is by the IP address. The IP address acts as a very rudimentary form of authentication on the network. In fact, whenever you access the Internet, you are probably authenticating your IP address, and you don't even realize it. Moreover, many of the Web pages you access will keep track of your IP address as a way to know where to send back information that you request. Essentially, the IP addresses of all the workstations on your network are flying around the Internet. Anyone can get the address of your computer, and that is the first step toward entry into the network.

What Makes Up a Firewall?

The first major component of a really good firewall is planning. There are dozens of firewall packages, some costing tons of money, others available as shareware or with the purchase of hardware. But what really separates one firewall from another is the planning that went into the installation and the follow-through after the system has been up and working for a period of time.

Firewall hardware can be just a router. Many routers have advanced security features built in. In other instances, firewalls are hardware and software. Because a firewall is a pass-through mechanism, the hardware does not need to be state-of-the-art for most implementations. The main job a firewall does is accept or reject a packet.

Types of Firewalls

As mentioned above, firewalls come in all shapes and sizes. There are two main implementations of firewalls: a router-based, packet-filtering device or an application-based, proxy firewall/gateway.

Router-Based, Packet-Filtering Firewalls

Router-based, packet-filtering firewalls work at the point of entry into the network. The router examines every packet that comes into the network and decides whether to allow the packet access or to discard it. This decision is based on a scheme laid out by the network administrator and is usually based on the source address of the packet.

The router can be configured to allow all packets into the network if they come from a particular network address, thereby disallowing everything else. The flip side of this coin is to allow everything into the network, unless is comes from a particular network.

In the first example, imagine you have two offices connected by TCP/IP through a router. In addition, your network has Internet access, but it is through the remote office. Figure 18.2 shows you what I mean.

Figure 18.2   Sample office layout with Internet connectivity

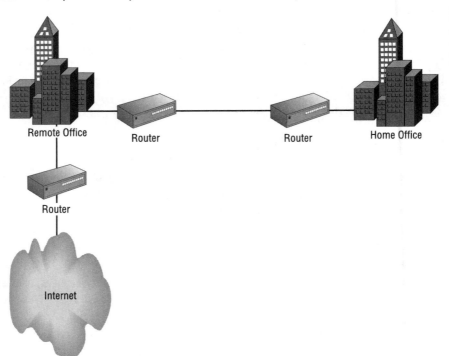

As you can see from this layout, any packet coming into the network at the home office must come through the remote office to be valid. In this case, you would configure packet filtering to allow any packets into the network, as long as those packets were coming from the remote office. Anything with a source address other than the remote office would be rejected.

In the second example, let's say that your network is hooked into the Internet, and you want to make sure that no one is going out and looking at dirty pictures from the site dirtypictures.com. In this case, you configure the system to accept all packets unless the packets come from dirtypictures.com.

The advantage to a router-based firewall is speed and not having to configure another computer to be the firewall. High-end routers use packet filtering based on source address, destination address, protocol, and port number. A low-end router can base its packet filter solely on a source address.

Although the speed of the system is a benefit, it is also a detriment. Packet filtering looks at the source address of the packet. The source address of the packet is relatively easy for crackers to fake. In the case of the forged address, the firewall may provide only the illusion of protection. This is why many of the software designers have improved on packet filtering to take advantage of the other attributes of a packet, such as filtering protocols, ports, or even the time of day.

How can you filter protocols? Assume that your network portal was not going to be used by your e-mail servers. In this case, you would be assured that you would not need any Simple Mail Transfer Protocol traffic coming through the firewall. You could then safely block SMTP by denying access to port 25.

Firewalls Using Ports

How can a firewall improve security by using ports? First of all, you have to understand how a port works. Think of the host IP address as the phone number of your company. This is the front-desk phone number, the one that rings on the desk of the temp receptionist. If someone dialed the main number and asked the temp some very specific questions about your network, they probably would not get much information. However, if the caller reached the number of the main desk and asked for your extension, now all the mysteries of the network would be available. When you think of a port, think of an extension number.

Just like an extension number, a port can be a window through the firewall. At each IP address, certain default services use certain ports. For example, port 80 is commonly used by HTTP, and ports 20 and 21 are used by File Transfer Protocol. Table 18.1 shows some commonly used ports, otherwise known as *well-known services*.

Table 18.1   Well-Known Services

Service Name	Port Number	Protocol	Alias
netstat	15	TCP	
ftp-data	20	TCP	
ftp	21	TCP	
telnet	23	TCP	
smtp	25	TCP	mail
name	42	TCP	name server

Table 18.1   Well-Known Services *(continued)*

Service Name	Port Number	Protocol	Alias
name	42	UDP	name server
whois	43	TCP	
domain	53	TCP	name server
domain	53	UDP	name server
bootp	67	UDP	
tftp	69	UDP	
finger	79	TCP	
pop3	110	TCP	postoffice
nntp	119	TCP	usenet
snmp	161	UDP	snmp
snmp-trap	162	UDP	snmp
exec	512	TCP	
login	513	TCP	
router	520	UDP	router routed
kerberos	749	TCP	kcd
kerberos	749	UDP	kcd
nfs	2049	UDP	Sun NFS
queue	10001	TCP	
gateway	10003	TCP	

When these services are started, they listen on these ports for messages, and when a message comes in, the protocol acts on it. Letting these well-known services go through your firewall is like opening a window in your home. It makes it easier for anyone trying to break in.

One way of working around the port problem is to reassign them, something you as the administrator can do when configuring the firewall. HTTP defaults to port 80, but like most good defaults, it does not have to stay there. You can change the port to whatever you like, as long as your users also know how to make the necessary changes to the browser on their workstations.

Finally, packet filtering can be time-sensitive. We mentioned that SMTP uses port 25. Suppose that you are managing the firewall and you leave the default port address at 25 for SMTP. Your boss comes to you and says that too many people are sneaking into work early to send e-mail to their kids. You can put a stop to this, if your firewall will allow it, by simply limiting SMTP access to the network to between the hours of 8 A.M. to 5 P.M.

There are some other limitations to packet filtering that you should take into account before choosing this method for your firewall. Remote Procedure Calls (RPCs) form two-way communication between hosts. They are difficult to filter because they negotiate the ports they are going to use. The ports are randomly assigned at system start-up. Because the assignment is random, there is no way to filter the RPCs effectively without blocking all of UDP. Blocking all of UDP also blocks necessary services such as DNS.

Application Gateways as Firewalls

Application gateways, as the name implies, are software-based firewalls. They function in a totally different fashion from routing-based firewalls. A gateway is in the business of changing things. It takes a perfectly good piece of data that a PC can understand and changes it so that a mainframe can chew on the data for a while. The gateway may also take that same information and translate it into something only a Mac can deal with.

An application gateway that acts as a firewall works in the same way. It processes each piece of information it receives. It not only decides whether that piece of information is valid for the network, it also changes it before sending it on to the final destination. This is important because it means the IP packet may come out the other side as something completely different, such as IPX.

Application gateways have other advantages, as well. Because the application gateway is doing so much work to the data already, it really isn't a problem to have the gateway write log files also. These gateways usually come with a rather impressive set of utilities to make the gateway do exactly what you want.

The disadvantages of this type of gateway include its increased workload and corresponding loss of speed. An application gateway usually has to be configured for each type of network service. In addition, because all this work is being done on the packets, you can anticipate that the speed is going to take a major hit.

Firewall Issues

After you install a firewall, you shouldn't have any issues, right? Really, they should all be solved! After all, a firewall is what keeps your network safe from the outside world.

It is just that type of attitude that creates one of the biggest fallacies related to firewalls. Too many people take the attitude that once it has been constructed, it can be forgotten. That is simply not the case. Firewalls tend to be like living, breathing organisms, needing attention for the first few formative stages of their lives.

Because a firewall is the first line of defense that your network has from the work of the cracker, it must be built strongly and be restrictive. You have to be very careful about what you let into your network. Unfortunately, the more restrictive you become, the more the services that your network provides may suffer. Somewhere there is a fine line, and it usually takes several attempts before the line is drawn.

Because the firewall is the first line of defense in our arsenal, some administrators tend to make it the only line of defense. They spend so much time on the firewall that they forget there are challenges inside the network, too. When this happens and once the firewall has been penetrated, it is almost like open season on data. Again, the best tool you have in constructing a good firewall is planning. That planning should concern all areas of your security scheme: firewall, passwords, logon names, logon times, domain layouts, trust relationships, etc.

What about those times when even planning isn't going to help? Services on the Internet seem to change daily, and the protocols that access these services change with them. It is bad enough that the services change and the protocols change, but sometimes there are different variations to work around. A prime example would be the recent Microsoft/Sun spat about Java. Sun licensed Java to Microsoft, and Microsoft changed it. For a while, there were two "versions" of Java to contend with. If you use an application gateway, that means someone has to write a new application gateway for the different versions. Chances are this will not happen overnight. You, as a network administrator, will also have to make a major decision while these applications are being written: Do you open up the firewall to take advantage of these nonprotected services, or do you close the firewall to protect your data and have a whole bunch of angry end users? It sort of makes you wonder, is this the reason you make the really big bucks?

Be Alert!

Firewalls fail. It is an unfortunate fact, but they do. The reasons they fail are many, and most revolve around keyboard operation in some way. The firewall may not have been properly installed and configured, or it may not have been properly maintained. Sometimes, however, it is the hardware that fails.

Firewalls are not impenetrable. Hackers and crackers are very good at what they do; otherwise, we wouldn't need this section of the book. There are utilities the hacker/cracker can use to determine what type of firewall you are using. Once that information is known, it is a matter of checking to find out how good the administrator really is. Depending on the platform the firewall runs on, administration may not be an easy job. A firewall running on a Unix box has literally hundreds of applications, protocols, and commands that can point to a hole in the system. After the firewall is in place, be diligent by making sure all the latest patches are applied and keeping up-to-date on the latest types of security attacks. All firewalls do the same types of things; how they do these things depends on the manufacturer. Be sure to read and study the documentation.

Computer Viruses

One of the greatest threats to computer networks today are computer viruses. The United States appears to be at the forefront of defeating these pests, but it is far from immune. Recent outbreaks of e-mail viruses have caused slowdowns of networks and renewed concerns about ways to stop this threat. For the first time recently, an alleged author of a virus was pursued by law enforcement with the aid of electronic and print media.

The existence of viruses and the need to protect against them are a fact of life. It is hard to remember a time when they didn't exist, but it wasn't long ago that computer viruses were unknown. The first viruses were created in university computer laboratories to demonstrate the "potential" threat that such software could provide. By 1987, viruses began showing up at several universities around the world. Three of the viruses still around today—Stoned, Cascade, and Friday the 13th—first made an appearance in 1987. Serious outbreaks of viruses began to appear over the next few years. Viruses became media events, with the Datacrime virus and Friday the 13th getting a lot of ink and air time. In 1990, Bulgaria became known as the world's virus factory: the NCSA found that Bulgaria, home of the notorious Dark Avenger, originated 76 viruses that year.

You may be wondering why Bulgaria was the hotbed of viruses. At the time, there was an abundance of trained, but out-of-work, computer programmers with time on their hands. When these programmers proved to be exceptionally prolific, the computer industry decided that it was time to take some defensive action. IBM created the High Integrity Computing Laboratory to lead the antivirus research effort. About the same time, Symantec began offering Symantec Anti-Virus. By 1991, the first polymorphic viruses—those that change their shape to avoid detection—began to spread and attack in significant numbers. That was also the year that the number of viruses topped the 1,000 mark for the first time.

Virus production began to proliferate, and that explosion continues today. Increasing populations of intelligent, computer-literate young people who appreciate the challenge of writing and releasing new viruses fuel the proliferation. Cultural factors play a role, also. At this time, the United States is the second-largest source of infection. Elsewhere, Germany and Taiwan are the other major contributors of new viruses.

As the number of young people who find the creation of viruses to be a challenge increases, the creation of viruses is getting easier. The same technology that makes it easier to create legitimate software is being applied to virus creation. The so-called Mutation Engine appeared in 1992, facilitating the development of polymorphic viruses. In 1992, the Virus Creation Laboratory, featuring online help and pull-down menus, brought virus creation within reach of even nonsophisticated computer users.

Increasing Numbers of PCs Means Increasing Numbers of Viruses

Because the number of PCs and the number of networks are growing so rapidly, it fuels the process. After all, there are more potential victims. With the shift of computing power moving from mainframe-based networks to PC-based and client/server-based networks, the temptation is almost too great. The current rapid growth of client/server computing is providing fertile ground for the virus writers. Some server-based solutions are precisely the type of computers that are susceptible. Because these servers act as the focal point for data exchange, it makes them an even more attractive target. A virus on one PC in the enterprise is far more likely to communicate with and infect more PCs and servers than would have been true several years ago.

The computer explosion is also helping virus creators because computers are ending up in the hands of relatively inexperienced computer users who are less likely to understand the virus problem. Because they don't understand it, they are more prone to pass viruses along or even be susceptible to scares. One study has shown that if a virus infects a single networked computer, the average time it takes to infect another workstation is 10 to 20 minutes.

The Cost of Virus Infection

When a computer virus hits, how much does it cost? What is the price tag of having to combat a computer virus that runs rampant through the industry? In the United States, someone is always around to put a price tag on a natural disaster. The largest outbreak of a virus in the recent past has been the Melissa.A virus, and unfortunately, there have been no formal estimates. It doesn't take much imagination to realize that Melissa saddled companies, universities, and governments with one very big bill.

Melissa.A was a new virus that rapidly spread around the world, infecting many computers and bringing down networks. It was a Word Macro virus and used Microsoft Outlook to send infected documents across the Internet. The Melissa virus belongs to the so-called Class Infectors and resides in the module "This Document." The module is renamed by the virus to Melissa. When an infected document is opened in Word 8, the virus removes the Tool/Macros menu item and then turns off three options: ConfirmConversion, VirusProtection, and SaveNormalPrompt.

When an infected document was opened in Office 2000, it set several registry keys and then proceeded to execute the most dangerous part of the code. Using Microsoft Outlook, the virus found the first 50 entries from the user's Address Book and sent the infected document as an attachment to those selected recipients. This meant that if a mailing list was one of those first 50 entries, more than 50 users would receive the virus. The subject line in all the sent messages read, "Important Message from—UserName." The text of the message read, "Here is the document you asked for, don't show anyone else ;-)." This somewhat innocuous virus literally brought companies and the Internet to their knees. Mail servers around the world were bogged down handling the sudden influx and expulsion of messages.

Melissa had two kinds of impact: the initial snowball effect and the ripple effect. If the end users opened the attachment that caused the problems, corporate systems were flooded with resource-hogging e-mails in exponentially increasing numbers. As the snowball gathered momentum, more e-mail servers were affected. This interruption in their service was likely to ripple through corporate networks, causing any number of consequences—some obvious, some subtle.

It Wasn't Just Outlook!

Despite the virus's connection with the Outlook client, Microsoft's Exchange Server wasn't the only e-mail server at risk from the Melissa virus. It was capable of striking non-Exchange servers, as well. As a result, e-mail servers of all types experienced outages that crippled everything from corporate networks to Internet service providers. This was especially true for small businesses and ISPs that were keeping costs in check by running multiple applications on one server. In such cases, shutting down the e-mail server may also involve shutting down other mission-critical software, such as database, remote-access, and print servers.

Given this range of failures, putting a price on the impact on a per-user or per-company basis, let alone a nationwide or worldwide basis, is impossible. However, if such a figure were to be computed, it would include some direct as well as indirect costs, not to mention, in some cases, some very subtle costs.

On the direct side of things, there are costs associated with IS personnel time, lost productivity on behalf of end users, and products purchased in an attempt to implement a solution. So far, thousands of network administrators, systems specialists, and consultants have been called, beeped, and paged.

Think of it: If the virus hit on Friday, phones and pagers would be incessantly ringing. Immediately, you would have the cost of engaging an immediate response over the weekend with more follow-up. For the larger companies that employ an IT staff, the cost is immense but may not involve overtime. For the small business owner who depends on a consultant, there is a ton of unbudgeted consulting costs connected with this virus. The ancillary cost of this problem can spread far, even so far as to look at the opportunity cost of dedicating these personnel to an emergency while other projects go unattended.

With the Melissa virus, money was spent on hardware and software to solve the problem, temporarily circumnavigate it (in an attempt to keep other systems running), or both. In the meantime, many end users were left in the lurch with an interruption of some, if not all, of their services. Companies were not only spending money on idle workers but also experiencing a temporary loss of those employees' contributions to company revenues.

For consumers, an interruption in e-mail service is probably not as severe as an interruption in phone service. The effect of e-mail interruptions on businesses, however, carries with it a greater risk of loss. Businesses are now dependent on e-mail systems to communicate critical management information and transaction details that are time-sensitive. Tasks that once took hours with a fax machine now take seconds with e-mail. A catastrophic failure of either a sender's or recipient's e-mail system can have a paralyzing effect on business communications. The results included the delay of a transaction, the cancellation of what might have been a profitable business deal, or worse yet, the loss of customers. After all, time is money.

Finally, the role of the e-mail server has changed over the years. It has evolved from the electronic equivalent of a post office (storing and forwarding text messages) to a facilitator of group collaboration and offline database transactions. In terms of their "groupware" aspects, these servers have grown to support other group collaborations and communications around topics (for example, company happenings), processes (workflow applications, where a document goes through ordered steps of review and approval), and projects (a new product launch). Companies that depend on teams of people, who in turn depend on the collaboration services provided by these servers, felt the pinch more than those companies that were less team- and technology-dependent.

On the transaction end of things, many corporations now depend on e-mail systems to handle the capture and distribution of database transactions. A typical situation involves a mobile worker who cannot directly access the corporate database to enter an order taken in the field. Instead, the order is taken offline on a notebook computer and then e-mailed directly to the database. Through an API designed explicitly for this purpose, the database is notified of the inbound mail. It then opens the mail, decodes the transaction, and enters the information into the database—just like someone sitting at a terminal. To the extent that companies rely on their mail servers to handle these e-mail-bound trans-actions, they run the risk of closing their doors should the system go down—the costliest of all catastrophes.

Suffice it to say, despite the relatively benign nature of this macro virus, the worldwide cost of dealing with it easily escalated into the hundreds of millions of dollars. Like all viruses with the potential to reach epidemic proportions, the key to stemming the cost is educating users on how to prevent infection in the first place.

Throughout this section, I have been referring to this virus as "benign" and "innocuous." It could also be described as a prank gone amok: there was no damage-causing agent, such as destroying data on a hard drive or rewriting a BIOS. This was a virus that let you know it was there and moved on. From that point, it could be a whole lot worse.

Virus Prevention—Practice Safe Computing

The spread of computer-virus infections can be stopped through the practice of "safe computing." The following is a list of some dos and don'ts of safe computing:

1. Always use legal software. Although it is not unheard of for software coming from the original manufacturer to have a virus, the chances are reduced.

2. Never boot your computer system from a diskette that is not write-protected. When the diskette is created, it should be checked for viruses.

3. When you boot from a fixed disk, make sure you have a virus-protection program installed and working, with an up-to-date virus-definition file.

4. If you must use a diskette, always check it for viruses, or format it before using the disk on your computer system.

5. Always be on the lookout for strange occurrences:

    a. If you do a folder listing, look carefully at the contents of the folder.

    b. Observe whether your computer system is slowing down.

    c. Watch for files that disappear.

    d. Keep a lookout for decreases in the main memory or reduction of disk space.

    e. Watch for unusually large sizes on program files.

    f. Watch for recent creation dates on old program files.

    g. Watch for unusual displays on the computer screen.

6. Use caution when using any new software. There have been instances where commercial software has been sold with a virus.

7. If you are downloading software from the Internet, make sure your browser and virus-protection program will scan the data before it is saved to the local hard drive.

8. Teach end users about computer viruses so that they can recognize them. End users need to be able to identify viruses so that they will be able to prevent their spread.

9. Make sure there is virus-protection software not only on the local host but on any application or file servers, as well.

10. Make sure there are appropriate reporting procedures in place if a virus is found.

11. Make sure the network SWAT team responds immediately to any infestation of a virus, before it spreads to the rest of the network.

Remote-Access Security

As far as a network administrator is concerned, the good old days may have been back before remote access. These were the days of closed networks, where very few commercial businesses had an Internet connection or wanted one. Web pages were unheard of, and if an advertising agency put a URL in an ad, they would be run out of the building for wasting precious space. My goodness, how times have changed. Not only do you have to provide security from the outsiders breaking in over the Internet, some people need to dial in to the network to get access over telephone lines.

Providing network access to people who want to dial in over public telephone lines has added an entirely new dimension to the task of keeping business-critical information secure. Conventional telephone systems are public; anyone can dial a number and reach the portal to your company's network. The primary concern of remote-access security is to make sure that only known, authorized users can enter that door.

Remote-Access Security for the Enterprise

If you work for a global organization that has multipoint-access requirements, chances are you are not going to trust remote-access security to just any product. You are going to be looking for something that is specifically designed to provide security for the information that is going to be distributed over remote networks.

Centralized Security

One approach to this problem is called "centralized" security. With centralized security, a terminal or communications server will authenticate a dial-in user's identity through a central database stored on an Authentication server. As the name implies, this server stores all the necessary information about users, including their passwords and access privileges. By using a central location for authentication data, you are providing a greater degree of security for sensitive information. Because this information is all stored in one place, the management is simplified, and you have a more scalable solution as the size of the network increases. Authentication servers can be configured in various ways, depending on the network infrastructure and the corporate security scheme. Common schemes for centralized security are based on Remote Authentication Dial-In User Service (RADIUS) and Terminal Access Controller Access Control System + (TACACS+) technologies.

RADIUS

RADIUS is an Internet Engineering Task Force (IETF) draft that has emerged as a common standard for centralized security implementations. Almost all Remote Access server and security-application vendors have announced RADIUS support due to its robust capabilities, commonality between vendors, and extensibility. The RADIUS draft defines the protocol, but leaves implementation to the actual vendors. The RADIUS system operates in client/server mode, with the RADIUS client being the Remote Access server. The Remote Access server will then request authentication against a RADIUS "server." RADIUS servers have been developed on a variety of platforms ranging from Macintosh, Windows 3.x, Windows 95/98, Windows NT, and Unix implementations.

Why Use RADIUS?   RADIUS can provide a single point of authentication and authorization. When a RADIUS server is used as a stand-alone server, remote dial-in users are authenticated against the server, with authorization privileges also controlled by the server. Accounting information regarding session time, the protocols that are used, and the server utilization can be captured, and the output can be used for auditing purposes and/or for billing purposes.

RADIUS server implementations from a number of vendors can be blended together to act as "proxy clients" to other security servers. This allows for seamless integration with other security implementations. RADIUS products are being used for proxying capabilities in Windows NT implementations and with Novell Directory Services. It is anticipated that other products will be available soon to support evolving directory schemes such as X.500-based directories.

In the case of NT and NDS, proxy support means that the remote dial-in user can authenticate directly against the NT Domain or the NDS structure. There is no need to maintain a separate user list on the Remote Access server. When an administrator adds, deletes, or modifies user privileges directly in an NT Domain or NDS structure, these changes are reflected in the Remote Access server privileges. Figure 18.3 shows you the layout of one type of system.

Figure 18.3 RADIUS system layout with Remote Access servers and Authentication servers

NT Server

Minneapolis

Novell Server

London

RADIUS Server

UNIX Host

Sydney

Remote Access
Servers

Authentication Servers

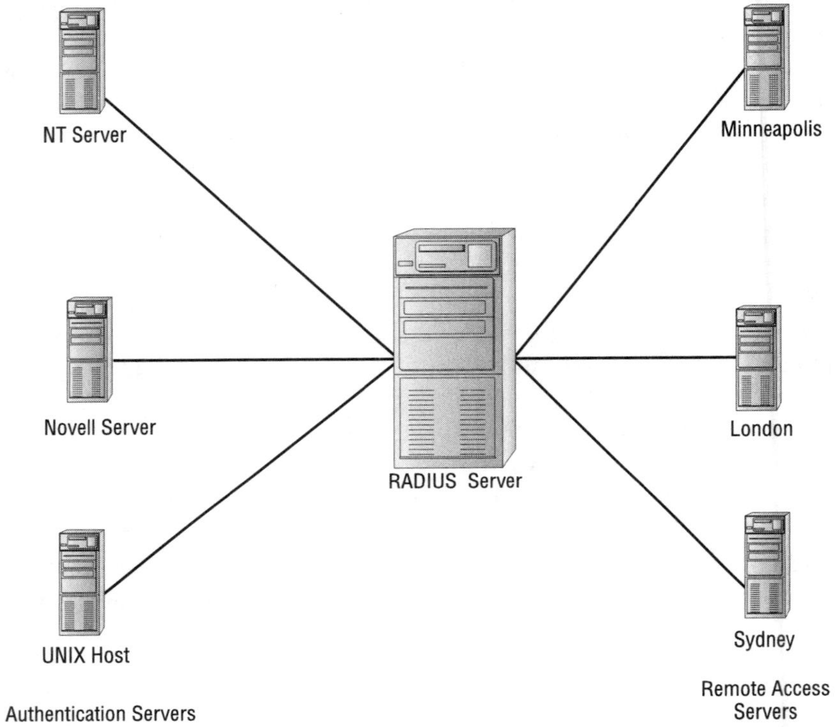

Interoperability Because RADIUS has received multivendor support, it defines the general parameters for Remote Access servers. Remote Access–server manufacturers have had to extend RADIUS to address additional device-specific capabilities that are not included in the IETF draft. By providing the functionality of vendor-attribute dictionaries, many vendors can easily extend the RADIUS product to address these requirements. In a mixed environment, multiple dictionaries have resulted in some confusion. Vendors are now working to extend common parameters within the RADIUS specification, guaranteeing interoperability.

TACACS+

TACACS+ is another protocol from the IETF. Like RADIUS, it is designed for third-party authentication. The Terminal Access Controller Access Control System (TACACS) is a security protocol that communicates between network devices and an authentication database. The TACACS Protocol was originally written by Cisco Systems. There are three variants of the original:

- Standard TACACS supports authentication.
- TACACS+ is an enhancement to the TACACS Security Protocol.
- XTACACS (Extended TACACS) supports authentication, authorization, and accounting.

Due to the limitations of standard TACACS, most Network Access Servers (NAS) in the market that support standard TACACS and XTACACS also support TACACS+. In effect, TACACS and XTACACS are in the process of becoming obsolete.

User Authentication   Your Network Access Server (NAS) functions as a proxy TACACS client for dial-in users. When a user logs in, the NAS prompts them for their username and password. To authenticate a dial-in user, the NAS then sends a request for user authorization to a TACACS server elsewhere on the network. The TACACS server returns either a permit or a deny response to the NAS, which then forwards the response to the user. This process is entirely transparent to the dial-in user.

TACACS can serve as a front-end Security Protocol to other authentication databases, such as `/etc/passwd` files. For more information about TACACS, refer to RFC1492, *An Access Control Protocol, Sometimes Called TACACS.*

User authentication in both TACACS and RADIUS goes through the following steps:

1. A user dials into the network through a Remote Access server.
2. The Remote Access server forwards the user identification and password to the Authentication server.
3. The Authentication server validates and provides access privileges to the user.

Token-Based Security

Another method of remote-access security revolves around the theory of "security by obscurity." In the security-by-obscurity method, the users must have a specific object in their possession to access the network. The "obscurity" of that object creates a huge problem for attackers.

The Credit Card Approach

Talk about security by obscurity! Fred Hendra, an Information Systems Analyst with Morrison Knudsen Corporation of Boise, Idaho, uses a system from Security Dynamics of Bedford, Massachusetts. When a member of the M-K staff dials in to authenticate into the network, they have to pull out this little credit card–sized device that will provide them with the secure ID necessary to access the system. This secure ID changes every two minutes, and when you dial in, you have one chance to enter the correct ID. If you are a fat-fingered typist, kind of like the author of this book, and you screw up the authentication, you are out of luck. You have to wait for the two minutes to expire to try again.

The cards are all synchronized, so they are not people-dependent; they are system-dependent. You can buy as many of the cards as you want to provide remote access for as many users as you can connect.

This type of security is referred to as token-based security. If anyone were to come in contact with the credit card, they still couldn't use it, because there is a password required.

There are other variations on this theme, but in each case this concept of a one-time login involves having the security server know that the information is not going to be transmitted over insecure channels. In other methods, when a user connects, he or she receives a challenge from the security server. The user takes the challenge information and uses it to calculate the response from the password. The security server then calculates the response and compares its answer with that received from the user. The password never goes over the network, nor is the same challenge used twice.

Solutions such as the two discussed here are driven by the fact that the electronic information that travels over the telephone line is subject to security threats and can be "stolen." Integrating mathematical computations into the login process helps ensure that the information traveling across the telephone system is worthless after a single login, as opposed to the character string in a user password, which can be used repeatedly.

Other Token-Based Solutions

Another token-based solution is AssureNet Pathways. It is the philosophy of AssureNet that user authentication forms the basis of sound network security. If authentication is compromised, it may lead to other security functions being compromised, despite the fact that those other security processes are well designed and are still intact.

Other Token-Based Solutions *(continued)*

Reusable passwords are the weakest security link in most networks. To improve on that situation, many companies are looking for better authentication techniques. The token-based authentication and access-control systems provide a reasonable balance between security and lower cost. The basic premise of the token-based system is two-pronged authentication based on something you know and something you have. These systems work to eliminate many of the risks inherent in the use of static passwords by generating a dynamic password that can be used once for authentication.

One of the most popular types of tokens falls into the category of challenge/response. This type comes in both a hardware and a software version. Both types of systems perform the same type of challenge/response authentication. Software tokens are easier to use. With this technology, when a login is attempted, the server challenges the client with a random number. This challenge is encoded using the token. Both the server and the client perform the encoding. The resulting value is used by the client as a one-time password. The server then compares the received response with its expected response, and if the two values match, the client is authenticated.

AssureNet Pathways works with existing communication APIs where appropriate and works with its partner companies where no standard APIs exist.

Transaction Encryption

Remote-access communication suffers from being forced to use public telephone lines. Even though authentication has been assured with several of these products, what about the actual data that is moved back and forth?

Data encryption is of great importance to industries such as financial institutions, governments, and other organizations with highly sensitive data. With data encryption, users need an encryption key to access data. Without this key, the data is meaningless. This makes the data listen-proof and offers good protection against network access. But it does have drawbacks. There is significant CPU overhead as the server encrypts the data.

Remote-Access Security Suggestions

If you are getting ready to implement a Remote Access server, here are some issues to think about. First of all, when approaching the topic of security, try to break things down into processes. For example, when a user dials in, he/she has to authenticate to the Remote Access server, so that would be our first process.

At the RAS, the points you should look for in your solution include

- Support of industry-standard name services.
- Local database support for smaller sites.
- The ability to include token-based security, either now or in the future.

Once these items have been handled, the end user should be authenticated by the RAS server. Now they need to authenticate into the actual computer network.

For network security, consider a network-oriented solution rather than a peer-to-peer solution. The security pieces that networks such as Novell NetWare with NDS or Microsoft NT Domains use will help make managing security that much easier.

Once the user has been authenticated into the network, there is still one more authentication process to complete: validation at the application. Make sure that you have password-protected applications such as

- E-mail
- Scheduler
- Document management solutions
- Workflow solutions
- Workforce automation
- Accounting applications
- Human resource applications
- Other productivity applications.

Sounds like a lot of passwords, doesn't it? In some cases, these can be streamlined into a single login, depending on the risk level. The important thing here is to work that fine line between security and overburdening people with passwords so complicated they have to write them down.

User Validation for Remote Access

As you plan your remote-access system, there are several ways, other than the token-based method, to provide for secure user validation. Password features, such as expiration, grace logins, and allowing users to change personal passwords, can provide flexibility to both users and administrators.

Password Protection   It seems like everything is networked today. The Computer Emergency Response Team (CERT) recommends that organizations concerned about security and the integrity of their systems consider moving away from standard, reusable passwords. CERT has documented several security breaches involving the capturing of host names, account names, and passwords, which intruders can now use to gain access to those hosts and accounts.

Location Validation and Call Level Security   Location validation employs various callback methods to confirm a user's location. One of these methods is Caller Line ID (CLI). CLI validates an incoming call phone number against an internal database of approved numbers. CLI works with ISDN calls by providing the called site with the ISDN telephone number from which the call is being made. This allows the called site to verify that the call is coming from a location that is authorized.

Besides using callbacks as a security feature, it can also be used to take advantage of lower-charge plans from various locations. For example, you have a branch office that has one call rate per minute, and the home office may have a lower cost-per-minute rate. In this case, the remote office will call the home office, and the home office will call back and establish the longer conversation.

Another callback method involves fixed dial-back numbers, in which the system dials a preassigned number. Fixed dial-back numbers help reduce costs, in that they enable the system to assume remote-access line costs. Again, this gives the company the opportunity to centralize its expenditures. This method also allows the company to control dial-back access. Because the system dials a known number, an intruder would not be called back.

This scenario works great, as long as your remote users aren't mobile. For example, if a user travels from motel room to motel room, organizations can use a roaming dial-back. In this case, the remote user can specify a number at which he or she should be called back. This is primarily a cost-savings device, not a security enhancement; however, the call is no less secure than any other regular dial-in procedure.

Point-to-Point Protocol (PPP) Security Authentication   PPP has several methods of validating a caller's identity. The most common are Password Authentication Protocol (PAP) and the Challenge-Handshake Authentication Protocol (CHAP).

PAP is the simplest security method used for a dial-up connection to be established. Once the link is established, an ID/password pair is repeatedly sent by the sender to the authenticator until authentication is either established or the call is disconnected.

PAP is a very weak authentication method. Passwords are exchanged, but they are sent over the circuit in an unencrypted format. There is no protection against playback or repeated trial-and-error attacks. In addition, the dial-up station is in charge of the frequency and timing of the attempted logins. Fortunately, there are stronger methods available.

CHAP Security Authentication   CHAP, for example, uses a three-way handshake. After the link establishment phase is complete (meaning the modems are talking to each other), the authentication method sends a challenge message to the peer. This authentication method depends on a "secret" known only to the authenticator and the peer. The secret is not sent over the link.

CHAP provides protection against playback attacks through the use of an incrementally changing identifier and a variable challenge value. The use of repeated challenges is meant to limit the time of exposure to a single attack. With CHAP, the authenticator is in charge of the frequency and timing of the challenges, not the peer.

Both PAP and CHAP can be used on any dial-up service, including ISDN lines that do not support CLI.

Access-Control Authorization

Now that the remote user has connected to the Remote Access server, they are in the building. How do they get on the network? The access-control piece refers to what parts of the network, resources, and services the user can actually make use of. There are a number of remote-access authorization models. For example, access may be controlled on a user-by-user basis or on a group basis. The Remote Access server may control access by the connecting port or even by the protocol. In other words, the network administrator has the flexibility of defining the control based on either a people model or a hardware model. Some of the more common authorization scenarios are

- Dial-in, dial-out, and LAN-to-LAN settings that allow specific users to gain access only to features they actually need, further closing security loopholes and minimizing exposure.

- Dial-back that can be configured to authorize different users for either fixed or roaming dial-back. Roaming dial-back is less secure than fixed dial-back.

- Administrator privileges that are used to designate which administrators or groups can track usage, change users' rights, or administer Remote Access servers.

- Setting a maximum connection time. This ensures that users are not staying connected for too long.

- Setting the times when a user may dial in will prevent off-hour access to network services. This may work to protect the network during periods of backups, compression, processor intensive/disk intensive, or I/O intensive tasks.

- Using a firewall for network and device filtering. This can prevent specific users from accessing particular networks, devices, or services.

Accounting and Auditing

Accounting is used to track, audit, and report on security and usage activity on any network segment. In a dial-up environment, accounting enables administrators to determine usage patterns and traffic patterns, so they can identify unusual activity. Accounting can also detect attempts to access protected files.

Whenever I hear the word *accounting*, I think of billing, which is a common use. For example, by using the accounting features of some remote-access software, the accounting department can divide up the phone bill for the outgoing calls by corporate division. Now, don't even think about asking me to handle that nightmare of paperwork, but some accounting person somewhere would love the task.

Web Page Security

This section is not written for the Webmaster; this section is written for the person that has to support the hardware that the Webmaster actually uses. Now, just suppose your boss has decided that Web commerce is the way of the future, and your company is going to be at the forefront of this bursting technology. When your boss calls you in to tell you of this great revelation, it is also made clear that the success or failure of this program depends on you keeping the Web site secure. Web site security is really important, as customers need to feel comfortable leaving personal information and credit card numbers on the Web.

As you begin to research how in the world you are actually going to pull this off, two acronyms keep popping up: SSL for Secure Socket Layer and S-HTTP for Secure Hypertext Transport Protocol. These two protocols do similar things, but they work with different parts of the standard Internet transaction. SSL is extremely flexible but not as granular as S-HTTP. SSL provides encryption and user authentication at the OSI Transport layer, allowing it to secure not only HTTP messages but also applications such as FTP and Telnet. SSL processes all the data flowing between the applications, not just certain parts. With SSL, you can selectively encrypt a field on a form; this may increase processing time. Another SSL shortcoming is that it only authenticates between server applications. In applications that need to authenticate a client, such as online banking, SSL should not be used.

S-HTTP is an extension of the HTTP protocol. By invoking S-HTTP, you can selectively encrypt single fields of data. Unlike SSL, S-HTTP also supports client-to-server authentication, making it ideal for applications that provide access to untrusted sources such as the Internet. Because S-HTTP is a derivative of HTTP, it can only be used to secure Web transactions; S-HTTP does not work with applications such as FTP or Telnet.

Credit Card Processing

But what about that credit card thing? How can a user authenticate into your Internet site, give their credit card number, and know that the transaction is *really* safe? You may have heard the stories about the cracker Kevin Mitnik, who managed to get up to 20,000 credit card numbers from the Internet service provider Netcom. You obviously don't want this happening to your company.

There are basically two ways of taking and clearing credit card transactions over the Internet. The first is the local-save scenario, and the second is a remote transaction using Common Gateway Interface (CGI) scripts. A CGI script is a program that allows a server to communicate with users on the Internet using forms. For example, when a user enters information in a form on a Web page, a CGI script interprets the information and communicates it to a database program on the server.

Local-Save

In the local-save scenario, the credit card information is sent from your Web page using a secure, encrypted session. This is where S-HTTP comes into play. As it travels from the client to its final destination, the credit card number goes through several processes. The first step is to verify that it really is a credit card number and not just a string of numbers that someone typed in trying to get your product for free. To check this information, you would run the number through the same algorithm that is used to generate credit card numbers in the first place. There are two possible outcomes of this process: either the number is really a potential credit card number or it is a fake.

Once the number your system has been given matches the algorithm, you still need to verify that the number really belongs to the applicant. After all, if you can run a number through an algorithm that would check to see if the card meets all the normal specifications, someone else could get their hands on the same algorithm and generate a batch of fake credit card numbers. Once the potentially correct information is received, it is written to a local disk where it is stored for later verification.

If you are the type of business in which you can retrieve the credit card number and run it through your local bank before shipping the product, this is an ideal situation. If, however, you have information that is readily available on the Web for download, you have a period of time where your company could be vulnerable.

Another problem with this approach is if you are storing other people's financial information on your server. Therefore, you are depending on your security plan to be strong enough to protect not only your information but your customers' information. If your system is breached, you are putting your most valuable resource at risk: the spending lists of those credit cards. This could be a massive amount.

Banks don't look favorably on money being stolen, and other companies are not particularly enthralled when they end up giving away goods or services. Therefore, investigating agencies become involved, and sooner or later, it will come out that some of those stolen credit cards had one thing in common, your server. Once that information is made public, your attorneys will be spending a lot of their time defending lawsuits.

Remote Saves Using CGI Scripts

In the case of remote saves using CGI scripts, your company is more or less just the front for the transaction. In other words, your Web site hosts a form provided by a credit card verification service. When the customer fills out the form and sends it off, the information is sent to a remote server at the credit card clearing company for confirmation. Once the number has been confirmed, you are free to send out the goods or provide for Web access.

This scenario sounds really good for the selling organization, except that the company will never have any of the credit card information on file about the customer. If ever there were a dispute about the product or the credit card billing, your company would have no local record of the credit card number that the products were charged to. They'd have to obtain, usually for a price, verification of the transaction from the credit card clearing company.

19

Troubleshooting TCP/IP

I suppose that before I start this chapter, I should define exactly what I mean by troubleshooting TCP/IP. In my definition, troubleshooting TCP/IP is making sure that an acceptable level of service is restored in a timely fashion. Now that may sound like a very simple statement. (I am beginning to feel like President Bill Clinton here, when he kept insisting that there were different definitions for the word *is*.) To get a bit more specific in reading the definition, I should define what is an *acceptable level of service*. Unfortunately, however, the definition of an acceptable level of service is out of your hands. An acceptable level of service is whatever the end user—in this case your customer—says it is! To put this more simply, if you are working on a problem, the problem is fixed when the users involved say it is fixed.

When someone first starts working with protocols, operating systems, or computers in general, troubleshooting is probably 95 percent science and 5 percent art form. After the person has been around the proverbial block a few dozen times, troubleshooting moves to about 15 percent science and 85 percent art form. Troubleshooting is a science when you are stumped and are forced to go back to the basics of removing everything and starting over, one step at a time, until something fails, and then you fix whatever fails. Troubleshooting is art form when the troubleshooter takes one look at the problem, smiles inwardly, walks over and makes one or two changes, and things begin to work smoothly again. It is that experience thing kicking in and coming to the rescue.

The Troubleshooting Model

The folks at Novell Education came up with a great troubleshooting model that transcends hardware, operating systems, and applications and gets right to the heart of the model. Although it is true that there can be no single troubleshooting model that applies to every situation, the model displayed in Figure 19.1 is useful for a point of discussion.

Figure 19.1   The six-step troubleshooting model

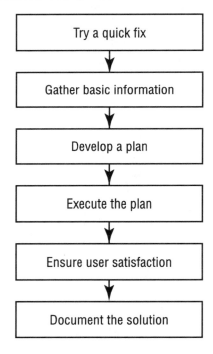

Step One: Try a Quick Fix

Isn't there an old saying that says even a blind squirrel can sometimes find a nut? Really, there are some things that you can try before attempting anything else. Take a look at the most probable causes of the problem first. Before starting out, take along your two most powerful tools: patience and the knowledge that you can always find the on/off switch.

1. *Always* remember the first rule of network computing: End users lie! They may not be aware that they are lying, but they probably are. If you ask the first question of troubleshooting, "Okay, what has happened to the machine lately?" and are told "Nothing," you *know* the end user is lying! Something always has happened, even if it was inadvertent. So eliminate end-user error. This means you can start with three possibilities:

   a. The end user did not do something properly.

   b. The end user did something just right and got the appropriate results, but the end user doesn't realize it. This is the "that is the way it is supposed to work" approach.

   c. A problem really exists.

2. Check the inventory.

   a. If you are working with hardware, is everything there that is supposed to be there, and is it plugged in?

   b. Is it the right stuff? Are you using the right drivers for the right network cards, using the right frame type, with the right addresses?

   c. Is everything connected the way it is supposed to be connected? Sometimes network-card problems can be alleviated by simply taking the card out, putting it back in, and making sure it is seated tightly and correctly in the slot.

3. If a hard disk is involved, back up your data, and verify the backup before proceeding. This is an important step that is often forgotten, and usually the repercussions of skipping this step can be severe. Remember, Murphy's Law is always in place: If anything can go wrong, it will, at the worst possible moment.

4. Turn everything off and turn it back on again. This routinely solves about 75 percent of problems.

5. Simplify the system by removing unneeded elements. This is the step that is really a pain in the anatomy. For example, I have systems that run both Windows 98 and Windows NT. My network has NetWare servers and NT servers. Because I have a mixed environment, if I click on Network Neighborhood and then look at properties, I see almost every type of adapter and driver invented loaded. There are a ton of them. Besides, I have a laptop, and that means all the drivers and configurations are also loaded for the modem. So, if a tech-support rep tells me to remove all the drivers for the network card, take the network card out of the system, and reinstall it, this is *not* a small task. It is really a pain, but unfortunately, it is necessary. This is where patience comes into play.

6. If you can run one network application but other applications won't run successfully, it's probably a network-rights issue. When this situation occurs, the symptoms may differ, and the error messages you get may be useless, but try to log on to the network using root, administrator, or admin and see whether that will give you access to the application.

7. Know what versions of software and patches are being used and what effect that each should have on the network. If you have to call any tech-support outlet, they will ask for that information and probably will want you to apply the latest patch.

8. RTFM. Read the fine manual. Check out the knowledge base, the technical information documents, and the company Web site. You would be surprised how many times the answers are already documented.

Step Two: Gather Basic Information

When the easy stuff doesn't fix the problem, now it is time to get to work.

1. Determine what the symptoms are, and determine how many people are affected. If you have just one person who is having a problem, the troubleshooting scenario is a lot different than if you have an entire subnet that is affected. Also, are the symptoms random, or are they easy to re-create?

2. Determine the amount of usage when the problems occur. Is the network simply overloaded with work?

3. Check the logs to find out whether something has changed since the last time everything worked correctly.

4. Check user groups, online forums, listserves, and usenet groups for information.

Step Three: Develop a Plan to Isolate the Problem

1. Using the information gathered in Step Two and your inherent knowledge of the situation, decide whether this is an end-user problem, application-software problem, operating-system software problem, or equipment problem. Keep in mind that you too are an end user, and there are times when you (if you are like me in any way) are capable of doing some really incredibly dumb things. It is okay, because that is how we learn. When it comes to determining whether an end user may have caused the problem, check out the person in the mirror, too.

2. Once you have a list of two or three things that could be causing the problem, take a look at which one is the most likely. For example, if you're having a problem pinging another host, the chances of the other host being simply turned off is more likely than a network cable being severed.

Step Four: Execute the Plan

1. Break down the first theory into the smallest reasonable, testable concepts. For example, if you cannot ping between Node 1 and Node 2 on your network, the problems could be among the following:

   a. Node 2 is down.

   b. Node 1 or Node 2 is not configured to use TCP/IP correctly.

   c. Node 1 or Node 2 has a bad network card.

   d. Node 1 or Node 2 has a cabling issue.

   e. There is a problem at the concentrator, hub, or MSAU.

   f. The router is having a problem routing the signal.

2. Begin to test your theory by changing one thing at a time. If you change more than one thing, you will never know which change solved the problem, and you may end up making the problem worse. After you have made one change, test the system to find out whether the problem has been fixed.

3. You can eliminate network-communication issues by moving forward one step at a time. This is called *forward chaining*. For example, look at the diagram in Figure 19.2. Suppose I am at host 10.1.2.3 and I am attempting to contact the Microsoft Web site at www.microsoft.com. If I am having problems, I need to find out where the problems are stemming from. I know that if I am using Ethernet, my signal goes from my host to the hub. I can start pinging the hub (if it has an address) at 10.1.2.2. If I get a successful response, then the next step is to find another system on my subnet, so I may ping 10.1.2.5. If that is successful, the next step forward would be to the first interface on the router, so I would ping 10.1.2.1. If that were successful, I would ping the other interface on the router at 10.5.2.1. If that were successful, the next step in the chain would be to ping the first interface on the next router, and so on, until I either hit www.microsoft.com or found which interface on my network was causing the problem.

Figure 19.2   An example of forward chaining

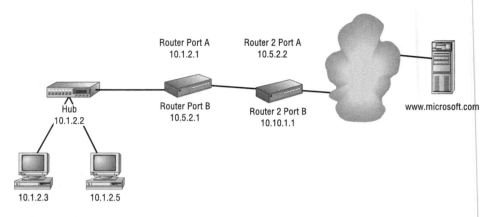

a. There is also *backward chaining,* which starts with you attempting to contact the destination host and then slowly working your way back to the source, one step at a time.

b. The last type of chaining is called *binary chaining.* With binary chaining, you start in the middle, isolating problems to one of the halves. Once that half has been discovered, you can continue by dividing the isolated segment in half, isolating that problem to one of the halves, and so forth, until you find the problem.

4. When executing your plan, make sure you use test equipment, software, hardware, and procedures that are known to be good. If you test a system using a cable that has a loose wire, you may become more confused!

5. If the plan doesn't work, seek existing help. This may come in the form of calling for tech support or doing what I call a *brain dump.* In many cases, while involved in the actual process of troubleshooting a problem, I may find that I have lost my way or become sidetracked, and the next step is lying right below the surface of my subconscious waiting to get out. All it needs is a proper forum. So I will call my wife, my father, or a friend and lay some ground rules. The ground rules are for them just to listen and not say one word! I then start talking about what I have done and why, what I have tried and the results, what I think I should try next, and somehow, the fog clears, and another potential plan begins to form. The person you use may think you are somewhat crazy, but in my case, that wasn't a shocking revelation.

Step Five: Ensure User Satisfaction

The problem isn't fixed until the end user or the customer says the problem is fixed. Just because you know the problem has been fixed, doesn't mean that it is fixed in the end user's mind, so that person may require some training, hand-holding, or selling on the fact that the system is operating exactly the way the system was designed to operate. Some end users have more of a problem with this concept than others do. Some seem to think that the system should operate the way they *want* it to operate, not the way it really works.

The road to this step can be rocky, also. Many times you will be facing a difficult network problem on many levels, and the end user will simply expect you to be able to walk by their desktops to resolve the issue. We all know that does not happen in every case. Sometimes I get stumped. Sometimes, I have to gather other information. Sometimes, I simply have to leave the person for a few minutes so I can think. In any case, I leave with a message saying that I will be back, and I give them a specific time or day. I then go about my business. If something unavoidable happens so that I cannot keep my scheduled "appointment," I make it a point to call the user and tell them exactly why I will not be there. It may be something like, I have contacted tech support and they have not returned my call, or the part I am waiting for simply hasn't arrived. I find that as long as I tell the end user what is going on and why it is taking so long, the frustration level stays down, and they are not as likely to go ballistic.

Step Six: Document the Solution, and Take Steps to Ensure It Doesn't Happen Again

I know, I know. Documentation is not your favorite task in the whole world. Mine neither. But it is necessary.

1. Document the cause of the problem and the solution. The record will provide a quick fix if a similar problem occurs again.

2. Do whatever can be done to prevent or prepare for a recurrence. For example, if you solved the problem by applying a patch, make sure the patch is available for other hosts. If possible, proactively roll out the patch to other hosts.

3. Test the system periodically to make sure there are no recurring problems.

4. Keep an updated network map and floor plan to help you spot potential problems or recurring problems in a particular zone.

Quick Fixes

If you are new to TCP/IP, or if you have been doing it for a while and just need a reminder, here are some quick fixes that you may need to check when you run into problems. Some of these quick fixes use commands, such as ping. If you aren't familiar with these commands, don't sweat it, we will cover them later in the chapter.

Network Connectivity

Now because this is not a book on hardware troubleshooting, I will not go into all the different things that can go wrong with network connections. Suffice it to say that one of the first things you should check are the simple things, such as is it plugged in? Are you seeing the network?

Is This a New Installation?

If you are installing TCP/IP on a host for the first time, some problems can crop up because of fat-finger typing.

Incorrect IP Addresses in Configurations   You know what happens when *type* comes out *tpye*. This problem can manifest itself in several different ways, but each of them can bring communications to a halt. For example, you attempt to add the following information to a host that will be using a static address:

- Correct IP address of 192.15.187.24
- Correct subnet mask
- Correct gateway
- Correct DNS server

An error in any of the entries can bring communications to a halt.

How Does It Do That Anyway?

When a computer wants to send a packet to another host, it puts the remote host's IP address in the destination-address area of the packet. The system must then decide where to send the packet. If the destination address is on the same subnet as the sending host, the packet is sent directly to the receiving computer. However, if the host address is on a different subnet, the packet is automatically forwarded to the subnet's default gateway for its trip around the network.

How does the computer determine whether the destination address is local or remote? It uses a process called *ANDing*. The ANDing process is based in Boolean logic. ANDing takes the destination address and converts it to binary. It then applies the subnet mask and begins to work its magic to see whether the two network addresses are the same. For example, when ANDing compares the number *0* AND any value, it is always a *0*. A *1* AND another *1* is always a *1*.

How Does It Do That Anyway? *(continued)*

Let's take a look at how this works on a grander scale. Take a look at Table 19.1.

Table 19.1   ANDing Process for 187.26.36.210 to Determine the Network Address

IP Address/ Subnet	1	2	3	4
187.26.36.210	10111011	00011010	00100100	11010010
255.255.240.0	11111111	11111111	11110000	00000000
Result	10111011	00011010	00100000	00000000
Decimal of result	187	26	32	0

We have an IP address of 187.26.36.210 and a subnet mask of 255.255.240.0. Suppose that this computer was sending a message to the host at 187.26.30.16. Judging from the fact that both are Class B addresses, it is possible that their hosts could reside on the same subnet. The ANDing process will find out whether the target host is on the right network. Table 19.2 shows the ANDing process for this address.

Table 19.2   ANDing 187.26.30.16 with a Subnet Mask of 255.255.240.0

IP Address/ Subnet	1	2	3	4
187.26.30.16	10111011	00011010	00011110	00010000
255.255.240.0	11111111	11111111	11110000	00000000
Result	10111011	00011010	00010000	00000000
Decimal of result	187	26	30	0

After we have done the ANDing process on these two addresses, we find that one is on subnet 187.26.32.0 and the other is on subnet 187.26.30.0. Because they are on different subnets, the packet will be forwarded to the default gateway for transportation through the network.

So, if you are a fat-fingered typist working with a static IP address, a small error can really screw up the works. Symptoms of this problem can be

- An operating-system warning that you have assigned an address that is already being used.

TIP   Some operating systems are aware enough of their surroundings to let you know when you have tried to steal another host's IP address. Other operating systems just ignore the configuration and don't give you any indication as to why. If you can't get the IP address to bind and if you have the luxury of another host that is configured correctly, you may want to try to ping the address you are attempting to assign.

- A DNS lookup failure. If you are pointing to a computer that doesn't have the DNS service running, you will definitely have a problem finding your way around the Web.
- A gateway failure. Again, if you enter in the wrong address, the system will truly believe that you know what you are doing. It will forward any packets going to a remote network to a host that has no clue about what it is supposed to do with them. The packets will be discarded, and you won't have a clue as to why.

Part of the problem with the misaddress adventure is that it is so easy to overlook your mistake. It usually takes someone who has very little system knowledge to come by and peek over your shoulder and point out your mistake.

To start the troubleshooting process, try pinging 127.0.0.1, which is a reserved address called the *loopback*. It basically checks to make sure that TCP/IP is configured properly on this host. If pinging 127.0.0.1 works, try accessing other areas using another protocol. For example, if you are trying to access an area using FTP and it doesn't work, try going somewhere using Telnet. If that works, then your network card and cabling are okay. You can also try the ping command.

The ping command will report packet loss. Some packet loss is expected but not all. If no other protocols work and ping reports a 100 percent packet loss, check the cables and the gateways. Are all the cables plugged in? Are all the gateways up and working?

Problems with Configuration Files

Depending on the operating system you are using, some configuration files are probably being parsed as TCP/IP loads. For example, in Windows NT, there is a chance that the system is accessing the HOSTS file or the LMHOSTS file for information. If you are using NetWare, the file server will be accessing the SYS:\etc\resolv.cfg file to find the DNS servers it needs to operate; it will access the SYS:\ETC\gateway file to find the gateway, and it may also access the SYS:\etc\HOSTS file to locate individual hosts.

Read through the configuration files. Almost all TCP/IP programs store configuration information in plain English. Read through the files related to your problem, and make sure they are correct. Check the last modified date on the files to see whether they have been changed recently. It is also a good idea to make sure the entire IT staff knows to document any changes to *any* configuration file. The documentation can consist of a comment line, including any changes made, the date the changes were made, who made the changes, and *why* the changes were made. Sometimes correcting one problem may create another. Sometimes the best-laid plans can cause unexpected, wide-ranging problems.

Check all the configuration files. If you are working in a Unix environment, there are a bunch to go through. Table 19.3 shows the typical configuration files in a Unix system and what they are responsible for.

Table 19.3   Typical Unix Configuration Files

File Name	Description
/etc/syslog.conf	Defines message type and the path to the log file.
/etc/bootptab	Defines addresses and load files.
/etc/snmp.conf	Defines communities and allowable addresses; may also define hosts to receive trap messages.
/etc/inetd.conf	Defines servers to be run by inetd.
/etc/resolv.conf	Name service; defines local domain name and the next server in the chain.
/etc/named.boot	Defines locations of databases, other nameservers, and domain served.
/usr/local/domain/named.fwd	Name server database for normal requests.
/usr/local/domain/named.rev	Name server database for in-addr.arpa requests.

Table 19.3   Typical Unix Configuration Files *(continued)*

File Name	Description
/usr/local/domain/named.ca	Name server database to prime the cache.
/etc/services	Database for service name/number translation.
/etc/protocols	Database for protocol name/number translation.
/etc/networks	Database for network name and address. This file is not needed if you are using named.
/etc/hosts	Database of host names and addresses. This file is not needed if using named.

Check Log Files

Windows NT has the System Error log. NetWare has the SYS$LOG log file, and Unix has a variety of log files that get written to whenever things happen on the system. If you are having problems, it may help the troubleshooting process to find out what the log files can tell you. They will sometimes provide helpful clues to the problem. They can also provide interesting riddles and error codes that can never be deciphered, but that is another story.

Service providers, like the System Error log, are noted for the amount of information they can provide. In the case of programs or services that will not start, check to see whether there may be an optional switch setting that will output information directly to the screen. In the Unix world, this is the –d switch, which turns on the diagnostic information screens. Server programs will usually run in the background and write information directly to a file.

Some useful Unix log files include those shown in Table 19.4.

Routing

If you are having problems getting information from point A to point B, you may have to check the routing information on the gateways in your system. If you are using TCP/IP and you are hooked to the Internet, you have at least one gateway for your network. When a change is made to the network, the routing information may not have been

Table 19.4 Typical Unix Log Files

File Name	Description
`/etc/bootplog`	Log of bootp transactions.
`/usr/adm/errlog`	Log of hard-disk errors.
`/usr/adm/messages`	Default name of the `syslog` data file; check your `syslog` configuration file for the actual filenames.
`/usr/adm/sulog`	Log of superuser or root logins.
`/usr/lib/cron/log`	Log of commands executed by `cron`; shows who, what, and when; may also show error messages.
`/usr/spool/mqueue/syslog`	Log of sendmail transactions and error messages.

forwarded to all the gateways in a timely manner. Protocols exist specifically for moving the routing changes automatically, but the movement of those changes takes time. In cases like this, a great troubleshooting tool is *lunch*. By the time you get back, the problem may have solved itself, and you can take all the credit.

Depending on the types of routing protocols you are using, routing updates may not happen at all. In some cases, the only way the routing information is updated is if someone enters the information manually. Not all gateways will use router update protocols. If that is the case on your network, you will need to check the routing tables on as many gateways as you can to make sure they all point to the right place for your eventual destination.

Each gateway should have a default route. If no specific route exists for the network or for the host you are trying to reach, the gateway will then forward the packet to the default route. The gateway that receives the forwarded packet, and then checks its own routing table, and the process continues until the data is delivered. If there is a problem, follow the trail of the routes, and watch for loops or other misdirections.

Keep in mind the Time to Live or TTL. Most packets should reach the destination in under twenty gateway hops, even on the Internet. If your chain of gateways goes over 20, you probably have a misdirected route. The data may make it to the target eventually, but the odds will be great that time has been wasted. You will also want to keep an eye on the Internet Control Message Protocol (ICMP) redirect notice. This message is sent when a gateway forwards packets to a successor router when a shorter path is available.

A loop in the routing of packets ruins any chance of accessing your target host. For example, Gateway A sends the packet to Gateway B, which sends the message to Gateway C. Gateway C checks the routing table, and instead of sending the packet off to Gateway D, it sends the packet back Gateway A, and the circle starts all over again. It is not long before the TTL is invoked, and the packet is discarded. This will show up in the ICMP TTL Expired messages.

DNS and Name Service

The letters for www.microsoft.com are so much easier to remember than a bunch of silly numbers, aren't they? Sometimes you can actually reason out what a URL should be by taking a wild guess.

Although names are much easier to remember for humans, computers gag on such things. Computers want numbers, and they are not happy until they get the numbers they require. This is where the domain name system, or DNS, steps in. The problem is that the name service sometimes lags on updating the appropriate records. In some cases, you may have actual connectivity to the machine you are trying to get to, but because DNS has not been updated, it may not be obvious. In this case, try running the program or application using the IP address instead of the URL to see whether that solves the problem. If it does, you know you have a DNS issue and not a TCP/IP issue. If you can find the system with the IP address and not with a URL, you may want to run a utility to check the number address against its name stored on the Name server. It might be wrong there.

Check the Daemons or Services

If you are trying to get services from another computer and you are not being successful, perhaps you should find out whether that host is running the daemons or services needed to complete the request. For example, if you were to try to ftp to a site that was not running the FTP daemon, you may be able to find the host, but you would not be able to connect or perform any useful FTP-based tasks. In this case, this is not usually something you can do yourself. For example, you are looking for the latest patch for NT. You try to access the ftp.microsoft.com site to get the latest file, but it will not respond. There is probably little you can do to solve Microsoft's problem, so that patience thing comes back into play once again.

Solving Problems

This section is going to look at some of the methods you can use to solve various types of problems. Because I have to be somewhat generic here, your particular problem may not show up, but I will do my best to show you how to use some of the basic TCP/IP utilities and commands to give you the information you need to make informed decisions.

The troubleshooting scenarios I will look at include testing basic network connectivity, troubleshooting access to the network, checking routing, checking name services, figuring out protocol problems, and covering the SNMP (Simple Network Management Protocol).

Testing Basic Connectivity

Whenever you have a host that has TCP/IP installed, and it won't connect or communicate with other hosts, the first command used for testing is the `ping` command. The `ping` command simply indicates whether a remote host can be physically reached. `Ping` can also display statistics about packet loss and delivery times.

ping

The `ping` command tests whether a remote host can be reached from your computer. It allows you to check the network connection, independent of the applications in which the problem was discovered. `ping` can help you determine whether further testing should be directed toward the network connection or to the application.

For example, let's say you are having problems with a browser getting to the www.sybex.com Web site. To check the network connectivity, you may ping either the IP address of the Sybex Web site (if you know it), or you may ping www.sybex.com. If the packets can travel to the remote system and back, you don't have a connectivity problem, you have a browser problem. If the packets cannot get to the remote system and back, you have a connectivity problem and not a browser problem. Either way, your troubleshooting has narrowed the areas of consideration and testing.

The following code shows the syntax of the `ping` command. Look at Table 19.5 for further `ping` command options.

```
ping [-t] [-a] [-n count] [-l size] [-f] [-i TTL] [-v TOS] [-r count]
[-s count] [[-j host-list] | [-k host-list]] [-w timeout] packetsize
destination-list
```

Table 19.5   `ping` Command Options

Option	Description
-t	Ping the specified host until stopped. To view statistics, press Ctrl + Break. To stop ping, type Ctrl + C.
-a	Resolve addresses to host names.
-n count	Number of echo requests to send.
-l size	Send buffer size.
-f	Set Don't Fragment flag in packet.
-i TTL	Time to Live.
-v TOS	Type of Service.
-r count	Record route for counts hops.
-s count	Timestamp for count hops.
-j host-list	Loose source route along host-list.
-k host-list	Strict source route along host-list.
-w timeout	Timeout in milliseconds to wait for each reply.
packetsize	Defines the size in bytes of the test packets. This field is required only if the count field is going to be used. Use the default packet size of 56 bytes.

NOTE   Be very careful of messing with the packet-size parameter. A commonly known hacker DOS (Denial of Service) attack is known as the Ping of Death. The Ping of Death is used to issue a simple `ping` command to an unsuspecting host, using a packet size of something other than 56 bytes. Some NetWare servers and NT servers stopped working with either an ABEND or a Blue Screen of Death.

Using ping   An end user calls to say that they have a network problem, and they cannot ftp or telnet to a certain host. The end user will then say something like "It used to work!" The next question out of your mouth should be of the "what have you done to the system" variety, to which you will get the standard answer of "nothing." Time to troubleshoot. Once you get the host name from the remote user, you can ping the remote host. If your ping is successful, have the end user try to ping the remote host. If the user's ping is successful, you can concentrate on further analysis of the specifics of the application the user is trying to use. For example, your user may be having problems with the syntax `ftp://ftp.microsoft.com`, in which case you have solved the problem with deductive reasoning and a mastery of spelling. If that doesn't work, perhaps the user is trying to ftp to a host that does not have the FTP service running. Perhaps the host was down when the user originally tried, and now it has come back online. Have the user try the application again, while you watch or listen to every detail of what they are doing. If the user is doing everything right and the application still fails, you may have to use a more detailed analysis or coordinate with the remote system administrator.

If your ping works and the user's ping fails, try to concentrate testing on the user's system configuration. Find out what is different about your system from the user's. Concentrate on why the path to the remote host is different for the two of you.

If your ping fails and the user's ping fails, pay close attention to error messages. The error messages displayed by ping are helpful guides for planning further testing. The details of the error messages may vary from operating system to operating system, but these are the most common types of errors:

Unknown host   The remote host's name cannot be resolved by DNS into an IP address. The name servers could be at fault, the name could be at fault (check spelling carefully), or something could be wrong between your system and the remote server. If you know the remote server's IP address, try to ping that. If you can reach the host using the IP address and not the DNS name, the problem is associated with the name service. Use `nslookup`, or dig to test the local and remote servers. Also make sure to check the accuracy of the host name the user gave you.

Network unreachable   The local system does not have a route to the remote network. If the numeric IP address was used on the `ping` command line, reenter the `ping` command using the host name. This eliminates the possibility that the IP address was entered incorrectly or that you were given the wrong address. If a routing protocol is being used, make sure it is running, and check the routing table with `netstat`. If RIP (Routing Information Protocol) is being used, `ripquery` will check the contents of the RIP updates being received. If a static default route is being used, reinstall it. If everything seems fine on the host, check its default gateway for routing problems.

No answer   The remote system did not respond. Most network utilities have some version of this message. Some ping implementations print the message "100% packet loss" or "Request timed out." Telnet prints the message "Connection times out." All these errors mean the same thing: the local system has a route to the remote system, but it receives no response from the remote system to any of the packets it sends. There are many possible causes to this problem: the remote host may be down; either the local or the remote host may be configured incorrectly; a gateway or circuit between the local host and the remote host may be down; the remote host may have routing problems. The only way to solve this is to implement additional testing. Carefully check the local configuration using `netstat` or `ifconfig/winipcfg/ipconfig`. Check the route to the remote system with `tracert`. Contact the administrator of the remote system, and report the problem.

Figure 19.3 is a sample of the results that come from the use of a `ping` command.

Figure 19.3   `ping` command results

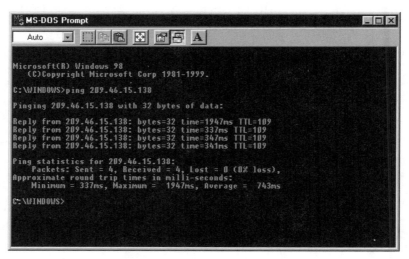

A successful `ping` command will show moderately low datapacket loss and a fast response time. The definition of "moderately low" and "fast" will depend on various conditions. For example, if I am hooked into your company WAN and I am checking a connection to the server room using 100MB Ethernet, I would expect significantly faster results than if I was pinging `www.microsoft.com` from a dial-up connection through my ISP.

If packet loss is high and response time is slow, there could be a network hardware problem. If you see these conditions when communicating over great distances on a wide-area network, there is nothing to worry about. TCP/IP is designed to deal with unreliable networks, and some wide-area networks suffer a lot of packet loss. If these problems are seen on a local-area network, they indicate trouble.

On a local-area network cable segment, the round-trip time should be near 0, and there should be little or no packet loss. If the packet loss is high, there is probably a problem with the network's hardware. On an Ethernet network, the problem could be a bad cable segment or a bad piece of communication hardware, such as a hub, switch, or transceiver.

Bad cables can be diagnosed with an inexpensive cable tester. If you have an intelligent hub or switch, it should have some form of diagnostic software built in. If you have purchased the less expensive pieces of hardware, you will probably have to troubleshoot using the old-fashioned grunt method, which is disconnecting individual pieces of equipment until you come to the one that is causing the problem.

The results of the ping test, even if it is successful, can help you direct further testing toward the most likely causes of the problem. Other diagnostic tools are available that may help you locate the underlying cause.

Troubleshooting Access to the Network

If you have tried to use the ping command and have received any kind of response that indicates the ping command did not leave the building, you probably have a problem in the lower layers of the network protocols. If the preliminary test points to this type of problem, concentrate your testing on routing and on the network interface.

Troubleshooting with the ipconfig/ifconfig/winipcfg Commands

Sometimes, it just pays to know where to start. Starting may be as simple as making sure that TCP/IP is configured on the workstation and is doing what it should. This is especially true of systems that are using DHCP to pass out information. At this point, the ipconfig, ifconfig, or winipcfg commands come in handy.

> **NOTE**   ipconfig, ifconfig, and winipcfg all perform relatively the same functions, but each works with a different operating system. ipconfig works well with Windows NT and Windows 98, ifconfig works well with Unix, and winipcfg works well with Windows 95/98 only.

Take a look at Figure 19.4; it shows the results of the winipcfg command from a recent session I had using my dial-up connection to the Internet. This IP address, subnet mask, and gateway were provided by my dial-in, on-the-road ISP, Earthlink.

Figure 19.4 The results of the winipcfg command

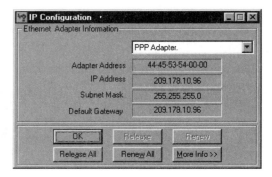

I can get similar results, but not as fancy, using the ipconfig command-line utility. The results are shown in Figure 19.5.

Figure 19.5 The results of the ipconfig command

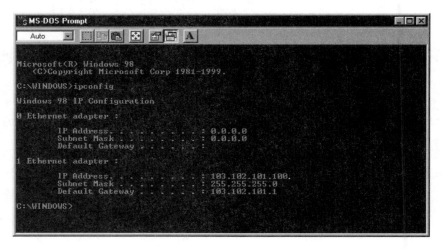

In Figure 19.5, you will notice that it shows Ethernet card 0 with no addresses assigned and Ethernet card 1 with an IP address and gateway assigned. Ethernet 0 is my dial-up adapter, and because I was not connected to an ISP at the time, nothing is registered.

When I received this information, I entered in the command ipconfig. The command can be used to do other things, such as release or renew a DHCP request. Table 19.6 shows the ipconfig options.

Table 19.6   The ipconfig Options for Windows 98

Option	Result
/All	Display detailed information.
/Batch [file]	Write the information to a specific file or to ./winipcfg.out.
/renew_all	Renew all DHCP IP addresses for all adapters.
/release_all	Release all IP addresses for all adapters.
/renew N	Renew the DHCP IP address for adapter N.
/release N	Release the DHCP IP address for adapter N.

ifconfig is like ipconfig in that it checks the network interface configuration. You would use this command to vary the user's configuration if the user's system has been recently configured or if the user's system cannot reach the remote host while other systems on the same network can.

When ifconfig is entered with an interface name and no other arguments, it displays the current values assigned to that interface. For example, checking interface le0 on a Solaris system gives a report that looks similar to

```
le0: flags=863<UP,BROADCAST,NOTRAILERS,RUNNING,MULTICAST> mtu 1500
inet 192.34.55.105 netmask ffffff00 broadcast 192.34.55.255
```

ifconfig provides two lines of output. The first line shows the interface's name and its characteristics. Options to look for include

UP   This option lets you know the interface is enabled for use. If the interface is "down," have the superuser on the system bring the interface "up" with the ifconfig command (ifconfig le0 up). If the interface will not come up, replace the interface cable, and start again. If it still fails, it may be time to check the network interface card.

RUNNING   This option lets you know the interface is operational. If the interface is not "running," the driver for this network interface card may not be properly installed.

The second line of ifconfig output shows the IP address, the subnet mask in hex, and the broadcast address. This is the line you would check to make sure the network card is properly configured.

These utilities or commands are helpful in troubleshooting some configuration problems. Some of the more subtle problems, such as a misconfigured IP address, may be more difficult to troubleshoot. A system that is experiencing difficulties may *not* be the system with the problem. For example, if I am on a host that has been working just fine using IP address 192.54.25.123 and all of a sudden my system starts having problems, the problems may stem from someone misconfiguring a new host on the subnet and giving it "my" IP address of 192.54.25.123. Some desktop operating systems are sophisticated enough to warn the user that the address is already in use. Others simply don't attach the IP address to the card and never give an explanation as to why. In cases like this, you may have to rely on the arp command.

Troubleshooting with the arp Command

In Chapter 2, we discussed ARP as the Address Resolution Protocol. The developers of TCP/IP were working very hard to confuse people when they designed and programmed a utility called arp that will check the results of address resolution.

The syntax for arp looks like this:

```
arp -a [ipaddress][-N target_address]

arp -d [ipaddress][target_address]

arp -s [ipaddress][ethernet_address][target_address]
```

Table 19.7 explains what each of the options accomplishes.

Table 19.7   The arp Command Options

Option	Description
Ipaddress	Specifies the IP address to resolve.
Ethernet_address	Specifies the MAC address to resolve.
Target_address	Specifies the IP address of the network interface card whose ARP table should be changed.

Table 19.7   The arp Command Options *(continued)*

Option	Description
-a	Displays current arp table data.
-d	Deletes the host specified IP address.
-s	Adds the host specified by the IP address using the ethernet_ address as the MAC address. The MAC address should be 6 hexadecimal bytes separated by hyphens.
-N	Displays the ARP address for the NIC specified by the target address.

With these options you can view the contents of the address resolution table, delete the problem entry, and install a corrected entry. The ability to install a corrected entry is a stop-gap measure while you search for a permanent fix.

You should use arp if you think there are incorrect entries getting into the address-resolution table. One clear indication of an arp table problem is when the wrong host responds to commands such as FTP or Telnet. Intermittent problems that affect only certain hosts can also indicate the arp table has been corrupted. arp table problems are usually caused by two systems using the same IP address. The problem seems to be intermittent, because the entry that appears in the table is the address of the host that responded the quickest to the last ARP request. Sometimes, the right host is the first to respond. Sometimes, it is the imposter that responds first.

If you suspect that two systems are using the same IP address, display the address-resolution table with the arp -a command. This is the easiest way to verify that the IP and Ethernet address pairs are correct if you have a record of each host's correct Ethernet address. For this reason, your network documentation should include each host's Ethernet and IP addresses when the host is added to the network. If you have that kind of documentation, you will be able to correct the ARP records or, at least, locate what is wrong with the table.

If you don't have a record of all the Ethernet addresses on your network (and let's face it, many of us can't keep track of where the IP addresses are, much less the Ethernet addresses), the first three bytes of the Ethernet address can help you look for a problem. The first three bytes of the address identify the equipment manufacturer. A list of these prefixes is found in the Assigned Numbers RFC, in the section titled *Ethernet Vendor Address Components*. This information is also available at ftp.isi.edu/in-notes/ iana/-assignments/ethernet-numbers.

As an example, an arp -a listing might look something like

Device	IP Address	Mask	Flag Physical Address
e0	abc.stuff.com	255.255.255.255	08:00:20:05:21:33

If you were to look up the first three bytes of this address, you would find that it is assigned to Sun. You wouldn't be able to tell which particular Sun device you were accessing, but if you thought abc.stuff.com was on a Cisco system, you would recognize that you might have a problem.

If checking the record for the correct assignment of the manufacturer prefix doesn't help, you could also try to telnet to the device. If the device supports Telnet, you may be able to get some information off the login banner to find out whether you are at the right place.

netstat

Another utility that can be used to troubleshoot network-access problems is the netstat utility. netstat should be brought out of your toolkit whenever you suspect that your local-area network connection is unreliable. The syntax for netstat is:

```
netstat [-a][-e][-n][-s][-p protocol][-r][interval]
```

Table 19.8 explains the netstat options.

Table 19.8   The netstat Options

Option	Description
-a	Displays all connections and listening ports.
-e	Displays Ethernet statistics. This may be combined with the –s options.
-n	Displays addresses and port numbers in numerical form
-p	Shows connections for the protocol specified by the Protocol option.
protocol	Protocol can be TCP or UDP when used with the –p parameter. If used with the –s parameter, the protocols can be TCP, UDP, and IP.
-r	Displays the routing table.

Table 19.8   The netstat Options

Option	Description
-s	Displays preprotocol statistics. By default, statistics are shown for TCP, UDP, and IP; the –p option may be used to specify a particular subset of these protocols.
interval	Redisplays selected statistics, pausing interval seconds between each display. Press CTRL+C to stop redisplaying statistics. If omitted, netstat will print the statistics once.

The output of the netstat –i command is shown next.

Name	MTU	Net/Dest	Address	Ipkts	Ierrs	Opkts	Oerrs	Collis	Queue
le0	1500	stuff.com	morestuff	45022	2	68234	2	5067	0
lo0	1536	loopback	localhost	2456	0	3443	0	0	0

The second line for the localhost loopback can be ignored. The first line, dealing with a real network access, is significant, and only the last five fields will give you any useable troubleshooting information.

Starting at the far right side, take a look at the Queue column. This statistic will be incremented when a packet has to wait before being handled. This statistic should be at 0. If the interface is up and running and the system cannot handle the packet immediately, suspect a bad cable or a bad network card. Replace the cable and see if the problem improves. If the new cable doesn't work, look at replacing the network card.

The columns for input errors (Ierrs) and output errors (Oerrs) should be close to 0. Regardless of how much traffic has passed through the interface, 100 errors in either of these fields is probably too high. High output errors can indicate a saturated local network or a bad physical connection between the host and the network. High input errors can indicate that the network is overworked, the local host is overworked, or there is a physical network problem. If there is a physical problem, use ping or a cable tester to check it out. Evaluating the collision rate can help you determine whether the local Ethernet segment is saturated.

If you look at the collision field (Collis), don't be surprised to find a high value. That is normal. What is not normal is that the percentage of output packets that result in collisions is too high. This means that your network segment may be too big and may need to be segmented. If the ratio between collisions and output exceeds 5 percent, you may want to keep an eye on the expansion assigned to the segment.

Collision rates are a percentage of output packets. Don't use the total number of packets sent and packets received; look at the values on the Opkts and Collis fields when looking at the collision rate. In the example above, our collision rate is operating at about 7 percent, so the network may need to be segmented.

Segmenting an Ethernet Network

In the previous section, segmenting an Ethernet network was suggested several times. Changes in technology is making this less and less of a problem, but it still does occur.

Ethernet specifications call for media access to be accomplished using a CSMA/CD (Carrier Sense Multiple Access/Collision Detection) approach. This means that when a system wants to move information on the network, it checks the wire to make sure there are no other packets flying around the network. If the wire is available, it will then put its packet on the wire and have the packet start its journey. Because each and every interface can sample the wire and put information on the wire at the same time, the chances of two systems putting a packet into motion at the same time increases with the number of hosts on the segment. Having two machines put information on the wire at exactly the same moment may not be a problem. Problems arise when a host samples the wire, finds it free, and then starts to send a packet. Meanwhile, the host next to our original host may have just put a packet on the network, and there is a collision. Obviously, the more hosts on the network, the greater the chances are for this to occur. When this occurs with too much regularity, you have to reduce the number of hosts on the segments. That can be done by either changing the concentrator or hub to a switch or by dividing the segment.

The easiest and most efficient method of dividing the segment is by swapping the old concentrator for a switch. A concentrator works by concentrating or centralizing signals. A packet sent by System A has access to every other system on the network at the same time.

A switch, on the other hand, creates a virtual path between the switch and the host, eliminating any chance of a collision. When a host wants to send a packet, the switch creates a dedicated path between the switch and the host, so collisions are a thing of the past. On most switches, the ports can be used in several modes. For example, if you have five systems that are rarely used, you can connect those five to a concentrator and then plug the concentrator into one of the switch ports. A server, or another demanding host, can be given a dedicated port so it doesn't share a segment with any other system.

Some switches do double duty. For example, you may have a switch that works with a 10Mbps network card or a 100Mbps network card. Figure 19.6 shows how a switch and a concentrator may be combined in an Ethernet network.

Figure 19.6   Switches and concentrators in the same network

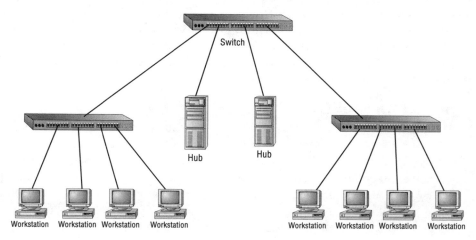

In this figure, you have two Ethernet hubs connected into the switch as well as two high-priority, high-demand systems.

Before deciding on this strategy, it is a good idea to spend time planning. Switches, especially the new 10/100 auto-sensing switches, are expensive. Before allocating a port on your new switch, take a look at what services are in demand and who is communicating with whom. Then try to develop a message-flow plan that will reduce the amount of traffic traveling over any segment. For example, if one of the high-demand systems that is plugged directly into a port spends most of its time communicating with a system that is plugged into one of the concentrators, the system on the concentrator should be moved into one of the switch ports. Another alternative would be to add another concentrator for the high-demand system and its favorite communications partner and then plug that concentrator into the switch port that the high-demand system is currently occupying. This is a sample of using planning to get the highest return on your investment in the switch and performing load-balancing at the same time.

Some networks are still using the old coax cable Ethernet, and the temptation is always there to break the cable and add a bridge or a router. You won't want to do that. If your network is that old, it is time to consider upgrading. If you are considering moving to a router or a bridge, the saturation rate with a coax cable on the network should be high. Whenever you are using a coax cable, you are using shared media because everyone is using the same cable. In most cases, this is an accident waiting to happen. You should alter the design of your network to something in which a single user cannot bring down the entire network by disconnecting the wrong wire. It is time to move to Category 5 unshielded, twisted-pair (UTP) cables and create a 10BaseT Ethernet or a 100BaseT Fast Ethernet network. In this case, the wire that goes from the computer to the wall connects into a protected (and locked, hopefully) wiring closet. This isolates the network components in the user's cube to the point that if the user does something, only their system will be affected. The new network may help to solve your collision problems and reduce the amount of hardware troubleshooting you need to do.

Network Hardware Problems

As I talk about troubleshooting TCP/IP, there are times when the hardware is mentioned. If there is a hardware problem, in many cases, the problem and the solution will be out of your hands. For example, you may be perfectly capable of replacing network cards, concentrators, switches, and some cabling, but when you check your hardware-problem priority list, these things don't fail all that often. The chance of a leased telephone line having a problem or a link on your wide-area network going down is probably greater than a network card all of a sudden going south. When this situation happens, you will need to contact the telephone company or the company that is in charge of managing your network.

Many times when there are communication problems between sites, the administrator may take a wait-and-see attitude. I think this comes from all those times we have been trying to fix something while constantly answering pages to tell us the network is down. We don't want to put the burden on the tech trying to solve the problem. That attitude is admirable, but the tech may not know they have a problem until you tell them. So get on the phone, because the worst thing that can happen is the triage desk will tell you they already know the line is down.

If your communication problem is on the local-area network, it will be up to you to handle the troubleshooting and the solution. When troubleshooting network problems, documentation, and log files, knowledge of the network and common sense will often be your most useful tools. A cable tester can come in handy, but chances are the right answer to the question of "What has changed on my network lately?" will provide many of the tips necessary to solve the problem. Often the best or quickest way to solve a problem is to start unplugging things. You keep unplugging one thing at a time until the problem goes away. When that happens, you are probably holding the culprit in your hand. Because this technique of unplugging things is usually done at a switch or a concentrator, you may be left holding a cable that leads off to a computer somewhere on your network. This is where good documentation comes into play. If you have the documentation, you can see which host is plugged into which port. If you don't have good documentation, the next step is to wait for the phone to ring with a person telling you they just lost their network connection! This is not the most scientific method of determining the next step in the troubleshooting process.

Troubleshooting Routing

When a user receives the error message that a network is unreachable, there is a routing problem somewhere. If the problem is in the local host's routing table, it is easy to detect and to resolve. For example, the first thing to try would be to use the `netstat -r` command to access the host's routing table. Figure 19.7 shows the routing table that is currently maintained on my laptop, when I am connected to the Internet from my daughter's home in Illinois.

Figure 19.7   Results of `netstat -r`

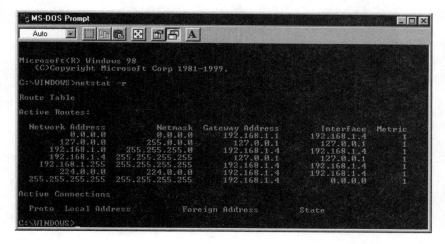

`netstat -r` issues fairly transitive results. For example, I first tried to go out to my POP3 server, and when I did, I received the routing discovery shown in Figure 19.8.

Figure 19.8   Finding how to get to `mail.psconsulting.com`, using the `netstat -r` command

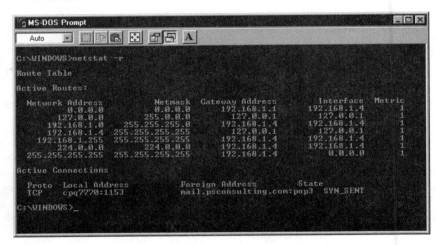

A second later, I tried to clear out my other e-mail account on the Earthlink network, and the results that I received to the same command are shown in Figure 19.9.

Figure 19.9   Finding how to get to the `mail.earthlink.net` host, using the `netstat -r` command

As you can see, the information on mail.psconsulting.com is gone. Be aware that when you use the netstat -r command, history is very short-lived.

Based on a *Network Unreachable* error message, you would start by checking the routing table on the host that is making the attempt. Suppose you are trying to reach the host at 192.68.1.4. This is a Class B address, and because netstat is interested in the network address and not the host address, we would be looking at the route to the NETWORK 192.68.1.0. If you were working on a Unix host, you could use the command netstat -nr | grep '192.68.1.0'. Grep is a utility that would be used to display the specific route to the destination. Because there is no specific route to the destination, look for a default route. If netstat returns a correct route to the host or a valid default route, the problem is not in the routing table. It is probably beyond the local machine, and another command, tracert would be used to locate the problem. I will discuss tracert later in the chapter.

If netstat does not return a valid route, it is a local routing problem. When that has been determined, you have two ways of approaching the problem, depending on whether your network uses static or dynamic routing. If you are using a static routing table, you will need to install the missing route to the routing table by using the route add command. Because most of the systems that rely on a static routing table will be depending on the default route, this is the one that will usually be missing. Besides using the route add command to temporarily replace the route in the routing table, it would probably be wise to check which configuration files are supposed to add the route to the table at boot.

If you are using dynamic routing, make sure the routing program is running, or the gateway is properly configured in the TCP/IP configuration. On a Unix host, if you are checking for a route with a dynamic-routing table, you will want to make sure the gated daemon is working.

If the correct daemon is not running, restart it, and specify tracing. Tracing will allow you to check for problems that might be causing the daemon to terminate abnormally.

TIP   Now, let's be honest here. If the host having the problem is not a server, the way that you are going to solve most of the problems that I have been discussing is to simply reboot the host. If the routing configuration usually works, something strange has happened to cause this abnormality. It may just be a sporadic occurrence, so the quickest way of getting everything back to normal would be to shut down the host and restart it. If the configuration is correct and hasn't been corrupted, that should solve the problem.

Using tracert to Solve Problems

If the local routing table is correct, the problem may be occurring outside of your local network. Remote routing problems can cause the *Unreachable Host Error* message or the *Network Unreachable* error message. Just because you receive either of these error messages does not mean that this is *your* problem. It may be a problem that is occurring on someone else's network segment. The way to determine where the problem is occurring would be to use the tracert utility.

The syntax for the tracert command is

```
tracert [-d][-h maximum hops][-j host_list][-w timeout]target_name
```

Table 19.9 explains the options.

Table 19.9   tracert Options

Option	Description
-d	Putting in the -d switch tells the command not to resolve the addresses to host names.
-h maximum hops	Maximum number of hops to search for the target. Default is usually 30.
-j host_list	Loose source route along host_list.
-w timeout	Timeout in milliseconds to wait for each reply.
target_name	The name of the target host for the trace route.

tracert tracks the route that UDP packets take from the local host to a remote host. It prints the name and the IP address of each gateway along the route to the remote host.

tracert tracks the packets using two techniques. First, it will use a small TTL to determine the intermediate gateways. The TTL values start at 1 and increase in increments of 1 for each group of three UDP packets sent. When a gateway receives the packet, it decrements the TTL by 1. If the TTL reaches 0, the packet is not forwarded, and an ICMP *Time Exceeded* message is returned to the source of the packet. tracert then displays one line of output that is displayed for the gateway, and it shows the meaning of each field in the line.

Along with the TTL methods, the packet also has an incorrect port address. The incorrect port address comes into play when the packet finally reaches the appropriate destination host. Because the port address is wrong, the destination host will return an ICMP *Unreachable Port* message. When tracert receives the *Unreachable Port* message, it knows that it has reached the destination host, and it stops the trace. It then displays the final line, showing the actual route taken to the destination. In other words, tracert is able to develop a list of gateways starting at the default gateway and moving one step at a time through the network. Figure 19.10 shows the result of a tracert from a dial-in connection to the host networksolutions.com.

Figure 19.10 tracert from a dial-in connection to networksolutions.com

Tracing route to networksolutions.com [198.41.0 8]

over a maximum of 30 hops:

1	198ms	176ms	176ms	maxl.dsll-ca-us.earthlink.net [207.217.150.213]
2	183ms	202ms	179ms	f5-1-0-ar0l-pas.neteng.itd.earthlink.net [207.217.150.1]
3	177ms	179ms	180ms	f2-0-br02-pas.neteng.itd.earthlink net [207.217.50.61]
4	235ms	192ms	179ms	Hssi2-0-0.GW1.LAX4.ALTER.NET [157.130.226.153]
5	196ms	209ms	177ms	121.ATM2-0.XR2.LAX4.ALTER.NET [146.188.248.102]
6	192ms	177ms	178ms	192.ATM3-0.TR2.LAX2.ALTER.NET [146.188.249.6]
7	258ms	234ms	242ms	111.ATM7-0.TR2.DCA1.ALTER.NET [146.188.136.209]
8	250ms	256ms	237ms	198.ATM6-0.XR2 TCO1.ALTER.NET [146.188.161.177]
9	*	237ms	235ms	192.ATM8-0-0.GWI.TCO1.ALTER.NET [146.188.160.37]
10	254ms	270ms	265ms	Internic1-gw.customer.ALTER.NET [157.130.32.242]
11	264ms	265ms	268ms	networksolutions.com [198.41.0 8]

Trace complete.

This trace shows that it took 11 intermediate gateways to reach the Network Solutions host. It also shows that round-trip travel time for packets to reach the host average 264 milliseconds.

How much can you trust these displays? Well, as you know, there are several different variations of the TCP/IP suite, so there are several variations on ICMP. In addition, the path that a packet may take to reach a destination may change, depending on the configuration of the intermediate gateways. This can lead to some "interesting" results. For this reason, don't depend on the output of `tracert` too much. The things to look for in the results of a `tracert` are

- Did the packet get to where it was supposed to go?
- If the packet did not make its final destination, where did it stop?

When a `tracert` fails to get packets through to the remote end system, the trace dies. It displays a series of three asterisks at each hop count until the count reaches 30. If this happens and you know whom to contact, you can contact the administrator of the destination host and the administrator in charge of the last gateway that was displayed. They may be able to help or the problem may be out of their control.

Troubleshooting Using Name Service

One of the most common error messages displayed in the world of TCP/IP is the *440: Host Unknown* message. Again, this error message can be a "real" message, or it can be a temporary condition that implies that your packet somehow lost its way in the maze of the Internet. Certainly, if you are trying to reach the Whatever Company, and you are not sure of the URL and start plugging things in at random, the *440: Host Unknown* message is probably true. However, if you are looking for `www.microsoft.com`, the chances are the message could be a false reading.

Name server problems can usually be diagnosed with the `nslookup` command. `nslookup` is a command-line utility, but it also finds its way into many of the popular TCP/IP shareware utility suites. It is designed to help you locate information on a particular DNS name or to find out information on all the records for a particular host.

`nslookup` has two execution modes, Interactive and Noninteractive. Noninteractive mode is best for looking up information about a single record and for scripting. Interactive mode is less commonly used, but it is convenient if you are looking up multiple records at a single time or need to make use of the extended command set.

Noninteractive Mode

To use this mode, you will have to provide the `nslookup` utility with all the information it needs at the command prompt. These are provided in the standard way, as command-line parameters. For all the parameters, preface the option with a hyphen. If the parameters require a string argument, follow it with an equal sign and a value.

Table 19.10 explains what each of the `nslookup` Noninteractive options accomplishes.

Table 19.10   nslookup Noninteractive Options

Option	Description
-all	Shows the default DNS server and any options you have enabled during the session.
-class	Changes the class of the query you wish to submit. This is normally set to Internet, the default.
-d2 or -nod2	Enables or disables exhaustive debugging. This will show you all of the information that is retrieved about the sites you query during your session.
-debug or -nodebug	Enables or disables Debugging mode. When enabled, information from some of the packets will be displayed. This option is more commonly used than set d2, which shows more information than most people are interested in.
-defname or -nodefname	Enables or disables, automatically appending a dot and the domain name (specified with the set domain option) after each host name entered into nslookup that does not already include a domain name.
-domain	Modifies the domain nslookup appends to the end of the host names.
-ignore or -noignore	Enables or disables acceptance of packets with truncation errors.
-port	Sets the default TCP/UDP port. This is only used in the very uncommon circumstance of a DNS server that is operating at a port other than the default port of 53.
-querytype	Sets the type of information query that will be submitted to the DNS servers. This command is the same as set type.
-recurse or -norecurse	Enables or disables asking the DNS Name server to query other servers if it does not have the information in its cache or zone files.

Table 19.10 `nslookup` Noninteractive Options *(continued)*

Option	Description
`-retry`	Sets the number of times `nslookup` will try the same DNS server before giving up. When `nslookup` queries a DNS server, it will try *x* number of times. The timeout value between each query doubles until the retry value is reached.
`-root`	Sets the name of the Root server.
`-search` or `-nosearch`	Enables or disables the parsing of the `srchlist` parameter.
`-srchlist`	Allows you to configure a list of domain names that `nslookup` will automatically append to each host name you query. It parses the search list.
`-timeout`	Controls how many seconds `nslookup` waits to hear a response from a DNS server. By default, this value is set to 2.
`-type`	Sets the type of information query that will be submitted to the DNS servers. This command is a synonym for `set querytype`.
`-vc` or `-novc`	Enables or disables, forcing `nslookup` to use a virtual circuit when submitting queries to the DNS server.

Interactive Mode Settings for nslookup

The Interactive mode for `nslookup` allows you to perform queries for several servers in sequence. It also allows for more flexibility within the command-line arguments. To enter the Interactive mode with a Windows NT machine, simply execute the `nslookup` command without any parameters. Your command prompt will change to a > sign, indicating that `nslookup` will be interpreting everything you type. The options are similar to those for the Noninteractive mode, and there are several additional commands shown in Table 19.11.

Table 19.11   Interactive Mode nslookup Arguments

Command	Purpose
exit	Quits nslookup.
finger	Connects with the Finger server on the current host. The current host is defined when a previous lookup for a host was successful and returned the address information.
help or ?	Shows you a list of the available options with a short description for each.
ls	Retrieves a list of all DNS entries for a domain. The fields returned by default contain host names and IP addresses. Many domains have hundreds or thousands of hosts, so this could be a pretty big list. To make the output a little more manageable, redirect it to a file just as you would DOS. nslookup will echo # signs, marking every fifty records.
lserver	Changes the default server to the specified DNS domain. lserver uses the initial server to look up the information about the specified DNS domain. This command is in contrast to the server command, which uses the current default server.
root	Changes the default server to the server for the root of the DNS domain name space. Currently, the host G.ROOT-SERVERS.NET. is used. (This command is a synonym for lserver g.root-server.net.) The name of the Root server can be changed with the set root command.
server	Changes the default server to the specified DNS domain. Server uses the current default server to look up the information about the specified DNS domain. (This is in contrast to the lserver command, which uses the initial server.)

Table 19.11   Interactive Mode nslookup Arguments *(continued)*

Command	Purpose
set all	Shows the default DNS server and any options you have enabled during this session.
set class	Changes the query class. This is normally set to Internet, the default.
set d2 or set nod2	Enables or disables exhaustive debugging. This will show you all of the information that is retrieved about the sites you query during your session.
set debug or nodebug	Turns Debugging mode on or off. When enabled, information from some of the packets will be displayed. This option is more commonly used than set d2, which shows more information than most people are interested in.
set defname or set nodefname	Enables or disables, automatically appending a dot and the domain name (specified with the set domain option) after each host name entered into nslookup that does not already include a domain name.
set domain	Changes the default DNS domain to the name specified. The default DNS domain name is appended to a lookup request depending on the state of the defname and search options. The DNS domain search list contains the parents of the default DNS domain if it has at least two components in the name. For example, if the default DNS domain is mystuff.mycompany.com, the search list is mystuff.mycompany.com and mycompany.com. Use the srchlist command to specify a different list. Use the set all command to display the list.
set ignore or no ignore	Enables or disables acceptance of packets with truncation errors.

Table 19.11   Interactive Mode nslookup Arguments *(continued)*

Command	Purpose
set port	Sets the default TCP/UDP port. This is only used in the very uncommon circumstance of a DNS server that is operating at a port other than the default port of 53.
set querytype	Changes the type of information query.
set recurse or set norecurse	Enables or disables asking the DNS name server to query other servers if it does not have the information in its cache or zone files.
set retry	Sets the number of times nslookup will try the same DNS server before giving up. When nslookup queries a DNS server, it will try *x* number of times. The time-out value between each query doubles until the retry value is reached.
set root	Set the name of the Root server.
set search or set nosearch	If set and the lookup request contains at least one period but does not end with a trailing period, appends the DNS domain names in the DNS domain search list to the request until an answer is received.
set srchlist	Changes the default DNS domain name and search list. A maximum of six names separated by slashes (/) can be specified. This command overrides the default DNS domain name and search list of the set domain command. Use the set all command to display the list.
set timeout	Changes the initial number of seconds to wait for a reply to a request. When a reply to a request is not received within this time period, the timeout is doubled, and the request is resent. (The numbers of retries is controlled with the set retry option.)

Table 19.11 Interactive Mode `nslookup` Arguments *(continued)*

Command	Purpose
set type	Changes the type of information query. More information about types can be found in RFC1035. (The set type command is a synonym for set querytype.)
set vc or set no vc	If set, forces nslookup to use a virtual circuit when sending requests to the server.
view	Sorts and lists the output of previous ls commands.

If you are having a problem resolving a name, try directly querying the Authoritative servers returned by the NS query. Don't rely on information returned by non-Authoritative servers. If the problems that have been reported are intermittent, query all the Authoritative servers in turn and compare the answers. Intermittent Name server problems are sometimes caused by the remote servers returning different answers to the same question.

The ANY query returns all records about a host, thus giving you the widest range of troubleshooting information. Simply knowing what information is available can solve many problems. For example, if you are trying to send an e-mail to a particular company and the e-mail keeps coming back, finding the MX record would help you to check whether the mail server is really operational. By the same token, if you have the MX record and there is no A record listed, you have found the explanation as to why a user could not telnet to the host.

If you are unable to locate any information about the host name that you have been given, perhaps the host name is incorrect. Given that the host name you have is wrong, trying to find it will be like searching for a needle in a haystack. nslookup can help. You can use the nslookup ls command to dump the remote zone file and then redirect the listing to a file. If you use the nslookup view command to browse through the file, you can search for another name that is similar to the name you were provided. Many lookup problems are caused by either incorrect host names or correct host names that have been entered incorrectly.

Examples of Troubleshooting Using nslookup

Suppose users of your network are having trouble resolving a specific host name from one computer, while the resolution works fine from another. Meanwhile, the first computer had no problem resolving other host names.

This is obviously a DNS lookup problem. If you are using external DNS lookups, the solution would seem to be to make sure that the computer with the problem is querying the same DNS system as the computer without the problem. Once the reconfiguration of the DNS system is completed, the lookup problem should go away. What happens if you are not going to the outside world for resolution? What happens if all resolution is taking place on *your* side of the firewall? In that case, you had better find the DNS system with the problem! You start by finding the Authoritative servers for the host name in question.

Start by setting the `nslookup` type to NS to get the name server records for the domain in question. This should return several name servers, so now it is just a question of finding out which name server has the problem. You can do this once you know which Authoritative servers service the domain in question. Then you can query those servers for information on the host. This should return the address record for the host. Keep testing each of the authoritative servers, until you find the one with the record that is incorrect.

The next step is to get the SOA (Start of Authority) records for each server and see whether they are the same. This is done by setting the `nslookup` type to SOA and querying the servers again. If the SOA records have different serial numbers, perhaps the zone file and the host name have not been downloaded yet to the secondary server. It may be a patience problem, where if you wait long enough the problem goes away. If the serial numbers are the same and the data is different, then there is a definite problem.

Now it is necessary to contact the remote domain administrator and provide notification that there is a problem. If you are not sure of the identity of the network administrator, it should be shown in the Mail Addr field of the SOA record.

Primary and Secondary Servers Not Synchronizing

If your network provides for DNS lookup and you have multiple DNS servers scattered about the land, it is inevitable that you will have an occasion where the secondary server does not synchronize properly with the primary server.

This problem usually manifests itself in a fashion similar to the problem reported in this scenario. A host accessing the primary name server can resolve a name or names without a problem. When the host tries to access the name from a secondary name server, the resolution fails. When the administrator examined the cache table, they found that the entry was right, but the name would still not resolve properly.

This problem rarely happens with just one secondary server. It will usually show up on several others. All the servers had the same SOA serial number, and a dump of the cache on each server showed that they all had the correct address records for the host name. In this case, the problem will usually be the way that zone file transfers occur. Primary servers load the data directly from local disk files. Secondary servers transfer the data from the primary server via a zone-file transfer. If the zone file was getting corrupted, that would account for the problem.

If you display the zone file and notice an odd display of information, the data may have been corrupted in the transfer, or it might be bad on the primary server. You can use nslookup to find out where the problem originated. When you check the records, a corrupted entry may exhibit a packet-size error message. This indicates that nslookup was having trouble retrieving a record from a server. At this point, it is time to get on the phone or send an e-mail to the remote administrator, specifying which records you are having problems with.

Cache Corruption

The problem described previously was caused by a bad record corrupting the cache on the secondary servers. Cache corruption can occur even if your server is not the secondary server. Sometimes the Root server entries in the cache become corrupted. In this case, dumping the cache and examining the output can help you locate the problem.

For example, let's say there are intermittent name server problems being reported. A user may not have a problem resolving names within the local domain or even resolving the name of some hosts outside the local domain. There may, however, be names in some domains that will not resolve. In this case, nslookup tests may produce no clues, so dumping the name server cache is the next step. When it is examined, you may discover that the Root server entries were corrupted. If information in cache is corrupted, you should stop and restart the DNS server process to clear the cache and reload the appropriate information.

Troubleshooting with SNMP

In this section, the approach to troubleshooting will come from another aspect. The previous examples all pointed to problems that were reported, meaning the administrator is being reactive. By using SNMP, the administrator may be able to avoid some problems.

There is a full-blown discussion of SNMP in Chapter 10, but for those of you who just wanted the *Reader's Digest* approach to SNMP, I will review it here. SNMP is a Client/Server Protocol. Like most things in computing, any time you get into something a little more specialized, a new batch of terminology goes with it. In this case with SNMP, the components are named managers and agents, instead of clients and servers. The agent, or *server piece,* runs on the system that is being managed. It is then referred to as the *managed network entity*. The agent software monitors the status of the device and reports that status to the manager.

The manager (the client) runs on a host called the *NMS* (Network Management Station). The NMS is assigned to collect the information from all of the different devices that are being managed. The NMS then consolidates this information and presents it in some usable form to the network administrator. This design places all of the data manipulation tools and most of the User Interface on the NMS. Concentrating the bulk of the load on the manager means that the agent software is small and easy to install. Correspondingly, most TCP/IP network equipment will come with an SNMP management agent.

SNMP is a request/response protocol. UDP port 161 is the well-known port used by SNMP. SNMP uses UDP because there is none of the inherent overhead that comes with TCP. Reliability is not an issue with SNMP because each time a system makes a request, a response is generated. If the SNMP application does not receive a response, it simply reissues the request. The TCP overhead of sequencing is not needed because each request and each response travels a single datagram.

The request and response messages that SNMP sends in these datagrams are called *PDUs* (Protocol Data Units). There are five PDUs used by SNMP, and they are listed in Table 19.12.

Table 19.12   The Five SNMP PDUs

PDU	Use
GetRequest	Manager requests an update.
GetNextRequest	Manager requests the next entry in a table.
GetResponse	Agent answers a manager request.
SetRequest	Manager modifies data on the managed device.
Trap	Agent alerts manager of an unusual event.

These message types allow the manager to request management information and, when appropriate, to modify the information. The messages also allow the agent to respond to manager requests and to notify the manager of unusual situations.

The NMS will request the status of each managed device. Making periodic requests is called *polling*. Polling reduces the burden on the agent because the NMS decides when polls are needed, and the agent simply responds. Polling also reduces the burden on the network because the polls originate from a single system at a predictable rate. The shortcoming of polling is that it does not allow for real-time updates. If a problem occurs on a managed device, the manager does not find out until the agent is polled. To handle this, SNMP uses a modified polling system called *trap-directed polling*.

A trap is an interrupt signaled by a predefined event. When a trap occurs, the SNMP agent does not wait for the manager to poll. Instead it immediately sends information to the manager. Traps allow the agent to inform the manager of unusual events while allowing the manager to maintain control of polling. SNMP traps are sent on UDP port 162. The manager sends polls on port 161 and listens for traps on port 162. Table 19.13 lists the trap events defined by RFC.

Table 19.13 Trap Events Defined by RFC

Trap	Meaning
coldStart	Agent restarted; possible configuration changes.
warmStart	Agent reinitialized without configuration changes.
enterpriseSpecific	An event significant to this hardware or software.
authenticationFailure	Agent received an unauthenticated message.
linkDown	Agent detected a network link failure.
linkUP	Agent detected a link coming up.
egpNeighborLoss	The devices EGP neighbor is down.

The most important trap may be the enterpriseSpecific trap. The events that signal this trap are defined differently by every vendor's SNMP agent software. Therefore, it is possible for the trap to be tuned to the events that are significant for that system. SNMP used the term *enterprise* to refer to something that is privately defined by a vendor or organization as opposed to something that is globally defined by an RFC.

Object Definition

The Structure of Management Information (SMI) defines how data should be presented in an SNMP environment. The SMI is documented in RFC1155 and RFC1065. The SMI defines how managed objects are named, the syntax in which they are defined, and how they are encoded for transmission over the network.

Each managed object is given a globally unique name, called the *object identifier*. This object identifier is part of a hierarchical name space. The name structure is used, just like in DNS, to guarantee that the name is globally unique. In an object identifier, each level of the hierarchy is identified by a number.

If this naming sounds pretty formal, it is. The objects are defined just as formally as they are named. The syntax used to define managed objects is Abstract Syntax Notation One (ASN.1). ASN.1 is ISO standard 8824. It is a very formal set of language rules for defining data. It makes the data definition independent of incompatibilities between systems and character sets. ASN.1 also includes a set of rules for encoding data for transfer over a network. The Basic Encoding Rules (BER) define that bit 8 of an octet is sent first, that the 2s complement is used for signed integers, and other nitty-gritty details of data transmission.

Every object managed by SNMP has a unique object identifier defined by the ASN.1 syntax and encoding defined by BER. When all of these unique objects are grouped together, they are called the MIB (Management Information Base). The MIB refers to all information that is managed by SNMP. You may hear the term *MIBs* (plural) because there are special databases for different types of devices.

The MIB I standards and the MIB II standards are defined by RFC. MIB II is a superset of MIB I and is the standard MIB for monitoring TCP/IP. It provides information, such as the number of packets transmitted into and out of an interface and the number of errors that occurred sending and receiving those packets, that is useful in spotting usage trends and potential trouble spots. Every SNMP agent supports MIB I or MIB II.

No matter what MIBs are provided by the agents, it is the monitoring software that displays the information for the system administrator. A private MIB won't do you any good unless your network monitoring software also supports that MIB. For this reason, most administrators will purchase monitor software from the vendor that supplies the majority of their network equipment.

Other features of network monitors include troubleshooting tools such as the following:

Network maps   Some monitors automatically draw a map of the network. Colors are used to indicate the state (up or down) of the devices on the network. At a glance, the network manager sees the overall state of the network.

Tabular data displays   Data displayed in tables or rendered into charts is used to make comparisons between different devices. Some monitors output data that can then be read into a standard spreadsheet or graphing program.

Filters   Filters sift the data coming in from the agents in order to detect certain conditions.

Alarms   Alarms indicate when thresholds are exceeded or special events occur. For example, you may want an alarm to trigger when your server exceeds some specified number of transmit errors.

Index

Note to the Reader: Page numbers in **bold** indicate the principal discussion of a topic or the definition of a term. Page numbers in *italic* indicate illustrations.

Symbols

@ (at sign) in zone files, 122
:: (colons) in IPv6 addresses, 392

A

AAA (Authentication, Authorization, and Accounting) protocol, 282
Abilene Project, **271–272**
abstract syntax notation number one (ASN.1), 25–26, 507
acceptable level of service, 463
access rights
    assigning user, group, and file system rights, 430–432
    and deleting default accounts, 429–430
access-control authorization, 458
accessibility plans for network resources, 347, *347*
accounting features for remote-access security, 459
accounts, deleting default accounts, 429–430
active advertising, **25**
Address Service Organization (ASO), 22
addresses. *See also* IP addresses
    address records, 42
    ARP (Address Resolution Protocol), 41, 42–43
    destination addresses
        destination IP addresses, 40
        destination port addresses, 82–83
        in packet headers, 237
        in routing, 215–216
    DHCP address allocation, 93–94
    DNS addresses, 240–241
    documenting, 302
    Ethernet addresses, 485–486
    hiding internal addresses from the Internet, 360, *361*
    host addresses, 63
    IPv6 addresses, **389–396**
        address lifetimes, 400
        aggregatable global unicast addresses, 391
        anycast addresses, 389, 393
        architecture and notation, 389–390
        assigning, 391
        BGP (Border Gateway Protocol) and, 395
        Classless Interdomain Routing (CIDR) and, 394
        colons (::) in, 392
        interdomain routing and, 393–395
        Interdomain Routing Protocol (IDRP), 395
        interface identifiers and, 391
        intradomain routing and, 396
        IPv4-based addresses, 392
        link local addresses, 392, 397–398
        loopback addresses, 392
        multicast addresses, 389, 393
        NLAs (Next Level Aggregators) and, 391
        OSPF protocol and, 396
        overview of, 391
        provider-based addresses, 394
        RIP protocol and, 396
        site local addresses, 392
        SLAs (Site Local Aggregators) and, 391
        special address formats, 391–392

TLAs (Top Level Aggregators) and, 391
unicast addresses, 389, 391
unspecified addresses, 392
link local addresses, 397–398
loopback addresses, 472
MAC (Media Access Control) addresses, 28, 42–43, 80
pooled addresses for dial-up connections, 321
port addresses
  defined, **10**
  firewalls and, 10
  FTP (File Transfer Protocol) and, 153
  IP addresses and, 47–48, 82–86, *85*
  RFC (Request for Comment), 10
  source port addresses and destination port addresses, 82–83
TCP/IP addresses, 9–10
Addressing tab in DNS/DHCP Management Console, 96, *96*
advertising, **24–25**
aggregatable global unicast addresses, 391
alarms, 262, *507*
all ones, **52**
all zeros, **52**
allocating. *See* assigning
alpha code, **259**
Alta Vista Tunnel software, 277–278
always-on Internet connectivity, 286
analog signaling, **34**, *34*
ANDing process, **470–471**
anonymous FTP, **149**, 424
anycast IPv6 addresses, 389, 393
application gateways, 443, 444
Application layer in OSI model
  Application layer proxying
    caches and, 361
    configuring, 378–379
    defined, **374–375**, *375*

FTP (File Transfer Protocol) proxies, 379
    HTTP proxies, 378–379
  defined, **24–25**
  planning for Application layer changes, 324–325
application processes, **82**
applications
  client/server applications, **3–7**
    defined, **3–4**
    TCP/IP and, 6–7
  e-mail applications, 6–7
  groupware applications, 6–7
applying patches, 427
approach phase of project management, **333–338**
  assembling the team, 334–335
  collecting business information, 335
  determining the scope of the design phase, 336–337
  implementing, 337–338, *338*
  overview of, 333–334, *333*
  preliminary scheduling, 337
  training the team, 335–336
Archie service, **49**, **172–174**, *173*, *174*
architecture
  of Internet 2 Project, 269–270, *270*
  of IPv6 addresses, 389–390
  TCP/IP architecture, **36–50**
    DoD model and, 36, *36*
    host-to-host layer protocols, 36, 45–49, *45*, *48*
    ICMP (Internet Control Message Protocol), 44–45, 386–387
    Internet layer protocols, 36–40, *39*
    IP routing protocols, 43–44
    network access layer protocols, 36–37
    process layer protocols, 36, 49–50
    Unix and, 36
    Windows 95/98 and, 36

areas, OSPF protocol and, 227

A-records, **42**

ARP (Address Resolution Protocol), 41, 42–43

arp command, 484–486

ARPAnet, 17–18, 20, 41

ASBRs (autonomous system border routers), **226–227**

ASN.1 (abstract syntax notation number one), 25–26, *507*

ASO (Address Service Organization), 22

ASs (autonomous systems), **226**

assembling teams, 334–335

assessing risk. *See* risk assessment

assigning

   IP addresses, **316–321**

      point-to-point addressing, 320–321, *321*

      pooled addresses for dial-up connections, 321

      RFC 1219 strategies for assigning IP addresses, 316–319

      workgroup IP address allocation, 319–320, *320*

   IPv6 addresses, 391

   user, group, and file system rights, 430–432

AssureNet Pathways, Inc., 454–455

asynchronous bit synchronization, **34**

asynchronous communications, **28–29**

Asynchronous Transfer Mode (ATM), 279

at sign (@) in zone files, 122

ATM (Asynchronous Transfer Mode), 279

ATMARP and ATMInARP protocols, 43

attacks. *See* security

auditing

   information access, 435–436

   for remote-access security, 459

   security auditing tools, 424–425

authentication. *See also* security

   AssureNet Pathways, Inc., 454–455

Authentication, Authorization, and Accounting (AAA) protocol, 282

card devices for remote-access authentication, 454

in IPv6 protocol, 402

RADIUS (Remote Authentication Dial-In User Service), 451–452, *452*

SecureID authentication, 277

Security Dynamics, Inc., 454

S-HTTP and, 13, 459

TACACS+ (Terminal Access Controller Access Control System +), 452–453

auto-configuration of hosts with IPv6 protocol, **397–401**

address lifetimes and, 400

defined, **397**

IPv6 DHCP protocol, 400–401

link local addresses and, 397–398

neighbor discovery and, 398

router advertisements and, 398–399

stateful auto-configuration, 399–400

stateless auto-configuration, 398–399

automatic DHCP address allocation, 93–94

autonomous system border routers (ASBRs), **226–227**

autonomous systems (ASs), **226**

availability evaluation, 414

B

backbones

   defined, **227**

   vBNS (Very High-Performance Backbone Network Service), 19, 272–273

backing up

   DHCP databases, 239

   WINS databases, 243

backup bridges, 210–211

backup designated routers (BDRs), 225–226, *225*

backup domain controllers (BDCs), 203
backward chaining, **468**
bandwidth
    documenting bandwidth requirements, 296
    in virtual private networks, 286–287
Basic Encoding Rules (BER), 26
BBSs (bulletin boards), 7–8
BDCs (backup domain controllers), 203
BDRs (backup designated routers), 225–226,
    225
BER (Basic Encoding Rules), 26
Berkeley Internet Name Domain servers.
    See BIND
beta code, **259**
BGP (Border Gateway Protocol), 43–44,
    232–233, 395
binary digits, **52**
binary IP addresses, converting to decimal
    addresses, 53
BIND (Berkeley Internet Name Domain)
    servers
  BIND boot files, 128–129
  defined, **113**
bit synchronization, **34**
bits, **52–53**
Blowfish encryption algorithm, 285
BOOTP protocol, 87, 88
Border Gateway Protocol (BGP), 43–44,
    232–233, 395
BPDUs (Bridge Protocol Data Units), 206–207,
    208–211, *208*
brain dumps, **468**
brand name systems versus clones, 187–188
bridges, **201–214**. *See also* routers
    broadcasting and, 203–204
    defined, **201–203**, *202*
    domain controllers and, 203
    learning mode bridges, **203**
    looping problems, 204–205, *204*

    network design and, 342
    planning implementations, 313, 315
    as semi-intelligent devices, 203
    source-routing bridges, **212–214**
      defined, **212–213**, *212*
      hello packets and, 212–213
      source-routing transparent bridges
        (SRTs), 213–214, *213*
    Spanning Tree Protocol, **205–212**
      advantages of, 206, 212
      backup bridges and, 210–211
      bridge broadcast frames and, 207–208,
        207
      bridge elections and, 207–209, *207*, *208*
      bridge IDs and, 206–207
      Bridge Protocol Data Units (BPDUs) and,
        206–207, 208–211, *208*
      defined, **205–206**, *206*
      and designating bridges, 209–211, *210*
      ideal spanning tree configurations,
        211–212, *211*
      port costs and, 209–210, *210*
      root bridges and, 206–207, *206*,
        209–211, *210*
    transparent bridges, **204**
    as unintelligent devices, 205
broadcasting, bridges and, 203–204
Bullet Proof FTP software, 145, *145*
bulletin boards, 7–8
bus topology, **30**, *30*
buying SNMP managers, 253
bytes, **52**

C

cable modems, 287–288
caching
    cache corruption on name servers, 504
    Cache files, 125–128
    caching-only DNS servers, 117

hierarchical and distributed caching, **364–370**
    Cache Array Routing Protocol (CARP), 368–370, *369*
    defined, **364**, *365*
    Internet Cache Protocol (ICP), 367–368
    Novell example, 365–366
  Proxy servers, **361–364**
    Application layer proxying and, 361
    overview of, 361–362, *362*
    proactive caching, 363
    protocol caching, 362–363
    security noncaching, 363–364
calculating IP addresses, 74–75
call level security, 457
callback methods for remote-access security, 457
Caller Line ID (CLI), 457
card devices for remote-access authentication, 454
Carnegie-Mellon University, 273
CARP (Cache Array Routing Protocol), 368–370, *369*
Carrier Sense Multiple Access/Collision Detection (CSMA/CD), 488
case studies
  Data Systems West (DSW), 254–255
  experts, 199
  internal network security, 407–410
  misplaced ports, 198
  Novell Proxy server, 365–366
  Proxy servers, 357, 365–366
  SNMP case studies, **254–261, 263**
    customizing off-the-shelf software, 259–260
    enterprise management, 255–257
    Hewlett-Packard OpenView system, 257–259

    multinational, multivendor networks, 257–259
    NASA network, 257–259
    network integration (Data Systems West), 254–255
    Nortel Optivity system, 263
    Y2K compliance checking with SMS, 260–261
  virtual private networks, 290
cellular topology, **32**, *33*
centralized remote-access security, 450–453
CERT (Computer Emergency Response Team), 21, 456–457
certificates, digital, **13, 139–140**
certifying users, 189
CGI scripts for credit card processing, 461
changes. *See also* planning
  documenting, 298, 305
CHAP (Challenge-Handshake Authentication Protocol), 458
checking. *See also* troubleshooting
  daemons or services, 476
  hard disk usage, 294–295
  log files, 474, 475
checklists
  for network changes, 325–326
  for project management, 328–329
Checksum field
  in IP packet headers, 40
  in UDP protocol, 49
CIDR (Classless Interdomain Routing), **69**, 394
circuit-level proxies, **380–382**
  defined, **380**, *381*
  port redirection and, 380–381
  SOCKS Proxy server, 381–382
Cisco L2TP (Layer Two Tunneling Protocol), 281–283
Class A IP addresses, 54
Class B IP addresses, 54–55

Class C IP addresses, *55*
Class D IP addresses, *55*
Class E IP addresses, *55*
classic application proxies. *See* Application
    layer in OSI model, Application layer
    proxying
Classless Interdomain Routing (CIDR), **69**, 394
CLI (Caller Line ID), 457
client/server applications, **3–7**
    defined, **3–4**
    TCP/IP and, 6–7
clients
    DHCP clients, **88**, **89–92**, **105–107**
        defined, **88**
        options DHCP servers can pass to DHCP
            clients, 89–92
        Unix configuration, 107
        Windows 95/98/NT configuration,
            105–107, *105*, *106*
    DNS clients, 129–131, *130*, *131*
clipboard trick, 249–250
clones versus brand name systems, 187–188
CNAME records in zone files, 125
collecting information for troubleshooting, 466
colons (::) in IPv6 addresses, 392
commands. *See also* software; utilities
    arp, 484–486
    finger, 50, 423
    FTP session commands and parameters,
        148–152
    ipconfig, ifconfig, and winipcfg, 481–484,
        482
    netstat, 486–488, 491–493, *491*, *492*
    nslookup, 496–503
    showmount, 424
    tracert, 494–496
compacting
    DHCP databases, 239
    WINS databases, 243

components, standardization of, 187–188
compression in tunneling, 277
Computer Emergency Response Team (CERT),
    21, 456–457
Computer Oracle Password and Security
    System (COPS), 424–425
confidentiality evaluation, 413
configuring. *See also* implementing; installing
    Application layer proxying, 378–379
    auto-configuration of hosts with IPv6
        protocol, **397–401**
        address lifetimes and, 400
        defined, **397**
        IPv6 DHCP protocol, 400–401
        link local addresses and, 397–398
        neighbor discovery and, 398
        router advertisements and, 398–399
        stateful auto-configuration, 399–400
        stateless auto-configuration, 398–399
    Cache Array Routing Protocol (CARP),
        369–370
    DHCP clients
        in Unix networks, 107
        in Windows 95/98/NT networks,
            105–107, *105*, *106*
    DHCP relay agents
        in NetWare 5 networks, 107–108
        in Windows NT networks, 108–109,
            108, *109*
    DHCP servers
        in NetWare 5 networks, 94–101
        in Unix networks, 103–105
        in Windows 2000 networks, 103
        in Windows NT networks, 101–103, *102*
    documenting TCP/IP configurations,
        301–302
    FTP servers, **159–172**
        in NetWare 5 networks, 165–169, *166*
        overview of, 159

Index

in Unix networks, 169–172
in Windows NT 4 networks, 160–165,
    160, 161, 162
quick fixes for configuration file problems,
    472–474
spanning tree networks, 211–212, *211*
connection-oriented versus connectionless
    protocols, **38**, **229**, **322**
content filtering on Proxy servers, **371**
contention access method, **28**
control bits field in IPv6 headers, 386
converting binary IP addresses to decimal IP
    addresses, 53
COPS (Computer Oracle Password and
    Security System), 424–425
corrupted caches on name servers, 504
costs
    default OSPF costs, 227–228
    port costs of bridges, 209–210, *210*
    of virtual private networks, 278
    of viruses, 446–449
Count to Infinity problem, 222
Counterpane Systems, 284–285
creating
    migration strategies, 348
    network resource accessibility plans, 347,
        347
    project implementation schedules, 348–349
    teams, 334–335
    zones, 133, *133*
credit card processing on Web sites, 460–461
cryptography. *See* encryption
CSMA/CD (Carrier Sense Multiple Access/
    Collision Detection), 488
customizing off-the-shelf software with SNMP,
    259–260
CuteFTP software, 145–146, *146*

D

daemons, 476
data compression in tunneling, 277
Data Encryption Standard (DES), 433–434
Data Link layer in OSI model, **27–29**, **313–315**
    bridges and, 313, 315
    defined, **27–28**
    Ethernet switches and, 313–315, *314*
    LLC (Logical Link Control) sublayer, 28–29
    MAC (Media Access Control) sublayer, 28
    Token Ring switches and, 315
data risk assessment, 420–421, *420*
Data Systems West (DSW) case study, 254–255
databases
    DHCP database maintenance, 239
    synchronizing
        link-state advertisement databases,
            225–226, *225*
        mobile computing and, 6
    WINS database maintenance, 243
datagrams, **80–87**. *See also* frames; packets
    BOOTP protocol and, 87
    datagram format in UDP protocol, 48–49,
        48
    IP (Internet Protocol) and, 37–38
    MAC (Media Access Control) addresses
        and, 80
    protocol numbers and, 80–82, *82*
    RARP (Reverse Address Resolution
        Protocol) and, 86
    service numbers and, 82–86, *85*
decimal IP addresses, converting binary
    addresses to, 53
default accounts, deleting, 429–430
default OSPF costs, 227–228
deleting default accounts, 429–430
demultiplexing, **81**
denial of service (DoS) attacks, 12, 478

Department of Defense (DoD)
   ARPAnet, 17–18, 20, 41
   DoD network model, **35–36**, *35*
DES (Data Encryption Standard), 433–434
design, **178–197**. *See also* planning
   clones versus brand name systems, 187–188
   finding problem areas, **178–184**
      expectations and, 181–184
      help desks and, 180–181, 184–187
      Murphy's Law and, 182–183
      overview of, 178–180
   help desks, **180–181**, **184–194**
      and finding problem areas, 180–181,
         184–187
      finding trends, 185–188
      help desk software, 190–192
      McAfee Total Service Desk (TSD)
         software, 190–191
      NetManage software, 191–192
      training, 188
      and training and certifying users, 189
      Web-based help desks on intranets,
         192–194
   of Internet 2 Project, 268–269
   project-design phase of project management,
      336–347
      creating network resource accessibility
         plans, 347, *347*
      designing network infrastructure,
         340–341
      determining the scope of the design
         phase, 336–337
      DNS configuration, 344, *345*
      FTP tasks, 344
      Internet connectivity, 342, *343*
      IP addressing, 343, *343*
      ISDN tasks, 342, *343*
      overview of, 338–340, *338, 339, 340,*
         341

      routers versus bridges, 342
      routing strategies, 344–346, *345, 346*
      SNMP tasks, 342, *342*
      virtual private network option, 346, *346*
   and saving money, 187–188
   and standardization of components,
      187–188
   system-design life cycle (SDLC), **329–331**
      detailed system design, implementation,
         and operation, 331
      general system design and systems
         evaluation, 331
      maintenance, 331
      overview of, 329, *330*
      system analysis and specification, 330
   wide area network (WAN) design, **235–248**
      DHCP database maintenance, 239
      DHCP implementation planning,
         237–239, *238*
      DNS implementation planning, 239–241
      final plan, 248
      and future of networks, 235–237
      HOSTS file implementation planning,
         245–247
      IP (Internet Protocol) and, 236
      LMHOSTS file implementation planning,
         243–245
      Multiprotocol Label Switching (MPLS)
         standard and, 236–237
      WINS database maintenance, 243
      WINS server installation planning,
         241–243
designated routers (DRs), 225–226, *225*
designated servers, 132–134, *132, 133*
designating bridges, 209–211, *210*
destination addresses
   destination IP addresses, 40
   destination port addresses, 82–83
   in packet headers, 237
   in routing, 215–216

Destination Port field in UDP protocol, 49

Destination Unreachable error messages, 44

detailed system design, implementation, and operation, 331

device drivers, sockets drivers, *355*

DHCP (Dynamic Host Configuration Protocol), **73–74, 79, 87–110**

address allocation, 93–94

BOOTP and, 88

defined, **79, 87–88, 109–110**

DHCP clients, **88, 89–92, 105–107**

defined, 88

options DHCP servers can pass to DHCP clients, 89–92

Unix configuration, 107

Windows *95/98/NT* configuration, 105–107, *105, 106*

DHCP database maintenance, 239

DHCP relay agents, **88, 107–109, 237–238**

defined, **88**

NetWare *5* configuration, 107–108

wide area network design and, 237–238, *238*

Windows NT configuration, 108–109, *108, 109*

DHCP servers, **88, 89–92, 94–105, 237–238, 240–241**

defined, **88**

DHCP Manager, 101–103, *102*

DNS addresses and, 240–241

DNS/DHCP Management Console, 94–99, *96*, 117, *118*, 132–133, *132, 133*, 138, *138*

NetWare *5* configuration, 94–101

options DHCP servers can pass to DHCP clients, 89–92

Unix configuration, 103–105

wide area network design and, 237–238, *238*

Windows 2000 configuration, 103

Windows NT configuration, 101–103, *102*

documenting, 302–303

how DHCP works, **109–110**

IP addresses and, 109–110

IPv6 DHCP protocol, 400–401

Network Address Translation (NAT) and, 73–74

planning DHCP implementation in wide area networks, 237–239, *238*

diagrams of networks, 297–298

digital certificates and signatures, **13, 139–140**

digital signaling, **33**, *33*

directories, user directories, 432

disclosure of information, 12

disk drives

monitoring usage, 294–295

removable disks and drives, 434–435

distance in networks, *56, 57–59, 58, 59*

distance-vector routing, **219–222**, *220*, 223

distributed caching. *See* hierarchical and distributed caching

DNS. *See* Domain Name System

DNSO (Domain Name Service Organization), 22

documentation, **293–305, 309–312**

bandwidth requirements, 296

current network environment, 294–295

defining functional requirements, 295–296

documenting changes, 298, 305

documenting solutions, 295, 469

e-mail policies, 301

finding, 300–301

and implementing solutions, 299

and integrating multivendor networks, 296–297

Internet policies, 301
IP address worksheets, 300
network diagrams and specifications,
    297–298
and planning for Physical layer changes,
    309–312, *309, 310, 311*
policies, 300
security policies, 301
software licenses, 301
TCP/IP documentation, **301–305**
    addresses and subnets, 302
    configurations, 301–302
    DHCP, 302–303
    HOSTS and LMHOSTS files, 304
    routers, 305
tracking hard disk usage, 294–295
virus protection policies, 301
WAN/LAN maps, 61–63, *61, 62,* 300, 507
DoD. *See* Department of Defense
domain controllers, 203
Domain Name System (DNS), **40–42, 50,
    111–140**
    BIND (Berkeley Internet Name Domain)
        servers
        BIND boot files, 128–129
        defined, **113**
    Cache files, 125–128
    defined, **40–42, 50, 111**
    digital signatures and, 139–140
    DNS clients, 129–131, *130, 131*
    DNS servers
        DNS server roles, 117
        linking, 117–118, *118*
        wide area network design and, 240–241
    DNS/DHCP Management Console in
        NetWare, 94–99, *96,* 117, *118,*
        132–133, *132, 133,* 138, *138*
    Domain Name Service Organization
        (DNSO), 22

domain name space, **114**
domain names and, 111–113
future of, **137–140,** *138*
implementing, **322–323**
    planning DNS implementation in wide
        area networks, 239–241
Incremental Transfer Protocol, 139
installing, **131–137**
    on NetWare 5 networks, 132–134, *132,
        133*
    on Windows NT networks, 134–137,
        134, 135, 136
IP addresses and, 323
IPv6 protocol and, 388–389, 403
name server queries, **118–121**
    defined, **118–120,** *119*
    inverse queries and reverse lookups,
        120–121
name servers
    defined, **42, 114**
    forwarders and, 117
    name server (NS) records in zone files,
        42, 124
    primary, secondary, and master name
        servers, **117**
    quick fixes, 476
    synchronizing primary and secondary
        servers, 503–504
    troubleshooting, 496–504
network design and, 344, *345*
nslookup utility and, 496–503
quick fixes, 476
registering domain names, **114–115,** *115,*
    137–138, *138*
resolvers, 114, 119
resource records, 121–122
Reverse-Lookup files, 125
security extensions, 139–140

top-level domains (TLDs), 21–23, 111–112, 114

versus WINS (Windows Internet Name Service), 113, 137

zone files, **116, 121–125**
    CNAME records, 125
    defined, **116, 122**
    host records, 124
    mail-exchanger (MX) records, 42, 124
    name server (NS) records, 42, 124
    resource records and, 121–122, 123
    at sign (@) in, 122
    SOA (Start of Authority) records, 122–123

zones
    creating, **133,** *133*
    defined, **112, 116,** *116*
    designated servers and, 132–134, *132, 133*
    DNS server roles and, 117

domain names
    defined, **21–23**
    domain name space, **114**
    Domain Name System and, 111–113
    fully qualified domain names (FQDNs), 112–113, 120–121
    Internet Corporation for Assigned Names and Numbers (ICANN) and, 22
    registering, 114–115, *115,* 137–138, *138*
    TLDs (top-level domains), 21–23, 111–112, 114

domains, **113**

DoS (denial of service) attacks, 12, 478

dotted decimal notation for IP addresses, 40, 53

downloading files with FTP, 152, 155

drivers, sockets drivers, 355

drives
    monitoring usage, 294–295
    removable drives, 434–435

DRs (designated routers), 225–226, *225*

Dynamic Host Configuration Protocol. *See* DHCP

dynamic routing, 219–223. *See also* routers
    Count to Infinity problem, 222
    defined, **219**
    distance-vector routing, 219–222, *220,* 223
    link-state routing and link-state packets (LSPs), 222–223

dynamically allocated ports, **86**

E

Echo and Echo Reply messages, 44

e-commerce, 12–13, 459–461

educating. *See* training

EGPs. *See* Exterior Gateway Protocols

EIGRP (Enhanced IGRP) protocol, **231**

e-mail
    e-mail applications, 6–7
    e-mail migrations, 418–419
    e-mail policies, 301
    e-mail security, 432–433

employee education, 428–429, 436

encryption. *See also* security
    Blowfish encryption algorithm, 285
    cable modems and, 288
    Data Encryption Standard (DES), 433–434
    internal network security and, 433–434
    in IPv6 protocol, 402
    PPTP (Point-to-Point Tunneling Protocol) problems, 284–285
    RSA cryptography, 276
    S-HTTP and, 13, 459
    transaction encryption in remote-access security, 455
    tunneling and, 276–277

end users. *See* users

Enhanced IGRP (EIGRP) protocol, **231**

enterprise network management case study, 255–257

error messages
- Destination Unreachable, 44
- Host Unknown, 479, 496
- Network Unreachable
  - in netstat command, 493
  - in Ping command, 479
- in Ping command
  - Host Unknown, 479
  - Network Unreachable, 479
  - No Answer, 480
- in tracert command
  - Time Exceeded, 494
  - Unreachable Port, 495

Ethernet networks
- CSMA/CD (Carrier Sense Multiple Access/Collision Detection), 488
- Ethernet addresses, 485–486
- Ethernet switches, 313–315, *314*
- segmenting, 488–490, *489*

examples. *See* case studies

exchanging information. *See* sharing information

expectations, 181–184

experts case study, 199

Exterior Gateway Protocols (EGPs), **231–233**.
  See also routing protocols
- BGP (Border Gateway Protocol), 43–44, 232–233, 395
- Exterior Gateway Protocol (EGP), 233
- versus Interior Gateway Protocols (IGPs), **231–232**

external security, **437–461**. *See also* security
- firewalls, **437–445**
  - application gateways, 443, 444
  - case study, 198
  - components of, 439
  - defined, **438**
  - firewall issues, 444–445
  - IP addresses and, 438–439, *438*
  - port addresses and, 10
  - positioning, 438, *438*
  - purpose of, 438–439, *438*
  - router-based packet-filtering firewalls, 439–441, *440*
  - using ports, 441–443
  - virtual private networks and, 275, 278
  - for Web sites, 9–11
  - well-known services, 81, 441–443
- remote-access security, **450–459**
  - access-control authorization, 458
  - accounting and auditing features, 459
  - callback methods, 457
  - Caller Line ID (CLI), 457
  - card devices, 454
  - centralized security, 450–453
  - CHAP (Challenge-Handshake Authentication Protocol), 458
  - location validation and call level security, 457
  - PAP (Password Authentication Protocol), 457
  - password protection, 456–457
  - PPP (Point-to-Point Protocol) security authentication, 457–458
  - RADIUS (Remote Authentication Dial-In User Service), 451–452, *452*
  - security-by-obscurity method, 453–455
  - suggestions, 455–459
  - TACACS+ (Terminal Access Controller Access Control System +), 452–453
  - token-based security, 453–455
  - transaction encryption, 455
  - user validation, 456
- viruses, **301, 445–450**
  - cost of, 446–449
  - history of, 445–446
  - increasing numbers of PCs and, 446
  - Melissa virus, 446–449

polymorphic viruses, 445, 446
safe computing practices, 449–450
virus protection policies, 301
Web site security, **9–11**, **13**, **459–461**
   credit card processing, 460–461
   firewalls, 9–11
   S-HTTP, SSL (Secure Sockets Layer) and,
     13, 459
extranets, **265–273**. *See also* virtual private
  networks
defined, **265–267**, *266*
Internet 2 Project, **267–272**
   Abilene Project, **271–272**
   applications, 270–271
   architecture of, 269–270, *270*
   design, 268–269
   overview of, 267–268
   participants' commitments, 269
   QoS (Quality of Service) and, 271
   vBNS (Very High-Performance Backbone
     Network Service) and, 19, 273
  vBNS (Very High-Performance Backbone
    Network Service), **19**, **272–273**

F

file system rights, 431
File Transfer Protocol. *See* FTP
files
   BIND boot files, 128–129
   Cache files, 125–128
   configuration file problems, 472–474
   downloading with FTP, 152, 155
   HOSTS files, 41, 245–247, 304
   LMHOSTS files, 243–245, 304
   Reverse-Lookup files, 125
   Unix configuration files, 473–474
   Unix log files, 475
   zone files, **116**, **121–125**
     CNAME records, 125
     defined, **116**, **122**

host records, 124
mail-exchanger (MX) records, 42, 124
name server (NS) records, 42, 124
resource records and, 121–122, 123
at sign (@) in, 122
SOA (Start of Authority) records,
   122–123
filtering on Proxy servers, **370–371**
finding
   documentation, 300–301
   problem areas, **178–184**
     expectations and, 181–184
     help desks and, 180–181, 184–187
     Murphy's Law and, 182–183
     overview of, 178–180
   trends in help desk reports, 185–188
finger command, 50, 423
firewalls, **437–445**. *See also* external security;
  hackers
   application gateways, 443, 444
   case study, 198
   components of, 439
   defined, **438**
   firewall issues, 444–445
   IP addresses and, 438–439, *438*
   port addresses and, 10
   positioning, 438, *438*
   purpose of, 438–439, *438*
   router-based packet-filtering firewalls,
     439–441, *440*
   using ports, 441–443
   virtual private networks and, 275, 278
   for Web sites, 9–11
   well-known services, 81, 441–443
FIRST (Forum of Incident Response and
  Security Teams), 21
flags
   in IP packet headers, 39–40
   in TCP protocol, 46
flow control, **38**
flow label field in IPv6 headers, 386

Forum of Incident Response and Security Teams (FIRST), 21
forward chaining, **467**
forwarders, 117
FQDNs (fully qualified domain names), 112–113, 120–121
Fragment Offset field in IP packet headers, 40
frames. *See also* datagrams; packets
  bridge broadcast frames, 207–208, *207*
  defined, **27–28**
FTP (File Transfer Protocol), **14, 49, 141–172, 324, 379**
  anonymous FTP, 149, 424
  defined, **14, 49, 142–143,** *143*
  downloading files, 152, 155
  FTP proxies, 379
  FTP server return codes, 156–157
  FTP sessions
    example, 155–157
    session commands and parameters, 148–152
  FTP User Interfaces, **143–152**
    Bullet Proof FTP, 145, *145*
    CuteFTP, 145–146, *146*
    FTP commands and parameters, 148–152
    FTP Control, 146, *147*
    FTP Voyager, 147–148, *147, 148*
    FTP-PM, 148
    Web browsers, 143–144, *144*
  implementing, 324
  installing and configuring FTP servers, **159–172**
    in NetWare 5 networks, 165–169, *166*
    overview of, *159*
    in Unix networks, 169–172
    in Windows NT 4 networks, 160–165, *160, 161, 162*
  mirror sites, 155
  network design and, 344

port addresses and, 153
Sun Microsystems Network File System (NFS), 142, 157–159, *158*
Telnet and, 153
TFTP (Trivial File Transfer Protocol), 141–142
User Data Transfer Process (User DTP), 153–155, *154*
User Protocol Interpreter (User-PI), 153
full-duplex communications, **322**
fully qualified domain names (FQDNs), 112–113, 120–121

G

Galaxy Scientific Corporation, 290
Gantt charts. *See also* project management
  defined, **338,** *338*
  for DNS and e-mail tasks, 344, *345*
  for IP addressing tasks, 343, *343*
  for ISDN tasks, 342, *343*
  for network resource accessibility planning, 347, *347*
  for routing tasks, 346, *346*
  for SNMP tasks, 342, *342*
gateways
  application gateways as firewalls, 443, 444
  defined, **25, 354**
  Proxy servers and, 353–354, *355*
geeks, 7
general system design and systems evaluation, 331
Get and Get-Next operations of SNMP managers, 251
global top-level domains (gTLDs), 21–23
Gopher utility, 49
group rights, 430–432
groupware applications, 6–7
gTLDs (global top-level domains), 21–23

Index

H

hackers, **422–425.** *See also* firewalls; internal
    network security
    anonymous FTP and, 424
    Computer Oracle Password and Security
        System (COPS), 424–425
    denial of service attacks, 12, 478
    finger command, *50*, 423
    hacking tools, 423–424
    Security Analysis Tool for Auditing
        Networks (SATAN), 423
    Unix showmount command, 424
Handshake Protocol in Secure Sockets Layer,
    13
hard disk drives
    monitoring usage, 294–295
    removable disks and drives, 434–435
hardware
    equipment/infrastructure protection,
        416–419
    equipment/infrastructure risk assessment,
        414–416
    SNMP compatibility, 254
    standardization of, 187–188
hashes, 433–434
Header Checksum field in IP packet headers, 40
header format in IPv6 protocol, 384–386, *385*
hello packets
    OSPF protocol and, 225
    source-routing bridges and, 212–213
help desks, **180–181, 184–194**
    and finding problem areas, 180–181,
        184–187
    finding trends, 185–188
    help desk software, 190–192
    McAfee Total Service Desk (TSD) software,
        190–191
    NetManage software, 191–192
    training, 188

    and training and certifying users, 189
    Web-based help desks on intranets, 192–194
Hewlett-Packard OpenView software, 254,
    257–259
hiding internal addresses from the Internet,
    360, *361*
hierarchical and distributed caching, 364–370
    Cache Array Routing Protocol (CARP),
        368–370, *369*
    defined, 364, *365*
    Internet Cache Protocol (ICP), 367–368
    Novell example, 365–366
High-Performance Backbone Network Service
    (vBNS), **19, 272–273**
hop-by-hop routing, 237
hops in routing, **216, 218**
hosts
    auto-configuration with IPv6 protocol,
        397–401
        address lifetimes and, 400
        defined, **397**
        IPv6 DHCP protocol, 400–401
        link local addresses and, 397–398
        neighbor discovery and, 398
        router advertisements and, 398–399
        stateful auto-configuration, 399–400
        stateless auto-configuration, 398–399
    defined, **53**
    host addresses, **63**
    host records in zone files, 124
    Host Unknown error message, 479, 496
    hosting Web sites on company versus ISP
        servers, 9
    IP addresses and host names, 52
HOSTS files, 41, 245–247, 304
host-to-host layer protocols, 36, 45–49, 321
    defined, **321**
    TCP (Transmission Control Protocol)
        defined, **45**

port numbers and, 47–48
segment format, 45–47, *45*
UDP (User Datagram Protocol), datagram
format, 48–49, *48*
HTTP (Hypertext Transfer Protocol)
defined, **50**
HTTP proxies, 378–379
Secure HTTP (S-HTTP), 13, *459*

I

IAB (Internet Activities Board), 21
IAHC (Internet International Ad Hoc
Committee), 22–23
IANA (Internet Assigned Numbers Authority),
21
ICANN (Internet Corporation for Assigned
Names and Numbers), 22
ICMP (Internet Control Message Protocol),
44–*45*, 386–387
ICP (Internet Cache Protocol), 367–368
Identification field in IP packet headers, 39
IEPG (Internet Engineering Planning Group),
21
IESG (Internet Engineering Steering Group), 21
IETF (Internet Engineering Task Force), 21
ifconfig command, 481–484
IGMP (Internet Group Membership Protocol),
386
IGPs. *See* Interior Gateway Protocols
IHL (Internet Header Length) field in IP packet
headers, 38
IKE (Internet Security Key Management
Protocol), 282
implementation phase of project management,
347–349
creating implementation schedules, 348–
349
creating migration strategies, 348
overview of, 347–348, *347*

implementing. *See also* configuring; installing;
planning; project management
Domain Name System (DNS), 322–323
planning DNS implementation in wide
area networks, 239–241
FTP (File Transfer Protocol), 324
project-approach phase, 337–338, *338*
Telnet, 324–*325*
InARP (Inverse ARP) protocol, 43
Incremental Transfer Protocol, 139
information sharing, **7–14**, 377–378, **459–461**
FTP (File Transfer Protocol) and, 14
Internet commerce, 12–13, 459–461
Internet information sharing, **8–12**
firewalls and, 9–11
hosting Web sites on company versus ISP
servers, 9
overview of, 8–9
TCP/IP security and, 11–12
intranet information sharing, 8
overview of, 7–8
with Proxy servers, 377–378, *378*
infrastructure protection, 416–419
infrastructure risk assessment, 414–416
installing. *See also* configuring; implementing
Domain Name System (DNS), **131–137**
in NetWare 5 networks, 132–134, *132,*
133
in Windows NT networks, 134–137,
134, 135, 136
FTP servers, **159–172**
in NetWare 5 networks, 165–169, *166*
overview of, 159
in Unix networks, 169–172
in Windows NT 4 networks, 160–165,
160, 161, 162
outsourcing VPN installation, 280–281
WINS servers, 242–243

integrating multivendor networks, 257–259, 296–297

integrity evaluation, 413–414

intelligent agents
    data risk assessment with, 421
    intruder detection with, 422

interactive mode options for nslookup command, 498–502

interdomain routing, 393–395

Interior Gateway Protocols (IGPs), **223–232**.
    See also routing protocols
    defined, **223**
    EIGRP (Enhanced IGRP), 231
    versus Exterior Gateway Protocols (EGPs), **231–232**
    IGRP (Interior Gateway Routing Protocol), 230
    OSPF (Open Shortest Path First), **43–44, 225–230**
        advantages of, 227
        areas and, 227
        autonomous system border routers (ASBRs) and, 226–227
        autonomous systems (ASs) and, 226
        backbones and, 227
        default OSPF costs, 227–228
        defined, **43–44, 225**
        hello packets, 225
        hops and, 218
        IPv6 addresses and, 396
        IS-IS (intermediate system to intermediate system) protocol and, 228–230
        OSPF redundancy, 227–228
        and selecting routes, 226
        stub areas and, 227
        and synchronizing link-state advertisement databases, 225–226, 225
        terms defined, **226–227**

RIP II (Routing Information Protocol II), 224

RIP (Routing Information Protocol), 43–44, 218, 223–224, 396

intermediate system to intermediate system (IS-IS) protocol, 228–230

internal network security, **407–436**. *See also* external security
    case studies, **407–410**
    employee education and, 428–429, 436
    hackers, **422–425**
        anonymous FTP and, 424
        Computer Oracle Password and Security System (COPS), 424–425
        denial of service attacks, 12, 478
        finger command, 50, 423
        hacking tools, 423–424
        Security Analysis Tool for Auditing Networks (SATAN), 423
        Unix showmount command, 424
    risk assessment, **410–422**
        availability evaluation, 414
        confidentiality evaluation, 413
        data risk assessment tools, 420–421, *420*
        defined, **412–414**
        equipment/infrastructure assessment, 414–416
        equipment/infrastructure protection, 416–419
        integrity evaluation, 413–414
        intrusion detection, 420, *420*, 421–422
        overview of, 410–412
        redundancy and, 419–420
        theft, 419
    strategies, **427–436**
        applying patches, 427
        assigning user, group, and file system rights, 430–432

auditing or logging information access, 435–436

deleting default accounts, 429–430

e-mail security, 432–433

encryption, 433–434

intruder-detection plans, 433

password policies, 428–429, 430

removable disks and drives, 434–435

segregating network segments, 434

trust relationships, **426**

Internet. *See also* Domain Name System; extranets; virtual private networks

always-on Internet connectivity, 286

domain names, 21–23

hiding internal addresses from, 360, *361*

history of, 17–20

information sharing via Web sites, **8–12**

firewalls and, 9–11

hosting Web sites on company versus ISP servers, 9

overview of, 8–9

TCP/IP security and, 11–12

Internet 2 Project, **267–272**

Abilene Project, 271–272

applications, 270–271

architecture of, 269–270, *270*

design, 268–269

overview of, 267–268

participants' commitments, 269

QoS (Quality of Service) and, 271

vBNS (Very High-Performance Backbone Network Service) and, 19, 273

Internet commerce, 12–13, 459–461

Internet policies, 301

management of, 20–21

National Science Foundation (NSF) and, 18–20

planning Internet connectivity in network design, 342, *343*

Proxy servers and Internet access, 354–355, *354*

Internet Activities Board (IAB), 21

Internet Assigned Numbers Authority (IANA), 21

Internet Cache Protocol (ICP), 367–368

Internet Control Message Protocol (ICMP), 44–45, 386–387

Internet Corporation for Assigned Names and Numbers (ICANN), 22

Internet Engineering Planning Group (IEPG), 21

Internet Engineering Steering Group (IESG), 21

Internet Engineering Task Force (IETF), 21

Internet Explorer

FTP User Interface, 143–144, *144*

tunneling and, 275–276

Internet Group Membership Protocol (IGMP), 386

Internet Header Length (IHL) field in IP packet headers, 38

Internet International Ad Hoc Committee (IAHC), 22–23

Internet layer TCP/IP protocols, **36–40**

Internet Research Task Force (IRTF), 21

Internet Security Key Management Protocol (IKE), 282

Internet Society (ISOC), 20

InterNIC, 21–22, 63

intranets. *See also* extranets; virtual private networks

defined, 8

information sharing via, 8

Proxy servers and, 355

Web-based help desks on, 192–194

intrusion detection, 420, *420*, 421–422, 433

Inverse ARP (InARP) protocol, 43

inverse name server queries, 120–121

IP addresses, 9–10, 21–23, 42–43, 47–48, 51–76, 80–87. *See also* addresses; IPv6 protocol
  Address Service Organization (ASO) and, 22
  arp command and, 485
  assigning, **316–321**
    point-to-point addressing, 320–321, *321*
    pooled addresses for dial-up connections, 321
    RFC 1219 strategies for assigning IP addresses, 316–319
    workgroup IP address allocation, 319–320, *320*
  bits and, 52–53
  CIDR (Classless Interdomain Routing) or supernetting, **69**, 394
  Class A addresses, 54
  Class B addresses, 54–55
  Class C addresses, 55
  Class D addresses, 55
  Class E addresses, 55
  converting binary to decimal addresses, 53
  defined, 9–10, 52–53, 70
  DHCP protocol and, **109–110**
  Domain Name System (DNS) and, 323
  domain names and, 21–23
  dotted decimal notation, 40, 53
  firewalls and, 438–439, *438*
  host addresses, **63**
  host names and, 52
  how IP addresses work, **70**
  InterNIC and, 63
  IP address worksheets, 300
  IP calculators, 74–75
  MAC (Media Access Control) addresses and, 42–43, 80
  Network Address Translation (NAT), **72–75**
    defined, **72–73**, *72*
    DHCP (Dynamic Host Configuration Protocol) and, 73–74
  network addresses, **53, 56–63**
    calculating IP network and host addresses, 74–75
    defined, 53
    defining networks, 56–60, *57, 58, 59, 60*
    determining how many networks you have, 60–63, *61, 62*
  network design and, 343, *343*
  port addresses and, 47–48, 82–86, *85*
  protocol numbers and, 80–82, *82*
  public versus private IP addresses, **359**
  RARP (Reverse Address Resolution Protocol) and, 86
  sending and destination addresses, 40
  subnetting and subnet masks
    and assigning IP addresses, 316–319
    defined, **64–69**, *67*
    documenting subnets, 302
    IP address calculators and, 74–75
    Subnet Options tab in DNS/DHCP Management Console, 96–97, *97*
  terms defined, **52–53**
  troubleshooting in network configurations, 470–472
  virtual private networks and, 286
  well-known services and, 81
  Windows 95/98 and, 71
IP (Internet Protocol), **37–40**
  datagrams and, 37–38
  history of, 18
  IP packet header fields, **38–40**
    Destination Address, 40
    Flags, 39–40
    Fragment Offset, 40
    Header Checksum, 40
    Identification, 39
    Internet Header Length (IHL), 38

Options, 40
overview of, 38, *39*
Protocol, 40
Source Address, 40
Time-to-Live (TTL), 40
Total Length, 39
Type of Service (TOS), 39
Version, 38
versus IPv6 protocol, **76, 384, 385, 402–403**
wide area network (WAN) design and, 236
IP routing protocols. *See also* routing protocols
BGP (Border Gateway Protocol), 43–44,
      232–233, 395
OSPF (Open Shortest Path First) protocol,
      43–44, 225–230
   advantages of, 227
   areas and, 227
   autonomous system border routers
         (ASBRs) and, 226–227
   autonomous systems (ASs) and, 226
   backbones and, 227
   default OSPF costs, 227–228
   defined, **43–44, 225**
   hello packets, 225
   hops and, 218
   IPv6 addresses and, 396
   IS-IS (intermediate system to intermediate
         system) protocol and, 228–230
   OSPF redundancy, 227–228
   and selecting routes, 226
   stub areas and, 227
   and synchronizing link-state
         advertisement databases, 225–226,
         225
   terms defined, **226–227**
overview of, 43–44
RIP II (Routing Information Protocol II),
      224

RIP (Routing Information Protocol), 43–44,
      218, 223–224, 396
ipconfig command, 481–484, *482*
IPng. *See* IPv6 protocol
IPSec security protocol, 279, 281, 282
IPv6 protocol, **75–76, 383–403**
   addresses, **389–396**
      address lifetimes, 400
      aggregatable global unicast addresses,
            391
      anycast addresses, 389, 393
      architecture and notation, 389–390
      assigning, 391
      BGP (Border Gateway Protocol) and, 395
      Classless Interdomain Routing (CIDR)
            and, 394
      colons (::) in, 392
      interdomain routing and, 393–395
      Interdomain Routing Protocol (IDRP),
            395
      interface identifiers and, 391
      intradomain routing and, 396
      IPv4-based addresses, 392
      link local addresses, 392, 397–398
      loopback addresses, 392
      multicast addresses, 389, 393
      NLAs (Next Level Aggregators) and, 391
      OSPF protocol and, 396
      overview of, 391
      provider-based addresses, 394
      RIP protocol and, 396
      site local addresses, 392
      SLAs (Site Local Aggregators) and, 391
      special address formats, 391–392
      TLAs (Top Level Aggregators) and, 391
      unicast addresses, 389, 391
      unspecified addresses, 392
   control bits field, 386

defined, **75–76, 383–384**
in Domain Name System (DNS), 388–389, 403
encryption and authentication, 402
flow label field, 386
header format, 384–386, *385*
history of, 383–384
host auto-configuration, **397–401**
address lifetimes and, 400
defined, **397**
IPv6 DHCP protocol, 400–401
link local addresses and, 397–398
neighbor discovery and, 398
router advertisements and, 398–399
stateful auto-configuration, 399–400
stateless auto-configuration, 398–399
ICMP (Internet Control Message Protocol) revisions, 386–387
versus IPv4 protocol, **76, 384, 385, 402–403**
path MTU discovery, 386
Ping utility, 387–388
RFCs (Request for Comments), 75–76
security, 401–402
transitioning to, 402–403
IRTF (Internet Research Task Force), 21
ISDN tasks in network design, 342, *343*
IS-IS (intermediate system to intermediate system) protocol, 228–230
ISO Development Environment (ISODE), 20
ISOC (Internet Society), 20
isochronous communications, **29**
isolating problems in troubleshooting, 466–468, *468*
ISPs (Internet service providers), hosting Web sites on company versus ISP servers, 9
iterative name server queries, **119**

J

JDL Technologies Proxy servers, 376

L

L2TP (Layer Two Tunneling Protocol), 281–283
LAN Emulation ARP (LEARP) protocol, 43
LAN (local area network) maps, 61–63, *61, 62,* 300, *507*
laws of network computing, 182–183, 307–308, 327–328
Layer Two Tunneling Protocol (L2TP), 281–283
learning mode bridges, **203**
LEARP (LAN Emulation ARP) protocol, 43
least significant bits, **52**
Length field in UDP protocol, 49
lifetime of IPv6 addresses, 400
link local addresses, 392, 397–398
linking DNS servers, 117–118, *118*
link-state advertisement databases, 225–226, *225*
link-state routing and link-state packets (LSPs), **222–223**
LLC (Logical Link Control) sublayer in OSI model, **28–29**
LMHOSTS files, 243–245, 304
load-balancing, 372–373
local area network (LAN) maps, 61–63, *61, 62,* 300, *507*
local-save credit card processing, 460–461
location validation, 457
log files
checking, 474, 475
in Unix, 475
logging
connections with Proxy servers, 371
information access, 435–436
Logical Link Control (LLC) sublayer in OSI model, **28–29**
loopback addresses, 472
loopback IPv6 addresses, 392

looping
    bridge looping problems, 204–205, *204*
    router looping problems, 222, 476
LSPs (link-state packets), **222–223**
lying by end users, 298, 308, 465

M

MAC (Media Access Control) addresses, 28,
    42–43, 80
MAC (Media Access Control) sublayer in OSI
    model, **28**
McAfee Total Service Desk (TSD) software,
    190–191
mail-exchanger (MX) records in zone files, 42,
    124
maintenance
    maintenance features in SNMP, 262
    in system-design life cycle (SDLC), 331
management. *See* design; network
    management; planning; project
    management; SNMP
Management Information Bases (MIBs), **251**,
    507
manual DHCP address allocation, 93–94
mapping networks, 61–63, *61*, *62*, 300, 507
master name servers, **117**
Media Access Control (MAC) addresses, 28,
    42–43, 80
Media Access Control (MAC) sublayer in OSI
    model, **28**
Melissa virus, 446–449
mesh topology, **32**, *32*
messages. *See* error messages
MIBs (Management Information Bases), **251**,
    507
Microsoft Internet Explorer
    FTP User Interface, 143–144, *144*
    tunneling and, 275–276
Microsoft Windows 95/98

DHCP client configuration, 105–107, *105*,
    106
IP addresses and, 71
Microsoft Windows 2000, DHCP server
    configuration in, 103
Microsoft Windows NT
    deleting default accounts, 429–430
    DHCP client configuration, 105–107, *105*,
        106
    DHCP relay agent configuration, 108–109,
        108, *109*
    DHCP server configuration, 101–103, *102*
    Domain Name Service Manager, 135–137,
        135, *136*
    HOSTS files, 41, 245–247, 304
    installing and configuring FTP servers,
        160–165, *160*, *161*, *162*
    installing DNS on Windows NT networks,
        134–137, *134*, *135*, *136*
    LMHOSTS files, 243–245, 304
    Service Packs, 134
    trust relationships, 426
    WINS (Windows Internet Name Service),
        113, **137**, **241–243**
        versus Domain Name System (DNS),
            113, 137
        overview of, 241–242
        planning WINS server installation,
            242–243
        WINS database maintenance, 243
migrations
    e-mail migrations, 418–419
    migration strategies, 348
mirror FTP sites, 155
misplaced ports case study, 198
mobile computing, 3–7
modems, cable modems, 287–288
Modify DHCP Options dialog box, 98, *99*
monitoring. *See* checking

most significant bits, **53**

MPLS (Multiprotocol Label Switching) standard, **236–237, 279**

multicast IPv6 addresses, 389, 393

multinational, multivendor networks
integrating multivendor networks, 296–297
SNMP case study, 257–259

multiplexing, **81**

multipoint connections, **29**

Multiprotocol Label Switching (MPLS) standard, **236–237, 279**

Murphy's Law, 182–183, 307–308, 327–328

MX (mail-exchanger) records in zone files, 42, 124

N

name servers. *See also* Domain Name System
defined, **42, 114**
forwarders and, 117
name server (NS) records in zone files, 42, 124
name server queries, **118–121**
defined, **118–120**, *119*
inverse queries and reverse lookups, 120–121
primary, secondary, and master name servers, **117**
quick fixes, 476
synchronizing primary and secondary servers, 503–504
troubleshooting, 496–504

NAPs (Network Access Points), 19

NASA network case study, 257–259

NAT. *See* Network Address Translation

National Scaleable Cluster Project (NSCP), 273

National Science Foundation (NSF), 18–20

NCP (Network Control Protocol), 18

neighbor discovery, 398

Net3 Group IP Subnet Calculator, 74–75

NetJunction software, 259–260

NetManage software, 191–192

Netscape Navigator FTP User Interface, 143–144

NetSource Partners Web site, 256

netstat command, 486–488, 491–493, *491, 492*

NetWare
deleting default accounts, 429–430
installing and configuring FTP servers, 165–169, *166*
installing DNS on NetWare 5 networks, 132–134, *132, 133*
NetWare 5 DHCP relay agent configuration, 107–108
NetWare 5 DHCP server configuration, 94–101
NetWare 5 DNS Management Console, 138, *138*
trust relationships, 426

network access layer TCP/IP protocols, 36–37

Network Access Points (NAPs), 19

Network Address Translation (NAT), **72–74, 358–361**
defined, **72–73**, *72*
DHCP (Dynamic Host Configuration Protocol) and, 73–74
Proxy servers as Network Address Translators, **358–361**
and hiding internal addresses from the Internet, 360, *361*
overview of, 358–360, *359*

network addresses, **56–63**. *See also* IP addresses
calculating IP network and host addresses, 74–75
defined, **53**
defining networks, 56–60, *57, 58, 59, 60*
determining how many networks you have, 60–63, *61, 62*

Network Control Protocol (NCP), 18

network design. *See* design

network diagrams and specifications, 297–298

Network File System (NFS), 142, 157–159, *158*

network integration case study, 254–255

Network layer in OSI model, **27**, **316–321**

  defined, **27**

  point-to-point IP addressing and, 320–321, *321*

  pooled addresses for dial-up connections, 321

  RFC 1219 strategies for assigning IP addresses, 316–319

  workgroup IP address allocation, 319–320, *320*

network maintenance features in SNMP, 262

network management, **194–197**. *See also* project management; SNMP

  case studies

    experts, 199

    misplaced ports, 198

  clipboard trick, 249–250

  communicating inside and outside the department, 194–195

  knowing and respecting your users, 196–197

  knowing your limitations, 184, 195–196

  outsourcing VPN management, 280–281

  prioritizing tasks, 194

Network Management Stations (NMSs)

  defined, **250–251**, **504–505**

  placing, 251–252

  polling devices, 505

network portion of IP addresses, **53**

network probes

  data risk assessment with, 420–421

  intrusion detection with, 422

network resource accessibility plans, 347, *347*

network services, **82**

Network Solutions, Inc. (NSI), 22

Network Unreachable error message

  in netstat command, 493

  in Ping command, 479

networks. *See also* design; wide area networks

  defined, **56–60**, *57*, *58*, *59*, *60*

  determining how many networks you have, 60–63, *61*, *62*

  future of, 235–237

  mapping, 61–63, *61*, *62*, 300, *507*

  planning with SNMP, 262

  troubleshooting network access, **481–507**

    with arp command, 484–486

    with ipconfig, ifconfig, and winipcfg commands, 481–484, *482*

    name server problems, 496–504

    with netstat command, 486–488, 491–493, *491*, *492*

    with nslookup utility, 496–503

    routing problems, 474–476, 491–496, *491*, *492*

    segmenting Ethernet networks, 488–490, *489*

    with SNMP, 504–507

    with tracert command, 494–496

Next Level Aggregators (NLAs), **391**

NFS (Network File System), 142, 157–159, *158*

NICNAME utility, 50

NLAs (Next Level Aggregators), **391**

NMSs. *See* Network Management Stations

No Answer error message from Ping command, 480

noninteractive mode options for nslookup command, 496–498

Nortel Optivity software, 254, 263

Novell Proxy server example, 365–366

NS (name server) records in zone files, 42, 124

NSCP (National Scaleable Cluster Project), 273

NSF (National Science Foundation), 18–20

NSI (Network Solutions, Inc.), 22
nslookup utility, 496–503

O

object identifiers in SNMP, 506–507
octets, **52**
Open Shortest Path First protocol. *See* OSPF
Open System Interconnection model. *See* OSI
   model
OpenView software, 254, 257–259
OpenView Web site, 255–256
Options field in IP packet headers, 40
Optivity software, 254, 263
OSI model, **19–20, 23–36, 307–326**
   Application layer, 24–25, 324–325
   Application layer proxying
      caches and, 361
      configuring, 378–379
      defined, **374–375**, *375*
      FTP (File Transfer Protocol) proxies, 379
      HTTP proxies, 378–379
   Data Link layer, **27–29, 313–315**
      bridges and, 313, 315
      defined, **27–28**
      Ethernet switches and, 313–315, *314*
      LLC (Logical Link Control) sublayer,
         28–29
      MAC (Media Access Control) sublayer,
         28
      Token Ring switches and, 315
   defined, **23–24**
   versus DoD model, 35–36, *35*
   history of, 19–20
   Network layer, **27, 316–321**
      defined, **27**
      point-to-point IP addressing and,
         320–321, *321*
      pooled addresses for dial-up connections,
         321

RFC 1219 strategies for assigning IP
         addresses, 316–319
      workgroup IP address allocation,
         319–320, *320*
   Physical layer, **29–34, 309–312**
      analog signaling, 34, *34*
      bit synchronization, 34
      bus topology, 30, *30*
      cellular topology, 32, *33*
      defined, **29**
      digital signaling, 33, *33*
      mesh topology, 32, *32*
      physical topologies, 30–32
      planning for changes in, 309–312, *309,
         310, 311*
      point-to-point versus multipoint
         connections, 29
      ring topology, 30, *31*
      star topology, 30, *31*
   Presentation layer, 25–26, 324–325
   Session layer, 26, 324–325
   Transport layer
      defined, **26–27**
      planning for Transport layer changes,
         321–323
      Transport layer proxies, 357, 373, 380,
         381
OSPF (Open Shortest Path First) protocol, **43–
   44, 225–230**. *See also* routing protocols
   advantages of, 227
   areas and, 227
   autonomous system border routers (ASBRs)
      and, 226–227
   autonomous systems (ASs) and, 226
   backbones and, 227
   default OSPF costs, 227–228
   defined, **43–44, 225**
   hello packets, 225
   hops and, 218

IPv6 addresses and, 396
IS-IS (intermediate system to intermediate system) protocol and, 228–230
OSPF redundancy, 227–228
and selecting routes, 226
stub areas and, 227
and synchronizing link-state advertisement databases, 225–226, *225*
terms defined, **226–227**
Other DHCP Options tab in DNS/DHCP Management Console, 97–99, *98*, *100*
outsourcing VPN installation and management, 280–281

P

packets, **27–28**, 80–87. *See also* datagrams; frames
BOOTP protocol and, 87
defined, **27–28**
destination addresses in headers, 237
hello packets
OSPF protocol and, 225
source-routing bridges and, 212–213
link-state packets (LSPs), 222–223
MAC (Media Access Control) addresses and, 80
Multiprotocol Label Switching (MPLS) standard and, 236–237
netstat command and, 487–488
Ping command packet size parameter, 478
protocol numbers and, 80–82, *82*
RARP (Reverse Address Resolution Protocol) and, 86
router-based packet-filtering firewalls, 439–441, *440*
routing, 215–216
service numbers and, 82–86, *85*
PAP (Password Authentication Protocol), 457
Parameter Problem messages, 44

paranoia, 182, 308, 327, 328
passing tokens, **28**
passive advertising, **24–25**
passwords
PAP (Password Authentication Protocol), 457
password policies, 428–429, 430
remote-access security and, 456–457
patches, 427
path MTU discovery, 386
PC Medic module of McAfee Total Service Desk software, 190
PDCs (primary domain controllers), 203
PDUs (Protocol Data Units)
Bridge Protocol Data Units (BPDUs), 206–207, 208–211, *208*
in SNMP protocol, 505
Pennsylvania State University, 273
performance of virtual private networks, 278–279
Physical layer in OSI model, **29–34, 309–312**
analog signaling, 34, *34*
bit synchronization, 34
bus topology, 30, *30*
cellular topology, 32, *33*
defined, **29**
digital signaling, 33, *33*
mesh topology, 32, *32*
physical topologies, 30–32
planning for changes in, 309–312, *309*, *310*, *311*
point-to-point versus multipoint connections, 29
ring topology, 30, *31*
star topology, 30, *31*
Ping of Death attacks, 478
Ping utility
cable problems and, 481
command options, 477–478

defined, 50
IPv6 Ping utility, 387–388
packet size parameter, 478
troubleshooting with, 477–481, *480*
PKI (Public Key Infrastructure), 280
placing SNMP managers and agents, 251–252
planning, **307–326**. *See also* design; network
    management; project management
    for Data Link layer implementations,
        313–315
        bridges, 313, 315
        Ethernet switches, 313–315, *314*
        Token Ring switches, 315
    DHCP implementation in wide area
        networks, 237–239, *238*
    DNS implementation in wide area networks,
        239–241
    HOSTS file implementation, 245–247
    LMHOSTS file implementation, 243–245
    for network changes, **307–309, 325–326**
        checklist, 325–326
        documenting changes, 298, 305
        overview of, 307–309
    for Network layer changes, **316–321**
        point-to-point addressing, 320–321, *321*
        pooled addresses for dial-up connections,
            321
        RFC 1219 strategies for assigning IP
            addresses, 316–319
        workgroup IP address allocation,
            319–320, *320*
    networks with SNMP, 262
    for Physical layer changes, **309–312**, *309,*
        310, 311
    for Session, Presentation, and Application
        layer changes, **324–325**
        FTP (File Transfer Protocol), 324
        SMTP (Simple Mail Transfer Protocol),
            325
        Telnet, 324–325

    for Transport layer changes, **321–323**
        Domain Name System (DNS), 322–323
        TCP (Transmission Control Protocol),
            322
        UDP (User Datagram Protocol), 322
    WINS server installation, 241–243
pointer records, 42
point-to-point connections, **29, 60,** *60*
point-to-point IP addressing, 320–321, *321*
Point-to-Point Protocol (PPP), 37, 457–458
Point-to-Point Tunneling Protocol (PPTP),
    275–276, 284–285
Poison Reverse routing, 222
policies, 300
polling access method, **28**
polling in Network Management Stations, 505
polymorphic viruses, 445, 446
pooled IP addresses for dial-up connections,
    321
POP3 (Post Office Protocol 3), 7
port addresses
    defined, **10**
    firewalls and, 10
    FTP (File Transfer Protocol) and, 153
    IP addresses and, 47–48, 82–86, *85*
    RFC (Request for Comment), 10
    source port addresses and destination port
        addresses, 82–83
ports
    dynamically allocated ports, 86
    firewalls using ports, 441–443
    misplaced ports case study, 198
    port costs of bridges, 209–210, *210*
    port identifiers, 47
    port redirection and circuit-level proxies,
        380–381
    TCP protocol and port numbers, 47–48
    Unreachable Port error message in tracert
        command, 495

positioning firewalls, 438, *438*
Post Office Protocol (POP3), 7
PPP (Point-to-Point Protocol), 37, 457–458
PPTP (Point-to-Point Tunneling Protocol),
   275–276, 284–285
Presentation layer in OSI model, **25–26, 324–
   325**
primary domain controllers (PDCs), 203
primary name servers
   defined, **117**
   synchronizing with secondary servers,
      503–504
private IP addresses, **359**
proactive caching, 363
process layer TCP/IP protocols, 36, 49–50
project management, **327–349**. *See also*
      network management; planning
   checklist, 328–329
   Gantt charts
      defined, **338**, *338*
      for DNS and e-mail tasks, 344, *345*
      for IP addressing tasks, 343, *343*
      for ISDN tasks, 342, *343*
      for network resource accessibility
         planning, 347, *347*
      for routing tasks, 346, *346*
      for SNMP tasks, 342, *342*
   implementation phase, **347–349**
      creating implementation schedules,
         348–349
      creating migration strategies, 348
      overview of, 347–348, *347*
   Murphy's and William's Laws and, 327–328
   overview of, **332–333**, *332*
   project-approach phase, **333–338**
      assembling the team, 334–335
      collecting business information, 335

   determining the scope of the design
      phase, 336–337
   implementing, 337–338, *338*
   overview of, 333–334, *333*
   preliminary scheduling, 337
   training the team, 335–336
project-design phase, **336–347**
   creating network resource accessibility
      plans, 347, *347*
   designing network infrastructure, 340–
      341
   determining the scope of the design
      phase, 336–337
   DNS configuration, 344, *345*
   FTP tasks, 344
   Internet connectivity, 342, *343*
   IP addressing, 343, *343*
   ISDN tasks, 342, *343*
   overview of, 338–340, *338, 339, 340,
      341*
   routers versus bridges, 342
   routing strategies, 344–346, *345, 346*
   SNMP tasks, 342, *342*
   virtual private network option, 346, *346*
system-design life cycle (SDLC), **329–331**
   detailed system design, implementation,
      and operation, 331
   general system design and systems
      evaluation, 331
   maintenance, 331
   overview of, 329, *330*
   system analysis and specification, 330
Protocol Data Units (PDUs)
   Bridge Protocol Data Units (BPDUs), 206–
      207, 208–211, *208*
   in SNMP protocol, 505
Protocol field in IP packet headers, 40
Protocol Service Organization (PSO), 22

protocols
connection-oriented versus connectionless
protocols, 38, 229, 322
Handshake Protocol in Secure Sockets
Layer, 13
history of, 17–20
protocol caching, 362–363
Record Protocol in Secure Sockets Layer, 13
reliable versus unreliable protocols, 38
provider-based IPv6 addresses, 394
Proxy servers, **241, 353–382.** *See also* servers
advantages of, 356, 358
Application layer proxying
caches and, 361
configuring, 378–379
defined, **374–375,** *375*
FTP (File Transfer Protocol) proxies, 379
HTTP proxies, 378–379
caching, **361–364**
Application layer proxying and, 361
overview of, 361–362, *362*
proactive caching, 363
protocol caching, 362–363
security noncaching, 363–364
circuit-level proxies, **380–382**
defined, **380,** *381*
port redirection and, 380–381
SOCKS Proxy server, 381–382
defined, **241, 353, 356**
examples, 357, 365–366
filtering, **370–371**
gateways and, 353–354, 355
hierarchical and distributed caching,
364–370
Cache Array Routing Protocol (CARP),
368–370, *369*
defined, **364,** *365*
Internet Cache Protocol (ICP), 367–368
Novell example, 365–366

Internet access and, 354–355, *354*
intranets and, 355
JDL Technologies Proxy servers, 376
logging connections with, 371
as Network Address Translators, **358–361**
and hiding internal addresses from the
Internet, 360, *361*
overview of, 358–360, *359*
network effects of, 356–357
proxying methods, **373–378**
Application layer proxying, 374–375,
375
information exchange, 377–378, *378*
overview of, 373–374
Proxy connection and communication
process, 376–377, *377*
Proxy server placement, 375–376
reverse proxying, **371–373**
defined, **371–372,** *372*
load-balancing and, 372–373
redundancy and, 373
uses for, 373
as routers, 358
sockets drivers and, 355
Transport layer proxies, 357, 373, 380, 381
PSINet, 290
PSO (Protocol Service Organization), 22
PTR-records, **42**
public IP addresses, **359**
Public Key Infrastructure (PKI), 280
purchasing SNMP managers, 253

Q

QoS (Quality of Service), 271
quick fixes, **464–466, 469–476.** *See also*
troubleshooting
ANDing process, 470–471
checking daemons or services, 476
checking log files, 474, 475

for configuration file problems, 472–474
for DNS and name services, 476
IP addresses in network configurations, 470–472
for network connectivity problems, 470–472
overview of, 464–466, 469–470
for routing problems, 474–476

R

RADIUS (Remote Authentication Dial-In User Service), 451–452, *452*
RARP (Reverse Address Resolution Protocol), 43, 86
Record Protocol in Secure Sockets Layer, **13**
recursive name server queries, **119**
Redirect messages, 44
redundancy
    OSPF redundancy, 227–228
    reverse proxying and, 373
    RIP redundancy, 224
    risk assessment and, 419–420
    router redundancy, 201, 216–218, *217*
registering domain names, 114–115, *115*, 137–138, *138*
relay agents. *See* DHCP
reliable protocols, **38**
remote connectivity in virtual private networks, **286–288**
    always-on Internet connectivity, 286
    bandwidth, 286–287
    cable modems, 287–288
    IP addresses, 286
remote save credit card processing, 461
remote-access security, **450–459**. *See also* authentication
    access-control authorization, 458
    accounting and auditing features, 459

callback methods, 457
Caller Line ID (CLI), 457
card devices, 454
centralized security, 450–453
CHAP (Challenge-Handshake Authentication Protocol), 458
location validation and call level security, 457
PAP (Password Authentication Protocol), 457
password protection, 456–457
PPP (Point-to-Point Protocol) security authentication, 457–458
RADIUS (Remote Authentication Dial-In User Service), 451–452, *452*
security-by-obscurity method, 453–455
suggestions, 455–459
TACACS+ (Terminal Access Controller Access Control System +), 452–453
token-based security, 453–455
transaction encryption, 455
user validation, 456
removable disks and drives, 434–435
reporting features in SNMP, 262
resolvers, **114**, 119
resource accessibility plans, 347, *347*
resource records, 121–122, 123
restoring
    DHCP databases, 239
    WINS databases, 243
Reverse Address Resolution Protocol (RARP) protocol, 43, 86
reverse lookup name server queries, 120–121
reverse proxying, **371–373**
    defined, **371–372**, *372*
    load-balancing and, 372–373
    redundancy and, 373
    uses for, 373
Reverse-Lookup files, 125

RFCs (Request for Comments)
Ethernet addresses, 486
finding, 139
IPv6 protocol, 75–76
on port addresses, 10
RFC 1219 strategies for assigning IP
addresses, 316–319
Site Security Handbook (RFC 2196), 11–12
TACACS+ (Terminal Access Controller
Access Control System +), 453
Web sites for, 139
rights
assigning user, group, and file system rights,
430–432
and deleting default accounts, 429–430
ring topology, 30, *31*
RIP II (Routing Information Protocol II), 224
RIP (Routing Information Protocol), 43–44,
218, 223–224, 396
risk assessment, **410–422**. *See also* internal
network security
availability evaluation, 414
confidentiality evaluation, 413
data risk assessment tools, 420–421, *420*
defined, **412–414**
equipment/infrastructure assessment,
414–416
equipment/infrastructure protection,
416–419
integrity evaluation, 413–414
intrusion detection, 420, *420*, 421–422, 433
overview of, 410–412
redundancy and, 419–420
theft, 419
road warriors, 3–7
root bridges, 206–207, *206*, 209–211, *210*
routers, **201, 214–223**. *See also* bridges
autonomous system border routers (ASBRs),
226–227

defined, **201, 214–216**
designated routers (DRs) and backup
designated routers (BDRs), 225–226,
225
destination addresses, 215–216
documenting, 305
dynamic routing, **219–223**
Count to Infinity problem, 222
defined, **219**
distance-vector routing, 219–222, *220*,
223
link-state routing and link-state packets
(LSPs), 222–223
hop-by-hop routing, 237
hops, 216, 218
interdomain routing, 393–395
looping problems, 222, 476
Multiprotocol Label Switching (MPLS)
standard and, 236–237
NetJunction software, 259–260
network design and, 342
Poison Reverse routing, 222
Proxy servers as, 358
quick fixes for routing problems, 474–476
route metrics, 218
router advertisements and host auto-
configuration with IPv6 protocol, 398–
399
router redundancy, 201, 216–218, *217*
router-based packet-filtering firewalls,
439–441, *440*
routing packets, 215–216
routing strategies in network design,
344–346, *345, 346*
routing tables and, 215
Split Horizon routing, 222
static routing, **218**, *219*
troubleshooting routing problems,
474–476, 491–496, *491, 492*

routing protocols, **43–44, 223–233**
Exterior Gateway Protocols (EGPs), **231–233**
BGP (Border Gateway Protocol), 43–44, 232–233, 395
Exterior Gateway Protocol (EGP), 233
versus Interior Gateway Protocols (IGPs), **231–232**
Interior Gateway Protocols (IGPs), **223–232**. *See also* OSPF
defined, **223**
EIGRP (Enhanced IGRP), 231
versus Exterior Gateway Protocols (EGPs), **231–232**
IGRP (Interior Gateway Routing Protocol), 230
RIP II (Routing Information Protocol II), 224
RIP (Routing Information Protocol), 43–44, 218, 223–224, 396
OSPF (Open Shortest Path First), 43–44, 225–230
advantages of, 227
areas and, 227
autonomous system border routers (ASBRs) and, 226–227
autonomous systems (ASs) and, 226
backbones and, 227
default OSPF costs, 227–228
defined, **43–44, 225**
hello packets, 225
hops and, 218
IPv6 addresses and, 396
IS-IS (intermediate system to intermediate system) protocol and, 228–230
OSPF redundancy, 227–228
and selecting routes, 226
stub areas and, 227

and synchronizing link-state advertisement databases, 225–226, *225*
terms defined, **226–227**
RSA cryptography, 276

S

safe computing practices, 449–450
SATAN (Security Analysis Tool for Auditing Networks), 423
saving money, 187–188
scheduling
preliminary scheduling in project-approach phase, 337
project implementation, 348–349
SDLC. *See* system-design life cycle
secondary name servers
defined, **117**
synchronizing with primary servers, 503–504
Secure HTTP (S-HTTP), **13, 459**
Secure Sockets Layer (SSL), **13, 459**
SecureID authentication, 277
security, **407–461**
AssureNet Pathways, Inc., 454–455
auditing tools, 424–425
authentication, 13
AssureNet Pathways, Inc., 454–455
Authentication, Authorization, and Accounting (AAA) protocol, 282
card devices for remote-access authentication, 454
in IPv6 protocol, 402
RADIUS (Remote Authentication Dial-In User Service), 451–452, *452*
SecureID authentication, 277
Security Dynamics, Inc., 454
S-HTTP and, 13, 459
TACACS+ (Terminal Access Controller Access Control System +), 452–453

of cable modems, 288
case studies, **407–410**
denial of service attacks, 12, 478
disclosure of information, 12
DNS security extensions, 139–140
employee education and, 428–429, 436
encryption
    Blowfish encryption algorithm, 285
    cable modems and, 288
    Data Encryption Standard (DES),
        433–434
    internal network security and, 433–434
    in IPv6 protocol, 402
    PPTP (Point-to-Point Tunneling
        Protocol) problems, 284–285
    RSA cryptography, 276
    S-HTTP and, 13, 459
    transaction encryption in remote-access
        security, 455
    tunneling and, 276–277
firewalls, **437–445**
    application gateways, 443, 444
    case study, 198
    components of, 439
    defined, **438**
    firewall issues, 444–445
    IP addresses and, 438–439, *438*
    port addresses and, 10
    positioning, 438, *438*
    purpose of, 438–439, *438*
    router-based packet-filtering firewalls,
        439–441, *440*
    using ports, 441–443
    virtual private networks and, 275, 278
    for Web sites, 9–11
    well-known services, 81, 441–443
hackers, **422–425**
    anonymous FTP and, 424
    Computer Oracle Password and Security
        System (COPS), 424–425

    denial of service attacks, 12, 478
    finger command, 50, 423
    hacking tools, 423–424
    Security Analysis Tool for Auditing
        Networks (SATAN), 423
    Unix showmount command, 424
internal network security strategies,
    427–436
    applying patches, 427
    assigning user, group, and file system
        rights, 430–432
    auditing or logging information access,
        435–436
    deleting default accounts, 429–430
    e-mail security, 432–433
    encryption, 433–434
    intruder-detection plans, 433
    password policies, 428–429, 430
    removable disks and drives, 434–435
    segregating network segments, 434
for Internet commerce, 12–13, 459–461
IPv6 security, 401–402
Ping of Death attacks, 478
remote-access security, **450–459**
    access-control authorization, 458
    accounting and auditing features, 459
    callback methods, 457
    Caller Line ID (CLI), 457
    card devices, 454
    centralized security, 450–453
    CHAP (Challenge-Handshake
        Authentication Protocol), 458
    location validation and call level security,
        457
    PAP (Password Authentication Protocol),
        457
    password protection, 456–457

PPP (Point-to-Point Protocol) security
authentication, 457–458
RADIUS (Remote Authentication Dial-In
User Service), 451–452, *452*
security-by-obscurity method, 453–455
suggestions, 455–459
TACACS+ (Terminal Access Controller
Access Control System +), 452–453
token-based security, 453–455
transaction encryption, 455
user validation, 456
risk assessment, **410–422**
availability evaluation, 414
confidentiality evaluation, 413
data risk assessment tools, 420–421, *420*
defined, **412–414**
equipment/infrastructure assessment,
414–416
equipment/infrastructure protection,
416–419
integrity evaluation, 413–414
intrusion detection, 420, *420*, 421–422
overview of, 410–412
redundancy and, 419–420
theft, 419
Security Analysis Tool for Auditing
Networks (SATAN), 423
Security Dynamics, Inc., 454
security noncaching, 363–364
security policies, 301
security-by-obscurity method, 453–455
Site Security Handbook (RFC 2196), 11–12
trust relationships and, **426**
of tunneling, 275–277, 281, 284–285
unauthorized access, 11
virtual private network security protocols,
281–283
AAA (Authentication, Authorization,
and Accounting) protocol, 282
IKE (Internet Security Key Management
Protocol), 282
IPSec, 279, 281, 282
L2TP (Layer Two Tunneling Protocol),
281–283
of virtual private networks, 279, 281,
284–285
viruses, **301, 445–450**
cost of, 446–449
history of, 445–446
increasing numbers of PCs and, 446
Melissa virus, 446–449
polymorphic viruses, 445, 446
safe computing practices, 449–450
virus protection policies, 301
Web site security, **9–11, 13, 459–461**
credit card processing, 460–461
firewalls, 9–11
S-HTTP, SSL (Secure Sockets Layer) and,
13, *459*
segment format in TCP protocol, 45–47, *45*
segmenting Ethernet networks, 488–490, *489*
segregating network segments, 434
selecting
routes, 226
SNMP managers, 253
sending IP addresses, 40
Serial Line Internet Protocol (SLIP), 37
servers. *See also* Proxy servers
BIND (Berkeley Internet Name Domain)
servers
BIND boot files, 128–129
defined, **113**
designated servers, 132–134, *132, 133*
DHCP servers, **88, 89–92, 94–105, 237–
238, 240–241**
defined, **88**
DHCP Manager, 101–103, *102*
DNS addresses and, 240–241

Index

DNS/DHCP Management Console,
    94–99, *96*, 117, *118*, 132–133, *132*,
    133, 138, *138*
NetWare 5 configuration, 94–101
options DHCP servers can pass to DHCP
    clients, 89–92
Unix configuration, 103–105
wide area network design and, 237–238,
    238
Windows 2000 configuration, 103
Windows NT configuration, 101–103,
    102
DNS servers
    DNS server roles, 117
    linking, 117–118, *118*
    wide area network design and, 240–241
FTP server return codes, 156–157
installing and configuring FTP servers,
    159–172
    in NetWare 5 networks, 165–169, *166*
    overview of, 159
    in Unix networks, 169–172
    in Windows NT 4 networks, 160–165,
        160, 161, 162
name servers
    defined, **42, 114**
    forwarders and, 117
    inverse name server queries and reverse
        lookups, 120–121
    name server (NS) records in zone files, 42,
        124
    name server queries, 118–121
    primary, secondary, and master name
        servers, **117**
    quick fixes, 476
    synchronizing primary and secondary
        servers, 503–504
    troubleshooting, 496–504
Proxy servers, 241
WINS server installation, 241–243
Service Packs in Windows NT, 134

services
    acceptable level of service, 463
    checking, 476
    QoS (Quality of Service), 271
Session layer in OSI model, **26, 324–325**
Set operations of SNMP managers, 251
sharing information, **7–14, 377–378, 459–461**
    FTP (File Transfer Protocol) and, **14**
    Internet commerce, 12–13, 459–461
    Internet information sharing, **8–12**
        firewalls and, 9–11
        hosting Web sites on company versus ISP
            servers, 9
        overview of, 8–9
        TCP/IP security and, 11–12
    intranet information sharing, 8
    overview of, 7–8
    with Proxy servers, 377–378, *378*
showmount command in Unix, 424
S-HTTP (Secure HTTP), **13, 459**
signatures, digital, 13, 139–140
Simple Mail Transfer Protocol (SMTP), 7, 49,
    325
Simple Network Management Protocol.
    See SNMP
Site Local Aggregators (SLAs), **391**
site local IPv6 addresses, 392
Site Security Handbook (RFC 2196), 11–12
size of networks, *56, 57–59, 58, 59*
SLAs (Site Local Aggregators), **391**
SLIP (Serial Line Internet Protocol), 37
SMI (Structure of Management Information),
    506
SMTP (Simple Mail Transfer Protocol), 7, 49,
    325
SNMP (Simple Network Management
    Protocol), **50, 249–263, 504–507**. *See also*
    network management
alarms, 262
case studies, **254–261, 263**

customizing off-the-shelf software, 259–260

enterprise management, 255–257

Hewlett-Packard OpenView system, 257–259

multinational, multivendor networks, 257–259

NASA network, 257–259

network integration (Data Systems West), 254–255

Nortel Optivity system, 263

Y2K compliance checking with SMS, 260–261

defined, 50, 250, 262, 504–506

maintenance features, 262

Management Information Bases (MIBs), 251, 507

NMSs (Network Management Stations)
    defined, 250–251, 504–505
    placing, 251–252
    polling devices, 505

object identifiers, 506–507

PDUs (Protocol Data Units), 505

planning networks with, 262

reporting features, 262

SNMP agents
    defined, 251, 504
    placing, 251–252
    Trap operations, 251, 505–506

SNMP communities, 252

SNMP managers
    defined, 250–253
    Get, Get-Next, and Set operations, 251
    hardware and software compatibility, 254
    how SNMP managers work, 252–253
    placing, 251–252
    purchasing, 253

SNMP tasks in network design, 342, 342

Structure of Management Information (SMI), 506

troubleshooting network access with, 504–507

SOA (Start of Authority) records in zone files, 122–123

sockets
    defined, 47
    Secure Sockets Layer (SSL), 13, 459
    sockets drivers, 355

SOCKS Proxy server, 381–382

software. See also commands; utilities
    Alta Vista Tunnel software, 277–278
    applying patches, 427
    customizing off-the-shelf software, 259–260
    help desk software, 190–192
    Hewlett-Packard OpenView software, 254, 257–259
    McAfee Total Service Desk (TSD), 190–191
    NetManage, 191–192
    Nortel Optivity software, 254, 263
    SNMP compatibility, 254
    software licenses, 301
    standardization of, 187–188

solutions
    documenting, 295, 469
    implementing, 299

Source Address field in IP packet headers, 40

source port addresses, 82–83

Source Port field in UDP protocol, 48

Source Quench messages, 44

source-routing bridges, 212–214
    defined, 212–213, 212
    hello packets and, 212–213
    source-routing transparent bridges (SRTs), 213–214, 213

source-routing transparent bridges (SRTs), 213–214, 213

Spanning Tree Protocol, 205–212
    advantages of, 206, 212
    backup bridges and, 210–211
    bridge broadcast frames and, 207–208, 207
    bridge elections and, 207–209, 207, 208

bridge IDs and, 206–207
Bridge Protocol Data Units (BPDUs) and,
    206–207, 208–211, *208*
defined, **205–206**, *206*
and designating bridges, 209–211, *210*
ideal spanning tree configurations, 211–212,
    211
port costs and, 209–210, *210*
root bridges and, 206–207, *206*, 209–211,
    210
specifications for networks, 297–298
Split Horizon routing, 222
SRTs (source-routing transparent bridges),
    213–214, *213*
SSL (Secure Sockets Layer), **13**, **459**
standardization of components, 187–188
star topology, **30**, *31*
Start of Authority (SOA) records in zone files,
    122–123
stateful host auto-configuration with IPv6
    rotocol, 399–400
stateless host auto-configuration with IPv6
    protocol, 398–399
static routing, **218**, *219*
Structure of Management Information (SMI),
    506
stub areas, 227
subnetting and subnet masks. *See also* IP
    addresses
    and assigning IP addresses, 316–319
    defined, **64–69**, *67*
    documenting subnets, 302
    IP address calculators and, 74–75
    Subnet Options tab in DNS/DHCP
        Management Console, 96–97, *97*
Sun Microsystems Network File System (NFS),
    142, 157–159, *158*
supernetting, **69**
switches

Ethernet switches, 313–315, *314*
Multiprotocol Label Switching (MPLS)
    standard, 236–237, 279
Token Ring switches, 315
synchronizing
    bit synchronization, 34
    databases, 6
    link-state advertisement databases,
        225–226, *225*
    primary and secondary name servers,
        503–504
synchronous bit synchronization, **34**
synchronous communications, **29**
syntax, OSI model and, 25–26
System Management Server (SMS) Y2K
    compliance checking, 260–261
system-design life cycle (SDLC), **329–331**. *See
    also* design; planning; project management
    detailed system design, implementation, and
        operation, 331
    general system design and systems
        evaluation, 331
    maintenance, 331
    overview of, 329, *330*
    system analysis and specification, 330

T

TACACS+ (Terminal Access Controller Access
    Control System +), 452–453
Tattletale protocol, 44–45
TCP (Transmission Control Protocol)
    defined, **45**, **322**
    history of, 18
    port numbers and, 47–48
TCP/IP protocol, **36–50**. *See also* IP addresses;
    IP (Internet Protocol); IPv6 protocol
    client/server applications and, 6–7
    defined, **23**
    groupware applications and, 6–7

history of, 17–20
mobile computing and, 6–7
TCP/IP architecture, **36–50**
   DoD model and, 36, *36*
   host-to-host layer protocols, 36, 45–49,
     45, *48*
   ICMP (Internet Control Message
     Protocol), 44–45, 386–387
   Internet layer protocols, 36–40, *39*
   IP routing protocols, 43–44
   network access layer protocols, 36–37
   process layer protocols, 36, 49–50
   Unix and, 36
   Windows 95/98 and, 36
TCP/IP documentation, **301–305**
   addresses and subnets, 302
   configurations, 301–302
   DHCP, 302–303
   HOSTS and LMHOSTS files, 304
   routers, 305
uses for, 3
teams
   creating, 334–335
   training, 335–336
Tech Help Computer Services (THCS), 75
technologies and defining networks, 56–57, *57*
Telnet
   defined, **49**
   FTP (File Transfer Protocol) and, 153
   implementing, 324–325
Terminal Access Controller Access Control
   System + (TACACS+), 452–453
TFTP (Trivial File Transfer Protocol), **141–142**
THCS (Tech Help Computer Services), 75
theft, 419
Time Exceeded error message in tracert
   command, 494
Timestamp and Timestamp Reply messages, 45

Time-to-Live (TTL) field in IP packet
   headers, 40
TLAs (Top Level Aggregators), **391**
TLDs (top-level domains), 21–23, 111–112,
   114
token passing access method, **28**
Token Ring switches, 315
token-based remote-access security, 453–455
Top Level Aggregators (TLAs), **391**
top-level domains (TLDs), 21–23, 111–112,
   114
topologies, **30–32**
   bus topology, 30, *30*
   cellular topology, 32, *33*
   mesh topology, 32, *32*
   ring topology, 30, *31*
   star topology, 30, *31*
TOS (Type of Service) field in IP packet
   headers, 39
Total Length field in IP packet headers, 39
Total Service Desk (TSD) software, 190–191
Traceroute utility, *50*
tracert command, 494–496
tracking. *See* checking
training
   and certifying users, 189
   help desk personnel, 188
   security and employee education, 428–429,
     436
   teams, 335–336
   virtual private network staff training, 281
transaction encryption in remote-access
   security, 455
transitioning to IPv6 protocol, 402–403
Transmission Control Protocol. *See* TCP
transparent bridges
   defined, **204**
   source-routing transparent bridges (SRTs),
     213–214, *213*

Transport layer in OSI model
 defined, **26–27**
 planning for Transport layer changes,
  321–323
 Transport layer proxies, 357, 373, 380, 381
Trap operations in SNMP, 251, 505–506
Trivial File Transfer Protocol (TFTP), **141–142**
troubleshooting, **178–184, 463–507**
 acceptable level of service and, 463
 defined, **463–464**
 finding problem areas, **178–184**
  expectations and, 181–184
  help desks and, 180–181, 184–187
  Murphy's Law and, 182–183
  overview of, 178–180
 network access, **481–507**
  with arp command, 484–486
  with ipconfig, ifconfig, and winipcfg
   commands, 481–484, *482*
  name server problems, 496–504
  with netstat command, 486–488,
   491–493, *491, 492*
  with nslookup utility, 496–503
  routing problems, 474–476, 491–496,
   491, 492
  segmenting Ethernet networks, 488–490,
   489
  with SNMP, 504–507
  with tracert command, 494–496
 with Ping utility, **477–481,** *480*
 quick fixes, **464–466, 469–476**
  ANDing process, 470–471
  checking daemons or services, 476
  checking log files, 474, 475
  for configuration file problems, 472–474
  for DNS and name services, 476
  IP addresses in network configurations,
   470–472

 for network connectivity problems,
  470–472
 overview of, 464–466, 469–470
 for routing problems, 474–476
 troubleshooting model, **465–469**
  backward chaining, 468
  brain dumps, 468
  collecting information, 466
  documenting solutions and preventing
   problems, 295, 469
  ensuring user satisfaction, 469
  forward chaining, 467
  isolating problems, 466–468, *468*
  overview of, 464, *464*
  trying a quick fix, 464–466
trust relationships, **426**
TSD (Total Service Desk) software, 190–191
TTL Exceeded messages, 44
TTL (Time-to-Live) field in IP packet
 headers, 40
tunneling, **275–278, 284–285.** *See also* virtual
 private networks
 Alta Vista Tunnel software, 277–278
 data compression and, 277
 defined, **276**
 encryption and, 276–277
 and integration with private networks, 277
 Internet Explorer and, 275–276
 L2TP (Layer Two Tunneling Protocol),
  281–283
 managing, 277–278
 PPTP (Point-to-Point Tunneling Protocol),
  275–276, 284–285
 RSA cryptography and, 276
 SecureID authentication and, 277
 security and, 275–277, 281, 284–285
Type of Service (TOS) field in IP packet
 headers, 39

U

UDP (User Datagram Protocol)
  datagram format, 48–49, *48*
  defined, **322**
unauthorized access, 11
unicast IPv6 addresses, 389, 391
University of Illinois at Chicago, 273
University of Michigan, 271
University of Pennsylvania, 273
Unix
  Computer Oracle Password and Security
    System (COPS), 424–425
  configuration files, 473–474
  deleting default accounts, 429–430
  DHCP client configuration, 107
  DHCP server configuration, 103–105
  HOSTS files and, 41
  installing and configuring FTP servers,
    169–172
  log files, 475
  showmount command, 424
  Sun Microsystems Network File System
    (NFS) and, 159
  trust relationships, 426
Unknown Host error message, 479, 496
Unreachable Port error message in tracert
  command, 495
unreliable protocols, **38**
unspecified IPv6 addresses, 392
User Data Transfer Process (User DTP) for FTP,
  153–155, *154*
User Protocol Interpreter (User-PI) for FTP, 153
users
  ensuring user satisfaction after
    troubleshooting, 469
  lying by, 298, 308, 465
  training and certifying, 189
  user directories, 432
  user rights, 430–432

user validation for remote-access security,
  456
utilities. *See also* commands; software
  Archie, 49, 172–174, *173*, *174*
  Gopher, 49
  NICNAME, 50
  Ping
    cable problems and, 481
    command options, 477–478
    defined, **50**
    IPv6 Ping utility, 387–388
    packet size parameter, 478
    troubleshooting with, 477–481, *480*
  Traceroute, 50
  Whois, 50

V

vBNS (Very High-Performance Backbone
  Network Service), **19**, **272–273**
VeriGuard, Inc., 285
Version field in IP packet headers, 38
virtual private networks (VPNs), **274–290**.
  See also extranets
  alternatives to, 289
  ATM (Asynchronous Transfer Mode) and,
    279
  case study, **290**
  costs of, 278
  defined, **274**, *274*
  disadvantages of, 281
  ease of use, 279–280
  firewalls and, 275, 278
  MPLS (Multiprotocol Label Switching)
    standard and, 279
  network design and, 346, *346*
  outsourcing installation and management,
    280–281
  performance of, 278–279
  PKI (Public Key Infrastructure), 280

Index

remote connectivity issues, **286–288**
    always-on Internet connectivity, 286
    bandwidth, 286–287
    cable modems, 287–288
    IP addresses, 286
security of, 279, 281, 284–285
security protocols, **281–283**
    AAA (Authentication, Authorization,
        and Accounting) protocol, 282
    IKE (Internet Security Key Management
        Protocol), 282
    IPSec, 279, 281, 282
    L2TP (Layer Two Tunneling Protocol),
        281–283
training staff, 281
tunneling, **275–278, 284–285**
    Alta Vista Tunnel software, 277–278
    data compression and, 277
    defined, **276**
    encryption and, 276–277
    and integration with private networks,
        277
    Internet Explorer and, 275–276
    L2TP (Layer Two Tunneling Protocol),
        281–283
    managing, 277–278
    PPTP (Point-to-Point Tunneling
        Protocol), 275–276, 284–285
    RSA cryptography and, 276
    SecureID authentication and, 277
    security and, 275–277, 281, 284–285
    versus wide area networks, 280
viruses, **301, 445–450**
    cost of, 446–449
    history of, 445–446
    increasing numbers of PCs and, 446
    Melissa virus, 446–449
    polymorphic viruses, 445, 446

safe computing practices, 449–450
virus protection policies, 301
Visa code, **259**
VPNs. *See* virtual private networks

W

WANs. *See* wide area networks
Web browsers as FTP User Interfaces, 143–144,
    144
Web sites, **8–12**
    DNS security extensions, 140
    firewalls and, 9–11
    hosting on company versus ISP servers, 9
    Microsoft white paper on Cache Array
        Routing Protocol (CARP), 370
    NetSource Partners, 256
    OpenView, 255–256
    overview of, 8–9
    for RFCs (Request for Comments), 139
    security, **9–11, 13, 459–461**
        credit card processing, 460–461
        firewalls, 9–11
        S-HTTP, SSL (Secure Sockets Layer) and,
            13, 459
    Site Security Handbook (RFC 2196), 11–12
    TCP/IP security and, 11–12
    Tech Help Computer Services (THCS), 75
    Windows NT Service Packs, 134
Web-based help desks on intranets, 192–194
well-known services, **81, 441–443**
Whois utility, 50
wide area networks (WANs), **235–248**.
        See also networks
    DHCP database maintenance, 239
    DHCP implementation planning, 237–239,
        238
    DNS implementation planning, 239–241
    final design plan, 248
    and future of networks, 235–237

HOSTS file implementation planning,
245–247
IP (Internet Protocol) and, 236
LMHOSTS file implementation planning,
243–245
Multiprotocol Label Switching (MPLS)
standard and, 236–237
versus virtual private networks (VPNs), 280
WAN/LAN maps, 61–63, *61*, *62*, 300, 507
WINS implementation planning, **241–243**
planning WINS server installation,
242–243
WINS database maintenance, 243
WINS overview, 241–242
William's Law, 182, 308, 327, 328
Windows. *See* Microsoft Windows
winipcfg command, 481–484, *482*
WINS (Windows Internet Name Service), **113,
137, 241–243**
versus Domain Name System (DNS), 113,
137
overview of, 241–242
planning WINS server installation, 242–243
WINS database maintenance, 243
Winsock Proxy servers, 381–382

workgroup IP address allocation, 319–320,
320

Y

Y2K compliance case study, 260–261

Z

Zero Administration Client module of McAfee
Total Service Desk software, 191
zone files, **116, 121–125**
CNAME records, 125
defined, **116, 122**
host records, 124
mail-exchanger (MX) records, 42, 124
name server (NS) records, 42, 124
resource records and, 121–122, *123*
at sign (@) in, 122
SOA (Start of Authority) records, 122–123
zones
creating, **133**, *133*
defined, **112, 116**, *116*
designated servers and, 132–134, *132*, *133*
DNS server roles and, 117

Index

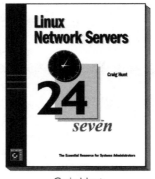

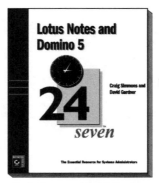

TAKE YOUR CAREER TO THE NEXT LEVEL

with 24seven books from Network Press

- **This new series offers the advanced information you need to keep your systems and networks running 24 hours a day, seven days a week.**
- **On-the-job case studies provide solutions to real-world problems.**
- **Maximize your system's uptime—and go home at 5!**
- **$34.99; 7½" x 9"; 544–704 pages; softcover**

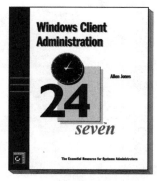

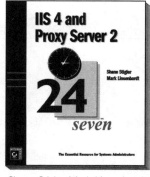

SYBEX BOOKS ON THE WEB

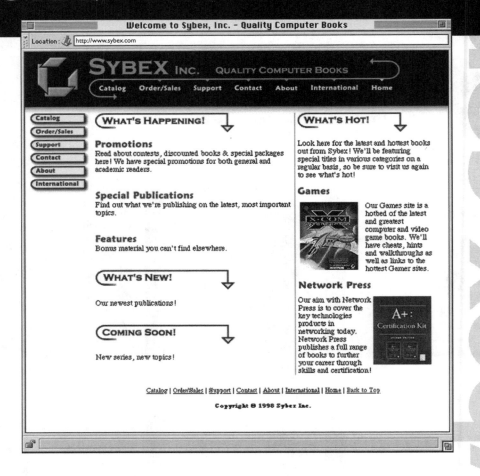

Welcome to Sybex, Inc. - Quality Computer Books

Location: http://www.sybex.com

SYBEX INC. QUALITY COMPUTER BOOKS

Catalog   Order/Sales   Support   Contact   About   International   Home

Catalog
Order/Sales
Support
Contact
About
International

WHAT'S HAPPENING!

Promotions
Read about contests, discounted books & special packages here! We have special promotions for both general and academic readers.

Special Publications
Find out what we're publishing on the latest, most important topics.

Features
Bonus material you can't find elsewhere.

WHAT'S NEW!

Our newest publications!

COMING SOON!

New series, new topics!

WHAT'S HOT!

Look here for the latest and hottest books out from Sybex! We'll be featuring special titles in various categories on a regular basis, so be sure to visit us again to see what's hot!

Games

Our Games site is a hotbed of the latest and greatest computer and video game books. We'll have cheats, hints and walkthroughs as well as links to the hottest Gamer sites.

Network Press

Our aim with Network Press is to cover the key technologies products in networking today. Network Press publishes a full range of books to further your career through skills and certification!

Catalog | Order/Sales | Support | Contact | About | International | Home | Back to Top

Copyright © 1998 Sybex Inc.

At the dynamic and informative Sybex Web site, you can:

- view our complete online catalog
- preview a book you're interested in
- access special book content
- order books online at special discount prices
- learn about Sybex

www.sybex.com

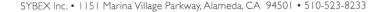

SYBEX Inc. • 1151 Marina Village Parkway, Alameda, CA 94501 • 510-523-8233

From the Experts...

Who bring you Mark Minasi's #1 best-selling *Complete PC Upgrade & Maintenance Guide,* Sybex now presents...

Nearly a million copies sold!

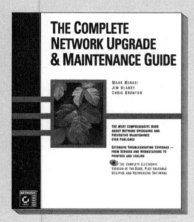

The Complete Network Upgrade & Maintenance Guide

BY MARK MINASI, JIM BLANEY, CHRIS BRENTON

The Ultimate Networking Reference—this book is a practical and comprehensive guide to implementing, upgrading, and maintaining networks, from small office LANs to enterprise-scale WANs and beyond.

ISBN: 0-7821-2259-0
1536 pp., $69.99

The Complete Website Upgrade & Maintenance Guide

BY LISA SCHMEISER

Destined to be the industry's ultimate Website reference, this book is the most comprehensive and broad-reaching tome, created to help you turn an existing site into a long-lasting sophisticated, dynamic, effective tool.

ISBN: 0-7821-2315-5
912 pp., $49.99

The Complete PC Upgrade & Maintenance Guide, 9th edition

BY MARK MINASI

After selling nearly <u>one million copies</u> of its previous editions, the 9th edition carries on the tradition with detailed troubleshooting for the latest motherboards, sound cards, video boards, CD-ROM drives, and all other multimedia devices.

ISBN: 0-7821-2357-0
1600 pp., $59.99

www.sybex.com

SYBEX

How to...

Work with SNMP agents	**Chapter 10**
Set baselines using SNMP	**Chapter 10**
Design an extranet	**Chapter 11**
See into the future of the Internet	**Chapter 11**
Design and use a VPN	**Chapter 11**
Document your entire network	**Chapter 12**
Evaluate your current network	**Chapter 12**
Document TCP/IP settings	**Chapter 12**
Use the seven layers of the OSI model to plan change	**Chapter 13**
Use switching hubs	**Chapter 13**
Increase performance of a Token Ring	**Chapter 13**
Design a time line for change	**Chapter 14**
Implement the phases of a project	**Chapter 14**
Use Proxy servers	**Chapter 15**